SEEDS *of*
DESTRUCTION

Elizabeth Abbott Green

Because of the dynamic nature of the Internet, any web addresses or links contained in this book may have changed since publication and may no longer be valid. The views expressed in this work are solely those of the author and do not necessarily reflect the views of the publisher, and the publisher hereby disclaims any responsibility for them.

King James Version, Oral Roberts Edition, Oral Roberts Evangelistical Association, Tulsa, OK

This book is a work of non-fiction. Unless otherwise noted, the author and the publisher make no explicit guarantees as to the accuracy of the information contained in this book and in some cases, names of people and places have been altered to protect their privacy. Any people depicted in stock imagery provided by Getty Images are models, and such images are being used for illustrative purposes only. Certain stock imagery © Getty Images.

ISBN: 978-1-959483-01-4 (sc)
ISBN: 978-1-959483-02-1 (hc)
ISBN: 978-1-959483-03-8 (e)

Library of Congress Control Number: 2022914360

I dedicate this book to
The memory of my wonderful mother,
Who kept all my cards and letters
Over the years and passed away
Christmas morning, 1996.

I dedicate the story of our family
To my devoted husband,
Our three children,
And our three grandchildren,
As a reminder of our happy times together
Before the world tried to drive us apart.
My true love always.

I dedicate the writing of this book
To the glory of God
For His abiding love, guidance and grace,
And for all His blessings and miracles,
Which sustained us through all the
Trials and tribulations of life.
I owe my inspiration to Him.

To God be the Glory!

Amen.

Table of Contents

Foreword

Elizabeth Abbott Green has written a compelling narrative of the life of a family, lived well but not without struggle…a life that spans the last half of the 20th Century and into the millennium, a life of equal parts of joy, heartache…and faith. I've known Libby for 61 years, the last 60 of which she's been the bride of my youth. The story begins on a south Alabama beach in 1956 where a couple of 19-year olds meet…and begin an unlikely odyssey they could not have dreamed! She, a lovely beach girl who had stars in her eyes, and would have been perfectly happy to have spent her life there on that beautiful place by the sea…and he, with mountains to climb and no thoughts of settling down…anywhere! Not being able to see too far down the road, they married a year later, and their horizons were about to expand significantly…they had places to go, and many life lessons to learn…and they had to do it in an ever-changing world.

Two years later, they hitched a trailer onto the back of their '55 Chevy Bel-Air, tenderly placed their one- and two-year old baby boys on a mattress in the back seat and drove away from a small southern college town into the West, and the world beyond, to seek their fortune. They were armed with an engineering degree, a commission in the Army, and the '55 Chevy… and more than a little excitement, wonder…and confidence that they could, with God's guidance, meet any challenges out there. What lives the four of them…to become five two years later with the birth of their only daughter… would lead, and what magic places they would see!

The first part of the family's life thrust all five of them headlong into something that was unique to them all…the life of a Military Family! There were professional challenges for me, and, for the family, excitement and fun, with lots of travel and an opportunity that most young families don't have to see a foreign land, and to see most of the great country that is the USA! But there were also the alter egos of excitement and fun… pressure, responsibility and discipline. A Military career, unlike most others, requires an oath, and that oath demands that lives be lived in accordance with those attributes. Elizabeth had those qualities, and became as close as one can come to the "perfect Army wife, mother and American", and later, a great Ambassador for the United States in every part of the world she lived. Even though the rigors of a military life impose unique requirements on the family…the added pressures of a foreign war, extended absence from the family unit by the military member, unexpected and frequent family moves and changes of schools…our family seemed to adapt well, and, for a time, to thrive.

The teenage years for the family, however, coincided with the growth of societal stress in the '70's, and began to reflect values from outside creeping in. My Army career took me to DC for the last six years, which was great for my career but not so good for the family's life. Elizabeth was quick to discover the family pressures that resulted. She took most of them on herself, and made an almost untenable situation survivable. The catalyst for the book "Seeds of Destruction" was a major incident that almost took the life of our second son Greg. The outcome of those years – 1976-1982 – was my premature retirement from the Army, our (Elizabeth's and my) movement overseas to take advantage of my training in the Middle East and Africa, and the emancipation of our three children to allow them some "growing up time and space!"

God's hand in this story became clear when, after I accepted a position with a major US firm that had a contract to build military facilities in the Middle East, Libby and I were privileged to make our first visit to Europe. We were to go to Frankfurt, Germany to allow me to work with German engineers who were designing the work, and when the design was mature, to go in-country to manage the construction of the facilities. As retired military, we were allowed access to a major US base, Rhein-Main Air Force Base, and Libby shopped there, arranged for travel tours, and sought out the on-base chapel. In tune with most of our life until then, she could never have imagined that, not only was a group of Women of the Chapel about to begin a major Bible study…but they had only eleven ladies signed up, and needed a 12th to hold the course! Thus, as I embarked on 22 years of exciting work in the Middle East, Libby threw herself into the unexpected opportunity to join the group Bible study available, while intensifying her individual study that persists today, and is the vehicle for this book.

The 23 years that we worked, lived and travelled Europe, the Middle East and Africa was a period of time that could only be inspired! The experiences of seeing places to which we likely would never have been able to travel are priceless, as are the friends we made in all the countries we touched. Particularly, the lands of the Bible came alive to us – John's cave on Patmos, the sites of Paul's travels in Corinth and Ephesus, the Roman catacombs and the Egyptian deserts where the Holy Family sojourned for four years.

The book should be interesting to many audiences: young military families trying to cope with the almost constant overseas demands placed on them in today's military; people of all ages who love travel and are willing and able to accept the challenge; and Christians everywhere who are interested in Bible prophecy.

Seeds of Destruction is the work of a lifetime, not only of the entire family who lived it, but especially a work of total commitment for over 30 years by the author, and the focused study of Christianity and the signs of our times. Elizabeth Abbott Green's analysis of the true path to God's will for us is exemplary, and I believe it should be read by all who feel that much of today's world is taking us in the opposite direction.

Introduction

This is the story of a military family as we traveled our great country during the early years of family life and later overseas to Rabat, Morocco, when our kids were in their teens, for my husband's in-country training as a Foreign Area Officer specializing in the Middle East and North Africa. We were a close-knit family because we moved so often and we needed one another, as we left old friends behind and made new ones in new locations. It was hard on our children, and, as a mother, I felt all their hurts and pain as we tried to make the best of every situation always looking forward to the new adventure. It was always a major adjustment having to *learn the ropes* of a new place and make a home for our growing family. Trying to create some *normalcy* out of all the upheavals of moving was quite a challenge, but we seemed to flourish as we made many new friends and learned to fit into many different cultures.

My husband was committed to his Army Career, having received his BS degree in Civil Engineering and his Commission in the US Army upon graduation from the University of Mississippi in January 1960. After having his high school band in Memphis, John was hired by *The Downbeats*, a very popular dance band at Ole Miss, to play saxophone and clarinet. I worked all over campus in various jobs as secretary, typist and two summers, after the births of our two boys, filling orders for football tickets. My last job at the Alumni House trained me to operate an Addressograph for mailing out literature to the Alumni. We left Oxford with two baby boys pulling a U-haul trailer behind us on our trek across the desert to his first assignment at Ft. Bliss, TX where John learned to fire a missile in preparation for his two-year assignment at Fort MacArthur's Air Defense Control Center, San Pedro, CA. It was my first move out of the South where I had grown up and spent all my summers on the beautiful white sandy beach of Gulf Shores, Alabama. John just happened to be playing a job with the Downbeats in August 1956 at the Canal Lounge when we met right there on the beach at Gulf Shores.

Since John decided to drive all night from Houston, where we spent the night with my oldest brother, Franklin, and his family, I crawled in back with the boys to sleep on a baby mattress, which covered the whole back seat. Around dawn, John called me up front to see the lively wild rabbits hopping around on both sides of the road. Overnight, the landscape had changed dramatically from vegetation to desert with picturesque table top mountains as far as the eye could see. It was the most beautiful sight I could have imagined as the desert came to life with shifting shadows falling across the landscape and a roadrunner crossing the road in front of us. After stopping for gas and coffee, we continued our exciting adventure amidst blowing tumble weeds all the way to Ft. Bliss. While checking in, John received a list of places where we might find temporary lodging for his three-month assignment, and we selected a duplex within view of the lovely El Paso mountain range. I was happy to find a nursery on post where I could leave the boys for the morning while I boarded a bus, with a few other wives, out to the firing range to watch as John and his hand-picked team fired the class missile for a direct hit.

After serving his two-year commitment, John chose to leave the Army and try out civilian life, so we borrowed a typewriter and started writing letters to send out with his resume to various companies across the nation. When the responses started pouring in through the mail slot of our front door, our 3- and 4-year-old boys had a regular field day, laughing and jumping all around as they gathered the mail to bring to us. John set up a few interviews as we crossed the country back to the Gulf, where we stayed with my folks for about a month while the boys and I enjoyed the beach. John flew to a few interviews and visited his folks in Ohio. Then he flew down to get us and drove us to Columbus, where Margaret was born July 2nd. John's first job as a Sales Representative with a major glass company took us to Richmond, where the kids and I were snowed in for five days at a time while he made his rounds over to Norfolk and down to the Carolinas. Neither of us were happy with this situation, so John followed up on another job for which he received an offer back in California as Civil Engineer for a major oil company. So we re-crossed the country again, visiting all the relatives along the way, back to California when Margaret was about 9 months old, and we found a cute little house in San Pedro overlooking Catalina Island. Still, we were not satisfied with this arrangement and felt like something was missing: John missed Army life and decided to come back in as a Regular Army Officer. His orders took us back to Ft. Bliss and the Air Defense Artillery School. We felt like we were home again.

After several attempts to write our story, I feel compelled to follow through this time because the time is short. Like prior to WW II, it now appears that we could be headed for World War III, or worse if we don't take back our Country and fight for liberty once again. The purpose of my book is to share my testimony of how God brought us through some very difficult times common to all people who are struggling to make it through life's incredible journey. In spite of all the odds against us as a military family, we were greatly blessed to have enjoyed many wonderful adventures together while the kids were still young and living rather sheltered lives. I remember telling people that *"Our kids discovered the world in Morocco"* because that's where they all three seemed to rebel against our parental authority to keep them safe.

Due to a tragic accident involving our second son, Greg, I promised God that I would denounce a study which I had fallen into several years earlier to please a friend. I thought it was beneficial to me in understanding the characteristics and personalities of our family members. The course teaches that *we are only fated by our lack of understanding* and that, *in knowing these esoteric truths,* we can *avoid pitfalls* and *make the most of our opportunities.* I eventually learned that this study is listed in the Bible under the *occult,* along with many other *abominations,* all of which can open the door to demonic attack. As I was preparing for bed the night of Greg's accident, I removed a piece of jewelry I had been unaware of wearing that day. It was a Christmas gift from John, a golden pendant with three small diamonds, which I never intended to wear because of what it represented. As I looked down in total disbelief at the object I was holding in my hand, I heard *the still, small voice* booming out loud and clear: *"Thou shalt have no other gods before me ... and no graven images!"* This is my testimony.

CHAPTER ONE

A Time for the Unexpected

1981

It was a Thursday, that cold fifth day of February 1981, a day our family would never forget. Early that morning, John and I had dropped our 21-year- old son off at an Arlington bus stop to ride the short distance over to the employment office on our way to work telling him to *"Get a job!"* In fact, it was the fourth day we had done this, hoping that he would *get a life.* John worked at the Pentagon, and I worked on the eighth floor of a high-rise office building in downtown Rosslyn overlooking the lovely Potomac River with a fantastic view of the Washington Monuments. John and I drove in together each morning from our home in Alexandria, and we usually had our family business meeting on our way to work. He would drop me off in front of my building and continue his drive over to the Pentagon parking lot. Sometimes, if he was running late, I would take the subway over to get the car and pick him up out front for the drive back home. Usually, however, I would busy myself in the office until he pulled up in view of our side office window. This back and forth drive was always a rat race and cost us 30-45 minutes through heavy traffic depending on where we lived, but it gave us time to hear the news and some of our favorite popular music. After two tours of duty in Saigon as an Intelligence Analyst/Briefing Officer at MACV Headquarters and several years of training as a Foreign Area Officer (FAO), John was now serving as one of the Army's top specialists in the Middle East and North Africa.

I was secretary to the Recreation and Tourism scientist in Forest Environment Research, a branch of the Forest Service under the Department of Agriculture. I loved my job and all the people I worked with in FER. On this particular afternoon, everything was proceeding along as usual and I was totally absorbed in my office duties when a phone call from John sent a shock wave throughout the entire office. Our second son, Greg, had been struck by a subway train in a tunnel near Metro Center around 2:30

pm and was rushed to George Washington University Hospital. John had just given the emergency room doctors permission to amputate his badly crushed right foot and lower leg. My mind rushed back to that morning when we dropped Greg off at the bus stop wearing his fleece-collared sheepskin coat and Pepsi stocking hat to keep his ears warm while looking for a job that day. What on earth was he doing in a DC tunnel? With Greg, anything was possible, and we could only speculate! Whatever it was, we prayed it would somehow change his life for the better.

The emergency room doctor said Greg would be in surgery for hours and there was nothing we could do but wait, so he suggested that we drive on home and get some rest. He told John that because Greg's blood-alcohol ratio was so high, they couldn't give him an anesthetic for fear of an overdose. He promised to call that evening with an update. Our drive home was reflective and quiet, as we thought back over the weeks and months leading up to this terrible accident. Nothing Greg did ever came as a total shock to us because we knew that if he didn't change his impulsive behavior something dreadful was a real possibility. He had come close to death so many times and owed his life to the quick actions and hard work of the many people who saved him.

We were not hungry that evening, so John and I just nibbled a bit on whatever we could find in the kitchen. Finally, the call came in from the young emergency room doctor with the update. We were very thankful to hear that the surgery had gone as well as could be expected and they had saved as much of his right leg as possible. They only removed the crushed portion around mid-calf, which the doctors thought would be ideal for the future fitting of a prosthetic device. They also removed his badly crushed left big toe, which was crushed inside his shoe. Only his tight shoe string kept the skin from ripping further up his foot. They searched for internal bleeding and found none. Except for a large, round puncture wound the size of a baseball on the upper side of his right thigh and a broken front tooth, everything else seemed to be intact. We were very thankful that once again his life had been spared by the grace of God.

While getting ready for bed that evening, I removed a piece of jewelry I hadn't been aware of putting on that morning. It was a Christmas gift from John, a golden pendant with three small diamonds, which I thought I would never wear because of what it represented. As I stood there looking down in total disbelief, I heard *the still, small voice* from God booming out loud and clear, *"Thou shalt have no other gods before me … and no graven images.*" In my haste to get ready for work that morning, I remembered looking around in my jewelry drawer for something which might go with the neckline of my blouse. I must have tried it on absentmindedly to see how it looked and then totally forgot about it. It was *an image* of my *sun sign, Sagittarius, the Archer,* with drawn bow and arrow, and it represented *Astrology*! I believe God allowed this to happen in order to make a strong point with me about something I already knew deep within my heart, but wasn't quite ready to face up to. I promised God right then and there that I would denounce this abomination once and for all and that I would get into deep Bible Study at my first given opportunity.

One of my Christian friends had told me quite matter-of-factly *"Astrology is of the occult, and it could have opened the door to satanic attack."* She went on to say that the practice of astrology is *"an abomination to God"* and advised me to burn everything I owned associated with it. I looked up the scriptures she gave me and found it listed among many other abominations in Deuteronomy, where God refers to one who consults the stars as *an observer of times.* In Jeremiah, He makes it very clear about *those who consult, or worship, the host of heaven.* I thought back over the years of Greg's rock idols and the demonic records he owned with vibes which drove us up the wall. I remembered his affair with the rock world, Circus Magazine, the grotesque posters covering his walls, and his desire to attend every rock concert which came to town. It was all abominable!

Since I had never really studied much of the Old Testament, I questioned what my friend told me, but I looked up the verses she gave me and started reading. I had once heard a TV preacher say *"If the Bible is indeed the infallible word of God, then every word of it must be true, or then none of it is true."* My friend referred me to Deuteronomy and Jeremiah. Was it a coincidence that all of these terrible things started happening after I got involved with astrology? I didn't get much sleep that night, and, around dawn, the phone was ringing. It was Greg! He was calling to let us know that he was in the hospital, so we wouldn't worry about him, as he had done so many times before. He seemed totally unaware of what had happened! We thanked him for calling and said we would drop by to see him on our way to work. It was a long drive through heavy morning traffic to Georgetown, but, when we finally arrived at the hospital, I noticed a Metro sign at the entrance. On future visits, the subway would be the way to go because Greg was bound to be in the hospital for a very long time.

When we walked into his room and saw him lying there without his right foot under the sheet, I could only think of one thing to say — something my mother might have said — *"I'm so glad to see those toes,"* as I gently brushed my fingers across the four remaining ones of his left bandaged foot sticking out from under the sheet. I couldn't bear to think of the ones that were missing! They had started the morphine early that morning and Greg wasn't feeling a thing, nor did he seem aware of what happened. We visited for a short while and then it was time for us to leave for work. We hugged him goodbye and promised to come back for a longer visit on the weekend. I told him about seeing the Metro sign out front and mentioned that I might be able to hop on the subway once in a while to ride over from Rosslyn on my lunch hour and have lunch with him. Of course, this became a habit as the weeks passed and Greg always expected me to bring him *a Big Mac, large fries and a chocolate shake* in exchange for his hospital food. He looked forward to our weekly visits!

John and I drove over the first Saturday for a long visit and met his roommate, Ronald, a Baptist minister, who had been scheduled for back surgery when Greg was brought in. Ronald's surgery was postponed until the next day, and he called all the Christian doctors and nurses together to pray for Greg. He told us that he thought this was why God arranged for him to be at this hospital at this particular time. He tried to get into a hospital closer to his home in Woodbridge, but couldn't find one which had the right equipment for his particular type of back surgery. He said GWU was the only hospital he could find with the right equipment and the availability. He requested that Greg be assigned to his room. Ronald tried to get through to Greg regarding the dangers of alcohol and his obvious need of salvation. However, Ronald was only able to put up with Greg's rock music for a day or two and then asked to be moved to another room. Once Greg discovered his bedside radio and learned how to tune in the rock station, the nurses couldn't get him to keep the volume down.

Considering his injuries, Greg looked good and seemed happy when we visited him. We could see where the skin had been ripped off the top of his left foot and where the doctors had stapled skin grafts from his thighs. We could also see the large puncture wound on the back upper side of his right thigh where something, maybe the protruding rod of the approaching train, had miraculously pushed him aside and quite possibly saved his life. This open wound had to be cleaned out and repacked daily until it healed. Still there was no sign of Greg's awareness that something tragic had happened. A Metro representative arrived while we were there one day and told us that the driver of the train said that when she rounded the bend and saw him on the tracks, *it looked like he was bending over looking for something.* She said that when he looked up and saw the approaching train, he turned to run but there just wasn't time to get out of the way.

Greg's continuous apathy over his lost limbs caused the doctors to question his mental stability over the next few weeks. Then, one night as John and I entered the apartment, the phone was ringing. It was Greg and he was hysterical, *"Mom, I've lost my foot, and my big toe is gone! I won't be able to walk down the beach anymore! And the skin was ripped off the top of my foot!"* We must have shared his agony over the phone for an hour, as we tried to think of ways he could have a new leg made in the form of a prosthetic device that would look real. He thought of snakeskin boots that would fit over the rest of his right leg and his disfigured foot. He seemed more concerned about his disfigured left foot than the missing right one. We thought of ways his big toe might be replaced. Finally, he got it all out and seemed comforted enough to relax and get some sleep. I called the nurse's station and found they had taken him off the morphine that day and started him on Tylenol III. He later told me that he liked the morphine so much he just didn't care about what had happened to him.

Many weeks later, Greg would recount his story of that fateful day: After we left him at the bus stop to take the bus to the employment office, he boarded one headed for the Pentagon where he caught a subway train into the District. He was headed for the radio station to pick up some records he had won during the Christmas holidays. He said he was having a good day and joked around with the disc jockeys. Then he left with his records to walk back to Metro Center for the trip home when he passed a liquor store. He had no intention of buying anything and *"just walked in to look around"* when he noticed a large bottle of rum on sale. He walked out! Half-way down the block, something made him turn around and go back. He knew it was wrong, but without consideration for lessons learned, he bought the bottle of rum anyway and continued his walk to Metro Center. While waiting for his train, he placed his records down against the wall of the platform, opened the bottle and took a drink. When he saw the train coming, he placed the bottle inside his coat pocket and boarded the train. He found a seat, opened the bottle and drank some more. Somewhere along the way, he remembered his records leaning against the platform wall and decided to go back to get them. He remembered getting off at National

Airport and crossing over to the other side to wait for the next train. While standing there, he remembered offering a man a drink. Many people must have seen him in that intoxicated condition. Why didn't someone get help?

CHAPTER TWO

Prior to the Accident
1980-1981

When John and I moved from our townhouse in Vienna to the seventh floor of our high-rise apartment building in Alexandria, we were welcomed by the wonderful sounds of Hawaiian music wafting up from the swimming pool below and a gorgeous full moon overhead. We were too tired to go down to the luau, although our sweet landlady had encouraged us to join them. We were just too worn out from our long, tedious moving day! John and I preferred relaxing outside on our balcony where we could hear the music and watch the incoming air traffic into National Airport in the far distance. It was so wonderful to find peace in our new apartment which just seemed to fit our needs and was much closer to our jobs in the northern Virginia-DC area. It was a wonderful change from our recent life in Vienna: Greg was making progress in a drug rehab program at the State Hospital; Maggie was enjoying her new apartment in Vienna and her job at the Penguin Feather; and Jim was about to graduate from the University of Mississippi the following spring and get married in August. He was planning to bring his fiancée home with him for Christmas so we could get to know her. We hoped to spend some quality time with Jim and Kathleen and get better acquainted before the wedding.

Sometimes on weekends, I would sit out on the balcony and reminisce over the recent years trying to figure out just where our family had gotten so fouled up. We were such an all-American family while the kids were growing up and enjoyed all the normal activities of life: the beach, all sports events, traveling, pizza night or an occasional dinner at a good restaurant. However, when our kids reached their teens, it seemed like something took place inside them to bring out rebellion in one way or another to be like their peers. They had been raised as Christians, although we were not always in a good church environment, but they were taught right from wrong and encouraged to believe in God and have faith. What had gone wrong? Were they born with these seeds of rebellion already in them ready to blossom out at puberty? With Greg, it seemed that they developed into *seeds of destruction* as he plunged headfirst into other things, such as alcohol and drugs, which he knew were totally against us and all we believed in.

Our second son had always been the most daring of all three of our children and was bound to get himself into trouble sooner or later. When John was in Vietnam and we were living in Mobile, he told Maggie at the age of three to stand still and hold a paper cup of water on her head while he shot it off with his little bow and arrow. At six years old, it never occurred to him that he might miss. It could have put her eye out! But, thank God, it only grazed the top of her head. Jimmy, our oldest, took Greg's arrow and broke it into pieces and threw it on top of the apartment building. We were expected at my parents' home for dinner that Sunday, so I drove Maggie by the clinic first. Thank goodness, it only required a butterfly bandage. When Jimmy started to school in El Paso, Maggie became Greg's little sidekick and followed him around in her Indian outfit. One day while they were playing Indian, Greg found some matches and started a fire behind a bush in our front yard. Our next door neighbor had a better vantage point to see the whole thing and telephoned me to bring it to my attention. Sometimes, they would play Camelot, and he would tie her up in her little rocking chair in the pretense of burning her at the stake. Around the age of 10, Greg made a miniature guillotine and started cutting the heads off of Maggie's dolls, which I believe he got from watching his favorite TV show, *Dark Shadows,* when he came home from school. John came home from work one day just in time to save him from a beating by a very angry young man of 16, who was chasing him down for throwing rocks at his go-cart in front of our house. He was always daring and mischievous as a young boy, which we figured was just a natural part of growing up. However, as he grew into his teens, it was as though Greg thought himself invincible and that he could get away with just about anything. He began to *push the envelope* a little further in each situation, which seemed to increase his boldness and self-confidence but also, at times, put his life in jeopardy.

I tried to think of places we could take Jim and Kathleen while they were home for Christmas. I thought they might enjoy coming down to my office to see where I worked and then have lunch in one of the *trendy places* in Rosslyn where the young people seemed to flock in the afternoon.

After lunch, they could catch the subway into the District of Columbia to visit the museums and monuments and then meet us back at the Pentagon to ride home. They might like to visit John for lunch at the Pentagon on another day and resume their tour of Washington. We could take them to our favorite dinner theatre in Woodbridge one evening and to the Kennedy Center another. There was always something going on in the DC area, so I would have to scan the newspaper and make reservations. Kathy could have the second bedroom and Jim could sleep on a small bed behind the couch in the living room. Maggie could drive over from Vienna to spend Christmas Day with us, and I would serve my usual turkey dinner with dressing and all the trimmings. We looked forward to their visit and planned on spending our entire holiday vacation showing them around Washington.

As stated earlier, the accident hadn't come as a great surprise to either John or me. We knew that if Greg continued his dangerous lifestyle, something dreadful, out of the ordinary, was likely to happen to him. We had tried for years to get him into a substance abuse treatment program through the county court system, however, everything seemed to fall through and nothing was accomplished. Now we thought we could rest assured that he was in the right place for treatment. However, after about a month in the program attending daily meetings and receiving counseling, he became very ill with a severe stomachache and was released to the University Hospital in Charlottesville. They found an obstruction in his stomach, which needed emergency surgery, and called John for permission to operate. Of course, John gave his permission, and, a couple of days after the surgery, the hospital called to ask if we could drive down to Charlottesville to pick him up and bring him home to recuperate. We figured that our short lived peace would be shattered sooner or later, but we didn't expect it to be quite this soon. All we could do was bring Greg home and hope for a new beginning.

It was a beautiful fall day and the trees were at the peak of the season, turning to rustic shades of browns, red and gold. It was really the loveliest time of the year in the Shenandoah Valley, so we enjoyed our hour's drive through the lovely scenery to Charlottesville. John and I used this time on the way down to devise a new plan for Greg, one which we hoped would give him time to heal and a new beginning for his life. But first, there were a few very important things we had to get straight. In order for him to stay in our apartment while we were at work, he would have to remain drug and alcohol free for the safety of those who lived in our building. We needed his promise that he would spend his time studying the GED manual in hopes of passing the test as soon as possible to get his high school graduation certificate. We would also expect him to scan the daily newspaper to seek a job and a place to live in the area after his recuperation.

We enjoyed meeting the hospital staff who had taken such good care of Greg, and we were glad to see him looking so well and feeling well with a good attitude about getting on with his life. On our drive back to Alexandria, we discussed our plans for a new beginning and Greg said he was willing to cooperate. He said he wanted to pass the GED test to get his diploma from high school and that he wanted to get his own apartment and become independent. The Director of Forest Environment Research, where I worked, suggested that Greg apply for a job in one of our National Parks. He said there were wonderful opportunities for young men and great training programs to work in the National Forests. I took Greg to see a great documentary about the possibilities of working for the Forest Service, and, although it would have presented him a great opportunity and a very interesting career, he wasn't at all interested.

About a week before Thanksgiving, Greg found *a room for rent* advertised in the paper, and I drove him over to Falls Church to have a look. He would be sharing expenses with two other young men who were looking for another tenant. He could ride the bus into the city to work each day. Of course, he had to first find a job. Without hesitation, I paid the deposit and one month's rent, and we moved him in expecting him to keep his word, find a job and budget his money to pay his support. At the end of the first week, he was kicked out with all his belongings which were strewn all over the backyard. They shoved his furniture down the back stairs, and one chest of drawers was broken beyond repair. When they called me to come and get him, I had no recourse but to drive over in our station wagon and retrieve what I could. It was the most miserable day of my life and what a letdown! Greg was heavily intoxicated! He had just walked through his landlords' living room, picked up a bottle of their liquor and wolfed it down. No wonder they were throwing him out.

Greg thought he was helping me load our station wagon with all his things, but he was picking up piles of clothes mixed with dirt and throwing them haphazardly into the back of our car. What a mess! I tried to organize and reposition everything in order to get it all in the car, and, when I saw his ungodly magazine collection he had purchased with our "expense money," I immediately deposited it on top of the garbage to be picked up the following morning. When we finally got in the car to leave, the engine wouldn't start! It was so embarrassing. I had no alternative but to swallow my pride and knock on the landlords' door to borrow their phone and call a taxi. I had to leave the packed station wagon there in their driveway overnight until John could take me back the following morning to get it started and bring it home.

Greg's second committal resulted the first week of January when he dropped a lighted cigarette onto a stuffed chair at the second rooming house. He found another *room for rent* shortly before Christmas, and I drove him over to see it. The guy showing us the room looked rather shifty and didn't make a good impression, however, we were desperate to find Greg a place before Jim and Kathy arrived home for Christmas. We just didn't have enough beds to go around otherwise in our small apartment. As it turned out, Greg slept in our apartment anyway in a sleeping bag on the thick carpeting of the living room floor, so our family could all be together during the holidays. We took Kathy and Jim to see *"Oklahoma"* at the Lazy Susan Dinner Theatre, and John brought them over to meet me for lunch one day in Rosslyn. They also enjoyed having lunch with him at the Pentagon and rode the subway into the District to see the monuments and tour some of the museums. Maggie brought a friend with her for Christmas Day to share our turkey dinner, and we all enjoyed our special day together. Then a few days after Christmas, Jim and his best friend, Gill, from Morocco, who was also living in the Washington area by this time, helped Greg move into his new rooming house. Then it was time for Jim and Kathy to take off on their drive back to Ole Miss.

Greg was scheduled to start work two days later at Toys-R-Us, restocking shelves for the *after Christmas sales*. However, just when we were hoping that Greg would be able to get on with his life and his new job, and also learn some responsibility, we got a phone call from the police that he had been arrested for starting a fire at the rooming house. Again, we had paid the deposit and a full month's rent to a man who reeked of alcohol when Greg moved in. Greg wasn't sure of how the fire started, but this shifty little man pulled the chair out into the yard and watched the wind whip up the flames. According to Greg, he never even tried to put out the fire. Instead, he called the landlord, who immediately called the police to have Greg arrested. Greg said this guy already had the rum and was drinking when he offered him a drink, and he didn't really know what happened after that. Since Greg didn't drive or have access to a car, I guess we'll never know what actually transpired that day, but it sounded like a trumped up charge to me. I called the Crisis Squad to intervene and had him set up for another Court Hearing. The Judge sentenced him back to the VA State Hospital to finish the program from which he had recently been released.

The Hospital released Greg after only a couple of weeks and sent him home on a bus exactly one week before his tragic, and *near-fatal, accident,* because *they did not consider him a danger to himself or others.* Greg said it was because he was spending too much time in the restroom having to blow his nose due to a bad cold, and he said that someone locked him in there for a while before they released him. Since John had laid down the law that Greg wouldn't be allowed to come home until he completed a drug program, I had to meet his bus alone and decide what to do with him in all that freezing weather. Since we still had a few days to go on his month of paid up rent, all I could think of was to drop Greg off at the rooming house for the remainder of the time for which we had already paid. I didn't feel good about the situation, but at least he would be out of the cold for the night and that would give us time to come up with a better plan. Since John was adamant about not allowing him back into our apartment and it was getting late, I really had no alternative. Since he was told that his room was already rented on his first knock on the door, Greg knocked on the door a second time due to my insistence that he try again. This time he insisted that he be allowed to sleep on the couch in the den until we could find another place. After he was allowed inside and I drove away, the shifty little man punched him in his stomach where his stitches had been a few months earlier. Again, he called the landlord, who called the police. It was well after midnight when the policemen knocked on our front door to ask if our son could come in for the night to get out of the freezing weather.

Due to the circumstances, John reconsidered and allowed Greg to come in and stay overnight until we could devise a new plan. We could not allow him to stay in the apartment while we were at work because of his alcohol and drug addiction and the danger it presented to those who lived in our building. John said that Greg would have to leave every morning when we left for work, and he would have to spend his time looking for a job. If he managed to find one, he would be expected to work a regular work day before coming home to meet us in the lobby. Then he would be allowed to come up with us for dinner and overnight in the apartment. Greg agreed. So we dropped him off at the employment office Monday morning and left him there to register. We were very anxious to hear the results of his day of job hunting when we got home each evening, but there was not much he could tell us. He said that he had applied for a job at a nearby Mexican restaurant, but we heard no more about it. Once he had a job, we expected him to work all day and not come home until we did. He appeared to be cooperating and was ready to get in the car every morning. After the first two days, John started dropping him off at a bus stop to ride the short distance over to the employment office. However, as he told us much later after the accident, he never even entered the employment office to request a job. Each evening, we would find him sitting in the lobby waiting for us to come home, so he could come up for dinner and spend the night. He said he spent his daytime doing other things he enjoyed more than job hunting.

On Thursday, the fourth day, our worst fears were realized when John received a phone call from the emergency room at GWU Hospital asking his permission to amputate Greg's badly crushed right foot and lower leg. We prayed that somehow God would use this terrible tragedy to turn Greg's life around for the better and get him the professional help he needed to overcome his addictions. Our son was sick, and he needed help to get his life back on the right track. This time we would not allow him to come home until the hospital found him the proper treatment facility which could lead to his rehabilitation toward a good future and a productive life.

CHAPTER THREE

A Sequence of Events
1964-1973

During all our moves around the Country, when the children were most vulnerable, they became engulfed in the lifestyles of their peers. It was as though they were individual *barometers* measuring *the moral climate* of all the places we lived. They were affected by their friends in one way or another, and all the while, their characters were being molded and tested. We loved traveling around our beautiful country when our kids were small seeing all the wonderful sights together as a family, and we always took advantage of our opportunities to stop and see the interesting places along the way such as Carlsbad Caverns, the Painted Desert, the Petrified Forest, Yosemite National Park, the Grand Canyon, and the Sonora Desert. Later, when they were in their teens, we took them to Disneyland, Hawaii and Morocco. As our military life took us overseas, it was great to experience life in another country, as we learned some of the history and customs and quite naturally picked up some of the language. We also learned to appreciate the charm of our differences as foreigners in another land, and we tried to teach our kids to be good Ambassadors for God and Country. We had always been rather close knit as a military family because we needed one another when we had to leave old friends and family behind and move on to a new place.

El Paso, Texas:

When John returned to Army life in 1964, he was again assigned to Ft. Bliss. It was like coming home again, and this time, we were assigned to on- post family housing on Scott Avenue. Jimmy started to school that fall and caught the school bus right in front of our house. Greg looked so sad when Jimmy left on the bus that day because it was the first time the boys had been separated. Maggie became Greg's little sidekick and followed him around playing Indian or Camelot, etc. Jimmy learned a few words of Spanish in the first grade, so when anything was accidently broken, they blamed it on Maggie's doll and said, *the mal baby did it!* We had a double birthday party for the boys in April because their birthdays were just two weeks apart, and we invited all the kids in the neighborhood plus a couple of Jimmy's first grade classmates. My mother and dad, who had visited our relatives in Houston, drove out for a few days, and we had fun driving them around El Paso and taking them out for their first taste of Mexican food. We also drove them to White Sands Missile Range for a picnic in the National Park and then up through the beautiful mountains to Cloudcroft. While John was working one day, I drove them over to *La Posta, at Old Mesilla,* a famous Mexican restaurant just outside Las Cruces, NM where *Billy the Kid* was captured over a century earlier. They loved walking around the small town and seeing the jail where Billy was imprisoned.

John received orders for Vietnam about the time Jimmy finished his first year of school. His teacher impressed upon me the importance of spending that first year of school with one teacher in one school, because she said, "It sets the pattern for the remainder of the school years." John would be trained in Baltimore, MD as an advisor to the South Vietnamese Army, so we made the decision to keep our family together as long as we could even though the boys' school year 1965-66 would be divided between three different schools. After leaving Baltimore, John thought it important to detour by Washington, DC for a couple of nights to visit the national museums. The kids loved the Museum of Natural History and were greatly impressed with the dinosaurs and all the animals displayed in their natural habitats. The boys did fine walking all the way through the museum with their pent up energy, but John had to carry Margaret who was only three and couldn't keep up. We walked across the street to the Smithsonian where John and the boys loved seeing the airplanes and were able to buy some sandwiches and drinks for a picnic lunch on the Mall. After a brief rest, we walked down the mall area to the Washington Monument and a little further on to the Lincoln Memorial and took many pictures along the way. Then it was time to head back to the motel and prepare for our long drive to Columbus where we spent Christmas in Ohio with John's mom and dad.

Mobile, AL:

John left us in a very nice apartment on Spring Hill Avenue to be near my folks during his first year in Vietnam. As a result of Greg's interrupted first grade, he was having trouble adjusting to the new location just as Jimmy's first grade teacher had warned us about. Greg's first grade teacher at Old Shell Road School, Miss Inge, recognized his lack of self-confidence, discovered his interests and told him to bring his dinosaur collection to school for *Show & Tell.* It worked so well she had him take his display over to the other first grade class, which was taught by her sister, the other Miss Inge. Greg loved showing his dinosaur collection to his classmates, and, as a result, he became very popular with both first grade classes. Both Miss Inge are to be highly commended for their great success.

I was relieved to learn that John was not an Advisor in the jungles of Vietnam. Miraculously, he was working 16 hour days at MACV Headquarters in Saigon, and he was gaining valuable experience as an Intelligence Analyst/Briefer. It was an answer to my prayers: The position just seemed to open up for John at just the right time and the guy he replaced had been sent home early due to security issues. Many of our friends were being shipped over late in 1965 during the first big build up, and reports coming back from the wives I knew were just horrible. Most of the guys had never known combat, and, once over there, they learned the enemy was deeply entrenched in the mountains by the thousands and had been for years. Their orders were: "Find the enemy and kill them." The heartbreaking movie taken from the book, <u>We Were Soldiers,</u> tells the story of what happened to our brave young men who were given this assignment on their first mission to Vietnam in 1965. When John returned home at the end of December 1966, he was given an assignment near Mobile where we could remain a while longer near my family and enjoy our Gulf beach.

Montgomery, AL:

When John arrived home shortly after Christmas 1966, my mother and dad drove over from their home on the eastern shore to go with the kids and me to meet his plane. After having Christmas all over again in our small apartment, we enjoyed our family get-togethers until it was time to move to Montgomery where John was assigned to the Armed Forces Examining & Entrance Station (AFEES). Hoping to remain settled for a while, we purchased a new home in a new housing development near Bear School with easy access to Maxwell Air Force Base. Our family flourished that year with the boys' involvement in Little League Baseball and Cub Scouts, and, on the first day of school, I found myself volunteering as a den mother for Den 8, which would meet at our house every Wednesday afternoon from 3:30-5:30. I benefited as much as the boys from all the projects assigned to us each month. John purchased a second car, a cute little green Volkswagen to drive to work, so I would have the big car to transport the kids to their various activities, including a carpool for Margaret's kindergarten class.

I learned to dye rice and macaroni, make kites, weave baskets, and discovered many crafts I had never experienced before. I helped the boys make emblems and a giant eagle, as a centerpiece, for our dinner table at the Cub Scout's Blue & Gold Banquet, which was the highlight of the year. The second highlight was the Box Car Derby, which all the guys looked forward to because it was both fun and competitive to see who could make the fastest race car. Of course, it had to look good, too, and we had all sorts of designs and colors. To start off the year, we had a tour of Barber's Dairy where we saw how the milk got from the cows into the bottles and then into the stores, and everyone was happy when we received a round of ice cream at the end of the tour. Maggie was our little *mascot* because she went everywhere we went and even collected garbage along the highway, which we used to make our *garbage monster* that hung on a large poster in our den. The boys worked hard to earn their badges: we tackled two assignments in one when we studied *Rivers* of the world and made *Kites*. Each Cub drew the shape of his assigned River on his kite, as shown on the map, and then put the kites together themselves and flew them in our backyard. Later, each Cub drew a scene depicting a *Montagnard house or farm in Vietnam* and held up his poster at the monthly Cub Scout Pack Meeting. As each one stepped up to the microphone to tell his story, most of the guys shied away from the mike and you couldn't hear a word they said, but Greg, when it was his turn, and understanding the problem, stepped boldly up to the microphone and spoke directly into it. You could hear his voice clearly all over the auditorium.

John was the Adjutant of AFEES and was kept busy running the station and dealing with operational problems and guys coming in from all over the State of Alabama and Northwest Florida. He was able to make some changes which proved very beneficial to everyone, including more pay and better hours for the secretarial pool, which was overworked having to type all the information from all the guys coming into the Service through AFEES. John signed the boys up immediately for Little League Baseball and he played Softball and Basketball in the adult leagues. We did all our shopping at Maxwell AFB Commissary and BX and our medical needs were met at the AFB clinic or hospital. We also attended the AFB Protestant Chapel. Their baseball team, "The Eagles," with Jimmy as pitcher and Greg as catcher, won their little league tournament that year with trophies for all the players right there, too, at Maxwell Air Force Base. The boys did very well at Bear School, which was just a short drive from our home, and Margaret finished kindergarten. She learned to sprout peas and grow them in our little patio garden along with our tomatoes and bell peppers. Life was good! On Halloween night, we picked up our first pet and named her "Spookie." Then one day the following spring, after she gave birth to her first litter of kittens, John informed us that it was time to move again. The Army thought he should have some *command time* and was sending us to Milwaukee, so he could command a nuclear missile battery on Lake Michigan.

Before we left Montgomery, a funny thing happened regarding our five-year-old daughter, Margaret, who we had jokingly nicknamed "Yacky Duck," because she was always talking. John told me I could drop her off at AFEES while I had a doctor's appointment on base. Some of the secretaries at his office wanted to see Margaret because they had heard so much about her, so John took her into the Colonel's office and sat her down at his desk with some pencils and paper while he was at lunch. When the Colonel came back in unexpectedly, his secretary warned him that Margaret was in his office sitting at his desk. He had not met her either, so he gently opened the door to peek in and smile. He said that she boldly spoke up and said to him, "My daddy told me I could sit here, and do you know what he is? He's a Captain!" John said everyone in the office cracked up, especially Colonel Marcou. Wish I had been there.

Milwaukee, WS:

We arrived in Milwaukee towards the end of June 1968 and checked into the BOQ with no air-conditioning until we could find appropriate housing before school started in August. It was probably the hottest summer on record, and our cat, "Spookie," was climbing the screens of our room trying to get out. She must have gone into heat about that time after having given birth to a litter of kittens a few months earlier. Perfect timing! Eventually, she did get out! And we could hear her moaning as she circled the barracks beneath our open windows. Knowing she was probably keeping people awake, I went outside to try to coax her back in or, quite possibly, into our little Volkswagen, which was parked alongside our larger car. However, she played a game of cat and mouse with me and would come almost within my reach and then run back up under the cars. To my horror as I was sitting outside on the steps in John's bathrobe in tears with curlers in my hair, Reveille sounded! I had no idea what was happening as the doors flung open and guys dressed in fatigues came running out of the building headed for God knows where! It wasn't even dawn yet!

We celebrated Maggie's 6th birthday on the 2nd of July, 1968 in the BOQ with small chocolate cakes assembled together with toothpicks and candles. While remaining there for a couple of months, we chose to eat our main meals at Old Dutch because we loved the shakes, chili, bean soup, hamburgers and fries. However, on mornings, we ate our breakfast in the Mess Hall. Finally, we found our end unit in an apartment complex a couple of blocks from the school and registered the children. The winter was extremely cold with piercing winds like needles and pins hitting in our arms and legs. We had to bundle up and wear long, heavy pants and coats. Maggie got stuck in a snow drift on the way home from school, and the boys said they had to pull her out. She would walk out into the snow as far as she could go until she started freezing and then start screaming for someone to come and get her. I would drive them every morning, and the other kids in the neighborhood would pile into our car until it was jam packed. John had a hard time getting back and forth each day in the heavy snow with the Volkswagen. However, on Thanksgiving Day, he drove us all into Battery B on Lake Michigan in our larger car, and we finally got to see where John worked. The cook for B-Battery turned out to be a New Orleans Master Chef, and he and his crew were up all night preparing the traditional Thanksgiving Dinner. It was so good and so special for us to be there with the troops and their families! It was truly a day we would never forget! John said the Thanksgiving Prayer and blessed the food as he led all of us in the Lord's Prayer.

Ft. Bliss, TX:

The following March, just after his promotion to Major, John was released from duty in Milwaukee with new Orders to attend the Air Defense Officers Advanced Course at Ft. Bliss. On our trip from Milwaukee to El Paso, John hooked up the Volkswagen to the big car, and it served as a temporary *home* on the road for our cat. To passersby, it looked like she was driving the VW with her paws on the steering wheel, and they would laugh and point to her as they passed us. Once again, the kids' schools had to fall in place, but this time, all three almost made it all the way through the entire school year: Maggie's first grade, Greg's fourth and Jimmy's fifth. With good memories of Ft. Bliss, we felt like we were home again for the third time. We celebrated Maggie's 7th birthday in July with a birthday party and invited all the kids in our new neighborhood. The boys rode their bicycles to school on post from our new home on Snow Street, while Maggie rode the school bus with her friends.

There were a lot of good things about Ft. Bliss. We all loved Mexican food, except for Margaret, who always ordered a hamburger until she was older and decided to try a taco. We discovered Pancho's Mexican Restaurant, where the food was good and the prices right, and the owner came to know us very well that year. The kids always looked forward to Armed Forces Day, which allowed them to walk around the grounds, look at all the military vehicles and equipment and try some of them out. The boys were on their first football team, coached by one of John's best friends, and the Ft. Bliss Falcons won the El Paso City Championship. Maggie, the smallest cheerleader, also earned a trophy along with the other girls who cheered for the Falcons. Once they threw her up in the air and none of the girls thought to catch her. We have a great picture of Maggie sitting on the ground plaiting her hair totally oblivious to the football game. The coach set both boys up for a touchdown before the season was over, and, of course, Dad got a great picture of both of them. I learned a marvelous technique of oil painting over acrylics from a retired Colonel's wife, who taught me how to lift the oils in just the right places for the highlights to show through. We also put a man on the moon that year of 1969 and John bought us the largest Magnavox Color TV console he could find, so we could see the whole magnificent event from beginning to end; a truly incredible accomplishment projected by President John F. Kennedy in 1960.

John was totally absorbed in all his courses that year and was an honor graduate of the Officer's Advanced Course. He also led the winning missile design team at the end of the Guided Missile Systems Course. The two courses ended with graduation exercises in May 1970 and John was now officially an *expert* in his field of Artillery. We traded in our old Chrysler Newport for a new yellow Chrysler Town & Country Station Wagon, which came with an 8-Track tape of Tom Jones singing "Sittin' by the Dock of the Bay." Just as always, when things seemed to be going well, John received new Orders! This time, they were for his second tour of duty in Vietnam, and John would be in God's hands once again and far away from his family.

Mobile, AL:

This time, John left us in a nice apartment on Old Shell Road to be near my family and Maggie would be in the third grade at Old Shell Road School. The boys' 6th and 7th grade classes were several miles away at the middle school. Since I had to drive the boys early, I dropped Maggie off on my way back and she could walk home to go with me to pick up the boys later in the afternoon. At least they would all be able to start school at the beginning of the school year along with their classmates. When John arrived in Saigon, he was automatically assigned to his old job as Analyst/ Briefing Officer at MACV-J2 Headquarters. My youngest brother, Joseph, 12 years my junior, dropped out of college to enlist in the Army and was sent to I Corps near the DMZ to drive an armored personnel carrier. My brother, Michael, 9 years my junior, was awaiting orders for Vietnam at Ft. Benning. Our father suffered a fatal heart attack in November at the age of 69 while fishing with a friend in a small boat on Mobile Bay within sight of his home. We believe it was triggered by worry and anxiety over his sons' involvement in Vietnam. The Red Cross brought Joe home for Daddy's funeral and informed John about his death. Michael and Ginger took Joseph and Mother on a retreat to Stone Mountain to get them away for a while, so they could have some quality time together before Joe had to return to duty back in his old unit.

I spoke to the office manager of our apartment complex about breaking our lease so we could move over with Mother because she was alone and I thought she needed us. Mother never learned to drive and totally depended on our dad for transportation, so we moved across the bay to be with her.

Not wanting to break up another school year for the kids, I neglected to tell the school officials about our move, which meant I had to drive them back and forth to school each day regardless of the weather. I wrote a letter to the Army explaining our family's involvement in Vietnam, and they respected my wishes to relieve my brother, Michael, of being called to duty and allowed him to serve out the remainder of his time at Ft. Benning. He was assigned to the Accounting Office and received good experience while he and Ginger awaited the birth of their first baby. About a month after returning to duty, Joe's Unit took a direct hit while they were assembled in a bunker for an awards ceremony. John was aware of what happened but didn't know of Joe's involvement. Joe later told us that he was standing in the doorway of the bunker finishing his lunch when he heard the sound of a 122mm rocket coming straight at them. He was blown out the door with a wooden beam landing across his legs and lower back. Most of the young men inside the bunker were killed, and Joe helped dig them out. After he came home a few months later, Mother found his Purple Heart hidden in the back of a drawer.

In early February 1971, GEN Creighton Abrams, Commander of US Forces, dispatched John and a colleague to brief the flight crews aboard the US Aircraft Carriers Kitty Hawk and Ranger and the US Marine Landing Force aboard the Iwo Jima. John said that standing on the LCO platform of the Kitty Hawk watching the planes come in for a landing at midnight was a thrilling experience he will never forget, and this assignment was the highlight of his second tour in Vietnam. John's mission was to provide the intelligence assessment of the enemy's capabilities and probable course of action. His colleague would present the Army of the Republic of Vietnam and US support forces involvement in the general battle plan to strike into the panhandle of Laos to neutralize the North Vietnamese logistics base. They would do carrier landings for the first time in their lives, and they loved it! Just being aboard the Carriers was exciting as they watched the fighter planes coming in for landings and taking off on the short landing strips. After briefing the flight crews of the two Carriers and making on-board videos for the crews out on missions, they were ferried to the Iwo Jima via US Navy helicopter to brief the US Marine landing forces, which would be required to go ashore if needed. John said that he faced a totally committed landing force of American fighting men with their total focus on the mission they might be asked to perform. He said it was a very sobering moment for him, and he realized once again that American men of war, whether Army, Navy, Air Force or Marines, were truly "brothers in arms," and he was very proud to be a part.

Towards the end of February, John met me in Hawaii for his R&R, and we stayed on the 35th floor of the Hilton Hawaiian Village on the beach at Waikiki for five days. We ran into some of his friends on the beach and usually ate lunch in one of the beach restaurants with lots of melon ball salads and some really great Mahi Mahi dinners. John rented a beautiful gold Camaro and drove us all around the Island of Oahu to visit the Pineapple Plantations, lovely Waimea Falls and the very exciting Waimea Bay, where we watched surfers riding in on the waves. We drove up to the highest point of Nuuanu Pali Lookout, where John made many beautiful pictures of Diamond Head and the city of Honolulu below. We enjoyed several dinner shows, including one by Don Ho, but we especially enjoyed our leisure time on the beach listening to the music and songs sung every evening by the popular young lady singer at the Hilton Beach Pavilion. John and I had a wonderful time together those few days, although it ended much too soon. Mother and the kids stayed with Aunt Kate at her home in Mobile, so it would be easy for her to drive them back and forth to school. I returned home to find a large *Welcome Home* sign stretched across Mother's living room which the kids had made, and we left it up for John's return in May. He came home just in time to ride with me to pick them up from their last day of school.

White Sands Missile Range, NM:

For his next assignment, John requested White Sands Missile Range, New Mexico because it was the center for development and testing of the new Safeguard Anti-Ballistic Missile System, which was John's specialty. We had heard from friends that it was a great place to raise a family and had very good schools with many activities for the kids. Joe returned home just a few weeks after we left Mother alone in her house. Our family flourished for a year and a half at White Sands from the summer of 1971 through the end of 1972. Jim 14, Greg 13, and Maggie 10 were all able to settle down into a more *normal* way of life. Our original plan was to stay there for as long as we could, and the boys were very active in sports: Jimmy won MVP in Basketball; Greg won MVP on his junior league baseball team; and Maggie went on her first overnight camping trip with the Girl Scouts. John took us on a special vacation that summer to see the

Grand Canyon, and we spent about a week driving around a portion of its southeastern rim. Everyone enjoyed the functions of the Officers' Club, and I became active in the Officers' Wives Club.

It was here in this environment that I became involved in the study of astrology with one of my friends who held an office in the Officers' Wives Club. Lani was a very attractive and colorful lady of Chinese descent from Hawaii, and a very good cook. She loved entertaining in their beautifully decorated home with Chinese red carpeting and taught me how to make Chinese spareribs, wontons, bacon wrapped water chestnuts, egg rolls and many other authentic Chinese dishes which she often served at her parties. Her husband and son often played golf with John and Jimmy and all the kids loved swimming in the large O-Club swimming pool, just a short distance from our house. Lani called on me to help in her preparation and delivery of the OWC Newsletter, which we delivered with the help of our kids, and our SAFSEA Cookbook containing the favorite recipes of all the ladies. She coaxed me into having a New Year's Eve party at our small home to welcome in the New Year, which turned out to be a lot of fun.

White Sands Missile Range was located just a short drive over the winding mountain pass to Las Cruces and a couple of hours north of Ft. Bliss. We had a fantastic view of the lovely Organ Mountains from our fenced-in backyard and our kitchen window. We had a small garden of tomatoes and bell peppers, of which John traded a few to one of his colleagues for Poblano peppers to use in our Mexican cooking. Greg sold Christmas cards around the neighborhood to earn a small red ball & chain radio and a set of bow and arrows, and he became very good at hitting the bull's-eye. His target was carefully set up inside our redwood fence. John and I made long-lasting friends there at White Sands Missile Range, and we enjoyed having people over for backyard barbecues. The kids had a Halloween party and invited all the kids on post. They had a great time and the kid who won first prize for best costume had an arrow going through his head. It was a friendly family environment and we loved living there.

In spite of our plans to stay settled for several years to give the kids a chance for a more normal way of life, the Army, as usual, had other plans. Congress was in the process of shutting down the whole Anti-Ballistic Missile Program, and John was hoping to be selected as Commander of the first site being built in North Dakota. When construction on the site was permanently halted, he contacted the Military Personnel Center to inquire about his possibilities. Because there was no place for advancement in his field of training in Guided Missile Systems anymore, he elected to switch over to Intelligence and started attending Seminars at the University of Oklahoma working towards a Master's degree in Public Administration. He also made the decision to become a Foreign Area Officer (FAO), and the Army issued new orders for John to attend the University of Arizona to earn his Master of Arts degree in Oriental Studies. They were lacking specialists in that area of the world. He would specialize in the Middle East and North Africa. We had mixed feelings about leaving our home at White Sands, but it was time to move on to our next assignment: Tucson, AZ.

Tucson, AZ:

Tucson was an exciting new place for our growing family although we came at mid-year and the kids were in three different schools. It was Jimmy's first year of high school, Greg was in junior high, and Maggie, still in elementary school, was able to ride her bike. I volunteered as *another mother* to work in the school office, and I also drove our station wagon loaded with kids on numerous school outings. Maggie's 5th grade teacher was happy to inform me that she would be promoted the following year to teach 6th grade, and Maggie would be promoted along with her to the next level. I took my tape recorder to Margaret's end of year graduation ceremony, when all the kids were promoted to the next grade level, and the program was so beautiful it brought tears to my eyes as it ended with "Sunrise Sunset." I felt the years drifting by so rapidly, and I was overwhelmed with emotion every time I listened to it.

It was here in this apartment, while making the beds one morning after everyone had left for school, that a feeling of depression and gloom came over me, and I had what I believe might have been a prophetic vision of the future. As I lay there across the end of one of their beds looking out over the desert, I felt so far from home and was left with a feeling of insecurity for our family because our kids had absolutely no roots to keep them firmly planted in good soil for a good and solid upbringing. I felt helpless because the world was changing and there was nothing I could do about it. Someone had stolen Greg's wooden chest from his wood working class, which he was so proud of, and then someone stole Maggie's bike, which she rode to school every day and had been locked in the bike rack behind our apartment. We drove all over the neighborhood looking for the bike but couldn't spot it anywhere. I always believed that God was watching out for us and with Him all things are possible. I knew I had to hang on to my faith so He could bring us through all these unpleasant situations. Then one of Maggie's friends brought over two little white mice in a cage to give her and told me "not to worry! They would never have babies because they were both girls." In a matter of days, there were tiny white mice going right through the bars of the cage, and I found them all over the apartment … but somehow, most of them ended up in the dirty clothes basket in the bathroom, which made them somewhat easier to collect. I had no choice but to take them to the pet store hoping they could be sold: at worst, they might become food for the snake, a horror the girls were quick to warn me about. I worked to improve my Mexican cooking and tackled one of my, and John's, favorites, *Chilies Relleno.*

On a trip one day to buy groceries at the Air Force Base Commissary, I signed John up to coach a Pony League baseball team, and he was assigned to coach the Cardinals. It gave him a break from his constant studies and also a little exercise, which he badly needed. And it gave the rest of the family a change of pace to get out of the apartment and root for something. Both boys were on John's team: Jimmy as pitcher and third baseman, and Greg as catcher and outfielder. It was fun watching the games and the Cardinals did very well, but the parents were always arguing and I wondered whatever happened to good sportsmanship. Jimmy was selected to the All-Star team for the League that year, but the best part of the game for Maggie and me was going out to Shakey's when the game was over. She and I learned to secure our two pieces of pizza on our plates before the guys devoured them all right before our eyes! We all loved the player piano and the draft root beer! It seemed strange to wake up to snow on the ground around the swimming pool that winter in Tucson.

I loved working at the elementary school a few days each month and felt secure when things were going well for the kids. I drove a carload of Maggie's classmates through the beautiful Sonora Desert to the Sonora Desert Museum, which included a guided walking tour. It was one of the highlights of the year for me and a very memorable day for the kids. I learned as much as they did about animal life on the desert from what we found along the trails, and I found everything the guide shared with us very interesting and somewhat amusing. The boys attended their first rock concert and Greg won his first prize over the rock radio station. The first rock music I heard was "Joy to the World," and I saw no harm in that. It sounded almost Biblical!

John worked hard getting his Master's degree at the University of Arizona, and I typed all his papers and theses (with hardly any errors.) They were beautiful! And I joined him in learning much about the Middle East. The kids remember my typing all night long that last night, as he handed his handwritten pages to me as soon as he finished writing them, including a very long report on "Lawrence of Arabia." That last night turned into the next day with me still typing as the movers were hauling out our furniture. The kids found the branch of a Christmas tree on their way home from school, and we put it in the back of our station wagon, which we named "The Yellow Submarine." We planned to detour over to Anaheim for four days at Disneyland, and they placed the tree in the middle of a table at the Cosmic Age Motel and propped it up with all our Christmas gifts. We decorated it beautifully with candy and gum wrappers. Breakfasts were especially good with great coffee at Hills Brothers' Café and Christmas Dinner was absolutely fantastic. I learned to add sliced water chestnuts to my turkey dressing.

CHAPTER FOUR

A Sequence of Events II

1974-1975

Ft. Bragg, NC:

Leaving California on our way to Ft. Bragg was a real drag. We were three hours behind when we arrived and had to get up in what seemed like the middle of the night to get the kids off to school their first day. Jim was in high school, Greg in middle school and Maggie still in grammar school. John had to be at the orientation of the FAO Program early that first Monday morning, so it was my job to get all three kids off to their correct schools on busses going in three different directions, which proved very embarrassing for Jim. For some reason, I thought he was on the wrong bus, so I chased it down to find out that it was the right bus. When I climbed the steps of the bus, looked in and said, "Jimmy, you're on the wrong bus!" he was nowhere to be seen, so I assumed the bus driver was right and Jim had gone into hiding mode somewhere on the bus. Greg adjusted quickly and made a couple of friends at his school, but Maggie's school was a big letdown for her after the wonderful school year she experienced in Tucson. She wasn't at all happy until she signed up for girls' softball at the beginning of the season. However, it was time to move again before the season was over, and she suffered another big letdown. Jim did very well on his high school's golf team, and one of his best friends went on to become a very successful "Pro."

John had classes every day in the FAO Course, and I was able to join him in the French Course one day each week. Since it was a rather condensed course, it required us to study as often as possible, especially those of us who had never studied French. Since it was totally foreign to me, I really needed to study after getting the family settled in temporary quarters and off in three different directions to school. However, John insisted that I attend the home maintenance course the previous day, which I had taken at every military post we had lived on and already knew how to patch screens and clean ovens, etc. I was not at all prepared that first day, so, naturally, the teacher called on me to read. I turned to the guy on my right and asked, "Where are we?" Not only was I embarrassed, but I was a little peeved at John for not allowing me to stay at home the previous day to study. Anyway, Gary, the guy on my right, and his wife, Nancy, who was sitting to his right, became two of our best friends at Ft. Bragg, and we have tried to keep in touch over the years through our Christmas cards and letters.

Our French class was hilarious! We had more fun that day than any other day of the week, I guess because we, the wives, were involved. Also, we owe a lot of our fun to a wonderful guy who was a very good sport. He had received a Master's degree in Spanish, and every time the teacher called on him to read, it came out that way... like Spanish. We tried not to laugh at first, but, it was so funny, we just couldn't help it, and, after a while, we were practically rolling in the aisles. John, who has a very high language aptitude, passed our French refresher course with a 2-1, although he had many more subjects to study. I was very happy to pass with a 1-1. We attended many FAO functions together and made many long lasting friends. When we left Ft. Bragg, all the guys were talking about which country they wanted to select for their in-country training. The time passed quickly, and soon it was time to head West again for the next leg of our journey: Language School at the Presidio of Monterey. After leaving Ft. Bragg, we drove west to Ohio and then south to Alabama to see all the grandparents before heading back across the country for another year in California. First, though, we took time out to take the kids for a week's vacation on our beach at the Gulf.

Monterey, CA:

We took our time driving across the lovely deserts of Texas, New Mexico and Arizona and enjoyed stopping for Mexican food in a few places we remembered along the way. Then we headed up the California coast to the Presidio of Monterey, where John was scheduled to begin classes in Arabic. Now we were venturing into new territory, and, after spending the first night in a motel, we took the short drive around the Peninsula to get the layout of the Presidio and the lovely white, crescent-shaped sandy beach of Monterey. John checked us into the BOQ at Ft. Ord for a few days and applied for on- post housing. When he found out that a house would not be available for another month, we decided to look for temporary lodging at Asilomar Beach, just a couple of blocks from the Pacific Ocean and only a short drive over to the Language School. Nearby was historic *Cannery Row,* once famous for its sardine canning industry, which now lay abandoned except for a few dilapidated old warehouses, some of which had been renovated and turned into modern-day shops or restaurants; among them, *The Spaghetti Factory,* loaded with atmosphere and great Italian food. In a Spanish style building with a fantastic view of the harbor, we discovered our favorite Mexican Restaurant, *Tia Maria.* Also nearby was famous *Fisherman's Wharf,* alive with all sorts of wiggly sea creatures and the pungent smell of fish. The quaint little shops of Carmel, the wind-blown Cypress trees on the misty ocean drive and the rocky shoreline containing hundreds of seals swimming and sunning themselves on the rocks, were all part of the charm of the Presidio of Monterey.

We were surprised to find a very nice home in our on-post housing at Ft. Ord and two great golf courses. Our new home was quite roomy with beautiful parquet floors and a nice enclosed patio. I bought the end of a bolt of white rice cloth for making drapes for its many full-length windows and some remnants of carpeting to cover some of the floors. Plants seemed to flourish in the cool, moist climate, and I noticed Swedish Ivy and Asparagus Fern in hanging baskets everywhere. Another beautiful plant, Fuchsia, which Mother said was my grandmother's favorite, also seemed to thrive beautifully and did very well in hanging baskets. I placed our lovely basket of Swedish Ivy in front of the large sliding glass door of our living room where it could get the morning sunlight and it also did very well. Jim helped me finish the boys' bedroom suite in an antique green with new brass drawer pulls, and their bedroom looked great with their large brown, gold and green striped bedspreads and light brown curtains with dark brown trim. We purchased a corner group for Maggie's bedroom with a table, lamp and two twin beds to go with her small chest of drawers which Jim also antiqued in the same green and brown. John turned our largest walk-in closet at the end of the hallway into a study where he could keep his language books and tapes, and, with the aid of a headset, he could drown out the noise of our active family with his favorite classical music and language tapes during his many hours of study. He did very well in learning the Arabic language and became quite fluent.

During Christmas vacation 1974, we drove over to Yosemite National Park where we reserved a cabin and took a bus tour around the lake. The scenery was incredible with majestic "El Capitan," the gigantic waterfall, "Mirror Lake" and the surrounding mountains, all breathtakingly beautiful. We saw people sledding in the snow and a nearby wolf walking through the same area seemingly unnoticed. It was a great trip thanks to the coaxing of our next door neighbors who loaned us their winter boots, jackets and gloves to make the trip. John's mother and dad visited us in February, and we enjoyed showing them around the Presidio and the shops of Carmel along with the historical places around Fisherman's Wharf and Cannery Row. We took them out to eat at our favorite restaurants there, and I think they enjoyed the Spaghetti Factory most of all because of the atmosphere and, of course, the great Italian food. They made lots of pictures of Monterey's white sandy beach and the lovely drive around the Presidio. We also drove them up the Pacific coastline to the Presidio of San Francisco where we had a long rest stop and took many pictures of the famous Golden Gate Bridge... then turned around to come back to Monterey. It would have been nice to drive across the bridge, but we didn't want to get caught up in all the heavy afternoon traffic.

John bought a second-hand Toyota for our use as a second car soon after our arrival, so I would have the station wagon to drive as needed, and, when we left the following summer, he was able to sell the smaller car for the same price. A family moved in next door on the other side of us, and the mother asked *"How do you get your boys to dress so nicely in slacks?"* Her 12-year old son, just back from Germany, wouldn't wear anything but jeans. She confided that her niece was coming for Christmas, and she was planning to have a taco party for her, so she invited Maggie and the boys over to meet her. Her sister's family had been having a lot of trouble with her, and she thought meeting our boys and Maggie might set a good example. Looking back, the opposite may have been true: Greg was very impressionable at the age of 15, and the girl was cute! The kids enjoyed the taco party and all seemed well for a while, but the impression had been made.

Jim was a major golfer on his high school's golf team shooting par or better, and he and his dad played a lot of golf several times a week. Greg was off to a good start in his second year of high school and was doing very well in all his courses. The father of the three children who lived next door to us on the other side was impressed with Greg and hired him to child-sit his three children while he and his wife enjoyed an occasional outing. One of his sons was crippled due to a childhood illness and he needed a little extra help in getting around, so he hired Greg to fill in while they occasionally enjoyed getting out to a movie or having dinner. They took the family to Yosemite for a wonderful vacation around Christmas and inspired us to do the same during the holidays after Christmas. Greg was a responsible teenager at that time and enjoyed wood working... he finished some beautiful boards for me at the woodshop out of wormwood, which I used in making some decorative wall plaques for our kitchen. One of my new friends, Rhoda, a former classmate of John's from Ole Miss, lived a few houses down and taught me how to make *Garbage Art* out of cereal boxes.

Garbage art was a clever technique of drawing the designs for *fruit* or *vegetables* in three dimensions from patterns on the plain side of cereal boxes. After cutting out the parts and gluing them in layers on pieces of finished wood forming a 3-D effect, I put my oil pallet to good use in painting the formations on the plaques for the finished product. They turned out very well and even looked quite professional for decorating the kitchen with fruits, vegetables and berries. Some of the berries were in lattice worked baskets and looked quite decorative. Rhoda taught me to make NFL quilts using NFL sheets on one side with a plain color on the other, which folded over to make the binding. She also gave me the directions for making *Sock Monkeys* out of men's work socks and I made one for each of the kids. Rhoda was very talented and just the person I needed to get me motivated again after making all our drapes and antiquing the boys' bedroom furniture. We went to OWC meetings together and drove around the area looking for antiques. We found some beautiful *Tiffany-style lamp shades* in a variety of colors at *Little Baja*, a Mexican import store, and I bought two of them to take with me to Morocco.

While John was heavily engaged in learning Arabic, he kept us informed about the country we were assigned for his in-country training. Jim 16, Greg 15, Maggie 12 and I plunged into the study of his first assigned country: Ethiopia. It seemed intriguing and had a Christian background, but, before we could really get deeply involved, the Army notified John that this country was cancelled because their President, Haile Salassi had been overthrown. Now it was considered too dangerous for a family tour, so he was assigned Lebanon. Again, we were given material to study and were looking forward to living in Beirut, *the Paris of the Middle East*, when war broke out in Lebanon on an even greater scale, and that country was cancelled. Finally, John received orders for Morocco, and we looked forward to living in the Capitol City of Rabat. This country was more stable and had a strong French influence. Since both of us had taken the French refresher course during the FAO program, it seemed a good choice. He tried to teach us a little basic Arabic to go along with the French, and we all became interested in learning everything we could about life in Morocco.

John's Lebanese language instructor took us to a nearby park where he demonstrated how to prepare Arabic food. Some of our favorite dishes, which I still prepare today are as follows: *Arabic Moussaka:* In a large casserole dish, place layers of fried sliced eggplant, which have been cooked in hot olive oil, slices of one large onion, 1 lb. ground beef, or lamb, seasoned with salt and pepper and browned in skillet, thick slices of 2 large tomatoes; strips of one green bell pepper and covered with 1 cup hot water with 1 Tbsp. lemon juice. Bake 45 minutes in 350-degree oven. This is great served over Rice accompanied with Pita Bread. *Arabic Cauliflower:* Break cauliflower into florets and sauté in hot olive oil seasoned to taste with garlic salt, pepper and lots of cinnamon sprinkled liberally over florets as it is cooked until just tender and serve hot. *Arabic Rice & Fried Chicken:* Fry chicken in hot vegetable oil and set aside. Place one cup rice with some broken Vermicelli in drippings with several thinly sliced green onions and chopped bell pepper. Brown slightly in skillet and add 3 cups chicken broth to simmer until rice is done (about 20 minutes), then season to taste with salt and pepper. John's instructor went on to tell us that *Lamb* and *Chicken* are the preferred meats in the Middle East. *Tagines* are very popular in Morocco and usually served with couscous. *Shawarmas*, consisting of layers of thinly sliced lamb, chicken, and veal rotating on vertical rotisseries are very popular all over the Middle East. They are kept hot and moist by the frequent swabbing of sauces, as layers are continuously sliced off and served inside pita bread.

John and Jimmy played golf every chance they got after work or on holidays, and I was always busy with my projects. Greg and I would usually watch the afternoon movie while he did his homework and I worked on quilts or other projects, and Maggie was usually reading, doing homework or working on art projects in her room. One afternoon, Greg was not there to see the second part of a movie I knew he wanted to see.

I called him but he was nowhere to be found. Half an hour later, Greg's next-door friend, Jack, knocked on our front door and told me to come quickly to help Greg. Not having any idea of what he was trying to tell me, I followed Jack outside and around the house where I bumped into Greg all covered with dirt trying to come in through the patio gate. I had never seen him like that before, and he was quite obviously intoxicated. He could hardly stand up to walk and was bumping into everything. I ushered him inside the patio and through the kitchen door to our bedroom where he passed out on the carpet. As soon as John pulled up out front, I ran out to prepare him for what he was about to find on our bedroom floor.

We both assumed that Greg was experimenting, as some teenage boys are prone to do, and hopefully, he would learn from this a valuable lesson of what not to do in the future. John helped him into the bathroom, where Greg threw up most of the concoction he had been drinking in the desert behind our house. John got him into the bathtub for a bath and then into his pajamas before putting him to bed. The next day, Greg told us that he and Jack mixed together all the different kinds of liquor they could find in both their houses and took it out to the desert in back of our houses to drink. Jack was supposed to be involved in the experiment, too, but when he saw what it was doing to Greg, he very wisely backed out. Greg said he had some weird hallucinations which really scared him. We didn't go back there along the firing range to see what they had left behind. As far as we were concerned, *the experiment,* which we considered a total disaster, was over and done with. We didn't think Greg would ever try that again.

After Greg's experiment with alcohol, everything returned to normal for about a month. Then one afternoon as I was busily engaged in my work, the doorbell rang, and I discovered a couple of long-haired boys standing at the front door, one wearing sunglasses. They asked for Greg, and, before I could turn around, Greg appeared behind me as though he were expecting them. They were the guys he had met at the bus stop. Normally, he would have introduced me, but this time, they all entered the house and walked back to his room. The door closed! No sooner had it closed than it reopened and all three of them paraded out the front door. About 20 minutes later, I heard Greg trying to climb in through his bedroom window and suggested that he come in as usual through the front door. I knew by his odd behavior that something was going on. I noticed a rustling sound underneath his jacket, as he entered the house and quickly walked down the hall to his room closing the door behind him. Quickly, I opened the door and walked in to find him trying to hide something in the top of his closet. It was a potato chip bag and, inside the bag, a large wad of what I assumed to be marijuana. Greg told me that it belonged to one of the boys who wanted him to hold it for a while, so he wouldn't get into trouble. Greg had just turned 16 and I had never known him to smoke anything or to have been in any kind of trouble, so I told him to take it back to the boys and let them worry about it. In hindsight, I should have called the MPs to *nip it in the bud* and just let the chips fall where they may. Greg told me later that it was his, but he had been ripped off and it was only oregano. Whatever it was, I never saw another trace of anything that looked like marijuana again as long as we lived at Ft. Ord.

Towards the end of the year, John's Iraqi language instructor invited us to his home where his wife had been cooking for days preparing many wonderful dishes for us to sample of the many typical foods prepared in the Middle East. Her table was literally covered with these well-prepared dishes. The most popular dips were *Hommous and Baba Ghanoush*, served in flat bowls with triangles of pita bread. My favorite was Hommous, which was made out of chick peas, lemon juice, minced garlic and tahini sauce all blended together and spread out in a bowl, then dribbled with a little olive oil with tiny slivers of green onion and black olives around the edges and a little cumin sprinkled on top. *Baba Ghanoush*, a little harder to make, consisted of roasted, peeled and mashed eggplant mixed with minced garlic and tahini sauce dribbled with olive oil. Most dinners are preceded by dips, pita bread and condiments already on the table.

We learned that *Kofta* is one of the most popular dishes in the Middle East and is a blend of minced lamb, finely chopped onions, parsley and fresh mint leaves mixed with a little salt and cumin and formed into patties, or kebabs molded around skewers, and grilled or fried in hot oil and served as a meat dish with rice or vegetables. *Falafel* is also a very popular dish and is very similar to the above, but it is a meatless dish made of chick peas blended together with olive oil, garlic, coriander, cumin, salt and black pepper and formed into patties and cooked in hot oil and drained well before serving inside pita bread with sauces; or it can be served like a hamburger with the usual condiments. *Stuffed Grape Leaves* are also very popular and are usually served as an appetizer or side dish. These are made from ground lamb or beef, with or without rice, and seasoned with similar spices mixed together and rolled inside grape leaves before dropping into hot oil to cook meat mixture and drained before serving warm. *Kebabs* are skewered strips of lamb, chicken or beef which are broiled, or grilled, until done and usually served with rice as a main dish and a salad such as Tabouli. *Tabouli* is a very popular salad made largely from parsley, mint and prepared cracked wheat, and is served all over the Middle East. The following recipe is for a large gathering: Three medium cubed tomatoes, 1 cup minced scallions, ½ cup chopped mint leaves, 2 ½ cups chopped parsley. Add 1 cup bulgur, *cracked wheat*, which has been twice soaked and pressed well. Mix in with vegetables. Just before serving, add the following *Salad Dressing*: 6 Tbsp. olive oil, 4 Tbsp. lemon juice, 2 tsp. salt and ¼ tsp. pepper. This large salad keeps well and is very popular at picnics or other large gatherings.

Greg obviously succeeded in his next attempt to buy *pot* from the boys at the bus stop! We could tell by his appearance every afternoon when he came home from school. It didn't take us long to recognize the symptoms of his addictive behavior. Our kitchen displayed evidence of Greg's craving for food known to that generation as *the munchies*. Once he got started, he plunged into it *whole hog* and everything about him changed. He was fired by our next door neighbor from child sitting because of his unreliability. Greg regressed back to the age of his 12-year-old neighbor. At the end of the school year, his Geometry teacher called to say that he was passing Greg but strongly advised that he take Geometry over the following year if he planned to go to college. He said Greg had done well the first half of the year, but, for the last few months, he seemed to be day dreaming out the window and was not paying attention. We hoped the upcoming move into a new environment would produce enough change in Greg's life to bring him out of it.

Vacation Time: Hawaii

Since we had the entire summer to travel to New York to catch our plane for Morocco, we decided to catch a hop to Hawaii while we were on the West Coast. We had promised the kids that someday we would show them Hawaii, where we had met on John's R&R from Vietnam in 1970. We drove to Travis AFB hoping to get a lift to Hickam AFB. It was a long drive and we arrived late and checked into the BOQ for a good night's sleep before boarding a plane for Hawaii the following day. John signed us up early, but there were only single seats, or doubles, available all day long, and we were just about to give up and head back to the BOQ when we heard over the intercom that a C- 141 Starlifter transport plane was scheduled for takeoff with plenty of seats available. So we took them and boarded. It had little insulation, if any, and we had to ride backwards all the way, but at least we were on board -- for the slowest and most miserable flight of our lives! Maggie and I each took one of my nerve pills because she was about to have a panic attack and we needed sleep. It was impossible! The sound and vibrations of the airplane were just awful, and I wondered how our troops ever made it across the ocean and landed in combat readiness. It had to be the longest night of our lives, and, after we finally arrived at Hickam several hours later, the sun refused to come up and the busses were not running. We sat there and waited for a bus to show up for another couple of hours, then loaded all our suitcases on board for Ft. De Russey.

Thank goodness Ft. De Russey could provide us with the information we needed to find a good hotel suite for a family of five at reasonable cost. We selected the Royal Aloha just two blocks behind the Hilton Hawaiian Village and were finally able to get some rest. From the next day on, we had a fabulous time and everything was great! For ten glorious days, we rode busses all over the Island of Oahu and saw everything from the Rain Forest to the Pineapple Plantation and, in between, the Arizona Memorial, Paradise Park, Sea World, and the Polynesian Cultural Center plus all the free shows at Ft. De Russey. We just happened to arrive in time for the Army's 200th Anniversary and enjoyed a wonderful Luau on the beach at Waikiki with free shows and spectacular fireworks. The view of Diamond Head was fantastic and the water was cool, clear and sublime. Our main pastime was fun in the sun just walking the beach looking for shells and souvenirs. We discovered the *free Kodak Show* downtown which turned out to be a wonderful historical movie about Hawaii, the native Hawaiians and a short narrative about the bombing of Pearl Harbor. We walked around Honolulu shopping for souvenirs to bring home with us: shirts, sandals, and lots of shell jewelry for Maggie and me. Even the boys liked the *Puka Shells* which looked great with a suntan. Then we would select our favorite restaurant for the evening, which usually turned out to be Chinese because the Chinese food in Hawaii is the best you can find anywhere. Jim, Greg and Maggie were finally able to see where John and I had spent his R&R from Vietnam several years before, and Greg was his old self again and enjoying every bit of it.

After the first week, John made a couple of trips out to Hickam AFB to try to get us a hop back to the mainland but quickly found that it was a losing battle and he was losing valuable vacation time with us on the beach, so he bought us all airline tickets on Pan Am for our trip back to San Francisco. From there we took the shuttle from the airport back to Travis AFB to pick up our car. Once back home again at Monterey, it was time to wash clothes and repack for the cross-country trip. The movers packed our household goods for storage, and we packed the shipment of our personal belongings to be shipped to Rabat. Then it was time to clear quarters, pass inspection and head south for Anaheim, where we celebrated Maggie's 13th birthday and the Fourth of July at Disneyland. It was another fantastic vacation!

After leaving Disneyland, we drove east to visit our families in Mobile, Memphis and Ohio before arriving in New York to visit John's brother, Mark, who lived right in the heart of Manhattan. We checked into our lodging at Ft. Hamilton where John called Mark to get directions to his apartment. Mark ordered pizzas for all of us to share that evening as we visited and made plans for the following day. He took us on a *walking tour* of New York City and showed us great places to eat on the way to the Twin Towers, the UN Building and many other great places of interest. We stopped for lunch in a small *bistro*, where Mark advised us on what to order and then we walked by Central Park. We enjoyed our whole day with Mark. Then it was time to head back to our quarters at Ft. Hamilton to get a good night's sleep before our overnight flight to Morocco.

John was up early the following morning to find an auto repair shop in Brooklyn, which could fix the back window of our station wagon, so it would close tightly before its overseas journey. The kids and I were ready to go to JFK, where John left us in the Pan Am Terminal while he drove our '69 Chrysler Town & Country down Long Island to the Port of Bayonne, NJ for its transatlantic voyage. After taking care of that very important issue, John caught a bus to Grand Central Station, and then transferred to another bus to bring him back to the airport. When he found us, our flight to Morocco was right on schedule and we boarded within the hour. The kids and I were all excited about our first trip across the Atlantic Ocean, and we were ready for Morocco, the mysterious country we had learned so much about.

CHAPTER FIVE

A Time for Morocco

1975-1976

Our flight across the Atlantic Ocean touched down very early the following morning in Lisbon where we managed our baggage through Portuguese Customs and then had to re-board our plane for the remaining short flight to Casablanca. Still half asleep, we then had to pass through Moroccan Customs. There to meet us was our driver from the US Embassy to take us to our new home in Rabat. It was a very interesting drive through the lovely countryside with all sorts of new sights which kept us fascinated all the way in spite of our jetlag. We were driven to a stately old French Villa located on a main thoroughfare overlooking the lovely Bou Regreg River valley. There to greet us was the Defense/Army Attaché, COL Lawrence Thompson, and his lovely wife, Laura. They had completely stocked our large kitchen and supplied us with linens until our shipment of household goods had time to arrive. There also to meet us was our houseboy, Ali, who sort of came with the house to tend the gardens and take care of our needs. He would be there every morning at 8:00 am. After this warm welcome, the Thompsons left so we could get some rest and settle into our new home.

COL Thompson gave John general instructions for his year of in-country training and provided him with books and information to study at home. On his first morning of duty at the Embassy, John met the US Ambassador and his staff and was introduced to the other Embassy personnel. They also arranged for our temporary transportation to get around the country while awaiting our station wagon's arrival at the port of Kenitra. As a FAO, John had his own separate budget under the Embassy's Budget Officer. He would use that budget to visit the major countries in North Africa and the Middle East, meet the US Ambassadors and the government officials, and he would familiarize himself with their political and military structures. He would also enjoy sampling the food and life styles of each country and, of course, tour the historical places. When he returned from his trips, he would write lengthy reports describing what he experienced, who he met, how he was treated, and what he accomplished in each country.

Our family would experience life in Rabat, and they would have stayed there well past our one year had they been given the choice. During the year, we would visit all the large cities and important places: Casablanca, Tangier, Fez, Meknes, Oukaimaden, high in the Atlas Mountains, and Maggie would visit Marrakech with her 8th grade class. We would visit the famous ruins of *Volubilis*, where an historic battle took place in Roman times and where a scene was filmed of the Roman ruins in the movie, *Patton*. We would make many new friends associated with the American Embassy and have many memorable adventures. Our sons, Jim 17 and Greg 16, would attend Kenitra High School, located about 20 miles north of Rabat on a US Naval Base, and they would be picked up in front of our house around 7:00 am and dropped off in the afternoon by a Kenitra School Bus. Maggie, age of 13, would attend the Rabat American School and would be provided school bus transportation leaving around 7:30 am.

A few days after our arrival, we were invited to a welcoming party at the home of the Naval Attaché who lived next door to the US Embassy. Our house was just around the corner and quite convenient to both the Embassy and the Marine House, which was located next door to the home of the Naval Attaché. His son Gill, and Jim became good friends over the year, and, like clock work, Jim would disappear after dinner every evening. At first we didn't know where he was going, but it soon became apparent that all the young people were flocking to the Marine House. With the young Marines there to keep charge, it was like a Teen Center with juke box and tile floors for dancing, a welcoming place where all the teens loved to hang out. On special occasions, they would have catered parties and send out invitations. They were great hosts and always had good food, dancing and socializing for all the teens and the older crowd, too. It took about a month for our station wagon to arrive, so walking around the corner was very convenient. All the kids enjoyed movies shown at the Embassy on Friday and Saturday nights. Finally, one of the guys John worked with at the Embassy arranged for him to use an extra pickup truck, a bright green Dodge Ram, and we were able to drive over to Kenitra Naval Base for shopping at the Commissary and BX.

John and I were invited to occasional dinner parties at COL Thompson's home, but we were not invited to dinner parties of the others due to the nature of John's in-country training. One evening upon our arrival at the Thompsons' home. Laura met us at the door and asked if I would help her greet the guests because her husband was tied up in a meeting with King Hassan regarding a war going on in the desert against the "Polisario, the rebels seeking independence for the Western Sahara." When COL Thompson arrived, of course, everyone was interested in finding out what was going on in the Desert. Even then *the rebels* were causing trouble in southern Algeria, and, a few years later, we learned of many training camps in that region.

Laura proved to be an excellent hostess and a very dear friend. I valued her friendship immensely. She and her driver picked me up one day and took me along with them to the vegetable soup. It was the first time I had ever seen such a vast display of so many kinds of vegetables, fruits and flowers in such large quantities with so many people flocking in to barter for the produce. Since I didn't intend to hire a cook, as many did at a very minimal cost, or have large dinner parties, I would do all my shopping at the Kenitra Naval Base Commissary, or sometimes at the Embassy convenience store around the corner. We were instructed to soak our leafy vegetables in Clorox water for about 20 minutes and then rinse well before using in salads. I invested in a 2 gallon electric coffee maker, which I filled each morning to the top with tap water, and I kept hot all day for coffee, tea, drinking water and rinsing purposes.

Laura and her driver picked us up one Sunday morning to introduce us to the small Protestant church which held weekly services a short distance away. It was held by missionaries, and I was very impressed to find Christian services in this Muslim country. I thought we would start attending this church and was anxious to tell John about it, however, circumstances crept in and I never had transportation. By the time the weekend rolled around, everyone had plans: John and Jimmy played golf with their golf buddies, Maggie was usually visiting her friend, Janet, at her house, and Greg had plans of his own. So I busied myself with reading, working on hobbies or cooking and just tried to keep up with our family. Dinner was usually at a set time in the afternoon when all the family would be home. Sometimes, Maggie, Greg and I would enjoy the pool with other families at the Royal Dar Es Salam Golf Course while the guys played golf. This was a good time for us to get to know some of the families who worked with the Embassy in some capacity. One of my new friends, Marilyn, whose husband played golf with John and Jimmy, was the 7th grade teacher at the Rabat American School and she had a daughter Maggie's age. Her best friend, Dottie, had come over from the States to teach the 8th grade class at the Rabat American School and she would be Maggie's teacher.

When Marilyn learned this, she insisted on driving over to pick us up and take us to meet Dottie and see her incredible apartment in the *old Kasbah* section of Rabat, known as *the Oudiah*. It looked as though the houses were built on top of one another, and you really couldn't tell where one ended or another began. It provided an atmosphere similar to the movie, *Casablanca*. After parking the car, Maggie and I followed Marilyn down narrow passageways until we came to Dottie's heavily bolted front door. Then we had to wait while she unlocked several deadbolts to let us in. I was very impressed with the interior of her very old, but very lovely and totally refurbished, apartment. It was not at all what I expected, but it was nicely furnished with a very modern Moroccan motif. Dottie was a delightful person with an exuberant personality! She invited us in and whisked us out on her balcony where we were amazed to view the sprawling wide mouth of the Bou Regreg River, which from our house on the high bluff overlooking the river valley below, looked like *a tiny silver band in the moonlight winding its way through*. The view was spectacular with lovely flowering vines growing up both sides of her very large balcony.

After a few minutes of enjoying the exotic atmosphere outside on the terrace, Dottie invited us back inside for her delicious *Moroccan Mint Tea,* which she served with assorted Moroccan cookies. I learned that it takes quite a bunch of fresh mint leaves to make real Moroccan Mint Tea and it was sweetened to perfection. Dottie asked Maggie about her interests, talents and what she would like to study during the year. She told us that this year for their annual school play, they would perform *The Wizard of Oz*, and everyone would have a part. Marilyn was also very talented and played the piano for all the school activities and special events. She would conduct the music and Dottie would be the producer, instructing the students in their roles and costumes. "The Wizard of Oz," toward the end of the school year, turned out to be one of the school's greatest productions, and a mixture of people of all ages came to see it.

Soon after our arrival, we had our introduction to the Muslim holy month of *Ramadan*. The people fasted from morning until sunset when they would break the fast with a feast, or large meal which they referred to as a *Fete*. Ali came to work as usual every day at 8:00 am and worked all day without food. He was totally worn out before he left at the end of the day. That's about the time I told him that he didn't have to wash the floors every day, and that every other day would be fine. He also did our laundry in an old ringer washing machine in the back courtyard and hung the clothes out to dry. He would start with the light colors and end with the dark colors all in the same water and then rinse them in a tub of fresh water. It was not a perfect setup, but it did suffice, although the colors of our clothes faded much quicker. Ali worked very hard and did a great job of keeping the house clean, and he also tended the yard and flower beds. When John was away on a trip, he was very helpful to me in watching over our family and making sure we were safe. On occasion, I would cut the beautiful long stemmed roses along the wall of the entrance way to put in a tall vase and then feel guilty about not getting his permission. At first, we wondered why he cut the big beautiful blossoms of the lovely cacti growing in front of our villa but later learned that he had to do this to keep them healthy and not become overgrown.

When our station wagon finally arrived from its voyage across the ocean, it took us quite a while to find our way around Rabat. Since it was an old French-styled City, very much like Mobile, with streets going out from the center in all directions, it wasn't easy for us to find a particular address. Since we were new and didn't know our way around, just having the street addresses did us no good. Everyone knew where the American Embassy was and that we lived just around the corner on the main street, so it was more convenient for the kids to just hitch a ride with a friend. We had established rules for the boys to be home before midnight, but Maggie, who had just turned 13, hadn't begun to start dating yet or going out to parties. So John and I set a time for her to be home by 11:00 pm, which seemed reasonable as long as we knew where she was and who she was with. School nights were off limits for all the kids.

One night soon after our arrival, a mother came to pick up all three of our kids for a party she was having at her home for her teenage daughter, who was leaving for school in Rota, Spain. She picked them up on the street in front of our house before I had a chance to run down the steep incline of steps to meet her and tell her of our house rules. Maggie called around midnight to tell us that she didn't know what time she or the boys would get home because the mother had gone to bed and she saw no sign of her. She called again around 1:00 am to tell us not to worry, the party was still going on and they would be home as soon as they could. They came in around 2:30 am. The mother dropped them off in the street in front of our house and drove off quickly, and I never did get to meet her. Of course, John and I tried to reestablish the house rules, but it seemed impossible making them stick because they were all running in different directions. I heard Maggie tell one of her friends over the phone one day when our reading was interrupted by a telephone call, *"Don't come to our house. Our house is gross."* In other words, Mom and Dad are always here.

Since we were in a Muslim country and really had no church life, John respected my wishes to read to them something of a Christian nature on Saturday afternoons after lunch before they all dispersed in different directions. I would read something of a Christian nature either from the Bible or a Decision Magazine, which we received each month, or a good Christian book such as <u>The Hiding Place</u>, which told the story of Corrie ten Boom and her family's involvement in helping the Jewish people escape the Nazis. We realized that their peers were obviously allowed more liberties, and our discipline seemed old fashioned; however, I'm glad we kept them safe for as long as we could. It seemed like time and the ways of the world had caught up with us, and, all of a sudden, we were faced with open rebellion on all fronts. Our kids, at the most vulnerable time of their lives, discovered a new and exciting world, a different world from the one they had known before, a world free from family rules and discipline.

One Sunday morning on his way to the golf course, John came across Greg staggering down the street with one of his friends on their way to meet up with some of their other friends. He had stayed at his best friend's house overnight and they had quite obviously gotten into his dad's liquor cabinet. John whisked him into the car and brought him home where he *read him the riot act* and grounded him. Over the following year, Greg got together with his friends for various parties, some of which included alcohol. Hashish was quite prevalent on the Moroccan market and very easy for them to come by. We learned from other parents that most of the kids were experimenting, and hash had become a serious problem. In fact, it was so serious that they had planned to shut down Kenitra High School and send the kids off to private schools in Spain. When they learned that we were coming and preferred that our boys attend high school from home, they decided to keep it going for one more year. If only we had known about the drug problem, we would probably have chosen to send the boys off to school. However, there was no way of knowing that this would have solved the drug problem because they would probably have been exposed to them anyway.

When I tried talking to other mothers about the problem, it seemed to be a *taboo* subject! No one wanted to talk about it for fear of being deported. One mother told me she would be glad when her family left Morocco to get her son away from it. We were involved in many things that year and in no position to solve the problem either, so we tried to handle it personally as problems arose within our family. When Ali found things in the boys' room which he thought we should know about, he placed them on top of their beds so we would be sure to see them. When I found paraphernalia, I would take it across the street and throw it over the bluff. Magazines would be taken down to the basement and burned in the furnace which Ali tried to keep going. One day, he came to work to find it all clogged up and the fire out, so he had to really work to clean it out and get the fire going again.

We noticed Ali throwing the garbage over the bluff across the street instead of placing it neatly in the garbage can on pickup day. John instructed me to tell Ali not to do that anymore but to put the garbage in the can and place it out front of our house for pick up at the appropriate time. I composed my French into a sentence stating this thought as well as I could, *Mettez vous le garbage a cote de la rue,* and I thought he understood. Yet he kept on throwing it down the bluff. Finally, we realized that he knew what he was doing when we noticed the animal tenders prodding their goats up the embankment to eat the scraps. After trying so hard to figure it out, we laughed when we realized that my word for garbage was wrong anyway. I must have remembered it from an old Jonathan Winters' commercial. But even that wouldn't have done any good because Ali spoke only Arabic and he knew what he was doing: he was feeding the animals below the bluff.

Sometime in early fall, there was a much publicized golf tournament at the "King's Royal Dar Es Salam Golf Club." Of course John and Jimmy signed up to play in the tournament. It was a really big event to be played on *the Red Course,* considered the toughest of the three 18-hole golf courses of Dar Es Salam. Since their golf clubs were in the overseas shipment, John and Jimmy had to borrow clubs from the American Embassy, and, by the time of the tournament, they had learned to use them quite well. John always played a good game of golf and had tried out several times for some of the professional tournaments in the States. This time both John and Jimmy entered with some of their friends, and Jimmy won the Tournament! He received a very nice set of golf clubs, which he really needed and used for many years afterwards. After that spectacular event, John became known as *the golfer's dad*.

I joined the English-Speaking Women's Club of Rabat at their Annual Fall Tea just after the start of school. Immediately, I became involved in making items to sell at the Annual Spring Fair to be held in April. It was a lot of fun meeting with the ladies each week at the Thompsons' home to get acquainted and organized into groups. I volunteered our home for weekly work sessions and placed my order for a dozen men's work socks to make a dozen *Sock Monkeys,* which I had learned to make from my friend, Rhoda, back in Monterey. We had a dozen women in our group, and each one was in charge of making one sock monkey to be cut out and sewn together on the sewing machine at Laura's house and then finished by hand at our house. I took Jimmy with me down to Sale, a little town below us in the valley where they made beautiful cane furniture to furnish our veranda with some comfortable chairs for the ladies to sit on while we worked outside in our front yard. I served coffee or tea and cookies every Wednesday morning while the project was in progress, and we enjoyed ourselves immensely sewing and chatting outside watching the cars go by. We really hated for our meetings to end when our project was finished. We had ladies in our small group from all over the world, including two from England who kept us in stitches. One of them exclaimed when we were just getting started, *"I've heard of stuffing a turkey or a chicken, but I've never heard of stuffing a monkey."* She went on to tell us about running over a chicken in an alleyway near her home in the outskirts of London, and picked it up and took it home with her to cook for dinner. She said it was delicious!

In early November, John made his first Orientation Trip to Casablanca, the largest city in Morocco, to familiarize himself with the port city and the important commercial and industrial centers. He paid a courtesy call on the American Consulate where he received an informal briefing on current topics of interest. He found Casablanca to be a *Western city* in many ways, especially the downtown commercial areas, and he visited *the Medina,* the "Old City," usually busy with tourists, but this trip was during the off season so he said Tourism was light. John also toured the city's periphery including the northern industrial area with the petroleum refinery and the Royal Golf Club at Mohamedia, where he and Jim later played in another Tournament. John said he drove along the beach and entertainment areas of *the Corniche,* which were very popular in summer, only to find very light population in winter, and he scanned the southern suburban area including the Royal Golf Club at Anfa.

In the latter part of November, John made his second Orientation Trip to Meknes and Fez, Morocco's two most important Imperial Cities. This time all four of us accompanied him for an exciting tour of these very old, historical cities. We spent the first night at a hotel in Meknes where John hired a tour guide to show us around the following day. I remember standing in front of a café down the street from our hotel very early one morning drinking small cups of extremely strong Arabic coffee as we waited for our tour guide in the exotic atmosphere of old Morocco. The guide took us to the King's Palace where we walked around the race track where the beautiful Arabian horses once raced. There was a huge wall around the track to keep the people out, and we found a few pieces of pretty blue mosaic tile which once trimmed the wall. Afterwards, John drove us around Meknes to various points of interest and we visited the "New City," with its Commercial area and Administrative Center, and also the Medina, the "Old City."

When we arrived at the holy city of Moulay Idriss, a tour guide showed us the tomb of Moulay Ismael and the vast underground Christian prison which was filled to capacity during the Islamic takeover. Then he drove us out to the Roman ruins at Volubilis, where we were met with another guide to escort us around the ruins. This was the highlight of our trip as we walked over the stone roads in which the chariots had made grooves hundreds of years before and tried to visualize amidst the ruins what the ancient city must have been like. It was the scene of many historic battles and was, in fact, the exact spot where a major scene from the movie, "Patton," was filmed. After our second night in Meknes, we drove around Fez for a very brief skirt of the gigantic city on our way back to Rabat. Since we ran out of time, John planned a three-day trip to come back in the spring for a more thorough tour of Fez.

In mid-December, John caught a flight out of Casablanca to fly to Tunisia for his third Orientation Trip. Tunisia is the smallest and most centrally located of the North African countries and shares both the Berber-Arabic heritage and the French Colonial experience with her neighbors to the West, Algeria and Morocco. After half a day at the US Embassy in Tunis visiting with the Ambassador and other government officials, John toured the city extensively, including the Medina, the administrative center and the downtown commercial and entertainment areas. He also toured several tourist attractions including the historic city of Carthage, coastal towns, and the American Memorial Cemetery at La Marsa. During this 7-day trip, he took a three-day driving tour around a large portion of the country and visited many of the historical ruins and the massive Roman aqueduct located near La Mohamedia, south of Tunis. He said the weather was very good during his whole time in Tunisia: This latter part of his trip was the most enjoyable as he toured the country and visited the very impressive historical sites, especially the numerous and well-preserved Roman ruins.

In February, John planned another Orientation Trip to familiarize himself with the scenic portions of the High Atlas Mountains in the vicinity of Marrakech and the Alpine ski-resort town of Oukaimaden. Just past Marrakech, we ascended up an increasingly steep and winding road with all sorts of vendors along the way selling snails, fruits, baskets, hats and all sorts of Moroccan delicacies including snakes. About halfway up, we started getting glimpses of snow on the ground, and, looking up, we could see the summit totally covered with beautiful white snow. At the time of our planned weekend trip, the Rabat American School was having *Ski Week* at the French lodge and those students who had registered for the whole week had been up there since the previous weekend taking skiing lessons. We were there for only two nights and had to be fitted for ski equipment the afternoon of our arrival which was Friday. We were fortunate enough to get there just in time for a blizzard which came during the night and supplied us with new fresh snow. Just as we all got ready in our ski attire and were at the bottom of the slopes, Maggie's friend, Sonja, met us and escorted us up to the top of the mountain to instruct us on how to ski back down. We were all set to follow her instructions when she saw her ski instructor and said, "Oh, there's my ski instructor." and left us there to figure it out ourselves. Needless to say, since none of us had ever skied before, we were all destined for a *wipeout*.

On my first trip down, I found myself going down headfirst with my ski poles spread out in both directions, when a man with a small boy stopped to help me up and showed me how to place my skies pointed inward so I could have some control. I inched my way all the way down. John, however, took off going down full speed ahead and crashed into something at the bottom, breaking a ski and badly twisting his ankle. He wasn't about to go up again until he knew it wasn't broken. I tried coming down one more time with a little more speed following my previous instructions, but found myself plummeting down the slope dragging my ski poles and my derrière in the snow as I came all the way down screaming. It was fun! I was sorry we had never had a chance to learn when we were younger. I noticed Greg and Maggie doing much better than I, and they were actually maneuvering themselves down without any major catastrophes. Jim was coming down the higher slopes like the other skiers, but, after all, he was the *jock* of the family and had friends up there with him showing him how.

One-night John and I returned home to find the nearly finished monkeys all over the living room in total disarray, and the ladies had to find their monkey and mend it if necessary. It seems the kids came in earlier than we did after one of the parties at the Marine House, and Greg and his friends had a monkey party in our living room. When the dozen monkeys were finished, we started making felt eye glasses holders with Moroccan designs to sell at the Fair. Time was getting short and we were ready to turn in our wares. I think everyone was sad when our work was finished, but we still had our monthly Coffees and Teas to attend. The Fair was a great success and all the profits went to Moroccan charities, so all our fun was for a good cause. Our "Sock Monkeys" were a big hit and sold out quickly. They were cleverly displayed on hanging baskets and planters and in many other artistic arrangements. It was a great pleasure to see them in the arms of little children as they walked around the grounds with their mothers or fathers. I purchased two International Cookbooks from the ESWC which I value very much even today, and I'm forever looking up something I need to know.

Towards the end of the school year, the adventurous spirit of Dottie Layton took her 8th grade class on a bus trip over to the edge of the Sahara Desert where they would camp out overnight and cook their food over a campfire. Terry, one of the young Marines, volunteered to accompany the group to help out in supervision, putting up tents and building fires for cookouts. They planned to turn south at the edge of the desert and drive to the large city of Marrakech, travelling by day and seeing all the sights along the way. The weather was getting warm and they hoped for a good trip, however that was not to be the case. Things started going wrong right off the bat when they drove off in the bus and left their teacher behind waving goodbye. Dottie thought the bus driver was just moving the bus to another place, and the bus driver thought she would be traveling with her husband in their car behind them. When he realized they were nowhere to be seen, the bus driver finally stopped the bus to wait for Dottie and called the school to get his instructions. Maggie said they waited a very long time in the hot bus with no air conditioning, and finally, Dottie's husband caught up with the bus, so she could climb aboard. And off they went on their adventurous journey. The first evening seemed to go as planned, except the tents kept falling down during the night, and they didn't get much sleep. During their cookout that first evening, Maggie said they saw people with swinging lanterns coming slowly towards them from across the desert. They were all scared to death, but it turned out to be a group of harmless nomads passing by. However, for a few minutes, they imagined all sorts of things.

The second day, the bus broke down and all the kids, including Terry, had to get out and push. Finally, a Moroccan bus came along and gave all of them a ride into Marrakech, where a compassionate hotel owner allowed them to stay overnight with several rooms in his hotel. Maggie said they were all so tired and dirty from pushing the bus, the blowing sand and no sleep the previous night, they welcomed a place to bathe and a bed for a good night's sleep. The next morning, after a complimentary breakfast at the hotel, they toured the City of Marrakech and were able to ride camels, watch a snake charmer and see many exotic attractions. They also shopped for souvenirs and Maggie bought a camel skin hat, which she wore for years after leaving it outside to dry out in the sun for a few weeks to get rid of the terrible odor. Dottie bought tickets for all the kids on the overnight train back to Rabat. Again, they didn't get much sleep, but they were very thankful to be heading home. John and I were there to meet them early the next morning with some of the other parents. And, as John would later describe them, *"They were one surly bunch of kids getting off that train."*

In May, John flew out of Casablanca via Paris on his way to Jeddah, Saudi Arabia to begin his two-week Orientation Trip to the Middle East. He would meet with Ambassadors, Defense Attachés, foreign officials and other dignitaries to discuss important issues concerning the conditions which existed at that time in the Middle East. In addition to Saudi Arabia, he would visit Sudan, Egypt, and Jordan, and, after meeting with the governing officials, he would have tours of each country. In Jeddah, he visited the port, the central market place and the commercial areas before driving through some of the residential areas. In Khartoum, he visited the downtown commercial areas and government buildings, the confluence of the Blue and White Nile Rivers, and the People's Palace. In Cairo, he visited the administrative and tourist centers bordering the Nile river, the Egyptian Museum, Cairo University and Tower, the pyramids and sphinx of Giza, the Citadel with its Mohamed Ali Mosque and the Sultan Hassan Mosque. In Amman, he visited the University of Jordan, the Roman Amphitheater, and the Roman ruins at Jerash in addition to the downtown commercial and tourist centers.

Jim graduated from Kenitra High School the first week of June. It was very small with under a dozen graduates, but it was very nice and we made many pictures of the important event. We invited Jim's friends and his graduating class down to the beach with food and drinks for his graduation party. It was just a short drive over to the coast and was what he wanted to do to end our year in Morocco. The water looked awfully rough that day, but all the kids had a great time and there were no major problems. Everyone went swimming and played games of Frisbee and touch football on the beach. We ate our fried chicken and potato salad picnic style with paper plates, plastic forks and canned drinks. In spite of his indulgences, Greg actually had a good time at the party and passed his Junior year. Both he and Maggie seemed to be looking forward to their following year of high school back in the States. Jim was ready to enter college in the School of Engineering at Ole Miss, and we were hoping for Greg to follow him there the following year. Then, hopefully, Maggie would follow them both.

During the first week of July, we accompanied John on his Orientation Trip to Tangier to become familiar with the internationally-oriented city, its harbor and general vicinity including the rich agricultural areas of the Gharb plains. We stayed in a nice hotel on the beautiful white sandy beach of Tangier and enjoyed its international cuisine and a beautiful ocean view. We toured the city with its many souks and shopping areas, filled with tourists at this busiest time of the year. We purchased a three-metal pot of silver, copper and brass, which was obviously handmade and quite interesting. I must have seemed fascinated with it because the salesman followed us out the door and made us a very good deal. We drove over to the isthmus and got a glimpse of the huge Rock of Gibraltar and its very busy English port.

Finally, it was time to leave the beautiful coast of Tangier and head east along the recreational coastline of Morocco where colorful tents covered the beaches. We turned south and drove through Tetouan, heading back to our home in Rabat, when our station wagon went out on us in the foothills of the Rif Mountains. It was early afternoon and we had just passed the small town of Chaouen, so John decided to jog back to find an auto mechanic who could fix it. He told us to stay in the car and keep the doors and windows locked, and he gave me his hunting knife to protect us, as though I could fight off intruders. It was the Fourth of July 1976, our Country's Bicentennial, and the kids and I were cutting wild wheat on a Moroccan hillside in the Rif Mountains. John returned a couple of hours later with a small group of men to repair our car.

John said no one in the small town of Chaouen spoke English, and the main languages spoken in that part of coastal Morocco were Spanish and Berber. This gave John a good opportunity to use his high school Spanish, Arabic and practice his Moroccan dialect. While he was meeting with some men at the Police Station to discuss what might be wrong with our disabled car, they served him mint tea and sent a runner over to the Service Station to bring back their chief mechanic. In checking everything that could be wrong with our disabled car, they discovered a loose fuel line under the car, and one of them crawled under there and caught the gasoline in his mouth, then spit it into a bottle to save for putting back into the car when their work was done. They connected the fuel line, and, to everyone's amazement, the engine started immediately. Everyone applauded, and, after a few words of appreciation in three languages, we were on our way waving good-bye to all the men we left standing there with big smiles on their faces waving back at us. What a great experience!

Before the end of July, the boys and I accompanied John on his second trip to Casablanca. Maggie stayed with Janet's family. The purpose of this trip was for John to experience the city in a different season and tour other sections not seen on his previous trip. The tourist season was in full swing and city life was going on all around us. We didn't get much sleep with all the noise in the street below our hotel. We visited the Medina and just happened upon an auction taking place in the town square. We found a great restaurant down the street *loaded with atmosphere* and enjoyed delicious Pepper Steaks with spaetzel. It was fun being in Casablanca with the boys, walking around at night, drinking in the joyous atmosphere and blending into the *western city* with tourists from all over the world. We drove around the entire city before leaving town and passed along the heavily populated beach areas where we noticed many colored tents covering the beach as far as the eye could see. It was indeed prime time for vacationers and tourists, and Casablanca had a lot to offer them all.

As we were packing all our things to ship back to the States, I noticed a few extra items in Greg's suitcase which I promptly removed and threw over the bluff... they were obviously paraphernalia he wanted to bring home. One was a rather large water pipe and there were a few smaller pipes... but I didn't find any hashish. I searched through everything. Years later, he told me he had hidden it in baggies rolled up in his socks the night before we left. We checked all the suitcases and thought everything looked good, so we closed them up early the following morning and had them ready for packing into the van for our drive to Casablanca and our morning departure for New York.

We all had mixed feelings about leaving Morocco. We had enjoyed many wonderful adventures and made many new friends, but it had been quite a different experience and lifestyle from anything we had ever experienced before and one that we wanted to change. The kids had gained in many ways from life in a foreign country and learned so much about Morocco, but we hoped to get back to a more normal way of life for their sakes. John and I felt an urgency to get back to the way we were as a family. We hoped that our move back to the States and a new school and church setting would be enough to straighten them out. We hoped to put down roots in Northern Virginia and provide a more stable way of life, so the kids could finish growing up, finish high school and go on to college to make good lives for themselves.

CHAPTER SIX

A Time for Washington
1976-1977

After the long flight back across the Atlantic Ocean, we arrived in New York in early afternoon, where we struggled through US Customs and found our pickup van for our ride to New Jersey to pick up our new Malibu. It was a pretty blue Malibu Classic Chevrolet; which John had ordered from Rabat so we would have transportation upon our arrival in the States. After all the years of our kids growing up in the *Yellow Sub,* the smaller car was just too small to hold three nearly grown teenagers and all our baggage, so John took Jimmy with him to shop for a *top loader,* which would hold the large bags on top of the car. After a good night's sleep in a motel, we loaded up and took off on our long drive down to northern Virginia, where we planned to look for a home. I realized as I was getting dressed that first morning that I had left my skin freshener sitting on a shelf in our bathroom back in Rabat. While John was calling a realtor, I looked up Mary Kay Cosmetics in the telephone book. The lady who answered my call was a Mary Kay Director who just happened to live in Vienna, one of the areas in which we were interested. When she heard that we were looking for a house to buy, she said "Well, why don't you look at my house?" Not only did she sell us the skin freshener and her house, but she recruited me as a Mary Kay Beauty Consultant.

Our realtor took us all out to Godfather's Pizza for lunch the first day, which scored a big hit with all our kids, but, after several days of looking around at other houses, they were growing tired of house hunting. We decided to take a vote, and *"the Mary Kay House"* won. It was located just a couple of blocks from a high school where Greg and Maggie could walk to school. We drove down to Mobile to stay with Mother while waiting for Alicia and her family to move out. They had been planning for some time to move to Montana with their two small children to start a newspaper business, and we gave them the opportunity. Alicia gave me some of her

Mary Kay customers to get me started and, of course, shared some with her other recruits. On our way back to Vienna, we dropped Jim off at Ole Miss for Registration and Fraternity Rush. We were a little sad to leave him there, but we knew this was a very important move for Jim, and he would be coming home for Christmas and summer vacation.

While we were getting settled and ready for school to start, John flew out to Ft. Leavenworth for a two-week course at the Command & General Staff College, then had to attend a two-week course in the area before starting to work at the Pentagon. He would begin his new assignment as Analyst/Briefer for the Middle East and North Africa and also serve as the all-source briefer for Current Intelligence. John would be at his desk by 4:00 am to read all the incoming data and prepare the morning briefing. Arising at 2:30 am was not going to be easy with two teenagers in the house, and it was a long drive to the Pentagon where he had to park the car and walk a very long way through its corridors to his office.

John had never been one to retire early, but this job required it if he were to get enough sleep to do his job properly. Every night as soon as John's head hit the pillow, Greg was out the front door, and I was right behind him in the car to bring him back home, usually from the Seven Eleven down at the corner where he would meet up with some of his new friends. In our new split-level home, John's bed was located downstairs in the Mary Kay office, away from the rest of the family in what we thought would be a quiet place for him to sleep. Right away we knew we had a problem! The house was not exactly new and had developed a few creaks in the flooring. Since the kitchen was right above John's bed, he could hear every move Greg made into, and out of, the kitchen, and that created more than a few confrontations. Since John never got enough sleep during the week, he tried to make it up on weekends. He said it was worse than his long 16-hour days of working in Vietnam in a warzone.

We thought we had picked a good neighborhood near the high school where Greg and Maggie would have easy access walking back and forth to school. The house was perfect for a growing family and the downstairs basement was made into a very nice, large carpeted den with built-in bar and a cozy fireplace, and plenty of chopped wood in the backyard to keep it going all winter. We put our corner group in the far corner near a small half-bath to serve as an extra bedroom for Jim while he was home on vacation. It was really very comfortable for our needs and had the cutest Mary Kay office and pink storage room, which was built into a small downstairs hall closet. However, where Greg was concerned, we just hadn't expected to *jump from the frying pan into the fire!* But that's what we did! We had no idea of the terrible drug problem which existed in the whole Washington, DC area.

Since our new area was notorious for its high-cost of living, many military wives held jobs to supplement their husband's low income. If my consultant job with Mary Kay didn't suffice, I planned to find a secretarial position. Our neighbors were wonderful and came over to welcome us to the neighborhood. Right away, one lady, who lived a few houses down and across the street from us, called it *"a trashy neighborhood."* I thought she was kidding at first, but then realized she meant it sincerely. She offered to hold my first Mary Kay party and quickly became one of my closest new friends. I could always count on Martha for an honest opinion. She told me outright that we didn't want Greg to meet her son, *"He's a bum,"* she said quite matter-of-factly. He had dropped out of high school several years earlier and couldn't hold a job, so she took him down to Alabama to visit her mother, and, while he was there, he got into some trouble and the State Court forced him into a strict drug program which confined him for a year to dry him out and teach him a trade. Now, she said, he's a brick layer, and he loves his job and can support himself.

We discovered a wonderful little Methodist Church down a lane off Flint Hill Road, which I referred to as *the little Church in the wildwood.* It was just a couple of miles down the road from our house, and I was so anxious to get my family there as an important part of our *new beginning.* When we finally did get there one Sunday morning and entered the church, Greg disappeared immediately and we didn't know where he went. Of course, the usher took us to our seats in the congregation which were down in front, and, when Greg finally appeared, he didn't know where we were and walked down the center isle to the very front of the Church, where he turned around to look for us and mouthed an obscenity, which anyone could have read from his lips. Then he saw us and came over to where we were sitting. I could have died from embarrassment! We didn't go back! John and I continued our TV church schedule on Sunday mornings watching our TV preachers with Greg and Maggie. In retrospect, we should have gone back to the little Church in the wildwood trusting God to do his work and make some changes in our lives. We needed the prayers of the Church and the wonderful Pastor, who came out to our home for a visit.

Martha told me that her son had caused her so much trouble she had to get help from somewhere because she had no control over him, and she had to work full time to pay her house notes. Her husband had deserted them when he was just a little guy, which was probably part of his problem. Eventually, the Alabama Court System got him straightened out and she was very thankful. I considered what she told me about their situation and filed it away in my brain. Martha also told me about her job at Vega Labs just a couple of miles away in Vienna, which specialized in component parts for computers and modern day technology. It was just a short distance from our neighborhood, so Martha promised to let me know if a secretarial job became available. It would be a good place for me to work if we wanted to share expenses, and I could drive home for lunch if I chose to drive myself.

Maggie seemed to be off to a good start her freshman year and, always trying to compete with the boys, signed up for "Auto Mechanics." But her real love was Art, and some of her beautiful sketches were later published in the High School Year Book. Her home room teacher gave her a beautiful little black and while kitten, which we all fell in love with when she brought her home. We called her "Kitty," and the name stuck. She was the most lovable cat we ever knew and had a way of bringing her head up under one's hand to encourage someone to pet her. She left our house and was lost for a couple of days but soon found her way back and, not long afterwards, gave birth to six beautiful kittens. Maggie's friends came over to see them, and the three who looked like Persians went quickly, then the others, which were also adorable, found homes.

We received letters from Jimmy, and he told us of running into a young man whose parents lived pretty close to Vienna, and he would be able to get a ride back and forth with him for Christmas. He had joined a fraternity and was doing very well in his classes. He liked it there at Ole Miss and tried to attend all the sports events that year. When he came home for Christmas, he was able to get a job working full-time at Burger King, where Greg was working until he was fired for being high after getting his first paycheck. This became a pattern with Greg. He would do well for a couple of weeks and then blow it all to get high and lose his job. Jim proved himself to the manager and assured himself of a job when he came home the following summer.

John's parents, Hannah and Cyrus, flew in from Ohio for Christmas and we all enjoyed visiting around the warm fireplace downstairs in the den. Jim liked sleeping in his cozy section of the den while Greg slept upstairs in his small front bedroom. Maggie allowed the grandparents to have her large bedroom while she slept on a comfortable bed we made for her on the living room couch. John's folks told us about a house they were planning to buy in a small town in northern Mississippi, which Hannah had admired while working there as a young woman with the Civilian Conservation Corps (CCC). This organization, formed under President Franklin D. Roosevelt during the Great Depression, set up hundreds of camps all over the country and provided food and low-paying jobs to keep our nation going until we could come out of the depression. John offered to drive their car and tow his dad's boat down in the spring to help them make the move. Cyrus had bought a small fishing boat in Ohio, and they used it practically every weekend during the summer to keep their freezer packed with fish all year. Now he needed John to help him get the boat down to the recreational lake near the home they were buying, where they could resume their love of fishing in northern Mississippi. I baked the largest turkey I could find in the Commissary, and we all enjoyed a big Christmas Dinner with all the trimmings and a roaring fire downstairs in the den to keep the house warm. It was great having the family together, and we hated to see the grandparents off on their trip back to Ohio, but they had to get back to work with great plans for their retirement. We enjoyed having Jim home with us through New Year's weekend, and he and Greg enjoyed seeing some of their friends who had moved to our area from Morocco.

It wasn't long before we realized that Martha was right about the "trashy neighborhood." The young people seemed to be running wild, and we came to find out that a drug dealer lived two houses down from us. Open beer parties were very popular in the area, and strangers were welcome to just drop by. Greg was forever trying to find one he had heard about at school and would badger me into driving him around looking for it. I never did find one to drop him off but had to make the attempt anyway. Cars would speed by our home at all hours of the night, especially on weekends, and all sorts of vandalism took place. Someone shot a hole in our Chrysler station wagon, just missing the gasoline tank by a couple of inches, and another shot shattered our side window and exited through the windshield. A beautiful Moroccan planter on our front steps was totally demolished, and several mailboxes were knocked down. It was indeed a trashy neighborhood! But what could we do about it? Everyone was disgusted but had investments in their homes and couldn't just pick up and move without taking a loss.

John had approved my two big Mary Kay orders to get me started in my new business as a beauty consultant, and I had fun unpacking the boxes and stacking the products in my cute little pink stockroom. Several neighbors were gracious enough to hold parties for me to introduce the product and give facials, but it was still off to a very slow start. I called my customers on a regular basis, which Alicia had left with me, and I usually got some reorders. However, the growth of my business seemed to be at a standstill. Martha told me about an opening for a secretary at Vega Laboratories which would give me a monthly paycheck, so I decided to apply for the job and was hired to start work immediately. Commuting back and forth to work each day with Martha was fun, and we got to keep up with each other and what was going on in the neighborhood and at Vega. I liked my job as Secretary to one of the Department Managers and made a few new friends at Vega. While Martha was gone on vacation, I drove myself to work in the Yellow Sub and decided to come home for lunch. I found Greg and a couple of friends downstairs in our den having a "pot party." His two new friends had just moved into our area from an overseas assignment where their father had worked with an American Embassy in Africa, so their situation was very similar to ours. I had to chase them out and tell them not to come back! About a month later, these same two guys stole a car and stopped by our house to pick up Greg, but he declined the offer. Thank goodness! A policeman came by our house to ask Greg questions, but he didn't have any information to give them about what they were planning to do.

One day on one of my deliveries, I mentioned the marijuana problem to one of my customers and found her very open to discussion. She lived in a very affluent neighborhood and said many families there were having the same problems with their teens. In fact, her neighborhood was holding regular meetings to discuss the situation and determine what needed to be done to establish order. She promised to give me a copy of the study they were conducting as soon as it was available. Another customer confided that her son was causing them similar problems, and, although he was working to save money to buy a car, they were on the verge of asking him to move out to save their three young daughters from his bad influence.

Maggie, too, started changing during the year. She no longer wanted to wear the clothes I bought her, especially the cute, lacy blouses I made for her to wear with her jeans to give her a more feminine look. She wanted to dress like "the hippy generation," shunning the cute clothes she had always worn before and once felt good about. I had always bought cute patterns and material to make clothes for her and myself, which never seemed to be a problem before, but since we moved to Vienna, her personality seemed to change, and she wanted to dress like her peers to fit in with her new friends. It was heartbreaking! I ended up wearing some of the clothes I had made for her, especially two very cute lace-trimmed cotton blouses.

One day, I walked into her room and discovered an ash tray filled with cigarette butts, and I asked her if her friend, Gracie, had been there because I hadn't seen her come in. She said, "Mom, I smoke!" I couldn't believe it! Maggie had always hated cigarette smoke and said she would never pick up such a filthy habit. Then one night after being with their friends, Gracie came in with her quite early to "put her to bed" because she said, "Maggie's sick." I found out the next day that her "friends" had poured beer down her throat to force her to drink it. Peer pressure persisted the whole time we lived there in Vienna, and Maggie learned to drink beer and smoke cigarettes before the age of 15. Her whole demeanor and personality changed. I was just sick!

Greg's habit to leave the house right after his dad went to bed never ended. John averaged about 3 hours sleep each night, while I desperately tried to keep things quiet. Maggie kept her radio on low volume all the time to avoid hearing any disruptions or confrontations between Greg and his dad. She and I were "walking on eggshells!" Greg would try to slip off quietly into the night to party with friends. Then he would come in and head straight for the kitchen to satisfy his "munchies." It was a never ending battle which repeated itself night after night. The confrontations grew worse! Something had to change. Towards the end of the school year, Greg was lagging behind in several subjects, and we tried every way possible to prod him into getting his work done and hand it in on time so that he could graduate with his class.

The school assured us that he would be able to take part in the Graduation Ceremony if he made up his work during the summer. We paid for his "Cap and Gown Package," which included his announcements, which we mailed out to all the family just as we had done the previous year for Jim. Then I received a phone call from the school that Greg would not be allowed to graduate with his class because he failed the third subject, and they could not let him make up three subjects during the summer. Needless to say, we were all disappointed and very embarrassed because he was already receiving checks in the mail from family and friends and cashed them before we ever got home from work. We had no way of knowing what gifts he received in the mail nor to whom he owed Thank You notes. On the day of the Ceremony, Greg walked over to the school and sat in the bleachers to watch the Graduation of his classmates. It was so disappointing and heartbreaking!

On my next Mary Kay delivery to one of my customers who was open about their community holding weekly meetings to determine what needed to be done about the drug problem in their area, I received quite an extensive report. It was from the committee composed of doctors, scientists, and other professionals who lived there and were so concerned about the drug problem that they compiled the following information from very reputable sources, which stated that:

[Parents not only have the right to establish rules for their children and young adults as long as they remain under their roof, but they have an obligation to society as well as their other children to administer proper discipline and teach responsible conduct. If young people fail, or refuse, to abide by reasonable rules established for their welfare and the welfare of others, they should be held responsible and confronted and dealt appropriate, and fair, punishment. The punishment should be consistent with a firm follow through. It should never be administered in the heat of anger, and it should always be well thought out to fit the deed. If the young person continues to disregard the rules, the parents have every right to make that person leave their home.]

A short time later, my friend and her husband did make their son leave their home, and he drove away in his car with all his things. They were terribly worried until her brother called to say that he was with them at their Christian Camp Retreat, and their son had agreed to abide by their rules as long as he stayed there. On my next delivery, I noticed they had a "For Sale" sign in front of their beautiful home, and her husband was taking a leave of absence from his job to spend the summer working at the camp while they got their family back together and solved their family problems.

I mentioned to one of my customers over the telephone one day that I needed to find *something spiritual* because our attending Church didn't work out for us under our present circumstances. She invited me to a ladies' prayer group which met every couple of weeks for prayer and worship. It was wonderful! A lovely lady with long blonde hair started off our meeting by singing a beautiful Christian song with a rather deep sultry voice, which had once belted out ballads in a night club. Now, here she was praising God in a wonderfully gentle way with lyrics she had written herself. Her Testimony was one of miracles which saved her husband's life and brought them both together in a new and spiritual way as they were both filled with the Holy Spirit. They had been in a terrible automobile accident which almost cost them their lives. Her husband had been near death when rushed to the hospital and they didn't expect him to live when she cried out to God to save him. She called on all the Christians she knew to pray. Her Christian group joined together in prayer for many days, and, by a miracle, he finally pulled through! Now they are both devout Christians truly dedicated to God and serve Him through their Church. They are both on the prayer team!

I remember reading beautiful words of hope, faith, love and even some scriptures, including the Ten Commandments, around the top of my homeroom when I was in high school. Now they were taking prayer out of the schools and trying to eradicate all our Christian beliefs, which had once been the foundation of our lives. I noticed again the grotesque pictures of rock stars decking the walls of Greg's room. Rock magazines were filling his head with all kinds of garbage and indecent behavior setting an example for others to follow. No wonder he was so lost and confused! The blaring vibes with the garbled messages of his stereo penetrated the walls of our home. What were they telling him? What could we do to save him? Here we were trying to establish a good lifestyle for our family after all the instability of so many moves, only to find that it was too late. Our innocent children had become part of the world system. Our good intentions were not good enough to change them back to the way they were. God tells us,

> **"And be not** conformed to this world: *but be ye transformed by the renewing of your mind that ye may prove what is that good, and acceptable, and perfect will of God."* (Romans 12:2)
> "Come out from among them, and be ye separate... and I will receive you. And will be a Father unto you, and ye shall be my sons and daughters." (2 Corinthians 6:17)

Our kids seemed to be lost and drifting down a road led by the Pied Piper of the Rock World. *They needed salvation!* Why was all this misery happening to so many good people who didn't deserve all this hell? Then

I remembered who was behind it: Satan and his fallen angels, who were kicked out of heaven and down to the earth to take as many of us with them as they can to their eternal destination. Now these fallen angels, referred to in the Bible as demons, have invaded our children to turn them against their parents. I turned to First Peter and started reading:

"Beloved, think it not strange concerning the fiery trial which is to try you, as though some strange thing happened to you; but rejoice, inasmuch as ye are partakers of Christ's sufferings; that, when his glory shall be revealed, ye may be glad also with exceeding joy. If ye be reproached for the name of Christ, happy are ye; for the spirit of glory and of God rests upon you: on their part, he is evil spoken of, but on your part, he is glorified." (1 Peter 4:12-14)

"For Christ also hath once suffered for sins; the just for the unjust, that he might bring us to God, being put to death in the flesh, but quickened by the Spirit. By which also he went and preached to the spirits in prison." (1 Peter 3:18-19)

"For as much then, as Christ hath suffered for us in the flesh, arm yourselves likewise with the same mind: for he that hath suffered in the flesh hath ceased from sin; that he no longer should live the rest of his time in the flesh to the lusts of men, but to the will of God." (1 Peter 4:1-2)

"Yet if any man suffer as a Christian let him not be ashamed; but let him glorify God on this behalf. For the time is come that judgment must begin at the house of God: and if it begin at us, what shall the end be of them that obey not the gospel of God?" (1 Peter 4:16-17)

"And when the chief shepherd shall appear, ye shall receive a crown of glory that fades not away… Yea, all of you be subject one to another, and be clothed with humility; for God resists the proud but gives grace to the humble. Humble yourselves, therefore under the mighty hand of God, that he may exalt you in due time; casting all your care upon him for he cares for you.

"Be sober, be vigilant, because your adversary, the devil, as a roaring lion walks about seeking whom he may devour; whom resist steadfast in the faith knowing that the same afflictions are accomplished in your brethren that are in the world. But the God of all grace, who has called us unto his eternal glory by Christ Jesus,

after you have suffered a while, he shall make you perfect, establish, strengthen and settle you. In him be the glory and dominion forever and ever. Amen." (1 Peter 5:4-11)

When I called my customers again, I discovered that two of them lived next door to each other. Joanne had taken me to the Christian ladies meeting and Amy had some suggestions for me because she sensed a demonic influence. I learned the story of how the two of them had become friends over their backyard fence one day after having some misunderstandings due to the disagreements of their children. But, after talking over the issues and using a more Christian approach to solving their problems, they got to know each other and realized they had the same Christian values. Now, they were the best of friends. On my next telephone call to Amy, I expressed my frustration over our neighborhood problems. Her answer was very impressive: *"We don't wrestle against flesh and blood, but against principalities and powers of darkness."* We have to learn *Spiritual Warfare!* She referred me to Ephesians, Chapter 6:

> *"Finally, my brethren, be strong in the Lord, and in the power of his might. Put on the whole armor of God; that ye might be able to stand against the wiles of the devil, for we wrestle not against flesh and blood, but against principalities, against powers, against the rulers of the darkness of this world, against spiritual wickedness in high places. "Wherefore take unto you the whole armor of God that ye may be able to stand in the evil day, and having done all, to stand: Stand therefore, having your loins girt about with truth and having on the breastplate of righteousness; and your feet shod with the preparation of the gospel of peace; above all, taking the shield of faith wherewith ye shall be able to quench all the fiery darts of the wicked one.*
>
> *"And take the helmet of salvation, and the sword of the Spirit, which is the word of God; and praying always with all prayer and supplication in the Spirit, and watching thereunto with all perseverance and supplication for all saints."* (Ephesians 6:10-18)

After we moved into our home on Flint Hill Road, I wondered why our cane furniture from Morocco was breaking up in places when it had arrived in seemingly good condition. Since it was quite evident that Greg had brought some "hashish" home with him, I thought that maybe he had stashed it inside the cane furniture, which was breaking up every time he tried to retrieve it. He later told me the story of how he got it in the first place from one of the Moroccan souks. He said he went into the souk to make a purchase, paid his money and was left sitting unattended on a couch while waiting for someone to return with his order. When they didn't come back, he thought he had been ripped off and found a package hidden under some pillows. He knew what it was because he had been there before, so he stuck the package inside his jacket and left. He said it was a very large amount of hashish, and he brought it home to hide behind a loose tile below their bathtub. Then Greg hid it in baggies and put some of it in the lower part of a lamp, which the movers packed for our move to the States. The rest he hid inside his rolled up socks shortly before we closed our suitcases for the trip home.

I believe I had a prophetic dream one night in which God told me to take Greg and Maggie to Alabama, like Martha had done to get her son away from the "trashy" neighborhood. The whole DC area from Virginia over into Maryland seemed to be a cauldron of drugs for those who sought them and were under bondage, and Greg's friends in Morocco had told him where and how to get them. John was not getting enough sleep at night with his intense schedule at the Pentagon, and the confrontations were getting worse and reaching the point of potential violence. We didn't understand the full extent of what was happening with Greg. He told us years later that he had been experimenting with PCP and LSD, which were causing him to hallucinate. Maggie continued keeping her radio on all night so she could sleep, and we both continued our "walk on egg shells" trying to keep the peace. John confronted Greg every time there was a major disturbance and was called to the school one day from the Pentagon in his uniform, which was very embarrassing. I told John about my dream, and, remembering what Martha had confided in us about her son, he thought it might have some merit. His job was very important and he needed sleep in order to function, and we all needed a break from the constant turmoil in which we found ourselves. We knew the neighborhood would probably never recover and was probably the reason Alicia and her husband sold their home and moved to Montana to start a newspaper business. They had two small children to think about, and they had done what they thought best to get them away from it.

I called the Army Hospital to try to get some help and made an appointment for Greg to be seen by a Psychiatrist. I got him there on time for his appointment but couldn't hold him in the waiting room long enough to be seen by the doctor. Greg just disappeared! I couldn't find him anywhere. When the time was up, I found Greg at the door waiting for his ride home.

John and I thought it was the same ole stuff, "pot" or "hash," and/or alcohol, but, although we didn't know it at the time, it was much more than that and something we could not control. His appearance changed and his hair became wiry and bounced when he walked. He wouldn't get a haircut and developed a heavy, furrowed look around his brow. He lost his old personality and the ability to smile naturally, or laugh, as he had always done in the past. Looking back, I can see that it was a blessing from God that we took measures to get him out of there before something really catastrophic happened. We had no alternative but to put our house up for sale and it sold immediately!

John found a one-bedroom apartment in McLean near the entrance to The Potomac Parkway, which would greatly shorten his drive into work each morning. He would appreciate this location during the snowy winter months ahead. We moved some of our furniture down to Mother's, and John kept all the furniture which would fit into his small apartment plus all the plants and the corner group which fit snugly into his small dining room. This made a small alcove with a window for letting in the morning sun and provided a second bedroom if ever needed. Maggie, Greg, and I all piled into the old Yellow Sub with Kitty and took off for Alabama. We left John waving goodbye from his car as we drove away in two directions. John would come back the following day with a friend to help him move into his apartment and do the cleanup. I could tell Greg had something in his mouth as we were driving away, but there was nothing I could do about it, so I didn't let it worry me and kept on driving. Finally, after a rest stop for a fill-up and a few snacks, we arrived at our motel around sunset. As Maggie and I were bringing in our overnight bags from the car, Greg dropped Kitty outside in the moonlight, and we had a very difficult time trying to coax her into our motel room. We finally did it, though, probably because she was hungry and wanted her food! Then she seemed happy to settle down in a stuffed chair for the night. We were all worn out and ready for baths and a good night's sleep.

CHAPTER SEVEN

A Time for Truth
1977

During all my years growing up as a Christian, I never heard anything about *the occult*. Then one day after we moved to northern Virginia, a Christian friend told me quite emphatically that *"Astrology is of the occult"* and it is listed in Deuteronomy as *"an abomination to God."* I had told her about my interest in astrology and the courses I had taken at White Sands which taught me to work the family's natal charts. She thought my delving into it, although I never practiced it professionally, could have opened the door for demonic activity in our family and could be the cause of all the trouble we were having with our son, Greg. She advised me to *"burn everything!"* She said *"instead of consulting the stars,"* I should be *"consulting God"* and referred me to Deuteronomy, Chapters 17 & 18. Astrology was very popular at the time and I found myself accumulating all sorts of books, charts, logarithms, round rulers, etc., for preparing *natal charts* and *horoscopes*. Even John encouraged me and bought beautiful hardbound books whenever he saw them on sale in the major book stores. People loved hearing *what the stars had to say* about themselves and their family members, and everyone wanted to have their natal charts done. Since I had never really studied the Old Testament, I questioned what my friend told me, but I did look up the scriptures and began to contemplate what they were telling me:

> Deuteronomy 17:2-3: God makes it very clear about *"serving other gods"* and *"worshipping the sun, moon and the host of heaven."*
> Deuteronomy 18:10-14: God refers to astrologers as *"observers of times."* In other places, they are mentioned as *stargazers.*

Isaiah 47:13: *"Thou art wearied in the multitude of thy counsels. Let now the astrologers, the stargazers, the monthly prognosticators, stand up and save thee from these things that shall come upon thee."*

2 Kings 21:1-6: Other abominations listed under the occult: *"Anyone who makes his son or daughter pass through the fire"* (the sacrifice of babies/infanticide/abortion); *"divination"* (witchcraft); *"an enchanter"* (sorcery, the use of drugs for magical powers); *"a witch"* (one who practices magic or sorcery); *"a charmer"* (one who casts spells, or sorcery); *"a consulter of familiar spirits"* (one who calls up spirits of the dead or the devil); *"a wizard"* (one who practices witchcraft); or *"a necromancer"* (one who summons up the spirit of a dead person, or the devil, by incantation).

Now after all these years, I'm convinced beyond the shadow of a doubt that my Christian friend was right and the devil does work through astrology, as well as the other abominations, to get strongholds in peoples' lives. And his mission is to *kill, steal and destroy*. I believe that any one of these abominations can open the door for the devil and his evil forces of demons to come in and do their dirty work, and it is not easy to get rid of them because they infiltrate every aspect of our lives. We need to build our lives securely upon *The Rock, the firm foundation of Christ Jesus,* which God provides for all believers, so that our families can be safe and secure from the sinking sands of the world and its demonic influences. Without this firm foundation, these demons will force their way into our lives and rob us of our peace and joy. They will take away our freedom and lead our children down the road to destruction. They will establish idols for them to worship instead of the one true God. My astrology paraphernalia at this time was conveniently packed away in a box, and I had lost track of just where we put it.

During my early years, I attended Sunday school at a Methodist Church, and when I turned 12, I was automatically promoted into the adult church. Although I learned Bible verses and heard many wonderful Bible stories, no one ever explained to me that I needed to be *born again*. I knew nothing about water baptism and the need to be fully immersed to signify dying to sin and being raised up a new creature in Christ Jesus. I didn't even know about the need for a changed life. It was as if everyone in our church was already saved and on their way to heaven just by being good people and attending church. I once heard a well-known evangelist say that Jesus said, *"If you won't confess me before men, neither will I confess you before the Father."* Therefore, it seemed to me that commitment before others is a very important part of confessing one's faith, and there should be a moment in time when one actually *"receives Jesus as the Lord of his life."* Many people believe they are saved because they were raised in the church. However, their parents' commitment is not their commitment, and they must make this decision for themselves.

Around the time I was promoted into the adult church, one of my friends from a Birmingham suburb came down to the Gulf one summer with her dad on vacation. Her mother had recently died from cancer, and they were coming down to the beach to have a change of pace following her funeral. Sally and her dad wanted me to go back with them to be with her while she made the adjustment to life without her mother and her dad started back to work. Her Baptist Church was having a pep rally on the way to an old fashioned *"tent meeting,"* and we had a great time parading through the streets singing some really great songs I had never learned before: *I've got the Joy, Joy, Joy, Joy down in my Heart* and *I've got the Love of Jesus, Love of Jesus down in my heart, down in my heart to stay.* It was great! We ended up in a large tent, where I heard the Gospel message preached by a young evangelist for the very first time. Sally and I were sitting on the first row, and I jumped at the chance to *"go forward to receive Jesus."* My commitment was real, but I came back home and lapsed back into my old ways of talking during Sunday school and not paying attention. I remember my two teachers, Miss Rudd and Mrs. Baker, very fondly with great respect, although both of them passed on many years ago. I remember our Sunday school class walking down the street to Mrs. Baker's home for the Visitation of the funeral of her husband, who died of a long illness and was very old when I was about 12. I remember Miss Rudd working at a bakery a few blocks from our church. I was inspired by them to memorize two very important scriptures that remain with me today. They have always been a great source of strength and inspiration as we traveled around the world.

> *"Make a joyful noise unto the Lord, all ye lands. Serve the Lord with gladness: come before his presence with singing, know ye that the Lord, he is God: it is he that hath made us, and not we ourselves; we are his people and the sheep of his pasture. Enter into his gates with thanksgiving and into his courts with praise: be thankful*

unto him, and bless his name. For the Lord is good; his mercy is everlasting; and his truth endureth to all generations." (Psalm 100)

Years later, when I was 25 with two small boys in California and Maggie was still a baby, I couldn't resist the call to go forward again at an evangelical gathering in the Los Angeles Coliseum. We listened to a well-known and very famous Evangelist who gave the call to come forward, and I asked John to go down with me with the three children. However, he thought it best to stay seated with children so small and hard to keep up with, so I had to leave them sitting there in the bleachers and go down to receive the Lord for all of us. This time I was responsible for our whole family, and the seriousness of my commitment remained strong. I studied all the literature which I received in the mail from the evangelical association, and, the following year at Ft. Bliss, I checked out a book from the post library entitled, The Power of Prayer, which I read through a couple of times. I truly believed that God had the power to change things and heal my insecurities as a young military wife. I put the lives of all my family in his hands.

"The Lord is my Shepherd; I shall not want. He maketh me to lie down in green pastures: he leadeth me beside the still waters. He restoreth my soul: he leadeth me in the paths of righteousness for his name's sake. Yea, though I walk through the valley of the shadow of death, I will fear no evil: for thou art with me; thy rod and thy staff, they comfort me. Thou preparest a table before me in the presence of mine enemies: thou anointest my head with oil; my cup runneth over. Surely, goodness and mercy shall follow me all the days of my life, and I will dwell in the house of the Lord forever." (The 23rd Psalm)

When John received Orders for Vietnam the following year and I saw him off at the airport, I remember releasing him into God's hands and praying for his protection and guidance. I gave him a little red Bible with a note reminding him to read it every day, and, because he was such a negative person, I also sent a book along with him on Positive Thinking by Norman Vincent Peale. When one of his friends did a caricature of John, there were several big, thick volumes of *Things I don't like*, one small, thin volume of *Things I like*, and then there was this book on *Positive Thinking*. John said he read the Bible often, although he worked 16-hour days, and

I believe he also read this book on positive thinking. The Army trained him as an advisor to the South Vietnamese Army, and God answered my prayer when a job at MACV Headquarters opened up at precisely the right time. His new position at the headquarters in Saigon, in which he excelled brilliantly as an analyst/briefer, set the tone for the remainder of his Army career.

My involvement in astrology began in 1972 when a friend at White Sands Missile Range persuaded me to sign up for the course, *"just to keep it going,"* she said, *"or they will cancel the whole thing."* Lani was very anxious to continue her study of astrology after completing the first course which she found fascinating. I knew how much it meant to her, so I signed up for it, too, just to please her. Much to my amazement, I found it very interesting, and it seemed quite truthful in depicting the characters and personalities of my family members. Each individual *natal chart* seemed to be a type of *blueprint of each personality,* and you couldn't switch them around. It just wouldn't work because our kids were individuals and each one so different from the other two. Something lured Lani and me into it, and we were hooked. I, too, found it fascinating! But isn't that just like the devil? After distracting us from the truth, he tempts us with a similitude and very cunningly leads us away from the truth in another direction. *After learning how to prepare natal charts, we learned how to interpret them. Then we learned how to compare the natal charts with the daily transitions of the planets to get each individual horoscope.* After completing the first two courses, Lani and I signed up for the *Advanced Course,* although we had to drive half-way to El Paso to get to our teacher's house.

Astrology teaches that when a baby is born into the world and breathes in the atmosphere, he or she is magnetized by the positions of the planets: thus, the need for a natal chart to show us how we are held in bondage by the positions of the planets at the time of our birth. It also teaches that *we are only fated by our lack of understanding and that we can overcome our obstacles if we consult our daily horoscopes.* There are *"squares"* and *"crosses"* (bad aspects) and *"trines"* (good aspects) as the planets move around the zodiac, and things are always changing according to their positions in the solar system. By studying these aspects in relation to the individual natal charts, astrology teaches that people can make the most of their *"good times"* and avoid their *"bad times."* For instance, when one falls in love with another person, they should check their natal charts to see if they are compatible. God's advice is very simple: *"Don't be unequally yoked together, believers with unbelievers, because light and darkness cannot live together in harmony."* Therefore, for the sake of peace, joy and lasting happiness, Christians should marry Christians. Otherwise, there will surely be conflict. (2nd Corinthians 6:14)

According to Greg's natal chart, he had been born with a *"double square,"* which he would have to bear all his life. When my teacher saw his chart, she told me, *"This kid needs a lot of love."* Many years later after his accident, I couldn't resist checking his horoscope on the day it happened and found *"a grand trine,"* three good aspects, over his *"double square,"* which depicted a good day. How could knowing this beforehand have avoided the accident? It couldn't, because it only showed that his bad aspects were overcome by his good aspects, which astrologers would have said saved his life. Greg still lost his right foot, lower right leg and left big toe. It's only in looking back that one can see what happened on a particular day *according to the stars* and then point out what *the aspects* had to say about it. Only God knows the future and only he can work miracles in our lives. Things happen for a reason, and God is always in control. I reasoned that God, who created the heavens and the earth, knew what he was doing when he put the stars in place and created our solar system with powers, which cause the seasons to change and the oceans and rivers to ebb and flow with tides to purify the earth and keep it alive. He also does the same for us when we rely totally on him to produce miracles in our lives.

The Gospel in the Stars

On December 8, 1985, a Presbyterian minister in Ft. Lauderdale, Florida, gave a very unusual and interesting sermon about the galaxy. It was based on Psalm 19:1-6: *"The heavens declare the glory of God; and the firmament sheweth his handywork."* He also quoted Genesis 1:14: *"And God said, Let there be lights in the firmament of the heaven to divide the day from the night; and let them be for signs, and for seasons, and for days, and years...."* (Genesis 1:14)

God wrote the gospel in the stars starting with Virgo, depicting *the Virgin Birth,* moving clockwise around the zodiac, and ending with Leo, *the Lion of Judah,* Jesus, who came to destroy the works of the devil. In Scorpio, Satan is depicted as *a great Scorpion* whose tail is ready to strike the heel of a man, but the man is about to crush the Scorpion's head. (Genesis 3:15) Libra depicts *the Scales* tipped to one side, as we are *weighed in the balance and found wanting.* (Daniel 5:27) Sagittarius depicts the two natures of Christ as *the God-man* (a centaur with the body of a horse and the torso of a man) with a drawn bow and arrow aimed at the heart of *the Scorpion. "And I saw a white horse, and he that sat on him had a bow... and he went forth conquering and to conquer."* (Revelation 6:2)

> *"And I will put enmity between thee and the woman, and between thy seed and her seed; it shall bruise thy head, and thou shalt bruise his heel."* (Genesis 3:15)

God wrote the gospel moving clockwise around the zodiac, but Satan perverted it by moving counter clockwise starting with Aries, *the Ram,* who disputes God's word by saying, <u>*I am*</u>. Then he ends with one's own belief system, Pisces, *the two Fishes,* which says you can come to God this way or that way, it really doesn't matter. The Bible says there is only One Way to God the Father, and it's through his Son, *"the sacrificial Lamb of God who takes away the sin of the world."* He was *born of the Virgin Mary* from a *sinless seed,* supernaturally implanted by the work of the Holy Spirit, so Mary could give birth to a son born free from the *seed of sin* passed on from Adam. Because Jesus had no sin, death had no power to hold Him; *thus the resurrection.* When He died on the cross, our sins died with Him, and God said He will remember them no more. If we accept Jesus as Lord and His finished work at Calvary, the same power that raised Jesus from the dead will raise us up on the last day. It is appointed unto man once to die, and afterwards the judgment. (Hebrews 9:27) For those who receive Jesus as Lord, there will be no second death, and they will pass from death to life eternal. (Revelation 20:14-15)

I believe God allowed me to get involved with astrology to teach me about the reality of the spiritual realm. There are spiritual powers at work in the world today between God and the forces of evil, but God has it all under control. The Bible teaches that the things that are seen are *temporal,* but the things which are unseen are *eternal.* My friend, Amy, who first warned me about astrology, met me one evening at a Vienna shopping center to board a bus bound for a charismatic church about an hour's drive from Vienna. I really couldn't tell where we were going, but we did cross a bridge and wound round and around picking up people all the way. I didn't learn the denomination of the church, but I was under the impression that it was a large cathedral of some kind. It was an experience I will never forget! The air was charged with a magnetic force which had to be from God and seemed to move and flow in waves outward from the center of the church. I witnessed rows of people swaying in their seats as the power seemed to flow over them. Some were *slain in the Spirit* and fell to the floor. Some sat in their seats *laughing or praying in the Spirit.* Others were *running through the aisles or dancing in the Spirit.* A few *Prophecies* were given in tongues, and, each time one was given, a person from a different section of the church would give the *Interpretation* in English. There were *Healings* and *Words of Knowledge.* Someone with a word of knowledge came over to my friend and told her, *"Something is wrong with your heart."*

On the way back to Vienna after leaving the large cathedral, I sat beside a very nice middle-aged woman who shared her testimony and gave me a little booklet describing *the Baptism of the Holy Spirit.* The title of the booklet read *"Receive All God Has to Give."* She told me her story: her husband, hooked on pornography, eventually had an affair, so she divorced him and, being a good Catholic, never married again. Instead, she turned her life over to God and had a ministry of her own. I was so impressed with the events of the evening, I returned home with new vigor and a strong determination to get more deeply involved in Bible study. I came to the conclusion that when a person is truly *born again,* he or she is *set free* from the bondages of sin and has the power of the Holy Spirit to *cast out devils* which inhabit unsaved people. (Luke 24:49) The Bible tells us that Satan is *the prince of the power of the air* and *the god of this world.* (Ephesians 2:2) God has given believers power over him and his fallen angels to render them powerless if we rebuke them and cast them out in the name of Jesus. (Matthew 10:1; 12:28 & Titus 2:15) No longer should anyone be enslaved to a natal chart, a horoscope, or any other such thing to keep us in bondage to the evil forces of Satan. God has given us power in his name to take authority over the devil and rebuke him and his evil forces out of our lives.

Years later, when I got involved in an inductive Bible study course with the PWOC at Rhein-Main AFB, Frankfurt, Germany, I learned much more about astrology and its origin. It began at the Tower of Babel in the land of Shinar, today's Iraq (Genesis 10:8). Nimrod, who founded the first world empire in the city of Babel, was *a hunter of men's souls.* He and his people were of one language, one spirit, and in one accord to destroy God's people on the earth, and they built a spiritual tower, which reached up into heaven in an attempt to put Satan's throne above God's. God saw that their being *in one accord with one purpose, one mind and one goal,* they had the power to follow through with their plan. He had to stop them! So, he confused their language and scattered them over the face of the earth.

It is believed that around the top of the tower of Babel were signs of the zodiac and people gathered together to study the stars and began to worship them. They named the configurations they saw in the heavens as *signs of the zodiac,* and their superstitious natures aligned certain events on earth with the aspects they depicted in the heavens. They named the stars and the planets and studied their movements, which were always revolving around in the heavens. They believed certain aspects of the planets had power over events upon the earth and its inhabitants. They attributed these aspects to *good times* and *bad times,* and they assigned gods and goddesses over them. This study resulted in many false religions which sprang up over the earth and led to the worship of the sun, the moon and the stars. They also made images to represent these fictitious gods and goddesses, and the people worshipped these idols as they were led away from the One true God, the Creator of the heavens and the earth.

Nimrod, the grandson of Ham, who was cursed for defiling his father, Noah, hated God's people and went after them to slay them. Melchizedek, king of Salem, *the priest of the most-high God,* brought forth bread and wine and blessed Abram, who gave tithes of all he had and lifted up his hands *to the most-high God, the possessor of heaven and earth.* Then God made a covenant with Abram and changed his name to Abraham when he told him that he would be *the father of many nations.* God tested Abraham when he told him to take his son, Isaac, and some wood up to Mount Moriah and build a fire on which to sacrifice Isaac. Then the angel of the Lord held back his hand from slaying Isaac, *and God provided the sacrifice: a ram caught in a thicket by his horns.* Abraham offered up the ram instead of Isaac as a burnt offering. This is a *prophetic picture of Jesus dying as the lamb sacrifice for our sins,* when God, the Father, provided his only beloved Son to die in our place upon a wooden cross at Calvary. It is interesting to note that *the Crown of Thorns,* placed upon the head of Jesus was also represented in this prophecy by the ram's horns caught in the thicket. (Genesis 14:18-22 & 22:1- 18)

One Sunday afternoon as I continued my Bible study outside on our balcony, John brought me the rest of my glass of red wine left over from dinner. Somehow a tiny drop running down the stem of the glass dropped onto a page in my Bible. I just happened to be reading First Corinthians and it penetrated through the pages containing the Lord's Supper, Chapters 10-14. That little drop of wine will always be there in my Bible to remind me of my covenant with God to get into deep Bible Study as soon as possible and to denounce astrology. Later, as the Lord permitted, I would make other commitments to God, and I would give my testimony before the PWOC high in the Bavarian Alps at our Berchtesgaden Retreat. It would be one of the highlights of my life.

Covenants

A covenant is a solemn binding agreement between two or more people which can only be broken by death. The word, covenant, actually means *"cutting a compact by passing through pieces of flesh,"* and is used about 300 times in the Bible. In Biblical times, the covenant partners would split an animal in half and lay each piece opposite the other. Then they would walk through the pieces in the form of a figure 8, each one saying to the other, *"God do so to you if you break this covenant."*

1. The first covenant: Marriage, between a man and a woman, establish God as the foundation of a family to bring children into the world. (Ge 2:21-24)
2. God also established a covenant with Noah and gave him *The Rainbow* sign that he would never again destroy the earth with a flood. (Genesis 17)
3. God made a covenant with Abram when he told him to *"get out o country and from thy kindred… unto a land that I will shew thee: And make of thee a great nation…. And I will bless them that bless thee, and him that curseth thee: and in thee shall all families of the earth be bless* (Genesis 12:1-3)
4. God made a covenant with Abram one night when he passed through p of flesh of an animal sacrifice which was laid out before him. He pro Abram a son in his nineties and told him that his seed would be number the stars of heaven. He also promised Abram and his seed all the land the river of Egypt to the great river Euphrates. (Genesis 15:1-18)
5. God made a covenant with Hagar because he had heard her cries of affl and told her that he would *"multiply her seed exceedingly, that it shall n numbered for multitude."* She gave birth to Ishmael, who God

said wou *"a wild man; his hand against every man, and every man's hand ag him; and he shall dwell in the presence of all his brethren."* (Genesis 16)

6. God established the <u>Abrahamic Covenant</u> when he changed Abram's name to Abraham, which means *"the father of many nations,"* and as a sign of covenant, God told Abraham *to circumcise all his male children on the day after birth.* Then God told Abraham that this *covenant will be establish with Isaac, who Sarah shall bear unto thee at this set time in the next* God also changed Sarai's name to Sarah and promised to establish everlasting covenant with her son, Isaac, and his seed after him. (Ge 17:1-10)

7. In Genesis 21:1-21, Isaac was born to Sarah and Abraham, and he circumcised on the 8th day. God also promised Hagar that he would make son, Ishmael, a great nation.

8. In Genesis 22:1-8, God told Abraham to take Isaac and some wood Mount Moriah to offer him as a burnt offering. As Abraham was about this son, Isaac, the angel of the Lord stayed his hand and God provide sacrifice: a ram, caught in a thicket by his horns. This was symbolic o coming Messiah, God's only beloved Son, who would take our place o Cross to pay sin's debt.

9. <u>The Mosaic Covenant</u>: In Deuteronomy 29:1-9 & 30:19-20, Moses by the words of the covenant, which God told him to make with the child Israel, and told them to keep the words of the covenant and do them, so will prosper.

"I call heaven and earth to record this day against you, that I have set before you life and death, blessing and cursing; therefore choose life, that both you and your seed may live; that you may love the Lord thy God, and that you may obey his voice, and that you may cleave unto him; for he is thy life and the length of thy days; that you may dwell in the land which the Lord swore unto thy fathers, to Abraham, to Isaac, and to Jacob, to give them."

Four hundred years after the covenant with Abraham, *God gave The Law to Moses* to show the people what was causing the *enmity* between them. He instructed them on the building of *the Tabernacle* and established *the feasts and sacrifices.* Everything God told them was *symbolic of the coming Messiah* and his plan of redemption. It was divided into three chambers: In the center of the outer chamber, there was *a brazen altar* where the animal sacrifices were tied to the four horns of the altar and slain *(a picture of Calvary's cross where the Lamb of God would be slain)*. Then there was *the brazen laver* surrounded with mirrors where the priests washed daily and saw their reflections *(showing our need for a daily cleansing by the washing of water with the Word)*. Inside the holy place on the right side of the altar, was *the table of showbread (representing Jesus as the true bread from heaven)*, and on the left side of the altar, was *a seven branch lampstand*, fueled by oil and kept continuously burning *(representing the holy spirit and symbolizing Jesus as the light of the world and the Spirit without measure)*.

A thick heavy veil hung between God and the people, and, directly in front of the veil, was *the altar of incense (representing the prayers of the saints)* which the priest would wave before the altar so the sweet aroma could drift up over the curtain before God. Behind the veil, was *the third chamber (representing the throne of God) where his glory dwelt above the Ark of the Covenant*. The ark was made of acacia wood and covered with gold *(representing the humanity and deity of Christ)*. It contained three things: *Aaron's rod that budded, the pot of manna, and the tablets containing the Law*. Because the Law represented man's failures and condemnation, *God instructed Moses to build a mercy seat above the ark* so that a blood sacrifice could be placed there for the atonement of sins. Each year on the Day of Atonement, *the high priest would go behind the veil and place the blood from the sacrifice on the mercy seat*. God would look down, see the blood and tell the people their sins were covered for another year. This blood on the mercy seat was a temporary propitiation for sin, which would have to be repeated every year. Someday, the blood sacrifice of Jesus would be placed there on the mercy seat, and the sacrifices of bulls and goats would be no more.

Covenants were very popular in the days of Jonathan and David, and we see them making a covenant in 1st Samuel 18, where Jonathan gives David his robe, armor, sword, bow and belt because the Scripture says that *"he loved him as his own soul."* In those days, covenant partners would exchange robes, or coats, to symbolize putting on the other person's character. They exchanged belts, or girdles, to represent strength, and they exchanged weapons as a sign of taking on the other person's enemies. It was also customary to have a ceremony, *or covenant meal*, whereby each of the covenant partners would break off a piece of bread and place it in the other's mouth saying, *"This is me: you are eating me."* Sometimes the

Gentiles would mix a drop of their blood in their covenant partner's wine, but the Jews would never do this because they are forbidden to drink blood. Therefore, the wine is symbolic of the blood Covenant.

10. The New Covenant: In Hebrews, Chapters 8, 9 and 10: *The cutting of a Covenant through the "veil of his flesh"* did away with the Old Covenant provided a new and living way for people to come to God through Jesu the evening of the Passover, Jesus sat with the twelve disciples. As he the bread, he said to them, *"This is my body which is broken for you."* he held up the cup and said, *"This is the New Covenant in my blood who shed for you. Do this in remembrance of me."* (Matthew 26:26-38; 14:22-25; Luke 22:19-20; John 6:53-58)

When we enter into covenant with Jesus, we receive the same authority He received from God the Father, and He gave us His authority to act in His name. He said that we would do *even greater works than these after I go to the Father* (John 14:12). The power comes through the work of the Holy Spirit when we ask him, or allow Him, to do His work. In covenant, Jesus takes on our enemies, and His enemies become our enemies; He takes our weakness and gives us His strength; He bore our sickness and disease, so we could be in good health. When we are willing to remove our soiled garments of pride and self- righteousness, which to God appear as *filthy rags*, we are finally able to put on His *pure white, spotless robe of righteousness.*

At the moment Jesus died, as darkness covered the land and the earth quaked, the thick, heavy veil in the Jewish temple, which had kept the people away from God since Moses, *was ripped in two from top to bottom,* a fact well-documented in ancient Jewish records. This veil represented *the barrier of sin* which always existed between God and the people, *and it also represented Christ's flesh, which had taken on the sins of the world.* Symbolically, *God ripped the flesh of the sacrificial Lamb of God right down the middle in the cutting of the New Covenant, providing "a new and living way for people to come to God through the veil of his flesh."*

"This is the covenant that I will make with them after those days, saith the Lord. I will put my laws in their hearts and in their minds will I write them; and their sins and iniquities will I remember no more. Now where remission of these is, there is no more offering for sin.

> *"Having, therefore, brethren, boldness to enter into the holiest by the blood of Jesus, by a new and living way, which he hath consecrated for us, through the veil, that is to say, of his flesh."* (Hebrews 10:19-20)

In the Abrahamic Covenant, Abraham provided the sacrifice and God walked through the pieces of the animal sacrifice. Now God is providing the sacrifice of his Son, and he is asking us to walk through the pieces. It's God's responsibility to keep the *"Abrahamic Covenant"* with Israel, but it's our responsibility as Christians to keep the *"New Covenant." The Law* came by Moses, but *Grace and Truth* came by Jesus. On Judgment day, we will either stand before *a throne of Judgment* and be judged *according to our works,* or we will stand before *a throne of Grace* and receive *the free gift* of eternal life. (Matthew 27:50-51; Mark 15:38; and Luke 23:45)

The Kinsman Redeemer

In the Book of Ruth, we see the story of the widow, Naomi, and her daughter-in-law, Ruth, who after losing her husband decides to go with Naomi back to her people and said, *"whither thou goest, I will go; and where thou lodgest, I will lodge: thy people shall be my people and thy God my God."* From this story, we learn the importance of *the kinsman redeemer.* Our kinsman redeemer had to be:

1. A man;
2. A kinsman by blood (or blood covenant);
3. One willing to pay the price; and
4. One able, or worthy, to purchase our redemption.

He had to be totally without sin in order to be worthy to pay the price for our sin and buy us back. Because no sin could be found in Jesus because he lived a sinless life upon the earth, death could not hold him. Thus, the resurrection! What Jesus did that day, he did totally in his humanity as the son of man and not the Son of God. (Psalm 8:4-6) (Hebrews 2:5-9) While His body was in the tomb, his soul passed into Hades where he took the keys of hell and death from Satan and brought up with him out of *Paradise* all the Old Testament saints of the faith of Abraham, who had believed in the promise of his coming, and took them to the third heaven.

When Jesus went into the heavenly tabernacle, he placed his own blood on the mercy seat as the sacrificial Lamb of God. (Hebrews 9:11-15)

> *"For it is not possible that the blood of bulls and goats should take away sin. Wherefore when he cometh into the world, he saith, Sacrifice and offering thou wouldst not, but a body hast thou prepared me: in burnt offerings and sacrifices for sin thou hast had no pleasure…. He takes away the first that he may establish the second… by which we are sanctified through the offering of the body of Jesus Christ once for all…But this man, after he had offered one sacrifice for sins forever, sat down on the right hand of God… For by one offering he hath perfected forever them that are sanctified…*
>
> *"This is the covenant that I will make with them after those days, says the Lord, I will put my laws into their hearts, and in their minds will I write them; And their sins and iniquities will I remember no more… Having therefore boldness, brethren, to enter into the holiest by the blood of Jesus by a new and living way, which he has consecrated for us through the veil of his flesh, and having a high priest over the house of God; let us draw near with a true heart in full assurance of faith. (Hebrews 10:4-22)*
>
> *"Wherefore seeing we are compassed about by so great a cloud of witnesses, let us lay aside every weight, and the sin which so easily beset us, and let us run with patience the race that is set before us, looking to Jesus, the author and finisher of our faith; who for the joy that was set before him endured the cross despising the shame, and is set down before the throne of God."* (Hebrews 12:1-2)

Now when God the Father looks down from heaven and sees us through the blood of Jesus, the Lamb of God, which He placed on the mercy seat as an atonement for our sin, He sees us *in spotless garments, white and clean,* which have been *washed in the blood of the Lamb.*

CHAPTER EIGHT

Search for a New Beginning

1978-1980

My mother was a precious gem and always welcomed us home. She had been aware of our situation from the start and wanted to help if she could. Mother's bedroom with private bath was in the back of the house overlooking beautiful Mobile Bay. She allowed me the liberty of moving Maggie into the front corner bedroom and painting her walls a pretty blue to match the rest of her previous décor. We also sent her plush green carpet down to make her room comfortable and as much as possible like the one she had left. We knew this move was a big disruption for Maggie, but we hoped it would also get her away from the bad environment she fell into there in Vienna and somehow make us all stronger in the process. At the same time, we took our big sectional couch down to have reupholstered in Fairhope because John just didn't have room for it in his small apartment. I moved my clothes into the middle bedroom, which Mother always spoke of as "Libby's room," and Greg's things were taken upstairs to his attic bedroom where he and Jimmy had stayed while John was serving his second tour of duty in Vietnam.

For the first week, everything seemed to be going well. Greg got a job working at Ben's Barbecue on the causeway about half-way to Mobile, and he made pretty good wages for loading the dishwasher. Greg managed to get a ride with one of the workers at Ben's who also lived on the eastern shore. Ben was a wonderful man to work for, and he let all the guys eat well and even take home beer. I could tell Greg was buying pot again due to signs of the munchies, and he would stay upstairs in his room most of his off time. I would just have to be patient and let circumstances take care of themselves if I was going to succeed in getting him into treatment.

One evening Greg left the house early to meet some of his friends at a small park overlooking Mobile Bay. It was just a few blocks from Mother's house, and, some evenings, we could hear Greg coming home through the neighborhood by the sound of his small portable radio. Some of the young people seemed to gravitate to this place to hang out, and the police kept a close watch on it. Greg told me one evening that he was going to a carnival which had just come to our area, and a couple of hours later, I received a phone call from the police. They had arrested Greg for being drunk in public at the carnival and were taking him to the county jail to sober up. The policeman said he would be released the following morning, but I requested that he be held for evaluation by Mental Health. The doctor's report showed Greg had a "rigid," or "fixed," personality disorder which allowed him to make up his own rules and rebel against authority. He suggested that we make an appointment with a local mental health program which was supervised by a Christian minister in our area.

Pastor Jerry was doing a great job working with problem teenagers in the area. Maggie and I went to the first appointment, but there was no way we could get Greg to go with us. Eventually, the pastor came out to meet Greg at Mother's house and climbed the steep stairs up to his attic room to have a talk with him. Greg liked Pastor Jerry but refused to attend the weekly meetings. He enjoyed working at his job on the causeway and meeting with some of his friends at other times. Maggie and I continued attending the meetings which were good for her to express her grievance about having to leave school and all her friends in Vienna. I tried to make it up to her somewhat by buying her an electric guitar and driving her to Mobile for weekly guitar lessons. She had learned to read music in the 7th grade while taking clarinet lessons.

One day while Maggie stayed home with Mother to practice her guitar lessons, Greg accompanied me to the Naval Air Station to load up on groceries and do a little shopping at the BX. While I was in the Commissary, he had lunch at the Subway Station and then looked around the BX for a few things he needed. We made our purchases, loaded the car and drove on home to put up the groceries and have supper with Mother and Maggie. Later that evening, we heard a commotion upstairs in the attic. It sounded like Greg was having a party as the volume of his stereo climbed higher and higher. Maggie and I climbed the stairs to peek in to see what was happening, and, as we fearfully suspected, we saw a liquor bottle on the floor about three fourths empty. I had already decided what

I would do in such a case as this and called the police because we were both afraid that Greg might die from an overdose.

Two officers came out right away and found him comatose upstairs in the attic. Greg was unable to move, and somehow, the officers got him down the steep steps and into the back seat of our car. They told me to drive him to the nearest emergency room because they couldn't be responsible for him in that condition. Greg couldn't move his body at all and could only roll his eye balls to show that he was still alive. I had never seen him like that before. Maggie stayed home because there was no room for her in the car with Greg sprawled out over the back seat, so Mother and I drove him straight to Mobile Infirmary. They pulled him onto a stretcher and rolled him into the Emergency Room. She and I waited inside for a while, and, when we heard him starting to come out of it, we left him there overnight to be picked up the following morning. After getting him back home, he told us what happened. While I was in the Commissary, he took a walk over to the NAS Package Store and used his Military ID card to make a purchase. Since I had so many bags to bring in, I didn't notice when he took his bag upstairs.

Both Greg and Maggie were registered at Fairhope High School shortly after the Christmas break and caught the school bus every day from a little park near Mother's house. At first everything seemed to be going as planned, but Greg sought out the pot smokers. Maggie went to her classes and seemed to be adjusting fairly well, but, when it came to dissecting a frog, she rebelled against it and started skipping class. She found her place among the *gulley gang,* those who sneaked out of class and found their way down through the gulley to Fairhope beach. On the beach, they could play Frisbee and just hang around until it was time to catch the school bus back home. I had no idea about all of this until the Principal called me into his office one day. Maggie was put on *probation,* and Greg was *expelled* for smoking pot on the school grounds along with a few others. After this, Greg was picked up in Fairhope with some other kids in a truck and tested for marijuana. They found no drugs on him but his *pipe,* which they found in his pocket, contained residue. When his case came up before the court, I suggested to Greg that he offer to work off his fine by doing public service work. The Judge agreed and sentenced him to two weeks in the public jail while he worked it off.

Pastor Jerry was able to get Greg into an in-patient Mental Health Program in Mobile during the spring which he liked because he met a lot of other young people like himself. They all seemed to get along very well and had a lot of things in common. However, after a period of observing his sometimes bizarre behavior, the supervisor sent him home for the weekend. They were also having some construction work done on the building and were testing a few of the guys by allowing them to go home for Mother's Day weekend. I couldn't hold him there, and he took off hitchhiking to the Gulf. While drinking some beer down there, he made the mistake of asking a patrolman for a light for his cigarette. Of course, they determined his condition and took him to jail to sober up, and they allowed him to call me to come down and get him on Sunday morning. I took Greg back Monday morning as instructed, and, when they learned of his arrest at the beach Saturday night, they released him back to me saying that there was nothing more they could do for him there. Their analysis along with the recommendation from Pastor Jerry indicated that he needed long term treatment: They recommended that he be sentenced to the State of Alabama's Drug & Alcohol Treatment Program.

By this time, John had checked with The Army Hospital to see what they could do for Greg up there in the way of a drug treatment program. I reminded him that he had to be under a "Court Order" which would hold him for the duration of the Program because up there it had to be entirely "voluntary." They couldn't hold him against his will! John said that the doctor he spoke with assured him that they could take care of Greg up there just as well as they could in Alabama. John had been able to catch up on his sleep and wanted his family back up there with him. He thought if Greg was in treatment in a facility up there, we would be able to visit him occasionally. John drove down to go with us to Greg's second court hearing and met Pastor Jerry. I had requested the lady Judge, who I was told was very compassionate about helping young people like Greg, and they had assigned Greg's case to her. With the recommendations of Pastor Jerry and the Mental Health Program in Mobile, the Judge was ready to sentence Greg to one year in the State's long-term Drug & Alcohol Abuse Program.

John didn't like the idea of a *"Court Order,"* which in his mind would be equivalent to serving time and the beginning of a *"Record."* He wanted us back up there with him, and I had to break the news to Pastor Jerry who had worked so hard to get us to this point. John drove down for the last Court Hearing and told the Judge our plan to take Greg back with us and get him into treatment in Northern Virginia. After all we had been through, and the imposition on my mother and the upheaval it had cost

Maggie, I couldn't believe I let him talk me into it. The Court released Greg at age 19 back into our hands where we, once again, had to bear the responsibility of getting him into treatment.

The appointment which John had set up for Greg at the Army Hospital was with a young Psychiatrist who would evaluate our situation and make the proper arrangements for treatment. We all three met together in his office and then Greg met with him privately, as is usually the case when one has to volunteer. I couldn't believe it! My worst fears were realized! After all we had been through to get our son the help he so desperately needed, Greg had convinced this young doctor that it was just a *marital problem* between his mom and dad referring to our six-month *separation*. We didn't find this out until after Greg's accident when John tried to get some financial help through The Army Hospital. Then he was allowed to read the *"Summary of the Evaluation"* of the young Psychiatrist who interviewed us. He had diagnosed Greg as *"Normal"* and our family as *"Dysfunctional."* This young doctor referred us to *Crossroads* for *"Outpatient Family Counseling."* If John and Greg had been willing to attend these meetings, it might have proved beneficial after these professionals learned the severity of our case and were allowed to make their evaluation. However, I really didn't know of any State of Virginia in-patient program as good as the one in Alabama, which had the power of the Court to hold a young person in a long-term drug abuse program and teach them a trade after first drying them out. Their success rate was outstanding as I learned from others whose children had been in the Alabama State Program. We found ourselves right back where we started in the cauldron of drugs of the DC area.

Maggie registered at her old high school in Vienna at the beginning of the school year, and was able to spend the first three months with her best friend, Brenda, and her wonderful family. They practically adopted Maggie until we could bring her home. Brenda's twin sister had been killed in an automobile accident in which her grandmother was also killed. They took Maggie under their wings for those three months, which allowed her to get back into her old high school at the beginning of the year. Greg got a job stacking shelves in a McLean drug store, and all three of us, John, Greg and I, stayed in John's small McLean apartment until we could move into our new townhouse. It would mean a longer drive for John into work each day from Vienna, but his hours were now from 8:00–5:00, a normal work day and we would have much better sleeping arrangements. After a couple of weeks, Greg got his first paycheck from the drugstore and didn't come home from work as usual. Around 1:00 am, two patrolmen brought him to our front door and said they found him sitting cross-legged in the median of Chain Bridge Road. He was highly intoxicated.

I took advantage of my time in McLean while living so close to the Washington District, to take the Government tests and apply for a job. I had heard of the dire need for secretaries in the government agencies and thought it would be a good use of my time to see what offers I could get. My phone was ringing off the hook for a few days, and I must have gone to half a dozen interviews that first week, several in the Department of Agriculture. Then one day, as I was on my way up to the Personnel Office on the 9th floor of a high- rise office building in downtown Rosslyn, I met a young woman on the elevator who asked where I was going. I told her, and she said, "Well stop by my office on the 8th floor on your way down, Room 808, because we need a secretary badly." There had been a temporary freeze on hiring in the DC area, and the freeze had just been lifted. The Recreation Scientist in Forest Environment Research had just that morning told her to get him a secretary ASAP.

I did stop by Room 808 on the way down, and Peggy, the Staff Secretary for FER, met me at the door and escorted me around the offices introducing me to everyone. There were five scientists and three secretaries working in FER, under the Department of Agriculture, but Dr. Cramer, the scientist for *Recreation and Tourism*, was not there at the moment. Peggy introduced me to the fabulous *Wang* computer system with two terminals in the office for the secretaries to use, and I immediately fell in love with it. I had never typed on a word processor before, and it was a tremendous improvement over my old electric typewriter. The vibes of the office were right, and I knew this was it! I was totally at home in the office atmosphere and literally fell in love with the place, the people and the job. When Dr. Cramer returned from the South Building, he approved my application, and I was hired to start immediately.

Peggy and I had the first two desks on the left as one entered the office, and one station of the Wang was toward the windows in the open area between us. The office of my boss, Dr. Cramer, was to my right, and the office of the Director of FER was to her left. The secretary to the scientist for "Fish & Wildlife" was directly across the room from me, and the offices of the other scientists looked out over the beautiful Washington Monuments. Peggy and I synchronized our two small radios to our favorite radio station at a very low volume to produce a desirable stereo effect for a pleasant office atmosphere. On the eighth floor, we were practically level with the flight path of the airliners flying into National Airport over the Potomac River. It was very exciting!

John had picked out a beautiful new townhouse development right next to I- 66, which took us over to I-81, the Interstate System which ran all the way down through the beautiful Shenandoah Valley. He drove me over to Vienna to have a look at the townhouse available for lease and it was beautiful. We signed the lease immediately to move in sometime in November. It was a three-bedroom townhouse with two full bathrooms upstairs and a dining room with large bay windows overlooking the freeway both downstairs and upstairs in our master bedroom. It also had a nice living room with gold carpeting and a large eat-in kitchen and half-bath on the first floor. It would be perfect for our needs and our plants could flourish in the two large bay windows. We moved in before the end of November and were completely settled before Christmas. Jim came home for Christmas vacation and worked again at Burger King. It seemed like a new beginning for all of us. Maggie was already engaged in her studies, although she was a year behind her classmates and would have some catching up to do. Since our townhouse was located on the dividing line between the two school districts, both Greg and Maggie could have their new starts individually in two different high schools. Our reupholstered sectional couch in a lovely shade of blue was delivered to Mother's house with new pillows of bright yellow and matching blue just in time to be picked up with the rest of our shipment to Vienna. Mother was as happy about it as we to see what a good job they had done. It fit into our new small living room in three separate sections and blended in beautifully with the gold carpeting. The small dining room received our older set of living room furniture along with most of our plants and expanded the living area quite a bit. Our large kitchen with all the amenities also provided space for our dining table overlooking the Interstate. We were well equipped with our large Master Bedroom upstairs with private bath and large walk-in closet for John and me and two smaller bedrooms for Greg and Maggie and a large full bathroom for them to share. We also had a very nice half-bath downstairs for brushing teeth and last minute preparations before leaving the house. The kids and I even tacked up some leftover carpet padding on the boards in the unfinished basement to make a large den, a utility room with the W/D and a storage area. We put our corner group with the two small beds, table and lamp down there and some patio furniture. It was a great place for the young people to play their guitars and listen to their music, which John and I appreciated not being able to hear upstairs on the first two floors.

Maggie had a good dependable job working after school at MacDonald's just a few blocks from her high school, and Greg had a variety of new places to work in his new high school district before coming home in the evening. Sometimes, we would give him money in the morning to pay for our orders, and he would bring home Fish & Chips from Arthur Treacher's, or Chicken dinners from Kentucky Fried, etc. Later, as his jobs seemed to vary from one place to another, it might be pizza, barbecue or hamburgers. Sometimes, on rare occasions, John and I would pick up Chinese from our favorite Vienna *"Carry-Out"* on our way home, and that was always a happy occasion for all of us to share around our kitchen table. Usually, however, our reconstructed leftovers from Sunday dinner would last until the middle of the week.

I loved my job and told everyone that I came to work to get some rest. As time passed, they couldn't believe all the stuff we were going through at home with our irregular hours of sleep. Our drive into work each morning took about 45 minutes, but it gave John and me time to discuss our family business and the on-going problems which never ceased. In the afternoons, we enjoyed listening to our favorite music and hearing the evening news. Greg had many new starts, but not really a new change of lifestyle, as we continued with many revised plans for a new start and new *"Agreements"* which he signed over the two years we lived there at the townhouse development. His attitude remained the same as he continued to play his games with us. We knew it was a long shot that he would straighten up the way things were, however, we had no alternative but to try to make each plan work as best we could while keeping our jobs and our home together. We never quit hoping that Greg would get his life together.

Towards the end of June, Maggie told us that a friend from Fairhope was on his way up for a visit and needed someone to meet him at the Greyhound Bus Station. It was Saturday, so we all piled in the station wagon and drove down to the bus station to meet him. What else could we do? Marvin, a casual acquaintance of Maggie's from "the gulley gang" in Fairhope, stayed with us a few days and slept in our basement while he was making up his mind what to do next. They were like *"peas in a pod"* when he first arrived with lots to talk about, but then, after a couple of days, Maggie told him it was time for him to go because she was very busy getting on with her life and didn't need any more disruptions. She had a good job at a popular record store in Vienna and was making good progress catching up with her class in Adult Ed.

Marvin became friends with Greg, and I tried to drop them both off at the Army Induction Station, but they wouldn't get out of the car. Neither of them wanted to get a haircut! It could have been very good for both of them and given them a life. Marvin told Greg that he knew where he could get a job… on a shrimp boat out of New Orleans. If Greg would ride the bus back home with him to Fairhope, his dad would meet them and drive them over to apply for a job when the shrimp boats came in. Marvin said there were always plenty of jobs to go around because the guys coming in from the boats had lots of money to spend, and they would stay ashore as long as it lasted. It sounded good to us, so we bought Greg a bus ticket. Well, as the story goes, it was so hot ashore that all the ship hands returned to their jobs to go back out to sea where it was cool. There weren't any jobs! The boys returned to Fairhope with Marvin's dad, but Greg didn't want to stay at their house to wait on the next shrimp boat because he noticed spiders at Marvin's house, so he went to his grandmother's house. Mother's first thought was that we had sent him down to live with her, which was entirely ridiculous and out of the question. How could we ever have expected this plan to work when nothing else ever did? We bought him a bus ticket home immediately, and my brother, Joe, who had driven over to help Mother, drove him to the bus station to see him off.

On August 9, 1979, John had to leave on a very important mission to Egypt and left me with instructions to call LTC Jackson if there was an emergency while he was away and gave me his telephone number. When I arrived home that Friday evening, Greg had a message from his grandmother, Hannah, that John's dad, Cyrus, died that morning and funeral services would be held Monday morning. I had to call Robby to get the news to John so he could be turned around to come home for the funeral. The team of about 20 personnel, including senior representatives of all services, led by the Secretary of Defense, left Andrews Air Force Base at approximately 4:00 pm and was scheduled to arrive at Torrejon Air Force Base, Spain at 5:10 am for refueling on their way to Cairo. John got the message to call Robby about half way across the Atlantic. As Army Strategist on this team of "action officers" for the Secretary of Defense, John was involved in coordinating the Army portion of the total package of military assistance the US was prepared to give Egypt totaling over \$850M worth of military hardware, training and joint operations. This was a clear signal to the world that Egypt was no longer under the military umbrella of the Soviet Union, but now would receive close military assistance from the United States.

John hurried to the Operations Center at Torrejon to call Robby and received the news of his father's death. He had already experienced a long day and night without sleep, and now he had to turn around at 5:30 am Saturday morning to find a way home. His only possibility was a *freedom bird flight* out of Germany with a load of family members returning to the States. This flight to London Gatwick required verification from the US of Emergency Leave Travel Authorization. LTC Jackson and John's CO, COL Richards, got the Red Cross involved in order to get the authentication of his father's death in Mississippi to the Torrejon AFB Office in Spain in time for John to board the flight to London Gatwick. Thank goodness he made it! From Gatwick the following morning, he caught a flight to McGuire AFB, NJ. Since there were no connections to Washington, John had to ride the bus to the Philadelphia Airport and catch the first shuttle out Sunday morning at 8:20. There to meet him at Washington National Airport upon his arrival was his wife, his son, Greg, and his daughter, Maggie. Jim stayed home with Kitty to finish his summer job at Burger King before having to drive back to Ole Miss for the fall semester.

John called home from several places along the way to tell me what to do to get him ready for the funeral, then finally called early Sunday morning to give me his time of arrival at National Airport. I found his dress blues and had him all packed and ready to dress for the funeral Monday morning. Then Maggie and Greg helped me pack the car and prepare a bed for John in the full back portion of the Yellow Sub, so he could crawl in and get some sleep. But first, we stopped at MacDonald's for a quick breakfast and then hit the road over to I-81 for the long drive down through the Blue Ridge Mountains. John didn't wake up until we reached Roanoke about five hours later, where he took over the driving all the way to his mother's house in northern Mississippi. His mother was frantic because she didn't hear from us all day Sunday while we were driving. I had called her several times Saturday to let her know of John's difficulties in finding a way home but didn't have time to call Sunday morning when we were thrown into quick action. After our arrival, she finally understood what all he had been through to get there in the early hours of Monday morning.

We had time to get a little sleep before it was time to get up and dress for the 10:00 am funeral. We were glad to see that John's brother, Mark, and his wife, had arrived over the weekend to be with Hannah to comfort her during her time of sorrow and intense anxiety over John's very late arrival.

Back in Vienna, I continued calling my Mary Kay customers, and Maggie would sometimes ride with me to make deliveries. Although things had changed somewhat for the better in the neighborhoods which had taken control of their areas and kicked out some of *the bad apples,* they had gotten worse in others. The kids who attended church with their families had a much better chance of staying drug free and finishing school. However, many families chose to move to a better environment and try to get away from their problems, but, if their kids were already hooked, they would find a way to fill their needs one way or another. It was a terrible time for all of us!

> *"We looked for peace, but no good came; and for a time of health, and behold trouble! Is there no balm in Gilead?"* (Jeremiah 8:15&22) Yes, there is balm in Gilead: It's the Word of God.

John's mother spent Christmas of 1979 with us in our new townhome, and Jim didn't come home that year because of problems with the little Vega which was being repaired in Oxford. We experienced a blizzard which brought several feet of snow, and we were snowed in for several days. Our car was completely covered. I cooked a large turkey, and we had a big Christmas Dinner with all the trimmings, but it was interrupted when John was called into work unexpectedly due to Russia's invasion of Afghanistan. He had a hard time cleaning off the car and getting it out through the snow of our housing area to the main roads on his drive to the Pentagon. It was Hannah's first Christmas without her husband, and we all felt sadness at his absence from the dinner table before John was called back to work. This Christmas Day was very sad for all of us in spite of our poor attempts to make it joyful with Christmas music and TV Specials. The beautiful pristine snow did brighten it up a bit, although it kept us snowed in for a while. John made it back later that evening and we had plenty of good food to last all week. It was hard getting around for a while, but the snow melted enough the following week to drive Hannah to the airport for her flight back to Memphis. We hated to see her go but it was good for all of us to get back to work!

John started Law School at Catholic University with night classes now that he had regular hours which corresponded with mine, and somehow we continued to commute back and forth each day to work. In spite of our full- time jobs, John's Law School, and having to take care of a three story townhouse, we did very well. However, it was another two years of the same old games Greg played with us, pushing his luck more and more all the time, and looking back, I don't see how we survived it at all. John was forever kicking him out and Greg was forever finding a way to come back home. One day, he borrowed a ladder from our next-door neighbor to come in through one of our upstairs windows. He had all kinds of tricks and once covered his TV set with a black garbage bag so he could plug it into the back of our house and watch TV in the backyard. During our two-year period while living in our townhome, John would lay down the law and get Greg to sign an "Agreement" to get a job and keep our house rules in order to stay at home. This would work for a while and then we would find ourselves engaged again in a disturbance of major proportions, and I would call the Crisis Squad.

This usually resulted in our taking him to Court to try to force him into Treatment or getting a Restraining Order. Even under the *"Restraining Order,"* Greg found a way to come back: One night while we were asleep, we heard glass breaking downstairs and rushed down to find Greg trying to come in through a basement window. He cut his hand when a pane of glass broke and he was badly bleeding, so we brought him into the house to clean it up and bandage his wound. He seemed to try to straighten up for a week or two and then he would pull a really big one in which the Crisis Squad would have to be called out again. Crossroads got to know us very well those two years and listed us as a *Dysfunctional Family*, which probably resulted from our inability, or refusal, to attend their meetings. Maybe if we had gone to them, as they encouraged us to do, we could have handled everything differently and produced better results. However, neither John nor Greg were willing to attend these meetings. In retrospect, Maggie and I should have attended them anyway as a *lifeline of support*.

Saturdays were difficult for me because there were always the normal chores to be done in a three-story townhouse with a large family. I would go through it in the morning gathering all the clothes to be washed in the basement and vacuuming at least the top two levels as needed, then shopping for groceries and preparing the meal of the week with leftovers to see us through at least a couple of days. Some of our favorites were:

Beef Stew, Pot Roast, Baked Ham, Barbecued Chicken, Spaghetti, and Arabic Moussaka. But on Sunday morning, John and I needed our day of rest. We didn't have time to attend church, but we did watch our favorite TV churches and insisted that Greg and Maggie join us. Two of our favorite Pastors were Robert Schuller and Oral Roberts. We collected a few of Pastor Schuller's beautiful eagle statues with our contributions and practiced *"Seed Faith Giving"* with Oral Roberts. From Oral's teachings, we learned the importance of planting good seed in good soil, so God could bring the increase. And he also taught us to *launch out into the deep,* as God led us when John decided to retire from the Army and take a job overseas.

For a *dysfunctional family,* we certainly had a busy and productive life! Everyone had plenty of room to have his own space, but *the fly in the ointment* remained to destroy our peace and rob us of all the joys of life. Greg's jobs changed as often as he received a paycheck and spent it before we got home from work on enough *"pot"* to get him fired. However, he had one job vacuuming a furniture store in Tyson's Corner which lasted aver a month. They didn't seem to mind if he was a little stoned at times. While he was working, he seemed to feel good about himself, but, sooner or later, the cycle would be repeated. Maggie handled her money well and kept her job at MacDonald's for a couple of years until she started working at Penguin Feather. She received her diploma from high school by making up her work with night courses, and she used some of her money to equip the little Vega with a stereo system when Jim left it at home for her use at the end of the summer. A couple of years later, Maggie would hand it back over to him in exchange for our pretty blue Malibu.

On the 8th of March 1980, John left on an important mission to Tunisia as a member of a 5-Man Joint State/Defense Department Policy Assessment Team. In February, President Bourguiba of Tunisia had asked President Carter for arms to counter a revolt by rebels in the southern region which they believed to be instigated by Libya. The rebels had attacked the town of Gafsa, resulting in 41 dead and 111 wounded. The team was sent over to assess possible further defense requirements and to assist the Tunisian military in meeting such threats in the future. [Washington Post, Saturday, March 1, 1980, "US Provides Tunisia Arms to Offset Pressure by Libya."]

The US Team was welcomed by the Tunisian Minister of Defense and introduced to his staff which would be assisting them throughout the week. They were given briefings throughout the first day by key members of the Tunisian armed forces. The next two days were spent inspecting facilities in the northern part of the country, and attending a luncheon hosted by the Minister of Defense. On the fourth day the team was flown to the southern region of the country to inspect forces in that region. John said that one such unit, *the 1st Brigade,* featured a very impressive *Camel Corps,* which was lined up along the entrance to the post. After a briefing from the Brigade Commander and tasting the wonderful Tunisian food at dinner, they were presented very nice gifts and flown by helicopter to the island of Djerba, just off the eastern coast. In this luxurious seaside hotel, John said the accommodations were excellent; however, they seemed to be the only guests in the hotel and were heavily guarded by a unit of Tunisian armed forces. He said that during the entire trip, *"the security was very heavy and quite obvious."* They guessed the Tunisian Government had concerns over their safety in light of the previous month's attacks by the rebels around Gafsa.

After breakfast the following morning, they were taken to the small airport on the island and loaded aboard the Puma helicopter for the flight back to Tunis. John said it was a beautiful day to fly and all twelve seats were filled with his group of five, the US Defense Attaché and his Assistant Army Attaché and others of the Tunisian Ministry of Defense. As the pilot lifted the helicopter off the runway, he climbed steeply and started to roll right. However, at around 600 feet in the air, they heard a loud bang. John looked to his left and noticed the rear hatch door was gone and the aircraft started to shake and rotate back toward the ground. The pilot, who John understood to be the Defense Minister's personal pilot, fought with the controls and was able to land in an upright position. It was a miracle that no one was hurt! Apparently there was a malfunction in the closing mechanism of the hatch door, and, not only had it blown out the rear of the aircraft, but it had taken a good portion of the rear rotor blades with it. The US Army Assistant Attaché in John's group who had flown helicopters in Vietnam, took a look at the rear rotor and said to the aircraft commander, *"I've flown a lot of hours in damaged helicopters, but I'm not getting back in that one."* Land vehicles were dispatched from Tunis, and the team took the long way back to the hotel that night across the causeway back up the east coast to the Capitol. John enjoyed the long drive up the coastal road, which he had driven on his first trip to Tunisia, and said it was very beautiful.

Toward the end of the survey, the American Ambassador to Tunisia, Stephen Bosworth, invited the Team out to his residence for dinner on the Northern Coast of Tunisia near the ancient ruins of Carthage and the American Cemetery at La Marsa. John said the residence was located on one of the most picturesque vantage points along the Mediterranean Sea and the view was spectacular. In his capacity as Strategist for North Africa on the Army Staff, John had briefed Ambassador Bosworth when he was first appointed to Tunisia, where he served until 1981. Upon their departure from Tunisia, the Minister of Defense presented each of the five men with a very unique gift, a beautiful Tunisian Desert Sand Rose. The Sand Rose is a crystalline structure formed primarily of gypsum in the desert of North Africa by the action of water, wind... and *lots* of time.

One night during the freezing winds of March while John was gone to Tunisia, Greg brought a friend into our home to get in out of the cold and let him sleep in our basement. The following morning when he came up for breakfast, I was astonished! I didn't know who he was or where he came from. His name was Jeremy and he seemed to appreciate Greg's bringing him in with him from the icy cold weather which had just hit our area. I questioned him, learned his story and gave him breakfast. Jeremy said he had hitchhiked across the country from California starting out with a friend who stayed behind in Texas. They were both working there when Jeremy decided to leave and found a ride to Roanoke with a truck driver at a truck stop. From there, he got a ride to Vienna, and now he was looking for a job. He had been sleeping in a storage van below our townhouse before the ice storm hit and Greg met him at the Seven Eleven. Maggie told him about MacDonald's where she had worked before finding her present job at Penguin Feather. That afternoon, Jeremy was a big help to Maggie and me when Greg brought in a couple of friends and started passing around a bottle of whiskey which belonged to one of them. Although the guys were trying to get it away from Greg, Jeremy helped me chase them all out. I threatened to call the police if they tried to come back in or caused any more trouble. Greg wondered why I was allowing Jeremy to stay inside our house that afternoon while he was kicked out. Of course, Greg came in that evening to share the downstairs basement with Jeremy now that things were under control. The following day, it seemed to warm up a bit so I loaned Jeremy an old quilt to use in the van where he had been sleeping since the worst of the bad weather was over. I explained that John would be terribly upset about our breaking the house rules, which he had laid down so strongly before his trip, if I let him stay any longer.

Jeremy was a very likeable young man, and I found him to be very helpful and trustworthy. He did get a job at MacDonald's, and it didn't take him long to find a room to rent somewhere in Vienna. A few months later, he stopped by to ask a favor of John and me. He used his last pay check from MacDonald's to buy a bus ticket back to California when he learned his stepmother was dying of cancer, and he needed us to drive him to the main Greyhound Bus Terminal so he could catch the express bus to California. John found out where it was located, and we got him there on time and saw him off. I'll always remember Jeremy, as he was boarding the bus, turning around to say to John and me, *"Have a good life!"*

After one of our serious confrontations with Greg when we had to call the Crisis Squad for help, the Fairfax Judge sentenced him to The State Hospital's long term Drug & Alcohol Treatment Program. Also about that time, we learned that the owners of our townhouse were coming back to Vienna and wanted to move in the following month at the end of our lease. Everything seemed to be falling in place: Maggie and a girlfriend had found a nice apartment in Vienna where they could share expenses while she remained an assistant manager at Penguin Feather; Greg was busily engaged in a program at the State Hospital in the Blue Ridge Mountains; and John and I were more than ready for a new beginning. We found the ideal apartment in Alexandria on a hilltop overlooking National Airport! It would be much closer to our jobs with half the driving time. John set up our move! Maggie and Joanie secured their apartment in Vienna, and John and I were finally able to pursue a peaceful lifestyle of our own.

Maggie and her friend moved into their apartment with our old living room furniture, some of our drapes, Maggie's French Provincial bedroom suite for her bedroom and a few of our plants. Our newly reupholstered sectional couch fit beautifully into our new living room together as one large piece of furniture and our old, but still beautiful and faithful old Mediterranean-style TV console still worked. Our bedroom suite fit nicely into the large master bedroom, and our second bedroom served as a guest bedroom for anyone who might come for a visit. Our kitchen was furnished with a washer-dryer combination, our dinette table and chairs fit snugly in the small kitchen and we had plenty of cabinet space plus all the modern appliances. Kitty found her new home to her liking, too, and learned to climb all the way up to the top of the kitchen cabinets and sometimes found her place in the sun outside on our balcony. All we needed to purchase was a round glass top table for the dining room and four comfortable padded chairs. Our lounge chairs fit nicely outside on our L-shaped balcony which looked out towards Washington, and our new dining room had a lovely view of National Airport.

CHAPTER NINE

A Time for Recuperation
1981

After a couple of months had gone by and Greg was still in the hospital, I called one evening after coming home from work and heard that old familiar sound of a *cotton ball tongue*. I could tell he was intoxicated, so I hung up and called the nurse's station. They were already on to him and had tied him to the bed until he sobered up. He had taken a ride in a wheelchair that morning and found an unsupervised supply closet where he confiscated several bottles of rubbing alcohol to bring back to his room and mix with his soft drinks that day. The nurses had also discovered that he was not taking his medication but saving up his pills to take all at once to produce a *high*. They had to crush them up and stand by to watch him drink them down. It seemed to be part of the game he was playing with them at the hospital to see how much he could get away with, just as he had done with us over the years.

John and I were determined more than ever not to let Greg come home until he had completed a drug rehabilitation program. However, as time passed and the hospital could not find a facility which would take him in his immobile condition, John and I finally had to give in and drive over to pick him up on the day he was discharged from the hospital. Without a court order to hold him in a program, none of them were willing to take him anyway. Teen Challenge seemed to stand out above the others because it was the only one in which I thought Greg might be interested in long enough to follow through to completion. When he was in his preteens, he had seen the movie, <u>The Cross and the Switchblade</u>, and it made a big impression on him. It told the story of a Pentecostal preacher, Pastor David Wilkerson, who went to New York to save the lives of gang members, which he read about in the newspaper. He actually turned some of them around with his preaching of the gospel. They murdered people on the streets and were heavily into drugs and lives of crime. Greg also read the book, <u>*Run Baby Run*</u>, written by one of the gang members whose life was changed.

I called Teen Challenge and three of the guys came by the hospital to meet Greg and tell him about their program. He liked them and said he was interested, and I believe he did give it serious consideration. One of the guys told Greg about trying to kill himself because he was so lost and caught up in a miserable lifestyle which he hated but couldn't get out of. Greg agreed to volunteer for their program. However, there was one stipulation: he had to be ambulatory to take part in all their activities. They promised to put him on their waiting list while he was waiting for a prosthesis. We drove over to GWU Hospital on his discharge date and brought him home. A few days later, President Reagan and Jim Brady were brought into the same emergency room where Greg had received his emergency treatment. Both the President and Jim Brady were victims of gunshot wounds and also needed emergency surgery to save their lives. The President recovered but Jim Brady, who was shot in the head, was disabled for life.

Once again, we were faced with having to lay down the law and trust Greg to keep the house rules. We held onto the fact that Teen Challenge would be there waiting for him to enter their program as soon as he got his prosthesis. Through Social Services, I was able to arrange for a nurse to come by our apartment every morning for a couple of weeks to teach Greg how to wrap his stump to shape it for the future fitting of a prosthesis and how to do his exercises for firming up his leg muscles. I was also directed to the Virginia Department of Rehabilitative Services, and one of their counselors dropped by our apartment one afternoon to meet Greg and fill out papers requesting their services. A few days later, I received a phone call from Christine Ambers, Greg's newly assigned Counselor who made an appointment to come by after work to speak with John and me about Greg's *unlimited* possibilities. We were thrilled to learn about the new Woodrow Wilson Rehabilitative Center in the Shenandoah Valley which contained everything a handicapped person would need for a thorough restoration.

Christine told us that Greg could even complete a four-year college education while living at Woodrow Wilson if he had the desire and the ability. She said they would give him a College Aptitude Test upon the completion of his high school education and that would determine how much more education he would need. It would also help place him in the right courses for a suitable career. They would even help him find a job upon completion of the program. It seemed to be the answer to our prayers, and Greg seemed happy about the prospects of living in such a wonderful place where he could swim in the pool without feeling self-conscious about his missing limbs. She filled out the application but said it would first have to be approved by the Board before Greg could receive his entrance date. Christine proved to be an excellent Counselor and a dedicated professional who knew her business and would take no guff.

Several weeks after returning home, Greg started slipping out the front door of our apartment *to visit friends in the building.* He would leave the door slightly ajar, so he could go in and out. Many times, we would come home to find him slightly under the influence. He usually told us that he had been visiting friends. Later, he told us that one of his friends had put him in touch with a relative in New York City, who just happened to be *the best negligence lawyer on the East Coast,* and they were going to help him with a lawsuit against the Metro. We found out that this was true when the attorney came down to interview Greg regarding his case.

Eventually, Greg was making it all the way down the block to the Seven-Eleven on the corner to buy beer, drinking some of it there, and coming home with the rest of the *tall boys* stuck in his large coat pockets. After entering the apartment, he would head straight for the bathroom, lock the door and drink all the rest of the beer. Then we would hear him stumbling around before coming out and heading for the stereo to listen to his rock music. If it happened at night while we were asleep, John and I would be awakened by the sound of the stereo getting louder and louder, and we would get up and head straight for the living room to turn it down and try to keep Greg from dropping ashes or a lit cigarette on the rug or furniture. Usually when this happened, we would just give up trying to get any more sleep and turn on the coffee pot to get an early start to work after getting him to bed. Once again, Greg had the advantage! We were wearing out quickly and didn't know what to do about it. We couldn't just go on like this when we had to go to work and he was still recovering from surgery. We hoped that he would soon get his prosthesis and that Teen Challenge would have a place for him.

When Christine Ambers learned of Greg's recent escapades, she notified us that he would have to complete a long-term substance abuse program before he could be admitted to Woodrow Wilson. With all the seriously handicapped people living there at the Center, they simply could not take a chance on someone with a long history of drug abuse being admitted without first completing a long-term program. Greg maintained that he didn't need to complete a program because he wasn't addicted to anything. Christine responded that he *most certainly was addicted, if not "physically," then certainly "psychologically," and he most definitely needed a "long-term drug abuse program."* Otherwise, the lives of all the severely handicapped people at the Rehab facility would be in jeopardy, and the Department of Rehab would be held responsible if anything were to happen due to their negligence. Christine informed him that the Board would not approve his prosthesis until he volunteered for treatment. She promised to make an appointment for the fitting of a prosthetic device as soon as he showed signs of cooperating by attending an outpatient drug abuse program.

I received a phone call one day from a lady with Al Anon who invited me to attend a 6-week Workshop in Alexandria. I told her I was too busy with a full-time job and just didn't have the time, besides it was my son, Greg, who had the problem. She informed me that this program wasn't for him. It was for me! And it was for our family… to teach us how to handle family problems of addiction. She also made a good point: *"If one person in the family has a problem with alcohol or drugs, then the whole family has a problem and the whole family needs treatment."* She went on to say that each person in the family has a role to play in the life of the alcoholic, which revolves around the alcoholic every time there is an episode. It's like a *"merry-go-round"* that never stops. I thought it over and came to the conclusion that she was right. Eventually, after facing the facts, I was persuaded that I did indeed need to learn all I could about this important issue which seemed to be getting worse and worse. I reasoned that the program might provide us with *"a Life Line,"* which we might be able to use to bring us the professional help we needed. So, when the next course started during the summer and she called me back, I readily accepted. The Workshop would meet every Saturday morning for three hours from 9:00 am until noon.

Finally, Greg agreed to attend the Crossroads outpatient program, and Christine set up the Orientation. It would be his responsibility to attend the weekly meetings by riding the city bus which stopped in front of our building. Besides the weekly counseling sessions, they would keep a check on whether or not he was using drugs through urinalysis. After attending one of the meetings, he quit because he said it was too much trouble to get on and off the bus. Christine assured him that if he could haul beer all the way from the Seven-Eleven two blocks away up the steep incline to our building, then he could certainly manage to get on and off the bus which stopped right in front of it. Greg thought Christine would eventually give in and make the appointment, but Christine wasn't about to unless he was willing to cooperate. And he was in no hurry to leave our apartment. His escapades continued!

One Saturday morning, I invited Greg to ride along with me to buy a few groceries at the Commissary while he listened to the radio and watched the ducks on the lake. We had done this before without any trouble, and he seemed to enjoy getting out of the apartment. But this time, I returned to find him passed out on the back seat of the car with an empty mouthwash bottle on the floor. He had found a 32 oz. bottle of mouthwash in the trunk of the car and drunk every ounce. I was thrown into another state of *Emergency* and drove him directly to the nearest hospital where they pumped his stomach to save his life. His *blood ratio was .43* and could have been fatal. At one point, he stopped breathing and the medics really had to work on him to get him going again. The following morning, we were at the Court House for a re- committal hearing. This time, the Judge who tried him before gave him a stern warning that if it happened again, he would send him back to the State Hospital. The Judge told him that he would give him one more chance to make the outpatient program work, so I made another appointment for him with Crossroads within the week.

On the day of Greg's new orientation, I took the morning off from work, and the two of us enjoyed a nice, leisurely breakfast at IHOP before driving over to Fairfax for his 10:00 am appointment. He seemed happy and agreeable about making it work this time and showed renewed interest in being admitted to the Woodrow Wilson Rehab Center. It would only take about 6 months to complete the outpatient program, and then he could be admitted to WWRC. After signing in at the Crossroads admittance desk, we both talked to his new counselor, and then Greg talked with him privately. When we were being ushered out, Greg was told to call the office when he was ready to begin his new schedule. I thought it had already begun. Something was wrong. I realized then that he had not yet volunteered for the program. Once again, it was the same old thing as before! The program was voluntary, and it all depended on him to make it work. As soon as I arrived at my desk around noon, the phone was ringing. It was Greg, and I could tell again by his *cotton ball tongue* that he had been drinking and was well on his way to passing out. Immediately, I picked up my purse and headed out the door.

When I got home, I found Greg passed out on our 7th floor balcony with an empty bottle of rubbing alcohol lying nearby. I called 911 and the ambulance arrived within minutes to take him to the hospital where he went through the same procedure as before having his stomach pumped. This time, his heart stopped beating, and again, the doctors and nurses had to work hard to save his life. I called the Judge in Fairfax who promised to send him back to the State Hospital and arranged for another hearing, but this time, Greg was in Intensive Care and in no condition for a hearing. To show Greg's state of mind, he asked me to stay and have lunch with him just as I had done at GWUH following his accident. When I told him I couldn't possibly stay in the ICU and have lunch with him, he got peeved with me and said, *"Mom, what's wrong with you?"* I almost lost it as my voice became agitated, *"Greg, look at you lying there without your right foot and missing big toe. You almost died yesterday and the week before that, and you ask me what's wrong with me?"* The intensity of my voice brought the nurses quickly running in to usher me out because people were hooked up to respirators and other life-saving devices. They couldn't allow this kind of dispute between a hysterical mother and her totally disoriented son. After a few more days in the hospital, Greg was released to the Psychiatric Unit for observation and evaluation by the doctors of the hospital's Mental Health Unit.

During Greg's six weeks of observation, he shared a room with another young man in the Psychiatric Unit, which was located at the other end of the hospital. John and I were invited to visit on weekends during visiting hours, and we would sit around tables in the large recreation area where they served coffee and cookies. It was good to see him looking well and quite at home there as he took us around to see his room and introduce us to some of his friends. Of course, we also met with the doctors who were doing the evaluation, and they were quite forthcoming as they shared with us what they were learning about Greg. The patients attended group therapy sessions every day where they were led into discussions about what they thought had gone wrong in their lives and how they might change things for the better. This was very enlightening to us as they encouraged patients to take a good, honest look at their lives and discuss the consequences of their bad choices. Without a change in their behavior, they could not get well and live peaceful and productive lives. In denial, they passed the blame on to others to escape the responsibility of their behavior. They turned to alcohol and/or drugs to make themselves feel better and to try to feel *normal* again, however, this escape mechanism pushed them further into denial. Their relationships deteriorated as well as their minds and bodies, and they needed time out for healing mentally, physically, emotionally, and spiritually. The doctors called John and me in for a consultation and gave us the results of their analysis:

> [Greg had a *rigid mental attitude toward his environment and those in authority.* He lived *in a state of irresponsibility totally dependant on those around him to take care of him, even though he resented their authority over him. He showed no signs, or need, for a change in his lifestyle and was content to just go on day after day taking advantage of everyone.* The doctors had no alternative but to have him committed back to the State Hospital for the duration of their in-patient substance abuse program.]

They advocated another committal for long-term treatment, and they took it to Fairfax Court for a new court order. John and I were called upon once more to give our testimony as witnesses to Greg's apparent need for treatment, and we stated that we totally agreed with the doctors for his third committal. The Fairfax Judge kept his word and sentenced Greg to the completion of the State Hospital's Alcohol and Drug Abuse Program. Greg was in the program for about three days when he got himself kicked out on purpose to attend Jim's wedding. He and a friend left an AA meeting to buy beer at a Seven-Eleven and brought some back with them to the State Hospital. They were both asked to leave and were thrown out with all their things. The Highway Patrol found him and his friend hitchhiking back up the Interstate to northern Virginia with Greg still on crutches with his baggage strap over his shoulder.

I received a phone call at work from one of the officers who picked him up asking me to come down to the police station to get him. I told him I couldn't do that, since Christine, his Rehab Counselor, and the doctors had instructed all of us to stick together to be strong and not give in to him anymore until he completed a long-term substance abuse program. I tried to explain our situation, but the young officer just didn't understand and said, *"Well, have a nice day!"* as he slammed down the receiver. It was very hard those few days not knowing where Greg was or what he was doing. However, several times Christine assured us, *"Don't worry! He's a survivor!"*

After a few days, as we were preparing to drive down to Mississippi for the wedding, we received a phone call from John's mother that Greg was on his way to her house, and she had arranged for someone to meet his bus. He had stayed with a friend from the police station who bought him the bus ticket and put him on the bus for his grandmother's house in Mississippi. Greg was on his way to his brother's wedding. I'm sure this was his plan from the beginning: he knew the date of the wedding and that we would be there to pick up Hannah. He was also aware that we were planning on driving Maggie down for registration at Ole Miss at the same time. He knew we wouldn't leave him behind, so, once again, it all worked to his advantage just as he planned.

Greg attended the after-rehearsal dinner and ended up sharing our motel room. Maggie and her grandmother also shared a room together. Since Hannah had made Maggie's dress for her to wear for being in charge of the bride's book, she would be able to fit the dress on her before the wedding. My two brothers, Mike and Joe, and their families drove over from Mobile bringing Mother with them, and Uncle George and Aunt Grace drove down from Memphis. It was great seeing everyone and having them all together for this very happy occasion. Many of their college friends were there from Ole Miss, and we enjoyed watching Jim and Kathy open some of their wedding gifts sitting around the pool listening to the music coming from inside the restaurant.

The wedding at the First Methodist Church was beautiful, and Kathy looked radiant in her lovely white wedding gown. The reception followed at the Sheraton Motel where we and most of the guests were staying, and John and I were there to greet them along with Kathy's parents. The champagne fountain was flowing and an open bar was set up for the evening, the food was very good and everyone was having a great time dancing, eating and mingling in the crowd. Around 10 o'clock, the Bride and Groom made their *traditional getaway* under torrents of rice. Afterwards, John and I escorted his mom back to her room and we retired to our room for the evening. Maggie and Greg remained with the other young people who were still enjoying the party. Around 2:00 am, a highly intoxicated Greg was escorted to our room by a couple of Kathy's uncles; John finally got him to stay in the other bed where he soon passed out.

The party continued most of the night, and, just as we were about to get back to sleep, we heard people running and girls screaming. John put on his pants and went outside to find out what was going on. I got dressed and walked out to the pool area and found Kathy sitting in her father's lap crying. He was trying to console her! Jim had locked her out of the Bridal Suite and told her the marriage was off! I spoke to him through the door and convinced him to let Kathy into their room to get some sleep just before dawn. By this time, I was so wide awake I knew I couldn't sleep, so I just sat outside with Kathy's dad explaining about Greg's problem with alcohol and how we had suggested they not serve alcohol at the wedding. I told him that Greg was supposed to be in a 6-month program at the State Hospital and that he got himself kicked out on purpose to come to the wedding. Kathy's dad was very understanding.

Maggie decided that she didn't want to stay in Mississippi. She was embarrassed for getting into a squabble with Kathy and that, in a blackout, she threw a drink in Kathy's face. She confided that she did have a problem with alcohol... she experienced *tachycardia* when she drank now, and it scared her. She first learned what it was when she read some of my Al Anon workbook as a *symptom* of alcoholism. Since Maggie obviously needed treatment before going off to college, we brought her and Greg back home with us. We dropped off John's mother with some of Maggie's things at her house in case Maggie decided to come back to Ole Miss, and Jim promised to ship them to her later if she decided not to. We finally pieced together what had happened that night and how everything got so out of hand. Obviously, the bride and groom had returned to the party since they also had a room at the Sheraton. When Jim saw Greg's condition, he found consolation in talking to Maggie, who was glad to share some things with him that she had been keeping to herself. Still in her wedding gown, Kathy didn't understand why Jim wasn't spending more time with her on their wedding night. Maggie felt insulted by one of Kathy's remarks and threw a drink at her. Jim locked Kathy out of their room because he didn't like the way she was acting. All of this because of alcohol!!

After dropping off Hannah at her home, John, Greg, Maggie and I headed back to northern Virginia. Since nothing we planned had worked out, we needed that long drive home to discuss the possibilities of salvaging what was left of our lives. Greg seemed willing to try to get a job and also to study his GED manual for passing the test to get his diploma from high school. He had been studying the manual periodically over the past year, but we couldn't seem to make it over to the designated high school in time for him to take the test. Maggie finally admitted she had a problem and was ready to enter an alcohol treatment program. She had read parts of my Al Anon workbook during the summer, and I noticed her eyes fill with tears at one point. I asked if she thought she might be having a problem, but she wasn't ready to admit it then and avoided answering my question. The wedding, however, brought out the truth. She had been in a blackout when she threw the drink at Kathy and didn't remember a thing. She was embarrassed when she learned of her behavior and made the decision against attending college in Mississippi. Maggie felt she needed more time to think things over and make her decisions about what she really wanted to do with her life. She loved working at Penguin Feather and living in Vienna, but she wanted to go on to college to pursue her interests in Art and Literature. First, she had a problem to deal with back in Alexandria, and we were faced with the problems, anxiety and fears once again of not knowing what to do for Greg and Maggie.

My Bible reading became important once again outside on our balcony where I was able to enjoy my peace and solitude, and I brought it all up before the Lord asking for his guidance, wisdom and strength to see us through. I looked up scriptures dealing with *fear*, and there were many. Here is what I found:

Overcoming Fear

Jesus told us many times during his life upon the earth: *"Fear not!"* (Luke 12:32) The first kind of fear which comes to mind is the terrifying kind of fear which the terrorists use to instill in the hearts and minds of people to keep them in bondage. The second is the reverential kind of fear we have towards God, so his blessings can flow through us and out to others. In the Proverbs of Solomon, the son of King David, we learn that *"The fear of the Lord is the beginning of wisdom."* (Proverbs 1:7)

Fear is often described as the opposite of faith, but it is also the absence of faith. In order to understand fear and how it works, we must first understand faith. Faith is simply believing God and taking him at his word. Remember Job? He was a righteous man, but his friends told him that God was punishing him for sin in his life. However, God had removed his protection from Job and was allowing him to be tested. The devil spoke words of fear to Job, and Job said, *"The thing which I greatly feared has come upon me"* (Job 3:25), and his prayers stemmed out of that fear. Job's wife even told him to give up and die. Job's circumstances couldn't have been worse, but he never doubted God's goodness and said, *"Though he slay me, yet will I trust in him."* (Job 13:15) When Job finally stopped praying out of fear and started praying prayers of faith, his circumstances changed. Words of fear started the disasters, but words and prayers of faith ended them. In all these things, Job never blamed God nor failed to trust in him. God restored Job's health and gave him more than he had before.

> *"Faith is the substance of things hoped for, the evidence of things not seen...; But without faith, it is impossible to please him, for he that cometh to God, must believe that he is and that he rewards those who diligently seek him."* (Hebrews 11:1-6)

God has given to everyone *"a measure of faith"* (Luke 19:12-26), and if we don't use it, he will take it from us and give it to someone who will. Paul tells us, *"The just shall live by faith; but if any man draw back, my soul shall have no pleasure in him"* (Hebrews 10:35-38). Faith motivates us into action and causes us to trust God for wisdom and power to carry out our plans successfully. Unbelief produces doubt, apprehension and fear and can cause us to become so stymied we cannot move in any direction at all. We become so focused on our problem we cannot think of anything but the problem, and fear takes over to hold us in this bondage. In this case, our only hope is to break loose and *"launch out into the deep"* (Luke 5:4), putting all our faith to work in trusting God for a miracle and see what the Lord will do. The only way to let go of the problem is to put it in God's hands and pray for a miracle. We must first pray that he will lead us in the right direction and open the right doors. We must hope for courage and pray for strength to move forward in faith regardless of the circumstances. Fear and unbelief must go, or they will give place to the devil whose will is to destroy.

> *"Through faith we understand that the worlds were framed by the word of God, so that things which are seen were not made of things which appear."* (Hebrews 11: 3)

Where did fear originate? Fear made its entrance in the Garden of Eden when Adam hid from God trying to conceal his disobedience having eaten of the one tree in the garden which he was commanded not to eat thereof.

All fear stems from the fear of death. *"And the serpent said to the woman, 'Ye shall not surely die. For God knows that in the day ye eat thereof, then your eyes shall be opened and ye shall be as gods, knowing good and evil.'"* When Eve saw that the tree was good for food and that it would make one wise, she ate of the fruit and gave some to her husband, and their eyes were opened. Realizing they were naked, they tried to hide from God and conceal their disobedience. (Genesis 3:1-7) Death and the fear of death passed over all the earth as we all died spiritually in-Adam. *"The second Adam, Jesus, came to destroy the works of the devil"* and offers us eternal life. (1st Corinthians 15:21-22)

Faith in the word of God has the power to change things, regardless of the circumstances. Fear, on the other hand, has the power to paralyze, traumatize and hold us in bondage. Since *"faith cometh by hearing, and hearing by the word of God"* (Romans 10:17), so then must fear also come by hearing words of disbelief which contradict the word of God, including those *fiery little darts* of the devil (Ephesians 6:16). The Bible tells us *"Whatever is not of faith is sin"* (Romans 14:23). What we see with our eyes and hear with our ears enters our minds, and, if we meditate on these things, whether good or bad, they pass into our hearts and become part of our spiritual makeup. The Bible tells us, *"As a man thinks in his heart, so is he; for out of the heart proceed the issues of life."* (Proverbs 23:7) Jesus said, *"It's not what goes into a man that defiles him, it's what comes out of him."* (Mark 7:15-23) From Isaiah, we learn *"Thou wilt keep him in perfect peace whose mind is stayed on thee."* (Isaiah 26:3)

> *"Let not your heart be troubled: ye believe in God, believe also in me. In my Father's house are many mansions: if it were not so, I would have told you. I go to prepare a place for you. And if I go and prepare a place for you, I will come again, and receive you unto myself; that where I am, there ye may be also…. I am the way, the truth and the life: no man cometh unto the Father, but by me.*
>
> *"And whatsoever ye shall ask in my name, that will I do, that the Father may be glorified in the Son…. If ye love me, keep my commandments.*
>
> *"And I will pray the Father and he shall give you another Comforter, that he may abide with you forever; even the Spirit of Truth; whom the world cannot receive, because it sees him not,*

neither knows him: but ye know him; for he dwells with you and shall be in you....

"But the Comforter, which is the Holy Ghost, whom the Father will send in my name, he shall teach you all things, and bring all things to your remembrance, whatsoever I have said unto you.

"Peace I leave with you, my peace I give unto you: not as the world gives, give I unto you. Let not your heart be troubled, neither let it be afraid. Ye have heard how I said unto you, I go away, and come again unto you. If ye loved me, ye would rejoice, because I said, I go unto the Father: for my Father is greater than I." (John 14:1-31)

CHAPTER TEN

Back to Alexandria

1981-1982

Having heard of tremendous results through the Naval Hospital's Alcohol Recovery Program, I drove Maggie over the following Saturday morning ready to check her in for treatment. They quickly admitted her through the Emergency Room where they checked her heart and blood pressure and took down her case history. Then they made preparations for her to enter the program as soon as they found a place for her. First, she was admitted to the Detox Unit of the hospital where they put her in a nice room, gave her a gown and told her to get into bed. I helped her settle in and hugged her good- bye as the nurse came in to take her temperature. She assured me that Maggie would be well taken care of and they would call her dad when the withdrawal period was over. I was scheduled to fly to Ft. Collins the following day, Sunday, for a week's computer training course, since I had just begun my new job with the Department of Fire Distribution, still under the USDA Forest Service. John drove over the following Friday to pick up Maggie and all three of them, John, Maggie and Greg, met my plane Friday evening. I brought Maggie a gift from Colorado to show my confidence in her completing the program; a beautiful handcrafted turquoise and silver watchband with matching pendant. It was great to see her looking and feeling so much better.

We were up bright and early Saturday morning to drive Maggie into Maryland for the beginning of her recovery. The charming old country estate was situated off the main highway and down a country lane through fields which were still being harvested for use at the alcohol treatment facility. Finally, we arrived at the stately old manor where we were warmly greeted and ushered upstairs to the office where Maggie was admitted. We were then given a tour of the newly renovated old country home and the bedroom and bath Maggie would be sharing with two other women. The lovely old home provided a peaceful atmosphere for healing and restoration, exactly what Maggie needed. And it also provided the nourishing fruits and vegetables from the farm which she needed also.

The men's section of the program was on the other side of the house, and the younger men were housed in a more modern recreation building next door. Everyone ate around the large round tables in the dining room where they were encouraged to eat plenty of the fresh fruits and vegetables grown right there on the farm. All the meals were well-balanced and accompanied with vitamin and mineral supplements to rebuild their deficient bodies, which had become malnourished due to the ravages of alcohol. The cook was very busy in the large country kitchen preparing their mid-day meal when we quickly passed through to meet some of the workers. Outside the picturesque old home were acres of well-kept lawns covered with lovely shade trees, and everyone was encouraged to take long walks down the winding country lane or around the acreage surrounding the house out in the fresh air and sunshine. We were encouraged to come back on weekends to participate and learn all we could about the AA program and to attend the Al Anon meetings. Pitching horseshoes was a favorite pastime for everyone and the comfortable wicker chairs on the front porch were very inviting and led to many friendly chats gazing out on the peaceful surroundings.

On Sundays, there was a large open barbecue grill on the east side of the house where we could cook our wieners and hamburgers to perfection and a long serving table with the buns and condiments. It was also covered with all kinds of fresh salads, vegetables, barbecued beans, corn on the cob, watermelon, drinks and different kinds of desserts. We filled our plates and enjoyed a leisure lunch all spread out on the redwood picnic tables. The very atmosphere was therapeutic, and we were delighted with the wonderful food served in abundance. With so many scheduled meetings, lectures, movies and classes during the week, the patients were kept very busy, but, in their free time, they all seemed to find something they enjoyed doing. There was no time for boredom! They told us that Maggie was the youngest ever to complete the program. She developed her game of pool and pitching horseshoes, made many new friends and got along well with everyone. We looked forward to our Sundays at Melwood and drove over just about every weekend to spend time with Maggie. Greg enjoyed the visits, too, especially the food, and it was therapeutic and educational for all of us.

I was invited to join Maggie's group one Saturday morning to see a film and lecture about the harmful effects of alcohol on the internal organs. Maggie's physical showed her to be in the first stage of developing a *fatty liver*. An accumulation of fat was beginning to crowd and suffocate liver cells causing swelling and inflammation. Had she not stopped her intake of alcohol at that time, her condition would have worsened until she could have developed hepatitis or cirrhosis of the liver which could have taken her life at a very young age. John and I had no idea of how much or how often Maggie had been drinking after school when she was supposed to be at a friends' house or in the library doing her homework. With Greg and his friends coming and going at all hours, we told her not to go home until she knew we would be there after our workday when I would prepare supper for the family and we would try to have a normal family life. After her alcoholism became obvious, she confided in me that usually in the afternoon, she would buy some beer and drive over to the park to wait until it was time for us to come home. When she moved into the apartment in Vienna, she and her friend kept beer in the fridge. Although she always had a job and worked hard to complete her education, she turned to alcohol to relieve her anxiety so she could feel good about herself and escape the family problems.

One of the lectures was given by a rather stately old gentleman, a recovering alcoholic of many years, who shared his mistakes with alcohol and the toll it had taken on his body. He was very amusing and helped his students find the humor in their often decrepit conditions and taught them to laugh at themselves. We were very proud of Maggie's good attitude and wholehearted cooperation, and we were so thankful that it was discovered in time for a complete recovery. She would always be *a recovering alcoholic,* and, if ever she were to drink again, she knew the disease would pick up right where it left off. Her body was in a state of malnutrition, and it had a lot of healing to do. Her internal organs needed an extra supply of vitamins and minerals.

John and I were called in for a special meeting with Maggie's counselor about a week before she was to be released from the program to determine where she would go from there. She could have chosen to go to a half-way house because she knew Greg's problem still existed at home, but she chose to come home anyway. Since we had moved her bedroom suite into our second bedroom when she was planning to go off to college, we had room for her to come back home. Greg could sleep on the single bed we had moved into the living room behind the couch while Jim and Kathy were visiting, and we could put his things in the closet as we had done before. Maggie got her old job back with Penguin Feather, but, since it was a very long commute through very heavy traffic on the Washington Beltway, she decided to find another job closer to home. After a heavy rain, her car skidded off one of the exit roads on her way home from work one evening, and her dad had to retrieve her that night and the car the following day. This incident led to Maggie finding another job, and, since she wanted to learn the art of "silk screening," she found one silk-screening T-shirts. She seemed to enjoy the work, while deciding what she wanted to do about college.

I think Greg was impressed with the progress Maggie was making, and he began to show an interest in studying for his GED and finding a job. However, he was an alcoholic, too, and it was time for another major incident. We had hoped he would get the message from all we had learned during Maggie's treatment about the ravages of alcohol on a person's body, but, when a person is in denial, he cannot admit he has a problem. Therefore, whatever he has learned is rejected because in his mind it doesn't apply to him. Greg took the keys from my purse one day while the car was parked in front of the building and opened the trunk to find a large bottle of red wine which John had stored there because he didn't think it wise to bring into the house. We found Greg passed out on the back seat *comatose,* so we had to shift into high gear and drive him to a nearby hospital. Again, they had to pump his stomach to save his life. At one point, his heart stopped beating and they had to get it going again. They recommended a 28-day AA Program which they were in the process of starting the following week. John insisted that Greg sign up for the program before he would allow him back in our apartment. We had to think of Maggie who had just been released from a tremendous AA program and was doing very well at home with us. She had taken Greg with her to one of her AA meetings in the area, and we thought it could work out well for both of them to attend the meetings together. But Greg said that attending these meetings just reminded him of alcohol and made him want to drink more. John made it a priority to be with me for Greg's admittance into this program.

Sometimes it's hard to understand how *"all things work together for good"* because this was the very week of President Sadat's assassination, when John would be called upon by the Army Chief of Staff to accompany him as Middle East Specialist with part of a small group on Air Force II to Egypt to represent the US Government at his funeral. President Sadat had been shot at a Military Review in Cairo by elements of the Military opposed to the signing of the Peace Treaty with Israel. John was faced with the issue of doing his job and going on this very important mission, or getting someone to stand in for him. He chose the latter, and he was very sorry that he did because, after getting Greg there for the program with all his toiletries and clothes for a month, Greg refused to sign in as a *volunteer.* John was furious! And issued Greg an ultimatum: either have a job before the weekend or be out of our apartment.

The following Saturday morning when John reminded Greg of the ultimatum and was ready to *boot him out,* Greg responded, *"But I do have a job!"* Of course, we didn't believe him! *"Oh really?"* we answered. But it was true! He was all set up for an interview that afternoon with Better Home Insulators. It was incredible! Their office building was very conveniently located just a few blocks from our apartment. It was a telephone job booking appointments for estimates of home insulation, and his hours were established to catch people after they came home from work, which was perfect for me to drive him over each day at 6:00 pm. He could work all day Saturday, and he would receive an hourly wage plus a commission every time an appointment resulted in a contract. I drove him over to his interview that afternoon, and he was accepted for the position. Greg was a natural for this job, and he enjoyed it very much! He would be waiting downstairs in the lobby looking for us to pull up out front so he could get in the car as John got out, and I moved over to the driver's seat. Then I would drive him to work and return home to prepare dinner, then drive back to pick him up around 10:00 so he could come home for dinner. It worked perfectly! Our prayers were answered.

On the 13th of January 1982, an eerie snowstorm brought about a terrible tragedy to our area, another day which we shall never forget. Government employees were dismissed around noon due to warnings of heavy snow. I caught the subway over to the Pentagon to pick up the car and meet John out front as I usually did on similar occasions. When he didn't come out after circling a few times, I parked the car and tried to scrape the sticky snow off the windshield. It was so heavy and so thick, it just kept piling up and sticking to the windows. When John arrived, he had the same problem trying to clean off the snow, so he could see to drive home. It was impossible! The traffic wasn't moving at all! People were leaving their cars parked in the large parking lot and lining up at the bus kiosk. John and I made the same decision, and, as we were standing in line waiting to get on a bus, we heard what we thought was a rumor about a plane going down in the Potomac. But, as we finally boarded the bus, we could see lights flashing over toward the Potomac River, and we knew it must be true.

After what seemed like an eternity, we finally made it home and walked into our living room to find Maggie watching the tragic remains of Air Florida, Flight 90, in the Potomac River with people still being rescued. She had not gone to work that day because of the weather forecast telling people to stay home. Greg was not in the apartment when we arrived, but later came in after visiting friends in the building. He was obviously under the influence of something, probably alcohol, but was not out of control that evening. We watched the heroic efforts of those who saved the lives of the five survivors. One man actually stayed in the freezing water for about 20 minutes until the Park Police arrived in a helicopter to lift people out, and two more passersby jumped in the freezing water just in time to pull two people to safety. Out of six people alive in the wreckage, five were saved. One man was hooked in his seat and couldn't get out. He kept passing the lifeline to others, and, when the helicopter came back the last time to get him, he had already gone under with the shifting wreckage.

From news reports and the NTSB accident report, we learned that Air Florida, Flight 90, a Boeing 737 twin-engine plane, had been de-iced at 2:00 pm when the temperature was 67 degrees F. and again at 2:45 pm, but the plane had to sit in the long line piling up snow for almost an hour waiting to be cleared for takeoff, which was finally given at 4:00 pm when the temperature had dropped to 24 degrees F. Being so loaded with the sticky snow, the plane simply could not climb well enough to clear the 14th Street Bridge, which connects the District of Columbia with Arlington County, VA, and grazed the tops of seven cars at 4:01 pm. It also tore away a section of the bridge wall and bridge railing. Four people were killed on the bridge and four others injured. Of the 79 people on the plane, only 5 were rescued. [One of John's colleagues who had accompanied him and his 17-man inspection team to Sudan was one of the missing. He was flying down to the US Central Command, Tampa, FL to deliver the report of the Sudan inspection trip, which had taken place the previous November.]

I had made appointments for Greg to take the GED tests at Woodson High School on a Saturday morning once every couple of months starting in early September. We didn't even come close to being on time for the first appointment and aborted our mission before leaving home. We didn't quite make it the second time either. Finally, one Saturday morning in February, we made it with time to spare with the help of some *"No-Doze"* to keep him awake. As I dropped him off at Woodson, Greg saw several of his old friends from Madison High standing around waiting to go in. It turned out to be a very good day for him, and he enjoyed having lunch with his friends. When he found out a couple of weeks later that he had passed the test, he was elated and so proud of himself. He received his GED Certificate in March.

Christine was impressed. Now, having made two important accomplishments, she decided not to withhold his prosthesis any longer and made an appointment with Rehab's orthopedic doctor in Falls Church for his measurements. Within a few weeks, his temporary prosthetic device was ready for a fitting, and I drove him over to Fairfax Hospital and watched as he tried it on. A few adjustments had to be made, but it was wonderful to see his face light up with that big, handsome smile as he walked down the corridor for the first time without crutches. Greg became good friends with the young man who made his adjustments and gave him a good supply of prosthetic socks. He also taught him how to change the socks according to the fit of his leg and the changing temperature. Greg would have to keep extra socks with him to avoid getting blisters. He built up his leg muscles and gained a few calluses in the right places wearing the temporary prosthesis as his stump was being prepared to accommodate the more permanent one, which would be ready around the 1st of April.

One morning in March, I drove Maggie over to Melwood to receive her *six- month chip.* While she was attending the regular AA meeting, I attended the Al Anon meeting next door in a very large dining room where a large crowd of people were gathered around the tables. After the Speaker's address, the individual introductions began around the room with everyone sharing a bit about themselves and their alcoholics. When I stood up and introduced myself, everyone seemed very interested in what I had to say about our family situation and all the things we had been through, so I'm afraid I monopolized the floor for quite some time. After a while, one of the group leaders, an elderly gentleman, politely interrupted to ask me to bring it to a conclusion so the others would have time to speak. So I quickly wound it up and sat down. I was so embarrassed for monopolizing the floor that when he came over to apologize after the meeting, tears came into my eyes, and I started crying uncontrollably. Everyone came by to comfort me and they all said *"go ahead and let it all out,"* especially the wonderful compassionate speaker and his lovely wife, who had led the Al Anon meeting.

They were all so very nice and understanding; however, I was the one who didn't understand. I thought it was just my embarrassment over hogging the floor and taking too long to tell my story, not having been there before or knowing the proper procedures. I'm sure all of this was true to some extent, but when the tears started flowing, I couldn't hold them back. These good people stayed there with me and kept on telling me to *"go ahead and let it all out."* Now that I look back in retrospect, I know they understood more than I could realize at the time, how very important it was for me to tell our story and have a good cry and *"let it out."* I had been holding on to my composure for so long under such extreme conditions, I believe my subconscious took over and relieved me of the built-up pressure. God bless all those wonderful people who had been through what I had been through... maybe even worse. They understood! They had come closer to *walking in my shoes* than any other people on earth.

Finally, the first week of April, Greg received a call from the hospital that his permanent prosthesis was ready, and he would need a little time for adjustments after trying it on around 2:00 pm. Always trying to stretch out my vacation and sick leave, I rescheduled my eye appointment for the same afternoon. My only problem was that Greg would be in Fairfax, Virginia and my eye appointment was at Bethesda Naval Hospital in Maryland. I reasoned that Greg would have plenty of time for adjustments and could enjoy himself eating lunch in the hospital restaurant or just reading magazines while waiting for me. I left Greg there for his appointment and headed around the beltway to Bethesda for my eye exam. I had warned Greg that I might be a little late due to the heavy afternoon traffic, but to just have patience and wait for me in the lobby.

I had no idea they were going to put drops in my eyes which would blind me to the sunlight, and I left my sunglasses in the car. When I walked outside, the glare was so bad I couldn't see a thing. I thought if I can just make it to the car and find my sunglasses, I'll be able to make it home. However, God was taking care of me, although it would mean a little discomfort for a few days. As I was walking down the sidewalk on my way to the parking garage, I didn't see the curb and stepped right off into the air, twisting my ankle so badly I couldn't walk. I just sat there on the side of the road wondering what I was going to do. A lady coming out of the garage stopped her car to ask what was wrong. I told her, *"I can't see, and I can't walk."* She helped me into her car and drove me around to the Emergency Room. As I was sitting on the side of the examining table waiting for an x-ray, someone must have helped me call Fairfax Hospital to have Greg paged, so I was able to tell him where I was and what had happened. Then someone dialed John's office so I could tell him. He wasn't at his desk and I had to leave a message with my phone number. When he dialed the number, he heard *"Bethesda Emergency Room."* John didn't know what to expect, but, after hearing my story, he understood and left immediately to pick up Greg at Fairfax Hospital. After dark, I was able to drive myself home in the Yellow Sub and was hobbling around on my firmly wrapped right ankle for a month, while Greg was proudly wearing his new prosthesis and walking without the slightest limp.

Although Greg kept his job and continued to show signs of progress now and then, he still had his occasional bouts with alcohol, and the stereo continued to be our warning device. Somehow, *"getting high"* and *"heavy rock"* always went together. When it occurred, John and I would automatically rise up out of bed, rush out to the living room and resume our roles as enablers. I guess we had grown accustomed to the roles we had to play to keep the merry-go-round going. Maggie kept her radio on all night very low to drown out undesirable sounds. When John and I rushed into the living room, we would find Greg in some stage of getting highly intoxicated and turning up the volume of the stereo as he lit one cigarette after another. I would take over the cigarette ashes and volume control while John would try to control Greg and get him to bed. When this *merry-go-round* began years earlier, it occurred at random times and was somewhat sporadic, but, as time went by, it occurred more and more frequently, and we all had our *roles to play* in the life of the *problem drinker.* As I had learned in my Al Anon Workshop, it was taking more and more alcohol mixed with drugs for him to try to reach *the euphoria* he had first experienced, but now he was drinking to try to *feel normal and good about himself.* Now this *progressive disease* was taking its toll on his mind and body. And as long as we enabled him, the worse it would become and the worse the final outcome would be. We were fighting a losing battle. Something had to change!

One night, it all came to a head when John was preparing to attend a very important dinner for foreign dignitaries in a downtown Alexandria restaurant.

Greg came home under the influence and was very disruptive that afternoon. When his dad told him to get out, Greg threw a broken ashtray across the room which cut the back of John's hand so badly it required stitches. John made him leave the apartment, applied a bandage to stop the bleeding and finished getting dressed for his engagement downtown. Maggie and I drove him by the military hospital to have it stitched and properly bandaged before dropping him off at the restaurant. John and I knew we had to do something different because nothing else was working. We seriously considered retirement and moving out of the country where Greg couldn't find us for fear of another tragedy. We had seen the movie, *"Richie,"* whose father had shot him under similar circumstances, and we understood very well how it could happen. The doctors had told us that Greg would go on taking advantage of all of us while still expecting us to take care of him and bear all the responsibilities as the disease worsened.

I had applied for an *upward mobility* position in the Forest Service a few months before Greg's accident and heard nothing more about it until a couple of weeks before the accident. I was offered a position in Fire Distribution to be trained as a Computer Programmer. At the time, I thought it was great because of the upward movement into the field of computers, which seemed to be the way of the future. I accepted. However, when the time came for me to move up the street into my new office in Fire Distribution, I was in no condition to make the change and should have declined the offer. Maureen, my new Supervisor, was very understanding and had a very good plan for my training. After starting me off punching cards to teach me how the system works, Maureen taught me to write a program for the fire fighters in the field in which they would submit all their information via telephone regarding their aircrafts, retardants and other resources used to put out forest fires. I also learned to run off the Fire Report each week and submitted it to the office regarding the locations and sizes of forest fires across the Nation. It also included all the data and what was being done to put them out. It was a very interesting job, and I learned a lot about computers and how to make some beautifully colored graphs depicting all kinds of data regarding forest fires. However, after about a year in this wonderful job with Maureen and my new office environment, I had to inform her about John's decision to retire from the Army and take a job overseas. She was a very compassionate person and wished us well as she had seen me through thick and thin regarding this year of Greg's accident and recovery.

In April, I drove Maggie down to Virginia Beach to visit my sister, Amanda, and her family. She and her husband, Zachary, a retired Navy Commander, had raised a large family there, and their daughter, Cindy, Maggie's age, was planning to start college about the same time. They wanted us to come down to check out Old Dominion University in Norfolk, so Maggie would be near them while we were away and they could watch out for her. It sounded like a good plan, so we gave it some thought and decided to give it a try. Amanda drove us over to the college where we toured the area and Maggie headed straight to the office where she found out they offered all the courses she needed. The small growing college had a beautiful new Student Union Building and a very nice stadium with many activities which appealed to her. She was especially impressed with the English and Art Schools and planned to major in English with an Art minor. She spoke to someone in the Registrar's Office and picked up an application. It didn't take long for her to receive an acceptance, and she seemed happy about her opportunity to study the Arts and Literature. It was a good plan, and she looked forward to starting her classes in June. A couple of weeks later, I drove her down with a load of her things to leave with Amanda and Zach until she could move them into her dorm. She seemed happy, although a little apprehensive, because we would be so far away from her in Europe. Her counselor at Melwood had advised her not to make any major changes the first year of her sobriety, and there were still several more months to go.

John took his time about making the decision of taking his retirement after 20 years of Government service, because there was so much to consider regarding all the time and expense that had gone into his training as a Foreign Area Officer. He was regarded by the Army's leadership as one of their top Strategists on his area of the world and they didn't want to lose him. At military functions, I was often approached by one of his Commanding Officers, who would try to impress upon me the importance of his remaining in the service. They said the Army was greatly in need of his experience and he was assured of being promoted to full Colonel within the year. Also, according to one General Officer, he would be promoted *below the zone* thereafter because of the critical need for qualified Middle East specialists. He had written extensively on the existing political and security situations of the African and Middle Eastern countries and their threats to National Security. John wrote a very important paper on Libya and Muammar Qaddafi's threat to the stability of that region, and he also wrote a comprehensive Strategy Paper on the entire African continent that contributed significantly to subsequent US policy and strategy. In order to win the alliance of friendly countries like Egypt, which was establishing stronger ties with the US after several decades of cooperation with the Soviet Union, John felt it was very important to continue the direction we were taking toward the stability of these countries and also the stability of Israel.

In late 1981, The Army Chief of Staff issued orders for John to Fort Bragg, where the Joint Special Operations Command (JSOC) was being formed. The purpose of the JSOC was to provide the Country with an immediate response capability against terrorism, local wars that threatened the United States and the rescue of American hostages overseas. It would include Delta Force, the Navy Seals, Special Air Operations resources and other military outfits tailored specifically to the new warfare. However, due to our family situation, John felt he wasn't in a position to take the job which would require his instant movement to another country if needed and quite a bit of time away from home. He recommended a good friend and former classmate at the Institute for Military Assistance at Fort Bragg. When General Robert Schweitzer, Director of Strategy, Plans and Policy, was appointed to the National Security Council (NSC) as Deputy National Security Advisor by President Reagan, he expressed an interest in taking John with him to the NSC as Middle East-Africa Specialist, but that didn't work out due to the appointment of another highly qualified officer. Some positions they offered him were very appealing and one would have taken us back to Rabat, Morocco, others to parts of Africa. He was offered several top notch senior Attaché assignments and a teaching position at the Special Studies Institute at the Army War College, but none of them seemed appropriate at this crucial time of our life.

As John approached his Army retirement eligibility and we focused on our family situation, our decision became quite clear. We needed to make a change: Maggie needed to get on with college; Greg needed to learn responsibility and get on with his life; and John and I needed a new adventure away from family problems in order to save our sanity. In addition to all that, I needed to keep my promise to God to get into deep Bible Study as soon as possible. We decided to take Oral's advice and *launch out into the deep.* One of John's best friends and colleagues, Charles Rutherford, introduced him to a friend he knew from Vietnam, James McFarland, which led to a potential job with Litton Data Command Systems in Joint Venture with Philip Holzmann, Frankfurt, Germany for a job in Saudi Arabia.

After exhausting all possibilities in military assignments, John made his final decision. Having done his job at the Pentagon for six years as a FAO specialist in three critical positions, John felt he was leaving the Country in good shape and very strong militarily. He had done a good job! Now it was time for us to put our family in God's hands and make a major change in our lives by following up with one of these overseas jobs to discover our possibilities. We needed to try something different which would be exciting, and, at the same time, provide the finances we needed to get Maggie off to college and Greg out on his own, with the help of an escrow account to get him started. John flew to Los Angeles for an interview with Litton Data Command Systems and received an exceptionally good offer.

Over the previous months, John and I had discussed the possibility of his retirement with both Greg and Maggie, and we had mentioned the fact that he might accept a job which would take us overseas. We talked about college for Maggie, where she would like to be and what she would like to study. We also talked to Greg about finding a roommate for sharing the expenses of an apartment, so he could remain in the area and continue working at his job with Better Home Insulators. He didn't seem to take us seriously at first and wasn't showing any signs of progress toward finding an apartment or a roommate, so I drove him around the area looking for an acceptable place near his job. We found a nice two-bedroom apartment just a block from his job and across the street from a large shopping center with a grocery store, a bank and a bus stop. There were also two of Greg's favorite fast food restaurants and his medical doctor within two blocks of his apartment. Greg filled out an application, John co-signed the rental agreement and we put down the deposit. Through the Roommate Referral Service, Greg got in touch with a young man who had a job in construction and was looking for someone to share expenses. Although they had never met, they seemed compatible enough over the phone if they both kept their jobs and stayed straight.

We helped Greg make a small deposit to open his bank account at the bank in the shopping center across the street, so he could learn to handle his money and pay his bills. He needed to learn how to balance his checkbook and tend to his personal affairs. John also set up an escrow account for Greg to be handled by an attorney in Fairfax if he should need money for anything while we were out of the Country. Without depending on us so much, he might learn some responsibility and get on with his life. Of course, he would have to learn to budget his money, like we always had to do, to make ends meet each month. He seemed anxious to have his own place and make the plan work, however, it wasn't going to be easy living with another person he didn't really know. We thought it might be a good learning experience for him and his roommate to learn how to work out their problems and share expenses. His phone would be hooked up the following week, and we promised to call him before we left the Country.

At our apartment with shipments going in three different directions, it was chaos! John was on the phone getting insurance to cover the larger amount of furniture which was to be taken to Greg's apartment and another shipment of our bedroom suite and dining furniture to be shipped to Jim and Kathy in Jackson, plus the third shipment of clothing and personal items to be shipped to Frankfurt. On the days before our departure, we loaded the station wagon with our extra food, cleaning supplies and Greg's clothing and personal items and drove them over to his apartment. We also went shopping for groceries to get him started. He would receive the larger shipment of our household goods and furniture the following week. On Saturday morning, Greg was in the shopping center parking lot looking for us to pass by at the approximate time John had given him. We waved goodbye to him and gave him the *thumbs up* sign as our three-car caravan headed west toward the Blue Ridge Mountains on our way to Tennessee.

Before leaving Alexandria, John instructed Maggie and me to give him the thumbs up sign if everything was all right and to blink our lights if we needed to stop. He and Kitty, *the Captain,* in the Yellow Sub, with her front paws on the center front of the dashboard, led the way. Maggie, in the little Vega hatchback, was in second place, and I, in the Malibu, brought up the rear, as we headed west to the mountains and then south down I-81. The second day, John noticed Maggie blinking her lights as he headed us off the freeway to see what was wrong. Her muffler had been dragging along the pavement and finally fell off before we could safely stop. In spite of the irritating sound it was making, we finally made it to Memphis where John had a new muffler installed. John's mom, Hannah, was in Memphis to visit Aunt Grace and Uncle George for a couple of days so we wouldn't have to detour off the main route. We visited a few days there and attended one of John's high school reunions. Then we enjoyed seeing Kathy and Jim for a couple of days in Jackson and their new apartment near the Reservoir where they took us out for a wonderful fish dinner. We were pleased to see how well our bedroom suite and dining table and chairs fit into their apartment. Then we left the little Vega, which Maggie had equipped with a stereo system, with Jim and drove on to Mobile. He seemed happy in his job with the Mississippi Highway Department (MDOT), and Kathy had a good job as a legal secretary in a Jackson law office.

After about a week with Mother, where John had a safety check done on both cars, he flew to Frankfurt to begin his job with Litton. I arranged to have Maggie's wisdom teeth extracted by the same oral surgeon who extracted mine when I was about her age. Her orthodontist had recommended this be done when she reached 18 to preserve the work he had done with several years of braces. Somehow, John got permission from his boss to return to the States the middle of June due to a meeting in California, so I made a two-day reservation for us at the Gulf for our 25th Wedding Anniversary. I was very happy that John would be with me to drive Maggie to Norfolk to get her settled at ODU for the summer and then accompany me on our overnight flight to Frankfurt. It was only the beginning of the many flights I would make back and forth across the Atlantic Ocean in the next twenty-two years.

We told all the family good-bye, and, with the Yellow Sub safely parked in Mother's garage, we left Mother and Kitty at her home and took off in the Malibu for Old Dominion. Of course, we had to leave our Malibu with Maggie for her transportation around Norfolk, but she had no trouble finding an apartment to share with three other young ladies who were looking for another summer roommate. Maggie would get more permanently settled in the dormitory in the fall. John rented a car in Norfolk for a couple of days for us to drive while Maggie got the Malibu registered on campus and learned her way around. We spent a couple of days with Amanda and Zach before telling them all goodbye. Then we drove over to Norfolk and took Maggie out to lunch before leaving her there for summer school. We hugged her goodbye and took off on our drive to Dulles to return our rental car at the airport and board our 10:00 pm departure for Frankfurt.

CHAPTER ELEVEN

A Time for Frankfurt
1982-1983

Sitting in the Charles de Gaulle Airport in Paris the following morning, I was wide awake and excited as John sat napping while awaiting our connection to Frankfurt. He had barely adjusted to the time change when he had to turn around and leave the country again. There to meet us at the Frankfurt airport was Gretchen, a cute, vivacious red haired German girl about Maggie's age, who sped us around the autobahn in a Mercedes to our temporary apartment in Sachsenhausen. Our apartment, leased by Litton for people in transit, was right across the Main River from downtown Frankfurt, and we had a lovely view of the city from our balcony. John showed me around the apartment and then led me to a little market around the corner to buy a few groceries.

We were both very tired and in need of sleep, so I tried to figure out how the buttoned up sheet around the comforter worked and also the pillow cases with the large square flat pillows. Finally, we piled into bed and fell asleep as a gentle breeze wafted through our 20th floor window bringing with it the happy sounds of children playing on the playground below. The next thing we knew, it was midnight, and we were wide awake! Then I understood John's reasoning behind our marketing venture that afternoon: We were hungry and appreciated the food he had bought that afternoon for our midnight snack. John had learned on his first trip exactly what we would need. Feeling like morning had already begun, we tidied up the apartment, took our baths and prepared for our first day in Frankfurt. Sunrise found us out on the balcony watching the city come to life as we enjoyed our morning coffee, orange juice and cereal.

First Morning View in Frankfurt, Germany.

John caught a ride in to work that first morning and came back around noon with a company car, which we would be able to use until we could purchase one of our own. He took me riding through the city of Frankfurt and out to a small suburb to meet Greta, his real estate agent, a retired Lufthansa Airline stewardess, who showed us around the small town of Walldorf. The small town was situated on a lake, or *see*, as the Germans would say, and is a very popular place in summer. Right away, we loved the peaceful atmosphere of Walldorf, which was within walking distance of the *Bahnhopf*, where John could catch the train in to work whenever I needed the car. One of the houses around the corner from Greta and her husband, George, a retired Army general who also worked on the Litton-Holzmann project, would be available in August when the owners moved to the States for him to teach at the German school in the District of Columbia.

Greta introduced us to Herr and Frau Bergmann, who were very interested in learning about life in the Washington area because they would be living in McLean while he commuted into the District each day. They showed us around their lovely L-shaped home and explained all the features of the house and yard. Their beautiful backyard would be trimmed periodically by Frau Bergmann's father while they were away, and they would leave all the yard tools in the storage room for cutting the grass and shoveling the walks. When we came back a few days later to sign the lease, they opened a bottle of wine and invited us outside on their lovely patio covered by a mechanical awning as we toasted one another on our upcoming adventures. They invited us to their farewell barbecue to be held shortly before their departure when they would introduce us to their friends and our future neighbors. In the meantime, they would take us out one evening to show us around the city of Mainz, where the Main River flows into the Rhein. Greta and George joined us for a delightful evening of good food and wine tasting as we walked around the small city enjoying the jovial atmosphere of Mainz.

Over the next few weeks, Gretchen drove the wives on shopping trips to pick out furniture from Mobel Walter, a large furniture warehouse in the little town of Grundau, and to Herties, a downtown department store to shop for small appliances and household goods. It was also Gretchen's job to accompany us as translator when making our purchases. She was a delightful young lady whose apparel, at times, reminded me so much of Maggie, and, one day after moving into our new home, I gave her a Mary Kay facial and a few cosmetics. Litton had arranged for us to get special prices by doing all our shopping at the above mentioned stores plus a TV-video store in Frankfurt. John drove over to Grundau with me several times to look around and let me know which styles of furniture he liked best. We also picked out several Oriental rugs. We always ate lunch at Mobel Walter, where they served a great *Jaeger Schnitzel*, a chicken-fried veal steak, served with lots of *Pommes Frites* (french fries, served with mayonnaise). We also enjoyed eating lunch at Herties, the large downtown department store, where they served *Ziguener Schnitzel*, (a *Jaeger Schnitzel* covered with delicious mushroom gravy) and *Spaetzel* (noodles). John also enjoyed the large German sausages usually served in a bun with mustard and lots of french fries. It was probably our once in a lifetime buying spree to be able to furnish a whole house at one time having everything blend together so well. We loved the unique German furniture and selected it very carefully because we had plans to buy it from Litton at the end of the contract.

Within a couple of weeks, Greta managed to find us another temporary apartment in Walldorf that belonged to a young German bachelor who was soon going on vacation and was anxious to make some extra cash. When he returned a couple of weeks later, he moved into an extra room he had in the basement next door to his workout room. He rented his upstairs apartment to a young American woman stationed at Rhein-Main Air Force Base. It was rather small but very nice and we enjoyed living there until our house was ready in August. In the meantime, John and I took walks around the little town of Walldorf and enjoyed the delicious cones of ice cream, *Eis*. We also loved walking the nature trails which took us through the lovely forest. Across the street were many small, fenced-in plots of land owned by city dwellers, who came out on weekends to tend their gardens. We noticed many new and different kinds of vegetables in these gardens and learned some of their names. Soon we were stopping to chat with the very friendly German people usually starting out in German and ending up in English because most Germans speak some English. Sometimes we spoke a little of both languages, but we were always able to communicate beautifully one way or another.

John was delighted with the opportunity of buying a Mercedes to drive while we were living in Frankfurt and selected a beautiful light green three- year old automobile with beige and brown checked upholstery. He named it Max. One of the first things John had to do after getting his new car was to check out the Rheinblick Golf Course he had heard so much about. It was located in a mountainous area near Wiesbaden with a wonderful view of the Rhein River, and, when covered with snow in the winter, its steep fairways were also used for skiing. It became one of our favorite places to go on weekends. I sometimes walked the first nine holes for exercise but usually just relaxed on the patio reading or enjoying the view during his last nine holes. Besides the fantastic view from the golf course, I looked forward to having dinner before heading back home. They always served a wonderful buffet with a nice assortment of very well-prepared international cuisine. The German wines were very good, and our favorite was the dry white Riesling, one of the better German "*weis weins*," for which the area is famous. Their desserts were served a la carte and were exceptionally good.

Soon after our arrival, we were invited to a 4th of July party in a rather mountainous area east of Frankfurt where several of the Litton families had chosen to live. It was my first opportunity to meet everyone, and I was delighted to find that there were several of the ladies with whom I had much in common. One of the Litton wives volunteered to teach a class on basic German which lasted several weeks, so we found it convenient to ride together and meet the other ladies for lunch. Sometimes we all brought a dish to share, and it was great to get to know one another in that friendly atmosphere. John and I loved eating out in Germany and discovered many good restaurants near our home, so our little bit of German came in quite handy at times.

The Main River Cruise:

Scene at the Town of Seligenstadt.

Around the first of August, Holzmann invited the Litton group to join them for a day's riverboat cruise up the Main River. For Holzmann, this was the highlight of the year and the large two-deck cruise boat was very crowded with mostly Germans and, of course, those of us from Litton who joined their group. We were at the pier in downtown Frankfurt very early one Saturday morning and found ourselves standing in a very long line. Finally, we started moving forward and found our seats on the riverboat sitting at large tables in the hull where we could look out the window and enjoy the passing scenery of mountains, castles and small towns along the riverbank. Coffee and juice were served almost immediately followed by a very nice German breakfast of scrambled eggs, *"wurst"* (sausage) *"und brotchen"* (large rolls), accompanied by some very lively Dixieland music, which was provided by a small combo set up on the first deck. They had a game for us to play! They handed out pencils and paper to everyone, I'm sure to keep the children busy, and gave prizes for the best drawn Litton-Holzmann cow. It was a well- planned day of family fun and we enjoyed it tremendously!

A short time later, our boat docked at the small town of Hanau to tour a modern-day castle and its lovely gardens. Once back on board, we found our seats again for lunch and were served half a very delicious small roasted chicken with french fries and our choice of beverages and desserts, coffee or tea. About an hour later, we stopped at the small town of Seligenstadt for a tour of the historic site and the strategically placed ancient castle once used as a fortress. It was a very tall castle and well preserved with the original long dining table and chairs where the knights once sat and ate their meals. It was very interesting to hear the history and see all the other furnishings as well as a small cannon outside on the enclosed walkway still aimed at the river below. On the return trip, we found a place on the upper deck so John could get some good shots of the castles in the afternoon light. When it started getting cold on the river, we moved inside to the lower deck to warm up and hear the band playing the old German favorites. By this time, the people were enjoying themselves singing along with the music, drinking the German beer and dancing. We discovered the fun loving nature of the German people on this river cruise and appreciated their exuberant personalities and charm.

John and I collected a beautiful bouquet of flowers from our backyard to take to the Bergmanns' farewell party in August. We were impressed with the large number of people gathered around picnic tables in the small, brightly lighted backyard. There were two very long tables on the patio covered with all kinds of delicious German food and several kinds of meat which had been barbecued over the outdoor grill. A very professional bar, complete with bartender, was set up on the inside of the patio, and music from the stereo drifted softly around the neighborhood. We helped ourselves to the wonderfully prepared food and found a seat next to Greta who introduced us to our soon-to-be neighbors. We were welcomed to the neighborhood and felt accepted by these friendly German people immediately. After the food was cleared away, many people enjoyed dancing on the patio, but we continued enjoying the delightful conversation we were having with our new German friends. They told me about Farmers Market on Thursday mornings in front of the Court House, which usually had an abundance of fresh fruits, vegetables and flowers grown in the area. We wished the Bergmanns a very happy adventure in the US and they wished the same to us.

While moving into our new home, John and I watched the Mobel Walter delivery men unpack the truck and quickly assemble all the many pieces of furniture. We were impressed with the ingenuity of German craftsmanship and how uniquely everything fit together. Our oval patio table and chairs were similar to the Bergmanns', and we enjoyed sitting outside during the remainder of the summer and fall. The large mechanical awning completely covered the patio and added so much to the backyard. We had selected a very interesting six-piece schrank with matching dining table, chairs and chandelier named Dallas, which looked like it belonged in an old Spanish galley. And we love it! We also selected a Spanish style grandfather clock which blended right in. Our living room suite consisted of brown leather couch, loveseat, chair and ottoman with tiled top coffee table and end table. The lamps were trimmed with brown fringe and I picked out two unique pieces of furniture which I loved at first sight: a teacart and a telephone table. The bedroom suite, named El Paso, was a sort of rattan trimmed blonde wood, king-sized bed, three chests, a round glass top table and two comfortable rattan chairs. This provided us with a tranquil setting for having our morning coffee as we looked out our picture window or listened to our stereo. The center bedroom, which we called Maggie's room, was composed of one queen-sized bed with padded headboard and matching dark wooden chest of drawers. John's office consisted of a large desk and revolving leather chair with a very unique schrank, which contained a bookcase, a chest of drawers, a chifforobe and a pull-down single bed.

At first, living in Germany seemed a little difficult because we had to pay German taxes on everything we purchased, including US goods bought in US facilities. The government insisted that if we were living on their economy, we should pay taxes on everything, however, the active duty military were exempt from this obligation. Since we did most of our shopping at the Rhein- Main Air Force Base, we had to save all our receipts and take them over to the little town of Langen each month to pay our taxes. John drove us over the first time to find the Court House and meet the officials who set up our account. The jovial gentleman we met invited us into his office and seemed very happy to meet us and joked around about the US TV show he liked to watch, "Dallas." He spoke no

English, but it didn't take us long to feel right at home. It turned out to be a rather simple procedure, and, from then on, I could handle it myself: I would hand the clerk our receipts, and they would tally them up and tell me how much tax we needed to pay in Deutschmarks.

John and I enjoyed shopping in the German grocery stores and trying out their different brands of food, which were a little different from our American brands. And it was all part of the adventure. I sometimes enjoyed shopping at Farmers Market, which was within walking distance of our house, for vegetables in season. We continued to shop downtown at Herties Department Store, and always enjoyed their *Ziguener Schnitzel and Spaetzel* while we were there. We also loved walking around the Frankfurt mall, known as *the Zeil*, which consisted of closed off streets bricked over in unique artistic patterns with flowers and flower boxes everywhere, or planted in concrete containers. There was always something amusing going on downtown *on the Zeil*, such as musicians playing for money, or singers, or a mime or maybe an orator with a message. It was always fun to stop a while to watch or listen and maybe put a small donation in the pot for someone's good. All the people were friendly and eager to assist in answering questions or helping someone find his way around.

One day, we received a phone call from Greg and Ralph, his attorney. He needed a large sum of money to pay an attorney's fee due to a charge against Greg involving drugs. He had just been released from jail where he had been charged with four counts. John hit the ceiling and told him "No!" But, after thinking it over, he realized that we needed to help him because the charges were unjust. Greg had been arrested for something that happened back in February when his dad had kicked him out one night. A young undercover policeman had accosted him at a 7-11 and persuaded him to show him where he could buy some pot. Greg told him about a place he knew of in Vienna and showed him the way. That night, they were only able to get a very small amount, so he gave some to Greg and made arrangements to get a larger amount later. Again, he gave some to Greg as a payoff. Greg told his dad that after we left him, he tried to straighten up and got involved with VA Rehab, and, ironically, that is where he was arrested. The charges were very serious and he needed a good lawyer! Ralph said it sounded like a clear-cut case of entrapment. Although Greg had been a user for many years, we had never known him to deal drugs. John sent Ralph the money, and, when his case came to trial, his attorney proved entrapment and three of the charges were dropped.

Greg was found guilty of using only, and the judge put him on probation making him report periodically to a drug treatment facility as well as his probation officer.

Soon after we were settled, I decided it was time for me to start attending church services at Rhein-Main AFB and noticed the sign in front of the Chapel which said *"Gospel Services"* at 10:00 am. I was there a little early and in for a wonderful surprise: It was the Gospel Church, and the place literally rocked with the choir's energetic singing and movement. The people of this totally black Church were so friendly and welcomed me to come back. When I found the Chaplain's office to sign up for Bible Study, I realized that the *"Protestant Church Services"* started at 11:00, and so I had two delightful church services that morning. I had been so caught up in seeing Frankfurt and learning about German life, making trips around the area and shopping for furniture, I had neglected all summer to get involved with the Chapel. The following week, I received a phone call from a young Korean woman inviting me to join them every Thursday morning at 9:00 am. Her name was Jung, and she was the group leader of the inductive Bible Study Course at Rhein-Main Chapel. She told me that the group was about to end their study on Spiritual Gifts and they were planning to begin the study of Romans in a couple of weeks. When I told her that I would rather wait and start at the beginning of Romans, she exclaimed, *"So you're the one we've been waiting for!"* She went on to tell me that she had ordered twelve Romans workbooks in the spring and only eleven people had signed up all summer. When she asked if I would be interested in hearing the tapes they had finished on Spiritual Gifts, I told her that I would love to. That will give me something to do while John is gone to Saudi Arabia for two weeks.

The day John left Frankfurt for Riyadh, I drove over to meet Jung and to pick up the tapes. She was a young Korean wife who had left her family in Korea when her American husband received orders for Rhein-Main AFB, so she understood my concern for our family back in the States. She said that our group would also be an intercessory prayer group and that Romans would probably be postponed for an additional couple of weeks. I had time to hear all the tapes while John was gone, which started off with Church History. I placed all my study materials on our little round table in our bedroom which looked out over our tranquil backyard. I put in the first tape and sat there listening to it all the way through. Then I got my shorthand notebook and started jotting down all the information I learned.

I was amazed at what had transpired that first century after the death of Jesus and ran the tape back and forth to make sure of what I heard. Every day while John was away, I sat there listening and taking notes. Edict after edict was given by Roman Emperors to torture Christians and put them to death in the most horrendous ways. The wild animals kept under the Roman Coliseum were unleashed upon Christian gladiators for the amusement of the blood thirsty crowd who came to watch and laugh as people were torn apart and tortured to death. No wonder Rome fell! The people had grown so callous that life held no meaning whatsoever, so it meant nothing at all for them to bow down to Caesar and worship him as their Roman god.

The first Christians who did accept Jesus as Savior and Lord had to meet in catacombs underground, where they also had to bury their dead because Christians were not allowed to be buried within the city limits of Rome. Studying the history of the Church took me into parts of the Bible I had never read before, and I was amazed as the revelations of the prophets poured forth and proved the word of God as truth for me. I literally devoured all twelve of those tapes. It reinforced the book I once read at Ft. Bliss about <u>The Power of Prayer</u>, which I checked out of the Post Library and read over and over before John received his first orders for Vietnam. I felt the movement of the Holy Spirit filling me up with God's word and moving me into a new realm. I looked forward to each day and felt exalted above the problems of the world.

On my first day with the group, we introduced ourselves and then joined hands around the table to begin our meeting with prayer and asked God to open our spiritual eyes and to lead us into all truth. As I read the introduction to Romans, I felt so privileged to be taking this Bible course and to be part of this prayer group of young ladies under the leadership of Jung and the Holy Spirit. Our Bible Study Course had been authored by a well-known Bible teacher who began sharing her testimony with her patients as a registered nurse and then dropped out of nursing to begin her own ministry. I was surprised to learn that she had served as guest speaker at the two previous Berchtesgaden Retreats and had been so well received that Bible study groups had sprung up all over Europe throughout the US Military Community. As a gifted teacher, she encouraged all of us to be diligent students.

"Whom shall he teach knowledge? And whom shall he make to understand doctrine? Them that are weaned from the milk... For precept must be upon precept; line upon line...precept upon precept; here a little, and there a little." (Isaiah: 28:9-10)

She went on to quote Paul's message to Timothy, *"Study to show thyself approved unto God, a workman that need not be ashamed, rightly dividing the word of truth."* (2 Timothy 2:15)

During one of our monthly meetings with the American Women's Club of the Taunus, I sat next to a very nice young woman who asked if I had been down to Rhein Falls. Of course, we hadn't had time to do any traveling at that point, so I was very interested in finding out about her experience as she described the largest water falls in Europe at the mouth of the Rhein River. I listened to her with fascination and made notes of what sounded like a very exciting trip for us sometime in the future and the hotel which she highly recommended. We already had reservations for a three-day tour of Belgium during *All Saints Day* weekend in October, and I had taken the advice of my prayer partners in the Bible study to sign up for the November Berchtesgaden Retreat with the Protestant Women of the Chapel. It would be the highlight of the year for the PWOC and we were only allowed the privilege once so everyone would have an opportunity to attend. I signed up immediately.

A Tour of Belgium

Towards the end of October, John and I boarded a comfortable motor coach provided by the AWC of the Taunus for our tour of Belgium. It proved to be one of our most memorable trips of the year and one in which the AWC proved to be the most well-organized tour group of any to be found in the area. We enjoyed the scenery as we headed down the German autobahn and crossed the border into Belgium. We stopped in Brussels for lunch and selected a restaurant on one of the most picturesque squares in the world known as La Grand Place. Our guide pointed out buildings representing different periods of history, where "every façade is different and the whole is in perfect harmony." Around this historic square, we saw buildings of Romanesque, Renaissance, Gothic, Baroque, and Neo-Classical all standing side by side and dating back as far as 900 AD. All buildings are in striking contrast one to another and each depicts a different era of history. Later in the afternoon, we arrived in the medieval city of Ghent and quickly followed a tour guide through the streets as we viewed the historic buildings and walked along one of its lovely canals. As darkness fell, the beautiful old buildings were illuminated, creating an excitingly different atmosphere.

Five Facades of Buildings lining "La Grand Place"
Standing side by side in Perfect Harmony.

We drove on to romantic Brugge, Ghent's sister city, where we had dinner in our hotel dining room and spent the night. The following morning, we walked through the lovely, quaint streets of Brugge, famous for its beautiful handmade "bobbin lace," which we noticed exhibited in most of the downtown store windows. In strolling through Brugge, one can see majestic white swans all along her canals and river banks, a confirmation to her promise to be permanently responsible for their preservation. After a boat ride down one of its many canals, we were driven to the peaceful setting of the convent of the *Beguines,* secular nuns not bound by vows, who date back to the 13th century. *The Beguinage,* undoubtedly the most peaceful spot in Brugge, is still open to girls from all social backgrounds that choose to dedicate themselves to a mystical community life, under the leadership of a superintendent, and withdraw from society for a quiet retreat to find peace through devotion and prayer. Then we were driven to Market Square, where we had a walking tour of historical places. We were fascinated with the history of Brugge as our guide pointed out the famous Belfry, with its octagonal tower and 47 bronze bells. Standing majestically overlooking Market Square, The Belfry is the most important monument in Brugge and reflects the glory of the town's history. All the inhabitants of Brugge were once summoned from the Belfry Tower to gather on Market Square for very important announcements.

Lovely Canal Scene in the City of Brugge, Belgium.

Around the corner from Market Square, we visited the Burg, where the first country stronghold was erected in 864 AD as a defense against the Normans. Here we have another architectural anthology of Romanesque, Gothic, Renaissance, Baroque and Neo-classical in the various old, but very beautiful, buildings of government and the Basilica of the Holy Blood Church built in the 12th Century. The Archduke Maximilian of Austria was held prisoner in 1488 in one of these buildings when the town's people rebelled against his government. One of the rare works of Michelangelo to be seen outside of Italy, "The Madonna and Child," sculpted out of white marble in 1504, is housed in The Church of our Lady.

There are many famous churches in Brugge which house paintings by the Masters and other great works of art, including another famous Pieta of the 14th century housed in Our Lady of Charity. Also among them, Saint Basil's Chapel, built in the 12th Century and St. Savior's Cathedral, built in the 9th Century. We drove by the quite large St. John's Hospital and the very picturesque Old Toll House on the main Canal, covered with many beautiful swans. We plan to go back again someday to have a more thorough tour of all these very special places and also the two famous museums of Brugge: The Gruuthuse Museum and the Groeninge Museum.

The first settlement of Brugge grew up around a mouth carved out by the North Sea between the 4th and 7th centuries. Over time the shoreline moved to the west, and today, the seaport of Zeebrugge on the North Sea has developed into a harbor of worldwide stature. The following morning, we had a bus tour of Antwerp and a guided walking tour. We visited an old church which housed many famous paintings of the Masters, including Rubens, Van Dyck and Bruegel. Then we were dismissed to have lunch on our own right in the heart of Antwerp where, again, the architecture covered many eras of history and where the whole is in perfect harmony. John and I selected a restaurant in the very center of the city and enjoyed a fish dinner, although I wondered if my dried fish was really cooked. I assumed that it was and tried to eat it anyway. From Antwerp, we journeyed over to Zeebrugge to visit the Belgian seacoast where we had free time to walk around and take pictures of the busy seaport, the yacht harbor and the recreational areas. John and I selected a restaurant with atmosphere that evening for a romantic fish dinner on the seacoast before boarding our bus for the long drive back to Frankfurt. We arrived very late at the Rhein-Main AFRC parking lot, found our car and drove home. Our tour of Belgium had truly been an educational experience in learning the history of Europe and how the different nationalities and cultures spread across the continent. We fell in love with another country and the charm of its people, and we must go back again someday to spend more time and do it justice.

CHAPTER TWELVE

A Time for Berchtesgaden
1982

After beginning my Bible study course at Rhein-Main AFB, I became very active with the Protestant Women of the Chapel. John knew I would need the car on Monday nights to drive my sewing machine over to the church for sewing patches on uniforms and mending clothing for the troops, so he would ride the train that day and leave the car at home for me. Our Monday night PWOC volunteers were divided into two groups: one specialized in sewing and the other in cooking the Monday night meal for the troops while they waited for their sewing to be done. Afterwards, we workers would fill our plates to finish off what was left as we took time to visit. One of the young airmen brought his sewing machine to help us out for a while, and it was a great time for sharing our stories and testimonies. I was a few minutes late coming home one night, and, since we only had one key for the front door, I found John sitting on the front steps waiting for me with a few flakes of snow starting to fall. He had devoured a whole bag of liqueur flavored chocolate drops to keep warm, and I guess he was hungry, too.

John dropped me off at the Rhein-Main AFRC on his way to work the second Monday morning in November to board a bus for our trip to Berchtesgaden. We were told to bring a sack lunch because it was going to be a long day; however, we had no idea just how long it would be. Our bus broke down before it ever got to us, and the bus terminal announced a *slight delay* while they tried to find another bus. Around 11:00 am, we started buying drinks from the concession stand and began to eat our lunches. By the time our bus finally arrived around noon, we had finished eating our lunches and discarded our trash. At least we had time to get to know one another somewhat before finding our seats on the bus, and that made our time pass more quickly.

On the way down, I shared a seat with a very talkative young woman who quite matter-of-factly told me that her mother and father never liked her; they had always favored her sister. Her name was Rachel, and she was really hung up on it! I told her that she was probably mistaken about the way her parents felt about her. She could have misunderstood some small incident and allowed it to grow in her mind until it became larger than it really was. I advised her to get rid of it; just hand it all over to God and let it go. I must have thought of half a dozen ways to tell her to forgive her parents, because none of us are perfect, and let God handle it. Jesus is the healer! And he died to set us free! I finally said just roll it all up and throw it in the garbage. Our on-going conversation led to her telling me how she became a Christian, and it was very precious to me that she wanted to share it. Rachel said that she and her husband were lying in bed one morning, and they started talking about the existence of God. They had two precious children between the ages of two and four, and they came to the conclusion that there must be a God to make everything so perfect. Rachel dropped by the Rhein-Main Chapel that morning on her way to work to speak to the chaplain about the existence of God. Since she worked in a florist shop, they hired her to do all the floral arrangements for the church. She made many friends and was well liked by everyone she met. Then she and her family started attending church services every Sunday morning. I expressed how blessed she was that God had chosen her to raise her family in the church, so all of them would be blessed and her children would learn about the gospel of Christ Jesus. Rachel was quite a character and a person I will never forget! She was definitely one of God's chosen. (John 6:44)

This was my first trip down the autobahn driving south into Bavaria, so it was very special and exciting for me to see the occasional German castles on the hilltops. After a couple of hours, we could see the mighty snowcapped Alps off in the distance. They seemed to slowly rise, looming larger and larger until they towered all around us. I fell in love with the artistically designed Bavarian chalets which speckled the beautiful countryside. When we finally arrived at Berchtesgaden late in the afternoon, we found that all the rooms in the hotel where the conference was taking place were filled to capacity and we were stuck in a small hotel at the bottom. We would have to be transported back and forth each day up the mountain. Since we were all tired and hungry, we had dinner in the hotel dining room while they assigned us to our rooms and brought in our baggage. Then we boarded our bus for the drive up the mountain to the General Walker Hotel for the Welcoming Ceremony.

The Conference began with our guest speaker, April Moore, welcoming women from military chapels all over Europe. It was wonderful to hear Christian music wafting out over the large auditorium, once the scene of Nazi Headquarters during WWII. The theme of the conference was *"To God Be the Glory."* April gave a preview of what the week would be like and some of the topics she would cover, and our guest singer, Bobby Michaels, sang one of his beautiful Christian songs. We received our schedule for the week before we re-boarded our bus for the drive back down to Berchtesgaden. Then we had to get settled in our rooms and try to get some sleep, which was rather difficult to do after such a trying day and an exhilarating evening. I roomed with two very nice young women from Rhein-Main Chapel, and, when our wakeup call came so early in the morning, we had to laugh when the young chaplain's wife said, *"The spirit's willing, but the flesh is weak."* It was very hard getting up to make it down for breakfast @ 6:45 am.

Back at the conference that morning, it was wonderful to hear the beautiful Christian music flowing out over the auditorium. April's first message Tuesday morning was about the problems she faced as a young wife and mother who was always trying to save money by shopping in the bargain basements of large department stores. Then she would go home and tell her husband how much money she saved that day. She didn't realize it, but it was giving him a feeling of inadequacy, and he finally told her that he would work three jobs, if necessary, to get her out of the bargain basements. The message: *"God owns all the cattle on a thousand hills, and he can sell one, if necessary, to provide for his children."* Tuesday was somewhat chaotic because we had to learn our way around the General Walker Hotel to find the dining facilities for lunch, especially for those of us stuck overnight in Berchtesgaden. On Wednesday morning, April shared some of their other problems she and her husband had to overcome in raising their children and how God helped them through those troublous times. The message: *"If God is for us, who can be against us?"* and *"All things work together for good for those who love the Lord and are called according to His purpose."* (Romans 8:28-31)

Every morning we met in the large assembly hall where April started the day with prayer and her opening message. We would sing a few songs of praise and worship, hear a song by Bobby Michaels and then separate into our small groups to share on a more personal level. Our lunch break was around noon. Then we would return to our small group to finish up our personal testimonies, pray for our families and have free time to visit the book store to purchase Christian tapes and paperback books on our way back to the large assembly hall. We would hear April's afternoon message, sing a few songs of praise and worship, listen to another song by Bobby and then close with prayer. Bobby Michaels was a very nice looking young man, with a great soothing baritone voice, who once sang background for BJ Thomas. We would hear his testimony on the last morning of the conference. After our closing prayer around 4:30, we would re-board our bus for the ride back down the mountain to Berchtesgaden where we would have dinner in our hotel and sometimes share our testimonies.

On Wednesday, we started out the day the same as on Tuesday, but there was a forecast for snow. A few flakes started to fall around noon, so we had to board our bus after lunch for the ride back down to Berchtesgaden before the roads became dangerous. After most of us had found our seats, I heard a familiar voice coming from the front of the bus. It was Rachel! I could tell she was upset about the bus making it down the mountain with the snow starting to fall, and I heard the chaplain respond from outside the bus, "Well Rachel, if you don't make it down the mountain, I'll see you in heaven." A while later I heard her say to someone sitting in front of her as she was hanging onto the above railing, "Well, I used to feel that way, but now I just roll it all up in a little ball and throw it in the garbage." She was adorable! That evening, I sat for dinner with two ladies I had not met before, Carol and Margaret from California. They had been next door neighbors and worked together for the evangelical gatherings which came to Anaheim. We enjoyed our conversation as we shared our stories. Being stuck in Berchtesgaden all together as a small group from Rhein-Main gave us a better chance of getting to know one another.

Margaret, a bit older than Carol, was a retired widow who had lost her husband a few years earlier when Carol and her husband moved in next door. Every morning when Carol arose early, she noticed a candle burning through the window next door. Curious, she asked her neighbor about it and was very touched by her answer. Margaret was having her time with the Lord, and she started each day with prayer and lit a candle. It was a ceremony she had begun after her husband's death, and it helped her get through each day. She sought the Lord early in the morning by putting him first, reading her Bible and having time for prayer. Obviously, this had a tremendous effect on Carol because she began to start each day with Bible reading and prayer and lit a candle, too, if she was up before dawn. Eventually, they were going to church together and taking part in all the Christian activities. They always volunteered for the evangelical gatherings, so when Carol moved to Frankfurt with her husband's new assignment and learned about the PWOC Retreat to Berchtesgaden, she invited Margaret to come over as her guest to attend the Retreat and experience life in Germany.

Thursday morning, it was snowing so badly we couldn't get back up the mountain. The roads were covered with snow, and we were surprised to find the young chaplain stuck at the bottom with us. I believe he had come down later the previous day in case we couldn't get back up to the conference, and he brought with him a tape of what we had missed Wednesday afternoon. We had our own program in the small church next door to our hotel and listened to the tape. Then we walked over to the Riverside Church which President Eisenhower made famous during WW II, and I was able to stand on the bridge where he stood to take the same picture of the lovely little church in the snow. Rachel, Carol, Margaret and I all sat together in the church, and I took a picture of the three of them sitting together in one of the pews. Our ladies from Rhein-Main Chapel, all stuck at the bottom of the mountain, enjoyed having dinner together that evening and shared more of our testimonies.

Friday, the last day of the conference, was very beautiful and serene with the sun shining brightly all day to light up the lovely pristine snow which covered everything. The roads were now safe enough for us to be driven up the mountainside for the final day of the conference and the music was especially beautiful. Bobby gave his testimony about how he messed up his life with drugs and caused his family much worry due to his cocaine addiction. However, his Christian parents in Florida welcomed him home and helped him make a new start. He finally made the decision to hand his messed up life over to God, and, as a result, he was blessed with his own music ministry and a beautiful Christian wife, a very talented Swiss ballerina. Now they lived in Switzerland and took part in Christian seminars all over Europe. Bobby reminded me so much of my son, Jimmy, with his blonde hair and similar features, I hung around to speak with him at the end of the session and he wrote Greg's name down in his Bible to add his name to his prayer list. Bobby shared his testimony that morning about how he, BJ and some of the other singers had gotten involved with drugs: uppers and downers at first, which led to cocaine addictions, and how God moved in their lives to bring them out of it. They were thankful for the prayers of their family members and so grateful to be free from the bondage to cocaine, they promised God that they would devote the rest of their lives to serving him through their Christian songs and music.

I shared my testimony that day with my group since I had missed two days with them because of snow. The girls offered me good advice about how the power of prayer had worked for them under similar circumstances and escorted me to the book store in search of a book one of them recommended. I purchased the paperback and two of Bobby Michaels' tapes, *"God Cared Enough"* and *"He was there all the Time."* We closed our last meeting with arms around one another in a prayer circle as we tearfully prayed for our lost loved ones. Bobby Michaels lives on through his beautiful songs, and I'm sure his parents and lovely wife are thankful just knowing that he surrendered his life to God before it was too late for him. He died much too young just a few years ago from severe health problems.

> *"Confess your faults one to another, and pray for one another, that ye may be healed. The effectual fervent prayer of a righteous man (or woman) availeth much."* (James 5:16)

That afternoon, as we celebrated the Lord's Supper in a lovely Candlelight Ceremony, our hearts were brimming over with God's love. The songs of Praise we sang that day lifted our spirits as we felt his wonderful presence moving over the auditorium, filling the whole house with his glory. I knew in my heart, as I looked out over the grounds covered with the freshly fallen snow that if God could change that once horrendous Nazi headquarters into something so beautiful, which echoed his wondrous love and beauty, he could change the lives of my lost family members. He could draw them to himself and open their spiritual eyes so they could see him as he is, *The King of Kings and Lord of Lords.* (Revelation 19:16) Jesus said, *"I am the way, the truth and the life: no man cometh unto the Father, but by me."* (John 14:6)

Christians all over the world have come to know Jesus in many different ways because all lives are different, and no one can come to God unless the Father draws him. (John 6:44) As our bus headed back to Frankfurt, my heart was so filled with the joy of the Lord that I felt lifted up above all the problems of the earth. I longed for the day when my family would become *my brothers and sisters in Christ Jesus* and join together in sharing *his marvelous light.* As we passed through the countryside on our way home with artistic Bavarian chalets dotting the snow-covered mountains, my thoughts drifted back to one of our recent studies. I remembered hearing the story of Horace Greely and how he tried to prove Jesus a fraud: he actually staged a mock courtroom trial where all the evidence was presented before a court of law and a verdict was reached.

A Courtroom Trial

Horace Greely, the once famous New York newspaper reporter and Attorney at Law, set out to prove that Jesus was a fraud and launched a thorough investigation of all the known facts regarding his death and resurrection. He prepared his case as if he were preparing it for a courtroom trial to be heard before a jury. After months of research, investigation and deliberation, Horace Greely concluded that Jesus *is* who He claims to be, *the Son of the living God,* and that *the Resurrection* offers the most logical account of what happened to His body. Remembering His exact words, "After three days I will rise again", and giving the scriptural account, Greely begins to present his case.

> *Pilate commanded that the tomb be guarded for three days, and the Pharisees sealed the stone in place, which closed the only outlet to the tomb. Then he "commanded that the sepulcher be made sure until the third day, lest his disciples come by night and steal him away and say unto the people 'He is risen from the dead', so the last error shall be worse than the first. So they went, and made the sepulcher sure, sealing the stone and setting a watch." (Matthew 27:62-66)*

The Roman soldiers searched everywhere for the body of Jesus, and they would have found him if it were at all possible. His disciples had dispersed in all directions in fear of losing their own lives to the point of denying they ever knew Jesus. They were so dismantled and distraught that even an attempted removal of his body would have been unthinkable. They couldn't understand what had gone wrong because they had never fully understood what was to happen in the first place. (John 20: 9) In spite of what Jesus had told them, they still thought he would crush the

Roman Empire and restore the kingdom to Israel. Grieved by his death, they thought it was all over. The thought probably even occurred to them that he might have been an imposter.

The strong evidence of the case revolved around the *eye witness accounts* of those who had personally seen Jesus in the forty days which followed his death. Their testimonies corroborate the Biblical account of those who actually saw Jesus in his resurrected body with his visible wounds. (John 20:24-29)

> *"For I delivered unto you first of all that which I also received, how that Christ died for our sins according to the scriptures; and that He was buried, and that He rose again the third day according to the scriptures: And that he was seen of Cephas, then of the twelve: After that, He was seen of above five hundred brethren all at once… After that, he was seen of James then of all the apostles, and last of all he was seen of me also, as of one born out of due time."* (1st Corinthians 15:3-8)

What did Paul mean, *"as of one born out of due time?"* The Book of Acts tells the story of Saul of Tarsus, who became the Apostle Paul almost overnight, whose letters to the existing Churches in Italy, Greece and Turkey would make him the author of the largest segment of books in the New Testament. Although the lot fell upon Matthias, I believe God chose Saul, the most unlikely candidate, but the one chosen by God with enough zeal to take the gospel to the world.

Saul, a religious Pharisee, hated Christians and had witnessed the stoning death of Stephen, who had given his Testimony before the Council of the Chief Priests of the synagogue just before he was stoned to death for blasphemy. In Stephen's testimony, he gave an account of Jewish history and accused the Council of resisting the Holy Ghost and slaying the prophets who foretold of the coming of *"The Just One; of whom ye have now been the betrayers and murderers: Who have received the Law by the disposition of angels, and have not kept it. When they heard these things, they were cut to the heart, and they gnashed on him with their teeth."* (Acts, Chapter 7)

> *"But, he, being full of the Holy Ghost, looked up steadfastly into heaven, and saw the glory of God, and Jesus standing on the right hand of God, and said, 'Behold, I saw the heavens opened,*

and the Son of man standing on the right hand of God,'... and the witnesses laid down their clothes at a young man's feet whose name was Saul. And they stoned Stephen, calling upon God, and saying, 'Lord Jesus, receive my spirit.' And he kneeled down and cried with a loud voice, 'Lord, lay not this sin to their charge.' And when he had said this, he fell asleep." (Acts 7:55-60)

Saul was so filled with hatred for the Christians, he was on his way to Damascus to throw as many as he could find into prison when:

"Suddenly there shined round about him a light from heaven: And he fell to the earth and heard a voice saying to him, 'Saul, Saul, why are you persecuting me?' And Saul answered, 'Who art thou Lord?' And the Lord said, 'I am Jesus whom you are persecuting: it is hard for you to kick against the pricks.'" (Acts 9:1-28)

Saul was blinded for three days and led to Damascus where Ananias helped him receive his sight and prayed with him to be filled with the Holy Ghost. God miraculously took Saul away in the spirit to another place to teach him the Gospel, as depicted in his letter to the Corinthians: Paul said of himself,

"I knew a man in Christ who was caught up to the third heaven, whether in the body or out of the body, he could not tell: How he was caught up into paradise and heard unspeakable words, which it is not lawful for a man to utter.... And lest I should be exalted above measure through the abundance of the revelations, there was given to me a thorn in the flesh... For this thing, I besought the Lord thrice, that it might depart from me. And he said unto me, 'My grace is sufficient for thee: for my strength is made perfect in weakness.' Most gladly, therefore, will I rather glory in my infirmities, that the power of Christ may rest upon me... for when I am weak, then am I strong." (2 Corinthians 12: 2-9)

God changed Saul's name to Paul when he received the anointing of the Holy Spirit and entered into the New Covenant with Jesus and the Apostles. (Acts 13:9) To Paul, one of our chief witnesses for the defense, we ask the all-important question: "Who is Jesus of Nazareth?"

"And immediately there fell from his eyes something like scales, and he received his sight at once; and he arose and was baptized; and, when he had received food, he was strengthened. Then Saul spent several days with the disciples at Damascus. Immediately, he preached Jesus in the synagogues as the Christ saying, 'He is the Son of God.'" (Acts 9:18-20)

John, the Apostle, gives us an even greater account of Jesus as the Son of God, who brings the true Light into the world. In the same Chapter, John, the Baptist, as *"the voice of one crying in the wilderness,"* says to us that *"there is one coming after me, whose shoe's latchet I am not worthy to unloose."* ... *"I baptize with water,"* but *"he will baptize with the Holy Ghost and with fire."* Then John *saw the Holy Spirit descending from heaven like a dove, and it abode upon Jesus.* In the Book of John, we find the testimonies of two witnesses: John, the apostle, the author of this Book, and John the Baptist, *"the voice of one crying in the wilderness, Make straight the way of the Lord."* (Isaiah 40:3) When John saw Jesus coming to him to be baptized, he said, *"Behold the Lamb of God which taketh away the sin of the world."* ... *"And I saw, and bare record that this is the Son of God."* (John 1:9, 23-34)

"In the beginning was the Word, and the Word was with God, and the Word was God. The same was in the beginning with God. All things were made by him, and without him was not anything made that was made. In him was life; and the life was the light of men. And the light shineth in the darkness and the darkness comprehendeth it not.

"There was a man sent from God whose name was John, who came to bear witness of the Light; that all men, through him might believe. He was not that light, but he was sent to bear witness of that Light. That was the true Light, which lights every man that comes into the world.

"He was in the world, and the world was made by him, and the world knew him not. He came unto his own, and his own received him not. But as many as received him, to them he gave power to become the sons of God, even to them that believe on his name: Which were born, not of blood, nor of the will of the flesh, nor of the will of man, but of God.

"And the Word was made flesh, and dwelt among us, and we beheld his glory, the glory as of the only begotten of the Father, full of grace and truth. John (the Baptist) bare witness of him and cried, saying 'This is he of whom I spoke, he that cometh after me is preferred before me: for he was before me; and of his fullness, we have all received, and grace for grace.... For the law was given by Moses, but grace and truth came by Jesus Christ.'

"And this is the record of John when the Jews sent priests and Levites from Jerusalem to ask him, 'Who art thou?' And he confessed, 'I am not the Christ.' And they asked him, 'What then? What sayeth thou of thyself?' And John said unto them, 'I am the voice of one crying in the wilderness, Make straight the way of the Lord.'.... The next day, John saw Jesus coming unto him to be baptized and said, 'Behold the Lamb of God, which takes away the sin of the world.'... And John bare witness saying, 'I saw the Spirit descending from heaven like a dove, and it abode upon him.'... 'And I saw and bare witness that this is the Son of God.'" (John 1:1-34)

[Notice how the Book of John begins and how it correlates with the first words of God: *"In the beginning, God created the heavens and the earth. And the earth was without form, and void; and darkness was upon the face of the deep. And the Spirit of God moved upon the face of the waters."* (Genesis 1:1-2)]

Also, there may be proof of Christ's resurrection in a linen burial cloth known as the *"Shroud of Turin,"* which was seen by many lying in the empty tomb when the others came in to inquire about the body of Jesus. It is all explained in a book written about a burial cloth, which is believed to bear the scorched image of Christ and was hidden for hundreds of years. It was *"rediscovered in 525 AD when it was found in a niche above the west gate of the wall of the city of Edessa, now Urfa, in south central Turkey."* The story of the shroud plus the scientific evidence of its authenticity is explained in The Verdict on the Shroud. It was brought to my attention back in 1973 while living at White Sands Missile Range, NM when Greg brought home a book entitled, The Mystery of the Shroud of Turin. He found this book in a pile of books people were giving away, and he brought it home to me. Since then, I have studied everything I could find about this mysterious linen burial cloth, which has upon it what is believed to be the scorched image of a person crucified exactly like Jesus because all the wounds are the same as his wounds which were described in scripture. The image is believed to have been scorched onto the cloth at the time of the resurrection, which produced a certain kind of heat in combination with the burial ointments applied to his body. It was very similar to the snapping of a camera and could be a miracle of God left behind as proof of the resurrection. The picture on the cloth is the negative and shows up as light. All the wounds of Jesus are visible by the blood stains, and scientists have even determined the blood type. This burial cloth, in my opinion, could not be a forgery!

Next, we have a procession of four witnesses, Matthew, Mark, Luke and John, who all give their accounts and testify to these facts:

> *"On the first day of the week, Mary Magdalene came to the sepulcher very early while it was still dark and saw the stone was taken away."* She ran to tell Peter and John, *"They have taken away the Lord out of the sepulcher, and we know not where they have laid Him."* They both ran to the sepulcher, and *"looking in, they saw the linen clothes lying there, and the napkin, that was about his head, not lying with the linen clothes, but wrapped together in a place by itself."* (John 20: 1-9)
>
> *"When the evening was come, there came a rich man from Arimathaea, named Joseph, who also was Jesus' disciple: He went to Pilate, and begged for the body of Jesus. ... And when Joseph had taken the body, he wrapped it in a clean linen cloth, and laid it in his own new tomb, which he had hewn out in the rock and he rolled a great stone to the door of the sepulcher and departed.* (Matthew 27:57- 60)
>
> *"Now when the evening was come, Joseph of Arimathaea went in boldly unto Pilate and craved the body of Jesus.... And he bought fine linen, and took him down, and wrapped him in the linen and laid him in a sepulcher hewn out of a rock, and rolled a stone unto the door of the sepulcher. And Mary Magdalene and Mary the mother of Joses beheld where he was laid. And very early in the morning, they came unto the sepulcher ... And when they looked, they saw that the stone was rolled away: for it was very great.... And they saw a young man ... clothed in a long white garment... And he said unto them, be not afraid: Ye seek Jesus of Nazareth, which was*

crucified: He is risen. He is not here: behold the place where they laid him." (Mark 15:42-Mark 16:6)

"And Joseph of Arimathaea, a counselor and a good man, went unto Pilate and begged the body of Jesus. And he took it down and wrapped it in linen and laid it in a sepulcher hewn in stone where never a man before was laid. It was the day of preparation before the Sabbath, and the women which came with him from Galilee followed after and beheld the sepulcher and how His body was laid. And they returned and prepared spices and ointments." (Luke 23:50-56)

Next Greely calls four impressionable witnesses, God the Father and the apostles Peter, James, and John, who all testify together because these three were present when God the Father spoke from heaven when they were on the *Mount of Transfiguration: "This is my beloved Son, in whom I am well pleased." "And as they came down from the mountain, Jesus charged them saying, 'Tell the vision to no man, until the Son of man be risen again from the dead.'"* (Matthew 17:1-9)

"Moreover I will endeavor that ye may be able after my decease to have these things always in remembrance: For we have not followed cunningly devised fables, when we made known unto you the power and coming of our Lord Jesus Christ, but were eye witnesses of his majesty. For he received from God the Father honor and glory, when there came such a voice to him from the excellent glory, 'This is my beloved Son, in whom I am well pleased.' And this voice, which came from heaven, we heard, when we were with him in the holy mount." (2nd Peter 1:13-18)

After all these witnesses, Horace Greeley rests his case. The Verdict: *The Resurrection is the only conceivable explanation for the missing body of Jesus.* Therefore, the court concludes that Jesus *is* who he claims to be: *The Son of the living God, and He was resurrected on the third day just as He proclaimed.*

CHAPTER THIRTEEN

Paris, London & Kandersteg

1982-1983

As in Morocco, I found myself involved with the American Women's Club and managed to get a ride to the luncheons with some of the other wives. One of my friends, Annie, who lived in Morfelden, just down the road from Walldorf, invited me over to her house for lunch one day, so we could make plans for riding together to some of the luncheons and to our German language class, which was being taught by one of the Litton wives to give us enough basic German to get around Europe, order from a menu and do a little shopping, etc. The luncheons of the AWC of the Taunus were held at some of the most prestigious restaurants and castles around Frankfurt and the food was always great, so it was to my advantage to attend as often as possible. We also learned about the upcoming trips they were sponsoring, and we were able to sign up for the ones we wanted before they became overbooked. I felt greatly privileged to belong to the AWC and took advantage of our possibilities to travel with them. I also learned to book some of our bus tours at the Rhein-Main Armed Forces Recreation Center (AFRC) and signed us up for a four-day bus trip to Paris over Thanksgiving weekend.

A Tour of Paris

John and I left Rhein-Main early Thursday morning bound for Paris and stopped for lunch on the border, as we had done on our trip to Belgium. From here we took a route which took us into France, and we stopped in Reims for a wine tasting tour of *Moet & Chandon*, a champagne distillery where Napoleon once purchased his champagne. We arrived in Paris around sunset and settled into our room. On Friday morning, we boarded our bus for a city tour of Paris, and John was in high heaven taking pictures of all the famous places: *The Arch de Triumph; the Champs Elysees; the Place de la Concorde; the Eiffel Tower; and Notre Dame Cathedral.* After walking around to take more pictures, we selected a romantic little restaurant for lunch and then headed back to our hotel via the subway to get ready for our evening *Illumination Tour.* The atmosphere of Paris by day changed into an entirely different Paris by night. Our riverboat cruise took us around the small island where *the Louvre Palace* once housed the Royal Family and where the seat of the French Government is located. Like a large moat, it is completely surrounded by the Seine river. John was equipped with high speed film to capture all these incredibly beautiful places.

On Saturday morning, we joined our tour bus for our journey to *Versailles,* the magnificent country estate of King Louis the XIV, which was built to satisfy his hunting needs while living at the Louvre Palace. He liked it so well, he eventually stayed there permanently. It was also the home of Kings Louis XV and XVI. The latter, Louis XVI, was beheaded along with Marie- Antoinette at the beginning of the French Revolution in 1789. The large palace was also incredibly beautiful with oil murals covering the ceilings and walls, gilded with gold, and furnished with antiques of an early period of provincial French. It has tiled floors throughout with large rooms for parties and very large dance halls. The courtyards and picturesque gardens, endowed with lovely fountains, sculptures and pools of water, were embedded in a misty fog on the day of our visit lending an almost eerie atmosphere to the beautiful mansion as we learned its magnificent, and sometimes gory, history. After lunch, we visited the *Louvre Museum,* which houses Michelangelo's famous Mona Lisa and numerous other famous paintings by the Masters. We were transported up to *Montmartre,* where we had the most fantastic view of Paris in front of the Sacred Heart Church. From this hilltop, John captured his most artistic shot of the *Eiffel Tower* through the misty fog and the bare branches of a tree. We walked around to *Painter's Square,* where artists from all over the world set up their easels to paint while exhibiting some of their work. As incredible as it may seem, we bumped into two old friends we came to know quite well from the FAO Course at Ft. Bragg, Maurice and Annette, who were in our French class in 1974. We remembered how much Maurice wanted France as his country of choice for in-country training, and we were very happy to learn that he was now serving his second tour as US Army Attaché to France. Both he and Annette loved Paris! It was remarkable that our paths should cross at that particular time on that particular day, our one and only visit to Artist's Square on the hilltop at Montmartre.

Our bus tour stopped at a gigantic flea market on the way back to our hotel, and, since we preferred not to shop or mingle with the vast crowd of people, John and I found a little café for coffee and a brief rest stop from our hectic schedule. Instead of going on the cabaret tour that evening, we chose to stay in the hotel and splurge on a steak dinner to have with our bottle of champagne from Reims. We managed to top it off with a delicious chocolate mousse! We enjoyed great food and a restful evening, which we really needed. On the way home, we stopped again in Reims to see the beautiful Cathedral, *Notre Dame de Reims,* where John took many pictures. And we discovered a little bakery across the street, so we walked in to look around and bought a box of delicious French pastries to take home with us. We arrived at the German border around 3:00 pm, and enjoyed our delicious roasted chicken once again served with mixed salad and lots of French fries. This time we sat directly above the autobahn where we could watch the traffic pass directly below us. We arrived in Frankfurt around sunset.

When we returned from our trip to Paris, we were happy to find several letters from Maggie telling us about life in the Freshman dorm, and were happy to hear that she was doing well and determined to make all A's. However, reading between the lines, we could tell that she wasn't at all happy with dorm life because there was too much partying going on. We also had a letter from Ralph telling us that he and Greg had forced out Greg's roommate because of his failure to pay his share of the rent. Both he and his girlfriend were using drugs and neither of them were trying to get along with Greg. From Ralph's observation, it seemed like Greg was trying to shape up. However, the whole month's rent was now coming out of the rapidly shrinking escrow account. Greg thought he could make up the difference by working full time and said he didn't want another roommate. Maybe he was learning some lessons now that *the shoe was on the other foot.* Our plan had been to help him through the first year and then allow him to pay his own way. John told Ralph that he would send another check to replenish the escrow account and thanked him for his help with Greg.

I was very thankful for the support of my prayer group. I felt that God was working in our family, but sometimes it's hard not to worry, or at least be concerned, about our children when we are far away from them. I had learned that *worry* is not *of faith*, and, therefore, must be considered *sin*, because it is an unprofitable drain of one's energies and does no good for anyone. *Faith* cannot operate within the same realm as *worry, anxiety, and fear.* These opposing forces can *restrict and paralyze* those caught up in them. *Faith*, on the other hand, is *a positive, motivating force,* which can spur possibilities into action and, with God's help, *produce miracles.* This is a *spiritual law* of great importance, which I needed to learn!

> *"For God has not given us the spirit of fear; but of power, and of love, and of a sound mind."* (2 Timothy 1:7)
> *"Now faith is the substance of things hoped for, the evidence of things not seen."* (Hebrews 11:1)
> *"Therefore I say unto you, 'Take no thought for your life'...* *'Which of you, by worrying, can add one cubit to his stature?'...* *'your heavenly Father knows that ye have need of all these things.'* *'But seek ye first the kingdom of God and his righteousness; and all these things shall be added unto you.'"* (Matthew 6:25-34)

Since Thanksgiving had been such a tremendous blessing for John and me, we decided to do something really spectacular for Christmas. I booked us on a six-day tour of England with the AFRC. We decided to spend Christmas at home, since there were so many Christmas functions we needed to attend, and leave on our journey the following Monday. Greta and George invited us to their Open House quite early in the month, and we enjoyed meeting some of their German friends and also being with some of our Litton group. We enjoyed the Litton Christmas Pot-Luck Dinner when they presented all their employees a large Christmas basket of all kinds of goodies, including a Christmas turkey. John accompanied me to the PWOC Christmas Dinner and was finally able to meet some of my Christian friends from Berchtesgaden. He gave me the *ultimate compliment* on the way home when he said, *"They're just like you."*

Jim & Kathy called Christmas Day, and then Mother called to say Merry Christmas. Greg and Maggie were spending Christmas with Amanda, Zach and their large family, and Amanda always cooked a big turkey with dressing and all the trimmings, and we hoped they were all having a great family get- together. They had invited Greg to ride the bus down to spend Christmas with them for a few days, and Maggie drove him back to northern Virginia to find that his apartment had been vandalized. They called the police and reported it, but nothing was ever done about it, nor did they find out who did it. And no one thought to collect anything on our insurance, which John had purchased before we left the country. Maggie drove back to ODU the following day to try to get some rest before starting the next school semester.

A Tour of London

On Tuesday evening after Christmas, we boarded our bus around 9:00 pm for our long drive to Zeebrugge, Belgium, where we had to embark about 3:45 am aboard a huge four-deck ferry for the four-hour crossing of the English Channel. We ordered our first full English breakfast at the restaurant around 5:30. What a thrill it was to see the beautiful White Cliffs of Dover in the distance glowing through the dim light of dawn, and, the closer we came with the rising of the sun, the whiter and brighter they looked as they began to tower over us. After disembarking from the ferry at Dover, we were driven to the top of the beautiful cliffs to look down upon the port below and take pictures of Dover Castle and the spectacular view of the English Channel.

The White Cliffs of Dover, England.

We drove on to Canterbury where we stopped to walk through the historic old city, the cradle of English Christianity, and toured Canterbury Cathedral. We stood near the place where Thomas Becket was murdered while kneeling in prayer. From there we walked through the ancient Roman ruins where the Romans ruled from AD 43 until the fall of the Roman Empire in the 5th century. St. Augustine brought Christianity to England in the 6th century, and Canterbury has been the seat of the Archbishop, the Primate of all England, ever since. We enjoyed our drive through the English countryside as we neared London and arrived at our hotel in early afternoon. John inquired about theatre tickets and managed to buy two tickets for *Evita* that evening. While waiting for the theatre to open in the Soho District of London, we found an Italian restaurant right around the corner from the theatre. We enjoyed a great pizza and the wonderfully relaxing music of a very talented piano player. John enjoyed the play very much, but I found it very depressing. We took the subway back to our hotel and were in bed before midnight. It had been a very long day!

Our city tour of London the following morning took us to all the famous places: *Westminster Abbey; Piccadilly Circus; Trafalgar Square; St. Paul's Cathedral; the Houses of Parliament; the Tower of London; London Bridge; Tower Bridge and last, but not least, Buckingham Palace.* After lunch, a delightful young woman who reminded us of Mary Poppins, with her closed umbrella held high above her head to lead the way and an adorable Belgian brogue, took us on a walking tour of *Windsor Castle.* The castle, which dates back to the 11th century, is the oldest inhabited castle in the world and is still in use by the Royal Family. It is interesting to note that the Royal Children were housed in this castle during World Wars I & II. We followed her through the old town listening to the stories of King Henry VIII, who had passageways leading from his private chamber to different parts of town, and we stopped for tea and scones in a quaint little tea room to which one of the passageways led. Then it was time to return to London for the pub tour.

John and I ordered dinner at the first pub we visited, *The Swan*, along with most of the others on our tour because we were all very hungry. We had not had time to eat anything since lunchtime and we had worked up quite an appetite. We found that most of the British pubs serve both hot and cold food during dinner hours. The tour provided us with a free drink at each of the three night spots. Not having a taste for beer, I ordered soft drinks, but John enjoyed sampling the different English ales and lagers.

Both of us, however, enjoyed visiting the different places and sampling the various kinds of atmosphere. All of them were interesting and ranged from uptown to the mysterious waterfront where Jack the Ripper once stalked his victims. Our guide confided that Princess Margaret had been seen on occasion at the second pub, *The George*, which seemed to have a rather nice ambiance. However, I believe the last one, *The Prospect of Whitby*, was the most enjoyable and famous. It has the atmosphere! We noticed a framed newspaper article rating it *"in the top 10 of the best places to eat in London since 1968."* It is an old remodeled warehouse on the waterfront which was rebuilt with very large, old-fashioned stone floors and several open fire places throughout to keep it warm and cozy. The beautifully polished wooden bar, built on top of large wooden wine barrels, is very impressive, and the lovely river landing with hanging Chinese lanterns creates a peaceful and romantic atmosphere. We enjoyed listening to a vocalist singing folksongs accompanied by a small combo, as we sat by the fire sipping hot chocolate.

Early Friday morning, we boarded the bus for our *Stratford-Upon-Avon* tour and were delighted to find our witty guide from the pub tour. As we headed toward the heart of England, he cracked many jokes about Winston Churchill and did some very good imitations before stopping briefly at Winston's boyhood home. We were able to peek through the fence and take pictures. Then we journeyed on to Stratford where we visited the birthplace of William Shakespeare and toured the stately home of his mother, Mary Arden, and the charming thatched roof cottage of his wife, Ann Hathaway. While in Stratford, we were very surprised and impressed to stop for lunch at the *Swans Restaurant* for a formal five-course dinner, which was spectacular with excellent service. After a short break for shopping in Stratford, we headed out to *Warwick Castle*, which was just a short distance away. We were very impressed with this medieval castle, which represented the era of the English knights. It was furnished throughout with some of the original furniture, or replicas, and had many displays of the clothing, armor and weaponry of the knights.

When we arrived back at our hotel, we were happy to find tickets for *Camelot*, starring Richard Harris, awaiting us at the desk. Again we had to hurry to catch the subway over to Soho to find our theatre and our seats before the curtain opened. *What a fantastic performance!* Afterwards, we decided to find the same Italian Restaurant and have another wonderful evening with the same great pizza and music we had enjoyed so much before. It was New Year's Eve! And we wanted to spend it in this wonderful atmosphere, hoping the same piano player would be back on duty. And he was! We noticed several distinctive foreign languages being spoken all around us by the lively people who were obviously bringing in the New Year! *What a delightful evening!* We had to hurry to catch the last subway train back to the hotel.

On Saturday morning, we departed London and headed south to *Brighton*. Although it was cold and windy, we walked along the promenade of England's most popular seaside resort to *the Royal Pavilion*, built in 1778 by George, Prince of Wales. Before becoming King George IV in 1820, he had turned his old stately boyhood home into a very unique Indian-style castle decorated throughout with a Chinese motif. Now it is a very unusual palace and quite interesting to visit! John and I walked through the narrow, winding streets of the small town and, as we learned to do earlier, found a quaint little restaurant where we had the most memorable *sole meuniere*, which literally melted in our mouths along with their wonderful fresh steamed vegetables.

We departed Brighton shortly after noon for our journey to *Battle*, and, on the way, stopped to walk out on the highest cliffs overlooking the ocean. We were warned not to get too close to the edge because people have actually been blown off because of standing too close. The wind was blowing constantly and came in powerful gusts, which were unpredictable, so we took our guide's advice and stood way back. About mid-afternoon, we arrived at the historic site where the *Battle of Hastings* took place in AD 1066, in which King Harold was killed when William the Conqueror invaded England. The old fortress is very well preserved and completely enclosed within a beautiful high stone wall. Next door to the old fortress, in stark contrast, is a very inviting English Tea Room where we would have loved to stop for tea and scones or pastries, but, because it began to rain, we had to get on with our journey to Dover. Along the way, the light rain turned into a terrific downpour! Our rather rustic and old, drafty hotel was a welcome sight when we finally arrived that evening, and our beds were warm and comfortable.

Sunday morning, John and I ventured out into the drizzling rain with our umbrellas to find a coffee house for breakfast and discovered a marvelous old church and cemetery right in the heart of Dover. The pictures we made are loaded with the atmosphere of the church and cemetery on a rainy winter day. We enjoyed our last English breakfast and boarded our bus for the return trip across the English Channel. This time, our ferry would cross the shorter distance from Dover to Calais, and we would spend a large portion of our two-hour crossing outside on the deck watching the swarming sea gulls and taking pictures of boat activity. We spent our last half-hour inside the restaurant warming up with hot cups of coffee while gazing out the window at the numerous sea-going vessels crossing the channel. The drive back to Frankfurt from Calais was long, but our rest stop at the French-German border was a very welcomed sight. Being familiar with the procedure now, we automatically took our places above the autobahn with our plates of delicious roasted chicken, salad and fries.

Because I had previously signed us up with the AWC for the Switzerland trip in January, John and I only had time to read our mail and repack. I did manage to cook our turkey for having sandwiches on the trip and packaged the rest away in our freezer for later meals. Because our trip to Belgium in October had been so spectacular, we knew that Switzerland with the AWC would be just as great.

Kandersteg, Switzerland

John and I left Frankfurt at 8:00 am on Thursday, January 6, with a tour sponsored by the American Women's Club of the Taunus. We had a very comfortable motor coach with bathroom, bar for soft drinks, snacks, coffee and tea, and fantastic clean panoramic windows for picture taking. Our route south took us between the French Alps on the right and the Bavarian Alps on the left. We loved having hot tea with our turkey sandwiches as we drove along in comfort enjoying the beautiful scenery. We entered Switzerland around 12:30 just north of Basel, and the land was pretty much the same as Germany at this point, with the Swiss Alps still in the far distance. However, after leaving Basel, we started making a gradual ascent to higher ground with the snowcapped mountains of Switzerland getting larger and larger, and, as we ascended to higher altitudes, we arrived at Lucerne, the lovely Swiss city on the lake.

We were given a guided tour of Lucerne as we walked through its narrow streets and listened to our guide as he explained the ornate wrought iron fixtures above the doorways. Some were very elaborate and all were very unique, exhibiting the type of business within. We walked across a bridge to visit an old cathedral, which was very beautiful, especially on the inside, and, to get back across the lake, we took the old, wooden bridge which crossed Lake Lucerne diagonally and led from the city center to the lovely old chapel. This old rustic *Chapel Bridge*, partially covered to keep out the winter snow, has flower boxes on both sides for lovely flowers which flourish beautifully during the spring, summer and fall. During our years of travel, Lucerne became our favorite and most enchanting city with all the changing seasons of the year, and John and I were blessed to be able to come back time and time again to enjoy its beauty. The ducks, swans, and geese, which inhabit its cold waters and the sea gulls flying overhead tend to keep it alive all year. The cold water fish, *Plaice,* which we prefer above all others, is in abundance year round and is found on menus all over town. It is so delicious!

After our brisk walk around the city, we continued on our drive ascending gradually up into the higher mountains and passed many lovely lakes and green valleys. There were many farms and orchards in the valleys, and I fell in love with the adorable Swiss Chalet, the typical mountain cottage built with the beautifully carved, dark-stained wooden trim beneath the large eaves and brightly colored shutters, many with German lettering across the front. We drove around one side of a large lake on our way to Kandersteg, where we checked into Hotel Victoria about 4:30 pm. We had no idea that we were over 6,000 feet above sea level until two days later when we compared our location with other high areas around us. There was no snow on the ground when we arrived, and we had to look up to see snow on the highest peaks. We were told that this was very unusual for this time of year in Kandersteg.

Hotel Victoria, Kandersteg, Switzerland.

Hotel Victoria was very nice with a large living room, a few sitting rooms and a very large formal dining room with many long dining tables covered with fresh white linen table cloths and place settings already prepared for dinner. Our second floor bedroom was very comfortable looking out over a lovely chapel in the midst of town with a bell tower which rang out every hour and especially on Sunday morning when it was time for church. We would have a formal dinner every night and a full breakfast every morning.

Although the hotel was rather old and rustic, it was very well-kept and beautifully designed and decorated. It also was very clean and efficient with a heated pool and all the comforts of home. We found ourselves right in the middle of a small skiing resort town very near the slopes. We settled into our rooms to freshen up before dinner at 8:00 and were delighted with its wonderful food and efficient service.

Because of expected snow on Friday, our leaders decided to take our group over to visit another high mountain resort, which was already covered with snow. We left Kandersteg about 9:00 am and drove back around Lake Thune to Lauterbrunnen where we boarded a cable train which took us up to a mountain ridge, where we boarded a smaller train, which ran along the mountainside to the tiny town of Murren. This town was literally hanging on the mountainside with plenty of snow and skiers everywhere. The town was filled with Swiss chalets within sight of the mighty *high peak of the Eiger,* and John and I found it very exciting. We walked through the streets admiring its beauty and the artistic arrangements of even the chopped wood piles in front of the houses. We browsed through its shops, and, when it started to snow, we found Hotel Edelweiss to escape the cold and went inside to warm up a bit. We decided to sit down at a table and have lunch when we looked out the windows and saw nothing but a very long way down. The hotel was built out over a ledge with no visible signs of support and we wondered about the foundation and what was holding us up! It was beautiful just sitting there admiring the gorgeous view and the snow with the drop of thousands of feet below us. The food was very good, but we had to hurry to catch our train back down the mountainside to catch up with our group and return to our bus.

We thought surely that Murren was higher than Kandersteg due to the mode of transportation, the snow and the abundance of skiers. Certainly, it was up where the action was! But we found out that Murren is under 6,000 feet and not quite as high as Kandersteg, which is slightly above that altitude. On the way back, we stopped in a little town for shopping and a delicious hot Swiss chocolate, and we arrived back at Hotel Victoria early enough to relax and freshen up before dinner. Every evening, we enjoyed a delicious four-course meal in the large formal dining room starting with soup, salad and a very well-prepared entrée with assorted vegetables, and then a great selection of desserts served a la carte. The food was outstanding!

Ski Lodge above Kandersteg, Switzerland.

Saturday morning was terribly foggy, but we decided to walk from our hotel to the cable car lift and go up the mountainside to walk along a trail through the snow down to Lake Oeschinen. Our group leaders gave us the directions and loaned us snow boots if we needed them. John and I rode together in a two-seater cable car lift with a blanket over our legs, and it was terribly exciting to look down and see the tree tops below us. Once at the top, we set out following along behind some of our group along the trail, but, since neither of us had snow boots and only our leather boots, we couldn't get good footing for the steep paths, so we decided to turn around and go back to the lodge for hot chocolate. It started clearing right away, and, by the time we got there, it was completely clear and the sun was shining brightly. John managed to take a panorama of the mountains from where we were standing, and the high peak directly in front of us looked like *The Jungfrau*. Then we ran out of film just as we came upon a herd of goats grazing on the mountainside above the lodge where we had lunch. We thought we would go back down and get more film to come back while the sun was shining and take more pictures. However, on the way down, the sun disappeared behind the clouds, so we just walked around the town taking pictures of the chalets and stopped for hot chocolate. It began to snow and kept it up all night.

Sunday morning, the sun was brightly shining on the beautiful new fallen snow. One of the ladies supplied me with a pair of snow boots early that morning and insisted that we go back up and get those pictures while we still had time. John had to use a long pole to stay upright, but we both made it down the trail to the lake and got some wonderful pictures. He also got some more good shots of what we thought was another of the highest peaks, *The Jungfrau*. Then we stopped for hot chocolate one more time and had to leave before 11:30 am to get ready for our departure back to Frankfurt. The goats were no longer there, so we took pictures of the tracks they left behind.

We came back into Germany through the Capitol City of Bern, where we had a bus tour of the lovely city and drove by the city zoo, where we saw Switzerland's *mascots, the live bears,* which appear on all the emblems and crests. The banks of the river are extremely steep and very high with row after row of houses built on the sloping banks. During the summer, they celebrate a national holiday with people floating down the river in droves using all kinds of floats. We stopped late in the afternoon for lunch and arrived back in Frankfurt around 8:00 pm.

We were pleased to have letters from Greg, Maggie and Mother when we returned home, and I set to work writing letters and Trip Reports. I was happy to hear that Greg was doing well with LAS, an AA program, and his group leader was the same lady counselor I had come to know in my Al Anon Workshop years earlier. I knew she would be a great help to him since she already knew his case through me. He said he had quit drinking for good and maybe smoking pot. I hoped he was right. Maggie was making A's in all her courses that year and seemed to be doing well. We were looking forward to having her home with us for the summer and hearing all about her first year of college.

CHAPTER FOURTEEN

A Time for Learning

1983

Now that we were back from our trips, I knew I had to get deeply involved in my Bible studies to make up for lost time. We only had half a year left before our scheduled move to Riyadh, and Jung, our group leader, planned for us to begin the Book of Revelation in March. She invited me to meet her for lunch one day at a little restaurant between our two homes, and we shared a wonderful Hungarian Goulash along with our testimonies and a great European salad. She told me how she got involved in teaching *Precept Upon Precept* after hearing our Bible study teacher speak at one of the Berchtesgaden Retreats, and she considered it a blessing to be our group leader. She was a devout Christian and had left Korea when her American husband was assigned to Rhein-Main Air Force Base, Frankfurt, Germany. Jung told me that she knew what my *Spiritual Gift* was, but she would not tell me. She said that I had to find it out for myself. That really started my thinking about it, and I never did come up with the answer. Since then, I've learned that God supplies his people with what they need at the time they need it through the work of the Holy Spirit.

Our teacher had started us off back in October proving the Deity of Christ by cross-referencing the Old and New Testaments. We also used this method to prove the fulfillment of the prophecies given of the *First Coming of Christ* as the long awaited Jewish Messiah. I was surprised to learn that there are many more prophecies given of his *Second Coming* than of his *First*, which are yet to be fulfilled at the end of the Church Age. John said that I was spending so much time in Bible Study that I should be working towards a degree in Seminary. In fact, some Bible colleges do give college credits for studying this *Inductive Bible Study Course*. Beginning with John 1:1 and rotating through the Bible, we can prove the Deity of Christ:

Proving the Diety of Christ

"In the beginning was the Word, and the Word was with God, and the Word was God. The same was in the beginning with God..." (John 1:1)

"In whom we have redemption through his blood even the forgiveness of sins: Who is the image of the invisible God, the firstborn of every creature." (Colossians 1:14)

"I said therefore unto you, that ye shall die in your sins: for if ye believe not that I am he, ye shall die in your sins." (John 8:24)

"I and my Father are One." (John 10:30)

"Who being the brightness of his glory, and the express image of his person, and upholding all things by the word of his power, when he had by himself purged our sins, sat down on the right hand of the Majesty on high;" (Hebrews 1:3)

"For in him dwells all the fullness of the Godhead bodily." (Colossians 2:9)

"Who is the image of the invisible God, the first born of every creature: For by him were all things created, that are in heaven, and that are in earth, visible and invisible, whether they be thrones, or dominions, or principalities, or powers: all things were created by him, and for him: And he is before all things, and by him all things consist. And he is the head of the body, the church: who is the beginning, the first born from the dead; that in all things he might have the preeminence. For it pleased the Father that in him should all fullness dwell." (Colossians 1:15-19)

"And Thomas answered and said unto him, my Lord and my God. Jesus said unto him, Thomas, because thou hast seen me, thou hast believed: blessed are they that have not seen, and yet have believed." (John 20:28-29)

"And now, O Father, glorify thou me with thine own self with the glory which I had with thee before the world was." (John 17:5)

"I am the Lord: that is my name; and my glory will I not give to another, neither my praise to graven images." (Isaiah 42:8)

"Therefore the Lord himself shall give you a sign; behold, a virgin shall conceive and bear a Son, and shall call his name Immanuel." (Isaiah 7:14)

> *"Jesus answered and said unto them, Verily I say unto you, if ye have faith and doubt not, ye shall not only do this which is done to the fig tree, but also if ye shall say unto this mountain, be thou removed, and be thou cast into the sea; it shall be done. And all things whatsoever ye shall ask in prayer, believing, ye shall receive."* (Matthew 21:21-23)

In Ecclesiastes 4:12, the Bible says that *"a three-fold cord is not easily broken,"* and one thread of the golden cord, which ties the whole Holy Bible together from Genesis to Revelation, is *Jesus* the promised *"Seed of woman."* (Genesis 3:15) The other two golden threads are *God the Father* and *God the Holy Spirit.* It is interesting to note, and extremely important to understand, that *The One true God* is *God in three persons: God the Father, God the Son, and God the Holy Spirit.* And we are made in his image! Each one of us is one in three persons: s*oul, body and spirit.* The Hebrew word for God, *Elohim,* is plural meaning more than one: *"In the beginning God (Elohim) created the heaven and the earth."* (Genesis 1:1) In Genesis 1:26, it is stated even more emphatically, *"And God (Elohim) said, 'Let us make man in our image, and after our likeness.'"* Notice: God didn't use the plural word for "image" or "likeness" because we are all individuals, and we all have different characteristics. He is One God in three persons and each One holds a different office.

The Soul: is made up of the Mind, the Will, and the Emotions, and Love is the greatest emotion of all because *"God is Love,"* and the first Commandment that God gave us is to *"love the Lord our God with all our heart, with all our soul and with all our mind."* Jesus said *"If we love our neighbor as ourselves, we have kept all the Commandments."*

> The Mind: *"Let this mind be in you which is also in Christ Jesus."* (Philippians 2:5)

> The Will: *"Jesus said unto them, 'My meat is to do the will of him who sent me, and to finish his work.'"* (John 4:34)

> The Emotions: *"Beloved, let us love one another; for love is of God; and every one that loves is born of God, and knows God. He that loves not knows not God: for God is love."* (1 John 4:7-8)

<u>The Body</u>: *"The Word became flesh and dwelt among us, and we beheld His glory, the glory as of the only begotten of the Father full of grace and truth."* (John 1:14)

<u>The Spirit</u>: *"And I will pray the Father, and he shall give you another Comforter, that he may abide with you forever; even the Spirit of Truth whom the world cannot receive, because it sees him not, neither knows him: but ye know him; for he dwells with you, and shall be in you."* (John 14:16)

Melchizedek, King of Salem, the first priest mentioned in the Bible to worship the One True God, brought forth bread and wine and blessed Abram as he gave tithes to "the Most High God, the Possessor of Heaven and Earth." (Genesis 14:18-22) The Bible is the incredible story of a Nation, a people entrusted with the Oracles of God. They were given the burdensome task of preserving them and bringing them to the world, so that all mankind would have the same opportunity of knowing and worshiping "the Most High God." In order to understand this incredible story, one must first learn how to interpret scripture, which is not hard after we learn the fundamental rules handed down to us by Bible scholars over the years. We must begin with an attitude of prayer asking God to open our spiritual eyes and lead us into all truth. (Hebrews 7:1-2; 21-25)

First, we should read through the text quickly to understand the context and establish a general overview. Then we should search for clues which might reveal who wrote it, to whom it was written, where and when it was written, and the main topics, events, ideas or teachings included therein. After meditation about the first read, we are ready to begin reading through the text slowly with purpose, meditating upon one segment at a time and letting the text speak for itself to reveal its repeated emphasis or main points of interest. Then we will learn to mine the nuggets of gold we find there and store them away in our hearts. Scripture cannot be interpreted many different ways, as some people think. It can only be interpreted one way: the way God intended for it to be interpreted. In order to do this, we must know the mind of God and his precepts through regular Bible study. With the Holy Spirit as our teacher and guide, the precepts of God's word will be illuminated as he leads us. (John 14:16-26 & 16:13-15) (Romans 8:16)

"For we have not followed cunningly devised fables, when we made known unto you the power and coming of our Lord Jesus

> *Christ, but were eyewitnesses of his majesty. For he received from God the Father honor and glory, when there came such a voice to him from the excellent glory, 'This is my beloved son in whom I am well pleased.'...*
>
> *"We have also a more sure word of prophecy; whereunto ye do well that ye take heed, as a light that shines in a dark place, until the day dawn and the day star arise in your hearts:*
>
> *"Knowing this first; that no prophecy of the scripture is of any private interpretation, for the prophecy came not in old time by the will of man; but holy men of God spoke as they were moved by the Holy Ghost."* (2nd Peter 1:16-21)

Scripture must always support scripture, and, by this method, we can prove what is *"Biblical"* and what is not. Scripture cannot contradict itself. If there ever appears to be a contradiction, it is because something has been left out, misinterpreted, or taken out of context. In order to have the complete picture, we need to gather all related scriptures on a given subject, and, when we have fit all the pieces of the puzzle together, the whole matter should be thoroughly covered and clearly understood. For instance, God teaches us how to pray: if we *"pray according to his will"* and if *"we abide in him and his word abides in us."* (John 15:7) Jesus said, *"If you ask anything in my name, I will do it"*: however, all the other scriptures must also apply. If there is a lack of *"repentance"* (James 4:3) or *"an unforgiving spirit"* (Mark 11:25- 26), our prayers can be hindered. This *enmity,* which exists between ourselves and God, is a spiritual barrier which can only be broken through true repentance and forgiveness. We must get our house in order first and then come boldly before the throne of God in prayer and let our requests be made known. Sometimes God's answer will be *No* because it is not in our best interest, or it might interfere with his plan for our lives. Other times, something we've asked for is simply delayed because only he knows when the time is right for it to be answered. Someday, we will know all the reasons why.

God's word should always be taken literally as long as it makes sense. If it doesn't make sense, then it is because the writer never intended for it to be taken literally, but *symbolically.* If this is the case, we must try to identify the type of figurative speech used by the author so we can better understand its true meaning. Many times, the author will tell us the interpretation. If he has interpreted anything else in the text of a similar nature, we should be able to use that interpretation to aid us in that of another. The following are a few examples found in the Bible:

A *Parable* is a story that teaches a moral lesson or truth. It is true to life and designed to make a central point such as *"The Wise and Foolish Virgins."* (Matthew 25:1-13) Jesus used parables to describe examples of *"The Sower,"* and even interpreted them himself. (Matthew 13:1-52)

A *Simile* is an expressed or stated comparison of two different things that uses connecting words such as *like, as, or such as*: such as the description of the angel of the Lord: *"His eyes were like a flame of fire"* (Revelation 1:14).

A *Metaphor* is an implied comparison between two different things: For example, *"I am the vine, you are the branches"* (John 15:5); *"I am the door of the sheep"* (John 10:7); and *"I am the bread of life"* (John 6:48).

An *Allegory* is a story with an underlying meaning that differs from the surface facts of the story itself. It describes one thing by using the image of another such as in Daniel, where we find an exceptional Allegory of *Media- Persia* (the ram) being overthrown by *Greece* (the goat), and when *the long horn* is broken off (Alexander the Great), the Greek Empire is divided between *the four horns* which come up in its place (the four Generals) who took over after Alexander's death (Daniel 8:3-8).

If the Jews had known how to interpret prophecy, they could have known when Jesus would be presented to the world as Messiah because God had told them in Daniel, Chapter 9. This prophecy deals with *periods of time* as depicted in the *70 weeks of Daniel.* Since Israel's history has been broken down into *490-year periods*, this period of time, *70 weeks,* represents weeks of years, *70 periods of 7 years each* (490 years). *From the decree issued by Artaxerxes* in Nehemiah, Chapter Two, to rebuild Jerusalem *until Messiah the Prince,* there were *7 plus 62 weeks of years,* for a total of *69 weeks,* (483 years). It is believed that the remaining week signifies the *7-year period of great tribulation,* which is to come upon the whole world at the end of the Church Age followed by the end of the world as we know it. (Daniel 9:24-27) (Nehemiah 2:3-8)

> *"And while I was speaking, and praying, and confessing my sin and the sin of my people Israel, and presenting supplication before the Lord ... Gabriel, whom I had seen in the vision at the beginning ... touched me ... and said, O Daniel I am now come forth to give thee skill and understanding ... therefore understand the matter, and consider the vision.*

"Seventy weeks are determined upon thy people and upon thy holy city, to finish the transgression, and to make an end of sins, and to make reconciliation for iniquity, and to bring in everlasting righteousness and to seal up the vision and prophecy, and to anoint the most Holy.

"Know therefore and understand, that from the going forth of the commandment to restore and to build Jerusalem unto the Messiah the Prince shall be seven weeks and threescore and two weeks: the street shall be built again, and the wall, even in troublous times.

"And after three score and two weeks shall Messiah be cut off, but not for himself: and the people of the prince that shall come shall destroy the city and the sanctuary; and the end thereof shall be with a flood, and unto the end of the war desolations are determined.

"And he shall confirm the covenant with many for one week: and in the midst of the week, he shall cause the sacrifice and the oblation to cease, and for the overspreading of abominations, he shall make it desolate, even until the consummation, and that determined shall be poured upon the desolate." (Daniel 9:24-27)

According to the Jewish calendar, Sir Robert Anderson calculated from *Daniel's 70th week prophecy* that Jesus rode through the streets of Jerusalem on a donkey with a great multitude waving palm branches and crying out, *"Hosannah to the Son of David; blessed is he that cometh in the name of the Lord"* on Palm Sunday, April 12, AD 32. (Mark 11:1-10) (John 12:12-15)

"Rejoice greatly, O daughter of Zion; shout, O daughter of Jerusalem: behold thy King cometh unto thee: he is just, and having salvation; lowly, and riding upon an ass, and a colt the foal of an ass." (Zechariah 9:9)

"Blessed is he that cometh in the name of the Lord." (Psalm 118:26)

"Then sent Jesus two disciples, saying unto them, 'Go into the village

... and ye shall find an ass tied, and a colt with her: loose them, and bring them unto me. And if any man say ought to you, ye shall say, The Lord hath need of them; and straightway he will send them....

"And the disciples went, and did as Jesus commanded them, and brought the ass, and the colt, and put on them their clothes, and they set him thereon." (Matthew 21:1-9)

"And when he was come nigh, even now at the descent of the mount of Olives, the whole multitude of the disciples began to rejoice and praise God with a loud voice for all the mighty works that they had seen; Saying, 'Blessed be the King that cometh in the name of the Lord: peace in heaven, and glory in the highest.'

"And some of the Pharisees from among the multitude said unto him, 'Master, rebuke thy disciples.' And he answered and said unto them, 'I tell you that if these should hold their peace, the stones would immediately cry out.'

"And when he was come near, he beheld the city and wept over it saying, 'If thou hadst known, even thou, at least in this thy day, the things which belong unto thy peace, but now are hidden from thine eyes.

"For the days shall come upon thee, that thine enemies shall cast a trench about thee, and compass thee round, and keep thee in on every side, and shall lay thee even with the ground, and thy children within thee; and they shall not leave one stone upon another because thou knewest not the time of thy visitation.'" (Luke 19:37-44)

"O Jerusalem, Jerusalem, thou that killest the prophets, and stonest them which are sent unto thee, how often would I have gathered thy children together, even as a hen gathers her chickens under her wings, and ye would not! Behold, your house is left to you desolate. For I say unto you, Ye shall not see me henceforth, till ye shall say, 'Blessed is he that cometh in the name of the Lord.'
"(Matthew 23:37-39)

Why didn't the Pharisees recognize Jesus when he had fulfilled all the prophecies? They didn't know how to interpret prophecy, and they expected him to come as *The Lion of Judah* to take back their government from Rome and rule with a rod of iron. They did not recognize him as *the sacrificial Lamb,* when some of the old prophets had referred to him as such, especially Isaiah 53, where God presented Jesus as *"a lamb who was brought to the slaughter... and opened not his mouth."*

"Who hath believed our report? And to whom is the arm of the Lord revealed? For he has grown up before him as a tender plant, and as a root out of a dry ground, he hath no form nor comeliness; and when we shall see him, there is no beauty that we should desire him.

"He is despised and rejected of men; a man of sorrows, and acquainted with grief, and we hid as it were our faces from him; he was despised and rejected of men and we esteemed him not.

"Surely he hath borne our griefs and carried our sorrows: yet we did esteem him stricken, smitten of God and afflicted. But he was wounded for our transgressions, he was bruised for our iniquities; the chastisement of our peace was upon him, and with his stripes we are healed.

"All we like sheep have gone astray, we have turned everyone to his own way; and the Lord hath laid on him the iniquity of us all. He was oppressed, and he was afflicted, yet he opened not his mouth: he is brought as a lamb to the slaughter, and as a sheep before her shearers is dumb, so he opened not his mouth.

"He was taken from prison and from judgment; and who shall declare his generation? For he was cut off out of the land of the living: for the transgression of my people was he stricken. And he made his grave with the wicked and with the rich in his death; because he had done no violence, neither was any deceit in his mouth.

"Yet, it pleased the Lord to bruise him; he hath put him to grief: when thou shalt make his soul an offering for sin, he shall see his seed, he shall prolong his days, and the pleasure of the Lord shall prosper in his hand. He shall see of the travail of his soul, and shall be satisfied: by his knowledge shall my righteous servant justify many; for he shall bear their iniquities.

"There will I divide him a portion with the great, and he shall divide the spoil with the strong; because he hath poured out his soul unto death; and he was numbered with the transgressors; and he bare the sin of many, and made intercession for the transgressors."
(Isaiah, Chapter 53)

Even after his death, they didn't recognize Jesus as Messiah, even in the Psalms of David and the prophecies of Zechariah:

"'My God, my God, why hast thou forsaken me? Why art thou so far from helping me, and from the words of my roaring? ...

"'But I am a worm, and no man; a reproach of men, and despised of the people. All they that see me laugh me to scorn: they shoot out the lip, they shake the head saying, he trusted on the Lord that he would deliver him.... They gaped upon me with their mouths, as a ravening and a roaring lion.

"'I am poured out like water, and all my bones are out of joint: my heart is like wax; it is melted in the midst of my bowels. My strength is dried up like a potsherd; and my tongue cleaves to my jaws; and thou hast brought me into the dust of death.

"'For dogs have compassed me: the assembly of the wicked has enclosed me; they pierced my hands and my feet. I may tell all my bones: they look and stare upon me. They part my garments among them, and cast lots upon my vesture.'" (Psalm 22:1-18)

"And they shall look upon me whom they have pierced; and they shall mourn for him as one mourns for his only son." (Zechariah 12:10)

"And one shall say to him, 'What are these wounds in your hands?' Then he shall answer, 'Those with which I was wounded in the house of my friends.'" (Zechariah 13:6)

Since Israel, as a whole, did not receive Jesus as Messiah at that time, Paul explains to the Romans in Chapters 9, 10 & 11 that God is not finished with the Jew:

"I say then, hath God cast away his people? God forbid; for I am also an Israelite, of the Seed of Abraham, of the tribe of Benjamin. God hath not cast away his people which he foreknew.... Even so then at this present time also there is a remnant according to the election of grace. (Romans 11:1-6)

"I say then, have they stumbled that they should fall? God forbid: but rather through their fall salvation is come unto the Gentiles, for to provoke them to jealousy." (Romans 11:11)

"I say the truth in Christ, I lie not, my conscience also bearing me witness in the Holy Ghost, that I have great heaviness and continual

sorrow in my heart. For I could wish that myself were accursed for Christ for my brethren, my kinsman according to the flesh:

"Who are Israelites to whom pertains the adoption, and the glory, and the covenants, and the giving of the law, and the service of God, and the promises; whose are the fathers, and of whom as concerning the flesh Christ came, who is over all, God blessed forever. Amen.

"Not as though the word of God hath taken none effect. For they are not all Israel, which are of Israel: Neither because they are the seed of Abraham are they all children: but, in Isaac, shall thy seed be called. That is, they which are the children of the flesh, these are not the children of God: but the children of the promise are counted for the seed." (Romans 9:1-8)

"What shall we say then, that the Gentiles which followed not after righteousness, have attained to righteousness, even the righteousness which is of faith. But Israel, which followed after the law of righteousness, hath not attained to the law of righteousness.

"Wherefore? Because they sought it not by faith, but as it were by the works of the law. For they stumbled at that stumblingstone; as it is written, 'Behold, I lay in Zion a stumblingstone and rock of offense: and whosoever believeth on him shall not be ashamed.'" (Romans 9:30-33)

"Brethren, my heart's desire and prayer to God for Israel is that they might be saved. For I bear them record that they have a zeal of God, but not according to knowledge. For they, being ignorant of God's righteousness, and going about to establish their own righteousness, have not submitted themselves unto the righteousness of God.

"For Christ is the end of the law for righteousness to everyone that believeth; for Moses described the righteousness which is of the Law, That the man which doeth these things, shall live by them.

"But the righteousness which is of faith speaks on this wise, The word is nigh thee even in thy mouth, and in thy heart; that is, the word of faith which we preach; that if thou shalt confess with your mouth the Lord Jesus, and shalt believe in thine heart that God hath raised him from the dead, thou shalt be saved. For with the heart, man believeth unto righteousness; and with the mouth confession is made unto salvation.

"For the scripture saith, Whosoever believeth on him shall not be ashamed, for there is no difference between the Jew and the Greek: for the same Lord over all is rich unto all that call upon him. For whosoever shall call upon the name of the Lord shall be saved.

"How then shall they call on him in whom they have not believed? And how shall they believe in him of whom they have not heard? And how shall they hear without a preacher? And how shall they preach except they be sent? As it is written, how beautiful are the feet of them that preach the gospel of peace and bring glad tidings of good things!

"But they have not all obeyed the gospel. For Isaiah saith, 'Lord, who hath believed our report?' So then faith cometh by hearing, and hearing by the word of God." (Romans 10:1-17)

"For if the casting away of them be the reconciling of the world, what shall the receiving of them be, but life from the dead.

"For if the first fruit is holy, the lump is also holy: and if the root is holy, so are the branches. And if some of the branches are broken off, and thou, being a wild olive tree, were grafted in among them, and with them partake of the root and fatness of the olive tree; boast not against the branches; but, if you boast, you bear not the root, but the root bears you.

"Thou wilt say then, the branches were broken off that I might be grafted in. Well, because of unbelief they were broken off, and thou standeth by faith. Be not high minded but fear; for if God spared not the natural branches, take heed lest he also spare not thee.

"And they also, if they abide not still in unbelief shall be grafted in: for God is able to graft them in again: how much more shall these, which are the natural branches be grafted into their own olive tree: For I would not have you ignorant, brethren, of this mystery, lest you should be wise in your own conceits, that blindness in part is happened to Israel, until the fullness of the Gentiles be come in.

"And so shall all Israel be saved; as it is written, There shall come out of Zion, the Deliverer, and shall turn away ungodliness from Jacob: For this is my covenant to them, when I shall take away their sins.

"As concerning the gospel, they are enemies for your sakes: but as touching the election, they are beloved for the father's sakes.

For the gifts and calling of God are without repentance." (Romans 11:15 -29)

Jesus will come again at the end of the tribulation, but this time, he will come as *the Lion of Judah,* as Israel expected him the first time, to destroy all those who destroy the earth and are killing God's people. He will put an end to sin and establish his kingdom upon the earth when he divides the sheep from the goats. (Matthew 25:31-41). When the Book of Isaiah was handed to Jesus one Sabbath morning in a Nazareth Synagogue, he stood up to read the passage where it was written:

> *"The Spirit of the Lord is upon me because he hath anointed me to preach the gospel to the poor; he hath sent me to heal the broken hearted, to preach deliverance to the captives, and recovering of sight to the blind, to set at liberty them that are bruised: To preach the acceptable year of the Lord. And he closed the book, and he gave it back to the minister and sat down.*
>
> *"And the eyes of all them that were in the synagogue were fastened on him. And he began to say unto them, 'This day is this scripture fulfilled in your hearing.'*
>
> *"And all bare witness, and wondered at the gracious words which proceeded out of his mouth. And they said, 'Is not this Joseph's son?' And he said, 'Verily I say unto you, no prophet is accepted in his own country.'"* (Luke 4:18-24)

Why didn't Jesus finish reading the rest of the sentence found in the original text of Isaiah, Chapter 61, which reads, *"To proclaim the acceptable year of the Lord, and the day of vengeance of our God?"* He cut it off in mid- sentence because the rest was yet to come over 2,000 years later. He knew they would not accept him at that time, and, therefore, *"the day of vengeance"* would not come until the end of the Church Age, *"when the time of the Gentiles is full."* (Isaiah 61:1-2)

> *"O the depth of the riches both of the wisdom and knowledge of God! How unsearchable are his judgments and his ways past finding out! For who hath known the mind of the Lord? Or who hath been his counselor? Or who hath first given to him, and it shall be recompensed unto him again? For of him, and through him, and to him are all things: to whom be glory forever. Amen."* (Romans 11:15-36)

CHAPTER FIFTEEN

Italy & The Netherlands
1983

We had a very mild winter in Frankfurt that year, or so we were told by our German friends, with only a small amount of snow. John continued to ride the train in to work whenever I needed the car or when snow was expected. I learned my way over to Langen each month to pay our German taxes and also to the Rhein-Main Commissary to shop for groceries. Sometimes I preferred to shop at the nearby German markets and became quite familiar with some of their products, especially their wonderful *Kellogg's Hazelnuss Cornflakes*. I also continued driving by the AFRC to check on the upcoming trips and paid our deposits via my American Express card. I was thrilled to discover an eight-day trip to Italy in March and booked us for that one plus a weekend trip on the *Flying Dutchman Motor Coach* for a tour of Holland in April.

Towards the end of January, we received a very encouraging letter from Greg saying that he had gotten a fresh start after Christmas, although his apartment had been vandalized while he was in Virginia Beach. Maggie drove him back to northern Virginia and was with him when he discovered the damage. The two of them cleaned up the mess and reported it to the police. Maggie drove back to school the following day to rest up before her classes resumed, and Greg got back to work. He thought he could pay the other half of the rent and buy his food. His doctor also arranged to have corrective surgery done on his foot to give him more stability. He removed a joint in his longest toe, next to his big toe, and flattened it out a bit so it would line up with the other toes and do a better job of replacing his missing big toe. He told us about his attorneys picking him up and driving him downtown to answer the interrogatories in the deposition of their lawsuit against the Metro. They told him his case looked very good and the *status call* to begin the court hearing was scheduled for mid-April.

They encouraged him to attend his LAS meetings and, above all, to stay straight.

Spring seemed to come early with the sun shining brightly all day, and we loved setting out on our walking tour around our small city of Walldorf and through the nature trails of the forest. It was fun to see the vegetable and flower gardens being worked again by the city dwellers coming out on weekends to do their spring planting. Some would stay overnight in their small shelters built on their plots of land to enjoy their gardens and the surrounding countryside. About once each month, John would cut the grass in our small backyard, which had been trimmed immaculately by Frau Bergmann's father back in the fall, and I would help him rake up the leaves and bag the residue for pickup. The laws of our small community were very strict regarding proper bagging, or the garbage truck would pass us by. We found that out when we placed our bags of leaves next to our garbage can and left them there thinking they would eventually be picked up. One of our brusque, but well-meaning, German neighbors from across the street came over and insisted that we take our bags of rubbish back inside the gate and get them off the street! We thought she was quite rude, but reluctantly brought them back inside the gate. When we checked the instructions for the city pickup of garbage, we learned that it was just not the right day to put out the rubbish. We also found out that on one day each month, we could put out large assortments of whatever we wanted to get rid of, and they would take it all away. We had to take all our glass and paper to the proper locations for recyclables, and all glass had to be put in containers according to color.

A Tour of Italy

Before we knew it, March had arrived with our anticipated tour of Italy. We found ourselves on a motor coach early one Saturday morning heading southeast down the autobahn to Nuernberg, where we disembarked for lunch inside the huge stone walls of an enchanting old medieval city. Then our drive that day took us all the way down to Innsbruck, Austria where we spent our first night at Hotel Grauer Baer in the romantic old city across the street from the famous *Golden Roof*. The snowcapped mountains towering above Innsbruck were absolutely beautiful, and John was out at the crack of dawn walking briskly through the streets taking pictures. I chose to enjoy my breakfast and hot coffee from inside the restaurant as I watched through the window.

After a quick bus tour of the city of Innsbruck on Sunday morning, the second day of our trip, we continued our drive through Brenner Pass into Italy. As we neared Venice, we noticed hundreds of dilapidated old homes along the canal which obviously had been very beautiful during their prime. We checked into our hotel early in the afternoon and re-boarded our bus for the evening tour of Venice. We disembarked in a rather large parking lot and crossed over an arched bridge into the romantic old city, where we walked along the canals and noticed its mode of transportation. We looked into shops and read menus to find a place for dinner and finally selected "Bella Venizia," because of its ambiance and aromas coming from inside. We ordered Sea Bass, which was cooked to perfection and served with artichoke hearts, eggplant and peppers.

We strolled through the streets of Venice after dinner and boarded a small gondola with several others and started down the main canal seven gondolas abreast with some of the gondoliers singing Italian songs. Someone in the center gondola was playing an accordion along with the singing and it was very enchanting. Then we turned into the smaller canals where only one or two gondolas at a time could enter, and we could see people living in their homes having dinner or preparing their meals, while others were scurrying home for the evening. It was amazing to notice the steps of homes leading down under the water and to realize they were actually sinking. As we made the turn onto a smaller, darker canal, John took a terrific picture of the silhouette of our gondolier against the lighted background of a building. It was certainly an evening to remember!

On Monday morning, we crossed over the bridge again to enter Venice and hopped aboard a large canal boat used to transport groups of people around the city. Our tour guide led us off the boat at *St. Marks' Byzantine Cathedral* where our walking tour began. We toured the large cathedral in *the Piazza San Marco*, a very large public square, and the *Doge's Palace*, with its dark dungeons and gory history. Numerous political prisoners had been kept there for long periods of time and many had been tortured to death. Afterwards, we visited *a Venetian glass factory* and watched the skilled craftsmen blow balls of molten silica into beautiful forms of amethyst crystal. We purchased a beautiful carafe with six matching wine glasses trimmed in gold. Then we had time to walk through the city again to drink in the atmosphere and capture some of the charm of Venice on film. We found another restaurant with atmosphere for lunch and ordered pizza, salad and Chianti. Then we discovered an ice cream parlor on *the Square*, where we were introduced to our favorite raisin-rum *Italian gelato*: *Malaga*. About this time, we realized that our time was running out and we had to hurry to catch a boat down the main canal back to the arched bridge to cross over and board our bus for the next leg of our journey to Florence, through the lovely Tuscan hills.

Scene of the Harbor of Venice.

The Piazza San Marco, Venice.

After arriving in the beautiful city of Florence, we checked into our hotel and had a nice dinner in the hotel dining room. It was still early, so we re- boarded our bus for a drive to the hilltop overlooking the city, which was all spread out along the riverbank before us. Then we were driven to the *olde town*, where we disembarked to follow our guide through its streets as he pointed out the various points of interest. The historic *Ponte Vecchio* with its ancient shops built on top of the ancient bridge, where they used to sell fresh meats and fish, now specializes in jewelry and precious gems. Due to its antiquity, no vehicular traffic is allowed across this bridge any longer, so we had to walk to the *Piazza Michelangelo* to see his work, and then back across the bridge to the bus. Then we were driven through the city to the *Pitti Palace* and the *Palazzo Vecchio*.

Our tour of the city of Florence on Tuesday took us through *Medici Chapel* and the second largest cathedral in the world, *Santa Maria del Fiore,* with its giant Gothic dome and white, green and red marble exterior. The magnificent 14th century *Campanile, by Giotto,* rises almost 300 feet next door to the great cathedral and is thought to be the most beautiful bell tower in the world. We toured the famous *Baptistery of San Giovanni, with its magnificent bronze doors by Ghiberti, "Life of Christ" and "Gate* of Paradise," which took him 27 years to complete. At the *Accademia*, we saw *Michelangelo's original "a Pieta,"* the very beautiful statue of Mary holding Jesus in her arms, and also his very famous, and quite awesome, statue of *"David."*

After lunch, we left Florence and headed south to Rome where we checked into our downtown hotel. After dinner, we re-boarded our bus and were given an illumination tour of ancient Rome and saw the famous *Coliseum, the Circus Maximus,* where the famous chariot races were held, the *Roman Forum* and the *Palace of the Caesars.* Then we disembarked to visit the *Piazza Navono* and the famous *Trevi Fountain*, where John got many outstanding night scenes.

The Roman Coliseum.

The Church in the Catacombs, Rome.

On Wednesday morning, we rode along the famous *Appian Way* to visit the *Catacombs of San Sebastiano* and walked through the narrow underground passageways where hundreds of Christians were buried before the 5th Century. It was against Roman law to bury or burn a body within the city limits, and many Christians had been martyred during that time. Paul had been beheaded and Peter crucified upside down during the first century AD. After lunch, we toured *St. Peter's Cathedral*, the largest cathedral in the world, where we saw Michelangelo's most famous and beautiful *a Pieta*, his last and most perfect statue of Mary holding the slain Christ in her arms. It is absolutely breathtaking! And, of course, we stood in line to see the famous *ceiling of the Sistine Chapel*, which took Michelangelo four long years to finish, and, when the scaffolding was removed, everyone was astonished at his achievement. The Pope was so amazed that he commissioned Michelangelo to paint the scene of *The Last Judgment* on the huge wall behind the altar. Both are spectacular! Next, we toured the ancient *Coliseum*, where many Gladiators and Christians were martyred and killed by ferocious animals for the amusement of the bloodthirsty crowds who came to watch.

Underneath the Coliseum floor, one can see where the animals were kept. Today it is overrun with cats which live there to keep the rodents under control, and it looks antiquated all covered with mold. Before going back to the hotel, we took pictures of the *"Palatine"* where the city of Rome had its beginning around 735 BC.

On Thursday morning, we were off bright and early heading south for Naples and Pompeii. We noticed the twin volcanoes to our left as we neared Naples, one, the notorious Mt. Vesuvius, the eruption of which once buried the city of Pompeii with tons of volcanic ash and rubble. On a lovely hillside overlooking the Bay of Naples, we stopped for a fish dinner before driving on to Pompeii, just a short distance to the east. We spent a couple of hours walking through what once had been the most luxurious resort city of the Romans. Buried for almost two thousand years beneath tons of volcanic ash and rubble, Pompeii proved to be the most incredible excavation of the 20th Century and uncovered the most well preserved city of the ancient Roman Empire.

In August AD 79, almost ten years after the Romans destroyed the Temple in Jerusalem, Mt. Vesuvius erupted and took this small, exclusive community of 20,000 Romans and Hebrew slaves by surprise. Only those who ran quickly leaving all their possessions behind escaped with their lives through a dense fallout of ash before the larger explosion occurred sending larger stones and debris into the air. Someone, probably a Jewish slave, had hastily written "Sodom and Gomorrah" in Hebrew on the wall of a house before trying to get out. We noticed among the homes, restaurants and large basilicas for town meetings, many brothels as well as temples and statues erected to the astrological gods and goddesses. Some of the preserved bodies were found just as they had died in a panic situation, some clutching bags or pieces of jewelry, and some with small children trying to escape. None were ready for such a catastrophe! Closer to the water, Pompeii's sister city, Ercolano, was covered with a torrent of mud, and the remains of many bodies were found inside a cave near the shoreline where they died.

From Pompeii, we drove east and then turned to the northeast around the beautiful Bay of Naples as we began to climb upward into the higher hills where we saw many orange and lemon trees on the way to Sorrento. John and I walked around the lovely city and found an ice cream parlor where they sold our delicious Malaga ice cream, so we had to stop there for a few minutes. Then we visited a furniture store, which sold the lovely intricate in- lay wood products, and I fell in love with a beautiful blue music box which played *"Return to Sorrento."* John promised to buy it for me someday when we do return. The scenery on the way down was absolutely gorgeous with the sun starting to set in the west and the *Isle of Capri* in the bay as small drops of rain began to hit the windows of our bus. About halfway between Naples and Rome, we stopped for dinner at a restaurant where we were served a plate of spaghetti with tomato sauce and then some kind of a meat entrée with salad and a glass of Chianti. We arrived back at our hotel around 10:00 pm after a very adventurous, but tiring, day.

The Cathedral and Leaning Tower of Pisa.

Early Friday morning, we left Rome heading north for *Pisa* where we stopped within view of the *Tower of Pisa* and went into a small restaurant for lunch. We also purchased a couple of ceramic mementos and then walked across the street to tour *the Tower and the Baptistery,* where we got some really great shots of the *leaning tower.* Our guide told us that it is expected to fall sometime around 2004. However, I believe they have done some work to preserve it and keep it a while longer, because, as far as we know, it hasn't fallen as of this writing. We continued our drive through the mountains to Lake Como where we had dinner and spent the night at Hotel Continental right on the lake. We hope to go back again someday for a longer stay at this wonderful hotel and board one of their luxurious liners for a day's outing on the gorgeous lake. It looked like a great family vacation retreat. John and I walked around after dinner taking pictures and enjoying the atmosphere of this very beautiful place as we both had feelings of nostalgia at having to leave so quickly the following morning.

We were up bright and early for our long journey back to Frankfurt through Switzerland as we listened to our guide telling the many fascinating tales of Switzerland. Among them was the famous legend of William Tell who shot an apple off his son's head to save his life for refusing to pay the outrageous taxes placed on his land by the Austrian tyrant, Gessler. As the story goes, William Tell pulled two arrows out of his quiver and told Gessler that if the first arrow missed its mark, the second would be aimed straight for his heart. Of course, the arrow did not miss its mark and his life was spared, but Gessler would not spare his freedom and sentenced him to life in prison. As Tell was being taken to prison in Lucerne, the boat in which he was riding capsized. He was a giant of a man, so they loosened him to help upright the boat. Tell managed to escape and took a short cut to get ahead of Gessler where he ambushed him and finally did shoot him in the heart. With Gessler's death, all of Switzerland became free from the heavy taxes and has remained so ever since.

Switzerland has also remained a neutral zone from world wars and is considered a zone of peace and safety. We stopped in Lucerne for dinner and ordered *Plaice,* our favorite fresh water fish from Lake Lucerne, with the delicately steamed vegetables and chocolate mousse for dessert. In other parts of Europe, the fresh water fish is sometimes listed on the menu as *Trout Meuniere.* These fillets also melt in your mouth and are served with steamed vegetables and potatoes, noodles or rice. The recipe for this delicious fresh fish calls for it to be rolled lightly in flour with just a little seasoning and sautéed on moderately low heat in butter just a few minutes on each side until done. We arrived back at Rhein-Main AFB around dusk.

Having not heard from Greg since February, I tried calling him over the next several days, but to no avail. Finally, in desperation, I called Ralph, who was beginning to think that he had somehow become Greg's adopted father. He said that Greg had volunteered for a 28-day alcohol treatment program and was in Fairfax Hospital. According to Ralph, Greg had gotten along rather well after his new start in January until one night when a new assistant manager at work, unfamiliar with his drinking problem, brought some beer over to his apartment after work. Obviously, Greg had drunk just enough beer to be sociable, but it only takes one. He walked across the street to a convenience store to buy more beer when he was arrested for being drunk in public. Greg couldn't remember what happened that evening and was too embarrassed to go back to work. Eventually, he ran out of money and went to see Ralph about giving him some more from the account. Ralph saw that he needed food and gave him some money, but he also encouraged Greg to enter the Fairfax AA program and even picked him up and drove him over for admittance. Greg's attorneys with his lawsuit against the Metro also encouraged him to complete the program, and they kept up with him explaining that it would be very good for his case if he finished it entirely. We were very hopeful he would!

A Tour of the Netherlands

On the 3rd Friday of April, we left Rhein-Main AFB about 11:00 pm on the *"Flying Dutchman"* for our overnight ride to Holland. I was surprised to discover one of my prayer partners from Precept, a young lady and her husband, sitting directly behind us. After our rest stop at 2:00 am, I was able to get some sleep until we stopped for breakfast around 6:00 am. Our *hearty Dutch breakfast* consisted of slices of ham and cheese served on bread with a warm boiled egg sitting upright in a ceramic container. Carrie showed us how to crack the shell around the middle and peel it off, then eat the egg right out of the shell with our forks. We had assorted breads and jams served with hot coffee and juice. It was quite sufficient for the early morning, and by the time we were underway again, we were wide awake. First we visited the *International Flower and Bulb Center* in Hillegom with acres of beautiful tulips and other beautiful flowers grown from bulbs. They were gorgeous! Without my knowing it, John took a hilarious picture of me *tiptoeing through the tulips* from a distance.

"Parade of Flowers," Haarlem, Netherlands.

We were pleased to learn that our trip was at the *very peak* of the flower season, and we would stop in Haarlem to see the *Annual Flower Parade.* Scores of floats and vehicles were covered with thousands of the most beautiful, colorful flowers we had ever seen, and high school bands from all over Holland marched in the parade. Across the street, we could see many old people in wheel chairs. I was reminded of Corrie ten Boom, who had died the previous week at the age of 91, which just happened to be the number of her favorite Psalm. I wondered how many of those old folks had known Corrie and her sister, Betsy. How many of them had brought their clocks and watches to be repaired at their father's Haarlem clock shop? How many of them had known about their work with the *underground* to hide the Jewish people and help them escape the Nazis to a place of safety?

> *"He that dwells in the secret place of the most High shall abide under the shadow of the Almighty... He is my refuge and my fortress: my God; in him will I trust."* (Psalm 91:1)

When Hitler's Nazis started their rampage against the Jews in Haarlem, the ten Booms vowed to help them any way they could, and they began to take some of them into their home. Then they became involved with the *underground railroad* to get them to safety and allowed the members of their organization to build a secret hiding place in the wall behind Corrie's bed on the top floor where they had just enough time to get up the stairs and behind the wall before the guards could catch them. They practiced this procedure over and over and had to remove all traces of their being there at the same time. The ten Booms helped hundreds of Jews escape before they themselves were taken away as political prisoners; however, all their guests left hidden in the hiding place managed to escape to freedom. Father ten Boom died of pneumonia shortly after arriving at Ravensbruck, but Corrie and her sister, Betsy, survived for quite a while to minister to their inmates. With their hidden Bible undetected upon their admittance, which was a miracle in itself, they were able to hold prayer meetings and even thanked God for *fleas, or lice,* to keep the guards away.

Many people were saved before they were led away to the ovens or died of mistreatment by the guards. Betsy grew very weak because of this abuse and died after the first year, but Corrie was miraculously released soon afterwards to share their story with the world in her first book, The Hiding Place. She was well received by Christians all over the world and gave her testimony at evangelical gatherings and churches everywhere. Her books tell the story of the many miracles which happened during those years. Corrie and her sister, Betsy, were able to teach others how to have faith and love in spite of all the horrible abuse. After Betsy was beaten by one of the guards for not being able to do the hard labor, she had to remind Corrie not to hate and told Corrie and the others that *"no pit is too deep that*

God's love is not deeper still to reach down and pull them out." She also told Corrie that the Lord had shown her that they would both be out by the end of the year. And they were! Betsy died and was taken to heaven, but Corrie was released by *a technical error* to give her testimony to the world.

As we continued our bus tour of Holland, we drove to *The Keukenhof,* a beautiful, picturesque 70-acre park with millions of gorgeous blooming plants, most of them tulips, grown from the bulbs of Holland. Its century old trees and ponds were alive with numerous ducks, swans and geese amidst decorative bridges and a large windmill. It was truly a photographer's dream!

After taking many pictures of the Keukenhof Gardens, we had lunch on the way to Delft, where we visited a *Blue China factory* and watched the lovely patterns being drawn and hand painted on the many ceramic vases, plates, cups and bowls. Then we drove by *The Hague,* the seat of the Royal Dutch Government, and *the Peace Palace,* which houses the *International Court of Justice.* Adjoining The Hague is *Scheveningen,* Holland's famous summer sea resort, so we quickly drove along the beach area and past the casinos. Then we drove on along the North Sea to *Madurodam,* a miniature city complete with moving ships, vehicles, trains, and airplanes. The buildings are replicas of the famous places of Holland. It was built for one of the royal children many years earlier and is now a museum open to the public. Since a light rain began to fall while we were walking around Madurodam taking pictures, we were glad to finally arrive at our hotel in Rotterdam to change out of our wet clothing for dinner at the hotel. Afterwards, we walked around the vicinity of our hotel under our umbrellas taking more pictures.

The Keukenhof Gardens, Holland.

Sunday morning, we headed for Amsterdam and boarded our glass-topped boat for a canal tour of the city. Once a major world trading center, Amsterdam is still a large industrial city and world famous diamond center located on the Amstel River. Because there was a dam here on the river during the days of Napoleon, he officially named it Amsterdam and made it the Capitol of the Netherlands. In those days, it ranked with Paris and Venice as one of the leading industrial cities of the world. We toured a diamond factory and purchased a lovely dinner ring for me with two nice marquises and a few smaller diamonds. After our brief ride through the canals, we left Amsterdam and visited a *cheese farm* on the way out of town, where we learned how the different cheeses are made. We learned that cheese made from goat's milk contains half the cholesterol as cheese made from cow's milk. The goats were adorable!

Then we visited a w*ooden shoemaker* where we had a brief demonstration of how wooden shoes are made into exact sizes. There are only two kinds of wood that can be used to make authentic wooden shoes that Hollanders wear to work in the tulip fields. The other woods allow water absorption and will eventually soak through the wood. This particular kind of hard wood will keep the feet dry even in the wettest of fields, so, with my love of flowers and our future home in mind, I bought myself a pair of wooden shoes which I have to this day as a wonderful souvenir of Holland.

We drove on to the old world fishing village of *Volendam*, located on the *Ijssel Sea* where we walked along the dock and selected a restaurant for dinner and ordered a wonderful fish dinner. This small town, loaded with atmosphere, is a great place for tourists and good seafood. We enjoyed the fresh air as we looked out as far as the eye could see across the fresh water of the Ijssel Sea. It was hard to believe that the Dutch had created this gigantic fresh water sea by damming up the entrance to the North Sea and pumping all the salt water out and fresh water in. As they say in the Netherlands, *God created the earth, but the Dutch created Holland.* On the way home that afternoon, we noticed many large patches of color where different varieties of flowers and bulbs were being cultivated for export all over the world, and, of course, we saw many windmills and dikes. We drove to the German border, stopped for a snack in the afternoon and arrived back in Frankfurt around 7:00 pm.

CHAPTER SIXTEEN

From Romans to Revelation

1983

We were happy to get a letter from Greg telling us about moving into his new rooming house in Falls Church, however, we were disappointed to learn that he only completed 10 days of his 28-day AA program. He didn't tell us why he left early, only that he had gotten a lot out of the program and didn't think he would ever drink again. Ralph helped him get out of his lease a month early, and Greg packed only the things he needed and moved over to Falls Church via taxi. John had arranged for the packing and furniture pickup back in March with the actual date to be set by Ralph as appropriate. About the same time as his move, John replenished the escrow account to help him through the summer. Ralph kept a record of Greg's expenses and mailed us itemized statements. I don't know what we would have done without Ralph's help, and we were very appreciative.

We were very hopeful about Greg's determination to remain drug free for the sake of his winning the law suit, which had been rescheduled for a fall hearing. Ralph helped him line up a telephone job working out of his room with Purple Heart Vets to arrange pickups for donations along their scheduled routes. He also had a telephone installed in Greg's room along with a desk where he could work in a professional manner. With an air-conditioner and refrigerator in his furnished room and with the shared kitchen and bathroom down the hall, Greg seemed quite comfortable and was able to pay his rent. He also made friends with the other tenants with whom he shared the accommodations. He liked it much better than his old apartment.

Again, it was good to get home from our trip and back into my Bible studies. Paul plunged right into his letter to the Romans telling them about the upcoming Judgment of God because they were abiding under his wrath.

"For I am not ashamed of the gospel of Christ: for it is the power of God unto salvation to everyone that believeth; to the Jew first, and also to the Greek. For therein is the power of God revealed from faith to faith: as it is written. The just shall live by faith.

"For the wrath of God is revealed from heaven against all ungodliness and unrighteousness of men, who hold the truth in unrighteousness; because that which may be known of God is manifest in them; for God hath shown it unto them. For the invisible things of him from the creation of the world are clearly seen, being understood by the things that are made, even his eternal power and Godhead; so that they are without excuse: Because that when they knew God, they glorified him not as God, neither were thankful; but became vain in their imaginations and their foolish heart was darkened.

"Professing themselves to be wise, they became fools, and changed the glory of the incorruptible God into an image made like unto corruptible man, and to birds, and four-footed beasts, and creeping things. Wherefore God also gave them up to uncleanness through the lusts of their own hearts, to dishonor their own bodies between themselves: who changed the truth of God into a lie, and worshipped and served the creature more than the Creator, who is blessed forever. Amen.

"For this cause God gave them up unto vile affections: for even their women did change the natural use into that which is against nature: And likewise also the men, leaving the natural use of the woman, burned in their lust one toward another, men with men working that which is unseemly and receiving in themselves that recompense of their error.... And even as they did not like to retain God in their knowledge, God gave them over to a reprobate mind, to do those things which are not convenient;

"Being filled with all unrighteousness, fornication, wickedness, covetousness, maliciousness; full of envy, murder, debate, deceit, malignity; whisperers, backbiters, haters of God, despiteful, proud, boasters, inventors of evil things, disobedient to parents, without understanding, covenant breakers, without natural affection,

implacable, unmerciful: Who knowing the judgment of God, that they which commit such things are worthy of death, not only do the same, but have pleasure in them that do them." (Romans 1:16-32)

Judgment Day

The second chapter of Romans explains the judgment of God falling on the ungodly on the Day of Judgment, and Paul warns us about judging others.

"Therefore, you are inexcusable, O man, whosoever you are that judges another: for when you judge another, you condemn yourself; for you do the same things. But we are sure that the judgment of God is according to truth against them which commit such things. And do you think, O man that judges them which do such things and you do the same, that you shall escape the judgment of God? Or do you despise the riches of his goodness, forbearance and longsuffering; not knowing that the goodness of God will lead you to repentance? But after your hardness and impenitent heart, you are treasuring up unto yourself wrath against the day of wrath and revelation of the righteous judgment of God; who will render to every man according to his deeds." (Romans 2:1-6)

God tells us that Judgment will be according to five things:

1. "Truth," (Romans2:2);
2. "Our deeds," (Romans 2:6);

3. "Paul's gospel," (Romans 2:16) &

    (1 Corinthians 15:1-10);

4. "Our words," (Matthew 12:37); and
5. "The words of Jesus," (John 12:48).

"What advantage then hath the Jew? Or what profit is there of circumcision? Much in every way; chiefly because that unto them were committed the oracles of God. For what if some did not believe? Shall their unbelief make the faith of God without effect?

"God forbid: yea, let God be true, but every man a liar; as it is written, that thou might be justified in thy sayings, and might overcome when thou art judged. But if our righteousness commends the righteousness of God, what shall we say? Is God unrighteous who taketh vengeance? (I speak as a man.) God forbid: for then how shall God judge the world? (Romans 3:1-6)

"As it is written, there is none righteous, no, not one: There is none that understands; there is none that seeks after God. They are all gone out of the way, they are together become unprofitable; there is none that doeth good, no, not one.

"Their throat is an open sepulcher; with their tongues they have used deceit; the poison of asps is under their lips: Whose mouth is full of cursing and bitterness. Their feet are swift to shed blood: Destruction and misery are in their ways: And the way of peace, they have not known: There is no fear of God before their eyes." (Romans 3:10-18)

"Now we know that what things so ever the law saith, it saith to them who are under the law; that every mouth may be stopped, and all the world may become guilty before God... For all have sinned and come short of the glory of God." (Romans 3:19-38).

Daniel's Vision of Judgment:

"In the first year of Belshazzar king of Babylon, Daniel had a dream and visions of his head upon his bed... I beheld 'til the thrones were cast down, and the Ancient of Days did sit, whose garment was white as snow, and the hair of his head like pure wool: his throne was like the fiery flame, and his wheels as burning fire.

"A fiery stream issued and came forth from before him: thousand thousands ministered unto him, and ten thousand times ten thousand stood before him: the judgment was set, and the books were opened.

"I saw in the night visions, and, behold, one like the Son of Man came with the clouds of heaven, and came to the Ancient of days, and they brought him near before him.

"And there was given him dominion, his dominion is an everlasting dominion, which shall not pass away, and his kingdom that which shall not be destroyed.

> *"I beheld, and the horn made war with the saints, and prevailed against them; until the Ancient of Days came and judgment was given to the saints of the most High; and the time came that the saints possessed the kingdom."* (Daniel 7:9-22)

John's Vision of Judgment:

> *"And I saw thrones, and they sat upon them, and judgment was given unto them: and I saw the souls of them that were beheaded for the witness of Jesus, and for the word of God, and which had not worshipped the beast, neither his image, neither had received his mark upon their foreheads, or in their hands; and they lived and reigned with Christ a thousand years.*
>
> *"But the rest of the dead lived not again until the thousand years were finished. This is the first resurrection. Blessed and holy is he that hath part in the first resurrection: On such the second death hath no power, but they shall be priests of God and of Christ, and shall reign with him a thousand years....*
>
> *"And I saw a great white throne and him that sat on it from whose face the earth and the heaven fled away; and there was found no place for them. And I saw the dead, small and great, stand before God; and the books were opened: and another book was opened, which is the Book of Life: and the dead were judged out of those things which were written in the books, according to their works.*
>
> *"And the sea gave up the dead which were in it; and death and hell delivered up the dead which were in them: and they were judged every man according to his works.*
>
> *"And death and hell were cast into the lake of fire. This is the second death. And whosoever was not found written in the book of life was cast into the lake of fire."* (Revelation 20:4-15)

On Good Friday, the first of April, John and I drove down to Garmisch for three nights at the Von Steuben Hotel at the Armed Forces Recreation Center. While registering, we noticed the selection of available bus tours through the Bavarian countryside to visit *Oberammergau* and *Weis Kirche*. It was our first trip down into Bavaria to admire all the artistically designed buildings and to sample the food at the international restaurants of Garmisch. We were amazed at its beauty with all the lovely murals which covered the buildings, so we parked the car and walked through the city. We were pleased to find many good restaurants and finally selected one which listed *Chateaubriand for Two* on the menu outside its entrance. We walked in and were ushered to our table where we placed our order for the outside menu. We were delighted with the wonderfully prepared *Chateaubriand for Two* served with *Spaetzel,* freshly steamed vegetables, good bread, red wine and a delicious *Chocolate Mousse.* It was all very good and another evening to remember.

On Saturday morning, we boarded our bus for a drive through the lovely Bavarian countryside to the famous *Open Air Theatre at Oberammergau* and walked through the museum to see pictures and costumes of *The Passion Play* held every ten years. This tremendous production portraying *the life and death of Christ* began in the 17th Century when the townspeople promised God that if he would rid them of the terrifying *Black Plague* moving across Europe, they would honor him every year with this memorial. Since all the people involved in this production from actors and artists to seamstresses and stage managers live in this small town, all businesses have to close down for the entire year. This is the reason why they can only afford to do it once each decade. Oberammergau is also famous for its many beautiful wood carvings and silver crosses which they sell year round. John purchased a small silver cross and chain for me as a memento of this very enchanting small town, and we promised ourselves to come back for The Passion Play at our first opportunity.

We stopped on the way back to visit *Weis Kirche* (the White Church), a very beautiful Rococo-style church built in 1746 to house a statue of *Christ in chains,* which is said to have cried real tears. This statue, which was first assembled to be carried in a religious procession, was discovered in someone's attic after being left there for many years. It was re-discovered by a lady who started praying to it in her home and declared that it cried real tears. This beautiful Rococo-style church was built to house the statue of Christ and to accommodate the thousands of people from all over Europe who make pilgrimages to see and pray before the famous statue. Saturday evening, we tried another restaurant in Garmisch and ordered *Pepper Steaks,* which were delicious and served with *Spaetzel,* a large European salad, good bread, red wine and Crème Caramel.

On Easter Sunday, we attended church services at Ft. Sheridan Chapel and then returned to our hotel. Our afternoon drive through the Bavarian countryside took us past the castles of King Ludwig II, who had suddenly become king of Bavaria at the age of 18 when his father, King Maximillian, died unexpectedly. We saved the tours of these castles for a later date when Maggie would come over for summer vacation. We also stopped to visit *Weis Kirche* again and noticed people coming out after Easter services. On our way back to Garmisch, we stopped to tour a beautiful *14th Century Benedictine Monastery,* where monks conduct a school for boys and make the famous *kloster liqueur:* yellow for ladies and green for men. John purchased the green as a matter of curiosity to see what it was like. Sunday evening, he drove us into Garmisch for dinner, and we parked in front of our restaurant of Friday evening's choice. Again, we ordered the same meal, *Chateaubriand for Two,* topped off with *Chocolate Mousse* for dessert. What a great Easter weekend in Bavaria! After breakfast Monday morning, it was time to fill our thermos and head back to Frankfurt.

With our time getting short for finishing Romans, we had to start doubling up on our weekly meetings to have time to get started with the Book of Revelation before some of us had to leave Frankfurt. We were discussing how the *old man of sin,* inherited from Adam, must be allowed to die so the *new man* can be born of the Spirit of God.

> *"What shall we say then that Abraham our father, as pertaining to the flesh, hath found? For if Abraham were justified by works, he hath whereof to glory; but not before God. For what saith the scripture? Abraham believed God, and it was counted unto him for righteousness. "Now to him that worketh is the reward not reckoned of grace but of debt.... Even as David also describes the blessedness of man, unto whom God imputes righteousness without works. Saying blessed are they whose iniquities are forgiven, and whose sins are covered. Blessed is the man to whom the Lord will not impute sin. (Romans 4:1- 8)*
>
> *"What shall we say then? Shall we continue in sin, that grace may abound? God forbid. How shall we, that are dead to sin, live any longer therein? Know ye not, that so many of us as were baptized into Jesus Christ were baptized into his death?*
>
> *"Therefore, we are buried with him by baptism into death... For if we have been planted together in the likeness of his death, we shall be also in the likeness of his resurrection: Knowing this, that our old man is crucified with him, that the body of sin might be destroyed...*
>
> *"For he that is dead is freed from sin. Now if we be dead with Christ, we believe that we shall also live with him: knowing that*

Christ, being raised from the dead, will die no more; death hath no more dominion over him.

"For in that he died, he died unto sin once: but in that he lives, he lives unto God. Likewise, reckon yourselves to be dead indeed unto sin; but alive unto God through Jesus Christ.

"Let not sin therefore reign in your mortal body that ye should obey its lusts. Neither yield your members as instruments of unrighteousness unto sin; but yield yourselves unto God, as those that are alive from the dead, and your members as instruments of righteousness unto God. "For sin shall not have dominion over you: for ye are not under the law but under grace. What then? Shall we sin because we are not under the law, but under grace? God forbid. Know ye not, that to whom ye yield yourselves servants to obey, his servants ye are to whom ye obey; whether of sin unto death, or of obedience unto righteousness?

"But thank God that ye were the servants of sin, but ye have obeyed from the heart... Being made free from sin, you became the servants of righteousness. What fruit had ye then in those things whereof ye are now ashamed? For the end of those things is death.

"But now being made free from sin, and become servants to God, ye have your fruit unto holiness, and the end everlasting life. For the wages of sin is death; but the gift of God is eternal life through Jesus Christ our Lord." (Romans 6:1-23)

In Romans 7, we see a picture of the flesh warring against the spirit, and Paul tells us that it's possible for people to spend their entire lives in this very frustrating condition, always trying to keep the law of God through works of the flesh. If *"the old man"* isn't allowed to die to sin, he will keep on coming back through his old habits of the flesh. People want to be free, but their flesh wars against them.

"O wretched man that I am; who shall deliver me from this body of death? I thank God through Jesus Christ our Lord. So then with the mind I myself serve the law of God; but with the flesh the law of sin." (Romans 7:24-25)

In Romans 8:1-2, we learn to let go of "the Law," which keeps us in bondage to works of the flesh, and we receive a new law: *"The law of the Spirit of life in Christ Jesus"* which sets us free from *"the Law of sin and death."* God gave the Law *"to serve as our school master to bring us to Christ"* to show us our need for a Savior (Galatians 3:24-25). We cannot do it ourselves. Therefore, we must let go of The Law and put all our faith and trust in Christ. Only by the grace of God are we saved through faith. *"For the law was given by Moses, but grace and truth came by Jesus Christ."* (John 1:17)

> *"There is, therefore, now no condemnation to them which are in Christ Jesus, who walk not after the flesh, but after the Spirit. For the Spirit of life in Christ Jesus hath made me free from the law of sin and death."* (Romans 8:1-2)

> *"Wherefore the Law was our schoolmaster to bring us to Christ, that we might be justified by faith. But after faith is come, we are no longer under a schoolmaster."* (Galatians 3:24-25)

> *"For what the law could not do, in that it was weak through the flesh, God sending his own Son in the likeness of sinful flesh, and for sin, condemned sin in the flesh: That the righteousness of the law might be fulfilled in us, who walk not after the flesh, but after the Spirit. For they that are after the flesh do mind the things of the flesh; but they that are after the Spirit, the things of the Spirit.*
>
> *"For to be carnally minded is death; but to be spiritually minded is life and peace. Because the carnal mind is enmity against God: for it is not subject to the law of God, neither indeed can be. So then they that are in the flesh cannot please God. But ye are not in the flesh, but in the Spirit, if so be that the Spirit of God dwells in you. Now if any man have not the Spirit of Christ, he is none of his. And if Christ be in you, the body is dead because of sin; but the Spirit is life because of righteousness....*
>
> *"For as many as are led by the Spirit of God, they are the sons of God. For ye have not received the spirit of bondage again to fear; but ye have received the Spirit of adoption, whereby we cry, 'Abba, Father'. The Spirit itself bearing witness with our spirit, that we are the children of God: And if children, then heirs; heirs of God, and joint-heirs with Christ; if so be that we suffer with him, that we may be also glorified together. For I reckon that the sufferings of this present time are not worthy to be compared with the glory which shall be revealed in us....*

"For we know that the whole creation groaneth and travaileth in pain together until now. And not only they, but ourselves also, which have the firstfruits of the Spirit, even we ourselves groan within ourselves, waiting for the adoption, to wit, the redemption of our body....

"And we know that all things work together for good to them that love God, to them who are called according to his purpose. For whom he did foreknow, he also did predestinate to be conformed to the image of his Son, that he might be the firstborn among many brethren. Moreover whom he did predestinate, them he also called: and whom he called, them he also justified: and whom he justified, them he also glorified.

"What shall we say then to these things? If God be for us, who can be against us? He that spared not his own son, but delivered him up for us all, how shall he not with him also freely give us all things?" (Romans 8:3-32)

"But I would not have you ignorant, brethren, concerning them which are asleep... For if we believe that Jesus died and rose again, even so them also which sleep in Jesus will God bring with him.

"For this we say unto you by the word of the Lord, that we which are alive and remain unto the coming of the Lord shall not prevent them which are asleep. For the Lord himself shall descend from heaven with a shout, with the voice of the archangel, and with the trump of God: and the dead in Christ shall rise first.

"Then we which are alive and remain shall be caught up together with them in the clouds, to meet the Lord in the air: and so shall we ever be with the Lord. Wherefore comfort one another with these words." (1 Thessalonians 4:13-17)

"And if Christ be not raised, your faith is vain; ye are yet in your sins. Then they also which are fallen asleep in Christ are perished. If in this life only we have hope in Christ, we are of all men most miserable. But now is Christ risen from the dead, and become the firstfruits of them that slept.

"For since by man came death, by man also came the resurrection of the dead. For as in Adam all die, even so in Christ shall all be made alive. But every man in his own order: Christ the firstfruits; afterward, they that are Christ's at his coming.

"Then cometh the end, when he shall have delivered up the kingdom to God, even the Father; when he shall have put down all rule and all authority and power. For he must reign until he hath put all enemies under his feet. The last enemy that shall be destroyed is death....

"There is one glory of the sun, and another glory of the moon, and another glory of the stars: for one star differs from another star in glory. So also is the resurrection of the dead. It is sown in corruption; it is raised in incorruption. It is sown in dishonor, it is raised in glory; it is sown in weakness, it is raised in power; It is sown a natural body; it is raised a spiritual body....

"And so it is written, 'The first man Adam was made a living soul; the last Adam was made a quickening spirit.'... The first man is of the earth, earthy; the second man is the Lord from heaven... And as we have borne the image of the earthy, we shall also bear the image of the heavenly. Now this I say, brethren, that flesh and blood cannot inherit the kingdom of God; neither can corruption inherit incorruption.

"Behold, I show you a mystery: We shall not all sleep, but we shall all be changed, in a moment, in the twinkling of an eye, at the last trump: for the trumpet shall sound, and the dead shall be raised incorruptible, and we shall be changed. For this corruptible must put on incorruption, and this mortal must put on immortality. So when this corruptible shall have put on incorruption and this mortal shall have put on immortality, then shall be brought to pass the saying that is written, 'Death is swallowed up in victory.'

"'O death where is thy sting? O grave, where is thy victory?' The sting of death is sin; and the strength of sin is the law. But thanks be to God, which giveth us the victory through our Lord Jesus Christ. Therefore, my beloved brethren, be ye stedfast, unmoveable, always abounding in the work of the Lord, for as much as ye know that your labor is not in vain in the Lord." (1 Corinthians 15:17-58)

"Who shall separate us from the love of Christ? Shall tribulation, or distress, or persecution, or famine, or nakedness, or peril, or sword? As it is written, for thy sake we are killed all the day long; we are accounted as sheep for the slaughter. Nay, in all these things we are more than conquerors through Him who loved us.

"For I am persuaded that neither death, nor life, nor angels, nor principalities, nor powers, nor things present, nor things to come, nor height, nor depth, nor any other creature, shall be able to separate us from the love of God, which is in Christ Jesus our Lord." (Romans 8:35-39)

CHAPTER SEVENTEEN

Summer in Frankfurt
1983

We began our study of the great Book of Revelation by listening to three introductory tapes by the author of our study, and we looked through our thick Revelation workbook to get an idea of how vast and deep our study was going to be. I noticed that written on the front page was a quote by a gentleman who had been inspirational to her in writing the course. It read, *"I believe that no teacher should strive to make men think as he thinks, but to lead them to the living truth, to the Master himself, of whom alone they can learn anything, who will make in themselves know what is true by the very seeing of it."* We began our study with prayer asking God to open our spiritual eyes so that we might see and know in our hearts what is true. Our homework was to read through the whole book in one sitting to get the general overview as we had done in Romans. Our Revelation workbook was twice the size of Romans with many more illustrations and charts to fill out and many, many more questions to answer.

John was told to write *the things which he had seen, the things which are, and the things which shall be hereafter.* (Revelation 1:19) This is the only book of the Bible which promises a blessing to those who study and heed its message. *"Blessed is he that reads and they that hear the words of this prophecy and keep those things which are written therein: for the time is at hand."* (Revelation 1:3) It wasn't until the last few decades that these visions made any sense at all, and today, the book practically interprets itself as one compares John's visions to the actual happenings in the world today. God told Daniel to *seal up his visions until the time of the end* because he knew no one would be able to understand them in his day (Daniel 12:9). God gave these revelations to John and Daniel to warn the people of what is yet to come and to give the *testimony of Jesus* to *his bondservants,* so that we might recognize these things as they begin to happen and reveal them to others. God tells us to be prepared, and he has always warned his people when it was time for something big to happen on the earth like the flood which was coming in the days of Noah (Matthew 24:37). Once these things begin to happen, they will happen rapidly, and it will be too late for some to get their lives in order to escape *the great and terrible Day of the Lord.* Jesus promised to *catch away his bride,* the true Church, *without spot and blameless* (2 Peter 3:14) to *the marriage supper of the Lamb* before the tribulation which is to come upon the whole world (Revelation 19:7-8).

At first glance, this last book of the Bible looks like a conglomeration of *allegories,* but John was given visions far into the future of things he had never seen before and there were no words to describe them. He had to describe what he saw using the only words he knew, and, therefore, these visions are probably *similes.* For instance, in describing a helicopter with the blades spinning around in the air, John might have used the words, *"and they had hair as the hair of women,"* ... *"and they had breastplates, as it were breastplates of iron, and the sound of their wings was as the sound of chariots of many horses running to battle."* (Revelation 9:8-10) In the same chapter, we see the description of modern day warfare with weapons being used such as guns, tanks, missiles, mortars and bombs:

> *"And thus I saw the horses in the vision, and them that sat on them, having breastplates of fire, and of jacinth, and of brimstone: and the heads of the horses were as the heads of lions; and out of their mouths issued fire and smoke and brimstone. By these three was the third part of men killed by the fire, by the smoke, and by the brimstone, which issued out of their mouths. For their power is in their mouth, and in their tails: for their tails were like unto serpents, and had heads, and with them they do hurt.* (Revelation 9:16-19).

In Chapters 12 and 13, John's visions are revealed as *allegories.* For instance, *"a woman clothed with the sun and the moon under her feet, and upon her head a crown of twelve stars,"* appears to be a *simile* of Joseph's dream (Genesis 37:9), which first appeared in his dream as an *allegory,* depicting his mother, father, and brothers. Therefore, we must assume that this *woman,* who is about to give birth to *a male child,* is *Israel,* who gives birth to *Jesus,* and *Satan* is ready to devour him as soon as he comes into the world.

"And there appeared a great wonder in heaven; a woman clothed with the sun, and the moon under her feet, and upon her head a crown of 12 stars. And she, being with child cried, travailing in birth, and pained to be delivered.

"And there appeared another wonder in heaven; and behold a great red dragon, having seven heads and ten horns, and seven crowns upon his heads. And his tail drew the third part of the stars of heaven, and did cast them to the earth: and the dragon stood before the woman who was ready to be delivered, for to devour her child as soon as it was born.

"And she brought forth a man child, who was to rule all nations with a rod of iron: and her child was caught up unto God, and to his throne. And the woman fled into the wilderness, where she had a place prepared by God, that they should feed her there a thousand two hundred and threescore days.

"And there was war in heaven: Michael and his angels fought against the dragon, and the dragon fought and his angels, and prevailed not; neither was their place found any more in heaven. And the great dragon was cast out, that old serpent called the Devil, and Satan, which deceives the whole world: he was cast out into the earth, and his angels were cast out with him." (Revelation 12:1-9)

"Therefore, rejoice ye heavens, and ye that dwell in them. Woe to the inhabitants of the earth and of the sea! For the devil is come down unto you having great wrath, because he knows that he has but a short time. And when the dragon saw that he was cast unto the earth, he persecuted the woman, which brought forth the man child.

"And to the woman were given two wings of a great eagle, that she might fly into the wilderness, into her place, where she is nourished for a time, and times, and half a time, from the face of the serpent. And the serpent cast out of his mouth water as a flood after the woman, that he might cause her to be carried away of the flood.

"And the earth helped the woman, and the earth opened her mouth, and swallowed up the flood which the dragon cast out of his mouth. And the dragon was wroth with the woman, and went to make war with the remnant of her seed, which keep the commandments of God, and have the testimony of Jesus Christ." (Revelation 12:12-17)

These last verses of Chapter 12 seem to describe the Nazi Holocaust, however, it could be *a two-fold prophecy* which also describes *the last 3½ years* of tribulation when the people of the earth help *the woman* escape once again to *her hiding place* where she is nourished from the face of the serpent. And the dragon sends a flood after the woman and the remnant of her seed, *which keep the commandments of God and have the testimony of Jesus Christ.* If this happens again before the end of the world as we know it, the Church will be in heaven and the Jews will be preaching the gospel to those remaining on the earth. Finally, after 2,000 years, their blindness will be lifted and they will recognize Jesus, *the Lamb of God*, as their long-awaited *Messiah.*

> *"Here is the patience of the saints: here are they that keep the commandments of God, and the faith of Jesus. And I heard a voice from heaven saying unto me, 'Write, Blessed are the dead which die in the lord from henceforth.'"* (Revelation 14:12-13)

In order to understand the Book of Revelation, we must go back over 2,000 years and see what the world was like at the time of Christ: Rome was at its height of power and was a melding pot for many diverse peoples. Large numbers of the lower classes were totally dependent upon the Roman government. Prosperity became the weakness of Rome and resulted in moral decay. Many owned Jewish slaves and idolatry abounded. The Emperor was like god to the people, and they were forced to worship him as God. Some remained skeptical, but they worshipped the government as the absolute rather than face persecution, and the emphasis was on the philosophical rather than the spiritual. The coinage lost its value. Humanism was the religion which taught that man can make his own rules and, therefore, become his own god. Rome was a divided nation, and all the conditions of Rome apply to our country today: immorality; perversion; idolatry; callousness toward the suffering of others; rapid rise in divorce; craving of pleasure; rise in taxes and rapid spending; the rejection of Christians and Jews; and the rejection of God to rule over them.

> *"Seek ye the Lord while he may be found, call ye upon him while he is near. Let the wicked forsake his way, and the unrighteous man his thoughts: and let him return unto the Lord, and he will have mercy upon him; and to our God, for he will abundantly pardon.*

For my ways are not your ways, saith the Lord. For as the heavens are higher than the earth, so are my ways higher than your ways, and my thoughts than your thoughts." (Isaiah 55:6-9)

In May, John and I were eager to see Maggie after her first year of college, and we were pleased to hear that she had selected German as one of her classes that year in preparation for her trip to Frankfurt. She had worked hard to earn her B+ average, and I'm sure she needed her summer break to get in some R&R time. We had left her with a new passport, and, as a college student under the age of 22, she was eligible for her round-trip ticket to Europe. Litton Personnel made her reservations and mailed her the airline tickets. She would move out of the dorm, leave all her things with Amanda and Zach, park her car in their yard and they would drive her to the airport. We were very excited to be at the Frankfurt Airport to meet her when her plane landed, and I believe she was, too. It was so great to have Amanda and Zach watching out for Maggie that year, and I don't know what we would have done without them.

We drove her around the city of Frankfurt for a while to get the feel of Germany, and Maggie spotted a *McDonalds*. She was hungry after hardly any breakfast or sleep on the plane, so we pulled over to wait while she ran inside for a hamburger, fries and a Pepsi. John took a cute picture of her coming out with her order, which she ate in the car as we continued our drive through the city. Then we drove her through the countryside out to our little home in Walldorf. We had chosen Maggie's bedroom suite while we were buying our furniture at Mobel Walter, so we were all prepared for her to come home for a long visit. She really seemed to like it there and soon found her place in the warm Frankfurt sunshine of our small backyard. It was great having Maggie at home with us even if it was only for two months before we all had to leave Germany.

A Tour of Bavaria

We had plans for the weekend and I'm not sure Maggie was ready for it because of *jet lag*, but we packed the car and took off for Bavaria to take advantage of a German holiday. We told her she could nap on the back seat while making the gradual adjustment to our time zone, although we had learned that it was better to stay awake and adjust quickly. It really didn't seem to bother her though, and she adjusted beautifully after the first day.

We drove through parts of the Black Forest and stopped in Triberg to see Germany's highest waterfall. Maggie and I climbed half-way to the top, and John took a cute picture of her sitting on a huge rock in front of the falls. We combined several of the short trips we had taken over the previous months with a few new ones, and I think we came up with a fantastic tour of Bavaria.

The Triberg Waterfalls in Germany's Black Forest.

We spent our first night in Hotel Drachenburg and had a very nice dinner overlooking the headwaters of the Rhein River flowing out of Lake Constance. The following morning, we drove over to Rhein Falls, the largest water falls in Europe, which John and I had missed on our first trip to Lake Constance. They were magnificent! All three of us sat in the little restaurant in front of the falls having lunch and admiring their awesome beauty as they came billowing over large boulders of rock. After lunch, we drove to Mainau Island on Lake Constance, just off the mainland of Bavaria, over into Switzerland, the very heart of Europe. On our German map, Lake Constance was listed as *Bodensee.* The island is covered with many lovely flowers, tropical plants and imported cedars from Lebanon. Like on our trip to the Netherlands, we just happened to hit the gardens at the peak of season. They looked quite similar to Holland's *Keukenhof.*

Hotel Drachenburg at the Headwaters of the Rhein River.

217

Rhein Falls, Germany: Europe's Largest Waterfalls.

As we were returning to the hotel that evening, Maggie and I took the wrong staircase on our way upstairs to our room, and, realizing what we had done, I hastily turned at the top of the stairs to go back down to come up the other way. As I did, my heel got caught in the loose carpeting and sent me flying down the stairs headfirst. It made a terrible noise, and both the hotel manager and John came running to see what had happened. They found me lying at the bottom of the first tier the way I landed, on my stomach, and started bringing me ice. I had come down riding on the palms of my hands stretched out before me with my shins hitting every step all the way down. Needless to say, I went to our room with my ice and retired for the evening. Maggie's room was just across the hall, so it worked out well for all concerned. She and her Dad could enjoy TV and talk without disturbing me. I took three aspirin and went to sleep. I didn't break anything, but my shins sure felt it the following morning when I tried to climb the steep incline up to Neuschwanstein Castle. While I was slowly making my way up the hill, Maggie got some great, artistic shots of the castle through the grass of a meadow covered with beautiful long-stemmed golden dandelions.

Neuschwanstein Castle, Bavaria, Germany.

On our castle tour, we learned that Neuschwanstein Castle was built in the middle of the 19th Century by the very eccentric King Ludwig II who had suddenly become king of Bavaria at the age of 18 when his father, King Maximillian, died unexpectedly. His father had been a very good king and had done much for Bavaria, but both of his sons grew up in a *fantasy world*. The younger son was declared insane at a very early age, and King Ludwig II wasn't at all prepared to rule Bavaria. He became infatuated with castle building! Linderhof Castle was the first one he built with a single throne in every room, and his bedroom had a built-in trap door directly above the kitchen, so he could have his table lifted up to his room laden with food whenever he wanted it. Linderhof Castle became his home during the castle- building period, and he usually slept in the daytime with the courtyards and fountains all lit up at night for his personal enjoyment. King Ludwig became obsessed with *Wagner's Swan Lake* and had a simulated *Blue Grotto* constructed in a cave behind the castle. Ludwig's legend, widely known by the people of Bavaria, states that he hired someone to pull him around in his swan-like boat inside his Blue Grotto while he pretended to be in the starring role of the play as *Wagner's Swan Lake* played to accompany his fantasy.

Ludwig also had a *Japanese Tea House* built near the Grotto overlooking the lovely valley below as he sat for afternoon tea on his one-man throne. The Tea House was furnished with palms and jeweled peacocks.

Neuschwanstein Castle was never completed on the inside and represented a *fairy castle*. Ludwig had plans for building two more when the people of Bavaria had him declared insane and dethroned him at the age of 40. Legend tells us that his doctor and other prominent people of Bavaria kept him imprisoned in one of his castles with all the doorknobs removed on the inside, so he couldn't escape. One day while his doctor was visiting, he gave Ludwig permission to go outside for a walk around the lake, and, when he didn't return as promised, the doctor went after him. Neither of them ever returned and their bodies were found in the lake. However, no one witnessed what actually happened, but it is believed that Ludwig, who was much larger, younger and stronger than the doctor, tried to escape, and, in their struggle, both of them drowned. We also visited the beautiful Rococo-style *White Church* on the way to Garmisch, which housed a statue of Christ which was said to have cried real tears.

We had a room reserved at the General Patton Hotel at the Armed Forces Recreation Center in Garmisch for a couple of days, and Maggie loved seeing the beautiful Bavarian Alps still covered with snow. John and I loved sharing this beautiful city with Maggie and enjoyed taking her out for dinner in the great international restaurants we remembered from our first trip. She was especially impressed with the clever artistic murals on the lovely buildings and houses in the city and the adorable chalets dotting the mountainside on our drives through the lovely scenic countryside. From Garmisch, we drove to Oberammergau to show her the famous *Open Air Theatre* where we walked through the museum to see the pictures and costumes of the *Passion Plays* which had been held over the years. She was impressed with the memorial the town made to God to rid them of the black plague. The lovely scenic drive from Oberammergau to Berchtesgaden was absolutely breathtaking with the snow-covered Bavarian Alps surrounding us. While registering for two nights in our Berchtesgaden hotel, we signed up for the bus tour the following day to Salzburg to see where the movie, *The Sound of Music*, was filmed and to visit *Mozart's birthplace*.

First, our tour bus took us half-way up the mountain to an elevator which took us straight to the top of what once was Hitler's mountain retreat, *the Eagle's Nest*. It is situated on the crest of the very high mountain above the

General Walker Hotel, which was once the scene of Nazi Headquarters. The view from up there is spectacular overlooking the mountains and lakes in the direction of Salzburg. We just happened to run into an old friend from Language School, Lori, the wife of one of John's classmates. She recognized us and joined us for our walk around the Eagle's Nest as John took pictures. While in Monterey, their young daughter had been kicked in the head by a horse while they were out riding and had to be rushed to the hospital. The doctors had to install a metal plate in her head to protect her brain while she was growing up. We were happy to hear that she had fully recovered from the accident. We learned a few years later that she now has a very successful career in a branch of the US Government. While in Salzburg, we drove by the home of the Von Trapp family to see where the movie was filmed on the lake with its very large outer doors surrounding the lovely home. We discovered the gazebo in a place by itself quite a distance down the road on another property. It proved to be a lovely addition to the Von Trapp estate for the special dance scene of *Liesl* and *Kurt* as filmed for the movie.

Scene from Elevator to "The Eagle's Nest."

Scene from "The Eagle's Nest."

In Salzburg, we also toured the birthplace of Mozart at No. 9 Getreidegasse. The Mozart family resided on the third floor from 1747-1773, and Wolfgang Amadeus Mozart was born January 27, 1756. He was the seventh child of Leopold Mozart, who was a musician of the Salzburg Royal Chamber. Only Amadeus and his sister, Maria Anna, survived. Mozart's birthplace was turned into a museum in 1880 and introduces visitors to the early life of the composer and his first musical instruments. The third floor exhibits Mozart's childhood violin and his harpsichord. There are also records of his life in Vienna and of his wife and family, as well as portraits and early editions of his music. The second floor is devoted to Mozart's interest in opera and includes the clavichord on which he composed *The Magic Flute*. The first floor is furnished with the period of furniture of the Mozart era, and the paintings illustrate his life in Salzburg. Other items of interest are one of his most striking portraits, painted in 1789 by Joseph Lange, his brother-in-law, pictures of his childhood and early editions of his music. We also visited Mozart Square, known in Salzburg as *Mozartplatz*, in the heart of the old city, where we found the 19th Century statue of the composer. From a small nearby restaurant, John bought the three of us a round of delicious Austrian desserts served with tea, as we sat to rest under a large leafed tree in the midst of the beautiful Cathedrals of Salzburg. We walked by the lovely fountain shown in the movie with Maria and the Von Trapp children. The following day, we started the drive back to Frankfurt stopping for lunch in Nuernberg, so Maggie could see inside the lovely old Medieval Fortress.

Back in Frankfurt, John was busy finishing up his work with Holzmann before moving down to Riyadh, where the major portion of his job was ready to begin in the deserts and mountains of Saudi Arabia. My Bible group quite hurriedly finished up Romans as soon as possible and began the study of Revelation because several of us were scheduled to move that summer. We knew we didn't have time to do justice to this great book of Bible Prophecy, so we had to work overtime to finish what we could and take our studies with us. I planned to purchase a set of Revelation tapes to go along with my studies in hopes of completing my gigantic Revelation workbook in Saudi Arabia during John's two-year assignment.

Maggie seemed to enjoy her free time to do as she pleased reading and enjoying our backyard sunshine while I was at my morning meetings at the Chapel. We also enjoyed going into the city to shop at Herties so we could have lunch in the cafeteria-style lunchroom, which always served the delicious *Jaeger Schnitzel* with lots of *Pommes Frites*. They also served an assortment of desserts, including the very delicious *Black Forest Cherry Cake*. Maggie seemed to enjoy some of the activities at the Chapel, and, on weekends, John would take us out for a drive in the lovely German countryside to find a new quaint little place to have lunch. Sometimes, he would take us with him to Rheinblick Golf Course where we could sit outside on the veranda to relax and read, or just enjoy the beautiful view of the Rhein River in the far distance. After his golf game, we would enjoy having dinner in the restaurant where the German food was always very good and the desserts outstanding.

The Legend of Lorelei

In early June, I booked us on a two-day Rhein River Cruise similar to the one John and I had enjoyed the previous summer on our Litton-Holzmann cruise down the Main River. We had a very nice day on our river cruise Saturday, and we stopped occasionally to tour a castle or have a rest stop for lunch or a snack break. Mainly, we just enjoyed the lively German music and joyous atmosphere of the people on the boat.

We heard the story of the famous *"Lorelei,"* a German folktale about an enchantress who once lived above the steep rock on the eastern shore of the Rhein River. It was said that she dressed in white and wore a wreath of stars in her hair, but more than her physical beauty, was the song she sang — a song so alluring, no one could resist its pull. Of course, there were many lives lost because of the alluring Lorelei and there were many tales to tell and many poems and songs written about her. According to the folklore, anyone sailing close to the rock would lose his life for her song was so irresistible, it would draw them into the rock; no sailors who tried to reach Lorelei ever returned. Actually, it was a legend of sailors who lost their lives because of the swift currents of the water and the gigantic rock, which seemed to jut out at an angular turn of the river. The large rock gets its name from the old German word, "lureln" (Rhein dialect), which means "murmuring," and the Celtic term "ley," meaning "rock." It is believed that the heavy currents of the river and a small waterfall in the area, which was visible in the 19th Century, created a murmuring sound, all of which was amplified by the natural echo produced by the rock itself and its location on the river. All of this combined gives the rock its name: *"murmuring rock."* And from this sound arose the German folktale of the alluring *"Lorelei."* Another German verb, "lauern," means "to lurk" or "lie in wait." And with the same "ley" ending, this translation would mean "lurking rock."

We spent the night in a hotel in Rudesheim on the Rhein River and walked through the plaza to find a good restaurant for dinner. We finally found one brimming over with atmosphere and crowds of people out for a joyous Saturday evening. The German food was great and so was the lively German music. Our bus picked us up early Sunday morning for the return trip to Frankfurt, and we were surprised to stop at the Monastery of Eberbach in the Rheingau for wine tasting, where wine had been made by the Monks for over 800 years. Maggie was content to wait on the bus and read while we toured the winery, but she was more amused by a family of cats outside the winery, which lived there to keep the rodents away.

A Tour of London & Paris

With our time running short, I booked Maggie and myself on a 6-day combined tour of Paris and London leaving John at home to deal with the packers as he wound up his job in Frankfurt. He drove us to Rhein-Main

AFRC on the evening of June 20th to catch our bus for Zeebrugge, Belgium and the 4:00 am crossing of the English Channel. It was practically the same trip John and I had taken during the holidays on our tour of London, however, with Maggie, it was bound to be different. After breakfast on board the ferry, Maggie and I found a good place to sit and watched the beautiful *White Cliffs of Dover* as they first appeared in the distance and loomed larger and larger until we pulled into the port. This time our bus took us up over the cliffs directly to *Canterbury Cathedral,* where we had a brief tour, and then straight to London.

The first thing Maggie did after arriving in our hotel room was to pick up the telephone directory and look up *Rory Gallagher,* her favorite rock star. She had recently attended a rock concert at Hampton Coliseum back in Virginia and met Rory in person. She got his attention by holding up a lifelike portrait she had done of him from a picture on the cover of his newest album. As I entered the room, she was talking with his brother and business manager, who told her that Rory was in County Cork, Ireland visiting their parents for a few days. We had a nice dinner in the hotel and walked around the area to see what we could find and took a couple of pictures. Since we were both very tired from our long night on the ferry, we settled into our room and got to bed early to be ready for the *City Tour* the following morning.

The Guards of Buckingham Palace, London, England.

The second day with Maggie was exactly the same as my first day in London with John. The bus tour of the city with a local guide took us to all the famous places: *Piccadilly Circus, Trafalgar Square, Houses of Parliament, St. Paul's Cathedral, and stopping at Buckingham Palace to see the changing of the guards.* After our free time for lunch downtown, our bus tour took us out to *Windsor Castle,* where we heard the English history and visited the tea room. That evening, *the Pub Tour* was exactly the same. We placed our orders for pub food and soft drinks at the first pub, just as John and I had done because we were hungry, and I knew the food at this pub was very good. Maggie wasn't at all impressed with the second pub, which our guide told us was often frequented by a younger member of the Royal Family. However, she was very impressed with the atmosphere of *The Prospect of Whitby,* London's oldest riverside inn, once an old warehouse made famous by Jack the Ripper, who was said to have stalked his victims here. She bought a Prospect of Whitby T-shirt. We started out with soft drinks, or tea, and ended up with hot chocolate at the old riverside inn sitting around the fireplace listening to a small combo, just as John and I had done, where our tour seemed to linger a bit longer than at the first two pubs.

Maggie chose to keep the third day open to do our things of choice without being confined to a group. I let her plan our day: first, we rode the subway to the *Tower of London*, where we explored the large old castle and heard some of its gory history. Then we rode the subway over to Ghent where we got off and walked a mile or two in search of Rory Gallagher's townhouse. When we finally found it, Maggie was content to just snap a picture from across the street of his front door and have pizza on the corner where we listened to Rory's hit records and *hung out* for about an hour. Then we walked back to the subway and found *Madame Tussaud's House of Wax*. The lifelike figures were so real it was incredible! It gave us an eerie feeling to look at their faces and realize that the heads of these historical figures had been molded immediately after their beheadings, which is how Madam Tussaud got her start. We were particularly interested in the two small brothers at the Tower of London who had been kept there some time and were finally murdered to keep them from inheriting the throne. They looked so real and lifelike! We made pictures of them and many other famous people.

London Bridge over the Thames.

Our optional tour that evening took us to the cellars of *The Beefeater*, located next door to the *Tower of London*, where we enjoyed the atmosphere of a medieval meal typifying the era and reign of *King Henry VIII*. We had learned much of his history on the *Windsor Castle* tour, where we had tea in the tea house to which one of his secret passageways led. The food was rather bland at the *Beefeater* and served with large pitchers of ale. They showed us how to beat on the table with rolled-up fists if we wanted anything and told us to *call the wenches* if we wanted more ale. They were scurrying around from table to table as people were beating on the tables and shouting out, *"More ale!"* Maggie thought that was great fun and got right into the spirit of things. Before I knew it, she was drinking the ale and pounding on the table for more. We enjoyed all the entertainers who rotated around the room: *the jolly jesters, the knife throwers, the jugglers, the magicians, and the singers and dancers* all kept us amused. Finally, it was all over, and we had to *bunny hop* out the door to catch our bus back to the hotel. When we arrived, I became very concerned when a young woman of the Air Force group, who had been sitting next to Maggie at the Beefeater, invited her to come into the bar with her and her friends. I suggested very strongly that she come into our room and get some sleep because our tour left early the next morning.

Maggie didn't feel well the next day, but we had to catch our bus for the drive to Dover and the channel crossing to *Calais*. From there, it was a rather short drive to *Paris*, and we arrived at our hotel early in the afternoon. Since she still didn't feel well, we cancelled out of the Illumination Tour of Paris that evening and had dinner in the hotel. The following morning after a good breakfast, Maggie felt much better and we were able to enjoy the *City Tour* and a *Cruise on the Seine* in the afternoon. Our *Three Corner Tour* took us up to *Montmartre* where we wandered around *Artist's Square* looking at all the artists at work with their easels set up and using all kinds of tempera. A very young artist drew Maggie in charcoal, and, of course, we had to buy it, although it wasn't a good likeness. Then we stopped by the *Flea Market* on the way back and bought her a cute crinkled cotton lavender dress to take back to school. When we got back to the hotel, we were ready for a good dinner and a good night's sleep. Then it was time to board our bus and head back to Frankfurt. We stopped for lunch at the little restaurant on the German border where we enjoyed the delicious roasted chicken with lots of french fries and salad as we sat above the autobahn for the last time.

When we returned home, our shipments to the United States and Saudi Arabia were gone, but the Frankfurt items remained to be packed. Litton allowed us to purchase the furniture we wanted to keep at the end of the contract, so we chose to buy most of the German furniture, which would be put into storage and kept for us. The other items would be sold to whoever wanted to buy them or shared with the ones who stayed in Frankfurt. George and Greta bought our major appliances and our patio and office furniture. They invited us over for a patio dinner Sunday afternoon right before we left, and Maggie, who all her life had wanted a dog of her own, was in high heaven visiting their two large Golden Retrievers. After our last pick up, we moved into a nearby *Gasthaus* while John sold *Max*, our beautiful light green Mercedes with the tan interior and the tan and dark brown check seats. He borrowed the company car for us to use during our last days in Frankfurt and tied up all the remaining loose ends. On our last evening, Maggie's 21st birthday, we took her out for dinner and she ordered a German beer. She said she had given it a lot of thought, and it was her last chance to taste the German beer before she had to leave Frankfurt. Her dad didn't object! Instead, he ordered one for himself and a glass of white wine for me! The following day, we caught our Pan Am flight back to the States.

We arrived at Dulles in the afternoon, rented a car and drove straight to the Arlington Holiday Inn where we checked in and called Greg. John told him our plans for driving over to pick him up the following morning to spend the day with us at the hotel. Having brought with him all our European slides, John purchased a Kodak Carousel projector and some extra trays from a nearby discount store and got busy sorting, organizing and filling the trays while Maggie and I took baths and prepared for bed. The following morning, we were up bright and early for breakfast and called Greg before driving over to get him. He gave us a tour of the rooming house, and we were pleased to see his room looking so neat with an efficient desk for his telephone job. He looked well and was happy to see us! Down the hall in one direction was an efficient looking kitchen shared by all the tenants, and, in the other direction, a large community bathroom.

It was the 4th of July, so we picked up a sack of Kentucky Fried Chicken with the additional extra food for dinner and spent the rest of the day visiting with Greg in our motel room as we enjoyed looking at all the slides for the very first time. That evening, we enjoyed watching the DC Fourth of July TV Special with all the beautiful fireworks on the Mall. We had a great visit with Greg and were happy to find him content with his present setup living in the rooming house and working his job scheduling pickups for Purple Heart Vets. The following morning, we picked Greg up for a farewell breakfast at IHOP before dropping him off and telling him goodbye. Then we had to set out on our drive to Virginia Beach to pick up the Malibu, which Maggie had left with Amanda and Zach. That evening we had a slide show for our Virginia Beach family to share our adventures and enjoyed being with them again. The following morning, we had to tell Amanda and Zach goodbye again and thank them for all their help in taking care of Maggie and her car. John turned in our rental car, and we headed south in the Malibu.

As we had done the previous year, we headed first to Memphis to visit John's mom, Hannah, who was visiting Aunt Grace and Uncle George, and we had a slide show for all the family. Then we drove to Jackson, where we had another slide show for Kathy and Jim, and they took us out for a wonderful fish dinner. From there, we drove on to Mobile where we had our fifth slide show for our eastern shore family; Joe and Erin came over from Mobile to join us. Mother was always happy to have us home again and we were happy to be there. After only a couple of days, it was time for John to leave for Riyadh to begin his job as Construction Manager for the Litton- Holzmann project in Saudi Arabia. Maggie and I saw him off at the Mobile airport; then she and I visited with Mother for about a month before having to drive back to Norfolk to get her settled for the fall semester. We stayed a couple of days with Amanda and Zach while she looked around Norfolk for a suitable apartment near the campus. She wanted to avoid dorm life this year because of the partying, which had not been good for her. Finally, she selected a newly renovated room in the attic of a home not far from the campus. Because of no exits out of the upper attic room in case of fire, I ordered her a rope ladder.

After having lunch together and getting her resettled in her new apartment, Maggie drove me back to Virginia Beach where I hugged her goodbye. I knew she was anxious to get back to her adventurous college life after spending her whole summer with John and me. We loved every minute of it! And we would miss her! Maggie drove away in good spirits leaving me with Amanda and looking forward to registering for her new fall courses. Again, she was determined to make all A's. I was happy to be with Amanda and her family for a while after leaving Maggie, and Amanda was wonderful about helping me get to the airport on time for my flight back to Mobile.

CHAPTER EIGHTEEN

Back in the States Again

1983-1984

I don't know what I would have done without my wonderful sister, Amanda, and her husband, Zach, during all our transiting years. After getting Maggie settled in Norfolk for another year of college, Amanda drove me to the airport to see me off for Mobile where Mother and Ginger met me at the airport. What would I have done without all these wonderful people? I owe so much to all of them for always having someone there to meet me. Mother was always glad for me to be home for a while and she took good care of our station wagon, which we stored in her garage. I took a look at the *old Yellow Sub,* which had raised our family and wondered how we could ever get rid of it. It was like our family home on the road! I decided to have it fixed up like new and even had it painted. Mother adopted it as part of her garage, and her yard man started it up once in a while to keep it running. After a thorough safety check to make sure it was still road worthy, Mother and I planned a little trip up to northern Mississippi to visit John's mother, Hannah, for her birthday the first week in September. Mother was suffering from arthritis and needed a knee replacement to keep her ambulatory. It was bone on bone in one knee and getting very painful for her to go up and down the two steps into her living room. She only needed cartilage clipping in the other knee; however, she needed time to think about it so we planned the trip.

Mother had taken excellent care of Kitty, our beautiful black and white cat, while we were away in Germany. She was very healthy looking at 7 years old but had gained a little weight. Mother had fed her well, and Kitty had been a great companion for her, but now, with Mother's arthritis getting so bad, she may have become a burden. I took her to the Vet for shots and her annual checkup. The Vet said she was healthy but to cut down on her food. Aunt Rebecca had given Mother a leash so she could put Kitty out on the porch, but Mother was afraid of the leash and never used it. I arose early one morning and put Kitty outside on the porch wearing the leash to see how she would do while I got involved in my Bible studies. I totally forgot about her! Later, when we heard thunder, Mother said, "Where's Kitty?" She was afraid of thunder and would always run to hide. Then I remembered putting her outside on the porch and ran out to see about her. Too late! She had hung herself trying to come in and her leash had gotten caught on the back of one of the redwood chairs. About that time, Uncle Charlie and Aunt Susan dropped by for a visit and he started digging her grave. We buried her inside an old pillow case in the shade of a large Azalea bush, and I was just sick! I couldn't believe that I could be so irresponsible! But God always has a plan. Things don't happen by accident! Mother couldn't have taken care of Kitty any longer in her condition with the upcoming surgery, and I had to leave for Saudi Arabia.

I continued my Bible studies early in the morning, and, after Mother got up and turned on her stereo music, we would have breakfast together and I would sometimes read to her. She was gradually losing her eye sight and couldn't see well enough to read the large print of her Bible. Mother had always been a very cheerful person and usually woke up in the morning *singing with the birds* and would turn on her music. I was grateful to be able to enjoy her company for as long as I could. Sometimes, I would try to share with her some of what I was learning in my Bible studies and where the Book of Revelation was taking me. I felt it was important for everyone to know what the testimony of Jesus reveals in his *"Message to the Churches,"* as we are nearing the end of the church age. Mother told me that one of her family members once told her that she thought the book of Revelation *was written by some nut*! That must have been what it looked like in those days because not many people could make heads or tails of this mysterious last book of the Bible. I also tried to share a little of what I had learned about church history, but I don't think she understood my intentions. She somehow got the idea that *"I"* was judging the churches, but I tried to explain that it really doesn't matter what I think: it only matters what God *is trying to tell us through his Word and the testimony of Jesus* in this very important *message*. He wants us to know the truth so we can be ready in these last days for the *rapture of his Church, the true body of Christ,* and for *the second coming of Christ,* for which there are many more prophesies than the *first*. I decided that where Mother was concerned, it would be best for me to stick with Romans and the prophecies which were already fulfilled. She loved to hear the prophecies regarding *The Christmas Story,* which follows at the end of this chapter.

Mother's orthopedic surgeon recommended replacement surgery in her right knee but only planned to clip the cartilage in her left knee, which was being pinched with her every step and was quite painful. She decided to proceed with the clipping but wanted some time to think over the more serious knee replacement. So we planned the trip to visit John's mother for her 70th birthday and took her with us to Memphis to visit Aunt Grace and Uncle George. They drove us around Memphis to see the newly renovated downtown area on *Beale Street* and the large, new Memphis Convention Center, where Grace worked for many years as hostess for all the conventions which came to town. Since she highly recommended *The Rendezvous,* famous for its *Memphis Barbecue,* to all the people who attended the conventions, the owner knew her quite well and reciprocated when she brought us in. Mother had a hard time going down the steps but loved the food once she made it to her seat at the table. She especially enjoyed sitting in the lobby of the *Peabody Hotel* watching the ducks as they exited the fountain at precisely 5:00 pm every day and paraded over to the elevator for a ride up to their *Penthouse,* where they automatically walked right into their cages.

After driving Hannah back home and taking her out to dinner, Mother and I spent one night with her and left the following morning heading for Birmingham. We were on our way to visit an old friend who still lived in Fairfield Highlands, a small suburb on a rocky hillside between the big city and the industrial town of Bessemer. Mother's oldest and best friend, Fannie, still lived across the street from where we lived when I was born. Now Fannie was getting old, and like Mother, suffered with Arthritis, but she certainly cooked us a wonderful dinner while we were there for our two-day visit. She and Mother had a great time reminiscing about the old days and told many fascinating stories, which I always enjoyed hearing. It was fun to listen to them, and I loved hearing their laughter! One time, when I was a baby and they were sitting in our front porch swing, one of the chains broke and sent them over sideways and backwards with their feet up in the air holding me and laughing. Thank goodness, my father was at home to hear their cries and come to their rescue.

I decided to walk down the street to see our old house on the corner with the two large rocks on either side of the sidewalk leading from the street up to the front porch. They were still there! But they looked so small compared to the way I remembered them. A man driving by stopped to ask if I knew who owned the place. He was interested in renting the garage apartment in back of the house. I said, "No, but I know who built it. I used to live in this house, and, when I was 4 years old, I remember watching my grandfather help my dad raise the roof of the garage to build the apartment." It was during the war when our country was just starting to come out of the great depression. My granddad was in his fifties, and, shortly after this very strenuous work, he suffered a slight heart attack and was told by a doctor to go home and get some rest. He and my grandmother did go home on the train, but a few months later, he had a fatal heart attack, and we had to ride the same train down to Mobile for his funeral. He had been a skillful carpenter in Mobile for many years and had built two large homes for his wife and five children to live in over the years.

After our two-day visit with Fannie, we drove back home where Mother called her doctor and told him that she was ready to have the knee replacement. He took a picture inside her left knee as he did the clipping of cartilage, and it was amazing to be able to see what he was doing with the tiny inserted camera. It would take several weeks for this knee to heal before they would proceed with the right knee replacement. Mother loved riding in the Yellow Sub, so we planned another trip while waiting for her first knee to heal. Amanda had purchased a dinette table from my brother's furniture store in Mobile while she was visiting that summer, so we decided to take it with us and drop it off in Virginia Beach. First we had to drive over to Mobile so Joe could pack it into the back of the station wagon, and then we had to pack in our suitcases and get underway on the day we left. First stop: Chattanooga, to pick up the Revelation tapes I ordered from the ministry. Second stop: Virginia Beach to drop off the dinette table. I think we may have stopped overnight a couple of times along the way; however, I do remember being pulled over and told by the Highway Patrol to hold it down to below 80. I was in a hurry to get to an appointment in Fairfax with Ralph regarding the escrow account and I also had an appointment in Maryland with our storage facility to get rid of some of our furniture. I also had a few other errands to run in the Washington, DC area.

When Greg learned that we were coming back up there to tend to some business, he asked if he could come back with us to visit his grandmothers and be with me while I was still in the country. He thought he could be of some help to his grandmother, Hannah, who was having health problems and was not eating well since she had lost her husband. Her neighbors had put her in the hospital a couple of times when she became ill from drinking a little too much of her favorite Port and not eating properly. Greg thought he could help her by being there to keep her company and doing the heavy work around the house. They were very much alike: Greg resembled her in appearance as well as his dad, and they both smoked and enjoyed working cross-word puzzles. They enjoyed watching TV and they both had a great sense of humor. They would be good for each other. Now that Greg was doing well and proved that he could hold a job and stay drug free, it just seemed like the right thing to do. I mentioned the possibility to Aunt Grace to see what she thought about it, and she, too, thought it might be good for both of them. Hannah didn't cook for herself as she had done for her family, and we reasoned that if Greg were there, she would rediscover the joy of cooking and start eating again. We thought this just might be enough to bring her out of depression.

John and I had been concerned about his mom staying in that large, two- story house alone with large utility bills, and there had been quite a few break-ins around the area. Instead of giving them separate financial assistance each month, it seemed sensible for them to share expenses and, at the same time, enjoy their lives together for as long as the plan worked. Hannah was a great business manager, and we knew she would do a good job of handling their finances. When I broached the subject of Greg's wish to come down for a while to be with her, she perked up and I noticed a gleam of hope in her eyes and in the tone of her voice. She always loved Greg and enjoyed all her grandchildren. I suggested that we try it out on an experimental basis while I was still around to help him move back to Virginia if, for some reason, the plan didn't work out. Greg promised to start working from her house as he was doing in Virginia with Purple Heart Vets, and he promised to get started with the Mississippi Department of Rehabilitation.

I had to see Ralph regarding his role as attorney for the escrow account and Greg's leaving the area, which sort of got Ralph off the hook. Second, I needed to go by our storage warehouse in Maryland to take a look at the furniture which had been picked up from Greg's apartment and much of it was damaged. I told them to just put it out for whoever wanted it to make room for our new German furniture which would be arriving from Germany at a later date. After doing this, Mother and I drove over to pick up Greg and all his things to move down to be with his grandmother in

Mississippi. Back on the eastern shore, Greg enjoyed seeing all the family before it was time for me to drive him up to his other grandmother's house in northern Mississippi. When I returned, it would be time for Mother's knee replacement.

Hannah was happy to see us and, as always when family was coming, she had cooked us a wonderful dinner. I stayed a few days to get the feeling of how it might work out for them together in that big house. Hannah's master bedroom was on the first floor and Greg would have the large bedroom upstairs right above her room. In addition, there was another large bedroom upstairs above the living room, but they would have to share the large old fashioned bathroom on the first floor. Also on the first floor, there was a nice dining room and a very large country kitchen in back with a large freezer and a very nice large backyard where she grew a few vegetables. While there, I did a little investigating to find out what was available in the area for Greg to continue his Rehab. There was a mental health clinic within walking distance with an AA program, including special counseling, in which I encouraged Greg to become involved. I also drove him over to meet the counselor, who had graduated from Ole Miss about the time John was there. I also drove over to the Baptist Church and spoke with a lady in the office about sending some young people over to meet Greg and invite him to church. I explained that he was new in town and needed to make some new friends. I was not able to learn anything about the State Rehab Program and thought his counselor with mental health would be able to advise him once he became involved.

Hannah and I shopped for new curtains for her high kitchen windows, and I hung them for her as she handed them up to me. They were beautiful! Then we stocked her pantry and freezer with food to last a while. Greg had his archery set up in the backyard in a safe place with restrung bow, new arrows and a bundle of hay on which to place the target. Hannah was growing tomatoes and a few other vegetables and flowers in her backyard, and, most importantly, she was cooking again and getting her appetite back! Everything was looking good, and they seemed quite happy about their new lifestyle together. Finally, I had to leave for home and it was time to say our goodbyes. I would telephone them periodically and Hannah would call me if there was a problem. I left them with a great feeling of hope.

Mother's full joint replacement was performed the third week of November, and, once again, the two of us were together in the hospital on Thanksgiving Day, the day I was born back in 1936. She placed an order for my Thanksgiving Dinner to be served along with hers in her private room. We enjoyed that day together and the hospital food was exceptionally good. In fact, I ate most of my meals that week right there in the hospital cafeteria during Mother's stay in the hospital. Mother's doctor had assured me before the surgery that he would build her a solid joint which would last the rest of her life whether she lost any weight or not. He told me that Mother became conscious enough during surgery to ask what all the hammering was about. He laughed and said, *"We're building a house!"* She was walking the very next day with a walker. We had her room all ready for her to come home with a new innerspring mattress, a TV for her bedroom, and a *pottie chair* and *a wheelchair* close to her bed. The worst part of the whole ordeal was the physical therapy, which Mother had to endure every other day to keep her knee from freezing up. Her therapist had to push her leg back as far as he could, but, as Mother said later, those few brief moments of excruciating pain were well worth it. She could walk and climb stairs with no pain whatsoever and had full use of both her legs. It was wonderful to see her recovering so well.

To get all our family together with John's mom in northern Mississippi for Christmas, I bought Maggie a round-trip ticket to Atlanta and left Mother in the care of my two brothers and their families. I took off early on the morning of Maggie's afternoon arrival and couldn't believe my eyes when I saw her exiting from the plane. She had worn an old sloppy pair of jeans underneath the beautiful apricot leather jacket with the dark brown furry collar, which had been part of her college wardrobe. I was so disheartened to see it worn so sloppily over her jeans that I completely forgot that I was almost out of gas and failed to gas up before I got on the beltway around Atlanta. We ran out of gas in all that heavy traffic, and I had to pull over to the middle safe zone to get out of it. And as I pulled over, I said loudly to Maggie, *"Don't get out of the car!"* Immediately, she flung open the door, ran around the car and climbed upon the high cement medium which divided the two sides of the five lanes going the speed limit in both directions. Thank goodness she was not killed! Two highway patrolmen stopped and blocked off the fast lanes of traffic passing us while they put enough gas in our tank to get us off the beltway. They accompanied us to a service station where we filled up the gas tank and proceeded on our way.

I had brought all my Christian tapes with me for a well-planned Christmas program which I tried to share with my family while I had them all together. I had told them to bring their Bibles so we could have a family devotional and celebrate the Lord's birthday. However, my plan was not very well received, and I could tell by the looks on their faces that this was not what they had in mind. Anyway, I proceeded to play my Christian tapes, and I'm glad I did because I knew that I had good messages that they needed to hear and this might be my only chance to plant some good seed in the good soil of their hearts. I believe that God was working even then in their lives, and I had to trust the Holy Spirit to do his work. I needed to hold on to God's promise that my whole house would be saved, and I had to let go and allow God to do His work knowing that His word would not return void. (Isaiah 55:11)

We enjoyed Hannah's wonderful Christmas dinner tremendously, and I helped where I could in serving and cleaning up. She assured me that everything was all right with Greg remaining with her throughout the spring when John and I were planning to be back to re-evaluate the situation. It was great having all the kids together for Christmas and spending this precious time together with their grandmother. We missed John, of course, but we would have him with us many times in the years to follow. Of course, I had to detour back over to Atlanta to put Maggie on her plane back to Norfolk, but this time, I made sure I had plenty of gas. Mother was doing very well when I returned home and was able to maneuver the two steps into her living room without pain. My sister-in-law, Ginger, had driven her back and forth to physical therapy every other day, and now the sessions were down to only twice a week. She was expected to do her simple leg raises and knee bends at home each day to keep her joints flexible.

After a short time at home with Mother resuming her therapy sessions, it was time for me to call Litton and set up my flight to Riyadh. John was beginning to wonder if I was ever coming over at all, and he was tired of living by himself in our large two-story house with no one there to help him. I made sure Mother was well stocked with food and left her with a freshly made bed and a clean house. I knew Ginger would make sure she got to the rest of her therapy sessions and doctor's appointments. Her neighbors and family were always dropping by for visits, so I knew she wouldn't be too lonely. I would continue to write her about all our travels and family updates. After saying all my goodbyes to the family one more time, Mother and Ginger drove me to the airport and saw me off on my first trip to Saudi Arabia.

The Christmas Story

Prophecy, 700 BC, Isaiah 7:14: *"Therefore a virgin shall conceive and bear a Son, and shall call his name Immanuel;"* which means, *"God with us."*

Matthew 1:21: *"And she shall bring forth a Son, and thou shall call his name Jesus, for he shall save his people from their sins."*

Prophecy 700 BC, Isaiah 9:6-7: *"For unto us a child is born; unto us a Son is given; and the government shall be upon his shoulder; and his name shall be called: Wonderful Counselor, Mighty God, the everlasting Father, and Prince of Peace. Of the increase of his government and peace, there shall be no end."*

Luke 2:1-20: *"And it came to pass in those days that there went out a decree from Caesar Augustus that all the world should be taxed… And Joseph also went up from Galilee… to be taxed with Mary, his espoused wife being great with child. And so it was, the days were accomplished that she should be delivered. And she brought forth her firstborn son, and wrapped him in swaddling clothes and laid him in a manger because there was no room for them in the inn.*

"And there were shepherds abiding in the fields, keeping watch over their flock by night. And lo, the angel of the Lord came upon them, and the glory of the Lord shown round about them, and they were very much afraid. And the angel said unto them, 'Fear not, for behold, I bring you tidings of great joy, which shall be to all people: For unto you is born this day in the city of David a Savior, which is Christ the Lord. And this shall be a sign unto you, ye shall find the babe wrapped in swaddling clothes, lying in a manger.'

"And suddenly there was with the angel a multitude of the heavenly host praising God and saying, 'Glory to God in the highest and on earth peace and good will toward men.' And the shepherds came with haste and found Mary and Joseph and the babe lying in a manger."

Prophecy regarding the birth of Jesus: Luke 2:25-35: *"And behold, there was a man in Jerusalem whose name was Simeon, a just and devout man waiting for the consolation of Israel, and the Holy Ghost was upon him; and it was revealed unto him that he should not see death until he had seen the Lord's Christ. He came by the Spirit unto the temple when the parents brought Jesus in for the custom of the law. He took Jesus in his arms and blessed God saying 'Let thy servant depart in peace according to thy word for my eyes have seen thy salvation... a light to lighten the Gentiles and the glory of thy people, Israel.' Then he blessed Mary and Joseph and said to Mary, 'Behold, this child is set for the fall and rising again of many in Israel, and for a sign which shall be spoken against; (Yea, a sword shall pierce through thy own soul also) that the thoughts of many hearts may be revealed.'"*

Witness, John the Baptist: John 1:29-36: *"When John saw Jesus coming unto him for baptism, he said, 'Behold, the Lamb of God who takes away the sin of the world...' John bare record, saying, 'I saw the Spirit descending from heaven like a dove and it abode upon him... I bare record that this is the Son of God... I baptize with water, but he will baptize with the Holy Ghost and with fire.' The next day, he and two of his disciples stood looking at Jesus as he walked, and again, John said, 'Behold the Lamb of God.'"*

Isaiah 45:5-8: *"I am the Lord and there is none other, there is no God beside me: I girded thee, though thou hast not known me: that they may know from the rising of the sun; and from the west; that there is none beside me. I am the Lord, and there is none else. I form the light and create darkness: I make peace and create evil: I, the Lord, do all these things. Drop down, ye heavens from above and let the skies pour down righteousness: let the earth open, and let them bring forth salvation, and let righteousness spring up together; I the Lord have created it."*

Isaiah 15:9-13: *"Woe unto him that striveth with his Maker! ... Shall the clay say to him who fashioned it, 'What makest thou?'... Woe unto him that saith to his father, 'What begettest thou?' or to the woman, 'What hast thou brought forth?' Thus says the Lord, the Holy One of Israel, and his Maker, 'Ask me of things to come concerning my sons, and concerning the work of my hands command ye me. I have made the earth and created man upon it: I, even my hands, have stretched out the heavens, and all their host have I commanded. I have raised him up in righteousness, and I will direct all his ways.'"*

<u>John 3:5:</u> *"Verily, verily, I say unto thee, except a man be born of water and of the Spirit, he cannot see the kingdom of God... that which is born of the flesh is flesh, and that which is born of the Spirit is spirit."*

<u>John 3:16:</u> *"For God so loved the world that he gave his only begotten Son that whosoever believeth in him should not perish, but have everlasting life.*

For God sent his Son into the world not to condemn the world; but that the world through him might be saved."

<u>This is the Gospel:</u> *The Good News!! Hallelujah!!*

CHAPTER NINETEEN

An Introduction to Saudi Arabia

1984

My Pan Am flight from Atlanta arrived at London's Heathrow Airport early on the morning of January 12, 1984, and my connecting flight to Riyadh on Saudia Airlines was scheduled for mid-afternoon. It was cold in the airport, so I went shopping for a sweater to make my wait a little more comfortable. All I could find in the gift shops were sweat shirts covered with London motifs, so I bought one. Then I walked around looking for a good restaurant where I could relax and order breakfast or dinner. I chose a *Roast Beef Dinner and Vegetables,* something very *English* to go with my new sweat shirt and my growing appetite. The time passed quickly, and I found my way over to the International boarding dock at the very end of Heathrow where I was able to board almost immediately. I arrived in Riyadh at the King Khalid International Airport about four hours later. It turned out to be a good flight with a very good meal on Saudia Airlines. The passengers were mostly Saudis, foreign workers or family members coming into the country. When I entered the terminal, John was standing outside customs looking in through the door with a crowd of other spectators there to meet someone. First, we had to get in the right line for our customs check, and then our baggage was opened and searched to make sure we weren't bringing anything in which might be forbidden. If we had magazines, they used a black marker to cover all flesh which wasn't allowed to be exposed such as arms and legs, etc. They allowed my Christian books and Bible to come in after looking through them and finding no pictures.

Finally, my ordeal of entering Saudi Arabia for the first time was over, and, as I exited customs, John was able to take over my baggage and lead me to the car. On the way out of the airport, we encountered a dust storm and pulled over to the side of the road to wait for it to pass, which took about five minutes. John said it was a usual occurrence which happened mostly at night and rarely during the day. When we finally arrived at our house, I found the evidence of dust storms all over the house, especially upstairs and under all the furniture downstairs. It looked like no one had ever vacuumed the upstairs since John moved in a few months ago. On the way, he pointed out a landmark on the corner where we always had to turn to get to our compound: a wrecked car which had been there for months. John said that drivers of all ages would wreck their cars, pull them off the road and leave them there at the wreckage site. It took the Saudi Government several years to develop a good plan for removing these wrecks, but eventually they did. During our stay in Saudi Arabia, we would see many more.

I was surprised to find a very nice two-story house in a secure neighborhood, in a compound of other houses very similar to ours inside a gated area. He showed me around the house and the downstairs bedroom, where he had been sleeping, right behind the kitchen. He never went upstairs where all the other bedrooms were located because all the living area he needed was right there, and very compact the way he liked it, and very convenient for getting ready for work each morning. Since he was not ready for sleep that evening, and I was so tired from jet-lag, I went upstairs to crawl into bed where it was nice and quiet. However, the dirt seemed to be everywhere, especially inside my bed between the sheets. I tried brushing it out with my hands, but to no avail, so I gave up and crawled in anyway. Somehow, I fell asleep and the next thing I knew it was morning. After finding my way around the kitchen for breakfast, I found the vacuum cleaner and gave the upstairs a good cleaning before unpacking any of my clothes.

Then it was time to take stock of the kitchen to see what I would need for cooking the meals and getting the house in order. We had a small building across the street which also served as a convenience store, a quick-stop restaurant and a recreation area. John walked me around to meet a few people and buy a few groceries, and introduced me to the very small recreation center, which seemed to be the meeting place for the whole compound. It had a pool table where the guys often met in the evenings or on weekends to challenge one another in a game of pool. However, with my long grocery list, I needed to find a large grocery store. Eventually I got to know the other wives and joined them on weekly shopping trips into town to Safeway or the large European shopping center, *Euro Marche*, which had everything from groceries to household goods and clothing. On one of my first trips out to the downtown area, we decided to have lunch at McDonald's, and I totally forgot about having to sit in the family section. After picking a table right in the middle of the restaurant and sitting down to eat, one of the TCN's who worked there came over to politely usher us upstairs to the family section. That was something we had a hard time getting used to, but we finally got the message after a few embarrassing moments. These workers were very polite and they also seemed a little embarrassed to have to ask us to move, but they had a job to do to keep us in our place. I sometimes took my camera along to take pictures from the bus, in case I had an opportunity.

The first thing I had to learn before venturing outside the compound was very important: I had to learn the proper dress code of Saudi Arabia. Women had to be properly *covered,* or they could be switched by the Saudi religious police, the *Matawah,* for not having their heads covered or exposing their arms or legs. In that case, the husband or father of the uncovered woman could be picked up and put in jail. As soon as I could go shopping for *an abaya,* I purchased a pretty black one trimmed in gold, which I believe was supposed to be worn on very dressy occasions. However, since I didn't know any better, I began wearing it every time I went shopping or out in public with the black matching head scarf to cover my head. After a while, I realized that we could get by with long, modest dresses having long sleeves, or long pants, even without the head scarf if we had short hair. The younger wives with long hair tried to be covered whenever they were out for fear of the Matawa with their switches to chase them down the street. The Saudis hated to see the abaya worn sloppily over jeans or short dresses which might expose the legs.

One of my new friends on the compound was a hair stylist and did a great job of cutting my hair and later gave me a good frosting. Since we were both interested in prophecy, we enjoyed our conversations and shared our Christian books and tapes. Both of us had read <u>The Late Great Planet Earth,</u> by Hal Lindsey, and shared what we had brought with us of his entire paperback book collection. John signed me up for a pool tournament at the recreation center across the street from our house, although I wasn't aware of it and really didn't know the rules of the game. However, when time came for the *tournament,* I walked across the street to watch him play and found myself *paired up for the start of the game.* It was incredible!

I won the first two games! Then, in the third game, my eight ball rolled into the pocket a bit too soon, and I became *disqualified*. Art, John's boss on the compound, won the tournament!

Towards the end of February, we had a dinner party, and I served our favorite *Arabic Moussaka, salad, pita bread* and our own version of *Saudi Champagne,* a mixture of *Orange-Mango Tang and Perrier*. This was followed by coffee and *Mandarin Dessert*. James McFarland, John's boss from Frankfurt, was in Riyadh at the time, and it was all very casual. I think everyone enjoyed the food and the mixture of people. We invited just about everyone on the compound, especially all those who had invited John to dinner before my arrival, so we decided to have more dinner parties until we had invited everyone at least once. When Bill, one of the older guys, brought an alcoholic beverage to the house for John to try out and John said it wasn't good, Bill opened our kitchen door and threw the concoction out into the backyard. We had determined that we would not get involved in making *sidiki,* the alcoholic beverage some tried to make in their bathroom stills because alcohol was illegal in Saudi Arabia, and some who tried to get away with it were expelled from the country.

Art, a retired Marine, and his wife, Ellene, returned from their *Around the World* trip after vacationing in Hawaii and told us about their stay at *Hale Koa,* the newly completed luxury hotel at Ft. DeRussey. They said it was wonderful, and Art signed us up for two rooms for a week in June. We decided to do as they did and made reservations for the Pan Am *"Around the World"* special. I needed to be in Virginia for Greg's hearing in May and also to help Maggie move her things into mini-storage, so she could accompany us to Hawaii. Since she was still eligible to come over as a college student under the age of 22, we thought she might like to visit us in Saudi Arabia for the rest of her summer vacation. John would leave in June to join us for the trip to Hawaii and parts of Asia on the remainder of the trip back to Riyadh. However, we hadn't heard back from Maggie about the possibility of this plan, and it sounded as though she didn't want to make the trip. Since we already had family reservations for two rooms, we invited Grace and George to accompany us to Hale Koa if Maggie chose not to go. George had served in WWII for the US Army driving supplies into the Battle of the Bulge, and Grace had always been like a big sister to John being only 13 years older. They had never been to Hawaii, and the four of us had always enjoyed traveling together.

Another friend, Ethel, invited me over for coffee one morning to tell me about their wonderful trip through Greece and suggested that we call our travel agent and book this same tour through Greek Organized Tours. She said it was the most wonderful experience of their life and raved about the land tour as well as their wonderful cruise of the Aegean Sea. She said prices were very good from Saudi Arabia being this close to Greece, and their tour guides were excellent. John and I followed through with Ethyl's advice and made our reservations with G.O. Tours for both of these wonderful excursions in August. The land tour would be first with a two-day stopover in Athens, and then the cruise of the Aegean Sea would begin on Monday morning of the second week.

As time approached for me to leave on the 2nd of May for the States, I had an uneasy feeling about Maggie. Something was wrong! She had not responded to my letter telling her about Hawaii. When I finally got to Norfolk, I found out the reason why. I took one look at her and knew she was sick again. The door handle on the driver's side of the car looked like it had side-swiped something. I couldn't open the door and had to crawl in from the other side. "What happened?" I asked. I didn't wait for an answer but looked up AA in the telephone directory and called the number for help. They helped me get her into *Serenity Lodge*, another 28-day alcohol recovery program in Norfolk. Somehow, she had made it through the last semester and passed her courses. Again, she seemed relieved to be in *Recovery*, so I left her there in the program, turned in my rental car and drove the Malibu down to Mobile to have it repaired and repainted. Serenity Lodge was very much like her first AA recovery program at Melwood Farms two years earlier, and the leaders were very professional just as the others had been. They did a tremendous job of bringing Maggie through the program, and this time, her sobriety would last!

When John arrived early in June, we drove up to see how Hannah and Greg were doing and learned that his court hearing was postponed until a later date. So we decided to take both of them with us on our trip to Norfolk since we were encouraged to attend a few days of Maggie's AA program. We had plenty of room since we had to bring both cars with us to return the Malibu to Amanda's house for Maggie's use when she finished the program, and we appreciated their company on the way up. The four of us stayed in two rooms of a nearby Norfolk motel and attended several days of the Al Anon and AA meetings because, as we learned before in Maggie's first program, the family also needs to be involved in treatment.

Then we drove Hannah and Greg back home, leaving Maggie to finish the program. She had already made the decision to move into a half-way house upon its completion because she was encouraged to work and attend AA meetings for the rest of the summer. Hannah assured us that she and Greg were doing well together that summer, and John and I had reservations in Hawaii starting the 23rd of June. For the interim, we would be at Mother's house if they needed us.

Mother seemed happy to have us back home again for the short time we had to spend with her that summer, and we tried to get her house in order because she had received so much of our mail it had begun to pile up. I stored a few things in her large hall closet and left some clothes hanging in the bedroom closet for our use when we returned. It seemed to work out well because I could give her house a good cleaning while I was there, and she could tell me what to do with her plants, which were too heavy for her to move around anymore. However, our time was short this time because of our previously scheduled *Around the World* flight back to Riyadh and our vacation in Hawaii plus three overnight stops in Japan, Hong Kong and Singapore.

A Tour of Hawaii

Since our scheduled flight for San Francisco was out of New Orleans, John and I decided to go over a couple of days early to visit *The 1984 World's Fair.* We rode street cars around New Orleans and saw a few of the Exhibitions at the World's Fair, but all of this had to be cut short: our Pan American flight out of New Orleans left at 7:30 am on Saturday and was scheduled to arrive in San Francisco around noon. Since Maggie was unable to fly with us to Hawaii, we were scheduled to meet up with Grace and George in San Francisco later that afternoon at the airport. And, since John and I were so early, we caught a bus to *Fisherman's Wharf,* where we had a fish dinner at a very nice seafood restaurant. Across the street we discovered a lovely park overlooking San Francisco Bay and the Island of Alcatraz, where some of our worst criminals had once been imprisoned. We finally met up with Grace and George at the airport terminal and boarded our Boeing 747 about an hour later. We arrived in Honolulu around 7:00 pm and loaded our baggage into a taxi, where we had what was probably the scariest taxi ride of our lives through the fast-paced Hawaiian traffic to our hotel at Waikiki.

We were very impressed with this luxurious military hotel, *Hale Koa*, which was built at the site of old Ft. De Russey, where John and I had met on his R&R in 1970. After a good night's sleep, we were all up bright and early to watch the sunrise and to attend the *Welcome Breakfast*, where we were briefed on all the activities and available tours on the Island of Oahu. Within a couple of hours, we planned our entire week and booked our reservations. First on the agenda: *the Arizona Memorial!* We had to hurry to catch our ride to Pearl Harbor, where we saw the original film of the Japanese attack. Then we rode out to the memorial in small boats to stand on the platform above the USS Arizona where over 1,100 of our sailors remain buried inside her hull. It is always a very somber and awesome experience to stand on this memorial with the pungent smell of oil and gasoline to remind us of what happened on this spot almost eight decades ago! On our trip back to Waikiki, we visited *Diamond Head* and the *National Cemetery.* That Sunday evening, we ended our first day in Hawaii with dinner at the Polynesian Palace and found the star of the show very entertaining. We started off with Mai Tais and then a delicious dinner buffet before the show started at 9:30 pm and ended about an hour later. We were glad to retire to our beds a short time later after a very long day.

On Monday morning, John and I were surprised to learn that George had already enjoyed what was to become his regular morning routine, a walk on the beach before breakfast. The four of us would meet every morning in the Hale Koa *Coffee House,* where we became addicted to the wonderful macadamia nut pancakes and the heavenly coconut syrup, which came with the *Big Breakfast.* This became a habit with us as our way to start the day. John and George left on the morning shuttle to the golf course that second morning, while Grace and I walked down to the International Market Place to do a little shopping and have lunch. We visited a store where we received a gift of Chinese script written on beautiful red paper by a very charming Chinese lady using a brush pen and black India ink. We purchased different kinds of shell jewelry and table mats made from the dark brown beans of a Hawaiian tree to take home with us. Later, John and I found a couple of hard bound books of beautiful Hawaii to send home to our mothers. That evening, we walked over to the Hilton Hawaiian Village for the Don Ho Show which was a lot of fun and quite entertaining. While waiting for the show to begin, we were served Mai Tais and a fantastic dinner of grilled Mahi Mahi and Shrimp.

Tuesday morning, we caught the bus for *Paradise Park* and enjoyed the scenic drive as well as the beautiful jungle gardens and rainforest with many exotic birds and exquisite flowers. That afternoon while walking on rocks of Waikiki beach, I lost one of my *aqua jellies,* and it seemed to get lost in the undercurrent and was carried out to sea. I gave up looking for it and considered it lost! That evening, we enjoyed a beautiful sunset dinner cruise on board the *Alii Kai,* a large catamaran off the coast of Oahu, while enjoying the lovely scenic beauty of Waikiki and Diamond Head. We enjoyed the Polynesian singers and dancers during the evening show and also the popular dance music which followed. The sunset was spectacular! We returned to the Hale Koa rather early, so we walked down to the Hilton Hawaiian Village to see what was going on at the beach pavilion. The female singer John and I had enjoyed so much back in 1970 was no longer there. We missed her but enjoyed the music of a small combo and bought a round of drinks to sit at a table.

On Wednesday morning, Grace and George had booked the Polynesian Cultural Center, which turned out to be spectacular and we should have gone with them. However, John talked me into catching the 8:00 am golf shuttle to Schofield Barracks Golf Course, where he played 18 holes with three other golfers. I drove the golf cart. While they were putting on the green, I accidently backed the golf cart into a hedge just as the lady golfer was beginning to putt. Of course it made a terrible noise which really upset her. John thought she was going to have a fit. I thought I should have gone with Grace and George! That evening at dinner, they told us about their marvelous all-day experience becoming part of historical Hawaii and blending in with the Polynesian people in their native villages. They really got into the atmosphere of old Hawaii and were part of a gigantic *Luau,* which included a parade of villagers coming down the river in canoes with chants and fireworks. They enjoyed hula dancers, knife and flame dancers, Hawaiian singing and the beautiful Hawaiian music. Although John and I had quickly walked through the Polynesian Cultural Center with the kids back in 1975, we had missed this wonderful all-day experience. We must go back again someday and take part in this fabulous all-day adventure.

While taking his walk early Thursday morning, George found my aqua slipper which had washed up on the beach. After breakfast, we walked downtown to see the Kodak Hula Show and then over to the famous old Royal Hawaiian Hotel, which is still very beautiful and very well cared for even today. We walked over to the zoo and found a beautiful park to explore. Then we headed back to the Hale Koa where we got in some beach time before our next scheduled event. Our *Luau* started at 5:30 pm with cocktails and music on the grassy lawn before the serving of the traditional food, *poi and raw fish*, which everyone is encouraged to at least try once. Then, of course, the roasted pig was served with yams, vegetables and fresh fruits, topped off with coconut pudding cake. All of this traditional Hawaiian food was delicious, *except for the poi and raw fish*, for which one has to develop a taste. All the entertainment was spectacular with hula dancers, flame and knife dancers, and, of course, people from the audience who were called up on the stage to learn the hula. It was all fun and entertaining! We took our fresh fruit back to our rooms to add to our fruit collection, which was rapidly accumulating. Grace had a great plan for it later on. Again, it was early, so we walked back down to the Hilton Hawaiian Village to hear the music at the beach pavilion.

Friday morning, John and I were up early to catch our ride to the airport at 6:00 am for our all-day adventure: *The Panorama Air Tour* of all the islands starting with the *Big Island of Hawaii.* Our air tour would take us around the islands in a small plane, and sitting across from the pilot in the other front seat, was a small boy of about six. We flew down into the *Valley Isle of Maui*, where we had a bus tour of the island and stopped for lunch. As we got back into the plane to take off again, the little guy threw up and there had to be a clean up before we could take off again. I volunteered to move up front to take his seat for a better view while he sat in back with his parents looking out a side window. Next, we stopped in the *Garden Isle of Kauai*, where we enjoyed a ride in a small boat up the *Wailua River* to the famous *Fern Grotto*. It was very beautiful and we were able to stop for pictures. Again back in the air, we flew over coffee plantations, macadamia nut farms, pineapple fields, water falls, lava fields, leper colonies and cliffs descending hundreds of feet straight down to the ocean. We flew through valleys of tree topped mountain ranges and into canyons and were amazed at the beautiful changing coastline with its secret coves and lagoons.

Our plane was small and held only nine passengers, but the pilot was very good and tilted the plane so that all on board could see and have clear shots for some really great pictures. He flew us over *Mauna Loa* and down into the crater of *Kilauea*, a live volcano, which was erupting at the time with lava flowing out of it in several directions. On the way home, we had a fantastic view of Pearl Harbor and saw what the Japanese pilots had seen on that fateful day in 1941 when they took our US ships by surprise while they were safely docked in its harbor; outstanding, of course, is the Arizona Memorial representing all the ships lost that day and the sailors who remain buried in their hulls. It was a terrific day for John and me, and it was truly an experience we will never forget. Grace and George also had a very enjoyable day visiting *Sea Life Park at Makapuu Point* where dolphins, whales and sea lions perform in a fantastic sea show, which we and the kids had seen on our previous vacation in 1975. They also visited *the Reef Tank Exhibit and some really great museums while there at the Point.* When we arrived back at the Hale Koa, Grace and George were ready to take us out to a restaurant they had discovered just around the corner for a wonderful Mahi Mahi dinner.

On Saturday morning, we enjoyed our *Big Breakfast* and then got in some beach time before the guys watched an afternoon baseball game on TV. Grace and I wrote cards to send home with our mementoes to family members and also watched a little TV. Then we took a walk on the beach where we discovered a sign for church services on Sunday morning at 10:30. That evening we all enjoyed another Hale Koa Special: *A Salute to Hawaii's Silver Jubilee*, with a very talented lady singer who sang all the old traditional and patriotic songs of Hawaii and the USA. The dinner buffet that evening was exceptional and the show tremendous.

Sunday morning, we got up very early to have breakfast with George, who had booked himself for a special tour he wanted to take up to *Mt. Tantalus and Round Top National Park*. Around 10:00, Grace and I walked down the beach to the Hilton Hawaiian Village for the church service on the beach, *Sun and Soul Talk*. It was terrific! We sat on our beach mats and listened to spiritual songs and interesting testimonies of some of the visitors on the beach. Then a young minister gave a very meaningful sermon. Afterwards, Grace and I walked up and down the beach and enjoyed the water and sun while John enjoyed a TV golf tournament. Then we washed the fruit we had been collecting, and Grace made us a delicious fruit salad to enjoy outside on our balcony overlooking Diamond Head, our last afternoon together in Hawaii. That evening, we enjoyed a fantastic dinner in the *Banyan Tree Show Room* of the Hale Koa followed by *Tama's Polynesian Show* at 8:00. It was terrific and probably the high light of the week! We had the center front table in the midst of all the performers, who were mostly lovely young Hawaiian girls ranging in age from about 6 all the way up to maybe 15 or so. They were adorable and very talented as they performed various types of dances and chants to the sounds of Polynesian music. There were also hula dancers and knife and flame twirlers who also performed with chants. An older Hawaiian woman sang in the background while Tama, the Master of Ceremonies, sang the lead with a group of background singers. The show ended with the girls coming down into the audience to place leis over our heads and give us kisses on the cheek. What a beautiful way to end our very special Hawaiian vacation.

On Monday morning, July 2nd, we were all very sad when it was time for our pick up to the airport for John and me to catch our scheduled Pan Am flight for the remainder of our *Around the World* trip back to Riyadh with overnight stays in Japan, Hong Kong and Singapore to break up the long journey. John wanted me to get a taste of the Orient, which he had enjoyed on his first R&R from Vietnam to Hong Kong. We had our reservations and were looking forward to seeing a few more places we had never seen before and getting a taste of the different kinds of food and the uniquely different countries. However, John got on the phone and cancelled all our reservations, so we could be with Grace and George the rest of the day and see them off at 4:30 pm when they were scheduled to leave. This was a big mistake because our extremely long flight around over half the world took about 28 hours and was the most miserable flight of our lives, with entrees being served every four hours all the way from Honolulu to Riyadh. I had no idea just how large the circumference of Planet Earth until this very lengthy and tiresome trip.

CHAPTER TWENTY

Around the World
Back to Riyadh

1984

John and I were very sad to leave Hawaii on Wednesday morning, July 4th. We had such a wonderful time with Grace and George and also with our family back in 1975 before we left the country on our way to Morocco. We would have loved staying over another few days to enjoy all the activities of the Fourth, however, we had to make our rescheduled *Around The World* flight back to Riyadh. Our pick up time was 8:30 am, so we had to hurry with breakfast, get our baggage downstairs in the lobby and check out of the hotel. In our haste to be ready for pick up, John forgot his suit hanging in the closet. While checking our baggage at the airport, he remembered his suit, and I quickly got on the phone and called the hotel to have them send it to us by taxi. It arrived within the hour, and the taxi driver also presented us with a lovely Hawaiian flower. We left Honolulu at 11:30 am, stopped 2 hours in Tokyo; 1 hour in Hong Kong; 1 hour in Singapore; with an 11-hour time change between Hawaii and Riyadh. We lost a whole day when we crossed the *International Date Line*, and we finally arrived back in Riyadh at 4:20 am on Friday, the 6th of July. If we had it to do all over again, we would leave our original Itinerary as it was in the beginning visiting Japan, Hong Kong and Singapore for a total of three overnights to break up our extremely long trip. It would have made our Around the World Pan Am ticket more worthwhile and much more enjoyable.

Before John left the first of June to join me in the States, the Litton group had decided it was time to move from the Al Manar Compound, which had been built by Phillip Holzmann for Litton employees, over to a larger compound in Riyadh. They had to make room for a larger group of Litton employees coming over in July, as some of our present group would be phasing out and moving back to the States. It was good planning to keep the group of incoming families together on the same compound for the convenience of providing them with transportation while they learned their way around their new environment. They scheduled the move for a few days after our home trip, so we visited a few of the other compounds where we could be assigned and selected the one we thought best: the ROC Compound, built by Rashid & Omran Company, a much larger compound with a very nice restaurant, medical facilities and a convenience store. Since this plan to move was in the process while we were away, it was news to me after our return that we were scheduled to move that week. In spite of having to readjust to the time change and a terrible headache caused by *jet lag,* we had to get organized for the move to the ROC. It would be rather easy because we had used up practically all our food, and, since we had just returned, we left our clothes packed in suitcases so they could be easily transported over to the ROC. The rest of our household goods were taken over in boxes. All we had to do was unpack our suitcases, wash our clothes and hang them up or put them away in the chests of drawers. We had to get resettled quickly in our new compound and prepare for our next upcoming trip in August. We were extremely tired but kept ourselves awake all day Friday to adjust to the new time zone, hoping to be able to sleep our first night back in Riyadh; however, that was not to be the case!

John came home from work with some terribly disturbing news which kept us both awake all night. His mom's house burned to the ground early Thursday evening, ironically the day we lost due to crossing the International Date Line. John's brother, Mark, called him at work that afternoon to tell him about it. Everyone was all right, but the house was a total loss! Hannah had come home after attending a funeral and turned on the light switch to enter the house and fire shot down through the electrical circuit. She found Greg attempting to come down the stairs without his prosthesis to get away from the fire, which was rapidly spreading through the house. Somehow, by the grace of God, she was able to lead him the rest of the way down the stairs and out the front door. Thank goodness they were both able to escape the fire without injury!

Mark said his mom was hysterical when he spoke with her, but her insurance would pay off the full amount and he thought she would build a smaller house on the same lot or move to one of the newly completed senior citizen apartments in town. For the present, she was staying with her next door neighbor, Geraldine, until something could be worked out. To say the least, John and I were very concerned about his mom and wondered what we could do to help her rebuild from that distance. John called her the following day at Geraldine's house using the same number Mark had given him, which seemed to relieve her somewhat of the anxiety she was feeling. For the present, we had the responsibility of moving from one compound to the other and getting resettled before we could make another trip back to the States.

When we were finally able to make the trip home a few months later, we found John's mom, Hannah, living nicely in a one-bedroom apartment in the senior citizen housing development. Grace and George had driven down with their family members to help Hannah get resettled, and they made sure she had everything she needed. The ladies of the Baptist Church also came to her rescue, and soon she found herself taking minutes at church meetings. She developed many new friendships and became great friends with Ruby Gaye, one of the ladies of the church, who was also a widow about her age and had her own car to drive them wherever they needed to go. The two of them took us to their favorite restaurant for a great catfish dinner, which became a tradition whenever we visited Hannah over the next few years. Ruby Gaye came over often, and they did their grocery shopping together every week. They also attended church regularly and really seemed to enjoy each other's company. The Chief of Police of the small town just happened to be one of John's cousins, and he also watched out for Hannah and drove her to Memphis on several occasions and later to the hospital.

Hannah had been a heavy smoker most of her life, and we were very surprised and happy to learn that she had quit smoking! She looked healthy and seemed to feel so much better. Now she was involved with the ladies of the Baptist Church and went on many excursions with them, and later joined them on a fantastic trip to Europe. She had furnished her living room nicely with a sturdy sleeper couch, end tables, lamps and a very comfortable recliner, where she spent most of her evenings enjoying her crewel embroidery and her new stereo and TV. Her new deep freezer was full of frozen food, her kitchen cabinets were stocked with canned goods and all the glassware and dishes she needed, so all we had to do was thaw out something for dinner and cook it. We noticed, though, that her nice large bedroom was still void of furniture, so John and I went downtown shopping for the perfect bedroom suite. We found it on sale in the window of a local furniture store, and it fit in beautifully. It gave her the drawer space she needed for all her clothes, material and sewing equipment and provided her with a bedroom.

She had been sleeping on the sleeper couch in the living room. We left Hannah feeling good about her life in her small, but quite safe, apartment and all her new friends.

Greg was another concern for John and me, but there was nothing we could do about it. We knew that God had a plan for him, too, and it was all in his hands. On the day of the fire, Greg was taken to an alcohol treatment facility in a nearby city because there was no other place for him to go. We found out the truth of what happened that day many years later as Greg recalled the details of what precipitated the fire. When he called his attorneys about his lawsuit against the Metro, he learned that it had been thrown out of court, and he was so distraught that he got a friend to drive him across the Mississippi State line into Alabama to buy some rum. Hannah had gone to a funeral that day when he started drinking upstairs in his bedroom. He dropped a lighted cigarette onto his bed and wasn't able to pick it up in time to keep it from catching fire. He said the fan blowing overhead whipped up the flames. He couldn't put the fire out and was trying to get down the stairs when his grandmother came home and pulled him down the rest of the way and out through the front door. He said he found himself sitting in a police car watching the fire burn as he came out of a blackout and remembered asking someone for a cigarette. Thank God Hannah came home when she did, or Greg would have been a casualty of the fire. She saved his life!

Back in Riyadh, as I had always done in other countries, I joined the English Speaking Women's Club of Riyadh, along with many of my friends of the Al Manar and ROC Compounds. These meetings were held in beautiful palaces with some very interesting guest speakers and wonderful Arabic-style dinners served lavishly with well-set tables of pita bread, dips, and condiments. This would be followed by dinner starting with soup or salad, and then a delicious entrée with some kind of vegetables, and always ending with a very specially prepared dessert. Usually the guest speaker would begin her talk during the serving of desserts and coffee or tea. I remember vividly one of the guest speakers, a prestigious Saudi Arabian lady doctor, who spoke about *The Day*, in which all the Saudi women, in a pre- devised plan, took the keys from their drivers and just took off and started driving over the streets of Riyadh. Of course, the men put a stop to it immediately and rebuked the ladies and their well-organized plan. As far as I know, it has never happened again. This very articulate speaker shared many humorous stories about the first time she treated a Saudi male, who didn't believe in women doctors. It was hilarious! Usually, *the Litton ladies* sat together at dinner and sort of branched out afterwards to speak with other English-speaking women from all over the world. It was very interesting to meet these ladies and hear about their experiences, where they were from and what they were doing in Saudi Arabia. It was fun to meet them, and we had some really great conversations.

When we first moved to the ROC compound, I had a problem bumping my foot into the higher step coming down from the master bathroom and usually stubbed my toe. When our friend, Bill Voorwinden, one of John's engineers, heard about it, he built a ramp and brought it over to place in front of the bathroom step. It worked! And we were very grateful! Bill, the same guy who had thrown his concoction out our kitchen door at the Al Manar when John told him he didn't like it, was an older and very colorful gentleman who had already lived a fascinating life. In fact, he was *King* of one of the Samoan islands! He automatically became king, when he married the daughter of a former Samoan king, while visiting the island on vacation one year. Bill proved himself as a very kind and caring person in the short time John had known him while working together on this project. He often came by our house to drop off a beautiful rock he found somewhere out in the desert on one of his trips to inspect the sites. After one of his vacations back on the island, Bill brought John two very colorful Samoan shirts which he still keeps in his closet in remembrance of Bill. We still have the beautiful piece of petrified wood he brought back from the *Empty Quarter* of the desert, which he left on the side of our driveway one morning at the Al Manar compound.

Early one Sunday morning, Bill took off on one of his regular inspection trips to check the sites in the far south. This time he left his big Chevy Caprice at the car pool for service and took a smaller Toyota. He was a very impulsive man and it was his nature to drive fast. He preferred driving to the furthermost site first and then check the others on his way back to Riyadh. Usually, he would be gone about three days and check in to John when he returned to let him know he was back. John became concerned when Bill didn't show up as usual after three days and called the Saudi Police, who called him back that afternoon to tell him that Bill had been killed instantly when his car skidded in the sand on the highway and rolled over a couple of times. Bill was about half-way to his destination and had just passed the last gas station on his route. John concluded that Bill decided to turn around and go back for gas, and his impulsive decision to turn around, as he would have done in the larger Chevy Caprice, caused him to lose control of the smaller vehicle. The highway patrol had a hard time finding out where Bill worked and took him to a hospital in Layla where they pronounced him dead on arrival.

Finally, they were able to make the connection and notify Litton of his death. Then it became a long process of getting his remains out of Saudi Arabia and back to Samoa for burial. Someone had to sign all the official papers, make sure his body was properly prepared for burial and arrange for someone to accompany him all the way to Samoa. We will always remember Bill as a very kind and thoughtful good-hearted Dutchman who would have done anything for any of his friends. He was a little rough around the edges, a man of action rather than words, but, as John would say later, you always knew where you stood with Bill. He was one of John's most loyal friends.

Some of our friends from the Al Manar compound didn't move to the ROC but some of the ones we had left in Frankfurt did, so we resumed some of those friendships. Tanu and Sami, from California, moved into a house across the street from us, and we were glad to see them. I had only known Tanu slightly while living in Frankfurt, but John had known Sami well and said he was a brilliant engineer. Soon after they were settled, Tanu invited us over for dinner and we met their two young girls who were approaching their teens. They were a great addition to the neighborhood and we enjoyed their friendship tremendously. Everyone loved Tanu's Indian dishes which she brought to our German language class in Frankfurt and at some of the various Litton gatherings. That evening, she served her famous *Samosas*, followed by *Chicken Curry* served with rice and the appropriate condiments. It was so good, I cultivated a taste for curry right then and there, and chicken was always my favorite. Whenever we went out to dinner for a special occasion, I always requested the Intercontinental Hotel Restaurant in Riyadh because they served the best chicken curry in town with the best condiments; mango chutney, being my favorite, was simply out of this world!

Tanu invited me to come over one morning to watch her make Samosas. She taught me how to mix the Indian spices together to make *Gram Masala*, according to her mother's recipe and said it can be stored up to a year in a tight jar. She gave me some of hers to keep in a tight jar to get me started. In making Samosas, Tanu showed me how to make the crust, similar to pie crust, by rolling it out and cutting it in rectangles, then folding over each square and pressing the seams of the three sides together for making a pouch to fill with the spiced meat mixture. Then she sealed the fourth side and made sure all sides were tightly sealed before dropping them one at a time into very hot deep oil. When they were just the right shade of brown, she took them out of the hot oil and drained them on absorbent paper. She said they were best served while still warm. Tanu also made some very crispy flat breads cooked in hot oil and drained well to be eaten with her entrees. Tanu was a very good friend that year and invited me to go along with her and our Pakistani driver on shopping trips to find the various Indian foods she needed to prepare their meals. She showed me how to wear an *Indian Sari*, wrapping it around the waist, over the shoulder and around the waist again to hold it in place, and she gave me a pretty black sari trimmed with pastel embroidery. She also gave me a lovely ivory broach to help hold it in place and a jade necklace from India.

While still living at the Al Manar, John introduced me to Robert from Ohio, who had become one of his best friends on the project. He was waiting for his wife, Alice, who, like me a few months earlier, was trying to come over to Riyadh but had to get things worked out at home for her children to be taken care of first. She and I had a lot in common and much to share, although our family situations were somewhat different. When Alice finally arrived, I found her very attractive and enjoyed her friendship very much. Between the two of them, Robert and Alice had approximately ten children, due to their two marriages, and they supported the two homes where their children lived as two separate families. For that reason, Alice could only stay a few months and had to get back because her children were younger than Robert's and needed more supervision. Robert's children were practically grown and could pretty well take care of themselves. I believe Alice counted on her older two to watch over the younger ones when their sitter wasn't able to be with them, so she was very anxious to get back home.

As I said before, Greg was in God's hands now, and we prayed with faith and trust that God would work out everything for him. We received an important letter from his counselor at the AA half-way house, which said that he thought Greg needed more psychological treatment than he was able to get there at the AA facility. Since there was not much else we could do, we continued to believe God for a miracle! It was amazing that as we got deeper into our Bible studies, we were blessed with trips to many of the places the apostles had been to establish churches. And now we were scheduled for a trip to Greece and Turkey where Paul had preached and to the islands of the Aegean Sea where he had once been shipwrecked. We had been to Rome, where Peter and Paul were martyred, and we had visited the Coliseum, the scene of the lions and gladiators, and we had walked through the catacombs, where the first Christians worshipped underground and many were buried. We had visited *the Basilica of St. Peter* and seen the incredible work of Michelangelo on his magnificent painting of *the Ceiling of the Sistine Chapel* and his most famous *a Pieta* housed there. We had visited Florence to see many more of his incredible works, especially his awesome sculpture of *David.*

Now we were scheduled for a fantastic tour of Greece to visit the historic biblical sites of Paul's journeys to Athens, Corinth and Ephesus where he spoke to the people and established churches. His letters to these churches in Asia Minor would make up most of the New Testament, and we would visit *the Island of Crete* and see from a hilltop where Paul had been shipwrecked on his voyage to Rome and washed into a beautiful lagoon. We would visit *the Island of Patmos* and stand in the cave where John received *the Revelation of Jesus Christ* and visit the original church John had built there on the island. We would light candles in all these holy places and offer up prayers to our God.

Before we left for Greece, we received a long telephone call from Greg saying that he needed money to ride the bus from Mississippi to Virginia where he had learned through Amanda and Zach that his request for admittance to the Woodrow Wilson Rehabilitation Center had been approved. They had received the notification and called Hannah who gave them the phone number of the AA facility where Greg was staying. John talked to Greg's Counselor who recommended that Greg take advantage of this opportunity because there was not much they could offer him there at the half-way house. He helped Greg get ready for the trip and put him on the bus for Virginia Beach. Zach bought him the bus ticket, and John reimbursed him for Greg's expenses. He would stay with Zach and Amanda while waiting to get his new prosthesis and getting prepared for his admittance to WWRC. They wrote us regularly about his progress in Virginia Beach.

When Woodrow Wilson learned of the fire, they said he would have to complete a four-month AA program with counseling sessions before he could be admitted into their program. Amanda got him involved in every program available in Virginia Beach and said it looked good for him to be admitted in about four months if he cooperated with them and finished the programs. I'm sure this was a very big undertaking for Amanda and Zach, and we never intended for them to be involved; however, they seemed happy to report that he would get his new prosthesis in about three weeks! We'll never be able to repay them for all they have done, and I know that God has prepared a very special place for them in heaven. They have certainly earned their crowns for all they have done to help others upon the earth. With all the severely disabled living in this Virginia State facility for Rehabilitation, they had to be assured of providing a safe environment. Greg had to prove he was worthy of their trust before they could allow his admittance.

I continued my Bible reading and tried to follow Paul on his trips through the areas we would be visiting in Greece and Turkey. I was fascinated with Paul's message to the Galatians who were trying to keep *the Law* under *the New Covenant*, which went entirely against the liberty we have as Christians.

> "O FOOLISH Galatians, who hath bewitched you, that ye should not obey the truth, before whose eyes Jesus Christ hath been evidently set forth, crucified among you? This only would I learn of you: Received you the Spirit by the works of the law, or by the hearing of faith?
>
> "Are ye so foolish? Having begun in the Spirit, are ye now made perfect by the flesh? Have ye suffered so many things in vain if it be yet in vain? He, therefore, that ministers to you the Spirit and works miracles among you, does he do it by the works of the law, or by the hearing of faith? Even as Abraham believed God, and it was accounted to him for righteousness, know therefore that they which are of faith, the same are the children of Abraham.
>
> "And the scripture, foreseeing that God would justify the heathen through faith, preached beforehand the gospel unto Abraham, saying, 'In thee shall all nations be blessed'. So then they of faith are blessed with faithful Abraham.

"For as many as are of the works of the law are under the curse: for it is written, Cursed is every one that continues not in all things which are written in the book of the law to do them. But that no man is justified by the law in the sight of God, it is evident: for 'the just shall live by faith.'

"Christ has redeemed us from the curse of the law, being made a curse for us: for it is written, 'Cursed is everyone that hangs on a tree': That the blessing of Abraham might come on the Gentiles through Jesus Christ; that we might receive the promise of the Spirit through faith.

"Now to Abraham and his seed were the promises made, he said not 'And to seeds as of many; but as of one; and to thy seed, which is Christ.' ... Is the law then against the promises of God? God forbid: for if there had been a law given which could have given life, verily righteousness should have been by the law. But the scripture has concluded all under sin; that the promise by faith of Jesus Christ might be given to them that believe.

"But before faith came, we were kept under the law, shut up unto the faith which should afterwards be revealed. Wherefore the law was our schoolmaster to bring us unto Christ, that we might be justified by faith. But after faith is come, we are no longer under a schoolmaster. For all are the children of God by faith in Christ Jesus.

"For as many of you as have been baptized into Christ have put on Christ. There is neither Jew not Greek, there is neither bond nor free, there is neither male nor female: for you are all one in Christ Jesus. And if you are Christ's, then are you Abraham's seed, and heirs according to the promise." (Galatians 3:1-29)

"But when the fullness of the time was come, God sent forth his Son, made of a woman, made under the law, to redeem them that were under the law, that we might receive the adoption of sons. And because you are sons, God has sent forth the Spirit of his Son into your hearts, crying, 'Abba, Father,' wherefore thou art no more a servant, but a son; and if a son, an heir of God through Christ....

"But now, after you have known God, or rather are known of God, how turn ye again to the weak and beggarly elements, whereunto ye desire again to be in bondage? Ye observe days, and months, and

times, and years. I am afraid of you, lest I have bestowed upon you labor in vain....

"My little children, of whom I travail in birth again until Christ be formed in you, I desire to be present with you now, and to change my voice; for I stand in doubt of you. Tell me, ye that desire to be under the law, do ye not hear the law?

"For it is written, that Abraham had two sons, the one by a bondmaid, the other by a freewoman. But he who was of the bondwoman was born after the flesh; but he of the freewoman was by promise. Which things are an allegory: for these are the two covenants; the one from the mount Sinai, which gendereth to bondage, which is Agar.

"For this Agar is mount Sinai in Arabia, and answereth to Jerusalem which now is, and is in bondage with her children. But Jerusalem which is above is free, which is the mother of us all. For it is written, Rejoice, thou barren that bearest not; break forth and cry, thou that travailest not: for the desolate hath many more children than she which hath an husband.

"Now we, brethren, as Isaac was, are the children of promise. But as then he that was born after the flesh persecuted him that was born after the Spirit, even so it is now.

"Nevertheless what saith the scripture? Cast out the bondwoman and her son; for the son of the bondwoman shall not be heir with the son of the freewoman. So then, brethren, we are not children of the bondwoman, but of the free." (Galatians 4:4-31)

"STANDFAST, therefore, in the liberty wherewith Christ has made us free, and be not entangled again with the yoke of bondage... Christ is become of no effect unto you, whosoever of you are justified by the law; ye are fallen from grace....

"This I say then, Walk in the Spirit, and you shall not fulfill the lust of the flesh. For the flesh lusts against the Spirit, and the Spirit against the flesh: and these are contrary the one to the other; so that ye cannot do the things that ye would.

"But if ye are led by the Spirit, ye are not under the law. Now the works of the flesh are manifest, which are these: Adultery, fornication, uncleanness, lasciviousness, idolatry, witchcraft, hatred, variance, emulations, wrath, strife, seditions, heresies,

envyings, murders, drunkenness, revellings, and such the like: of which I told you before, as I have also told you in times past, that they which do such things shall not inherit the kingdom of God.

"But the fruit of the Spirit is love, joy, peace, long-suffering, gentleness, goodness, faith, meekness, temperance; against such there is no law. And they that are Christ's have crucified the flesh with the affections and lusts. If we live in the Spirit, let us also walk in the Spirit. Let us not be desirous of vain glory, provoking one another, envying one another." (Galatians, Chapter 5)

"Brethren, if a man be overtaken in a fault, ye which are spiritual, restore such an one in the spirit of meekness; considering thyself, lest thou also be tempted....

"Be not deceived; God is not mocked: for whatsoever a man soweth that shall he also reap. For he that sows to his flesh shall of the flesh reap corruption, but he that soweth to the Spirit, shall of the Spirit reap life everlasting....

"But God forbid that I should glory, save in the cross of our Lord Jesus Christ, by whom the world is crucified unto me, and I unto the world. For in Christ Jesus, neither circumcision avails anything, nor uncircumcision; but a new creature." (Galatians, Chapter 6)

A new creature! No amount of works of the flesh, whether they are of John and I, Amanda and Zach, nor Greg himself, would do any good except to keep him alive physically. He needed to be *born again* of the Spirit of God to be changed into *a new creature.* All we could do was pray for a miracle!

"There was a man of the Pharisees named Nicodemus, a ruler of the Jews: The same came to Jesus by night and said unto him, 'Rabbi, we know that thou art a teacher come from God: for no man can do these miracles that thou doest, except God be with him.'

"Jesus answered and said unto him, 'Except a man be born again, he cannot see the kingdom of God.' Nicodemus said unto him, 'How can a man be born when he is old? Can he enter the second time into his mother's womb and be born?'

"Jesus answered, 'Verily, verily, I say unto you, except a man be born of water and of the Spirit, he cannot enter into the kingdom of God. That which is flesh is flesh; and that which is born of the Spirit is spirit. Marvel not that I said unto thee, Ye must be born again.

The wind blows ..., and you hear the sound thereof, but canst not tell from whence it comes and whither it goes: So is everyone that is born of the Spirit.'

"*Nicodemus answered and said unto him, 'How can these things be?' Jesus answered, 'Art thou a master of Israel and know not these things? Verily, verily, I say unto thee, we speak that we do know and testify that we have seen; and ye receive not our witness.*

"*'If I have told you earthly things and ye believe not, how shall ye believe if I tell you of heavenly things? And no man hath ascended up to heaven, but he that came down from heaven, even the Son of man which is in heaven. And as Moses lifted up the serpent in the wilderness, even so must the Son of man be lifted up: that whosoever believeth in him should not perish, but have eternal life.'*" (John 3:1- 15)

CHAPTER TWENTY-ONE

A Tour of Greece

1984

John and I decided to take advantage of the Hajj, the Muslim holy month, and planned a vacation which would take us through Greece, the Greek Islands and into Turkey. On Monday, the 27th of August, we flew out of Riyadh on Saudia Airlines on a direct flight to Athens. Upon our arrival at the airport, our representative from Greek Organized Tours had us paged and helped us with our baggage to his car and drove us to our Hotel Herodion. After we checked in, he sat down with us in the lounge where we planned our entire two-week vacation. We were pleased to learn that our Hotel Herodion, which was located at the foot of the Acropolis, was also within walking distance of the downtown area. John wasn't feeling well when we arrived, so I walked downstairs to the restaurant and ordered Moussaka and salad. When John came down a little later, he ordered Shish Kebabs and Greek salad. We both loved the salad, which was mostly cubed cucumbers and tomatoes topped off with black olives and feta cheese. We were very pleased with the hotel, which provided a very comfortable room and a buffet style continental breakfast. Since we arrived rather early, we walked around the neighborhood that afternoon exploring the gift shops and taking pictures.

The following morning, we were up very early and found our table by a window in the dining room. Our bus picked us up around 8:15 for a tour of the city, which has grown up around the ancient ruins. We were intrigued with the *Arch of Hadrian*, which stands in its midst, and the *Temple of Zeus*. We passed by the *Presidential Palace* and many government buildings, museums and churches before we were driven up to the *Acropolis*, which was originally a fortress and religious center, honoring the goddess Athena. It is built high on a rocky hill and dominates the city of Athens. The *Parthenon*, the most famous monument in the Acropolis, was built in perfect proportion with eight columns across the front and back and seventeen columns on each side. It marks the *Classical age of Pericles*, the Golden age of the 5th Century BC.

The Parthenon, Athens, Greece.

We liked the Greek Moussaka and salad so much, we ordered it again for lunch before leaving on our walk into the city. We found the *Presidential Palace* just in time for the *Changing of the Guards*, which takes place every hour on the hour with much pomp and vigor. It was very impressive to see them in their uniforms with large tassels on their shoes, as they paraded in front of the palace and changed places. We walked quickly through the city to learn our way around for future walks we would be taking during our time between tours on the weekend. Then we had to hurry back to our hotel to get ready for *Athens by Night* and our pick up scheduled for 7:30. *The Sound & Light Show*, which took us to the top of *Pnyx Hill*, where *Pericles* and other famous orators *spoke to the Athenians during classical times*, was very enlightening as we learned the history of the great city. As they moved through different eras, parts of the Acropolis were lit up to depict where certain events took place. The lights were constantly changing and moving from place to place as voices could be heard telling the history of Athens and its destruction. It was from this hill, *Mars Hill* in the Bible, that the apostle Paul first preached to the people of Athens making reference to their *unknown god.* It grew quite cold that evening, and I wished I had brought my sweater. From Pnyx Hill, we were driven over to an *open-air theatre* where we watched a ballet company perform the *classical Greek folk dances.* I would have enjoyed them so much more if I hadn't been so cold that evening. Next time, I'll know.

Early Wednesday morning, we checked out of our hotel to be picked up for our *four-day classical land tour.* Our tour guide was a delightful young lady, *Alexandra,* and our bus driver, a very friendly and robust young Greek named *Aeneas.* It was to be one of our greatest adventures of all time and certainly one we would remember. Alexandra and Aeneas set the tone for our tour group, and, as we got to know one another, we just seemed to click together as a group and really enjoyed our time together. We even exchanged addresses at the end of the tour. On this three-day excursion into Greece, we had a long road ahead of us with much Greek mythology. Our first stop that morning was at the *Corinth Canal,* which cuts through the narrow neck of the isthmus and joins the Peloponnese peninsula to the mainland. After crossing the canal, we journeyed on to the ancient ruins of *Corinth,* dating back to 585 BC, and we saw where the apostle Paul spoke to the Corinthians and established a church. The marble pillars of the *Temple of Apollo* are still standing and the layout of the old city is still visible. The mosaic baths and marble toilet seats, which were a gathering place for the men to discuss the news and politics of the day, depict life as it was at that time. Conveniently located, the rows of toilet seats were built above an underground stream for the removal of waste as the men discussed their matters of interest. It was also interesting to see the ancient marble pillars of the temple where Paul first spoke to the Corinthians.

The Ancient Ruins of Corinth, Greece.

Next, we stopped at the ancient ruins of *Mycenae*, settled by the *Cretans* at the time of the *Minoan* civilization around 1400 BC. Built on a very high hill, it looks out over the *Plain of Argos* to the sea and protected them from surprise attacks by pirates. The famous *Gate of Lions* is in the northwest corner of the fortress and is obscured from view of passersby. A short distance away is the famous beehive tomb of *Agamemnon*, which was discovered by a shepherd in 1876, who thought he had found a well and removed the keystone on top of the tomb. It is a mystery how he did it because the keystone is believed to weigh approximately 120 tons, and, when the tomb didn't cave in, the entrance was located down below and dug out. Many priceless treasures were discovered in the tomb, which had been filled in with earth to prevent plundering.

We arrived at the lovely seacoast town of *Nafplion* around noon and checked into our hotel where we had lunch together. Then we re-boarded our bus for the afternoon drive to the famous theatre of *Epidaurus,* built during the 4th Century. It is believed to be the best preserved edifice of its kind with a seating capacity of 15,000 and superb acoustics, which carry a normal voice all the way to the top. And it is still in use today! Every summer, a festival of ancient drama is performed here by the Royal Theatre

Company. Epidaurus was the most important center for the worship of the *god of medicine, Aesculapius*. When a patient recovered after the treatment of the doctor priests, he would dedicate a replica of the body part which had been affected. The museum is full of these fascinating replicas. We returned to our hotel that afternoon and enjoyed some leisure time walking around the lovely grounds taking pictures. The old fortress, *the Acropolis*, above the small city of *Nafplion* beckoned to us to climb to the top, but we were just too tired and saved those very steep steps for another day. Then we enjoyed a very nice dinner in the hotel restaurant overlooking the lovely port and lighthouse all lit up at night with a beautiful full moon overhead.

The following morning, we began our drive through *central Peloponnese, Arcadia* and the towns of *Tripolis* and *Megalopolis*. We arrived at the ruins of ancient *Olympia* and found them very impressive. Alexandra told us the history and pointed out various places of interest. We looked out upon *the first racetrack where the Olympics originated in 776 BC.* It is from this racetrack that the sacred torch is carried to wherever the Olympics are held in the world today! Some of the guys in our group got out there on the racetrack and ran its full length! Alexandra told us that those who ran the first races ran them entirely nude. She said that the period of the games was always marked by a *sacred truce*, during which all the people of Greece forgot their differences for a while and united in the spirit of Hellenism. When we visited the *Olympia Museum*, she pointed out that all the Greek statues were standing alone whereas the Roman statues usually had to be propped up.

Olympia, Greece: "The Original 100 Meter Dash Track."

We arrived in *Olympia* a short time later and checked into our charming old hotel, surrounded with beautiful plants and flowers creating a lovely garden atmosphere. While standing in the garden waiting for our bags to be unloaded, our group decided to walk into town to do a little shopping and find a restaurant for lunch. After being assigned our rooms, we met again outside in the garden and started walking. Olympia proved to be a tourist town with many shops containing just about everything one might look for in the way of a souvenir or memento of Greece to take home with them. I fell in love with a beautifully carved wooden chess set, but I only purchased a couple of embroidered Grecian blouses and a woolen cape which would fit nicely into my suitcase.

Early that evening, Aeneas drove us out to a little restaurant on the side of town where he obviously knew the owner quite well, because he pulled the tables and chairs outside underneath the grapevines to form one long table. Then he ordered dinner for all of us and picked fresh flowers from the garden for our table. He even presented all the ladies with a flower from the garden and a lovely smelling herb. Aeneas was very much attracted to one of the young ladies in our group from California. It was a beautiful evening and one we would always remember. Almost immediately, our table was covered with hors d'oeuvres, dips, bread and

271

wine while Aeneas ordered what we thought was our entrée: Moussaka or Spaghetti. After gorging ourselves with all this delicious food for about an hour, we realized that they hadn't yet begun to cook our steaks, when the waiter came around to ask us how we would like them cooked. At this point, we had to tell Aeneas that we couldn't possibly eat another bite and to please cancel the rest of the meal. This wonderful, enchanting evening was accompanied by Greek music coming from inside the restaurant, while we enjoyed ourselves outside under the grapevines. I'm sure we will all remember this big-hearted Greek bus driver, who spoke very little English, but just bubbled over with love for everyone. When I asked him about his family, Aeneas said, "Ahhh! Tomorrow, we see Mama!"

Friday morning, we got an early start, and as we were driving through the plains of Ilia Akhaia, through Patras, the Capitol of the Pelopponnese, we passed through some beautiful farm country. As we approached a small town, Aeneas pulled the bus over to the side of the road, stopped and climbed down off the bus. And there we saw his Mama coming down the road with a big smile on her face with sacks of vegetables to be transported to the next town. He gave her a big hug, climbed back on the bus and off we went waving goodbye. About an hour later, the bus turned off the main road onto a side street and again stopped. Out of one of the nearby houses bounded his aunt and grandmother, waving and smiling, carrying more sacks of vegetables. He exchanged his mother's sacks for their sacks, and again, we all waved goodbye and off we went. This was so much fun!

Our drive that day took us along the *Dardanelles River* and through the lovely city of *Rion*, where we stopped to make pictures of a large floral clock which could be seen from the road. Then we boarded a ferry for crossing over the river to *Antirion*. We stopped for lunch at a French hotel and resort area on the river and then proceeded on our drive up higher into the mountains. The road became a series of sharp curves, and we noticed many small altars along the way, especially on the curves, where Alexandra told us people had been killed in accidents. These markers were left there to commemorate the spot where the accidents occurred. She said that sometimes they were put there by grateful people who nearly lost their lives but somehow escaped death. After swinging around one of the steep, sharp curves, one of our bags fell out the side of the bus, and Aeneas had to pull over, stop the bus and run back to get it.

It was late in the afternoon when we finally arrived at *Delphi* high in the mountains with a beautiful, breathtaking view looking down a deep, wild gorge to the *Gulf of Corinth*. The ancient Greeks had chosen this unique spot for their most sacred *Oracle of Apollo*, which influenced the fate of states and individuals alike for about a thousand years from the 7th Century BC until the 4th Century AD. During that time, it was considered the greatest sanctuary and spiritual center in the world. We were the last visitors of the day to walk through the ancient ruins of the *Sanctuary of Apollo*, built thousands of years before on that very steep mountainside. As we looked down from the top of this ancient theatre of Apollo over the marble ruins below and then again down into the very deep gorge which plummeted thousands of feet, an incredibly eerie feeling came over us as the sun began to set in the west.

The Ancient Ruins of Delphi, Greece.

It was almost dark when we re-boarded our bus for the drive to our hotel, which was just a mile away also located on the rim of the gorge. The town of *Delphi* was built right next to the ruins within easy walking distance of our hotel. The large patio in back of our hotel offered the same incredible view looking down the gorge to the distant sea. We decided once more to have dinner together, and, after getting settled in our rooms, we started walking down the street into town as a group because driving and parking the bus was such a problem on the very narrow streets. Alexandra directed us to a very nice restaurant right in the heart of town, and, again with the help of Aeneas, we pushed the tables together inside the restaurant. This time we ordered individually from the menu: John thought he ordered fish, but it turned out to be squid, and I ordered stuffed eggplant and stuffed tomato, two hors d'oeuvres. They were delicious, and I shared them with John. We also tried stuffed grape leaves, which someone passed around! A very interesting thing happened that evening, and we were all greatly surprised when Aeneas got down on one knee and proposed to Angie, the attractive divorcee from San Diego. Aeneas was serious! Angie was flattered, although quite taken by surprise. Of course she didn't take him seriously and passed it off as just kidding. I guess she turned him down as gracefully as she could under the circumstances.

After a great breakfast at the Delphi Hotel the following morning, we visited the ruins again, which looked altogether different in the sunlight, and we could see the large amphitheatre above the Sanctuary of Apollo. This time we toured the *Sanctuary of Athena* on the lower side of the road: although much smaller in area, it gave us the same awesome feeling with the deep gorge directly below and the sea of Corinth in the far distance. This portion of the ruins provided the mosaic baths which were supplied with water from the sacred *Castalia Spring* flowing from the foot of *the Phaedriades Rocks*. The huge aqueduct, which we had noticed on our way up the previous day, carried this water to the towns below. From the ruins, we were driven to the Delphi museum.

Alexandra walked us through the museum explaining the different periods of Greek History and their influences in the world. Built originally by the Greeks in Classical times, Delphi fell under the domination of conquerors during various periods of history. After the invasion of the *Dorians* from the north in about 1100 BC, warlike feudal kingdoms emerged from the dark ages at the dawn of recorded history in the 9th Century BC. In the following 600 years, the Greeks tried, or invented, every political system conceived by man, and most forms of government still bear the Greek name which is indicative of their origin. *Pericles* presided over the *Golden Age* of unparalleled intellectual and artistic achievements in 461 BC, the period leading up to the disastrous *Peloponnesian War.* In 334 BC, *Alexander the Great* stretched his world empire into *Persia* but died in 323 BC, having failed in melding Greeks and Persians into a new imperial master race. *Roman conquest* came in 146 BC, yet *Greece achieved a remarkable cultural conquest in reverse* when the Roman Empire became impregnated with *the higher art and thought of Greece,* and the Roman aristocracy sent its sons to the schools of Athens and Rhodes.

Alexandra said that *many priceless Greek statues were shipped to Hadrian in Italy* to embellish the centers of culture. In the 4th Century AD, Greece became part of the eastern empire's domain and *the spoils from Greece adorned Constantinople,* its new Capitol City. Pious Byzantine emperors closed the pagan universities and temples, and wave upon wave of barbaric tribes ravaged the country. The Byzantines were *overcome by the Turks* in 1460, and *the Greek peasants remained serfs, paying besides tithes, a poll- tax and a blood tribute of one-fifth of their male children to be brought up as Muslims. The Greek War of Independence,* which started in 1821, *was the beginning of their freedom from Turkish rule,* and the Protocol of London in 1832 established the frontier of the new Greek state, first a Republic, then a Kingdom, and finally in 1973, it again became a Republic. A military coup led to the return of former Premier Caramanlis who was sworn in as Premier of Greece in 1974.

Back at the Delphi Hotel around mid-day, we were served a wonderful Greek luncheon outside on the terrace overlooking the gorge and distant sea. The food was absolutely great: the best Greek Moussaka of the entire trip, served with a wonderful Greek Salad, great bread and a special Greek wine with Crème Caramel for dessert. While checking out, we purchased several tapes of Greek music as mementos of this fabulous trip, and, on the way down the mountain, we stopped for shopping in a small gift shop recommended highly by Alexandra. I bought a beautiful beige tablecloth with matching napkins. On our long drive back to Athens, Alexandra told us many tales of Greek Mythology. We arrived back at Hotel Herodion around 6:00 pm and checked in for a couple of nights before our scheduled cruise of the Aegean Sea.

John and I walked down the street to find a restaurant we had heard about where you can eat dinner and watch the Sound and Light Show of the Acropolis. Now the name of the restaurant had a special meaning for us since it was also the name of our Greek bus driver, so we decided to go there for dinner. The food was good, but the place was packed with people out to celebrate Saturday night. The only table we could find was in the cocktail lounge where we ordered a plate of hors d'eourves and a glass of wine hoping we could just sit there and watch the show. We could see it partially over the heads of the many people, but we couldn't hear anything but the din of chatter in the overly crowded room. However, it was a Saturday night to remember of having dinner in view of the Sound and Light Show of the Acropolis.

On Sunday morning, we walked into the city and heard beautiful sounds of classical music coming from a nearby park, so we sat down at a sidewalk café and ordered coffee. It was a lovely sunny day and we were delighted to hear the voice of a beautiful, vivacious young lady when she began to sing a few songs. Then we walked around to the *Palace* to take pictures of the *Changing of the Guards* because John had run out of film the first time. We took our time walking back to the hotel and discovered a very impressive excavation site right in the heart of town in what once was a lovely city park. We could plainly see that the ancient city lies directly beneath the modern city and probably covers the whole area, but modern buildings and landscaping prevent most excavations from taking place. Then it was time to head back to the hotel for lunch and our pickup for our afternoon tour down the scenic coast to Sounion.

We were picked up around 1:00 pm by a tour bus and headed down the southern coast to *Sounion*, where we found a large crowd of people high on a hill overlooking the Aegean Sea. The wind-swept cape was an obvious choice for the *Sanctuary of Poseidon*, where sailors might offer a last sacrifice to propitiate the mighty god of the sea before leaving the safety of the Saronic Gulf. It was from this lookout point that a runner would run all the way to Athens to warn the city of an approaching attack from the sea. In 490 BC, a soldier collapsed and died after running the 24.85 miles to Athens to announce the victory of the Greeks over the Persians in the Battle of Marathon. To honor him, the Athens Marathon race was originally established at that distance and was used in the 2004 Olympics held in Athens. On a lower hill stands the *Temple of Athena*. We would pass this way the following morning from the port of Athens, down the coastline and out into the Aegean Sea. That evening back at the hotel, we discovered again that we like lamb when cooked properly with the right combination of vegetables and condiments. We ordered the dining room special, a very tasty meal of lamb and vegetables, and we enjoyed it immensely. After dinner, we climbed the stairs to the rooftop where we had a clear view of the sound and light show while sitting comfortably at the foot of the Acropolis. Since we had already seen the show at Pnyx Hill and heard the history of Athens and Sounion, as the Greek Empire rose and fell, we didn't really need to hear it again; only to be reminded of its history.

Monday morning, we were up bright and early for breakfast, ready to check out of the hotel for our four-day cruise. Our tour representative transported us to the MTS Constellation, which was docked at Piraeus, the famous port of Athens. We boarded immediately and were underway by 11:30. Leaving our unpacked baggage in our stateroom, we hurried up on deck to wave good-bye to the city of Athens and snapped a picture of the ruins at Sounion as our ship quickly passed by on its way out to sea. Dinner was already being served in the dining room, so we hurried to find our seats at our assigned table to order from the menu.

Piraeus, the Port of Athens. Our Ship, "The Constellation."

On deck that afternoon, we went through the usual introductory meeting and life boat drill and purchased our tickets for the available excursions. At 6:00 pm we attended the *Captain's Welcome Aboard Cocktail Party* and were photographed shaking his hand as we passed through a long line of people. After drinks and hors d'eourves, it was time for the *Grand Buffet Dinner,* served buffet style in the bar and taken to the Leo lounge, where we found a seat to enjoy our food as we listened to the *Aegean Orchestra.* At 7:30, we arrived at the small Island of *Mykonos,* a popular tourist resort famous for its traditional windmills and whitewashed houses. John and I went ashore and walked around the small island getting the feel of it as John took some really great pictures. However, when we arrived back on board the ship, he realized that something was wrong with the camera and none of the pictures came out. Therefore, we would have to come back again someday to Mykonos to replace those pictures.

Tuesday morning, we arrived at *the Turkish port of Kusadasi* and boarded our bus for the half-hour ride to *the ancient ruins of Ephesus.* Our Turkish guide was excellent and spoke very good English as he gave us the history of the five different sites of Ephesus, once the center of world commerce, religion and culture. Its last site, dating back to about 1200 BC, is one of the most extensively reconstructed archaeological sites in the world. Built almost entirely of marble, the reconstruction which has already taken place is very impressive. The Library of Celsius, built in 135 BC, stands intact almost as it did then. The recently restored thermal baths of Sklastike were heated by steam circulation under the marble pavements. They are very interesting to see as well as the community toilets similar to the ones at Corinth with an underground stream for the removal of waste. These were also used as a meeting place about the same era, where people gathered to discuss matters of interest. Marble columns and stones depicting the fronts of houses line the main street which was only wide enough for one chariot to pass. Their marks are still clearly seen on the marble pavement. The type of statue in front of a house, or a carving, denoted the trade of the person who lived there.

Ancient Ephesus, Turkey: "The Library of Celsius."

From the Grand Theatre, "Looking down The Arcadian Way."

The main road takes you from the entrance of Ephesus to the famous ancient amphitheatre with a seating capacity of 24,000. Directly in front of the theatre is the famous *Arcadian Way* where *Cleopatra and Mark Anthony once rode in procession.* Next to it is the assembly hall, where the councils met to determine the fate of many people. It was here that it was determined to imprison the apostle Paul for fear that his teachings on Christianity would stir up riots and cause them to lose wealth from the sale of silver shrines made to the goddess Diana. Looking straight down the Arcadian Way, one can see a small building on a hilltop across a vast plain, which at that time was across an inlet of water from the sea, where Paul was imprisoned before being taken to Rome for imprisonment and martyrdom. From Ephesus, we stopped off in Kusadasi on the way back to our ship to see a demonstration of Turkish carpets. Buying a carpet in Turkey never crossed our minds, but we found one we really liked in a beautiful pattern of blue & beige wool. John found himself in a bargaining mode when they offered to pay the shipping cost to the States, and he made the purchase giving them Mother's address.

Back on board the Constellation, it was time for lunch as we plowed through the water towards the *tiny Island of Patmos.* Our tour guide told us the history of John, the apostle, who was living in exile on the island of Patmos when he received the Revelation of Jesus Christ. We would visit *the Grotto of the Apocalypse,* the cave in which John was living when he received the revelation, which has since been turned into a holy shrine. Then we would board a bus for our ride up to the monastery built high on a hilltop in the 11th century directly above the original small chapel, which John built in the 1st century. The view from the monastery was fantastic and gave us a panoramic view of the sea and the surrounding islands. Then we visited the cave where John lived when he received the visions from God. We left a candle burning there with our prayers. It was truly an inspirational moment! We looked out on the lovely meadow lands, now grazed by sheep and goats, and tried to imagine what it must have been like for John who had been banished there in his nineties. I read in The Search for the Twelve Apostles that after John received The Revelation of Jesus Christ, he took what he had written to Turkey to have each message sent to each of the seven churches in Asia, just as the angel of the Lord told him to do.

The Island of Patmos: St. John's Church.

Entrance to the Cave of "The Revelation."

We enjoyed a wonderful dinner that evening, *Greek Taverna Style*, with all the traditional Greek dishes served with red wine and assorted desserts. Afterwards, we were invited into the lounge for a special *Greek Night Show* featuring the *Ray Cornell Dancers*. They were fantastic and performed traditional folk dances ending with *Zorba*. On Wednesday morning, we passed through *the famous deer poised columns of Rhodes* and docked inside its guarded entrance. We boarded a bus for the city tour of *Rhodes*, the main island of *the twelve islands of the Dodecanese,* famous for their natural beauty and their classical medieval monuments. We passed by beautiful white sandy beaches, covered with tourists and vacationers and drove on up to the hilltop, which overlooked the city below and gave us an excellent view of the surrounding area. We drove on to the ancient marble ruins at *Kamiros* and then to the famous *Palace of the Grand Master,* where we disembarked for a guided tour of the medieval fortress.

Built during the 14th Century, this magnificent sandstone fortress, covering several acres of land, dominates the colorful harbor and crowns the hilltop where *the Colossus of Rhodes,* one of the *Seven Wonders of the World,* stood centuries earlier. Surrounding the palace is a series of three moats constructed so that invaders were not aware of more than the outer moat. It was built in 1310 as a recuperative hospital for knights wounded in the battles of the Crusades by the Order of the Hospitaler Knights of St. John of Jerusalem. These knights were selected from all parts of Europe and organized into groups by their native tongues. Applicants had to prove nobility on both sides of their families for at least four generations, eight generations for Germans. Their leader was selected *Grand Master* for his lifetime and ruled over the knights and the other inhabitants as *king*. *The Palace* served as his home, headquarters and rallying place. In 1552, the palace was under siege for over six months by the Turks, who lost over 90,000 men out of an army of 200,000 compared with the loss of some 200 knights of the Order of St. John. Through treachery, the impregnable palace was finally breeched and the surviving knights were permitted to leave for Malta.

During the four century Turkish occupation, the palace was used as a storehouse and a prison until 1856, when a meteor hit the arsenal and destroyed much of the edifice. It was totally restored during the Italian occupation of the Dodecanese Islands during the pre-world war days of WWII. After our tour of the palace with its medieval furnishings and parquet and mosaic floors, we walked through the narrow cobblestone streets of the old town within the fortress where the knights once lived. The quaint old town had been divided into sections according to nationality, and its old buildings and occasional courtyards echoed a medieval time of the past. At the end of the main street leading to the palace, we rounded a corner and discovered tourist shops selling everything from expensive fur coats and jewelry all the way down to post cards. We were told that Black Russian furs would go at a tremendous bargain!

Around noon, we headed for *Lindos,* the ancient capitol of the island before Rhodes was founded on the southeastern coast. We walked through this charming old town, with its unique narrow, winding alleyways and sidewalks separating the very old whitewashed buildings, on our way up to the acropolis to visit the *Temple of Athena*. We passed by many ladies lining the sidewalks selling lace tablecloths and other handmade items. It was quite a strenuous climb to the top, but it was well worth it. From there, we could see the beautiful bay and lagoon where Paul was shipwrecked on his way to Rome. The ruins were very interesting, but the view of the coastline was fantastic. After walking back down the sidewalk to board our bus, we were driven to Lindos beach where we received a box lunch and drink which was greatly appreciated after all our walking and climbing steps that morning. We noticed, or tried not to notice, that we were on *a topless beach* while eating our lunch there. After a couple of hours, we re-boarded our bus and headed back to Rhodes.

The *Captain's Gala Dinner* Wednesday evening was formal, although not many had brought along formal attire. We just dressed as nicely as we could and enjoyed the dinner, and it was fantastic. The first course: *Caviar*, I passed on to John along with the condiments. The second course: *Salad or Clam Chowder* was very good. The third course: *Filet Mignon or Baked Fish*, served with baked potato and assorted vegetables was also very good. And for dessert: *Baked Alaska*, everyone's favorite, and it was outstanding! Our dinner was obviously prepared by a great chef and we enjoyed it tremendously. Again, it was followed by *Showtime* in the lounge with the *Ray Cornell dancers* and *a special singer named Candy*, all wearing beautiful costumes and presenting very good and wholesome entertainment.

Thursday morning, we arrived at Crete, the largest of the Greek Islands and considered to be the most southern tip of Europe. We disembarked at the port city of Herakleion and boarded our tour bus. Within minutes, we were at the ancient site of *Knossos, the palace city of king Minos*, the oldest European Palace ever to have been excavated. These excavations, conducted by Sir Arthur Evans, an English archaeologist in the first part of the 20th Century, unearthed a flourishing, peaceful civilization, which existed 4,000 years earlier during the Minoan Age, the beginning of European civilization. It was the kingdom of *the Priest-King Minos, the legendary son of Zeus,* and the prehistoric ruler of the seas. From Knossos, he ruled the world's first naval empire until it was destroyed by a natural disaster which occurred around 1,500 BC. It is believed that this natural phenomenon was a gigantic tidal wave, or tsunami, caused by the eruption of a volcano, which completely engulfed the island destroying life and burying all traces of this remarkable ancient civilization.

The Ancient Ruins of Knossos on the Island of Crete.

Archaeologists have determined that the palace, which was built in the 19th Century BC, was destroyed by an earthquake and rebuilt in the 17th Century BC. Since the excavations, the palace has been mostly reconstructed, and it is very interesting to observe the still colorful murals on the walls, which depict life in that era. They tell stories of the priests and priestesses, animal sacrifices, and the death defying sport of *bull leaping*, where one would actually leap on the back of a bull and harness him. Portraits depict their style of dress, religion and customs. Pictures of mythological birds and animals symbolize their royal power. It is believed that Greek Mythology had its origin right here with the Minoan culture.

The palace was the center of a large town surrounded with trees and had a large courtyard with a small theatre consisting of properly placed stones in the form of a rectangle for the seating of the people. In the center of the theatre was a place for an orator to stand and speak. As one walks through this beautiful prehistoric *palace* with its complex architecture and numerous staircases and passageways, it is incredible to think that this had existed over 1500 years before Christ. This palace contains many chambers, altars for animal sacrifices, and two throne rooms, one for the priest and one for the priestess, each with a stone on which they would sit with stone benches lining the walls for the elders. A small colorful bathtub remains in one of the chambers, probably for the priestess, and clay pipes and an underground stream for the removal of waste from the bathroom. Man-size earthen vessels were used to store food in the storage room. Bright red and bright yellow were used in large quantities on the walls with some blue, black and cream colors. The pillars we first encountered at the entrance of the stone palace were painted bright red and trimmed with black.

After leaving Knossos, we visited the museum, where we were able to see the many beautiful artifacts discovered during the excavation period. There were many different shapes and sizes of pottery made out of clay and painted with the above colors in various designs. However, one thing stood out as very unusual: the cups were all cone shaped with handles as we have today; and there were many of them. The jewelry was very intricately designed and sometimes took the shape of insects such as the bee or grasshopper, and many were created with floral designs. The typical portrait of a Cretan noble was depicted with a bare chest and quite muscular with a wasp waist and long black curly hair. The bull was usually shown plowing the earth in harness, unless, of course, he was in the process of being harnessed. This is thought to represent a symbol of fertility for the growing of crops. Before leaving the island of Crete, our bus drove us around the outskirts of the city of Crete.

Back on board the Constellation, we were having lunch when we heard our tour guide's voice coming over the loud speaker giving us the history of the Island of Santorini. Then around 2:30 pm, we heard the Captain's voice calling everyone up on deck. Realizing that we were rapidly approaching the *Island of Santorini*, we rushed up to witness the most incredible sight of the entire cruise. We were passing through the great walls of the caldera, and we were right in the center of a live volcano. The walls of the caldera, we were told, are an archaeologist's dream because they contain all the layers and stages of creation over thousands of years.

As we moved into the harbor, we were amazed to look up and see the city of *Phira* built high above us on the very rim of the caldera. On the left hand side, we passed an islet of black volcanic rock and realized that this was the very center of the crater. We were told that it emits lava, gases and steam of 80 degrees C and is in the process of forming another island. Initially, there were three small islets of limestone rock in this corner of the Aegean Sea, and it was very interesting to note that through this region passes the line at which two large plates of the Earth's crust meet: The African and the Aegean plates. There has always been quite a bit of volcanic activity in this region, and over time, the limestone islets were surrounded by lavas brought to the surface from the very bowels of the earth. Slowly but surely, they were united and eventually formed one large, round island. About 1500 BC, the inhabitants of Santorini felt tremors and small eruptions: one which caused them to evacuate the island, but they returned and started to rebuild before another tremor caused them to leave again. Then an immense eruption occurred which shattered the island completely and its central section was submerged into the depths of the sea. What remains today are the crescent-shaped islands of *Santorini, Therasia and Aspronisi,* which, as seen from the air, give the outline of a large round island which once existed.

It is believed by many that this natural disaster is what happened to the missing continent of Atlantis, once thought to have been a myth which Plato wrote about. It is most likely that Plato wrote about a real continent he had learned about through stories handed down from generation to generation. Excavations at *Akrotiri,* further inland from Phira and the rim of the caldera, have uncovered a civilization very similar to Knossos, which is definitely related to the same era, the Minoan Age. Murals depict a large fleet of ships with warriors and a captain, and their houses, lifestyle and art closely resemble that of the civilization which existed at Knossos before the great tsunami.

The City of Phira on the Edge of the Caldera.

A Spectacular View of Santorini from the City of Phira.

It is believed that when the eruption of 1500 BC occurred, which blew away the central part of the island, the sea rushed in to fill the void and was immediately expelled by a second eruption which created the gigantic tidal wave which covered the civilization of Knossos. Santorini was entirely buried beneath a thick layer of pozzolana, and all traces of human activity vanished from the island for several centuries. Fragments of Mycenaean vases located in the region of Monolithos attest the resettlement of the island by the end of the 13th century BC. After the Captain anchored our ship in the bay of the crater below the very steep walls of the caldera, we went ashore in tenders since we were unable to dock at the landing site. Then we were given the choice of riding up to the city of Phira on the back of a donkey or going up in a cable car. We chose the latter. Once at the top, we found a restaurant overlooking the shimmering sea below and ordered a glass of wine to sit at a table and enjoy the view. I was able to get a terrific picture of John sitting there relaxing, as a donkey and rider surfaced coming up the pathway behind him. We plan to go back again someday to Phira and stay at a hotel for a few days to tour the museums and the ruins at Akrotiri.

Our last dinner on board the Constellation was sad because it was the end of our exciting tour of Greece. We enjoyed our last *Show Time* and took a walk around the beautiful Constellation before retiring to our room to get a good night's sleep so we could arise early for breakfast. When we did get up the following morning, we were amazed to find our ship already docked at Piraeus. We enjoyed breakfast and were already packed and ready to go when our tour representative met us on board to escort us off the ship and drive us back to our hotel in Athens. On the way, he drove us by the airport to check our bags and then dropped us off at the Herodion hotel, where we could rest in the lounge and have lunch before catching the shuttle back to the airport. Since our flight back to Riyadh was scheduled for departure around 7:00 pm, we had plenty of time to find a seat on top of the airport terminal to have a few snacks while we watched the air traffic. Then it was time for us to say goodbye to our fantastic Greek adventure and all the wonderful people we had met. We would remember it forever, and I knew I would have to write it all down in my Trip Report when I got home. Someday, I hoped to share it along with some of our other adventures and beautiful pictures of the world. We finally found our boarding gate at the very end of the terminal for the short flight back to Riyadh.

CHAPTER TWENTY-TWO

Switzerland & Ireland
1985

When we returned from Greece, it was hard getting back into a normal routine of life since we had not really had time to adjust to our new home before the trip. We had to shop for the things we needed to do the cleaning because we found our large terrace out front all covered with sand. We bought our first *squeegee* to clean off the water after hosing it off, and it worked very well. Sand storms came through occasionally, and it was something we had to get used to. We also learned that our house had a lot of windows with cracks around them which let in the sand, so we learned to put tape around all the windows to keep it out. Life was different at the ROC but somehow seemed better because of the large restaurant, which offered us a better variety of food on its monthly menu. Much of it was imported from the States, so the American food was always good. We could also depend on the Mexican food with good tacos and enchiladas. Also, I could walk down the street to my doctor's appointments and drop by the convenience store to buy a few groceries if I ran out of anything. For dental appointments, John drove us downtown to the American dentist, who did an excellent job of installing bridges or crowns and just basically took care of our dental needs under our company's insurance plan. John was furnished with a company car, so we always had transportation to wherever we needed to go. We were very happy to have letters from both our mothers when we returned and were very thankful to learn they were both doing well. Hannah had bought herself a new sewing machine and was busily making herself a new wardrobe. We looked forward to seeing her later in the year. Mother was also doing very well and looking forward to our trip report about Greece, so I got right to work on it and our correspondence to all the family.

I was so elated by all the marvelous places we had been and the things we had seen, which went right along with my Bible studies, that it took me a while to get back down to earth after our trip. Now I was anxious to get back into my studies and pick up where I left off, but here I was in Saudi Arabia where the *Call to Prayer* awakened me every morning at 5:00 am. Muslims all over the country were starting their daily routine of five prayers a day, so I got up to start mine. I was interested in learning more about their religion, so I picked up one of John's books which he had brought over with him on Middle Eastern history. I started reading about Islam and how it had its beginning in the 6th Century. Since all pagan religions believe in other gods, and some in many gods, I believe this religion had its roots in the other two major religions of that day. Christianity was moving rapidly across Europe and had reached Scotland and Ireland in the 6th Century. Although the Jews, as a whole, did not receive Jesus as Messiah, they were blinded so salvation could come to the Gentiles. God promises to remove their blindness at the end of the Church Age when *the time of the Gentiles is full.* This new religion of the 6th Century professes to believe in the one true God and the teachings of Jesus, but it rejects Jesus as *the Son of God.* It accepts him as *teacher* and *prophet* but does not understand *the lamb sacrifice as atonement for sin,* depicted by Abraham and Isaac on Mt. Moriah, when *God provided the sacrifice, a ram caught in the thicket by its horns, symbolizing the death of Jesus on Calvary's cross.* (Genesis 22:1-18)

We were happy also to receive letters from Amanda and Zach which brought us up to date on Greg and Maggie. Amanda said that Maggie was looking good and that she was more relaxed than she's ever been since starting to school at ODU. Maggie's letters were very positive, and she seemed to be solving her problems with self-confidence and taking charge of her life. Most of all, she seemed happy with her new courses and was enjoying them as she progressed. She rarely saw Greg, but she had a positive attitude about his eventual admittance into Woodrow Wilson. Both Amanda and Zach wrote us regularly to keep us informed about Greg's progress, and they encouraged him to get a haircut. Amanda arranged for one of her friends to come over to their house to cut his hair. They said it was a great improvement in his appearance, and they had hopes of getting him into the Woodrow Wilson Rehab very soon.

After about a month had passed and Greg had his new prosthesis, Amanda wrote that he was not cooperating with some of the programs. He seemed to be slowly drifting back into his old ways and didn't think he needed the programs. As he had done with us, he started slipping out to visit friends and was soon smoking "pot" again. We could tell by their letters that they were growing more and more frustrated. Zach tried talking to him and laying down the law like John had done, but it did no good because of Greg's *fixed attitude against authority*. He was taking advantage of Amanda and Zach exactly as he had done us over the years, when the doctors in the mental health unit of the Alexandria hospital told us that this could go on indefinitely. *The doctors had him committed* the third time through the Virginia Court system to a *long term drug and alcohol treatment program* in the State Hospital.

Three times, Greg was released from this State Hospital which never did work for him because of his *fixed attitude* against authority. He wasn't ready to admit he had a problem and therefore lived his life in denial depending on others to take care of him. AA had a much better chance of working for him, and we had dropped him off several times at an AA facility only to have him leave and appear back at our door. John had given up a good military career to save our sanity after many years of what they were just beginning to suffer with Greg, and I knew them well enough to know that they, like Christine Ambers, would take no guff. Finally, in one of her letters, Amanda said they had taken down the *Love Never Fails* sign, which had hung in their kitchen for as long as I could remember. We felt terrible about what they were experiencing with Greg, but what could we do from half a world away! After warning Greg of what would happen if he didn't abide by their house rules, they were finally forced into driving him over to Norfolk and dropping him off at the AA Shelter. John and I were somewhat relieved to hear this because they had chosen to do exactly the right thing. It got him out into the world where he could suffer the consequences of his actions, and it supported what I had learned in my Al Anon workshop!

Our next door neighbors, Dean and Dianne, invited us over to their house for Thanksgiving Dinner along with some of their younger Litton friends, and we enjoyed being with all of them and their two young boys. Litton provided each family with another large turkey for the holidays, so they were good enough to cook their turkey and invite their guests, allowing them to bring a side dish of vegetable, salad or dessert. It worked out beautifully! There was a great assortment of dishes which blended in amazingly well with the more traditional ones, producing a different, more exotic Thanksgiving Dinner than some of us were used to, but one that we all enjoyed tremendously. Everything was delicious! We enjoyed sampling all the different kinds of food all afternoon and exchanging recipes. We also enjoyed watching the kids play games, and, at the same time, we enjoyed watching one of our favorite old Broadway musicals, "*Brigadoon.*" It was a great Thanksgiving Day to remember.

Another friend, Eileen, who lived a few houses down from us on the ROC, was a lady from California, and we often rode the bus together for grocery shopping or just browsing around the souks. We seemed to enjoy each other's company and found that we had a lot in common. We were both adventurous spirits and enjoyed traveling, but we also had a love for cooking and knew how to use our computers and sewing machines. Also, I think we both had secretarial backgrounds. Over many trips to the souks, I ended up with many brass camels, ropes of camel bells, teapots, cups and other brassware mostly to give away after coming home because I could never use most of my accumulation. One day while looking around one of the souks, we just happened upon men's *thobes* in pastel solid colors of a pretty light blue and a light yellow, so we got the bright idea of buying one of each color and sewing lace around the collars and bodice to give them a feminine look. We each bought two of them and some pretty white lace and could hardly wait to get home to see what we could do with our projects. Our pastel dresses turned out very cute, and we wore them just about everywhere. We had learned that the Arabs consider it much nicer if *we Westerners* just dress modestly in long dresses with long sleeves or long pants, instead of *covering* with the abaya.

Eileen prepared a wonderful roasted *Leg of Lamb* for a small dinner party at their house before we all had to leave to go our separate ways, and it was so delicious served with *mint jelly* and the appropriate vegetables. John and I learned to love the flavors of the lamb mingled with the other complimentary foods, and I vowed to prepare it at home someday for our whole family. I prayed consistently for my family's salvation, so we could become a *normal* family and enjoy the good things of life once again. Now I know in my heart that Greg's problem went much deeper than physical, mental or psychological; it was a spiritual battle which only God could handle. We would have to get out of the way and have patience as we turned it all over to him and let God do his work.

In my new Bible group on the ROC Compound, I became friends with a very sweet young Korean woman, Soon-Bak, who asked me if John and I could babysit her precious four-year-old daughter, Joanie, while she and her husband attended a reception for a visiting Air Force Colonel. Of course, we were happy to sit with little Joanie, who attended her kindergarten class right next door to our house and we often saw her playing outside in the yard. She was very cute, and John and I had fun playing ball with her outside in our driveway and having a tea party in our living room. The following year, Soon-Bak gave birth to a baby boy, and John and I were happy to babysit both of them while they attended another Air Force function. When it was time for us to leave the following summer, Soon-Bak gave us a very nice farewell party at her house and our Bible study group brought some wonderful dishes to the party. She always called her husband, Barry, the Korean way, "Bally," with the "rs" making the "l" sound, and it sounded so cute. While I was visiting one day after the baby boy's arrival, Joanie decided to make her mother speak her daddy's name in English by holding her mother's cheeks between her two little hands and telling her to say *"Bar-r-r- y."* Joanie was very persistent, and it was so adorable, and fun for me, to watch her try so hard to get her mother to speak her daddy's name the English way. I felt so honored to be there with them to share this precious moment, but try as they may, Soon-Bak continued calling her husband Bally. And I believe she still does to this day!

When we lived in Vienna, I learned through our Christmas cards that Soon- Bak and her husband bought a house in Woodbridge. I dialed the telephone number she gave me and was so happy to hear her sweet voice when she answered. Soon-Bak is a delightful Christian friend! And I hope to see her again. We talked over the phone several times but never did get our husbands together before we sold our house in Vienna and moved away. A few years later, I tried calling her on the same number, and her grown son answered the phone. He told me that his mother and dad were back in Korea temporarily with the large company his dad worked for at that time. Today, Joanie is an accomplished designer with a large architectural firm in the DC area and has her own apartment. I was happy to speak with both of them while Joanie was visiting her mother at their home a few months ago, and we had a delightful conversation.

Since our time was getting short for John's original contract with Litton to run out, the company offered him a new contract which would keep us in Saudi Arabia a while longer and then a couple of years in California while awaiting another big project. It was quite appealing and would have allowed us to save a substantial amount of money, but John turned it down because he was more interested in coming back to the States to finish Law School. I was beginning to like living on the ROC, but I needed to be closer to our family. It was another important decision we had to make and one which would take us back and forth weighing all the issues and possibilities until it was resolved. I was reminded of other important decisions we had to make over the years, all of which would take us down different roads. We had to rely totally on God's direction to light up the pathway before us and lead us down the right road.

In January of our second year in Riyadh, I planned to be home for my mother's 80th birthday, and my brothers and sisters-in-law were planning a big birthday party. In her need to get home to her children, Alice seemed to be missing out on some of the trips others were planning; so I coaxed her into coming back to the States with me. I wanted her to see Switzerland on our way home, and I planned a trip on the *Glacier Express* between the two major cities, Geneva and Zurich, with overnight stops in Zermatt and San Moritz. It was something I needed to talk to John about, but he never could find the time. I never learned the reason why, but something went wrong with our husbands getting the payment in on time to our travel agent. All our reservations were cancelled the day before we were scheduled to leave! It could very well have been because the Glacier Express doesn't operate all year due to severe weather conditions, or it could have been the high-seasonal rates. However, I was finally able to reschedule our trip into Geneva and out of Zurich in a shorter amount of time taking the regular train between the two cities and cutting expenses considerably. Nevertheless, I had to try to make it home for Mother's 80th birthday at the end of January.

A Tour of Switzerland

Alice and I had a great time spending three days and two nights walking through the old town of Geneva and through the main parts of the downtown section. First, we took the city bus from the airport and placed our bags down inside the bus as we stood by and held on to the straps. Every time the bus turned, our baggage turned around on a circular device, and it was quite a surprise to us the first time it happened and so funny we had to laugh. Somehow we made it to our nice hotel on Lake Geneva where we could walk to all the interesting places of the downtown area. We visited the historic church with the magnificent view of the lake from the bell tower, and we dined at some of the great restaurants I remembered. I had learned a little French which helped us buy boots in Geneva and a little German which helped us on our way out in Zurich. Since we would be going up into the high Swiss Mountains via cable car and walking through snow, we decided to go shopping for snow boots. Of course, we both fell in love with the same pair of cute white furry-lined boots, which we bought and wore all the way through Switzerland. When we first arrived in our hotel room, I told Alice, *"Don't turn your hair dryer on 'High' or you'll blow out the lights, because they operate on a higher wattage that the US."* I had already learned my lesson on a previous trip. Well, guess what? *She forgot!* And while we were getting ready to go to dinner, out they went. But just for a few minutes and then they were back on again.

After our walking tour of Geneva, the second day, we rode the train around the lake to Montreux and checked into our hotel there just in time for lunch. We spent the rest of the afternoon touring the *Castle at Chillon*, made famous by Lord Byron in his poem, *The Prisoner of Chillon*. Then we walked back to the train station where we caught the cogged cable car up the mountain where John and I had enjoyed lunch one bright sunny day at *Rochers-de-Naye* and taken many gorgeous pictures of the beautiful view from the mountain top overlooking Montreux and the lake. I didn't know the cable car didn't go all the way to the top that late in the afternoon, so we had to get off at the highest point and walk around the small town to take pictures while searching for a restaurant to get in out of the cold. There were no restaurants here, but we noticed a tunnel which once served as a bomb shelter during WWII. While awaiting the last cogged train to take us back down the mountain, we discovered a small café on the boarding dock where we enjoyed a hot Cheese Fondue and a glass of white wine, which made this part of our journey a little more enjoyable. We also enjoyed a late dinner at the hotel that evening and retired early, anxious to get an early start the next day.

The City of Montreux, Switzerland. The Castle of Chillon, Montreux.

Alice and I were up bright and early for our continental breakfast and a nice walk through the park along the lake to make more pictures before check out time. John and I had stayed in this hotel before, and I remembered a great restaurant across the street from the train station where we were to board our train for Zurich. We were in the middle of the most wonderful Roast Beef Dinner when some German ladies learned that we were enroute to Zurich. They insisted that we leave right then to catch the *Express Train* scheduled to leave within minutes. So, reluctantly, we left our delicious half-finished dinner on the table of the restaurant to hurry across the street to buy our tickets for the *fast train* to Zurich. Since neither of us understood enough of the German language to know when the announcement was given, we sat there waiting with tickets in hand as we watched the express train pull slowly out of the station. All we could do was sit there laughing in astonishment!

Realizing our mistake, we became silly for the rest of the day as our *slow train* made all the stops along the way. However, the scenery was very beautiful with the freshly fallen snow as we rose higher and higher into the lovely Swiss Alps. We passed through the ski resort town of *Gstaad*, where John and I had once gotten off and found a wonderful restaurant for lunch, but Alice and I didn't have time to spare and we didn't know how much longer our trip was going to last. After numerous stops with signs announcing *Buffet,* we began to get very hungry and wished we had stayed longer to finish our delicious roast beef dinner. Finally, I was glad to see a sign I recognized, *Next Stop Lucerne,* a city I knew quite well. I coaxed Alice into getting off and promised her a great fish dinner of *Plaice,* fresh from Lake Lucerne, and always cooked to perfection, with *Chocolate Mousse* for dessert.

It was getting late in the afternoon when we disembarked at Lucerne and started walking through the downtown streets to get into the atmosphere of the lovely City. I pointed out the fixtures over all the doorways, which described the type of business found inside, and some of the other things I had learned on our city tour in 1984 when John and I were on our way to Kandersteg. Alice and I walked quickly through the city and across Chapel Bridge to the lovely old chapel I had told her about. Then we crossed the straight bridge back to the city where we found one of the restaurants I remembered. We found a table and placed our orders for a *Plaice* dinner and it was so delicious, just as I remembered, cooked to perfection and served with fresh steamed vegetables and a glass of white wine. We took time to just sit back and relax as we enjoyed our dinner and topped it off with a heavenly chocolate mousse and coffee. Then it was time to head back to the station to board the next train for Zurich.

We arrived at our hotel quite late in the evening only to find that our reservations had been cancelled and the hotel was full. I assumed this had something to do with our first reservations having been cancelled, and, knowing how they usually hold a room for special clients or situations such as this, I persuaded the hotel manager to find us a room. While waiting, Alice and I signed up for a sight-seeing bus tour early the following morning, which would take us up to the top of the highest mountain via cogged cable car. We had an early breakfast and caught our tour bus for a drive around the city, through the countryside and to the cogged cable car which took us up the mountain to the ski lift where we could enjoy the snow and watch the skiers. We enjoyed a hot chocolate in the snack bar of the ski lodge and found a place to rest while we enjoyed the atmosphere. We also walked around in the snow taking pictures of the lovely views from the mountain and it was very similar to Kandersteg.

The following day, Alice and I ventured out of our hotel after breakfast and toured some of the city of Zurich by foot. Then we hopped on a street car to ride around the very large city to see as much of it as we could during our last day. We noticed the park where the drug users hung out along the lake but avoided it and found a nice restaurant for dinner where we enjoyed *Jaeger Schnitzel and pommes frites* served with a great *European salad and Crème Caramel* for dessert. We were up early the following morning for breakfast and our scheduled pickup to the Zurich Airport. Our flight into New York was scheduled to leave sometime around mid-morning, so we could get through US Customs early and connect with our separate flights home. However, our plane had mechanical problems and was delayed several hours before takeoff, and Alice and I were both late in connecting with our scheduled flights home. Now Alice and I both had experienced the pros and cons of travel. She somehow managed to get through customs and make the late flight to Ohio, arriving at her home in a taxi well after midnight. I couldn't get a flight until early the next day and had no luggage for my overnight stay in the airport hotel. Without my pajamas to keep me warm, I couldn't get any sleep and caught the flu, probably from a glass in the hotel room, which I had to use for my three aspirin. Of course, I could have gotten it from the circulating air of the plane, but I had a bad case of something by the time I got home. *What a miserable day!*

I didn't make it home for Mother's 80th birthday, but they had a great celebration without me. And they made some great pictures! Our oldest brother, Franklin, and his wife, Jeanette, were there from Houston and all the others of our family. I remember calling someone *from the air* on my way home so there would be somebody at the airport to meet me; this time I think it was Joe. I am forever indebted to all my family for always having someone there for me. It was now a few days past Mother's birthday, and I took great precautions not to bring the flu home to her by keeping my distance and sterilizing everything. Thank God she didn't get it!

After being home a few days and getting over the flu, I called Amanda and Zach to learn something more about Greg. They figured he would stay at the AA shelter and get involved in their AA program which would allow him to stay in their half-way house; all of which would help him get into Woodrow Wilson Rehab Center. Greg told me later that he didn't go immediately into the AA shelter but spent Thanksgiving weekend on the vacant top floor of the building in which the AA shelter was located, eating his meals out of the vending machines on the lower floors. He said the nice, thick carpeting on the top floor was very comfortable and was vacuumed at least once while he was there. The following week he got involved with the Norfolk AA program and seemed to be cooperating when Zach and Amanda checked on him. Zach said Greg seemed to be off to another new start, with Woodrow Wilson hanging in the balance waiting for him to finish the AA program. Then he made friends with a couple of guys who didn't stay in the program and left to find jobs and share the expenses of an apartment. Greg told me later that they were really staying in a vacant house between renters which still had the heat on and the electricity on by somehow plugging into the house next door. Zach brought me up to speed about what he knew of the guys with whom Greg was living. They had moved to a house on a cul-de-sac in Virginia Beach when they were discovered and run out of the first place. Zach was a great detective and somehow kept up with Greg. He gave me his address and phone number. I decided to drive up there and find out what was going on with him.

I didn't want Amanda and Zach to get involved all over again if we could avoid it, so I stayed with them a few days while I called Greg and invited him out to lunch so we could talk. Then I drove him over to the Social Security Office to apply for SSI, hoping he could get some financial assistance. Greg was on his best behavior during this time and seemed to appreciate my help in applying for SSI. I also searched the paper to find him a job taking orders over the phone for a pizza restaurant. I drove him to his interview and he got the job to start working the following week, so I helped him pay his share of the rent. Although I didn't meet any of the guys, I left him there at the house on the cul-de-sac with the understanding that he would begin working his new job at the appointed time and pay the rest of his expenses himself. I bought him a few new clothes at the BX along with a small Bible and an Easter card. The card had little Easter bunnies hopping around on it, and I wrote, *"With each hop, you'll be making one more step up the ladder of success."* I didn't know it then, but both the Bible and the card would become very important to him over the next few years.

Greg was ready Easter Sunday when Amanda, Zach and I drove over to pick him up for their Methodist Church Services, and we enjoyed our Easter Sunday together in church. Although I never met any of the guys on the cul- de-sac, I hoped that Greg would keep his job and somehow be able to make a life for himself and pay his expenses. I saw Maggie before I left Virginia Beach and had a very good feeling about her. She was doing well in all her courses at ODU and seemed happy with her accomplishments. I drove away with high hopes for them both and headed back to Alabama.

I still had time to spend with Mother to open her mail, which was usually all piled up by the time I got there, and write a few checks to pay her bills. I would always go through the mail quickly and file away the important papers. Ginger was wonderful about helping Mother balance her check book and pay her bills while I was away, which was probably most of the time during those days. Her eyes were growing dim and she was developing macular degeneration. While I was home, I helped her with the checkbook and took her to doctor's appointments, and I would always give her house a good cleaning and check over her pantry to make sure there were no weevils in the flour, etc. This time, however, I was motivated to make her some blouses because her blouses were wearing out. Ginger had brought this to my attention when she tried to buy Mother some new blouses, but Mother didn't like the store bought blouses because they didn't fit. She was depending on me to make her some new ones by her favorite blouse pattern. I knew what she liked in the way of cotton material, so I went shopping for enough to make her about half a dozen blouses. Of course, I had to learn to use the embroidery setting of her sewing machine to make the button holes and I decided to do a little embroidery work around the collars and sleeves. They were beautiful! And Mother was so proud of them. Before I left the country again, Jim and Kathy drove over from Jackson for a weekend visit. Then it was time for me to pack up and leave on my flight back to Saudi Arabia to help John prepare for our move back to the States.

The Glacier Express

John had saved up some vacation time so we could leave early the middle of May and do some traveling on the way home. Knowing how disappointed I was at not making the Glacier Express with Alice, he checked with our travel agent and found that the best prices for the *Glacier Express* were for the *off-season*, so he set us up for a tentative trip leaving Geneva on the 16th of May for Zermatt and St. Moritz, taking us through the highest mountains of Switzerland with city tours in Geneva, Zurich and Amsterdam.

I remembered our first flight into Geneva which had been during the winter, and we descended into the city through a covering of dark clouds which seemed eerie, but we had a good landing and the next day was sunny. Our hotel at that time had been located on the lovely Corniche of Lake Geneva, so we made many pictures of the lovely park along the lake and found many good restaurants. The night before our scheduled departure, a large snow storm covered the area with several inches of snow and we found ourselves snowed in. Our flight to Riyadh was cancelled, and John had to call the Litton office to report our delay. Since our Hotel l'Arbalete was already booked, they transferred us up the hill to Hotel Les Armures in the Olde Town. The city was so beautiful and completely transformed with a fresh covering of snow, and it beckoned to us to get out and walk through the streets again to make more pictures and capture its entirely different atmosphere. It was fun! We enjoyed the wonderful *Trout Meuniere* in our hotel dining room, and we discovered a new restaurant, *a la Diligence,* in another location in the city, which served the most delicious *Pepper Steak, spaetzel and European salad.* And a great *Chocolate Mousse!*

On this trip into Geneva, however, we were looking forward to riding *the Glacier Express* up through the highest Swiss Alps, and I was glad to hear that John had paid the travel agent on time and our trip this time was a reality. First, we would spend a couple of days in Geneva where we would have a guided bus tour of the city and *Olde Town*; we would visit the historic places again including the *Church and Bell Tower,* where Calvin and Luther started *the Reformation of the Church* back in the 1500's; and we would have a tour of the United Nations building and other important government buildings we had not seen before. We would also launch out on our free time to find some of our favorite restaurants and hotels, which we remembered from before. Hotel l'Arbalete had been demolished and another building was going up in its place but Hotel Les Armures in the Olde Town was still there. We enjoyed another delicious *Pepper Steak* at *a la Diligence,* and it was great, exactly as we remembered, and another delicious *Chocolate Mousse.*

The *Glacier Express* took us through the low lying areas around the city of Geneva and began to slowly move us higher through the low hills and farm country into the higher plateaus where we noticed many farm animals, including many cows and goats grazing on the steep hillsides. We took a great picture of a cow, with a cow bell around its neck, which came right up to the train and looked in at us through the window while we were briefly stopped on the hillside. As we passed on through the lovely countryside, we began to see patches of snow here and there, and then more snow with the high snow-covered peaks in the far distance. We took many pictures! As we ascended higher and higher into the mountains, we passed through many long tunnels through solid rock. The scenery was absolutely breathtaking!

The Glacier Express at Zermatt, Switzerland.

Our first stop was *Zermatt,* where John and I spent one night in a hotel right in the midst of the town, with noisy people passing below our window at all hours. After breakfast early the next morning, we set out on foot to see as much of the town as we could and noticed the large cemetery in the center of Zermatt, where many people were buried who didn't quite make it to the top of the *Matterhorn,* or safely back down. We looked up to try to get a glimpse of the Matterhorn, but it was all covered with clouds that early in the morning. About an hour later, the clouds cleared away, and we rode the cable car as far up as it would take us. What a thrill! We were at the top of the closest mountain to the Matterhorn, and we got some great pictures all the way up and the way down and of the great mountain itself. We also took a great picture of the town of Zermatt below from that high vantage point. With no time to spare, we had to run to catch our train and made it just in time. As soon as we were on the train, the Glacier Express started moving out on its way to *St. Moritz.*

The Matterhorn, Zermatt, Switzerland.

On this portion of the trip, we would be passing through the highest mountains of Switzerland and we would be rising into higher altitudes while we had dinner. The glasses they used were tilted for going up the steep incline and had to be turned around in the other direction for going down. The food they served was absolutely delicious, but I was so busy taking pictures, I failed to eat it quickly enough to finish before my plate had to be removed. The sympathetic waiter looked at me with great compassion and said, *"I'm sorry,"* as he slowly took away my entrée and the delicious cauliflower, which had been steamed to perfection seasoned with a little butter, salt and pepper. I realized too late that they had a limited amount of time to serve each car, and the plates had to be removed before going on to the next car. We continued our journey still rising a bit more until it seemed to level off and go through the last long tunnel on the way to *St. Moritz*, where we stopped for overnight and managed to get a glimpse of the beautiful city all spread out surrounding one end of the lovely lake which was nestled beneath a gigantic mountain with many, many very high slopes perfect for skiing. It would require many cable car lifts to get up to the highest slopes for some great skiing and a breathtaking view. No wonder the peak season is so expensive!

We enjoyed our breakfast in this luxury hotel and walked around the close vicinity taking pictures. Like in Zermatt, we had to hurry back to the hotel for our baggage to catch our train for the last leg of our journey on the Glacier Express, which would take us into *Zurich*. Of course, we had to pass through many more long tunnels to get through some of the highest mountains in Switzerland and on the downward slope which took us down into the lower plateaus of Zurich. The scenery was gorgeous but the train ride seemed shorter in comparison with the two previous days. We stayed in Zurich two nights at a top notch hotel and enjoyed the guided city tour. During our free time, we walked around and rode street cars to see more of the city, as Alice and I had done, and ended up at the train station where we decided to have dinner. We would be back the following morning to catch our train for Amsterdam.

We spent two nights at the Amstel Hotel in Amsterdam with another guided bus tour of the City. We visited the *Rijksmuseum* where we viewed many beautiful works of the *Dutch Masters,* including some great oil paintings of Rembrandt. We also visited a diamond factory, where John bought me a beautiful diamond dinner ring with two marquises in the center surrounded by nine smaller diamonds mounted in yellow gold. Then we had a ride on the *Amsterdam Canal* through the city and visited the *Anne Frank House,* where she and her family had lived while trying to escape the Nazis. They would have made it if only an informant hadn't overheard them while trying to rob the downstairs office. Our trip ended here in Amsterdam having spent two nights in this lovely Dutch city, and, somewhere along the way, John picked up a virus and was feeling quite ill on our last evening, so we got to bed early.

A Tour of Ireland

From Amsterdam the next morning, we flew to *Dublin* where we checked into the *Dublin Airport Hotel* so John could get some rest and recover. I took this opportunity of taking care of the sick one to wash out a few items of clothing with our room's shampoo and hung them over the radiators to dry. We ate all our meals in the hotel restaurant, which we nicknamed *The Flying Circus,* because of all the families with small children and the dropped utensils and broken dishes. This was our first impression of Ireland where we came to know and love the Irish people, because I guess they reminded us so much of our own family when our kids were small. After a couple of days, John was feeling much better, so we took a taxi into Dublin to see the city. We conversed with the taxi driver all the way into town, and he very jokingly told us that all the good looking people went to America and the ugly ones stayed in Ireland. We enjoyed his Irish sense of humor as well as our bus driver's on the *City Tour*, which took us all over the city and by the *Post Office*, where we stopped to hear the history of the siege by British Troops in the *Easter Rising of 1916*. The post office was badly damaged and a few of the Irish leaders killed. An emerging hero of those captured during this siege was *Michael Collins* who became head of the *Irish Republican Brotherhood*, and, in 1921, took part in the *Anglo-Irish Treaty* negotiations which freed the southern counties from British rule.

Our city bus tour took us out from the city center to one of the largest walled city parks in Europe: Phoenix Park, which consists of 1,750 acres of grasslands and tree-lined avenues and, since the 17th Century, has been the home of a herd of wild Fallow Deer. It is also the home of the President of Ireland, *Aras an Uachtarain*, as well as the home of the American Ambassador, *Deerfield Residence*. Within the walls of the park, are many famous and historical places including the *Dublin Zoo, St. Mary's Hospital, the People's Gardens, Papal Cross, Wellington Monument, the War Memorial, a Military Cemetery and the Visitor's Center* with plenty of parking spaces at all locations. Before leaving the bus station, we signed up for a day tour to *Glendalough*.

Church and Cemetery at Glendalough, Ireland.

The following morning, we were up very early for breakfast and took a taxi back to the bus station to board our 8:00 am bus to *Glendalough*. We had heard from friends that this was one tour we didn't want to miss because this ancient cemetery contained so much history about Ireland and the Gaelic people. The memorials and markers throughout the cemetery, including the movie at the Visitor's Center, were all very interesting and explained so much about the origin of Ireland. We saw the movie and stopped to read some of the markers and then walked across a bridge to have lunch at the hotel restaurant, where our bus was parked. After a wonderful Salmon dinner in the hotel dining room, we just happened to run into a young couple from the Litton group who stayed in Frankfurt, the son and daughter-in-law of two of our good friends, Efram and Marge, who remained in Frankfurt.

As we were leaving, our bus stopped briefly at *the Meeting of the Waters*, where two rivers came together to flow as one large river. That evening, before going back to our hotel, we stayed in Dublin to see a play by *Sean O'Casey* and stopped by a pub for John to have one last Guinness before hailing a Taxi back to the hotel. The following morning, we checked out of the Airport Hotel and rode the tram over to Dublin Airport to check our baggage for the flight home. We enjoyed one last dinner in the airport restaurant before boarding our plane back to the States.

CHAPTER TWENTY-THREE

Back to Washington
1985

When we arrived back home, Zach was happy to report that Greg was now living at the Woodrow Wilson Rehab Center. It was complicated and Zach promised to give us the whole rundown when we came through Virginia Beach on our way to Washington. For the present, John and I were relieved to hear that Greg was finally in the best place he could be for getting his life in order and completing his education. We telephoned John's mother, Hannah, and Jim and Kathy, to let them know that we were home and of our plans to move back to the Washington area for John to finish Law School at Catholic University and for me to find a good secretarial job. They were happy to hear that we were home again and that Greg was finally in the program at WWRC. We assured them that we would come for a visit while staying for a few days with Mother awaiting our move in date. First, we had to find an apartment in Crystal City across from the subway, which we both intended to use for transportation back and forth each day. Zach gave us a telephone number where we could get in touch with Greg, so he could call us from the Rehab Center. When Greg called us at Mother's house, we told him our plans and promised to stop by to see him on our way through after we found an apartment. We also planned to stop by Virginia Beach to see Amanda and Zach to hear their amazing story of how they got Greg into the Rehab Center.

Zach taught ROTC at a boys' military school in the Tidewater area and worked with young men every day. Having raised a large family of six children, both he and Amanda knew how to handle young people in the Virginia area, and they certainly had gone out of their way to help Greg. Zach told us that he had a very bad opinion of the guys Greg was living with on the cul-de-sac because every time he drove by their house, he noticed odd things going on. On a hunch one day, he stopped by and knocked on the door to pay a visit and see how Greg was doing. Nobody answered the door, although Zach could hear them moving around inside. Finally, he called to them through the door and threatened to call the police to have the house raided if they didn't open the door and allow him to come in and see his nephew. Someone cracked the door to peek out, and Zach pushed it open and rushed in to find Greg lying unconscious on the floor obviously from an overdose. Zach had no idea what he had taken or had been given, and the guys weren't about to give him any clues. Zach said Greg's face was ashen and he knew he had to get him out of there quickly, so he picked Greg up bodily and carried him to his car. Then he drove Greg to their home in Virginia Beach.

Zach and Amanda saved Greg's life! Thank God, after a few days of liquids, good food and prayer, Greg came out of it and seemed very appreciative for their help. A few days later, after getting permission from the Woodrow Wilson Rehab Center, Zach drove Greg over to the cul-de-sac to get his things before driving him to Fishersville for admittance into Woodrow Wilson Rehab Center. Zach thought that the time Greg had spent in the Norfolk AA facility counted towards his acceptance into the WWRC program, and also I believe his former Rehab counselor in the northern Virginia area, Christine Ambers, might have had something to do with it. She had a long file on Greg and his accomplishments before he left the area: he had attended several AA programs, passed the GED test to get his certificate, held a job with Better Home Insulators for almost a year and he worked with Purple Heart Vets.

When I called to speak with Greg about the time we would be passing through Fishersville, I found that he was no longer there at WWRC. He had been released on his own recognizance. They couldn't hold him because it was entirely a *voluntary program*, and now the same old *merry-go-round* was trying to start up again. Greg knew that we were back in the country and was released because he remembered *how to play the game*. However, the rules of the game had changed, and we would never again allow ourselves to get hooked into such a losing battle. We drove on to Mother's house, and, a short time later, we received a phone call from Greg giving us his phone number and telling us where we could pick him up in Virginia Beach. John was furious! He absolutely refused! However, I promised to help him find a place to live in Virginia Beach on our way up to northern Virginia.

When our apartment was ready for us to move in about two weeks later, John, driving our new Cougar, went on up to meet the movers while I, driving our old faithful Yellow Sub, drove to Virginia Beach. I checked into a motel room and called Greg to meet me for lunch. Then I took him back to my motel room, and we looked in the *classified section* of the newspaper under *Rooms for Rent*. I found one almost immediately and dialed the number. The lady who answered the phone was very nice and explained that she had invested in a house with rooms to rent and needed people to share expenses. It turned out to be a good place with decent people living there and seemed to be the answer to our problem. I drove him over to meet her and arranged for him to move into his room that afternoon. It seemed too good to be true and had to be *the answer to prayer*. I was so very thankful! We shopped for a few groceries to get him started in the shared kitchen, and I paid his deposit and a month's rent. Then I left Greg there in his new rooming house feeling quite good about his new beginning, and he promised to get a job. I had a good rapport with his landlady and sent his rent in early each month. Greg and I communicated via their shared *community* telephone. When I arrived at the scene of our new apartment in Crystal City, the place was in turmoil and I had never seen such a scrambled up mess in my life! Everything was all mixed up and out of place. All the boxes had been shoved into the apartment haphazardly and just left wherever they landed. Of course some of this is to be expected, but this was undoubtedly the worst move-in I had ever seen or experienced! Probably because I had always been there to help John direct boxes to their proper places and plunged right into my job of unpacking the kitchen items first, getting things in place and the boxes out as quickly as possible to make room for new boxes coming in. Our success had always been using this method of organizing the kitchen first from which everything else revolves. John's job had always been to direct the furniture to the proper rooms and have it assembled properly as he kept track of the packing list for which everything is accounted as he checked it off. Eventually, everything found its place over the weeks and months ahead, but, temporarily in the process, it presented a topsy-turvy lifestyle and took much longer than ever before.

Around the first of October, I was ready to begin my job search typing letters and preparing a new resume. I applied for several Government secretarial positions and to a couple of law firms as legal secretary. I didn't bother applying for a job in computers since my former *upward mobility program* ended when John retired from the Army. Anyway, I realized that I was much happier working in a large office environment rather than being stuck in a back room with a computer. I attended several Government interviews and received several good offers: one from FER as Staff Secretary to replace Peggy, which would have been a promotion over my old job and was very tempting because I loved working in FER. However, they had changed to a new Lanier Computer System, which was foreign to me, and did away with the Wang. I felt the vibes were all wrong this time because the chemistry of the office had changed. Most of the people I had worked with were no longer there, so I decided to try something different with higher pay working in a law office as a legal secretary.

I was having a hard time making my decision when George and Grace came up for a visit towards the end of October, and they helped me decide simply by listening to me as I told them about each one of my offers. I turned down one because everyone in the office smoked and the air was filled with heavy toxic fumes when I walked in. Finally, I accepted a position with a reputable DC law firm working for a vibrant young woman attorney and her assistant. Our office was located on the 3rd floor of a high rise office building on 17th Street, one block over from the White House. It proved to be the right choice for me at this time of my life, and I enjoyed the atmosphere of working in the Capitol city with a wonderful assortment of good restaurants and very nice dress shops. John would meet me for lunch when he could or sometimes for dinner at one of our favorite downtown restaurants. I had a good rapport with my attorneys and all the others I came to know and work with in our law office environment.

A Tour of Washington, DC

After six years of living in the Washington area between 1976 and 1982, John and I had never really had a tour of Washington because we were always too busy with our jobs or solving family problems, so we decided to be well prepared for Grace and George when they came for a visit in October. We bought a tape, *Touring Washington by Auto*, and made reservations for all the places we wanted to take them. They arrived at National Airport on Wednesday afternoon, the 30th of October. We had a quiet dinner at home that first evening and got to bed early in preparation for our *Tour*, which began early the next morning. After a good breakfast, we drove over to *Arlington Cemetery* where we purchased two-day tickets for the *Tour-Mobile,* which would drive us through *the cemetery, the monuments, museums and government buildings* with stops all along the way and a tour guide on each bus describing points of interest and giving the history of the Capitol City. It was a great way to start our tour, and, at the same time, learn where everything was located. All we had to do was get off at the places we wanted to see and start walking through the museums, or large buildings, and especially through the monuments located throughout the mall area.

We began with a drive through Arlington Cemetery where we had a guided tour of the old *Custis Home* and enjoyed a fantastic view of the city with the cemetery below which had its start in the 19th Century with the bodies of soldiers who fell in the great Civil War. We visited the *Tomb of the Unknown Soldier* and watched the *Changing of the Guards,* then briefly stopped at the burial sites of *President John F. Kennedy,* with the *Eternal Flame,* and *Senator Robert Kennedy* buried nearby. Then we rode by the *Memorials* listening to the guide as he gave a brief history. After getting off the tram, we started with the *Space Museum* and had lunch in the *cafeteria of the Department of Agriculture,* before walking through the original *Smithsonian Building* and then across the mall to the museum of *Natural History* and next door to the museum of *American History.* We walked through the mall and rode the elevator to the top of the *Washington Monument* where we had a fantastic view of the entire DC area. Worn out from walking all day, John drove us down 23rd Street, just a few blocks down from our apartment, to the row of famous *international restaurants* to our favorite Thai restaurant, *the Bangkok Gourmet.* Since neither Grace nor George had ever tried Thai food, this was something different, and I think they enjoyed the *mild* version of *Shrimp, Almond Chicken and Chicken Curry* with lots of rice and appropriate condiments. My favorite was always *Mango Chutney.* In the same area was another one of our favorite all time restaurants where we would take them on another night, *Café Italia,* where the food was also great and above the tables were the signatures of the famous people who had once sat there for dinner.

Friday morning, we caught the 9:00 am bus for *Mt. Vernon,* the lovely historic home of *George and Martha Washington,* and the drive along the Potomac was beautiful although most of the autumn leaves had fallen. The walk-through tour of the old Washington Home was very beautiful with a marvelous view of the Potomac River from their front porch. The home had recently been restored to depict life as it was in the days of George and Martha with the slave quarters in back also restored. We visited their tombs just a short distance down the pathway from the home, and we ate our picnic lunch while awaiting our bus for the return trip to Arlington. That evening, John drove us out to Woodbridge to the *Lazy Susan Dinner Theatre* for their *Dutch Buffet* and their delightful production of *The Unsinkable Molly Brown*. Saturday morning, we deposited our *Tour by Auto* tape and set out following its directions through Washington. We started with *the Iwo Jima War Memorial in Rosslyn*, and crossed *Memorial Bridge* into DC which took us by *George Washington University* and the *GWU Hospital*, then down the main street of *Georgetown* and along *Embassy Row* all the way to *the National Cathedral*. Here we had a fantastic guided tour which took us all the way to the top of this very unique and impressive National Cathedral, which took several years in the building with many problems to overcome for a final completion of this very beautiful and ornate structure. From the high tower of the Cathedral, we had another fantastic view of Washington. On the way back to Arlington, our tour took us on a scenic drive through the downtown streets of the District and pointed out various points of interest along the way. After lunch, the guys watched TV football and snacked while the ladies watched a movie and prepared for an evening at the *Kennedy Center*. We had tickets with very good seats to attend a special concert by the *National Symphony Orchestra* featuring a world acclaimed violinist, Itzak Pearlman, whose performance was superb as always. The Kennedy Center was very beautiful and exciting.

Sunday was a quiet day of church, lunch and shopping for the ladies at Landmark Mall shopping center; for the men, a day of golf at Ft. Belvoir golf course with some of John's friends. On Monday morning, we rode the Metro over to *Capitol Hill* where we toured the *Capitol Building, the Jefferson Building and the Library of Congress*. We also visited the *Supreme Court* and found seats to watch the session in progress before it was adjourned for the day. Then we walked quickly through the *Madison Building*, found the Metro and headed home. That evening, we drove downtown to attend a play at *Ford's Theatre, Little Me*, which was very funny and cute. Then we visited the Lincoln museum on the ground floor of the theatre, which contains a unique display of various items pertaining to President Lincoln's assassination and the history of that ill-fated day.

Tuesday morning, we were up early to catch the Metro for our morning tour of the White House at 10:00. Then we walked down 14th Street to the *Commerce Building*, where we visited the *National Aquarium* and, from there, we walked to the *American History Building*, where we had a complete guided tour. Already worn out, we took a taxi back to a little pub near the White House where we were scheduled to meet Charles Rutherford, a good friend of John's, who worked in the Executive Office Building. While waiting, John ordered a round of Irish coffee for the four of us, which he ended up drinking because they were terribly strong. Then Charlie arrived to walk us over to the *west wing of the White House* for a special visit to *the Oval Office*. While still in the downtown area, we took Grace and George out for a fish dinner at our favorite restaurant in the District before catching the Metro back to Crystal City.

Wednesday morning, we drove Grace and George over to another part of town to visit some of their other relatives who also lived in northern Virginia and then back home for lunch and packing. We were sorry to see them off after spending such a great time together, but their plane was scheduled for departure at 3:00 pm. We had enjoyed a great *Tour of Washington,* but we were all exhausted and needed a little rest before it was time to get back to work. Two weeks later, I started my job with the DC law firm.

Maggie came home for Thanksgiving and a friend rode up with her to share expenses. John used our *Tour of Washington* tape again to take Maggie with us by *Lee's historic home in Alexandria* and then out to *Mt. Vernon* where we had reservations for Thanksgiving Dinner at the *Mt. Vernon Inn* for the three of us. The traditional sliced turkey and dressing dinner served buffet style was absolutely heavenly with many delicious salads and vegetables plus all kinds of desserts. I especially loved their cranberry muffins. After enjoying our wonderful dinner, we left the car parked at the restaurant and walked down the old country lane to the beautiful restored home of George and Martha Washington with the attached slave quarters. From the front porch, which stretched across the width of the house, we had a picturesque view of the lovely bend of the Potomac River as it turned to flow directly in front of us. After our tour of the home and slave quarters, we visited the tombs of George and Martha as well as the slaves' burial grounds. Maggie said she planned to come home again after the 13th of December, their last day of school, but would have to go back a week later to help her friend with his newspaper job. She wanted to be there to meet his parents when they drove down to spend Christmas with him and their daughter who lived in Norfolk.

Maggie was still enjoying her college courses and making good grades, and Greg seemed to be content to remain for the time being in the Virginia Beach rooming house where I left him. He said he was attending *Outreach,* a drug abuse program which met once a week, and that he was also meeting periodically with his Rehab counselor. He said he was due to begin a course in *Computer Programming* starting with *Key Punch* when he thought himself ready; however, he never did seem to get around to it. But at least he was taking care of himself and staying straight. The people in his rooming house shared the kitchen and did their own cooking, and they also shared the washer and dryer and chores to keep the house clean. Greg seemed content with the setup at first and got along well with the others, but then a few disagreements arose regarding the food in the refrigerator and chores left undone. They all pitched in for Thanksgiving Dinner and had plans for doing the same at Christmas. However, Greg decided that he wanted more privacy in preparing his meals and storing his food in the refrigerator, and he needed a private bathroom. He wanted me to help him find another place, but I told him that I was too busy with my new job to make the trip down there at that time.

In January, Greg called to tell me about a large check he received in the mail from Social Security, so I decided to drive down to check it out and help him open a checking account. Social Security required him to have an open bank account for his monthly checks to be automatically deposited. With the first deposit, he would be able to get his own apartment in Virginia Beach. We found the perfect place for him with a small kitchen and bathroom located on a main street in a good section of town. For the furniture he needed, he found *Aaron Rents* listed in the yellow pages of the telephone book. He had learned the importance of balancing his checkbook when his bank statement came each month from his first checking account while working with Better Home Insulators in northern Virginia.

I helped him find a good dentist to have his teeth cleaned and checked, and we discussed having his front tooth capped which had been broken in the subway accident. Having his front tooth capped certainly made an improvement in his appearance, and I believe it also added a lot to his self-esteem. Greg is the only one of our family who has never had a cavity (as of this writing), which I attribute to his drinking lots of milk while he was growing up. Now Greg could be responsible for his own life and not have to be dependent on us anymore. What a relief! He resumed his job with Purple Heart Veterans arranging charitable pickups in the Norfolk-Virginia Beach area, which gave him a little extra cash and something to do to keep him busy.

After about a month in his new apartment, Greg began calling me every few days with a few problems which I attributed to anxiety. His calls became more frequent, and I would usually call him back later in the evening to discuss what he thought was bothering him. At first he wasn't very forthcoming, but then one night he called from a mental hospital because of worry that someone was trying to poison him. Again, I attributed it to anxiety, but after listening a while, I realized that something was indeed very wrong and Greg was definitely afraid of something. He wanted me to come and take him away from that area for fear that something dreadful would happen to him if I didn't. He told me that one of the guys from his former rooming house, who he thought was a satanic priest, saw him walking down the street and followed him home. Now that he knew where Greg was living, he could drop by any time he wanted and come in over the balcony. Greg said that he was one of the guys who he thought tried to kill him when he lived on the cul-de-sac and Uncle Zach saved him. Now this guy was threatening him again and told him that his arms and legs might be found in the sack of victims' bones found on Virginia Beach after the satanic cult's sacrifices of Halloween night.

Greg was adamant about this and wanted me to come and get him from the hospital where he had checked himself in using his new Medicaid card. He told me about a satanic cult operating along the Virginia Beach area and he thought that this guy was one of its priests and had satanic powers. He suspected the other guys living in the house with him the previous year of giving him drugs which almost took his life and thought they might have been trying to poison him. After this guy left his apartment one night, after flicking his knife at him in a threatening manner, Greg told me that he went into his closet to find the Bible I had given him the previous Easter and picked up a Decision Magazine. He noticed on the cover a man holding his outstretched hands full of wheat and the scripture under it read, *"Ye reap what ye sow."* Greg promised to hand over his life to God that night if he would deliver him from this terrible satanic person and his accomplices who he felt were out to get him. He found his Bible and turned to Leviticus where he started reading about witchcraft and the abominations. It was Easter Sunday, and the Easter card I had given him the previous year was still inside his Bible.

It was hard for me to explain to John what had happened and why I needed to make another trip down to Virginia Beach. I felt I had to drive down and find out for myself what was going on. I went by the hospital to pick Greg up and take him home, and, after getting a pizza to carry with us, we spent that night in his apartment. I slept in his bed while Greg slept on the couch in the living room. I thought I heard voices coming from the other room, although it could have been the TV. Was it that satanic guy he told me about? Greg honestly believed that he had come into his apartment while he was at the hospital and poisoned his sugar. At that point, I didn't know what to believe, but I knew that something had happened before I came down to make Greg believe so strongly that this satanic person was out to get him and finish what he tried to do in the house on the cul-de-sac before Uncle Zach saved him.

Sunday morning, I looked up Teen Challenge in the phone book and made an appointment for us to drive over to Norfolk to meet with them about the possibility of Greg entering their program. They seemed to know about the satanic cult operating in the area, but they had a long waiting list of guys like Greg waiting to be admitted. All they could do was make an appointment for him with another Teen Challenge in the Piedmont area. I drove him over to see them, but they also had a long waiting list. I couldn't bring him back with me at that time and had to get back to Crystal City for work Monday morning. Greg told me about the "NIP" Shelter in Norfolk, another AA facility where he had stayed before, so I left him there for the week to give us time to decide what to do. I found an article from a newspaper I saved some years back about satanic cults operating at various locations up and down the eastern seaboard.

The following week, I informed the apartments that Greg would be moving out on Saturday and also Aaron Rents, so they could come by to pick up their furniture. Then I drove down on Saturday morning to pick up Greg from NIP and we loaded all his stuff in the Yellow Sub. We threw away all his food, which he thought might have been poisoned. Greg promised to get into Teen Challenge as soon as possible if I would take him back with me to Northern Virginia, so he could get a room back in his old rooming house and start working again for Purple Heart. Since I knew it would take some time to get him into Teen Challenge, I called John to explain what had been going on with Greg and asked him if I could bring Greg home for the weekend. John was very understanding and said if Greg would get a short haircut to prove that we could trust him, he could come back with me, but only for the weekend. Greg did get a haircut, and we arrived back in Crystal City before dark. We called his former landlady and found that she would have an available room for him sometime during the week. Greg did keep his promises, and we moved him over the following weekend.

The guys at Teen Challenge had impressed upon me the importance of getting Greg into a good Pentecostal church as soon as possible, so he could start hearing the infallible Word of God preached on a regular basis. He also needed the people of the church to lay hands on him to pray for his healing and to cast out demons. Finding a good Pentecostal church in his area would be a good place to start! I looked in the phone book and found an Assembly of God about a mile from his rooming house and drove over the following Sunday to accompany him. The people were so warm and friendly we kept on going back to this church every Sunday and sometimes on Wednesday nights. I tried to get back into Bible study on Sunday afternoons and started the first chapter of Revelation all over again. Working full time didn't give me much time to study. Still, I had to find the time. Greg began to study his Bible and watch Christian telecasts. I was amazed at the progress he was making.

CHAPTER TWENTY-FOUR

The Spirit of Prophecy
1986

In the Book of Revelation, we see Jesus as we have never seen Him before ... Like the unveiling of a priceless work of art, God is pulling back the curtain so we can see Him in all His brilliance as the very *Spirit of Prophecy* speaking through His angel, *the Angel of the Lord,* a very important message. These visions were given to John to reveal truths about what is coming in these last days so we will be prepared. It carries with it a special blessing for all who *read, hear and heed* the words of this prophecy. In his nineties, the last living apostle, John, having been banished to the Island of Patmos, was living in a cave when *One like the Son of man* appeared unto him and he was so overwhelmed by His brilliance, he fell at His feet as though dead.

> *"The Revelation of Jesus Christ, which God gave unto him, to show unto his servants things which must shortly come to pass; and he sent and signified it by his angel unto his servant, John: Who bare record of the word of God, and of the testimony of Jesus Christ, and of all things that he saw. Blessed is he that readeth, and they that hear the words of this prophecy, and keep those things which are written therein: for the time is at hand."* (Revelation 1:1-3)

According to John's testimony:

> *"I was in the Spirit on the Lord's Day, and heard behind me a great voice, as of a trumpet, saying, 'I am Alpha and Omega, the first and the last; and, what you see, write in a book and send it to the seven churches which are in Asia; unto Ephesus, and unto Smyrna, and unto Pergamos, and unto Thyatira, and unto Sardis, and unto Philadelphia, and unto Laodicea.' And I turned to see the voice that spake with me. And being turned, I saw seven golden*

candlesticks; and in the midst of the candlesticks one like unto the Son of man, clothed with a garment down to the foot, and girt about the paps with a golden girdle.

"His head and his hair were white like wool, as white as snow; and his eyes were as a flame of fire; and his feet were like unto fine brass as if they burned in a furnace; and his voice as the sound of many waters. And he had in his right hand seven stars: and out of his mouth went a sharp two-edged sword: and his countenance was as the sun shineth in his strength. And when I saw him, I fell at his feet as dead. And he laid his right hand upon me, saying unto me 'Fear not; I am the first and the last: I am he that liveth, and was dead; and, behold, I am alive for evermore, Amen; and have the keys of hell and death.

"'Write the things which thou hast seen, and the things which are, and the things which shall be hereafter; The mystery of the seven stars, which thou sawest in my right hand, and the seven golden candlesticks. The seven stars are the angels of the seven churches; and the seven candlesticks which you saw are the seven churches.'"
(Revelation 1:10-20)

The Message to the Churches

This *message* was given to John to show the people of all the churches which existed in that day and throughout all of church history, *the enmity,* the barrier of sin, which exists between ourselves and God the Father. It stands in the way of our prayers and is keeping us out of relationship with Him. Jesus opened the door for us to come in boldly and stand before the throne of God in heaven in the spirit of our prayers. We must ask Him to open our spiritual eyes so that we may see and pray in the spirit directly to God in the name of Jesus. John was told *to write* and *to send* this message to the seven churches in Asia. This message is believed to contain a *three-fold prophecy:* It describes (1) a church which existed at the time of John; (2) an era of time during church history; and (3) a type of Christian found in all churches.

[Note: The following messages within quotes are quoted from the King James Version of the Holy Bible. The summation is without quotes to give the historical account. The Holy Bible must accompany this study as well as the prayers of the students who want to be enlightened by the Holy Spirit who leads us into all truth.]

EPHESUS (30-100 AD): <u>Condemnation</u>: They left their first love for Jesus and exhausted the passion they once had for him. God tells them *"Remember therefore from whence thou art fallen, and repent, and do the first works; or else I will come unto thee quickly, and will remove thy candlestick out of its place, except thou repent."* <u>Commendation</u>: God gives them credit for their labor, their patience and sound doctrine, and for hating the deeds of the Nicolaitanes which he also hates. *"To him who overcomes, I will give to eat of the Tree of Life which is in the midst of the paradise of God."* (Revelation, 2:1-7)

SMYRNA (100-313 AD): There is <u>No Condemnation</u> for this church because they are the *suffering church* going through great tribulation. They endured ten terrible edicts placed upon them by cruel Roman emperors. The word, *myrrh*, from which this church gets its name, means *bitter*, and when crushed, it produces a sweet smelling aroma which comes up before God. <u>Commendation:</u> God tells them that he knows their works, tribulation and poverty, but to him they are *rich* because of their suffering and faithfulness. He tells them to fear not the blasphemy and the terrible things which they must suffer, but to *"be thou faithful unto death, and I will give thee a crown of life…. He that overcomes shall not be hurt of the second death."* (Revelation, 2:8-11)

PERGAMOS (313-590 AD): <u>Condemnation</u>: This church, which is betrothed to Christ, becomes married to the Greco-Roman empire under the emperor, Constantine, producing a bigamist relationship. Constantine had a vision of a large cross leading his armies into battle, and, being victorious, he made it very popular for his soldiers to become Christians. He changed the names of the pagan gods and goddesses to Christian names after Mary and the apostles and changed the pagan feasts and rituals to those of the Christian. Constantine made it so popular to become Christian that Christianity flourished in this bigamist relationship, and the world flocked in bringing with them all their pagan festivities and doctrines. They established two wrong doctrines which God tells us he hates: *the doctrine of Baalam*, which allows sin to flourish in the church (they had a popular saying, *If when we sin grace abounds, then let us sin more that more grace may abound*), and they had *the doctrine of the*

Nicolaitanes, which created hierarchy in the church (when God made us all to be *a kingdom of priests and kings unto God,* Revelation 1:5-6). The word, *Nicolaitanes,* means *to condemn or judge,* and, in this case, it means *to judge or rule over the people.*

As a result of these two wrong doctrines, the church almost died. God tells this church that he knows where Satan's seat is. Other false doctrines were ordained: prayers for the dead (AD 300); the worship of saints (AD 375); the worship of Mary and the rejection of the *second coming of Christ* (AD 431), which is prophesied throughout the Bible many more times than *the first coming of Christ;* the doctrine of purgatory (AD 593), which provides a place for sinners to be held after death until they are released by prayers and paid indulgences of the people to get them out. God tells this church: *"Repent! Or else I will come unto thee quickly and will fight against them with the sword of my mouth.... To him that overcomes will I give to eat of the hidden manna, and a white stone, and in the stone a new name written, which no man knows saving he that receives it."* (Revelation, 2:12-17)

THYATIRA (590-1517 AD): <u>Condemnation</u>: The name of this church means *continuous sacrifice* because sin flourishes in this church. Jesus died once to pay sin's debt, and since there is continuous sin in this church and no repentance, there can be no forgiveness. Jesus appears in Judgment as *"the Son of God, who hath his eyes like unto a flame of fire and his feet are like fine brass."*

<u>Commendation</u>: Jesus commends this church for their many good works, charity, faith, and patience, but they are dependent upon their good works. This church allows the prophetess, Jezebel, to teach and seduce God's people into immorality and to worship idols. God gives this church a stern warning to repent or else. *"Behold, I will cast her into a bed and them who commit adultery with her into great tribulation, except they repent of their deeds. And I will kill her children with death; and all the churches shall know that I am he who searches the reins and hearts; and I will give to every one of you according to your works."* This church lacks holiness and worship and practices moral compromise, which allows corruption and immorality to flourish, so they will be judged according to their works. Instead of standing before *a throne of Grace,* this church will stand before *a throne of Judgment,* unless they repent.

More false doctrines are added to this church: prayers are directed to Mary (AD 600); relics and bones of saints are worshipped (AD 610); prayer beads come into practice (AD 1090); the sale of indulgences (AD 1190); the doctrine of continuous sacrifice (AD 1215); the Holy Bible is forbidden to laymen (AD 1229); and Ava Maria is greatly accepted (AD 1508), in which Mary intercedes for those who pray directly to her. God says to those who have not allowed the evil prophetess, Jezebel, to seduce his servants into immorality and idol worship and to those who have not known the depths of Satan, *"I will put upon you none other burden, but that which ye have already; hold fast till I come. And he that overcomes, and keeps my works unto the end, to him will I give power over the nations: and he shall rule them with a rod of iron; as the vessels of a potter, they shall be broken to shivers: even as I received of my Father. And I will give him the morning star."* (Revelation, 2:18-29)

SARDIS (1517-1790 AD): <u>Condemnation</u>: This is the *dead church,* although it may have a little life left in it. There is no commendation for this church, yet God the Holy Spirit and the angels are saying to those who may still be alive, *"I know thy works, that thou hast a name that thou livest, and art dead. Be watchful and strengthen the things which remain that are ready to die; for I have not found your works perfect before God. Remember therefore how thou received and heard, and hold fast, and repent. If, therefore, thou shalt not watch, I will come on thee as a thief, and thou shalt not know what hour I will come upon thee. Thou hast a few names even in Sardis which have not defiled their garments; and they shall walk with me in white, for they are worthy. He that overcomes, the same shall be clothed in white raiment; and I will not blot his name out of the book of life, but I will confess his name before my Father, and before his angels."* (Revelation 3:1- 6)

PHILADELPHIA (1790 AD – end of age): <u>Commendation</u>: This is the *church of brotherly love,* with an open door into heaven that no man can shut. God tells them, *"I know thy works: behold, I have set before thee an open door, and no man can shut it: for thou hast a little strength, and hast kept my word, and hast not denied my name. Behold, I will make them of the synagogue of Satan, which say they are Jews and are not, but do lie; behold I will make them to come and worship before your feet and to know that I have loved you. Because thou hast kept the word of my patience, I also will keep you from the hour of temptation, which shall come upon all the world, to try them that dwell upon the face of the earth. Behold, I come quickly: hold fast that which thou hast, that no man take thy crown. Him that overcomes will I make a pillar in the temple of my God: and he shall go no more out: and I will write upon him the name of my God, and the name of the city of my God, which is new Jerusalem, which cometh down out of heaven from my God: and I will write upon him my new name."* (Revelation 3:7-13)

LAODICEA (1900 AD – end of age): <u>Condemnation</u>: This is the *luke warm church*, which has little or no passion for Jesus and is dependent upon its good works. Jesus is *outside this church knocking on the door*, waiting to be invited in for fellowship. God reveals that this church is weak and complacent. It is a *compromising* church, being neither hot nor cold; and he would rather have them hot or cold. Its *indifference* makes him so sick, he wants to *"spue them out of his mouth."* *"Because thou sayest, I am rich and increased with goods, and have need of nothing; and knowest not that thou art wretched, and miserable, and poor, and blind, and naked: I counsel thee to buy of me gold tried in the fire, that thou may be rich; and white raiment, that thou may be clothed, and that the shame of thy nakedness does not appear; and anoint thine eyes with eye salve, that thou may see. As many as I love, I rebuke and chasten: be zealous, therefore, and repent. Behold, I stand at the door, and knock: if any man hears my voice and open the door, I will come in to him and sup with him, and he with me. To him that overcomes will I grant to sit with me in my throne, even as I also overcame, and am sat down with my Father in his throne."* (Revelation 3:14-22)

"He that hath an ear, let him hear what the Spirit saith unto the Churches." (Revelation, Chapters Two and Three)

"When Jesus came to the coasts of Caesarea Philippi, He asked his disciples, 'Who do men say that I, the son of man, am?' And they said, 'Some say that thou art John the Baptist: some Elias; and others Jeremiah, or one of the prophets.' He saith to them 'But whom say ye that I am?' And Simon Peter answered, 'Thou art the Christ, the Son of the living God.' And Jesus answered, 'Blessed art thou Simon Bar- jona: for flesh and blood hath not revealed it unto thee, but my Father which is in heaven. And I say also unto thee that thou art Peter ("petros," a piece of rock) and upon this rock

("petra," this massive rock) I will build my church; and the gates of hell shall not prevail against it.'" (Matthew 16:13-18)

[NOTE: The above interpretation in the Greek Dictionary of New Testament Words found in Strong's Exhaustive Concordance of the Bible, which is listed in the Bibliography, can be found on Page 57, for Peter, #4074, and for rock #4073.]

In the controversial scripture of Matthew 16:13-18, Jesus called *Simon Bar- jona, "petros,"* which interpreted means *"a piece of rock."* Then he said, *and upon this rock, "petra,"* which interpreted means *"a massive rock,"* speaking of himself as in the revelation given to Peter that he, Jesus, is *"the Christ, the Son of the living God."* (1st Peter 2:1-10; Ephesians 2:8-22; Matthew 21:42- 44; Acts 4:8-12) Then in the following scripture, he went on to explain how the endued power from on high would work through believers.

"And I will give to thee the keys of the kingdom of heaven: and whatsoever thou shalt bind on earth shall be bound in heaven: and whatsoever thou shalt loose on earth shall be loosed in heaven.

"From that time forth began Jesus to shew unto his disciples how that he must go unto Jerusalem, and suffer many things of the elders and chief priests and scribes, and be killed, and be raised again the third day.

"Then Peter took him, and began to rebuke him, saying, 'Be it far from thee, Lord: this shall not be unto thee.' But he turned and said to Peter, 'Get thee behind me, Satan: thou art an offence unto me: for thou savourest not the things that be of God, but those that be of men.'

"Then said Jesus unto his disciples, 'If any man will come after me, let him deny himself, and take up his cross and follow me. For whosoever will save his life shall lose it: and whosoever will lose his life for my sake shall find it. For what is a man profited, if he shall gain the whole world, and lose his own soul?'

"For the Son of man shall come in the glory of his Father with his angels; and then he shall reward every man according to his works. Verily I say unto you, 'There be some standing here, which shall not taste of death, till they see the Son of man coming in his kingdom.'" (Matthew 16:19-28)

In Revelation Chapter 4, we have a glimpse into heaven while John was in the Spirit; and around the throne of God, there was *a rainbow like unto an emerald*. And round about the throne were 24 seats, and upon the seats were 24 elders sitting clothed in white raiment, and they had on their heads crowns of gold. And it looked like *a throne of Judgment* because out of the throne came lightnings and thunders and voices: and there were seven lamps of fire burning before the throne which are *the seven Spirits of God*. (The Holy Spirit, as depicted in Isaiah 11:1-5)

In Revelation Chapter 5, we have another glimpse into heaven with God on His throne holding a book in His hand sealed with seven seals. A strong angel asks in a loud voice, *"Who is worthy to open the book and to loose its seals?"* We see John crying profusely because no one in heaven, or on the earth, or under the earth could be found worthy to take the book and break the seals. Finally, one of the elders said to John, *"Weep not: Behold, the Lion of the tribe of Judah, the Root of David, hath prevailed to open the book and to loose the seven seals."* (Revelation 5:5) This book, or scroll, is believed to contain within it, *God's plan for the redemption of the earth*. It cannot go into effect until someone worthy can break its seals. Finally, the Lamb gets up from the mercy seat where He has placed His blood, walks up to God the Father, takes the scroll out of His hand and breaks the first seal. *Immediately, the Holy Spirit is sent to the earth.*

John describes his vision:

> *"And lo, in the midst of the throne and of the four beasts and in the midst of the elders, stood a Lamb as it had been slain, having seven horns and seven eyes, which are the seven Spirits of God sent forth into all the earth…. And they sung a new song, saying, 'Thou art worthy to take the book, and to open the seals thereof: for you were slain, and have redeemed us to God by your blood out of every kindred, and tongue, and people and nation; and hast made us unto our God kings and priests; and we shall reign on the earth.'"* (Revelation 5:6-12)
>
> *"And I saw when the Lamb opened one of the seals, and I heard, as it were the noise of thunder, one of the four beasts saying, 'Come and see.' And I saw, and beheld a white horse, and he that sat on him had a bow; and a crown was given unto him: and he went forth conquering and to conquer."* (Revelation 6:1-2)

The rider on the white horse is the *Holy Spirit,* who arrived in the upper room on the day of Pentecost bringing with Him *"the power from on high"* to empower the saints. The *bow* is the *rainbow,* which represents the covenant God made with Noah that He would never again destroy the earth with a flood. The crown is *the Victor's Crown,* which He brings with Him for all those who fight the good fight of faith, as we *"go forward conquering and to conquer."* As Paul told us in Romans, we are *"more than conquerors through Him who loved us."* (Romans 8:37) Since God is the author of this book, I don't believe He would allow the antichrist to make his entrance on a *white horse,* the symbol of purity.

"And when the day of Pentecost was fully come, they were all with one accord in one place. And suddenly there came a sound from heaven as of a rushing mighty wind, and it filled the house where they were sitting. And there appeared unto them cloven tongues like as of fire. And it sat upon each of them. And they were all filled with the Holy Ghost, and began to speak with other tongues, as the Spirit gave them utterance." (The Acts of the Apostles, Chapter 2:1-4)

The Olivet Discourse

"And Jesus went out, and departed from the temple: and his disciples came out to him to show him the buildings of the temple. And Jesus said unto them, 'See ye not all these things? Verily, I say unto you, there shall not be left here one stone upon another that shall not be thrown down.'

"And as he sat upon the Mount of Olives, the disciples came unto him privately saying, 'Tell us, when shall these things be? And what shall be the sign of thy coming, and of the end of the world?' And Jesus answered and said unto them, 'Take heed that no man deceives you. For many shall come in my name saying, I am Christ; and shall deceive many.'

"And ye shall hear of wars and rumors of wars: see that ye not be troubled: for all these things must come to pass, but the end is not yet. For nation shall rise up against nation, and kingdom against kingdom: and there shall be famines, and pestilence, and earthquakes in divers places. All these are the beginning of sorrows.

"Then shall they deliver you up to be afflicted and shall kill you: and ye shall be hated of all nations for my name's sake. And then shall many be offended, and shall betray one another, and shall hate one another. And many false prophets shall arise and deceive many. And because iniquity shall abound, the love of many shall wax cold. But he that shall endure unto the end, the same shall be saved.

"And this gospel shall be preached in all the world for a witness unto all nations; and then shall the end come. When ye therefore shall see the 'abomination of desolation,' spoken of by Daniel the prophet, stand in the holy place... then let them in Judaea flee into the mountains....

"For then shall there be great tribulation, such as was not since the beginning of the world to this time, nor ever shall be. And except those days are shortened, there should no flesh be saved: but for the elect's sake those days shall be shortened....

"For as the lightning comes out of the east, shines even unto the west; so shall also the coming of the Son of man be. For wheresoever the carcase is, there will the eagles be gathered together.

"Immediately after the tribulation of those days shall the sun be darkened, and the moon shall not give her light, and the stars shall fall from heaven, and the powers of the heavens shall be shaken.

"And then shall appear the sign of the Son of man in heaven: and then shall all the tribes of the earth mourn, and they shall see the Son of man coming in the clouds of heaven with power and great glory.

"And he shall send his angels with a great sound of a trumpet and they shall gather together his elect from the four winds, from one end of the heaven to the other.

"Now, learn a parable of the fig tree: when his branch is tender and it is putting forth leaves, you know that summer is near: So likewise, when you see all these things, know that it is near, even at the doors. Verily I say unto you, this generation shall not pass, until all these things are fulfilled.

"Heaven and earth shall pass away, but my words shall not pass away. But of that day and hour no man knows, no, not the angels of heaven, but my Father only. But as the days of Noah were, so shall the coming of the Son of man be....

> *"Watch therefore, for ye know not what hour your Lord will come…. Therefore, be also ready; for in such an hour as ye think not, the Son of man cometh."* (Matthew, Chapter 24:1-44)

As in the Olivet Discourse, there have always been antichrists, wars, famines and diseases, but in these last days, all these things will be on the increase. We are told to look to Israel as *the time clock*, and, when we see her surrounded by armies who want to destroy her, it's time to prepare to meet the Lord! As it was in *the Days of Noah*, so shall it be in the last days (Matthew 24:37). Peter tells us how it will be:

> *"Knowing this first, that there shall come in the last days scoffers, walking after their own lusts, and saying, 'Where is the promise of his coming? For since the fathers fell asleep, all things continue as they were from the beginning of the creation.'*
>
> *"For this they willingly are ignorant … that by the word of God the heavens were of old, and the earth standing out of the water and in the water; whereby the world that was, being overflowed with water, perished. But the heavens and the earth, which are now, by the same word, are kept in store, reserved unto fire against the Day of Judgment and perdition of ungodly men.…*
>
> *"But beloved, be not ignorant of this one thing, one day with the Lord is as a thousand years, and a thousand years as one day. The Lord is not slack concerning his promise, as some men count slackness; but is long suffering to us-ward, not willing that any should perish, but that all should come to repentance.*
>
> *"But the day of the Lord shall come as a thief in the night; in which the heavens shall pass away with a great noise, and the elements shall melt with fervent heat, the earth also and the works that are therein shall be burned up. Seeing then that all these things shall be dissolved, what manner of persons ought ye to be in all holy conversation and godliness?*
>
> *"Nevertheless, we, according to his promise, look for new heavens and a new earth, wherein dwells righteousness. Wherefore beloved, seeing that ye look for such things, be diligent that we may be found of him in peace, without spot, and blameless. And account that the longsuffering of our Lord is salvation; even as our beloved brother, Paul, according to the wisdom given unto him has written unto you."*
> (2nd Peter 3:3-15)

In the days of Noah, the people were warned to get in the boat, but they would not heed the warnings. Instead they scoffed at Noah and made fun of him! And they all drowned in the flood of the predicted rain which fell 40 days upon the earth. Two animals of each kind, male and female, and Noah's sons and their wives were saved in the ark which God instructed Noah to build, and the earth was replenished. And God made a covenant with Noah never to destroy the earth again with a flood and placed the rainbow in the heavens as a sign of this covenant. (Genesis 9:11-17)

> *"And when he had opened the fifth seal, I saw under the altar the souls of them that were slain for the word of God, and for the testimony for which they held: And they cried with a loud voice, saying, 'How long, O Lord, holy and true, dost thou not judge and avenge our blood on them that dwell on the earth?' And white robes were given to every one of them; and it was said unto them, that they should rest yet for a little season, until their fellow servants and their brethren, that should be killed as they were, should be fulfilled."* (Revelation 6:9-11)

> *"And I beheld when he had opened the sixth seal, and, lo, there was a great earthquake; and the sun became black as sackcloth of hair, and the moon became as blood; and the stars of heaven fell unto the earth, even as a fig tree casts her untimely figs when she is shaken of a mighty wind. And the heaven departed as a scroll when it is rolled together and every mountain and island were moved out of their places.*
> *"And the kings of the earth, and the great men, and the rich men, and the chief captains, and the mighty men and every bondman, and every free man, hid themselves in the dens and in the rocks of the mountains; and said to the mountains and the rocks, 'Fall on us and hide us from the face of him that sits on the throne and from the wrath of the Lamb: For the great day of his wrath is come; and who shall be able to stand?'"* (Revelation 6:12-17)

After the 6th seal is broken, we see for the first time the people of the earth running to hide in the rocks and dens of the earth *from the wrath of the Lamb*. We have never seen Jesus filled with such wrath!! We saw him turn over the tables of the money changers in the temple, but that was *justifiable righteous anger*. Now his *wrath* has grown to such proportions, it can no longer be held back. According to our teacher, W*rath is the well thought out and measured condition of a righteous and holy God toward sin.* From the prophet, Isaiah, we are told...

> *"Their land also is full of silver and gold, neither is there any end of their treasures; their land is also full of horses, neither is there any end of their chariots: their land is also full of idols; they worship the work of their own hands, that which their own fingers have made....*
>
> *"Enter into the rock, and hide thee in the dust, for fear of the Lord, and for the glory of his majesty. The lofty looks of man shall be humbled and the haughtiness of men shall be bowed down, and the Lord alone shall be exalted in that day....*
>
> *"And the idols he shall utterly abolish. And they shall go into the holes of the rocks and into the caves of the earth, for fear of the Lord, and for the glory of his majesty, when he arises to shake terribly the earth."* (Isaiah 2: 7-19)

> *"Who is this that comes from Edom, with dyed garments from Bozrah; this that is glorious in his apparel, traveling in the greatness of his strength? I that speak in righteousness, mighty to save: 'Why are you red in your apparel, and your garments like him that treads in the winepress?' 'I have trodden the winepress alone; and of the people, there was none with me: for I will tread them in mine anger and trample them in my fury; and their blood shall be sprinkled upon my garments, and I will stain all my raiment: For the day of vengeance is in my heart, and the year of my redeemed is come.'"* (Isaiah 63:1-4)

> *"For he said, surely they are my people, children that will not lie: so he was their Savior. In their affliction he was afflicted, and the angel of his presence saved them: in his love and in his pity he redeemed them; and carried them all the days of old. But they rebelled and vexed his Holy Spirit: therefore, he was turned to be their enemy, and he fought against them."* (Isaiah 63:8-10)

CHAPTER TWENTY-FIVE

From Ireland to Mobile
1986

After having a taste of Ireland on our way home from Saudi Arabia, John wanted to go back again for a golfing vacation during his summer break from Law School. Both of us were eager for a better tour of the country, especially the *Wild Ireland Tour* we had heard so much about. He listed all the golf courses he wanted to play, and Ballybunion was first on his list. Since it was also time for my two-week vacation, I made reservations for us on Pan Am using our accumulated mileage. John and I left New York at 8:45 pm on the 5th of June 1986 and arrived the following morning in Shannon at 7:30. Before leaving the airport, we stopped by the desk of the Irish Tourist Board and received a whole packet of information regarding Hotels and Bed & Breakfasts of Ireland. Then we signed up for a rental car the following morning and checked into the Shannon Airport Hotel. With our great road map which came with the rental car, we spent the rest of the day planning our trip. John used a felt tip marker to mark our first trip on this map and continued marking all our other trips over the years using different colored markers.

A Golfing Tour of Ireland

From Shannon, we drove to *Ballybunion* where John played 18 holes in the tallest and most rugged grass I had ever seen. I walked the first two holes with him as I nearly froze to death in the cold ocean wind, which blew constantly. I finally took refuge in the old club house, where I continued to plan our trip and wrote a few cards to send home. While I was looking around, I noticed the dining room open so I checked to see what they had on the menu. When John finally came in a couple of hours later, we were both hungry so we ordered a fried fish dinner and it was very good served with lots of boiled potatoes and fresh vegetables. Then it was time to drive to Adare where we had reservations for the night in the Woodlands House. The restaurant was offering a special dinner that evening which we couldn't resist: Roasted Leg of Lamb served with mint sauce, potatoes and vegetables with chocolate cake for dessert. It was well prepared and very good. Then John and I walked around the small town after dinner and made some fantastic pictures of the sunset. The following morning, John drove over to the golf course and played a round of golf with a young engineer who was looking for someone to play with before he had to get back to work. John came back raving about the beautiful course he had found which had been built around some old castle ruins of a previous century. Of course I had to see them, too, so he drove me over the following morning, and we drove around the whole area which had much potential for a very nice golf club, including a hotel and recreational area.

The next morning, we stopped by *the Irish Tourist Board* to make more reservations and they were very helpful in their recommendations of places we needed to see in Ireland. We had reservations that night at *Dundrum* after we visited the castle at Kilkenny and we planned to see *Blarney Castle* on the way to *Waterford* the following day. We left Adare sometime that morning and drove to *Kilkenny* where we had a tour of the castle and made pictures of the old medieval city. We had a quick lunch at Mulhall's restaurant and departed Kilkenny around 2:00 pm. From there, we had a very short drive to our reservations for the night at Dundrum and arrived around 5:00. It was a country hotel outside the city, so we didn't know what to expect, and, while checking in, we looked for a menu but couldn't find one, so we settled into our room, took our baths and dressed for dinner. Finally, we decided to go downstairs again and noticed the pub was open, so we went inside and sat at a table. It looked like a popular place because people began arriving and soon the place was crowded. The door to the restaurant opened precisely at 7:30, so John and I moved inside the restaurant. Much to our amazement, the special of the night turned out to be sirloin steaks served flambéed style in Irish whiskey with onions, mushrooms and garlic with baked potato and steamed vegetables. Our steaks were cooked to perfection and they were excellent! We ordered glasses of red wine and it turned out to be a lovely evening. However, our room was located over the bar with lots of noise until it finally closed around 1:30 am. Between the noise and our terribly sagging mattress, neither of us got much sleep and we hoped for a better night ahead. The next morning, we called room service for a pot of hot coffee and wheat toast with butter and preserves. We departed around 9:30 am.

On our drive south to *Waterford*, we encountered the cutest sight going down the road before us, a pack of small dogs with their little tails wagging high in the air in excitement as their trainer routed them up a hill below the great *Rock of Cashel*. John didn't want to stop at the Rock of Cashel so we drove on to Blarney where we had a tour of the castle but didn't kiss the Blarney stone. We arrived in Waterford around 3:30 pm and were disappointed to find that we were too late for the last tour which began at 2:30. We only had time to watch the movie and admired the beautiful crystal on display in the Gift Shop. We checked into our B&B and drove downtown to see the port and take afternoon pictures of the waterfront. It was beautiful down there, so we had dinner in a hotel restaurant where we could look out and admire the view of the harbor. We ordered Poached Trout with mashed potatoes and steamed vegetables followed by an Irish coffee and an Apple Tart. Our Waterford B&B was very nice and we enjoyed our full Irish breakfast before getting away around 8:30 am.

John stopped for pictures all along our drive through the countryside on the way to *Killarney* and we stopped for lunch in *Cahir.* We discovered a wonderful Irish pub on the corner of the square in the center of town which had great food, and, about a block down the street, was a well-preserved castle. We decided to take the tour of *Cahir Castle* and found it very interesting as we learned the town's history. We arrived in Killarney early in the afternoon and checked in for three nights at *Kathleen's Country House.* This was our first time to stay at Kathleen's and she was just getting started with a much smaller place than she has today. This was also our first time to visit *Killarney*, so John drove us around the town and out to beautiful *Killarney Golf Course,* where we walked around the grounds and took pictures of the many gorgeous hydrangeas, lovely gardens and the Lake of Killarney. John made reservations to play golf the following morning, and I took *the ring of Kerry* bus tour.

The second day, John drove us around the *Dingle Peninsula* and we stopped to take pictures of the lovely scenery and the historic beehive huts inhabited by the first dwellers of Ireland. It was a beautiful drive along the scenic Atlantic coastline and we also drove across the top of the large mountain above Dingle. At Kathleen's, we were delighted to find that her husband was a great cook and prepared dinner almost every evening. On our 30th anniversary, he prepared a wonderful Salmon dinner with garlic butter, served with delicious cauliflower, carrots, and potatoes, bread and wine with a delicious Raspberry Tart for dessert. It was very good! Every morning, we had a full Irish breakfast. When Kathleen learned that it was our anniversary, she went out of her way to drive me to my hair appointment at her hair salon and pointed out a good restaurant where we might have dinner on her husband's off night. It, too, was very good, but before we left Killarney, we would enjoy another of his great dinners: sliced Corned Beef with white sauce served with crisp steamed cabbage, baked potato, cream of vegetable soup and for dessert a delicious Minced Meat Tart.

"Slea Head," Dingle Peninsula, Ireland.

On our third day, John and I drove over to *Torc Waterfall* in light rain and up to *the Lady's View* of the Middle Lake of Killarney, which was *named by Queen Victoria* as a place for her ladies in waiting to sit for tea while they enjoyed the lovely view. Then we drove up to the restaurant at the top of the mountain where we had lunch and enjoyed another spectacular view of a beautiful rainbow encircling *the three Lakes of Killarney* and the city in the far distance. From there, we drove across the rock covered mountains to the small town of *Bantry* where we discovered many good restaurants, shops and some very nice looking B&B's. John also discovered a small 9-hole golf course where he played in light rain and I found a warm place in the snack bar to enjoy a bowl of hot soup. We would make this same drive many times over the years whenever we passed through Ireland. On one trip, we stayed in a Farm House on *Bantry Bay* with a very nice landlady who kept a roaring fire going in her fireplace and invited her guests to come down to meet one another as we sat for tea and scones or soda bread.

"The Ladies' View" of the Middle Lake of Killarney.

Rainbow over Killarney and the Three Lakes.

When we checked out of Kathleen's, we drove through Ennis over to the coast to see the beautiful *Cliffs of Moher* and through *the Burren* to the large city of *Galway* on beautiful *Galway Bay.* From there, we jutted over to the small town of *Portumna,* where we found a room at the hotel and had dinner. John signed up to play 9 holes the following morning at the Portumna golf club and was up at 6:00 am. He came back all excited to tell me about the hundreds of deer he had seen on the course that morning, and, after breakfast, he drove me out to see them. Not one of them was visible!

The Cliffs of Moher, County Clare, Ireland.

By this time, we were having some rain, so we drove the main road back to Adare and checked in again at Woodlands House. John met another young man at the Adare golf course and played another 9 holes. It was a beautiful course, and I enjoyed walking with them to take pictures of the old medieval ruins: the castle, an abbey and a 13th Century cemetery. They had great plans for the development of this beautiful golf course which included a hotel and recreational area. That evening for dinner at the Woodlands House we were having: Stuffed Trout with raisin & bread stuffing served with assorted vegetables and Trifle for dessert. We retired early to get a good start the next morning and checked out of Woodlands House about 7:30 am for our drive back to Ennis, where we stopped at a bakery for Irish soda bread and scones to take home with us. Our Pan Am flight was scheduled to leave Shannon early that afternoon, so we returned our rental car and had time for dinner at the airport restaurant before boarding our long flight home.

Back home again at Crystal Towers, we found out that Piedmont Teen Challenge also had a long waiting list. They advised Greg to get into an *Assembly of God* church which preached the inerrant Word of God truthfully and where the church members could lay hands on him to cast out demons and pray for him to be healed. We found a good Assembly of God church about a mile from Greg's house, and I would drive over on Sunday mornings to pick him up and take him to church. We both looked forward to Sunday mornings, and we loved the pastor and the people of this church. The pastor was a retired Navy Chaplain, who sang beautiful spiritual songs with his robust, but very mellow voice. One of the songs which he sang often was *"Sweet Holy Spirit"* and the lyrics of another, which he often sang, *"We are standing on holy ground, and there are angels all around."* I truly felt the presence of God in this church! And I looked forward every Sunday to hearing a prophecy. The pastor of this church always preached a wonderful spirit-filled sermon welcoming the people to come forward to receive the Lord, and for prayer and the laying on of hands for healing.

One gentleman, who laid hands on Greg when we first arrived, said he sensed the spirit of marijuana leaving him. A lady, who prayed for me to receive the Holy Spirit, said that I already had the Holy Spirit. She said I was *sealed* by the Spirit when I first believed and went forward to receive Jesus. She explained that this was *the earnest amount, "the promise of more to come,"* as I grew in Christ Jesus and was filled up more and more with the Spirit until it overflowed and produced the heavenly language. I just needed to keep on receiving more and more of the Spirit, *"speaking to myself in psalms and hymns and spiritual songs, singing and making melody in my heart unto the Lord."* (Ephesians 5:18-19) When Maggie came up for a visit, she joined Greg and me in attending this church, and she, too, went forward to receive Jesus.

When they filled the baptismal tank for Greg's baptism, I decided to be baptized with him and a few others, but he changed his mind and stayed home that day. I had been *sprinkled* as a baby, but that was my Mother's promise to bring me up *Methodist.* Now, I felt the need to be *fully immersed* as John baptized Jesus to set an example for us to follow, which symbolizes *dying to sin and being raised up in newness of life as a new creature in Christ Jesus.* For some reason, Greg was not quite ready to make this commitment and decided to wait a while longer.

During those first months of having so much to learn about the movement of the Holy Spirit, Greg was having some confusion about the differences of the denominations. He wanted to attend *Revelation Now,* a study of the Book of Revelation by another Christian denomination, *The*

Seventh Day Adventists, which believe Saturday is our true day of worship. It was a widely publicized event, so I picked Greg up and we both attended the teachings until a *red flag* went up according to Greg, and, being a new Christian, he was very legalistic about the interpretation of God's word. I realized that the first Christians met on Sunday, the first day of the week, because it was the day of our Lord's resurrection and is known in the New Testament as *the Lord's Day.* The first Christians were told to collect charitable donations on the first day of the week to help the poor widows and orphans and tend to the business of the church. I had wondered about this myself due to God's *Fourth Commandment to keep the Sabbath Day holy.* For the Jew, the Sabbath falls on the seventh day of the week and was the day Jesus worshipped in the synagogue. At the time of his death, the veil in the temple was ripped in two from top to bottom to provide a new and living way for people to come to God through the veil of his flesh; however he was resurrected on the first day of the week.

One day, I received a phone call from Greg who was worried that I had not burned all my astrology. I was glad that he brought it to my attention because I had forgotten all about it, and he was right! I needed to face up to something I should have done much earlier when I burned all the natal charts and horoscopes in my kitchen sink. The church was praying for him to be totally delivered from drugs and the rock world, which had led him down the road for many years to his near destruction, and he was rightly concerned that I hadn't gotten rid of all the demonic influences. I remembered that the box containing my astrology was put somewhere down in the basement of our apartment building mixed in with all our other belongings. I knew I had to go down into the basement to search for it and bring it up into the light so I could deal with it. It would be the final proof that my days in astrology were over, destroyed and denounced forever. As long as it remained, the spirit of the abomination still existed. John helped me look for it and placed it in the back of our station wagon as I suggested. Greg and I would have to find a place where we could burn everything which remained of the abomination. We found the perfect place in a little park being built across the street from the back of our apartment building. All the hard-bound books would have to be ripped apart and the pages burned in the small receptacle which was located there. However, after Wednesday night church service, our old faithful Yellow Sub refused to start.

Before we could get the box over to the little park, we had a problem. I couldn't get the back window all the way up and it began to rain. John was busy with Law classes and couldn't find the time to go over and charge the battery, and it continued to rain for the next two weeks. The cardboard box was literally falling apart in the church parking lot and my abomination was about to be exposed! How I wished I had been more responsible and gotten rid of all my astrology at the same time I meticulously burned all the charts, paperbacks and logarithms. John finally solved the problem by taking the subway to class so I could drive over in his car to pick up Greg, and the two of us finally got the box out of the station wagon and into the back of his car. We drove it over to the park where we managed to accomplish this tedious task and destroyed all the big hard-bound books. We were so relieved! After burning the pages, we deposited the heavy binders in the dumpster behind our building. By the way, we did finish Revelation Now all the way through, and Greg received a beautiful large King James Bible with a wooden chest to keep it in. The pastor, his wife and all his attendants were very dedicated people, and the pastor and one attendant came over to our apartment to pray for our family when the study ended. I bought a tape of songs sung by him and his wife and also a cookbook of meatless recipes. They must also be vegetarians.

During summer of 1986, Mother suffered a small stroke and Aunt Rebecca, Mother's only sister, with only a month left to live, saved Mother's life from her hospital bed. If she hadn't called 911 when she recognized Mother's slurring of speech over the phone as a symptom of an approaching stroke, Mother could have suffered a terribly bad one and become paralyzed, or even died, because she was all alone in the house. Aunt Rebecca had always been a great friend to Mother and all the rest of our family, especially to me. When I called her at the hospital, her first words to me were, *"I wish I had something good to tell you."* Aunt Rebecca died a few weeks later, and I wasn't able to make it down for her funeral. However, I knew I had to consider going down to spend some time with Mother to help her regain her strength and overcome the depression she must have felt in losing her only sister and her best friend.

About this time, we got some good news from Teen Challenge about an opening around the end of September in Greensboro, NC. The timing was perfect. I had shared with my attorney, Catherine, and her assistant, Lisa, our problems regarding Greg several months earlier when I made the trip down to Virginia Beach to bring him back to Falls Church. They couldn't have been more understanding and took me out to lunch before I left. Cathy gave me a lovely pearl necklace as a going-away gift and said not to worry about taking some time off, although they would have to find someone to replace me. They realized there was a good chance I might not be coming back.

It took several days to get everything in order for the drive down to North Carolina to leave Greg at the Greensboro Teen Challenge and then on to Mobile to spend some quality time with Mother. My plan was to come back to resume my job at the law firm while John finished law school, or, if they had already replaced me, I would find another job in the area. I sent out resumes before I left and John received several calls for interviews upon my return. Since the distance to Greensboro was slightly over a third of the way to Mobile, it was a good overnight stop for me and allowed time for meeting with those in charge to make sure Greg was properly admitted into the program. After breakfast, I drove him over for his admittance into Teen Challenge, and then it was time for me to get on the road to Mobile. I arrived at Mother's house that evening, and it was always good to be back at home again with her. Sometimes, when she was lying on the couch watching TV, she would wake up from a nap and look over to see if I was still there. She was growing old and needed me to be there with her to make sure she took her pills, ate well and drank her water. When I wasn't there, I always missed her.

Ginger came over to tell me their plans for spending Thanksgiving at Disney World with their two young teenagers, David and Donna. And she and Michael wanted Mother and me to go along with them. It was a marvelous idea, and I was looking forward to being with them and taking Mother out for a new adventure. We could all take turns pushing her wheelchair, and we always had a good time together. However, the following Saturday evening around dusk, something occurred which was entirely logical, yet quite unanticipated! Mother's doorbell rang! And guess what? There stood Greg with his baggage strap over his shoulder and a big grin on his face. He decided he didn't want to stay at Teen Challenge. No! He wanted to join me in Alabama to help take care of Grandma. He talked the guy in charge of the Greensboro Teen Challenge into buying him a bus ticket to Mobile. I couldn't believe it! Yet it was so typical of Greg. Teen Challenge was entirely a voluntary program, and I should have known something like this would happen. Now, as usual, I needed time to adjust and come up with a new plan.

What else could I do but cancel my plans for joining the others on the trip to Orlando and stay home with Greg because there just wasn't enough room for all of us in the car or in the motel rooms. Besides, he had already been to Disneyland three times and he was so unpredictable. As always, though, God had a plan and a reason for all these things falling into place the way they did. It was only a short time before Greg started noticing a small sore developing on the tip of his stump, where the tibia of his right leg was trying to protrude through the muscle. The doctors at GWU Hospital had removed the crushed portion of his leg exactly where the train had crushed the bone around mid- calf and saved as much as they could of the leg, thinking that would suffice. It worked for the first couple of years, but now the bone was starting to work its way through and it was getting very painful for him to walk. Greg had to revert back to his crutches for help with each step. I made an appointment through Alabama Rehab for him to see a doctor and was directed to the medical unit at the University Hospital of South Alabama. The Orthopedic Surgeon scheduled him for surgery to have the bone re-cut and the stump reshaped for a more comfortable fit of the new prosthesis.

In the meantime, Thanksgiving was rapidly approaching, and we had to decide what we would do while the others were at Disney World. Knowing how important it was for Greg to resume his church attendance and have the people of the church continue to pray for him, I again looked in the telephone book and found Knollwood Assembly of God on the west side of Mobile. Once again, we were warmly greeted by the people of the church and felt right at home with them just as in the Assembly of God in Falls Church. We attended faithfully every Sunday and made new friends at Knollwood. I found Greg outside one Sunday morning talking to a couple he had just met, and I believe he had just given them his testimony about how God saved him in his Virginia Beach apartment. Loraine and Will became two of our best friends that year and we always sat with them in church. They had lost a son about Greg's age while we were attending Knollwood and they took comfort in the fact that he had handed his life over to the Lord sometime earlier that year and had died in bed one night while reading the Bible. Greg made his decision to be baptized, and this time, it was for real. He was ready to make a full commitment to God, and, although he had a few setbacks from time to time, he considered himself truly *born again*. The pastor at Knollwood assured me that Greg was ready this time and God had a real hold on him. I kept going forward to receive more of the Holy Spirit hoping to receive the overflow of the heavenly language. Loraine impressed upon me that all people are different and God has plans for us all. She said that Jesus is the baptizer, and he will decide when the time is right for me.

"Likewise, the Spirit also helps our infirmities; for we know not what we should pray for as we ought: but the Spirit itself makes intercession for us with groanings which cannot be uttered. And he that searches the hearts knows what is the mind of the Spirit, because he makes intercession for the saints according to the will of God." (Romans 8:26-31)

I found my place among the women of the church and attended prayer meetings and Bible studies. One study on *The Gift of Prophecy* was very enlightening, and I include it at the end of this Chapter for all who want to learn more about spiritual gifts. Loraine gave me a marvelous little book by Francis J. Roberts, <u>Come Away My Beloved,</u> which I include in my Bibliography. It is full of prophecies given to the church over the years, and I took it with me along with my Bible while traveling overseas.

As my Bible studies continued, I gathered information from other Christian ministries, including three great sessions about *The Signs of His Coming,* by two ladies of a TV ministry team over a Christian TV channel. The first session was about *the Great Awakening,* which got its start at the *old Reformed Dutch Church in New York City,* when someone put a sign on the front door inviting people in for *a noon prayer meeting, which changed the world.* It tells about John and Charles Wesley preaching in the highways and byways of England and George Whitfield riding horseback all across America preaching to thousands. It is my prayer that we will experience another *Great Awakening* in our country like we had in the 1850's, when it was said that people were asking to be saved on ships coming into our harbors. The power of the Holy Spirit was so great; it was said that they could feel God's presence still miles out at sea. When Revival broke out in America, our country was greatly blessed and miracles abounded. When Billy Sunday preached in Chicago, all the bars closed down and people started going to church again. We need that kind of revival again in America today! The ladies also recommended the book, <u>Revival Fire</u>, and they discussed the *"Tetrad,"* the *four blood moons with an eclipse of the sun in the middle,* which has preceded many earth changing events over the centuries. There have been three of them in the last 500 years, one near the time Columbus discovered America, and that proved to be an enormous change in the history of the world and world commerce. It appears that the eclipse of the sun depicts a world event and the blood moons depict an event which affects Israel, such as the one around the time Israel was re-established as a nation in 1948.

The next teaching session of the lady's ministry was about the Jewish people returning to their homeland and the visions of two men who made it happen. This is another miracle of God and a very important sign of the times. After dispersing the Jews all over the earth, God began bringing them back to their homeland when the nation of Israel was re-established in 1948. This miraculous story is found in The Prince and the Prophet, written by Claude Duvenoy, and is listed in the Bibliography. It is about two great men, separated by two generations, who were brought together and used by God in a miraculous way to bring the Jews back to their homeland and fulfill Bible prophecy. William Heckler was a Jew who had a vision in a dream of the other as a child, Theodore Herzl. Heckler was searching for another *Moses* to bring his people back to their homeland for *The Rebirth of Israel.* Herzl was a prominent British statesman with great influence in Parliament and the United Nations who listened to Heckler and allowed God to work through him in presenting his case to the world.

> *"Now learn a parable of the fig tree; When his branch is yet tender, and putteth forth leaves, ye know that summer is nigh: So likewise ye, when ye shall see all these things, know that it is near, even at the doors. Verily I say unto you, This generation shall not pass, till all these things are fulfilled. Heaven and earth shall pass away, but my words shall not pass away. But of that day and hour knoweth no man, no, not the angels of heaven, but my Father only."*
> (Matthew 24:32-36)

The Gift of Prophecy

1. What is the Gift of Prophecy?

   A. It is God giving utterance through man in his native tongue. In this God sets aside the mind and words of man and superimposes his mi words in our language. (1st Peter 1:11-12)
   B. It goes beyond the ability to preach in an inspired manner. Proph angels did not understand many things which the Lord spoke throug but things which they desired to look into and understand.

C. It is man becoming God's spokesman. This has happened many time God has set aside our thoughts and words and imposed his.

D. Prophecy is the foretelling of Divine truth, as we are moved by th Spirit to speak. This is the most important part of the three gifts of utt which include tongues and the interpretation of tongues.

2. What is the purpose of the Gift of Prophecy?

A. Prophecy gives God a channel through which he can speak to supernaturally in an individual's own language. (1st Corinthians 14:1-2

B. It is for the edifying, or encouragement, of the Church. (1st Corinthian 4) *"He that speaks in an unknown tongue edifies himself; but prophesies edifies the Church."* There is no greater encouragement Church than to have God speak to us in our own language to rev Presence. Divinely dictated words not only reveal his Presence but br breath and sweetness of heaven into our midst.

C. To convince the unbeliever of the reality of God's Presence. (1st Cori 14:24-25) There is a difference between the unbeliever of verse 22 unbeliever of verses 24-25: the unbeliever of verse 22 is a sinn unbeliever of verses 24-25 is a Christian who is unlearned or does not in the Gifts of the Spirit. Prophecy is one of the most definite ways th has of revealing himself to the believer. Note the last part of verse verses 23-24.

D. Prophecy is exercised that all may learn. (1st Corinthians 14:31) Th many unlearned saved people in our midst today: Through prophec learn that God is able to manifest himself as he did in days of old.

3. How does the Gift of Prophecy work?

A. It works through the supernatural operation of the Holy Spirit.

B. In its simplest form, it operates apart from the other Gifts in stre present truth or fact.

C. Often it operates in conjunction with other Gifts:

    a.   As with the <u>Word of Wisdom</u> enabling us to know what to do in situation, as when they besought Paul and told him not to go to place, knowing what would happen. (Acts 21:10-11)

    b.   As with the <u>Word of Knowledge</u> in revealing a hidden fact, as wh told Ananias what he had done. (Acts 5:3)

    c.   As with the <u>Gift of Faith</u> in believing that God will keep his wor what he says, as when Paul spoke to Sergius Paulus and he was smi blindness. (Acts 13:6-11)

4.   All the gifts of the Spirit are supernatural and they are a <u>ministry o Church</u>. (Acts 2:4) *"For he that speaks in an unknown tongue speak unto men, but unto God: for no man understands him; howbeit in the spi speaks mysteries."*

5.   The person who speaks in an unknown tongue may also be grante second Gift of Interpretation of Tongues. (1st Corinthians 14:13) "Wher let him that speaks in an unknown tongue pray that he may interpret."

6.   *<u>"If there is no interpreter, let him keep silence</u> in the Church; and le speak to himself and to God."* (lst Corinthians 14:28) *"For God is n author of confusion; but of peace, as in all churches of the saints.* Corinthians 14:33)

7.   The Gift of the Interpretation of Tongues is <u>the supernatural showing for the Spirit</u> the meaning of an utterance spoken by a person in a lan which he does not understand. <u>The purpose of this Gift is to rende message from Christ</u>, which has been given in an unintelligible tongue made intelligible to those present.

8.   <u>This Gift exalts the Lord Jesus Christ</u>. It is the functioning of a miracle can be easily seen by the unbeliever and causes consternation to hi witnessed on the Day of Pentecost when the Church was born. (<u>Acts, Ch 2</u>)

9.   *"For if I pray in an unknown tongue, <u>my spirit prays</u>, but my understa is unfruitful."* <u>This Gift flows from the spirit and not the mind</u> Corinthians 14:14)

10. *"Wherefore <u>tongues are for a sign</u>, not to them that believe, but to them believe not: but <u>prophesying</u> serves not for them that believe not, but for that believe."* (1st Corinthians 14:22)

11. Tongues will cease at the end of this age when knowledge shall vanish the earth and the Church will be in heaven.

CHAPTER TWENTY-SIX

From Mobile to Seattle
1986-1988

From our friends at Knollwood, we learned of a *Camp Meeting* in Baton Rouge over Thanksgiving weekend at the *Family Worship Center* which some of them were planning to attend. Greg was thrilled because he had watched the pastor of this church on TV, even before he became a Christian. I had never seen him before, nor had I ever been to a camp meeting. However, Greg wanted to go, and it would solve the problem of finding something to do while the others were at Disney World, so I reserved a motel room for the four days of the camp meeting. The Family Worship Center was easy to find and there was a flock of people headed in that direction, so we just followed the crowd, parked the car and went inside to find a seat in the large octagonal building. We were warmly greeted and welcomed by the many attendants.

Camp Meeting 1986 got off to a great start Wednesday night with piano music and a string of talented singers, and the music could be heard all over the building. I was very impressed with the order in which we were received into the congregation and the whole atmosphere which prevailed throughout the evening. Even the restrooms smelled of a clean and sweet fragrance, and the loudspeakers worked very well. The singers were very talented and all of them were new to me. My favorites were a beautiful young lady singer's *"I Give You Jesus"* and the popular young male singer's *"There's a Light House."* Greg and I met many wonderful people over the four-day weekend and ran into our old friends from Knollwood, Loraine and Will, who sat with us and escorted us across the street to introduce us to the book store of the Bible College.

Thanksgiving morning found us back in the swing of the *Camp Meeting* at 9:00 am and stopped around noon for Thanksgiving Dinner, which was served across the street at the restaurant of the Bible College. Dinner was fantastic with the traditional turkey, dressing and all the trimmings and an assortment of desserts. We enjoyed it tremendously, especially sharing this very special day with Loraine and Will. In fact, we liked the restaurant so well we ate all our meals there for the rest of the week. The activities started up again after dinner with the pastor leading us in a Thanksgiving prayer followed by a guest speaker who delivered a great message. Then the pastor accompanied many of the singers of the previous night on the piano, backed up by the small orchestra and church choir. I was very impressed with the organization and talents of all these people. In fact, I learned that he actually wrote many of the beautiful songs he sang as he accompanied himself on the piano. I still love to hear these beautiful songs and could listen for hours to the beautiful messages they give to the world. I bought several tapes from the book store and have put them on disc for safe keeping. We enjoyed the humor of all the guest speakers as well as their inspiring messages.

The camp meeting was very exciting and entertaining as well as inspirational without one moment of boredom. Nobody went to sleep in this church! All the people we met were very friendly and ready to share their testimonies. And they were interested in hearing ours about the miracles God had done in our lives. Greg was not at all ashamed to tell his story about how the Lord saved him one day in his Virginia Beach apartment when he walked into his closet to find the little Bible I had given him one Easter. His testimony usually began with, *"I used to be a drug addict, but God saved me."* Then he would tell them about picking up a *Decision magazine* showing the outstretched hands full of wheat with the inscription below which read, *"Ye reap what ye sow,"* and how he found his Bible and started reading for the first time in Leviticus. A lady came up to me with a word of knowledge and said that I was *"a light shining in a dark place."* It all conveyed the same beautiful message about the life of Jesus, *"The promised Seed,"* and the need for us all to be *born again* of his *life-giving Spirit.* Greg and I loved every minute of visiting this church, and it seemed like the vibrant atmosphere he needed at this time of his life to continue his spiritual growth.

Greg's surgery at the University of South Alabama's Hospital was performed as planned in December, and it would take another month for his stump to heal and be reshaped for the fitting of a new prosthesis. He was not at all hampered by his inability to get around with the use of his crutches and looked forward to church at Knollwood every Sunday morning, and sometimes Wednesday evenings. Mother wondered why we had to drive all the way to the other side of Mobile to attend this church when her church was just around the corner. Then we started attending prayer meetings sometimes during the week at the houses of our friends at Knollwood. There was no way I could explain it to Mother or the rest of the family, so I didn't even try. John wondered if we were ever coming back to northern Virginia and started putting out resumes.

The Pastor at Knollwood told me that the Methodist Church was the forerunner of the Pentecostal churches. Its founders, John and Charles Wesley, were thrown out of the Anglican Church and driven to *the highways and byways of England to preach the Gospel of Christ* because their ways of receiving the Holy Spirit were foreign to the Anglican Church and, therefore, not accepted. The name, *Methodist,* was derived from their *method of praying through to receive the baptism of the Holy Spirit,* which overflows believers and produces a heavenly language, referred to as *speaking in other tongues.* This utterance first occurred on *the Day of Pentecost,* as described in *the Acts of the Apostles, and came in as "a great wind" with "tongues of fire"* which fell upon them in an upper room in Jerusalem, where Jesus told them to *"wait for the promise of the Father."* He told them they would be *"baptized with the Holy Ghost and with fire" and they would "receive power from on high."*

At the turn of the 20th Century, the Methodist Church was divided between believers and non-believers: those who believed in *"the baptism of the Holy Spirit and the gifts of the Spirit"* and those who did not. The Pentecostals, first called *the come outers,* left the Methodist Church and started their own churches all across the country. They continued their method of *praying through* to receive *the baptism of the Holy Spirit,* and they still believe in all *the Spiritual Gifts.* (1 Corinthians 14:13-33)

When I called Amanda to see how they were doing, Zach told me that he listened to Maggie every morning on WHRO FM Radio on his way to work. She was giving *the Morning Traffic Report,* and he thought she was very good and showed much potential in becoming a newscaster or reporter. Maggie hadn't said a word to us about it, probably because we hadn't talked to her in a while with all our energies going out in so many other directions. We were so caught up in all the things we were trying to accomplish, I'm afraid we had neglected her and also Jim. Maggie was making excellent grades in all her courses, and Jim was doing very well in his civil engineering job working with the Mississippi Department of Transportation (MDOT). His job was to inspect bridges all over the state to keep the roads safe, and he had just recently earned his PE Certificate, which qualified him as a *Professional Engineer.*

Since Greg and I seemed to be living with Mother again and John was getting antsy about my return to Virginia, we started looking for an apartment for Greg in the Mobile area where he could attend Knollwood and I could return to my old job in DC. John decided to drive down with Maggie, picking up his mother on the way, so all the family could be together at Mother's house for Christmas. Jim and Kathy drove over from Jackson, and I made Christmas stockings for everyone to fill with goodies Christmas Eve. Mother and I prepared a great turkey dinner, and it was great fun having all the family together again for Christmas. Of course, Jim and Kathy had to drive back the following Sunday to be ready for work on Monday and John and Maggie had to get back to their classes a few days later. They dropped Hannah off at her apartment in northern Mississippi and drove on to Virginia the following day.

It took Greg about a month to heal from his surgery and the temporary apartment we found for him in Mobile didn't work out, so he and I drove over to Baton Rouge to see what we could find for him near the Family Worship Center. We attended church services on Sunday and met some people who told us about the Dove Creek Apartments where many people of the ministry lived. It would be easy for Greg to get rides back and forth with some of the single guys who lived there. Following their directions, we found Dove Creek and applied for a one-bedroom apartment which would become available the third week of January. We made plans to move him over there and get him settled.

While Greg and I were trying to get him relocated in Baton Rouge, John informed me that he had an interview in New York with a company which might have a job for him with the Peace Shield Program in Saudi Arabia. It would be similar to his previous job with Litton, but this time he would be working for Boeing preparing communications facilities for the Saudi Arabian Air Force. Greg and I continued our project of getting him resettled at Dove Creek and bought him a few more pieces of furniture. We also registered him with the Department of Rehabilitation and changed his address, so he could continue receiving his SSI and Medicaid. Two of his new friends at Dove Creek were firemen, Brady and Jeff, who attended the Family Worship Center regularly and picked him up for rides to the ministry.

They also invited him to go along with them on fishing trips, and, on one occasion, they caught 84 fish, which they cleaned and packed inside milk cartons filled with water for easy storage in their freezers.

Greg said that Brady was a good cook and always invited him over to share his fish dinners. The two guys were faithful friends and good examples for Greg the whole time he lived at Dove Creek. However, after his lease ran out six months later, Greg and another friend moved over closer to the ministry to share expenses in a two-bedroom apartment. They even held prayer meetings in their living room, and I was impressed when I walked into his new apartment and saw their Christian pictures on the walls. The pictures I took of Greg at that time and the following years look absolutely *wholesome* compared to the way he looked before. I was thankful for his conversion and made many trips over to Baton Rouge to attend church services with Greg, and we always had dinner in the wonderful restaurant of the Bible College across the street.

When John arrived back in northern Virginia after Christmas, he continued to follow the Peace Shield Program and set up interviews: one in Philadelphia and three in Los Angeles. In the spring he wanted me to fly out to Seattle with him for an interview with Boeing, the primary contractor for the Peace Shield program. We stayed at Nendel's Motel on a small winding river in Tukwilla where we enjoyed watching the ducks during the two days of his interviews. As I recall, they had a good restaurant with very good food, and we would come back again and again. Feeling good about his prospects as Construction Manager of such a large Boeing project, which would follow up the job he had just completed with Litton, John had all our furniture and household goods moved into storage and cleaned out our apartment in Crystal City. In April, he received a phone call from Boeing stating how much they appreciated our visit and that things looked good. He received an offer in May and accepted it with a letter of confirmation the first week of June.

During this time, Maggie was enjoying her internship with WHRO-FM Radio in Norfolk. Upon her graduation from ODU the following year, she received two job offers as a result of her successful internship, which was well received in the area with her *Morning Traffic Report*. Maggie also served as *copy writer* for the news broadcast of her sponsor who gave the news on *The Morning Edition*. Her best offer was from the Tidewater Metro Traffic Control to become *their first on-air TV Reporter*, but she rejected it because she didn't want to begin her daily schedule so early in the morning.

Also, I think she shied away from having to appear in person on TV. Maggie's second offer came from a North Carolina radio station to do what she had done all year in Norfolk, but she rejected that also because she didn't want to move to North Carolina. Her boyfriend, Dave, had a good job in Norfolk and wanted her to stay there. She finally accepted a position making radio commercials with a company in Virginia Beach, supplying voice dialogue and background music in her main area of interest, *Creative Arts*. With all the turmoil of job hunting and moving after finally getting Greg settled in Baton Rouge, John and I seemed to be totally oblivious to the passage of time and lost track of Maggie's graduation at the end of the year. We were so proud of her and all her accomplishments, I wish we could have been there.

However, like a whirlwind, John moved us out of our apartment in Crystal City and was ready to take me off again in another direction. This time, it would be a drive across the expansive Midwest and the beautiful northern Rocky Mountains into Seattle. We called to tell all the family our news about our new venture which would take us back overseas and prepared for our trip across the Midwest bound for Seattle. John and I had never driven this route before across the northern Midwest, and it proved to be a much needed vacation for us both. We took time to see *the Black Hills and Badlands of South Dakota and Mount Rushmore,* with portraits of four great American Presidents. I was especially impressed with the profile of George Washington, which was quite visible from the highway as we passed below. We witnessed numerous tractors working at night with headlights harvesting the grain all across the farm lands of South Dakota as they cut and rolled the bundles of wheat, leaving them to be picked up, threshed and stored in the large granaries. With the lovely full moon overhead, it was a beautiful sight to behold!

The following day, we had a guided tour of the *Little Big Horn* in Montana, the scene of *General Custer's Last Stand,* when he was ordered to hold back hundreds of Sioux Indians with a military force of about 600 men. They had no idea that the number camped out across the river led by Chief Sitting Bull was around 6,000 men of three large Indian Tribes: Sioux, Cheyenne and Crow. We listened to the history, walked the area and saw the markers where Custer and his men had fallen and their bodies found on that fateful day in June, 1876. We visited the camp site of the scouts who observed Indian movement across the river but had no visibility of the great camp site where the majority of them were assembled inside the river bend a little further upstream. We noticed many buffalo breeding farms in Montana and even tried a *Buffalo Burger* one evening. It was a little bland compared to a beef burger, but probably healthier because of less fat.

A couple of days later, we arrived back at Nendel's Motel where John began his first day of work with Boeing on the 29th of June. While staying at Nendel's, we picked up the last brochure of a place called *Surprise Lake Village.* It sounded good and we needed to find a place quickly for our rather short stay in Seattle, so we drove out to have a look and were greatly impressed. We were pleasantly surprised to find a townhouse complex in the small town of Milton, which consisted of newly constructed, but rather rustic looking, buildings in a beautiful garden-like setting on a very lovely lake. The office and small recreation room were located on a wharf built out over the lake, where one could sit and enjoy the many ducks and geese. We noticed a nearby sign which read, *"Do NOT feed the Ducks."* It was there for a very important reason, which we later learned to appreciate. While living at Surprise Lake Village, we had the pleasure of inviting a few of our old Litton friends over, who still lived in the area, and some visitors from out of town, who were there for interviews. We would have time to get to know some of our new Boeing friends before our next venture overseas.

Our small one-bedroom house had a loft which served as a second bedroom, where we set up our computer and TV system, and this is where I started writing this book about 30 years ago. Half-way up to the loft, we had a small landing with a window where we placed our small rattan glass-top table and two rattan chairs. We often sat here to enjoy the view while having our morning coffee, or lunch, as we discussed our plans for the day. It was here in this setting, as we were having lunch one day that I got all excited telling John about my plans for the book. He seemed very interested in the project of my trying to reconstruct our lives as a military family while sharing some of our adventures around the world. It seemed to be a good use of my time since he would be away on short trips within the country before we were both scheduled to leave on his overseas assignment. I got so wound up with all my talking and enthusiasm that I finally said to John, *"Well that's enough about me. What do you think of my book?"*

Our little town of Milton was located between Seattle and Tacoma, and, when I rounded the bend to drive down into the valley to attend church on a clear Sunday morning, I could see the huge rounded snow-capped mountain top of Mount Rainier slowly rising in the distance as I made my descent. It was truly a beautiful sight to behold! Every Sunday morning, I would walk into the Puyallup Assembly of God and take my seat on the right side of the far left aisle about half-way back. And, every Sunday morning, Laurie and her husband would come in and take their seats on the row in front of me to the far left. After a while, we were exchanging smiles and *"Good Mornings,"* and, when the service was over, Laurie and I would sometimes stop to chat. We were always happy to see each other and decided to meet for lunch one day, and, when Laurie learned that I was starting to write a book about our family travels, she became very interested and wanted to read some of it. So I brought her home one day to sit on our landing for coffee and dessert and she read as far as I had written in the first Chapter. Of course, it was still in its primitive stage, but she became my chief supporter and encourager over the years. We shared many things about our families during our short stay in Seattle, and I was honored to meet her husband, James, and her mother and father, who also attended Puyallup Assembly. Laurie and I finally got our husbands together at our favorite Mexican restaurant before we left the country for Saudi Arabia. We have always kept in touch, especially at Christmas, and Laurie was always thoughtful enough to send me an Easter card. Whenever John and I pass through Seattle, we always give them a call and meet somewhere for lunch or dinner.

What I remember most about our life in the Seattle area is the lightly falling rain and the mist from the ocean which kept us cool at night and made the lovely plants flourish. The Puyallup Assembly was very much like the other Assemblies of God which I had experienced since leaving Falls Church, and I learned so much from the pastors of all these churches. The pastor in Puyallup was a fine gentleman who once told the congregation that he would *"tell the people the truth and let God do the changing."* The pastor's wife, a very petite and attractive brunette, conducted a week's Bible study on the Holy Spirit. Laurie and I didn't miss a night and found her teaching exhilarating. She began her study with a beautifully prepared table covered with a white linen table cloth and a big, round pitcher of cold water sitting in the middle of the table. She told the story about a Samaritan woman who was drawing water from a well when Jesus walked up and asked for a drink. She responded, *"How is it that you, being a Jew, ask a drink of me, a woman of Samaria, for the Jews do not deal with the Samaritans?"* Jesus answered,

> *"If you knew the gift of God and who it is that asks for a drink, you would have asked of him, and he would have given you living water.... Whosoever drinks of this water shall thirst again: But whosoever drinks of the water that I shall give him shall never thirst; but the water that I shall give him shall be in him a well of water springing up into everlasting life.... Ye worship ye know not what: we know what we worship; for salvation is of the Jews.... God is a Spirit: and they that worship him must worship him in spirit and in truth."* (John 4: 7-14)

Then she poured herself a glass of cold water and started drinking, making her point and, at the same time, making the rest of us very thirsty. She continued every night with more of her message, and, before her study ended, we all felt the well of water springing up inside. I enclose a copy of the study guide, which she handed out as she covered her teaching on the three main topics of the Holy Spirit.

The Office of the Holy Spirit

The Holy Spirit appears like a <u>Dove</u>, very gentle, and can easily be grieved or driven away. He is a symbol of peace. (John 1:32; Luke 3:22; Matt. 3:16, Mark 1:10);

Like the <u>Wind</u>, he cannot be seen, but we can sense his presence and feel his unseen power or force. (John 3:6-8; John 20:22; Acts 2:2);

Like <u>Fire</u>, he purges away impurity and has great zeal and passion for the spiritual things of God. (Matt. 3:11-12; Luke 3:16-17; Acts 2:3; Hebrews 12:29);

Like <u>Water</u> or <u>Rain</u>, he washes, refreshes and makes us clean. He is the source of life. (John 4:10-24 & 7:37-39; Isaiah 44:3; Hosea 6:3 & 14:5; Isaiah 28:11-12);

Like <u>Oil</u>, he anoints us with divine dedication to God and he is the source of God's healing power and light. (1 John 2:20,27; Acts 10:38; 1 Samuel 16:13;

Luke 4:18; Psalm 23:5; Isaiah 61:1; Luke 10:34; Matt. 25:3, 4, 8 &13);

He <u>Seals</u> us for God's protection and from the evil influences of the world, so that we may be filled with the Spirit of God. (2 Corinthians 1:22; Ephesians 1:13 & 4:30; 2 Timothy 2:19; John 6:27);

He is the <u>Earnest,</u> the down payment of more to come, of the fullness of God and a sample of the glory of God, which awaits us in-Christ. (2 Corinthians 1:22; 5:5; & Ephesians 1:14).

The Ministry of the Holy Spirit

First, he is the <u>Agent</u> or <u>Witness</u> of the new birth. (John 3:5-8);

He is the <u>Comforter,</u> or <u>Helper,</u> sent to empower believers and make them into the image of Christ. (John 14:16-19; John 16:7; Acts 1:4-8; Galatians 5:16; Romans 8:1-11, & 14; Psalm 103-14; 2 Corinthians 3:17-18);

He is the <u>Spirit of Truth,</u> our <u>Teacher,</u> and our <u>Guide</u> to lead us into all truth. (John 14:17, 26 & 16:13-15; Romans 8:14; 1 Corinthians 2:9-16; Luke 2:27);

He is our <u>Advocate</u> in heaven and intercedes for us. (Romans 8:34);

He is the <u>Restrainer</u> who convicts unbelievers and restrains the evil one and the work of demons upon the earth. (John 16:8-11; Isaiah 59:19; 2 Thessalonians 2:7-8);

He is the <u>Third Person of the Holy Trinity.</u> (1 John 5:7). All three Persons are truly God and equal in reign, but they all hold different offices.

The Baptism of the Holy Spirit

<u>Prophecies regarding His coming.</u> (Joel 2:28-29; Ezekiel 36:25-27) Jesus <u>breathed on the disciples</u> and told them to <u>receive the Holy Spirit</u> who was to come. (John 20:22) Jesus told them to <u>wait in Jerusalem for the Promise of the Father</u>. (Acts 1:4-5) He also told them that they would <u>receive Power when the Holy Spirit has come upon them.</u> (Acts 1:8; Luke 24:49);

We are <u>born of the Spirit of God</u> when we first believe. (John 3:3-8; 2nd Corinthians 5:17) <u>The Spirit gives Life.</u> (Romans 8:11; Ephesians 2:1, 18, 22) <u>The Holy Spirit is for all believers who ask the Father</u>. (Acts 2:38-39; Luke 11:11-13; Isaiah 28:11-12; Colossians 3:15) <u>Jesus, "the Baptizer," had to be glorified before the Spirit could come</u>, and <u>having received from the Father, He poured out His Spirit...</u> (Matt. 3:11; John 7:39; Acts 2:33) <u>This Baptism is for everyone, people of all ages.</u> (Joel 2:28-29);

All true believers will receive this baptism until the Lord returns. (Acts 2:38-39) Our body is the Temple of the Holy Spirit. (1 Corinthians 6:19; 2 Corinthians 4:7) Our "spiritual eyes," the eyes of our understanding, are opened through the work of the Holy Spirit so that we may see and understand spiritual things. (1 Corinthians 2:9-14) As we learn to walk in the Spirit, we will be gradually changed into the image of Christ. (Romans 8:1-6, 8, 9; Ephesians 5:8-10, 18);

We must ask the Father for the gift of the Holy Spirit. (Acts 2:38; Romans 10:9-10; Luke 11:11-13) The History of speaking in tongues. (Acts 2:1-4, 8:14-17, 10:44-46, 19:1-7) The Value of speaking in tongues. (1 Corinthians 14:2, 4, 14, 15; Romans 8:26-27; Isaiah 28:11-12) The Benefits of receiving the Baptism of the Holy Spirit. (Acts 4:13-14 & 31; 6:8; 9:33 & 40; 11:12; 12:7; 14:5; 10:22; 19:11-12) The Bible tells us to keep on being filled with the Holy Spirit. (Ephesians 5:18-21; 1 Peter 1:3-4; Ephesians 4:30) We must be prepared for Spiritual Warfare. (Ephesians 6:10-18; Matthew 4: 1-11; 1 Peter 4:12, 5:8; 1 John 4:4) The primary Evidence of the Holy Spirit working in a person's life is Love. (1 Corinthians, Chapter 13)

We tried to keep in touch with our kids and the rest of our relatives during our time in the Seattle area. Grace wrote us that Hannah was having some dental work done and got a great looking new hairstyle. She and Ruby Gaye were still enjoying traveling a bit with the church group and eating out at their favorite restaurant. John made several short trips and one long trip over to Saudi Arabia during the year and left me alone for a few weeks. I used this time to write down all I could remember about the sequence of events in the lives of our children, where we lived and the things we did. After my poor attempt at writing the first chapter, it became mostly a list of chronological events and the important things that stood out foremost in my mind.

It would take many years, and several new starts, of assembling all the information I had accumulated and then learning how to weave so many facets of our lives together in the creation of an interesting on-going story. God wiped the first version entirely off my hard drive by lightning to give me the last new start. Still, it would take many more years for this book to take shape and become worthy of being submitted to a publisher. As time passed, John and I had many more interesting trips and adventures to add to our story as we experienced life abroad and saw much more of the world after our children had lives of their own. When John returned from one of his short trips, we learned from Aunt Grace that his mom was not feeling well and was having trouble breathing. Her doctor referred her to a specialist to run some tests to find out what was causing her trouble. Grace promised to keep us informed.

Seattle was a great addition to our list of favorite places, and we celebrated our 31st Anniversary at the top of the Needle in downtown Seattle with dinner in the famous revolving restaurant. From there, we had a great view of Puget Sound and the surrounding areas. We could almost pin point the marina in the distance, which was owned and run by John's former boss with Litton, James McFarland, and his lovely wife, Samantha. Now they enjoyed operating the marina on the large expanse of waters and bays which covered Puget Sound. We enjoyed visiting them when we first arrived in the area and were invited to their Open House when Jim finished his latest project, the building of their lovely hillside home overlooking a valley with Puget Sound in the distance. John and I loved the gentle falling rain, which seemed to fall consistently at times, and the moist winds off the Pacific Ocean, which made the plants and wild vegetation flourish like the environment we remembered in Monterey. Occasionally, we would drive half-way up the mountainside of Mt. Rainier to the small town of Eatonville to visit our favorite wildlife park, *Northwest Trek*, nestled beneath the beautiful snow-capped mountain.

John and I discovered this animal sanctuary on our first attempt to drive to the top of Mt. Rainier, which was not available because the roads were blocked with snow. So we found our alternative in the small town of Eatonville: *Northwest Trek*, advertised as *a 50-Minute Tram Ride through a 600-Acre Wildlife Preserve.* It became our favorite Seattle attraction over the years, one which we would never miss on any of our trips through the Seattle-Tacoma area. The guided tram tours would take us through the lovely wildlife park where things are always changing according to the seasons. We learned the history of this lovely park, once privately owned and gleaned several times by forest fires, which always gave the park a new beginning having burnt up the undergrowth and produced a forest of new and healthier trees. Our guide pointed out the herds of caribou, elk, deer, bison, and a few moose as they freely roamed the area and grazed in the meadowlands.

On our first ride through the park, it was just past *rutting season* for the deer, and the winner, with his spectacular antlers, was resting with his harem on one side of the road, while a little further down on the other side, we saw the bachelors, with a few broken antlers here and there looking quite pitiful. Following the tram ride, we took the walking tour down the nature trail which took us past several outdoor exhibits where we visited the bald eagle, the golden eagle and the snowy owl. Then we stopped to observe the fishers, mink, wolverine and raccoons. We were also able to observe both below and above the waterline, the beaver and the otter. We noticed the black bear roaming around the forest and many gorgeous arctic tundra wolves, the major attraction of the park. They appeared to be living in their natural habitats, but they were actually living within fences with plenty of room to move around.

We would come back many times over the years to enjoy this wonderful natural habitat of animals which live in this region of the Northwest. And we would always eat our lunch in its small, rustic restaurant near the entrance.

Grace called us with sad news about Hannah's test results: The doctors at Memphis Baptist Hospital had found that she tested positive for lung cancer. She would be treated with radiation and chemotherapy to see if they could kill the disease before it spread. We hoped for a full recovery! During our short time in Seattle, we saw as much of the area as we could, and in no time, I was zipping around the freeways shopping at the commissary and other places while John was at work. On one occasion, I took my electric typewriter across town for repairs, and, as I was driving by a large church, I was prompted to turn off the road and check it out. There in the lobby, I found a booth set up to sell Christmas tapes of their special Christmas music, so I bought three of them and continued on my way. I had no idea what I was buying until I listened to them on my way home and found them to be full of the most exciting Christmas music I had ever heard, which tell the Christmas Story of the birth of Jesus in exhilarating movements. Right away, I went to work putting together a special 90-minute tape to give to all our family as a Christmas gift. On the cover, I used the picture of a beautiful little church in the snow of Kandersteg, Switzerland, a picture John took on our first trip in 1983. It is still our favorite Christmas tape, and we play it every year.

Hannah made several trips to Memphis for radiation treatments and spent some of the time with Grace and George. When we got the news that it didn't look good for her and the radiation treatments were only making her sick, John applied for a three-month leave of absence from the Boeing project. Hannah had stopped smoking for a couple of years and felt so much better, and we were so proud of her. And so was she! But she decided to go back to it because she liked it and found it comforting while doing her needle point or crossword puzzles. Almost immediately, she started having trouble with her lungs. John was granted his LOA and we prepared for the long drive to Memphis via Los Angeles. We left under bad weather conditions with the prediction of snow in the mountains of northern California. Sure enough, we ran into a blizzard as we were ascending up one of the highest mountains and wondered how we would get down on the other side and make it to our motel in Redding. We noticed a snow plow in front of us, so we crept along behind it all the way down, and, once at the bottom, we realized that there had been two snow plows in front of us. The next morning as we walked over to breakfast, we noticed little round cabbage–like plants protruding up proudly through the snow looking so elegant. I have a mental picture of them in case we move to Alaska.

When we reached southern California, we spent two nights at the Cosmic Age Motel where we had stayed that first Christmas at Disneyland with the kids after having left Tucson. It brought back many happy memories to John and me, as we took time to rest a while and reminisce of our happy times with our kids doing some of the things we had done with them and eating in some of the places we remembered. The next morning, we drove by the Crystal Cathedral on our way to the hospital to have my broken toe bandaged. During the night, I had bumped into a hotel fixture in the dark after turning out the light and my toe was obviously broken. John had straightened it out and tried to bandage it with a Popsicle stick, but that didn't work. The doctor at the hospital bandaged it properly and gave me a *walking shoe* to wear. The drive to Memphis would give it some time to heal and I would try to stay off of it for a while.

When we finally arrived in Memphis, Grace brought us up to date on Hannah's condition. She was in the hospital having more radiation treatments when we arrived that week, so, after visiting a couple of days, we left for Norfolk where Maggie was having exploratory surgery for a suspected cyst which they thought was causing a bladder infection. Thank goodness they didn't find anything, only an indentation where something could have been, and medication was all she needed to clear it up. When I saw her lying there in the hospital bed feeling so much pain from the tube they had inserted, I couldn't do anything to help her and I knew I was going to faint! As I was leaning over her bedrails to try to keep from falling, I heard her call out for somebody to *"Come and help my mom!"* The next thing I knew; I was lying on a lounge with a glass of orange juice being handed to me. The same thing happened in Morocco when Maggie was being treated for a dog bite she received from her best friend's bulldog. I had to drive her to the hospital in Kenitra for the deep puncture wound which had to be washed out with a strong solution to kill germs. Watching the solution shooting up out of her leg when I couldn't do a thing to help her, I fainted there, too, in the Emergency Room.

We brought Maggie home with us from the hospital to Amanda's house in Virginia Beach, where she was still in pain before starting our trip south to see her grandmother, who, by this time, was back in her home. Maggie didn't rest very well on the bed I made for her on the backseat of our car, and, when we finally arrived, we had to make a pallet for her on the living room floor, which was also uncomfortable. Hannah was still sleeping on her couch, which she preferred over her bed because she said it was more comfortable for her back, which gave it firm support. However, Maggie needed to be at home in her own bed and near her doctor, so we had to send her home where Dave could meet her plane and take care of her.

Hannah's freezer was packed with so much food; we didn't need to buy much of anything at the grocery for the remainder of the time we were there. After visiting a few days, it was time to take Maggie to Atlanta to put her on the plane back to Virginia for her doctor's follow up appointment. We met Dave on our first morning at the hospital, and he said he recognized me when I first walked in because of the family resemblance. We knew Dave would be there to meet Maggie's plane and take her safely back to her apartment where she could get some rest and finish healing. From Atlanta, after seeing Maggie off on her plane, we made a quick trip down to the Gulf to attend to some business regarding our condo *Rental Agreement* and arranged for a lady to stay with Hannah during the two days we were away, but she became ill and was taken back to the hospital where she died the following day. We felt just awful about not being with Hannah, the reason for our trip in the first place, but we had no idea she was that close to death. As always, we were just too thinly spread out.

After the funeral, John, his brother, Mark, and I cleaned out her apartment and tried to sell or distribute everything we could during the remaining time we had left of John's Leave of Absence. In retrospect, we should have cancelled our meeting with the condo rental program and put Maggie on a plane back to Virginia from Memphis. We should have had more time with both of them. Maggie needed her dad to advise her regarding her career possibilities following graduation. She had wanted to come out to Seattle for a visit, and we should have bought her a plane ticket. We should have been there for her graduation. Like they say, *"Life happens when you're making plans."* No matter what, even when we make mistakes or use bad judgment, we must believe that *"All things work together for good for those who love the Lord and are called according to his purpose."* (Romans 8:28 & 31) And we must continue to believe that everything is in God's hands and know that He is good. He always has a good plan for our lives.

Back in Seattle again, John's time was getting short for our leaving the country for our assignment in Saudi Arabia. We decided to do some of the things we hadn't had time to do and decided to take a day trip down the beautiful *Oregon coast*. We took many pictures of the beautiful Oregon beaches and shoreline, and we planned to come back to our area and take pictures of the Washington shoreline; however, it was too obscure to find. We drove west to the *Macau Indian Reservation* and around the *Kitsap Peninsula* to view the rocky coast. It was here that we discovered the more industrial side of Washington with its timber industry. We spent a couple of nights at Neah Bay, and, since salmon was quite plentiful in the area, we enjoyed many wonderful salmon dinners. However, we'll always remember the very special salmon dinner we enjoyed on the way home in Aberdeen the last day of our trip, which gave us a beautiful view of the river pouring out of Puget Sound as it made its way into the gigantic Pacific Ocean.

CHAPTER TWENTY-SEVEN

The Arabian Desert
1989-1990

We were sad to leave our little home at Surprise Lake Village on the 2nd of December, 1988, but it was time for another Saudi Arabian adventure. We headed south down Pacific Coast Highway, veering off to the east at Los Angeles on our way back to Alabama. John would go over first to get started with his job as Construction Manager with the Boeing project, and I would remain with Mother until he arranged for me to join him. I spent Christmas with Maggie and Dave that year in Norfolk, and we decorated a small Christmas tree in her apartment. Mother was with my brothers and their families and always enjoyed being with the grandchildren for Christmas. It was very cold that winter in Virginia, and I slept under a warm quilt I had made for Mother from scraps of material saved from clothing I had made for Maggie and myself over the years. I thought it would remind her of us while we were away and keep her warm with our love. However, Mother never used the quilt in south Alabama because the winters were usually mild and she said she was saving it for me, so I took it with me to Norfolk where I knew it could be put to good use. Maggie, Dave and I enjoyed Christmas together, and I finally got to know Dave and really liked him. They seemed happy and were planning to get married in the very near future. When I finally made it over to Saudi Arabia for the second time, I gave John the full report and we both felt happy for them.

John was at the airport to meet me and told me about our new compound on the way to our new home. He was happy to report that the AT&T Compound was a more settled compound surrounded with lots of green grass and the buildings were more tightly constructed than those we had in the past. Also, our apartment was on the second floor, and, therefore, the dust storms were no longer a serious problem. I liked the floor plan immediately with kitchen and living area on the left and two bedrooms on the right with two small bathrooms in between. It was smaller than we had before, but it was comfortable, adequately furnished, and quite compact. I could look out our kitchen window and see green grass and hedges which seemed to be occupied by a small family of peaceful looking cats. They looked well nourished, so I imagined our neighbors fed them very well. Our Seattle group, which had come over in early December, was already familiar with the place and seemed quite happy with their lives there. Our compound consisted of about eight two-story apartment buildings with well-kept grounds, two swimming pools and a couple of tennis courts. John and I would occasionally get out very early in the morning for a game of tennis before it became too hot.

Some meals at our little AT&T Restaurant were quite good and others didn't appeal to us at all. Since the cooks were usually Indonesian or Pakistani, the *"Curries," and "Chinese"* food was always very good and served with the appropriate condiments, egg rolls and rice. However, they tried to make the American food look like the pictures they saw on the menus, and, sometimes, we were in for quite a surprise! For instance, John and I once ordered *"Chicken Fried Steak"* from the menu, and found they had taken a chicken thigh which had been deboned and flattened out, rolled in egg and flour mixture and fried in deep oil. It looked like a chicken fried steak, but all they removed from the chicken thigh was the bone; everything else, the gristles, ligaments and membranes were left inside while they flattened it out. It was quite unappetizing, but always humorous, to see what they could come up with. We learned to check the menu first, and we hardly ever ordered *English* or *American*. As far as going out to eat was concerned, we sometimes drove over to the Al Manar Compound for *Mexican, Italian, English or American*. Occasionally, we drove downtown to a restaurant we discovered which served great *Arabic*. If we wanted to celebrate an important occasion, we might do as we did before, make reservations at the Intercontinental Hotel, where we could always depend on great *Chicken Curry or a Seafood Platter*. However, to resume our normal way of life, I cooked most of our meals at home.

John's *Inspection Team*, whose job it was to inspect the sites on the Arabian Desert, were all long-time Boeing employees from the Seattle office, however, because John was from *the South*, they gave themselves nicknames: Don was *Buford*, Maurice was *Virgil*, and Glenn, who grew up in Alabama, was *Joe Bob*. John's nickname was *Coach* because he coached the Peace Shield Project's basketball team. Glenn and his wife, Marianne, had three small girls which kept them very busy. Don and Kay were grandparents and corresponded with their family back in the States. Maurice and Rita also had family back in the States, and they loved to travel. In fact, they had spent several weeks living in India and were always ready to go somewhere. Also Maurice and Rita were very outgoing people and very brave in inviting everyone to their downstairs apartment for a big cookout during the year. We were all asked to bring a dish to add to their wonderful grilled steaks. They invited everyone, including some of the workers on the compound who they had come to know, who also brought some great food to add to the variety of dishes. It was amazing how well all of it went together and so did the mixture of people. We all had a great time!

John enjoyed coaching the basketball team and was over at the gym just about every evening after work. If one of the players didn't show up for a game, John was happy to take his place. One evening, I heard a commotion in our stairwell and opened the door to find two guys helping him up the stairs one step at a time. The *old man* had badly sprained his ankle in a very serious game of basketball that night and would have to keep it bandaged for the next couple of weeks. He went to work every day using his golf club, *"his 9 iron,"* as a walking cane, which he said fit so nicely into his right hand. Fortunately, we brought our ace bandages with us, which came in very handy that year because the coach used them quite often.

While overseas, I wrote Mother regularly and sent home trip reports, which she kept for me saying that someday she hoped that I would write a book. Now I have them chronologically filed inside sheet protectors and stored in a large hardbound notebook. They have proved indispensable in bringing the years back into focus. Hopefully, I will be able to finish this book someday, so our children and grandchildren will know what we did with our lives and what we accomplished with so much traveling and being gone so much of the time. We planned other trips from our home base in Riyadh as we took advantage of our time in the Middle East. We also had information from some of our military friends who had been to Kenya, which we had filed away for future use. They told us about going on safari and spending the night in a place they called *Treetops*. They highly recommended Kenya as a country we didn't want to miss if ever we wanted to experience the excitement of going on safari. While living this close, we decided to call our Riyadh travel agent to find out information about trips to Kenya. He sent us many brochures, and we finally selected one. Next on the agenda: Kenya, East Africa.

Our first East African Safari

In July 1989, John and I arrived in Nairobi, and were met at the airport by a Kenyan tour guide holding up a sign with John's name in big letters. He was very friendly and transported us and all our baggage to the Nairobi Hilton Hotel, where we would have dinner buffets and breakfasts for a two-night stay before our safari would begin. The first two days were spent at the hotel where we met with the travel agency next door to get our Itinerary and were introduced to our driver and tour guide. He started us off with a city tour of *Nairobi* and drove us to the *Nairobi Zoo* for pictures. He pointed out the best gift shops for buying souvenirs and drove us by the vegetable market, where we purchased two very large avocados just perfect for an afternoon snack. They were delicious and ready to be eaten right out of their shells with a little lemon juice, salt and pepper. Then we had a nice dinner at the hotel and got to bed early because our safari would begin early the following day.

On the 3rd day: After breakfast at the Nairobi Hilton, we boarded our van for our ride through *Kikuyu country* and stopped for *a tour of Karen Blixen's home where the movie, "Out of Africa," was filmed.* We drove on to *Nyeri* and arrived at the *Outspan Hotel* for lunch around noon, where we enjoyed a wonderful *Kenyan-style buffet while we watched Kikuyu dancers* and saw our first *witch doctor.* The food was very good at this hotel and was composed of many types of vegetables, leafy greens and a great assortment of desserts. I combined one of coconut and one of chocolate to make one outstanding dessert. It was delicious! Later in the afternoon, we were transported from the Outspan Hotel to *Treetops*, a small tree hotel built on stilts at a high elevation up in the trees. It was still rather early so we took pictures of animals at the salt lick, mostly elephants, and some beautiful birds up on our level in the treetops. We had a nice dinner that evening and spent the night in an end unit of the hotel, where we had great visibility. We got some really great pictures of the procession of animals passing by us under powerful floodlights. The lights didn't seem to bother them one bit. We could hear the lions and hyenas in the background as they came pretty close.

[NOTE: *While staying at Treetops on the night of February 5th, 1952, Princess Elizabeth became Queen of England due to the death during the night of her father, King George the Sixth.* She and her husband, Prince

Philip, the Duke of Edinburgh, were on their way to Australia and New Zealand by way of Kenya. They received the news of her father's death when they arrived back at their Kenyan Home, Sagana Lodge, the following day and hastily returned to the United Kingdom where they moved into Buckingham Palace.]

On the 4th day: Early the following morning as we were preparing to leave, we noticed many baboons coming to the back door of the Treetops kitchen, where scraps of food were thrown out to them each morning. When we exited Treetops to board our van back to the Outspan Hotel for breakfast, we noticed an armed guard standing by with a rifle. John got a picture of me coming out from behind one of the *blinds,* which were put there for the protection of guards and people who might need to get away quickly from one of the wild animals. After breakfast, we resumed our journey to *Nanyuki,* on the equator in the shadow of beautiful *Mt. Kenya,* arriving at the beautiful *Mt. Kenya Safari Club* in time for lunch. In the afternoon, we visited *the Animal Orphanage of Mt. Kenya Game Ranch,* made famous by actor William Holden in the 1970's. Then we walked back to the Safari Club and took our seats outside to watch Kikuyu dancers perform on the lawn in sight of lovely Mt. Kenya across the valley in front of us. We enjoyed a formal dinner that evening, and, when we returned to our suite, we found a fire going in our fireplace which was very nice and warm for our cold evening.

On the 5th day: After breakfast the following morning, John played nine holes of golf, and I took pictures from the vantage point of a small mound, which turned out to be an anthill. Red Ants!! They were crawling up my legs inside my pants! I was attacked all the way back to our room running as fast as I could and trying to squeeze them to death through my pant legs. John found a trail of clothes and dead ants all the way back to the bathroom, where I was trying to doctor my ant bites. After that ordeal, we walked over to the Animal Orphanage to say goodbye to the animals and take a few more pictures. We noticed some large funny looking birds walking around on the beautiful lawn in front of the Safari Club being fed by an attendant, who told us they are Maribou Storks and quite an attraction to visitors. Then it was time to check out of the Safari Club and head toward *Aberdare* and the very high *Thompson's Falls.* We stopped at *a Kikuyu village* to make pictures of the falls and purchased a hand-woven basket and three small ceramics. As we surfaced over a hilltop, we noticed in the distance *Lake Nukuru* with a pink coloration surrounding the lake and asked our driver what it was. He answered, *"Flamingo!"* We arrived at our hotel for lunch and checked into our small hut equipped with a draped mosquito net over the bed. Then we were driven through the bird sanctuary down to the lake teeming with hundreds of flamingo, pelicans and other rare birds. As we were passing through the underbrush, John just happened to have his camera ready and captured on film a fantastic, and perfectly focused, picture of a mother impala emerging from a thicket followed by her newly born baby fawn.

On the 6th day, we drove along the floor of the *Great Rift Valley* to the *Masai Mara Game Reserve* where we had dinner and spent the night in an obscure hut overlooking the waterhole, which was all lit up at night for the viewing of animals from the row of huts built on the hillside. We enjoyed an afternoon camera safari of wildlife in the park, famous for its black-mane lions. I have a mental picture of a group of giraffes walking through the tall grass, which I wasn't fast enough to capture on film. We did get a picture of a leopard hiding behind foliage up in a tree above its *kill*, probably an impala, dangling over a branch below him.

On the 7th and 8th days, we were up before dawn to board our van for very early morning safaris into the Masai Mara Game Reserve. It was cold at night on the African plain, so I learned to leave my pajamas on under my clothing. We took pictures of a *grey rhino* grazing a short distance away, considered a very rare species, and we saw dozens of *hippopotami* in the *Mara River.* On our way back to the *Serena Lodge* for breakfast, we just happened upon *a family of lions* lounging in the grass after what looked like a successful night of hunting their prey. We managed to get some really great pictures of the male lion with his beautiful black mane and his large family before having to return to the lodge. After lunch, it was back on the trail for an all-day safari into the wild with a wonderful dinner each evening at the *Serena Safari Lodge.* At the entrance to the lodge, there was a well-contained fire burning to keep the people warm as they entered or just stood around talking. They also had great entertainment, and we enjoyed watching the very tall Masai tribesmen demonstrate their incredibly high jumps in their dances. Our guide told us that some of the Masai men marry women of the Kikuyu tribe who are much shorter, and they build their houses out of mud and animal dung. The houses, built as high up as a Kikuyu bride can reach, have very low ceilings and doorways, so the Masai men have to stoop over to get inside their hut.

On the 9th day, we returned to the Nairobi Hilton Hotel for lunch and an afternoon of leisure as we walked around the shops looking for souvenirs. I had my eye on a nicely framed batik of two giraffes in a jungle setting. We enjoyed dinner at the hotel, and after a leisure breakfast the following day, we were driven to *Kenya's Cultural Center*, where the villagers performed their traditional dances in a setting of authentic villages, or *bomas*, representing sixteen ethnic groups depicting the traditions and daily life of the friendly and hospitable Kenyan people. We had dinner at the hotel and retired early.

On the 10th day, we began our second safari with a drive across the *Athi Plains, home of the Masai*, with lunch and afternoon game viewing in the park within sight of the beautiful *Mt. Kilimanjaro*. We took a picture of a mother hyena feeding her baby on the side of the road with the beautiful snow-capped mountain in the background. Our driver had to stop to help pull a car out of the mud so we could get through to *Amboseli* where we enjoyed a great dinner and spent the night at the very nice *Amboseli Lodge*.

On the 11th day, after an early morning game drive and breakfast at Amboseli, we proceeded to *Tsavo across the Chuyulu Hills and Lava Flow* where we had lunch in the largest park in East Africa. We continued our afternoon game drive on the way to Tsavo, where we had dinner and spent the night at the *Serena Lodge*. The next morning, we noticed baboon guards stationed at various locations as baboon families were coming up the trail. I was sitting outside on our porch when I noticed a small water hole which many of the animals were jumping with perfect reflections in the water. I was holding our broken camera which John had rigged with a safety pin to push down the shutter, so I calculated the timing of the next animal to jump the water hole. It worked! I got pictures of a baboon and also one of a young impala, both perfectly focused with their reflections in the water. After dinner, we watched a leopard, under floodlights, climb a tree to reach the lure of game placed there to attract them, and we got some great pictures that evening. Fortunately, we had two cameras working for us that night with fast film.

On the 12th day, we were transported to the airport at *Tsavo* to catch our flight to *Mombasa* where we stayed three nights at the *Serena Beach Hotel* on the beautiful Indian Ocean. They served wonderful buffet-style food in the restaurant and provided many activities plus beautiful gardens and a large swimming pool. The Arabic motif of this beautifully designed hotel was very plush and the lovely bright rose bougainvillea grew year round and overhung the sides of the beautiful *Mombasa Lodge & Restaurant*. They provided many optional tours around the area, and we selected a tour of the *Old Town of Mombasa* and the original settlement at *Fort Jesus*. But first we wanted to rest up from our safaris and just enjoy the peaceful atmosphere of the beautiful beach.

On the 13th day, we enjoyed the first day so much, we chose another day of leisure and began our day with a late breakfast in the hotel dining room, where we were fascinated by monkeys boldly entering the restaurant and hopping up on the tables to steal packets of sugar. We had to get pictures! Then we met the parrot in the lobby of the Lodge and took time to talk a while before walking down to the grassy area to sit under the trees to watch the catamarans passing by in the beautiful green Indian Ocean. We were also fascinated by the peddlers passing by, some with loads of merchandise on their heads, to set up shop at various locations on the beach to attract beachcombers to browse through their wares and make purchases. We spent the rest of the day just walking around the grounds taking pictures and enjoyed our casual buffet lunch and dinner.

On the 14th day, after our breakfast buffet, we were picked up for our tour of the *Old Town of Mombasa and Ft. Jesus*. We walked around the downtown area and found many places for shopping; however, we heard most of the history on the bus. We followed our guide around the ruins of Ft. Jesus and heard the history of the first settlement. Then we visited the museum to see some of the excavations. We were happy to get back to the Mombasa Lodge to enjoy more beach time before having to pack for our flight home the following day. We enjoyed our last dinner buffet and had time to speak with the parrot before walking around the grounds again at sunset.

On the 15th day, after our breakfast buffet, we told the parrot in the lobby goodbye and had a morning of leisure as we prepared for our flight back to *Nairobi* with our connecting flight to *Jeddah*. It was sad to leave the

Mombasa Lodge, but we had to get back to work in Riyadh. One of our old Litton friends, Dave, was there to meet us at the Jeddah airport that afternoon and furnished us with his company's car to drive to the Holiday Inn where we checked in for two nights.

On the 16th day, after breakfast, John drove me around the city of *Jeddah* and up the escarpment to *Taif* to show me the beautiful places he had visited on a previous trip. Then he drove us back to the city to find the international hotel and restaurant he remembered, which served a great Arabic seafood dinner starting with our favorite dip, *hommous* and pita bread. John ordered a seafood platter, and I ordered a fish dinner. It was a type of fish I had never eaten before from the local waters of the Red Sea, but it was very good, served with Arabic rice and *tabouli*, with crème caramel for dessert.

The 17th day: John drove me around a different part of Jeddah and we walked through a downtown souk where our friend, Dave, met us for lunch. We ordered *falafel*, served inside pita bread with sauce, condiments and a soft drink. Then he drove us to the Jeddah airport for our evening flight back to Riyadh. Our vacation in Kenya and the two days in Jeddah were absolutely fantastic. We had seen so many wonderful sights, but it was time once more to come back down to earth and get back to our normal work days.

Back at the AT&T Compound, Don made a hilarious video to send home to their kids which started off with him sitting at their kitchen table having his morning coffee, as he told about life in the compound. He started off very casually putting cream and sugar in his coffee and talking very seriously about one thing and then another, as he added a few more spoonfuls of sugar; then he would talk some more and add a few more spoonfuls of sugar. He did this for about five minutes and finally tasted it with a shrug to imply that it was awful. He quickly added another five spoons of sugar, tasted it again, and said, *"Ah, that's more like it!"* After taking us on a tour of their whole apartment, which was just like ours, Don made pictures of the whole AT&T Compound, showing the swimming pools and tennis courts and telling their story as he leisurely walked around, speaking to people as he went. He just happened to drop in on Rita, who had just made a beautiful *Pineapple Upside Down Cake*.

She invited him in, and, of course, Don had two pieces. Rita politely told him that she could make another one... and so it went.

Then Don walked back to their apartment where he found Kay sitting outside on their upper back porch balcony, casually knitting and talking to a neighbor down on the street below. Next on the video, Don included a trip he and Maurice made from Riyadh out to one of the desert sites driving us along the road they took and seeing the sights and scenery of towns, people, camels and mountains along the way. They finally met up with John and Glenn, who were just arriving as he was showing us the desert scenery from the escarpment of the site. Then Don gave us a tour of the living facilities at the camp where they sometimes had to stay overnight when they were doing their on-site work. Don also included a day trip out to watch the camel races on the outskirts of Riyadh.

Since I had never really understood John's job with Litton on his first trip to Saudi Arabia, I feel I must elaborate about the project now because it was quite an undertaking. In fact, as I look back and realize what the Litton- Holzmann Joint Venture accomplished, it was monumental! John tells me that his first trip in August 1982 was an *Orientation Trip* to see, and become familiar with, the work which was just getting started. He was only gone about two weeks that first time, but he made several other trips during the year to get accustomed to the Project and its environment and to monitor its early progress. While working in Frankfurt, he and his team of engineers monitored the Holzmann design of the system and signed off on several thousand of their project working drawings. Specifications for construction of the facilities were very tight, and they all had to be verified and eventually accepted by Litton, as meeting the requirements of the Contract with the Saudi Arabian Government. The job of the Litton Inspection Team was to verify all the work of the Holzmann Construction crews, including physical structures, communications and all electrical systems.

During the three-year project, the Litton-Holzmann Joint Venture built several Air Defense Operation Centers (ADOC), a number of radar sites, and the necessary long-range telecommunications systems which would efficiently tie everything together. All the facilities had to be built to strenuous specifications to accommodate the radars and high technology equipment that were to be installed. In addition to building the compounds where the workers would live while the work was being done at the radar sites, Holzmann was responsible for building the connecting roads and providing the water and power systems to all the sites. John said the guys building the roads were often harassed by nomads living near the sites, and some shots fired at them were reported from some of the mountainous areas. The sites were selected according to location and had to be spaced properly for the telecommunication system to work. All of this had to be planned out beforehand, and monitored regularly, so the parts would work together and the overall system would work effectively. Eventually, it did!

In his second job in Saudi Arabia, John worked with Boeing for the Royal Saudi Arabian Air Force (RSAAF) to build Operation Centers at the several air bases around the Kingdom. Boeing's work was similar to what Litton had done a few years earlier and it would complement the prior work done by Litton Data Command Systems for the Saudi Air Defense Forces. John had been Construction Manager on both critical projects. The Boeing Project Peace Shield established a Command, Control and Communications (C3) System for the Saudi Arabian Air Force, which involved the building of numerous long-range telecommunication centers, several Command Centers and a number of radar sites, all with uninterrupted power systems (UPS). John and his construction verification team drove, or flew, to all the sites regularly to inspect and verify that all phases of construction were built according to the approved working drawings. Theoretically, everything in the two Systems would mesh together and complement each other. Eventually, they did, and were quite valuable during Desert Shield and Desert Storm. We were about to realize the importance of having access to military facilities in Saudi Arabia from which Allied Forces of different countries could work together against a dictator, Sadam Hussein, who was about to invade Kuwait.

On the 20th of July, 1990, leaving @ 6:30 am from the compound gate, transportation was provided for all the families of the Peace Shield Program for an *Orientation Trip* out to the Al-Kharj Sector Control Center and Sector Operations Center for a slide show and tours of both sites. Around 10:00 am, we had a tour of the Command Maintenance Center, and around 11:00 am, we left for the Long Range Radar Site where we had a tour of the Command Security Building. The temperature was 120 degrees F. at mid-day, but it was *dry heat* and not too unbearable. Deep in the underground bunkers, it was rather cool but upstairs out in the Saudi sun, it was incredibly hot. This was our first opportunity to see work similar to the work Litton had done in the early years of their project, and now, with the additional work of the Boeing Peace Shield project, it was fascinating to see how the two projects would work together if ever needed to defend Saudi Arabia from would-be attackers. The Saudi Arabian Air Force would be trained to work the system and keep it in good operating condition over the years ahead, as the Air Defense forces had done after the Litton project was completed. Both the American and German construction companies were pleased in their combined efforts to provide an Air Defense System for the Kingdom of Saudi Arabia, which would strengthen the Kingdom with the ability to defend the peace and security of Saudi Arabia and their allies in the Middle East. If ever needed, the Air Defense System could be used to defend the peace and security of the whole world.

During his time in Saudi Arabia, John was a member of the Society of American Military Engineers (SAME), and we attended some of their very nice dinner parties while we were there and met engineers and dignitaries from all over the world. It was a privilege to enjoy the company of such interesting people as we shared dinner and got to know them on a more personal level. One of the most fascinating locations was the dining room on top of the *Riyadh Water Tower*, which afforded us a panoramic view of beautiful downtown Riyadh at night; truly a spectacular scene! Also while we were there in 1989, we were invited to attend the opening of the *International Stadium* in Riyadh, built under the supervision of Holzmann, the German construction company. It was another monumental task; a series of masts connected together with cables to give the appearance of Arabian tents. The stadium was gigantic with all the amenities of our greatest stadiums in the US; it was functional, desert-inspired and breathtaking!

In August, when Boeing learned of the invasion of Kuwait, the small country between Iraq and Saudi Arabia, most of the Boeing sites were still under construction, but several of them were almost finished. Boeing immediately sent over a brand new Boeing 747, fully equipped with test pilots, cabin crew, doctors and nurses, to evacuate all Boeing dependents. Our group was on that plane, but, before we could take off, those in charge had to get a correct head count of the passengers listed. So we sat there waiting on the ground for what seemed like hours. The small children had to be strapped in their seats and forbidden to move while they could get an accurate head count. Finally, we were in the air! When we landed in Shannon to re-fuel for the long flight over Greenland and Canada into Seattle, we heard a voice coming over the intercom: *"Welcome to Shannon! This is the first time we've ever seen a plane land here when all the passengers had pacifiers in their mouths."* The small children on the top deck of the airplane watching Disney movies, must have run to the windows to look out when we came in for a landing. Soon we were in the air again!

Rita and I were sitting together and she asked me some interesting questions regarding Bible prophecy. Years later, she reminded me of what we talked about that day and how she recognized that some of the predictions were already coming true. When we arrived in Seattle around 2:00 am, she and I waited for the mothers and children to get off the plane first and for the TV cameras to leave. Finally, we walked into our motel together and went to our separate rooms to get some rest. I turned on the TV and there we were, Rita and I, getting off the plane with baggage straps across our shoulders. All the large baggage was delivered to our rooms the rest of the night. In spite of no sleep, we were at breakfast early to receive our plane tickets home and make our phone calls to those who would be at the airport to meet us. I was so happy to see Mother and Ginger when I got off the plane, and I was very glad to get back to Mother's house where I could finally get some rest and a good night's sleep.

The following week, John insisted that I meet him in Ireland and started planning a golfing tour in September, since our original plan had been somewhat curtailed. As he requested, I bought him a new golf bag, filled it with his clubs and packed the golf bag and clubs inside his carrying case. I used my Delta mileage for my round-trip ticket to Dublin and planned to rent our car at the Dublin Airport, check into our hotel and meet John's plane when he arrived a few hours later. Needless to say, everyone was concerned that I would forget to keep the car on the left side of the road and have a wreck before John arrived to take over the driving. I solved that problem when I forgot to bring my driver's license and left it sitting on Mother's dresser. I had to ride the airport shuttle to my hotel and then back again to meet John's plane and leave the golf bag and my large suitcase at the airport. Then John was able to rent our car at the airport and load it as he usually did to get everything packed just right. Both he and Mother were so relieved!

We had a great tour of places we had never visited before up the northern coast of Ireland, and John played golf all along the way and I walked along with him some of the way just to get some exercise. We made reservations through the *Irish Tourist Board* and had a great assortment of hotels and guest houses. We enjoyed our Irish breakfasts every morning and bought a sack of apples to have on our drive through the countryside. Sometimes we stopped for fresh milk to go with our *Slim Fast* powdered breakfast drink, and we always enjoyed a nice dinner at the end of the day wherever we happened to be. We drove through Galway and spent the night in a hotel overlooking Galway Bay before driving to Connemara, where John played nine holes in very cold wind off the Atlantic. I enjoyed the warmth of the clubhouse with hot ham & bean soup. We discovered *The Moorings at Rosses Point, County Sligo,* which served a wonderful *Chicken Curry* and we always selected our table by the warm fireplace. We drove up the coast to *Bundoran* to *the Great Southern Hotel* and then on up to *Ballyshannon,* where we stayed several days at *Dorian's Imperial Hotel.* On our drive through the bogs along the shore line and around a lake near the northern border, we accidently drove through a bombed out check point of the IRA, which had been closed for years. Finally, we got back on the right road to Dublin, where we returned our rental car in time for one last dinner in the Dublin airport restaurant before connecting with our separate flights back to Riyadh and Mobile.

John remained in Saudi Arabia until the end of his Contract with Boeing and returned to Mobile in late December. The Allied Forces were in the process of building up for three months inside Saudi Arabia before they counter attacked in January 1991 under the Command of GEN Norman Schwarzkopf. John recalled the construction of several bases along the Saudi Arabian-Iraqi border from his Litton and Boeing jobs, and he felt it was likely that some may have been useful by the Allied Force in their counter attack into Iraq. When Desert Storm began, it found us sitting in our new high-rise apartment building in Crystal City, Arlington, VA watching the war on TV and having pizza and Chianti, *Compliments of Crystal Towers.*

CHAPTER TWENTY-EIGHT

A Time for All Seasons
1991-1993

As we watched the Gulf War taking place in January, 1991, a quarter of the world away, I wondered about our stance in the world. Could this be the first battle in the Middle East which leads to the last battle the Bible refers to as Armageddon? Could this be the beginning of the end of the world as we know it? It was over so quickly and the Allies won, but Saddam Hussein was still in power. As in all wars, it had been a war of good against evil and God was on our side. We won! However, the enemy still existed. I remembered a few months back when Kuwait was invaded by the Iraqi army and rumors were going around that we were to be evacuated: John received a phone call around 4:00 am, and I could tell by the nature of the call that the evacuation was on. Before the 15 minute call was over, I was dressed, packed and ready to go. Of course, we didn't leave until later in the day and I had time to repack and bring everything I could carry home with me. But I was ready!

Rita and I sat together on the beautiful brand new Boeing 747, redirected by Boeing to Saudi Arabia, to bring home all the women and children. She, too, was wondering about Bible Prophecy, which led us into a discussion about what was happening in the world. I remember quoting some of what I had learned in my Bible studies. Rita was interested and remembered years later our discussion that day about *the end times*. Even though this first battle with Iraq was a success, it took many years for Kuwait to overcome what the enemy had done to their Country. The oil wells were left burning, and it took many years for all of them to be capped and put back into operation. Also, much of the wildlife, sea life and birds had been destroyed or covered with oil, and they also had to be cleaned up and saved as much as possible. It took decades to clean up the terrible mess the Iraqis left behind, and the people of Kuwait were grateful for our help to run them out.

Now John and I were trying to get back into a more normal way of life by his finishing Law School and getting resettled in the Washington area. Our plan was to create an atmosphere of home life for our family and see more of Maggie and Dave while we were living that close to them. Dave had given her an engagement ring, and we needed to plan their June wedding. However, neither of them wanted a large church wedding and rejected the very thought of one, so it took some time to come up with a good plan. Since we had a condo on the beach at Gulf Shores and we wanted Mother and our closest relatives to attend the small wedding ceremony, I called the Gulf Shores Methodist Church and spoke with the Minister. He was very nice and agreed to hold the wedding ceremony in the church and requested that the two young people speak with him first as soon as they arrived at the Gulf. We agreed to purchase the flowers for the church altar. Dave and Maggie set the date for the June wedding and all was approved. The Reception would be held the following day at Mother's house overlooking beautiful Mobile Bay, where John and I were married in 1957. We ordered a beautiful *three-tier wedding cake and I prepared my Tuna Luau and punch* for our small gathering of family members. The happy couple would spend their honeymoon in our condo on the beach at Gulf Shores.

On March 2, 1991, John and I became the proud grandparents of a precious baby girl, Catherine Suzanne, born in Jackson, MS to our son, Jim and his wife, Kathleen. Of course, we had been ready to make the drive down to Jackson at any time, but the excitement of the new birth really set us into motion. Kathy's parents were already there, so that gave us a little more time to make the journey. I decided to have my hair frosted at a new salon in Arlington, which turned out to be a big mistake. It turned my hair different shades of blonde, with tinges of red and purple. In trying to make it look normal again, I lost the real color of my hair and started coloring it myself. When we finally arrived in Jackson, it didn't matter one bit what colors it turned out to be. Little Katie was such a joy just to hold in my arms and talk to, and I was so thankful that she, her mother and her dad had come through the whole procedure with flying colors. Kathy and Jim were ecstatic because they had waited so long for a baby, and here she was as beautiful as a baby girl can be. She had a little colic at first, and they had found that putting her car bed on the washing machine while it was going soothed her with its gyrations and made her stop crying and soon put her back to sleep.

Around the middle of May, we were surprised to get a long distance phone call from Florida calling us *collect.* It was Greg! He was on his way to Mexico City to marry Lorena. Shocked by another of his impulsive decisions, John and I responded adamantly, *"Greg, you can't do this! Turn around and go back to Baton Rouge! You're going to mess up your SSI and everything! Who's going to pay your rent... and the rest of your bills? You can't afford to get married now! You need to finish school first! And get a job! This is crazy!!!"* All of this to no avail, Greg was on his way and nothing could stop him. Before I left Mobile, I had driven over to Baton Rouge to take him to a very important appointment with his Rehab Counselor for him to get on with his program. We were very late because Greg was wrapping a gift for Lorena which he wanted to get in the mail that very morning, and he insisted on going by the Post Office first. He just could not be hurried up to make it to the appointment on time, and being so late, it was cancelled. Both his Rehab Counselor and I were very angry with him in refusing to put his appointment first, which had been set for over a month, and I did not have a good feeling about this, so I drove him back to his apartment and left Baton Rouge with him wondering why I wouldn't take him out to lunch that day.

We first met Lorena before John left the country in December 1989. She was visiting her sister and two nieces, who lived downstairs on the first floor of Greg's apartment building. When they heard of Greg's love for Mexican food, they invited him downstairs for a Mexican Dinner. The girls were fascinated with Greg's tree crabs and so was Lorena when she first saw them. Greg had named his menagerie of crabs after the prophets: *Ezekiel, Isaiah, Daniel, Job, Jacob, Micah,* etc., and, for some strange reason, took the largest one, *Jacob,* to church one day to show some people who had asked about them. The pastor noticed Greg holding the crab and came over to see what all the fascination was about when Greg automatically handed the crab to him. Someone took a picture of him holding the crab as the wiggly creature was partially coming out of its shell waving its claws in the air. I wonder what ever happened to that picture?!

Greg and Lorena attended church regularly at the Family Worship Center, and Greg taught Lorena some of the English language by reading the Bible together. She and her two closest sisters had been partially raised in a convent when their mother left them. Their dad arranged for them to live at the convent because he had no way to take care of them and they needed supervision. Lorena rejected what they taught at the convent but was open to Christianity as taught by the pastor of the church in Baton Rouge. When Lorena's visa was about to expire, she had to return to Mexico. Greg was terribly upset and ran up his phone bill calling her every day. He couldn't think of anything but Lorena and dropped out of his Rehab program. He just had to go to Mexico to get her back.

Greg and Lorena were also married in June 1991 at Lorena's Christian Church in Mexico City, and her step mother made her a beautiful wedding gown. They rode the bus to Cancun for their honeymoon and planned to take advantage of all the *freebies* at the hotels. We started getting phone calls from Greg every few days to send money orders to him in Cancun, and, when they finally returned to Mexico City, her very large family took turns putting them up for a few days at various places. Greg was able to get to know just about all of Lorena's relatives before he had to come home to get his finances in order to save his apartment. Some of his friends were taking care of his tree crabs, and some had even sent contributions in cash for him to make the trip to Mexico. I was trying to juggle his bills and save his apartment and his SSI. Finally, he had to fly home to get all these things in order and make plans for Lorena to come back into our country as his wife and a US citizen. Of course, we had to buy him plane tickets back and forth a couple of times for short visits while this procedure was taking place. About a year later, he flew down to Mexico City for the last time to bring her back to Baton Rouge on the Greyhound bus. They spent a couple of days in Juarez with a Christian family, arranged by Lorena's church, until they could board a bus to cross the border legally.

Around the same time Greg and Lorena were married in Mexico City, Maggie and Dave were married in Norfolk by a Justice of the Peace. Then they made the trip down to Alabama where they were married a second time by the pastor of the Gulf Shores Methodist Church. Ironically, both couples were married twice within a couple of weeks in two distant places without the other couple knowing anything about it. Of course, John and I wished all of them much happiness and hoped for a good future. All we could do at that late date was send out *Announcements* to all our family and a few good friends after their ceremonies had already taken place. It must have seemed strange to all of them, and they probably wondered *why didn't they just have a double wedding? But,* in our family, that's just the way it worked out!

Greg was working at *Fast Track*, the fast food hamburger take-out just a block away from their apartment, and Lorena had found a job working for a reputable widow in their area of Baton Rouge. Very soon, she would take a computer course and qualify as a bi-lingual Insurance Agent working for a large Insurance Company in Baton Rouge. Greg and Lorena were from different cultures and spoke different languages, so they had a lot of adjustments to make, however, they each had a great sense of humor and strong Christian beliefs to bring them through every situation. When they married, they were both in their thirties and quite set in their ways, so they had to depend on their faith and trust in God to help them solve their frequent misunderstandings. Greg learned some Spanish while Lorena was learning English, and when our only grandson, Joshua, came along a few years later, he seemed to enter the world already *bilingual*. They attended the Family Worship Center regularly while sometimes attending the Spanish Church in their area of Baton Rouge. They loved the Spanish music, and Lorena helped Greg understand the sermons if he had a question. They both found much joy in their Christianity, which was the foundation of their life.

Due to a rumor of the collapse of Pan American Airlines, which John heard going around law school, he scheduled our second trip to Kenya during summer vacation. Someone told him that we should take our mileage while we could, or we might lose it. So we made our reservations! This time, we planned to venture down into Tanzania and spend a few days in Frankfurt and Ireland on the return trip.

A Safari to Kenya & Tanzania

Thursday, July 25 1991: John and I landed in Kenya at the Jomo Kenyatta Airport and were welcomed by a very exuberant driver who drove us to the Nairobi Hilton Hotel. Our Itinerary into two East African countries, Kenya and Tanzania, was scheduled by Safari Tours as follows:

Friday, July 26: After breakfast and a morning of leisure, we were picked up for our afternoon tour of the *Nairobi National Park and Animal Orphanage* and then we were transferred to the railway station for the *overnight train to Mombasa*. This was quite an unusual experience having the late dinner on the train and then trying to sleep in our individual berths overland to *Mombasa* arriving early the following morning.

<u>Saturday, July 27</u>: With hardly any sleep, we found ourselves up at dawn looking out the windows of the small train watching the villages come to life with people walking to work and going about their morning business. We arrived at the Mombasa train station around 7:30 am, and were met by a driver who transferred us to the *Mombasa Serena Beach Hotel* where we had stayed before. This time, however, we were assigned to a cottage within sight and sound of a mosque, and it seemed quite different from our first time in 1989 when we stayed in the hotel. Of course, we still had the same easy access to the large restaurant, pool and activity center we remembered. After a leisure breakfast, we enjoyed our first day walking around the grounds and sitting out on the beach, watching the small boats go by as before.

<u>Sunday, July 28</u>: After breakfast, we enjoyed a bus drive through the countryside along the northern coast from Mombasa to *Malindi*, and we were able to view the lifestyle of the people who lived along the way. In the small village of Malindi, we boarded a glass bottom boat to view the coral reefs and the beautiful tropical fish. Some people having on bathing suits disrobed their outer clothing and dived into the water with their snorkels to swim among the fish. Around lunch time, we were dropped off at a beach hotel where they had a lunch buffet all spread out in the open. We were reminded not to order a drink with ice because of the possibility of getting sick from the water. It was okay to order a coke or beer in a bottle, but *no ice*!

<u>Monday, July 29</u>: We enjoyed another leisure morning of breakfast and beach time, followed by a buffet lunch in the restaurant. Then we were transported to the *Giriama Village* to watch the *traditional dances of Mombasa* and then visited the *Mombasa Craft Center*. We also stopped in *Gedi* for a tour of the ancient ruins on the way back to our hotel for dinner and overnight.

<u>Tuesday, July 30</u>: After a leisure breakfast and more beach time, we were picked up after lunch and taken to *Nyali* where we boarded an authentic *Arab dhow* for a brief *sight-seeing cruise down to Fort Jesus* and around the backside of *Mombasa Island* to moor in the calm waters *for a romantic starlit lobster dinner prepared on the dhow*, with many enjoyable condiments, drinks, and dancing. We enjoyed the *Mombasa music*, and returned to the jetty at 10:30 pm, where we were transferred back to our hotel.

<u>Wednesday, July 31</u>: We enjoyed our leisure breakfast and were again amused by the monkeys coming into the restaurant to steal packets of sugar. We took many pictures that day and enjoyed eating in the restaurant, but we spent most of our time on the beach watching the catamarans go by in the beautiful green Indian Ocean and the vendors selling their wares on the beach. We added some fantastic pictures of beach traffic to our collection.

While on the beach, we met a very nice Italian couple on vacation and learned to converse a little between our two languages.

<u>Thursday, August 1</u>: After breakfast, we were transported into the city for a walking tour of the downtown souks and bazaar, followed by a bus tour around the Island to watch the *Wakamba Wood Carvers* carving beautiful statues and wall hangings. We purchased two small statues: one of a rhino and one of an elephant with ivory tusks. We also purchased a lovely, and quite large, wall hanging of a *Masai Mama and Children*. Then we returned to the Mombasa Lodge for our last afternoon on the beach and noticed the Italian couple there also. When the gentleman made a purchase from one of the peddlers on the beach, John asked him on his way past us, *"Good buy?"* He answered, *"Goodbye!"* That was so cute and such a great way to say goodbye to our friends at Mombasa. We enjoyed our last dinner buffet and got a good night's sleep.

<u>Friday August 2</u>: We spent the day at leisure preparing for the next leg of our journey into the Serengeti. After dinner, we were transferred to the Mombasa Airport for our 10:15 pm flight to Nairobi. From there we were met at the airport and transferred back to the Nairobi Hilton Hotel.

<u>Saturday, August 3</u>: After breakfast, we met our driver and boarded our van for our *Tour of the Serengeti*. We departed at 9:00 am and headed for the *Amboseli Game Reserve*. We crossed the *Athi Plains*, passed the beautiful snow-covered peak of *Kilimanjaro,* and arrived at the *Amboseli Lodge* around noon. After lunch, we enjoyed a game drive through the park and returned to the lodge for dinner and overnight.

<u>Sunday, August 4</u>: We departed Amboseli around 7:30 am and soon arrived at the border where John and our driver left me in the van while they passed through Customs to have our Visa stamped. While waiting for them to return, I was approached by a Masai woman with very long earlobes,

who handed me a bracelet and said *"Take, bracelet for free!"* Then she posed and said, *"Take picture!"* I grabbed my camera and took her picture. Then she said, *"Bracelet for free. Picture not for free!"* She waited until John returned and paid her. The picture turned out beautifully! The roads were dry and very bumpy. We arrived at the *Arusha Hotel* for lunch and then proceeded on to the *Lake Manyara Hotel* for dinner and overnight.

Monday & Tuesday, August 5 & 6: After breakfast, we visited the *Lake Manyara National Park,* where we had lunch and proceeded on to the *Serengeti National Park* for a spectacular game drive. Our transportation was good, but the roads were very bumpy, and I found a strap hanging down from above which I held onto to lessen the impact of the bumps. It was also very dusty driving across the African plain and our driver pointed out an *ostrich school* moving slowly across the plain and explained that they travel together teaching the young as they go. We were covered with dust by the time we arrived at the *Seronera Wildlife Lodge* and badly in need of a bath and a change of clothes. There was no hot water. Of course, there was nothing we could do but bathe in the cold water provided by the hotel, and it was so good to feel clean again and refreshed in time for dinner. This beautifully constructed hotel was quite adequate and provided a restful and quiet night's sleep. We learned how the water system worked: we would have hot water in the evening and in the morning, but not in the middle of the day.

We had entered wildlife territory with lions and leopards among the many, many zebra, wildebeest, giraffe, topi, gazelle and Thompson's gazelle, which we would see on safari the next two days. We spent both days exploring the *Seregenti National Park* and enjoyed our morning and afternoon game drives. The food was very good at the Seronera Wildlife Lodge and we ordered dinner from the menu. While walking around outside the hotel, John saw a worker holding up a pole with a *large Rock Python* being carried away. It was very interesting to learn that this Rock Python is Africa's largest snake and lives mainly in the Seronera Valley. It has been known to live high in a tree for several months at a time as it digests its very large prey.

Wednesday, August 7: After breakfast at the Seronera Wildlife Lodge, we proceeded on to the *Ngorongoro Crater Lodge* where we had lunch and were assigned a cottage for the night. That afternoon, we visited the *Olduvai Gorge,* where the oldest skeleton of man was discovered by Dr.

Louis S. B. Leakey and his wife, Mary in 1959. They had been digging there for about a month when his remains were found. It was rather dusty down in the gorge, so we took baths and changed clothes before walking over to the very nice restaurant on the rim of the crater. We found the restaurant very crowded and were put on a waiting list. John and I walked outside to take pictures of the beautiful view, which looked down over the gorge into the crater. When we went back inside the restaurant, we were approached by a young African waiter with a big beaming smile and very white teeth who ushered us to our table. As he pulled out my chair, he thrust a menu into my hand and said, *"Sit here Mama! Take this menu!"* That was probably all the English he knew, but it was so cute the way it happened and a moment I'll never forget. As I recall, everyone got pretty much the same order from the menu, and it was probably either zebra or topi, but it was very good and quite enjoyable. When we left the restaurant to walk back to our room, we found we were in the midst of a herd of water buffalo calmly grazing all around us as we tried to calmly walk back to our cottage and close the door. They certainly were not there in daylight on our way to the restaurant, but now it was very dark and only the flashlights, which we were given at the restaurant to find our way back, lit them up to make them visible.

Thursday, August 8: The buffalo were gone the next morning when we walked over to the lodge for breakfast. Then we were picked up by a driver in a Land Rover to take us down into the very deep crater for game viewing. It was a little terrifying going down the steep cliff as we gradually descended all the way down the canyon wall to the very bottom of the crater. We were amazed to learn that down inside the crater, the whole area took on the same ratio of animals and predators as the upper portion of the Serengeti with the same vegetation, plains of grass and even a small river with water buffalo. Our safari found a family of lions and animals as noted above on the other game drives. We ascended back up the steep incline for lunch at the Ngorogoro Crater Lodge. Following lunch, John bought me a beautiful malachite necklace as a souvenir of this very exciting and adventurous excursion. Then it was time to leave the lovely Seronera Valley and drive back over the bumpy, dusty road to *Arusha*. Again, we were badly in need of baths and a change of clothes before dinner at the *Mount Meru Hotel* and in need of a good night's sleep.

<u>Friday, August 9</u>: After breakfast the following morning, we departed early for Nairobi arriving in time for lunch. We were sad our safaris were over and we would have to leave this beautiful country again, but we had a schedule to keep. During our afternoon in Nairobi, we walked around looking for souvenirs to bring home with us from our last trip to Kenya. I bought a beautiful batik of two giraffes among the trees, a couple of t-shirts plus some placemats of the animals. We enjoyed dinner that evening in the Nairobi Hilton restaurant and retired early to rest up from our safaris.

<u>Saturday, August 10</u>: We enjoyed a leisure breakfast in the hotel and walked around the gift shops one last time to buy a few gifts to take home with us and a few post cards. That afternoon we packed up all our souvenirs and walked over to the vegetable souk to buy two more ripe avocadoes for an afternoon snack. We enjoyed our last dinner at the Nairobi Hilton and checked out in time for our pick up to the airport. Our Pan Am flight was scheduled to leave at 8:00 pm for our flight to Frankfurt. We arrived around midnight and took a taxi to the Intercontinental Hotel overlooking the beautiful Main River. John made some beautiful night pictures of the river from our balcony.

After breakfast the following morning, we checked out of our hotel and rented a car for a drive to Walldorf to find a *Zimmer Frei* we remembered. It was still open to tourists, so we checked in for two days. From there, we could walk through the forest and by the gardens of the city dwellers. We visited the ice cream parlor for a cone of "Eis" and walked through the streets of the small town as we had done years before. We drove to some of the restaurants we remembered and ordered some of our favorite German foods, and, once again, enjoyed the European salads. John called George and Greta to let them know we were in Walldorf, and they met us for lunch at a restaurant, which just happened to be serving their famous *in season white asparagus*. It was served with a wonderful roast beef dinner and was very delicious. The following day, we drove out to Mobel Walter to look at furniture and enjoyed one of our favorite meals, *Jaeger Schnitzel*, served with lots of *pommes frites*, the German way, *with mayonnaise*. Then it was time to say good-bye to Frankfurt and catch our Aer Lingus round-trip flight to Ireland for a couple of days to see some of our favorite places around Killarney and then back to Frankfurt to board our Pan Am flight back to the US. It had been a fantastic vacation and one we would never forget!

In October 1992, Grace and George came up to Washington for another visit, and John and I had planned the things we wanted them to see. We had told her about the beautiful drive through the Shenandoah Valley and how safe it was, but she was adamant about not going up into the mountains. Grace was frightened at the very thought of driving through mountains because she was afraid of heights and had a misconception of the drive through them on an interstate highway. First, we took them through some of the battlefields of the Civil War beginning with *the Battle of Bull Run*, where hundreds of people went out with their picnic baskets to watch the battle begin, as if it were a sports event. They really had no idea of what was in store for our country and how long this battle would last, with great losses on both sides.

After leaving the Battlegrounds of Bull Run, Aunt Grace didn't notice our gradual ascent up to the highest mountains of the Blue Ridge Parkway and right through the middle of the Blue Ridge Mountains. Not until we turned to begin our descent half-way down the mountain to Monticello, did she realize that we had fooled her. It wasn't at all what she thought it would be, and it was fun and so beautiful! We had a wonderful tour of the old historic home of Thomas Jefferson and made some great pictures of Grace and George sitting together in the lovely picturesque gardens amidst the gorgeous colors of the fall leaves. We had a beautiful drive back home through Fredericksburg and Chancellorsville, two more famous Battle Grounds of the Civil War. In July 1863, the Union armies pushed back the Confederate forces at Gettysburg, the only battle fought on northern soil. On November 19, 1863, this great, shattered battlefield was dedicated as a *National Cemetery,* and, after a notable orator spoke for two hours, President Lincoln rose and gave his eloquent *Gettysburg Address* in less than three minutes.

The Gettysburg Address

"Four score and seven years ago, our fathers brought forth on this continent a new Nation, conceived in liberty, and dedicated to the proposition that all men are created equal. Now, we are engaged in a great civil war testing whether that nation or any nation, so conceived and so dedicated, can long endure. We are met on a great battlefield of that war. We have come to dedicate a portion of that field as a final resting place for those who died that that Nation might live. It is altogether fitting and proper that we should do this.

"But, in a larger sense, we cannot dedicate ... we cannot consecrate ... we cannot hallow this ground. The brave men, living and dead, who struggled here, have consecrated it far above our poor power to add or detract. The world will little note, nor long remember, what we say here; but it can never forget what they did here.

"It is for us the living, rather, to be dedicated here to the unfinished work which they who fought here have thus far so nobly advanced. It is rather for us to be here dedicated to the great task remaining before us ... that from these honored dead we take increased devotion to that cause for which they gave the last full measure of devotion.

"That we here highly resolve that these dead shall not have died in vain ... that this Nation, under God, shall have a new birth of freedom ... and that Government of the people, by the people and for the people, shall not perish from the earth." (Abraham Lincoln, 11/19/1863)

For thousands of years, slavery had been a profitable business throughout the world as one tyrant would take over another and make slaves of the defeated people. The Jews were enslaved to the Egyptians, the Babylonians and the Romans in different eras of history and many others are enslaved today in the slave trafficking of women, girls and young boys for evil purposes. However, in the US and England in the 1800's, Christians fought to abolish the slave trade: thus, the need for the great Civil War to free the black slaves who were brought to our country to work the farms and plantations by slave traders who bought them, sometimes from their own people in Africa. When it ended, thousands of our soldiers on both sides were dead and many more were maimed for life and came home on crutches. In fact, two of my great grandfathers, one on my mother's side with the Union army, and one on my father's side with the Confederates, came home on crutches, each with a missing leg.

In November 1992, Michael and Ginger came up for a visit to Washington with a group from Mobile to *March on Washington* to protest the staggering economy. We invited them to stay with us and enjoyed their visit tremendously. They enjoyed visiting Congress and the Capitol Building as well as the museums and monuments on the DC Mall and took loads of pictures. John and I took them on a driving tour of Washington using our *Tour by Auto* tape, and we parked the car at the entrance to Mt. Vernon and walked to the home of George and Martha Washington to see the lovely reconstructed home and slave quarters. Then we ate our picnic lunch on the lovely grounds before heading back to the car and continuing our drive. John and I joined them in their *march* around the White House with many people carrying signs and shouting slogans such as *Hold onto your Wallet! Or Give me Gridlock, or give me Death!* It was great fun having them with us, and we'll always remember our special time with Ginger and Mike in Washington for those few special days.

In April 1993, John and I drove down to Jackson to stay with precious little Katie and Jim, so Kathy could accompany two of her sisters to Germany to visit their third sister who was working as a teacher in Frankfurt with the Department of Defense Dependents School System (DODDS). They planned a European vacation, which turned out to be a great time for all. John and I loved every minute of our time with Jim and Katie, who had reached her first birthday in March and was walking very well. We took her to the Jackson Zoo, and she had the time of her life walking, or running, all over the place to see the animals. She was very intrigued with the lions. Her little mouth would drop open in awe every time she heard the lion sound, and she would take off running to find them. Of course, we had to keep up with her until she got so tired her Granddad had to pick her up and carry her. It was great to have this special time together with both Jim and Katie, and we cherish our memories. Katie was so adorable, and, when her mother returned a week later, she was overjoyed to see her, and, of course, Kathy was ecstatic to see Katie. John asked me beforehand, *"Are you ready to give up your baby?"* I must have looked very sad because little Katie, at that young age, sensed that her Grandma was feeling a little left out. She, Kathy and I were sitting at the dining room table, and I remember little Katie turning around to me and giving me a big pat on the arm as if to say, *"What's the matter with you, Grammy?"*

During the following summer, Jim brought them down to meet us at the Gulf, and Katie loved splashing the salty water and playing in the sand. She also loved wading in the surf and building drip castles. She was fascinated by the sand crabs cleaning out their houses and chased the sand pipers. She made everything new again for John and me as we saw it all through Katie's eyes. All the family came down to the beach to visit Katie, Kathy and Jim either at the condo or at Mother's house on the eastern shore. Mike and Ginger had a condo just a few miles from ours on the lagoon where Mike kept his boat, and he would sometimes take us riding around Ono Island. Mother would ride down to the Gulf with Joe and Erin, who had a home and business in Mobile, so it was convenient for them to stop by for her on their way down. They usually came down for the whole day, and we loved having all our family together. Mother was always excited when the little ones were there and loved holding them on her lap. She always loved Jimmy and Kathy and now Katie made their family complete. That first summer Greg and Lorena were back from Mexico, and they joined us for a few days. It was a great time for everyone to meet Lorena and welcome her to the family.

In late August 1993, Grace and George came up to Northern Virginia for another visit, and we took them on a driving tour of Old Town Alexandria and a Dinner Cruise on the Potomac River. We also drove them down to Williamsburg to visit the Visitor's Center where we saw two movies about the history of Williamsburg. We picked up Maggie at her apartment and caught the bus for a tour of historic Williamsburg beginning with the House of Burgesses, where we witnessed the enactment of a bill as it was presented before the House of Commons. Then we walked down Gloucester Street, visiting small shops along the way, and sat in the court house to hear an arbitrator, and then ended the tour there with a visit to the Anglican Church and cemetery. We drove over to Jamestown where we had another tour and experienced life in Colonial Williamsburg watching actors dressed in colonial attire depict the birth of the famous settlement of 1607 on the James River. After dropping Maggie off at her apartment, we drove down the Colonial Parkway to Yorktown where we saw a movie about the Revolutionary War and the surrender of Cornwallis. We then had dinner at *Nick's Restaurant,* a very good and famous restaurant right next door to the cave where Cornwallis was hiding before his capture; a real landmark in the area.

When I drove over to visit Greg and Lorena on one of my visits home, they had a surprise waiting for me. Lorena opened the door of a bird cage, and out flew a beautiful blue parakeet named *Ludivico.* He circled overhead and then landed on my shoulder and started kissing me all over my face with his tiny little beak and tickling me with his soft flapping wing feathers. He was so cute! He did this every time I came for a visit until Lorena put him back in his cage. Of course, Greg still had his tree crabs, which made chirping sounds to add to their family life during their first years of marriage. Later, while Greg and Lorena were away and someone else was feeding Ludivico, he flew out the door and they never saw him again! It was terribly sad and we always missed Ludivico when we came for a visit. We will always remember him and his sweet affectionate ways. Since they badly needed a car for transportation, John and I helped them buy a reliable second-hand car, and I taught Lorena how to drive. She passed the test to get her driver's license on the first try, and everything was working well for them, but it took several months before she felt confident enough to get out on the Interstate. Except for a few times before his accident, Greg had never driven a car, or gotten a driver's license, due to his disabilities, so we were very thankful that Lorena was able to assume the responsibility of driving them around Baton Rouge and later to Mobile.

John had received his JD degree from Catholic University Law School on the 24th of May, 1992, but it took him until the fall of 1993 to pass the Virginia State Bar. *The third time was the charm!* I helped by asking him questions all the way down to Roanoke, where the test was given, and felt like I had passed the Bar exam, too. Maggie drove up from Williamsburg to Richmond for the *Swearing-in Ceremony* at the Virginia Supreme Court on November 2nd. It was a great accomplishment for John, and now he was impelled to seek another overseas assignment. Now that he had his credentials as an attorney combined with his engineering qualifications, he just had to see what else he could find which might allow us more overseas travel. There were places we had yet to see before we settled down to open a law practice. John applied for a position advertised in the Retired Officer's Magazine as Legal Advisor to the Saudi Arabian Air Force. He received the offer from BDM International in McLean, VA on October 27th, accepted it on November 5th and started to work in the McLean Office on November 8th in preparation for movement to Saudi Arabia on the 1st of December. This time John would be working directly for the Royal Saudi Arabian Air Force.

With John's new endeavor, which caught me quite by surprise, we had to move quickly to have our furniture picked up and put back into storage with a shipment of our clothing and personal items being sent to our new address in Riyadh. I would remain with Mother as I had done before, and visit all the kids while awaiting my entrance into Saudi Arabia for the third time. In January, we learned of Maggie's pregnancy with Jenny, and the following year, of Lorena's pregnancy with Josh. During all these seasons of becoming a grandmother, I wondered how so many of these precious little lives could be lost to abortion mills before they ever had a chance to know love. What could they have given to the world? And what had been God's plan for their lives? Jesus said,

> *"Verily I say unto you, 'Except ye be converted and become as little children, ye shall not enter into the kingdom of heaven…. But whoso shall offend one of these little ones…, it were better for him that a millstone were hanged about his neck and that he be drowned in the depth of the sea. Woe unto the world because of offences!*
> *"Offences will come; but woe to that person by whom the offence comes!'"* (Matthew 18:1-7)

Mother lived to see three of her eight great grandchildren before her death Christmas morning of 1996. She would have five more great grandchildren in the years to follow through David and Donna, the son and daughter of Michael and Ginger. If it's possible for those who have passed on before us to look down from heaven and see the lives of their loved ones, I know Mother has enjoyed all of her grandchildren and is very proud of them all. Mother and I were able to share our last Thanksgiving Dinner together just a month before her death, and I was privileged to be there to feed her at the home of Michael and Ginger exactly 60 years to the day after she brought me into the world. Mother had a very hard delivery with me and she and I were in the hospital three weeks. The doctor told her not to have any more children. In fact, she and I were in the hospital so long, the nurses nicknamed me *"Pokey"* after Pocahontas because I looked so much like a little Indian baby with my long black hair. They say that every time you hear of a birth, you also hear of a death, and vice versa.

> *"To everything there is a season, and a time for every purpose under the heaven: A time to be born and a time to die; … a time to mourn and a time to dance."* (Ecclesiastes 3:1-2)

CHAPTER TWENTY-NINE

Back to the Book of Revelation

1991-1993

While John was occupied with Law School, I was back in my Bible study trying to figure out all the mysterious characters of this great prophecy. I was intrigued in trying to solve its many puzzles, obviously given to us for these last days so that we might recognize these things as they begin to happen. This book reveals that once they begin, they happen rapidly and they cannot be stopped because they are under God's control. As we begin again to study this great Book of the Holy Bible, we must ask God to *open our spiritual eyes so that we might see, and understand,* what John saw, and ask Him to *lead us into all truth.* After being away from my studies for a while, I found I had some re-reading to do to pick up where I left off and get back into a study mode. I learned to use my *Concordance to look up words in the Greek and Hebrew* to get a clearer meaning of the words used in scripture, so I could understand their true meaning. Since the Bible has been rewritten so many times over the years, the interpretations could have been lost, or misunderstood. Therefore, it is to our advantage to look them up if we have a question. My Concordance containing dictionaries of the *New Testament Greek* and *Old Testament Hebrew* words used throughout the *King James translation of the Bible* proved to be invaluable. Scripture must always support scripture, and there can be no contradictions, nor any stone left unturned, as we use scripture like pieces of a puzzle to put the whole picture together from beginning to end.

As we progress from our previous study into Chapter 13, we see a new empire coming into focus in a *beast rising up out of the sea, "having seven heads and ten horns, and upon his horns ten crowns, and upon his heads the name of blasphemy." ... "And I saw one of his heads as it were wounded to death; and his deadly wound was healed; and all the world wondered after the beast."* Strangely enough, this beast fits the same description as *that old serpent, Satan, the Devil,* which we saw in Chapter 12 waiting to devour *the male child.* Using Joseph's dream *describing his mother, father and brothers* as the *moon, sun and stars* (Genesis 37:9), we see a picture of *Israel* as *a woman, clothed with the sun, and the moon under her feet, and upon her head a crown of twelve stars,* who is about to give birth to the *promised Seed* (Genesis 3:15). Each head on *the beast with seven heads and ten horns* represents a *World Empire* which has come against Israel over the years to enslave her, or try to destroy her, and the *ten horns* are *ten kings or kingdoms*: 1. Egypt; 2. Assyria; 3. Babylon; 4. Media-Persia; 5. Greece; and 6. Rome.

For many years, students of the Bible believed the 7th World Empire, *the head with the deadly wound which is healed and comes back to life,* is the revised Roman Empire, and it very well may be. However, the progression of time has brought us much further along today and we see a shift in world affairs which is taking us back to medieval times when thousands of people were slaughtered in the most horrendous ways. And we see it happening again in the world today! Cities are being destroyed all over the Middle East and people are being tortured and killed, women and innocent children are being raped or sold into slavery, and some are being crucified to mock our Lord. This last *beast,* referred to us as *Mystery Babylon,* could very well be just that, *Babylon,* the head which comes back to life and tries to take the world by force. We can clearly see this ungodly force moving rapidly across the Middle East and they must be stopped! It is comforting to note that our Bible teaches, *"Absent from the body, present with the Lord."* (2nd Corinthians 5:1-8) All souls who lose their heads for Christ's sake go straight to heaven, while those of this demonic empire end up in the *Lake of Fire, their eternal damnation.* (Daniel 7:1-11 & 8:3-8; 20-22)

The first beast of Revelation 13 *rises up out of the sea,* which represents the nations, quite possibly the nations surrounding the Mediterranean Sea. *"And I beheld another beast coming up out of the earth; and he had two horns like a lamb, and he spoke as a dragon."* Could it be that, with the rise of Christianity, the devil came up with a new plan to divert God's people from the truth and force them to accept a new religion? (Revelation 13:11) God reveals the identity of this second beast as *the false Prophet,* which causes people to worship *the first beast,* who has the same description as that of the dragon in Chapter 12: *"And the dragon gave him his power, and his seat and great authority."* Normally, *horns* represent *kings* or *kingdoms,* but on the false prophet, they could stand for something entirely different. They could emulate something of a religious nature to give this false prophet some credibility and lure people into it quite subtly. If we judge this second *beast* by its works, *speaking as a dragon,* we must draw this conclusion because he is definitely in league with the devil.

That Old Serpent, Satan, the Devil

Where did Satan come from? How did that *old serpent, Satan, the Devil* originate? The prophets Isaiah and Ezekiel give us the story of this *created being,* which has caused so much trouble in the world and must be destroyed:

From the Prophet, Isaiah:

"How art thou fallen from heaven, O Lucifer, son of the morning! How art thou cut down to the ground, which didst weaken the nations! For thou hast said in thine heart, I will ascend into heaven, I will exalt my throne above the stars of God: I will sit also upon the mount of the congregation, in the sides of the north: I will ascend above the heights of the clouds; I will be like the most High.

"Yet thou shalt be brought down to hell, to the sides of the pit. They that see thee shall narrowly look upon thee, and consider thee, saying, 'Is this the man that made the earth to tremble, that did shake kingdoms; that made the world as a wilderness, and destroyed the cities thereof?'" (Isaiah 14:12-17)

From the Prophet, Ezekiel:

"Son of man, say to the prince of Tyrus, Thus says the Lord God: Because thine heart is lifted up, and thou hast said, I am a God, I sit in the seat of God, in the midst of the seas; yet thou art a man, and not God, though thou set thine heart as the heart of God. Behold, thou art wiser than Daniel; there is no secret that they can hide from thee.

"With thy wisdom and with thine understanding thou hast gotten thee riches, and hast gotten gold and silver into thy treasures: By thy great wisdom and by thy traffick hast thou increased thy riches, and thine heart is lifted up because of thy riches.

"Therefore thus saith the Lord God: Because thou hast set thine heart as the heart of God; behold, therefore I will bring strangers upon thee, the terrible of the nations: and they shall draw their swords against the beauty of thy wisdom, and they shall defile thy brightness. "Thou hast been in Eden the garden of God; every precious stone was thy covering... the workmanship of thy tabrets and of thy pipes was prepared in thee in the day that thou wast created. Thou art the anointed cherub that covers; and I have set thee so; thou wast upon the holy mountain of God; thou hast walked up and down in the midst of the stones of fire. Thou wast perfect in thy ways from the day that thou wast created, till iniquity was found in thee.

"By the multitude of thy merchandise they have filled the midst of thee with violence, and thou hast sinned: therefore, I will cast thee as profane out of the mountain of God: and I will destroy thee, O covering cherub, from the midst of the stones of fire.

"Thine heart was lifted up because of thy beauty, thou hast corrupted thy wisdom by reason of thy brightness...

"Thou hast defiled thy sanctuaries by the multitude of thine iniquities, by the iniquity of thy traffick; therefore, will I bring forth a fire from the midst of thee, it shall devour thee and I will bring thee to ashes upon the earth in the sight of all them that behold thee.

"All they that know thee among the people shall be astonished at thee: Thou shalt be a terror and never shalt thou be any more." (Ezekiel 28: 2-19)

Today, we are beginning to see another head on this beast, which could very well be the *eighth head, and* quite possibly a composite of all the other heads (Revelation 17:11). As demons are released from *the bottomless pit* to inhabit people without God, the evil deeds of this beast are becoming more and more horrendous. God describes this beast as *Mystery Babylon* and tells us that the time of this beast will be short because he will destroy it along with *the false prophet* before they can destroy the earth. (Revelation 17:8-12) The people living in bondage to this evil empire will be forced to pay homage to the beast or be killed. This is already happening in the world today! And soon they will be expected to receive *the mark of the beast,* or *the number of his name.* Our heavenly Father is the one true God of love and peace. Life is precious to him, and he would never tell people to kill others in his name, or any other name, but he would expect us to defend ourselves and others from these forces of evil. Therefore, there are times when God promotes war for the sake of righteousness to establish peace on the earth. The end result of this false religion, *depicted in the Bible as a spiritual adulteress,* is suffering and death for millions of people the world over. However, God will have the last word! He tells us the eternal destination of this beast and all those who follow after his false religion to try and take the world by force: *The Lake of Fire burning with brimstone.* (Revelation 17:1-18; Revelation 13:11-18; & Revelation 19:19-20)

> *"Here is wisdom: Let him that hath understanding count the number of the beast: for it is the number of a man; and his number is Six hundred threescore and six."* (Revelation 13:11-18) Man was created on the 6th day: What other numbers, pertaining to a man, come to mind?

Back in the 5th Century BC, King Nebuchadnezzar had a dream of a great image and called upon young Daniel to interpret the meaning of the dream because none of the magicians, astrologers, sorcerers or Chaldeans could give the interpretation. Daniel told the king *"But there is a God in heaven that reveals secrets and makes known to the king Nebuchadnezzar what shall be in the latter days."* Daniel explained that this great image of a man represented world empires which will follow Babylon, but he, the king, is the head of gold. The breast and arms of silver represent Media-Persia, his belly and thighs of brass represent Greece, his legs of iron represent the strong Greco-Roman Empire and his feet and toes, part iron and part clay, represent the last world empire which will not cleave together and will be broken in pieces. This last kingdom shall have the strength of iron, which breaks in pieces and subdues all things, but it will not mix together with the potter's clay and shall be *a divided kingdom, partly strong and partly broken.* This last kingdom upon the earth *will mingle together with the seed of men.* It shall be a divided kingdom and it shall not cleave together. Then we see *a stone cut out without hands* which *smote the image upon its feet... and the stone that smote the image of Babylon became a great mountain and filled the whole earth.* We see Jesus, *the stone that smote the image,* setting up his kingdom upon the earth and totally destroying the image of *Humanism,* when man becomes his own god. (Daniel 2:19-45)

Since the Book of Daniel is the companion book to the Book of Revelation, we must study Daniel and his visions of the end times. Daniel had many visions over the years of *beasts,* representing *world empires,* which would come to power against the Jewish people all the way until the end of the world as we know it. It started with Babylon, when Daniel, as a young boy, and his people were taken into bondage out of Jerusalem into the land of Shinar. Daniel was able to interpret the dreams of King Nebuchadnezzar and had many visions of world empires which would follow Babylon. When Nebuchadnezzar's son, Belshazzar, became king, he had a feast for his lords and commanded that *the golden and silver vessels taken from the temple in Jerusalem* be brought to him. Then he and his princes, his wives and concubines drank from them and profaned the holy vessels and *praised the gods of silver, and gold, of brass, iron, wood, and stone. "In the same hour came forth fingers of a man's hand, and wrote over against the candlestick upon the plaster of the wall of the king's palace.... MENE, MENE, TEKEL, UPHARSIN."* (Daniel 5:1-5; 22-25)

Daniel's interpretation:

"God hath numbered thy kingdom and finished it. Thou art weighed in the balances, and art found wanting. Thy kingdom is divided, and given to the Medes and Persians." (Daniel, Chapter 5:26-28)

In the Seventh Chapter, we see four great beasts, or empires, coming up from the sea, which are diverse one from another: The first *like a lion* describes Babylon, and King Nebuchadnezzar (7:4); the second *like a bear* describes Media-Persia (7:5); the third *like a leopard* describes Greece (7:6); and the fourth, *diverse from all the beasts that were before it,* describes Rome, with *ten horns, and a little horn, with eyes like the eyes of man and a mouth speaking great things,* believed to be the last antichrist (7:7-8). This seems to speak of the Roman Empire and its progression over the years, as God's Judgment falls upon the whole world.

"After this I saw in the night visions, and behold a fourth beast, dreadful and terrible, and strong exceedingly; and it had great iron teeth: it devoured and brake in pieces, and stamped the residue with the feet of it: and it was diverse from all the beasts that were before it; and it had ten horns. I considered the horns, and, behold,

there came up among them another little horn, before whom there were three of the first horns plucked up by the roots: and, behold, in this horn were eyes like the eyes of man, and a mouth speaking great things.

"I beheld till the thrones were cast down, and the Ancient of days did sit, whose garment was as white as snow, and the hair of his head was like pure wool: his throne was like the fiery flame, and his wheels as burning fire. A fiery stream issued and came forth from before him: thousand thousands ministered to him and ten thousand times ten thousand stood before him: the judgment was set and the books were opened.

"I saw in the night visions, and, behold, one like the Son of man came with the clouds of heaven, and came to the Ancient of days, and they brought him near before him. And there was given him dominion, and glory, and a kingdom, that all people, nations, and languages, should serve him: his dominion is an everlasting dominion, which shall not pass away, and his kingdom that which shall not be destroyed." (Daniel 7:7-14)

In Daniel, Chapter 8, we see the rise of Media-Persia and the rise of the Greek Empire, with the rise and fall of Alexander the Great. When Alexander fell, the kingdom of Greece was divided among his four Generals.

"Then I lifted up mine eyes, and behold, there stood before the river, a ram which had two horns... And as I was considering, behold, an he- goat came from the west ... and the goat had a notable horn between his eyes. And he came to the ram... and ran into him in the fury of his power ... and smote the ram. Therefore the he-goat waxed very great: and when he was strong, the great horn was broken; and for it came up four notable ones toward the four winds of heaven.

"And out of one of them came a little horn, which waxed exceedingly great, toward the south, and toward the east, and toward the pleasant land. And it waxed great, even toward the host of heaven; and it cast down some of the host and of the stars to the ground, and stamped upon them." (Daniel 8:3-10)

"And there was war in heaven: Michael and his angels fought against the dragon; and the dragon fought and his angels, and prevailed not; neither was their place found anymore in heaven.

"And the great dragon was cast out, that old serpent, called the Devil and Satan, which deceives the whole world: he was cast out into the earth, and his angels were cast out with him.

"And I heard a loud voice saying in heaven, Now is come salvation, and strength, and the kingdom of our God, and the power of his Christ: for the accuser of our brethren is cast down, which accused them before our God day and night. And they overcame him by the blood of the Lamb, and by the word of their Testimony; and they loved not their lives unto death.

"Therefore rejoice, ye heavens, and ye that dwell in them. Woe to the inhabitants of the earth and of the sea! for the devil is come down unto you, having great wrath, because he knows he has but a short time." (Revelation 12:7-12)

The end of Revelation (Chapter 12:13-17), seems to be a description of the Nazi Holocaust in the 1940's. God promised to bring the Jewish people back to their homeland, which he did in 1948, to the land he gave to Abraham and his seed through Jacob in the Abrahamic Covenant. God makes it very clear throughout the Bible that those who bless Israel will be blessed, and those who curse Israel will be accursed. We must obey God and do all we can to protect Israel and the Jewish people who have blessed the world in so many ways. They have become *streams in the desert* to make the desert bloom and produce food for the world, and they welcome everyone to share in their blessings as long as they are willing to live peacefully among them. Even more importantly, they have preserved *the Oracles of God,* the very foundation of our faith.

"And I looked, and lo, a Lamb stood on the mount Zion, and with him an hundred and forty and four thousand, having his Father's name written in their foreheads. And I heard a voice from heaven, as the voice of many waters, and as the voice of a great thunder: and I heard the voice of harpers harping with their harps: And they sung as it were a new song before the throne, and before the four beasts, and the elders: and no man could learn that song but the hundred and forty and four thousand, which were redeemed from the earth.

"These are they which were not defiled with women; for they are virgins. These are they which follow the Lamb whithersoever he goeth. These were redeemed from among men, being the firstfruits unto God and to the Lamb. And in their mouth was found no guile: for they are without fault before the throne of God." (Revelation 14:1-5)

"Behold, the day of the Lord cometh, and thy spoil shall be divided in the midst of thee. For I will gather all nations against Jerusalem to battle; and the city shall be taken, and the houses rifled, and the women ravished; and half of the city shall go forth into captivity, and the residue of the people shall not be cut off from the city.

"Then shall the Lord go forth, and fight against those nations, as when he fought on the day of battle. And his feet shall stand in that day upon the mount of Olives, which is before Jerusalem on the east, and the mount of Olives shall cleave in the midst thereof toward the east and toward the west; and there shall be a very great valley; and half of the mountain shall remove toward the north, and half of it toward the south. And ye shall flee to the valley of the mountains for the valley shall reach to Azal; ... and the Lord my God shall come and all the saints with thee....

"And this shall be the plague wherewith the Lord will smite all the people that have fought against Jerusalem; their flesh shall consume away while they stand upon their feet, and their eyes shall consume away in their holes, and their tongue shall consume away in their mouth." (Zechariah 14:1-12)

"And ye shall know that I am in the midst of Israel, and that I am the Lord your God, and none else: and my people shall never be ashamed. And it shall come to pass ... that I will pour out my spirit upon all flesh; and your sons and your daughters shall prophesy, your old men shall dream dreams, your young men shall see visions. And also upon the servants and upon the handmaids in those days will I pour out my spirit.

"And I will show wonders in the heavens and in the earth, blood, and fire, and pillars of smoke. The sun shall be turned into darkness, and the moon into blood, before the great and terrible day of the Lord come. And it shall come to pass, that whosoever shall call upon

the name of the Lord shall be delivered: for in mount Zion and in Jerusalem shall be deliverance, as the Lord hath said, and in the remnant whom the Lord shall call." (Joel 2: 27-32)

"And I saw an angel flying in the midst of heaven, having the everlasting gospel to preach unto them that dwell on the earth, and to every nation, and kindred, and tongue, and people, saying with a loud voice, 'Fear God and give glory to him; for the hour of his judgment is come; and worship him that made heaven, and earth, and the sea, and the fountains of waters.'

"And there followed another angel saying, 'Babylon is fallen, is fallen, that great city, because she made all nations drink of the wine of the wrath of her fornication.'

"And the third angel followed them, saying with a loud voice, 'If any man worship the beast and his image, and receive his mark in his forehead, or in his hand, the same shall drink of the wine of the wrath of God, which is poured out without mixture into the cup of his indignation; and he shall be tormented with fire and brimstone in the presence of the holy angels, and in the presence of the Lamb.'
...

"Here is the patience of the saints: here are they that keep the commandments of God, and the faith of Jesus. And I heard a voice from heaven saying to me, 'Write, Blessed are the dead which die in the Lord from henceforth': 'Yea,' saith the Spirit, 'that they may rest from their labors, and their works do follow them.'" (Revelation 14:6- 13)

"And I saw three unclean spirits like frogs come out of the mouth of the dragon, and out of the mouth of the beast, and out of the mouth of the false prophet. For they are the spirit of devils, working miracles, which go forth unto the kings of the earth and of the whole world, to gather them to the battle of that great day of God Almighty.

"Behold, I come as a thief. Blessed is he that watches, and keeps his garments, lest he walk naked, and they see his shame. And he gathered them together into a place called in the Hebrew tongue Armageddon." (Revelation 16:13-16)

The Bible indicates that *the bride of Christ* will come back with Jesus in his *Second Coming,* when he returns to set up his kingdom upon the earth. This time he will come as the *Lion of Judah* to rule the earth with a rod of iron. When the seventh trumpet sounds, *the kingdoms of this world become the kingdoms of our Lord and of his Christ. (Revelation 11:15) "The Mystery of God" is finished! (Revelation 10:7)*

And all Israel will be saved: God will bring Israel through the great tribulation for this is the *Abrahamic Covenant extended to Jacob, when God changed his name to Israel and gave him and his seed "all the land from the great river of Egypt to the Euphrates River."* (Genesis 15:18) Then Jesus will sit upon the throne of David and divide the sheep from the goats:

> *"When the Son of man shall come in his glory, and all the holy angels with him, then shall he sit upon the throne of his glory: And before him shall be gathered all nations: and he shall separate them one from another, as a shepherd divides his sheep from the goats: And he shall set the sheep on his right hand, but the goats on the left. Then shall the King say unto them on his right hand, 'Come ye blessed of my Father, inherit the kingdom prepared for you from the foundation of the world:*
>
> *"'For I was hungred and ye gave me meat. I was thirsty and ye gave me drink: I was a stranger and ye took me in: Naked and ye clothed me: I was sick, and ye visited me: I was in prison, and ye came unto me.' Then shall the righteous answer him, saying, 'Lord, when saw we thee hungred and fed thee? Or thirsty and gave thee drink? Or a stranger and took thee in? Or naked and clothed thee? Or when saw we thee sick, or in prison and came unto thee?'*
>
> *"And the King shall answer and say unto them, 'Verily I say unto you, Inasmuch as ye have done it unto one of the least of these my brethren, ye have done it unto me.' Then shall he say also to them on the left hand, 'Depart from me, ye cursed, into everlasting fire, prepared for the devil and his angels: ... For I was hungred and ye gave me no meat: I was thirsty, and ye gave me no drink: I was a stranger, and ye took me not in: naked, and ye clothed me not: sick, and in prison, and ye visited me not.'... 'Verily I say unto you, Inasmuch as ye did it not to one of the least of these, ye did it not unto me.' And these shall go away into everlasting punishment: but the righteous into life eternal."* (Matthew 25:31-46)

The devil will be bound for a thousand years, and, at the end of the thousand years, he will be set loose *to deceive the nations which are in the four quarters of the earth, Gog and Magog, to gather them together to battle,* and fire will come down from God out of heaven to devour them. And this will be followed by *the great White Throne Judgment,* when the books will be opened and the people will be judged according to their works. (Revelation 20:12) (Daniel 7:9-10 & Chapter 12)

> *"And I saw a great white throne, and him that sat on it, from whose face the earth and the heaven fled away; and there was found no place for them. And I saw the dead, small and great, stand before God; and the books were opened: and another book was opened, which is the book of life: and the dead were judged out of those things which were written in the books, according to their works.... And death and hell were cast into the lake of fire. This is the second death. And whosoever was not found written in the book of life was cast into the lake of fire."* (Revelation 20:10-15)

> *"And at that time shall Michael stand up, the great prince which stands for the children of thy people: and there shall be a time of trouble, such as never was since there was a nation even to that same time: and at that time thy people shall be delivered, every one that shall be found written in the book.*
>
> *"And many of them that sleep in the dust of the earth shall awake, some to everlasting life, and some to shame and everlasting contempt. And they that be wise shall shine as the brightness of the firmament; and they that turn many to righteousness as the stars forever and ever. 'But thou, O Daniel, shut up the words, and seal the book, even to the time of the end: many shall run to and fro, and knowledge shall be increased.'*
>
> *"Then I Daniel looked, and, behold, there stood two others, one on this side of the bank of the river and one on the other.... And one said to the man clothed in linen, which was upon the waters of the river, 'How long shall it be to the end of these wonders?'*
>
> *"And I heard the man clothed in linen, which was upon the waters of the river, when he held up his right hand and his left hand unto heaven and sware by him that liveth forever that it shall be for a time, times and an half (3½ years); and when he shall have accomplished to scatter the power of the holy people, all these*

things shall be finished. And I heard, but I understood not: then I said, 'O my Lord, what shall be the end of these things?' And he said. 'Go thy way Daniel, for the words are closed up and sealed until the time of the end.'

"*Many shall be purified, and made white, and tried; but the wicked shall do wickedly, and none of the wicked shall understand; but the wise shall understand. And from the time that the daily sacrifice shall be taken away and the abomination that maketh desolate set up, there shall be a thousand two hundred and ninety days. Blessed is he that waiteth, and cometh to the thousand and five and thirty days. But go thy way till the end be: for thou shalt rest, and stand in thy lot at the end of the days.*" (Daniel, Chapter 12)

CHAPTER THIRTY

A Return to Saudi Arabia
1994-1995

After spending two months with Mother and visiting all the family, I left Mobile the day after her 89th birthday to join John in Riyadh. He met me at the airport and drove me to our home bringing me up to date on his job and our new living arrangements. My first impression of the Phoenix Compound was that it was big! We had a two story villa with a beautiful winding staircase from the living room up to the second floor which consisted of three large furnished bedrooms and a luxurious master bathroom with bathtub, shower and bidet plus the vanity and other conveniences. John hired a house boy to clean for us once a week, which I appreciated very much. The workout room and library for books and tapes were located in the basement below us. Behind our villa was a large recreation center for get-togethers and a beautiful large swimming pool, which could be partially overseen by a nearby minaret. The door to our villa was just a few yards from the gated entrance, which was well guarded night and day. In front of our windows on the downstairs level were empty flower boxes which needed to be filled, so our first trip outside the compound had to be to find a nursery. We found several within a short drive, and it was fun picking out just the right assortment of plants to fill them. I chose petunias because they were very healthy looking in the Saudi sun, and they came in bright colors of rose, purple, pink, red and white. We planted a mixture and they were beautiful; just what our villa needed to brighten it up. I noticed a few of the TCN workers standing in front of them at various times to have their pictures made.

The first *Call to Prayer* came at 5:00 am, so I made it a habit to get up and begin my day at that time every morning. I would start off by reading a few scriptures and having my prayer time for our family back in the States, hoping that everything would work out for them and their lives would flourish as well as our beautiful petunias. Our kitchen was large and sufficient, although it needed some organization by the time I got there. I found joy in my cooking and dish washing just looking out my kitchen window and gazing upon our lovely flowers. I brought my Christian music with me and didn't hesitate to play my tapes at a reasonable volume. Even our Muslim workers seemed to enjoy hearing them. John had arranged to have our two-story villa vacuumed and bathrooms cleaned every week, and some of our young workers told me about their families and where they were from. They were working to send money home. One day after my arrival, I ventured downstairs to check out the books and videos and met a young woman, Maria, with her young daughter, Beth, who was about four years old. Maria was getting her morning exercise on the treadmill. We struck up a conversation and I learned about Christian activities going on right there on our compound. She encouraged me to get involved in the underground church and Bible study.

Our large water bottle had to be replaced several times each month for fresh drinking water, and we had brought with us our two humidifiers to keep the air moist. With our houseboy coming each week, I was able to devote my extra time to making Maggie's maternity dresses. We adjusted to our new life in Saudi Arabia and found it quite enjoyable. Soon my dining room table was all covered with material and patterns. Luckily, I had brought along my electric scissors. Since Maggie was expecting the first week of October, I plunged right into cutting out three adorable maternity dresses and had them ready for sewing within a couple of weeks. I assembled my sewing machine at one end of the dining table and finished sewing them together by the middle of March. John drove me all around looking for a store which carried sewing supplies, which I badly needed to finish the hems of the dresses, and we discovered *Everything for Sewing* in a small building off one of the main roads. Maggie had a job working in the gift shops in Williamsburg before the baby was born, and I estimated that she would need them sometime in April. While trying on the dresses and pinning in the hemline, I visualized how cute they would look on her. We packaged them up and got them in the mail around the end of March, and Maggie was very glad to get them. Dave made pictures of her wearing her new maternity dresses, and she looked so adorable! She said people were always complimenting her, asking where she bought them.

John was due for his first out-of-country vacation in May, so we planned a tour of Austria leaving on the 19th of May and returning on the 28th. Austria was one of the European countries we really wanted to see and had not yet had a chance to visit, so we called our Saudi tourist agent and set it up.

A Tour of Austria

We flew out of Riyadh on Austrian Airlines arriving in *Vienna* at 6:05 am and were met at the airport by an Austrian tour guide who drove us to our hotel. *Hotel Deutschmeister* was a small, rather quaint hotel located on the outskirts of Vienna inside a courtyard on a side street, but it was in a quiet section of town and had a great deal of Austrian charm. After checking us in and taking us to our room to get settled, the kind manager invited us into the small dining room for a breakfast while we were waiting on our city tour of Vienna. We found the hotel clean, comfortable, and more than adequate for our needs. About 9:00 am, we were picked up by a large van which transported us through the city to *Stadt Park*, where we boarded a large bus for the city tour just as it began to rain. Our tour guide pointed out all the places of interest in three languages as he gave us a brief history of Vienna. The rain let up a bit as we stopped to walk through the beautiful *Volksgarten, "the people's garden,"* where we took pictures from underneath our umbrella. By the time we arrived at *Schonbrunn Palace*, the rain had stopped completely, and we were able to walk around the Palace grounds. Fashioned after Versailles in 1692, Schonbrunn Palace served as the summer residence of *Empress Maria Theresa* and her family, including 11 daughters and 5 sons. Her youngest, *Marie Antoinette*, became *Queen of France* with her marriage to *Louis XVI*. Looking across the lovely gardens and upon the high hill above *Neptune's Fountain*, one can see the very impressive *Gloriett*, built in 1775 as a memorial to the Imperial Army and fashioned after a Roman arch of triumph. One of the most beautiful panoramic views of Vienna can be seen from this memorial.

Our tour bus dropped us off downtown across from the *State Opera House*, so we walked around looking for a good place for lunch. We settled on *Café Mozart* to get in out of the rain. It looked like a sidewalk café covered by a huge awning but inside was really a very nice restaurant with some of the best food in Vienna. I ordered *"Wiener Schnitzel,"* which came with sliced potato salad, and John ordered *"Bratwurst mit Pommes Frites, Brotchen und Bier."* Both of us had the delicious *"Erdbeere Torte"* for dessert, which was strawberry topping on a creamy chocolate torte flavored with Cointreau. It was delicious! Since we were so tired from our overnight flight and all our walking around on the city tour, we found the underground subway system and bought three-day passes with maps of the whole area, boarded our train and headed back to our hotel for some much needed sleep. We were pleased to find that the subway stop for Hotel Deutschmeister was just a block from the hotel.

The following morning, we were up bright and early for breakfast and found *our table* directly in front of a window beautifully set with fresh table cloth, flowers and a large thermos of hot coffee. We helped ourselves to the lovely buffet of fresh juices, cereals, boiled eggs and a large assortment of breads, cheeses, sliced ham and several kinds of preserves. We realized we had made the right choice of hotels when we noticed that our restaurant was patronized mostly by local Austrians. After breakfast, we walked down to the subway and used our passes to ride back into the city to take pictures of the beautiful church right in the center of town. Not far down the street from the large cathedral, we found the *Konzerthaus,* where we bought tickets for two concerts: *The Vienna Boys Choir and Mozart.* Again, we found *Café Mozart* around lunchtime to get in out of the rain and both ordered *Wiener Schnitzels.* The nineteen members of *the Vienna Boys Choir* paraded out on stage at precisely 4:00 pm and took their places around a large piano. They were introduced by their Director, a young man who played their introduction and accompanied them on the piano. The boys, composed of sopranos and altos, started off humming the notes of *Strauss* and were soon singing German lyrics to the music of many famous Austrian composers. Most of them were quite small boys, but four of them were rather tall with strong leading voices. The room was packed and about half-way through the concert, someone in the audience, probably an American, started clapping their hands in keeping time with the music during a lively Strauss number. The younger boys, who had been so composed and well disciplined, began to grin at one another, and this produced a series of grinning bouts for the remainder of the concert. It was so cute! We purchased a tape of their Strauss Concert, which we enjoyed tremendously on the remainder of our trip driving through the beautiful Austrian Alps.

It was pouring down when we exited the *Konzerthaus* around 5:00 pm, so we opened our umbrellas and walked over to the subway for our short ride over to *Café Mozart* for coffee and another *Erdbeere Torte,* while waiting for the Mozart Concert to begin at 8:00. The waiter said they were all out of Erdberre Torte and explained that they only prepare seven of these wonderful tortes each day. So, we ordered *Soup & Salad,* which was healthier for us anyway. Then he suggested we try their *Sacher Torte,* a chocolate torte with apricot filling, which we liked even better than the other. We later learned that this restaurant, *Café Mozart,* which we just happened into, is *the home of the world famous Sacher Torte*! Finally, it was time to return to the Konzerthaus around 7:00 to find our seats in the balcony for *Mozart in Historic Costumes.* The large concert house was very beautiful and the costumes made it seem like *the Mozart era* as the orchestra played his most beloved and well-known compositions. Our whole day was fantastic!

After breakfast the third day, we were transported to *Stadt Park,* where all tours seemed to originate. We boarded a large van for a drive through the lovely Austrian countryside to *Melk* where the history *of Osterreich* had its beginning as a *Roman fortress built on the bank of the Danube River where two smaller rivers, the Melk and the Pielach, flow into the mighty Danube.* Charlemagne is said to have granted the territory to a Frankish Herrieden abbot about 791, and it was later feudally acquired by the archbishop of Salzburg only to be overtaken by Leopold I around 976. Our guided tour of *Melk Castle* was very interesting as we walked through the large abbey and extensive library, both of which are especially beautiful with oil murals and gold leaf design throughout. Thousands of books cover the walls of the library all the way to the ceiling, and hidden doors were built into the library for secluded study. It was given to the Benedictine monks about 1112. The view of the rivers and valleys from the *Abbey Tower* is spectacular!

After lunch at the monastery restaurant located in the courtyard below the tower, we boarded our steamboat for a cruise down the lovely *Danube River* to the Austrian town of *Weissen Kirchen,* where we were met by a guide and driven the short distance to *Durnstein.* It was here that *Richard the Lion Hearted, King of England,* was imprisoned for two years for passing through on one of his crusades in 1193. He was imprisoned because the ruling monarchy of Osterreich wanted to prove he had the power over that territory. As we were walking along the cobblestone streets of this very charming ancient city, our small group stopped in a local pub for drinks and snacks as we chatted and took pictures. Then we continued our walk down the street and out into the gorgeous Austrian countryside to admire the vineyards, which seemed to be planted all over the mountainside.

Our guide met us along the road and transported us back to our hotels in Vienna. It had been a long, enjoyable day, and we noticed on our way back lots of fluffy white seed-bearing pollen from the trees floating in the air.

That evening, John and I rode the subway back into the city to find a place where we could get a good pizza. We had picked up a map on the Zeil the previous day advertising *DaVinci's Pizza* with great food and plenty of atmosphere! It had all those things, but it would have been very difficult to find without a map because it was in an out of the way place a couple of blocks over from the Zeil and around a dark corner. It was totally packed upstairs with people of all ages. We passed a large group coming out of the restaurant as we were trying to get in. The only table we could find was downstairs near the entrance, but it was well worth the wait and trouble because the food was outstanding, and we hope to go back again someday.

After our breakfast the fourth day, John made his last trip downtown to pick up our rental car, a Volkswagon hatchback, and we checked out before 11:00 am. We rode around the city of Vienna for a while before heading out of town to find the autobahn for our drive to Salzburg. Our drive took us back to the beautiful Danube Valley where we had been the previous day, so we stopped for dinner at *Restaurant Heinzle on the bank of the Danube River in Weissen Kirchen.* We had noticed this very inviting restaurant under the beautiful shade trees the day before and thought it looked like a place where we might find a good fish dinner. The fresh fish from the river was trout and was absolutely delicious! As we sat back and watched the river boats passing by, we saw our steamboat of the previous day coming in to dock as we had done. After enjoying our restful dinner on the bank of the Danube, we continued our drive along the Ybbs River and crossed over to get on the autobahn for Salzburg. To accompany the beautiful mountain scenery, we listened to our tape of the *Vienna Boys Choir singing Strauss.* It seemed so appropriate!

It had been a rather long day and we had reservations at a hotel in *Fuschl,* where we enjoyed a good night's sleep and took our time getting up the following morning. Since we were too late for breakfast, we found a small pizza restaurant open early for lunch and ordered our first *Calzone.* It was a rather short drive to *Salzburg,* but we wanted to get there early to have plenty of time to park the car and find the *old Stieglkeller Brewery Building,* where we were to pick up our tickets for *the Sound of Music Dinner Theatre.* A very kind Austrian gentleman directed us to the building just a few blocks away from the parking garage. Our walk took us through the cemetery which was filmed in the movie, and we tried to recognize the markers, or headstones, we remembered. Finally, we found the building and walked up three flights of stairs to get our tickets for the show scheduled for 7:00 pm. Since it was only 5:00, we decided to sit in the *Stieglkeller Bier Garten* to rest and have a drink while we looked out over the beautiful city of Salzburg with its many lovely buildings and cathedrals. After resting a while, it was still early and we were excited and energetic to get up and walk around, so we walked up higher into the surrounding countryside and found the old Abbey where Maria and Captain Von Trapp were actually married some 55 years earlier. We sat on the back pew for a few minutes and then descended down a very long stairway into the Olde Town where we passed by the large cathedral, which was shown in the movie, and around the corner to the little coffee house where we once sat with Maggie on a tour of Bavaria in 1983. Then we had to hurry back up the stairs of the Stieglkeller building to enter the Dinner Theatre and get ready for the show to start.

Salzburg, Austria.

After getting settled at our table in the dinner theatre, we placed our order, *Soup, Salad and Schnitzel with Noodles,* with *Crisp Apple Strudel* to be served at intermission. Before the play started, they showed a very interesting film of a recent interview with the real Maria Von Trapp in which she stated that the children had done the actual proposing, and she told much more of their real life story as a family. The movie and the play were very enjoyable and the food very good for being served by the actors in the casual atmosphere of a dinner theatre. After leaving Salzburg, we drove back to Fuschl where we had reservations for a second night at Hotel Mohrenwirt. This time, we were up very early to enjoy our continental breakfast and the wonderful assorted berry preserves, which we had missed the first morning.

Back on the autobahn, we headed east and then turned south through the beautiful countryside on our way to the mountainside town of *Hallstatt*. When we first entered the small ancient city through a tunnel built through solid rock, we had to find a place to park our car and then walk down the very narrow street to find *Hotel Gruner Baum*. It was during one of their annual festivities with people dressed in traditional attire while many activities were going on in the street. There was a roll of paper going down the street in one place for the children to draw pictures on and color. There was a band playing in the city square in front of our hotel, the back of which jutted out near the lake. After the majority of people left that afternoon, we were able to drive our car down the cobblestone street, which was just big enough for one car to pass down. Then we were able to park close to the hotel to bring in our baggage. The street was so narrow, the small trees had to be trimmed back flat against the buildings. Once situated in our hotel, we had to walk everywhere down sidewalks or upstairs to the next level to get around this lovely little town. The scenery was absolutely gorgeous from our hotel balcony overlooking the picturesque setting of the mountains and lovely tranquil lake. All our pictures turned out like picture post cards. We were there for two nights in this efficient hotel on *Hallstatter See* with a good restaurant and the most breathtaking views of the lake. The water was so still and placid, it reflected the mountains and changing cloud formations above it like the reflections in a mirror. It was so beautiful and truly an experience to behold at least once in a lifetime to walk out on our balcony and breathe in the atmosphere.

Hallstatt was *the Salt Mining Capital of the World* about a thousand years BC, and the following day, John and I rode an elevator hundreds of feet up the steep incline to the landing site of the old salt mine, where we were furnished a pair of coveralls before straddling a small train into the mining shaft where we slid down a chute to get inside the large chamber of the mine. Then we followed a tour guide to the large expanse of a bay-like area, where water had seeped in overtime to provide the world with the much sought after salt of that day. For half an hour, we stood there listening to the history of the old salt mining town and the mine itself with a sound and light show, which lit up the different areas as the story was told. When we exited the mine, we had a great view from that high vantage point above the small town and lake below. We rode the elevator back down and walked the narrow pathways back to our hotel in time for dinner. Upon our arrival, it looked like the houses had been built one on top of another, but, as we walked the pathways between them, which seemed to serve as streets, we realized that the first tier of houses had been converted into modern day shops containing every type of business needed to provide for a small city: a bank, stores and shops, a barber shop and hair salon, restaurants, museums, medical facilities, a church, a public square for the community to congregate and a transportation system around the lake.

The houses had been renovated many times over and provided homes for the small community of people making up the population. The town square was the scene of many parades and festivals taking place over the years during special holidays, historical events, ceremonies, graduations and funerals. We were fortunate enough to arrive just in time to witness one such festival or event each of the two times we visited Hallstatt. We also visited the old church and cemetery where hundreds of skulls were piled up inside a small house with dates written on them depicting the year in which each of their inhabitants died. On our second visit, we took the small boat around the lake to see the many other houses where the boat stopped to pick up and let off passengers.

The Austrian City of Hallstatt on the Lake.

On the road again, we headed for Zell am See and the high Alps, and, because of bad weather, we had to bypass the road leading up to the famous *Grossglockner,* the moving glacier of Austria's highest peak. Since we were disappointed in having to bypass the glacier, we found a room in a small hotel to check out the town and were delighted to find a cable car ski-lift to the top of the high snow-covered mountain above us. Our small hotel, which was located a little way between the town and the ski lifts, turned out to be one of our favorite places to stay in Zell am See because of the wonderful food prepared by the husband of our very hospitable landlady. In fact, he turned out to be quite a Chef and most of our favorite food was on the Menu. The atmosphere of the hotel was unpretentious and quite low-key which made us feel right at home. Since we ate all our meals there, we got to know both of them and took a great picture of them standing together in the restaurant before we left. We loved the location of this convenient hotel to all the available attractions around Zell am See and stayed several days enjoying the mountain and the lake.

Gasthof Schmittental at Zell am See, Austria.

John and I returned a second time to Zell am See at the same time we revisited Hallstatt a couple of years later and got pictures in summer and winter, and found it to be enjoyable at all times of the year. We tried another attempt to drive up through the highest mountains to see the Glacier, but again, the weather was not friendly and we were only able to stop in the high elevations for a snack at the park restaurant and, because of repairs being done on the road, had to turn around and drive back. We found the city of Zell am See quite modern with many good restaurants and places to shop. Also, there were many good hotels right on the lake. However, we always planned to go back to Gasthof Schmittental because we liked the owners, the atmosphere and the food.

*Lookout Point over the Lake at Zell am See
and the Surrounding Austrian Alps.*

Zell am See on the Lake and The Grand Hotel.

After leaving Zell am See, we found the road to Innsbruck through lovely meadowlands and small towns quite enjoyable with places to stop for lunch. We turned left off the main road to find our hotel which was situated on the bank of the Inn River at the entrance to the historic town of Hall. Once a wealthy salt mining trade center and mint, Hall has an enormous amount of charm and some very exciting history. The most impressive landmark, which towers above everything else, is the Castle of Hasegg, built in 1306 to protect the salt stores and the river bridge. In 1567, the Castle received the old mint transferred from the Castle of Sparberegg, and, with the minting of silver- talers, it achieved world-wide fame. The Rathaus, or Town Hall, once the residence of Tyrolean dukes, was donated to the citizens of Hall in 1406 by Duke Leopold IV of Habsburg and has served as the Rathaus ever since. The many blocks of ancient two and three story buildings, dating as far back as the 13th Century, have been reconstructed for modern day use and are very colorful and charming with many good restaurants in the area. Many beautiful churches date back to the 14th Century with a monastery and convent dating back to the 16th Century. The best tortes in town are found at the Rathaus restaurant and coffee shop, and the town square is a great place for making pictures or taking character shots of people caught up in the hustle and bustle of everyday life.

Our landlady asked about our plans for the day while serving breakfast and agreed that a trip up to Grossglockner through Gerlos Pass and Krimmer Falls would be a day well spent. The sun was brightly shining as we headed down the highway around mid-morning and turned south toward the Pass. The winding drive up to Krimmer Falls was beautiful, and we could see the falls after we crested the mountain and started our descent. John stopped to take pictures several times during the drive down into the valley where we were able to get a closer view. A couple of hours later, we were turning in the direction of the gigantic *Grossglockner,* which seemed to beckon us onward and upward as it offered us a wonderfully clear view when we finally arrived.

Drive to the Grossglockner in the Austrian Alps.

The Grossglockner Glacier, Austria.

It was rather costly to enter Hohe Tauern National Park for just a few hours, but it was well worth it since the network of roads, *Grossglockner Hochalpenstrasse*, takes you to the very heart of the largest national park in the European Alps with a nature conservation area of 1,080 square miles. It provides a beautiful panoramic drive for over 4 miles at altitudes of 7,200 feet and carries you far above Austria's longest glacier, *the Pasterze*. Built during the world's economic crisis between 1930 and 1935 by more than 3,000 workers, the project helped reduce the high level of unemployment and was very successful in providing entrance to the National Park. It was very cold in the higher altitudes, so we stopped at the *Glockner* restaurant for hot coffee and were happy to find *Sacher Tortes* on the menu. It was a perfect rest stop and we enjoyed the view and especially the tortes and hot coffee! Below the restaurant, we stopped to see *the Alpine Nature Show*, a great movie about the history of the building of the roads and the flora, fauna and geology. On the return trip to Hall, we stopped at a restaurant along the way and found another of our favorite Austrian foods listed on the dinner menu that evening, *Wiener Schnitzel with Spaetzel*.

After our adventurous drive to the Glacier, our landlady suggested that we might like to drive up to the top of the *Hinterhornelm*, a closer mountain with a nice restaurant and dairy farm on the summit. She had told us about it when we first arrived, but the heavy cloud cover kept us from going up at that time. Now it seemed to be clearing up a bit. So, around noon, we decided to go while we had the chance. We paid the entrance fee and started up the very narrow, rocky road as it crisscrossed higher and higher up the mountainside. After about half an hour of tedious driving, John wasn't sure we had enough gas to make it all the way to the top and back down again. We didn't expect the summit to be quite so high and the drive had become rather scary! Finally, as we almost reached the clouds and saw a place where we could safely turn around, John decided to take advantage of it and turn back. As we started our descent, we passed three bikers that we had passed on the way up. They smiled and waved as I took their picture. The drive was exciting and we got some great pictures in the sunlight, but we were glad when we finally made it safely down the steep mountain. We walked across the wooden bridge into Hall for another Erdbeere Torte only to find they were sold out, so we settled for an ice cream cone as we walked around the enchanting old town one last time before heading back across the bridge to our hotel. At dinner that evening, we told our Austrian landlady goodbye and promised to come back again someday. Then we prepared for our flight home the following morning from Innsbruck. We returned our rental car and boarded our small plane to Frankfurt where we had to move quickly between terminals to make our Lufthansa flight back to Riyadh. We arrived back in Riyadh around 8:30 pm.

Back at home in our villa, I started looking through some of John's books we brought over on Middle Eastern History. Some of the guys who worked for us were Muslim and some Hindu and one of them asked one day which religion we favored. Of course, they could tell by my Christian music that we were definitely Christian. They were always very respectful and asked about our family. Sometimes they would show me pictures of their mothers, sisters or girlfriends and it was obvious they were working in Saudi Arabia to send money home. Our flowers hadn't made it through the scorching summer sun and slowly started dying out in June, so I learned to cut them back early in May while they were still pretty. I knew they would miss the flowers, so I put them in large jars of water to leave with the TCN's downstairs for their room and also gave some to the guys at the gate to put in their guardhouse before John and I left on vacation.

Maria introduced me to Barbara and her husband, Matt, who led the Christian activities on our compound. Barbara taught Bible courses in a couple of the compounds, and Maria and I became her assistants that year. At the same time, I was trying to do some writing on our Apple II regarding my first attempt at writing this book. I had begun this venture back in Seattle and worked on it some during my second tour in Saudi Arabia, but, unfortunately, I was not quite ready for the project. First of all, I was spread out too thinly and lost my perspective with the births of our two grandchildren that year. A few years later, God wiped it off the hard drive entirely with lightning from a passing thunder storm which would force me to get a brand new start. Thank goodness I had saved my first manuscript with the chronological listing of facts, which helped considerably, but made for a pretty boring read. This particular year, however, besides being home in October for the birth of our second granddaughter, Jenny, I needed some quality time with Mother as she was growing old and needed me more than ever. What I really needed, though, where my book was concerned was a new perspective to weave in all the important things the first manuscript left out.

I was thankful for Maria and her family and for Matthew and Barbara, who had somehow arrived in Saudi Arabia at this particular time, when I desperately needed them to provide a meeting place to serve as *the church* while we were there. Barbara told me that Matt had quite a testimony of having been an accomplished American fighter pilot who experienced a mishap in the air while in training which sent his plane crashing into the ground breaking practically every bone in his body. While lying in his hospital bed recovering, he was brought to his *moment of truth* and became a devout Christian with a strong desire for the Ministry. Now he and Barb have a wonderful Christian family with four grown children all studying to make something meaningful of their lives and Matt pastors a large Christian church in the Northeast.

When their youngest daughter, Carol, came over at the end of the school year, something very significant happened when she and her mother went to the store for ice cream. She was wearing a dress covered by an abaya, and, when she exited the store, she heard *the Matawah*, the Saudi religious police, yell at the lady in front of her without her head covering to *"Cover!"* Automatically, the lady held up her abaya to cover her head and so did Carol, and, when Carol held up her abaya, it came up above her knees so you could see her legs. Of course, her father was arrested and not released until he signed a statement saying that he would keep his women covered. Matthew was finally released around midnight to drive his family home.

I never learned what happened to the ice cream, but this gave him an opportunity to witness to the other prisoners while he was in jail, and many of the nomads from the desert had never heard about Jesus. Matt would occasionally drive out to visit them in the desert, and, at times, I think he might have baptized some of them in our swimming pool.

Another dear friend, Josee, was in France visiting her mother when I first arrived and lived right across the street from us with her husband, Emory, who was a good friend of John's. They sometimes shared meals together while their two wives were away. When I went over to meet Josee to welcome her back to the compound, I told her that I was probably a descendant of the French because of my *Norman foot*. We laughed because her second toe didn't protrude out in front of her others like mine, and this was the only possible link I had to the Normans or the French. I fell in love with Josee right away because of her gentle nature, beautiful blue eyes and lovely smile, but we never could get our husbands together for dinner as we planned. Josee taught the ladies of our compound how to make *Crepes* by demonstrating the proper French technique. She allowed each of us to use her small, round *crepe pan* to follow her example and try to make one ourselves. They were very thin, and most of our first attempts were disastrous. Finally, each of us turned out a pretty good one, and we thought we had mastered the art of the French crepe making.

Harry and his wife, Sarah, lived around the corner, and we attended a large Birthday Party at their Villa which she gave to celebrate his 50th Birthday. Everyone was invited so there was a huge crowd! Harry worked with John as another attorney for the Saudi Arabian Air Force. One of the many dishes Sarah served was *Kugel*, a Classic Jewish dish of noodles, eggs, cottage cheese, sour cream and sugar with Graham cracker crumbs sprinkled on top. It was so good and quite easy and inexpensive to make. Years later, I would find the recipe for Kugel in <u>The Jewish Holiday Kitchen,</u> which another friend sent me after her visit just before John sold our condo at the Gulf.

Harry and Sarah joined us for a venture into town one evening for dinner at one of our favorite Arabic restaurants. We had been there several times before and had always enjoyed the well-prepared food. We had to sit in *the family section*, behind a very thin curtain separating the families from the majority of men. When it was time for us to leave and I got up to put on my abaya, it flew up into the air and hit a light fixture hanging from the ceiling.

Sparks flew out in all directions! And without thinking, I said, *Lord help me!* All of a sudden, several workers rushed over to ask if we were all right. One asked me, *"You Christian?"* I said yes, and they started telling me about miracles happening right there in Riyadh. I hope none of the Saudis overheard them, or it could have cost them their jobs...! The restaurant was soon closed and under renovation.

I learned the reason behind Josee's lengthy stay in France when it was revealed to us that her series of tests had come back *positive.* She had *cancer!* Josee would have to go back to France periodically for radiation and chemo. We were all saddened to learn the news, but, like Matt, she was drawn closer to God due to her circumstances. Barbara had prayed with Josee before she left for France with the fear of what might be causing her physical problems, and she accepted the Lord right away. The three of us, Barbara, Josee and I, all had lunch together in a downtown restaurant before we were scheduled to fly home in September. I was flying home for the birth of our second granddaughter, Jenny, and Josee was going home for more radiation and chemo. As she and I were saying our goodbyes standing in the street between our two houses, Josee looked up at me with those beautiful blue eyes and gave me a big smile as if to say don't worry about me, I'll be all right!... God is with me now.

Since Maggie was due the first of October, John planned on spending a couple of days of his vacation time in Ireland on our way to the States. We arrived in Mobile around the middle of September and called all the family to let them know we were home. Jim and Kathy were building a home in a suburb of Jackson, where Kathy had gone to school. She wanted Katie to have the same privileges she and her sisters had enjoyed growing up in a safe drug-free environment. Katie was very excited about the new house and wanted us to come and see it. They had sent us videos of the lot and the house in all its stages of development and now it was almost finished. They took Katie over to see *her house* every weekend, and the excited little Katie would run through the house from room to room and then hide in her closet until they found her. Then she would scream when they found her and run screaming through the house back to the front door, where she would start all over again. It was so cute! So first on our agenda, after visiting Mother, was to drive over to Jackson to see *Katie's house.* Next, we drove down to Baton Rouge to see Greg and Lorena and spent a couple of nights in a motel while we visited them in their apartment and took them out for dinner. However, this time we had to cut it short. Everyone was anxious about Maggie and knew we only had a short amount of time to get up there to be with her before the baby was born and for John to make it to Atlanta for his scheduled flight back to Riyadh.

When we finally got to Williamsburg, Maggie looked so cute and healthy in her maternity dresses, and Dave showed us all around the area, the hospital where the baby would be delivered and the gift shops where Maggie had worked until her last day the week before. Now she was ready to have a baby, and they were so excited! John took us to Olive Garden for Sunday dinner before we drove him down to Norfolk to catch his plane for Atlanta. Then he called us from the Atlanta airport to wish Maggie well before he took off on his flight back to Riyadh. Dave drove Maggie and me down to the James River to walk along the beach and look for shells and Indian relics. Dave found some sharp stones which he thought could have been used by the native Americans to scale fish and cut meat, which I brought back with me and still have in my rock collection. When we returned from our walk along the river, I left Maggie and Dave at their apartment to get a good night's sleep and gave them my motel room and telephone number, telling them to call me if anything started happening.

Of course, they didn't! Maggie said she started having what she thought might be labor pains that evening and Dave took her to the hospital. When I couldn't get her on the phone, I called the hospital to find that she had been admitted and drove over to find her in a hospital bed. Her labor pains persisted throughout the day, and Dave became the *ice man* giving her ice to hold in her mouth while I was the *cold rag lady* wringing out the wash cloth and wiping her forehead. She was so exhausted! And the doctor said that if she didn't give birth within a certain amount of time, he would perform a C- section. The three of us, Maggie, Dave and I, joined hands and I said a little prayer. All of a sudden, an older nurse came bursting into the room and told Maggie to turn on her side, then turn completely over in the opposite direction to the other side, and then quickly back again to the first side. It worked, the baby turned over and she was ready to be delivered. Her head had been upside down and wasn't able to come through. What a miracle! Our precious little granddaughter, Virginia, was born within minutes on October 3rd, 1994 and made her entrance with eyes wide open looking all around the room and actually looked each one of us in the eye. She was beautiful and had black hair like her Grammy at birth. I took pictures, and we all took turns holding and admiring her. Maggie was so tired she needed a good night's sleep, so I left early so she could get it.

The kind manager of the motel where I was staying agreed to charge me by the week, so I was able to drive over every day to spend time with Maggie and the baby. The first day Maggie came home with Jenny, Dave took a video of Maggie changing her diaper for the first time and me standing by giving directions. It was hilarious! I cooked a pot roast for dinner that first day with plenty of potatoes and carrots, and I rearranged Maggie's kitchen cabinets since Dave had arranged them from a man's point of view with all the pans on the top shelves and the dishes on the bottom. He was very kind when he noticed what I had done and said his mother would probably have done the same thing if she were living. A nurse stopped by to check Jenny every day for a week because she had a touch of yellow jaundice at birth and had to have a *blue light* over her bed for a few days. I noticed Dave sitting in the living room holding little Jenny in his lap for the longest time, just sitting there admiring her. He was a very proud daddy!

Amanda and Joanie drove up from Virginia Beach to visit with us at Wendy's, where we enjoyed an afternoon lunch and our short time just being together. Maggie had bundled up Jenny in a cute little white outfit Mother had made for her with a matching cap over her head, and she looked so cute sitting there in her car seat smiling at everyone. It was great to see Amanda and Joanie and to be with Maggie and the baby on their first outing. Jenny was doing well and wouldn't need the blue light anymore after another day or two. Then it was time for me to drive back to Mobile and spend some quality time with Mother before returning to Riyadh in November. This time I took back with me in my luggage ingredients which I couldn't find in the stores of Riyadh, such as pecans and chocolate chips, for making healthy oatmeal cookies for Christmas.

When I got back to Riyadh, I got into the Christmas spirit by making cookies and listening to my Christmas music. I gave some to the guys who worked on the compound with a Merry Christmas! I also gave some to Matt to take to his nomad friends out in the desert. John and I enjoyed attending the monthly Christian meetings held in one of the US assigned buildings downtown. Many Christians attended these dinners from all the compounds, and many of the TCN workers who served the food would sometimes hang around to watch the happenings and hear the wonderful spiritual songs and music. Before Matt and Barbara left Riyadh, they invited their Christian friends over for a special Sunday breakfast of Panini-style French toast filled with sliced fresh peaches and cream cheese served hot with warm maple syrup and lots of hot coffee. They were delicious! We were so blessed to have enjoyed this wonderful Sunday morning with such good Christian friends and such good food. Maria assisted Barb in the kitchen and actually prepared the French toast while Barbara served.

The following year 1995 was similar to 1994, although we got an earlier start in May to fly back to the States for John's home leave and got all the family together at the Gulf for Maggie to fly down with Jenny. She looked so cute in her little *watermelon outfit,* and we made loads of family pictures. We had to drive over to Jackson to see *Katie's house* again after they had moved in and made it their home, and, when we drove down to Baton Rouge to visit Greg and Lorena, they had some exciting news. They were very happy to announce that they were expecting our third grandchild the first of March. I had plenty of time to buy material to take back with me since I had everything I needed already over there to make Lorena a few maternity dresses. I could probably get them in the mail by mid-October. Greg was working at *Fast Track,* a fast-food hamburger carry-out just a block from their apartment, and they were both very happy about their expected arrival the end of February. Lorena got right to work preparing the nursery cutting out colorful material of animals and balloons to decorate the walls of the baby's room. She had learned to use the little *Elna* German sewing machine which I had given her, and she did a great job! The nursery was adorable!

CHAPTER THIRTY-ONE

The Last Homecoming
1996-1997

Since this was our *Grand Finale* and we were going back to DC to open a law office, John and I didn't expect to do much more traveling, so we planned our trip home to include some of the places we still wanted to visit before we settled down to a more permanent lifestyle. We had missed Spain entirely and promised ourselves that we would see Switzerland one more time, and, of course, we couldn't bypass Ireland! So, we planned our trip home through *Switzerland, Spain and Ireland* to spend about a week in each place. When we left the Phoenix compound around midnight on the evening of December 28th for the airport, we were amazed to find all the TCN workers of the compound lined up to shake our hands and wish us farewell as we boarded the bus. What a surprise! It was a very touching moment, and one we will never forget. Some of these guys who worked for us sent us Christmas cards the following year and wrote letters to let us know they made it safely back to their homes.

After boarding our plane around 2:45 am, we arrived in *Zurich* around dawn and headed straight for the train station where we purchased tickets for *Geneva* with stopovers in *Lucerne and Kandersteg*. The train ride to *Lucerne* was very beautiful through a winter wonderland of freshly fallen snow which continued falling throughout the day and night. John hailed a taxi to take us to *Hotel Balances*, located right in the heart of the city on beautiful *Lake Lucerne* with a fantastic view of *Chapel Bridge* and the historic chapel directly across from us. We had a fantastic view from our small balcony and the restaurant below where we sat to enjoy our meals. John had not brought his warm clothing to Saudi Arabia, so we had to venture out into the city to buy him a heavy jacket and some long-johns to keep him warm on the high slopes of *Switzerland*. He found the best winter jacket he ever owned in a Lucerne department store with gloves, hat and long-johns to keep his legs warm. We walked all over Lucerne that afternoon in the pristine snow to take our pictures, and then checked out of our hotel the following morning for our ride to the *Bahnhopf* to catch our train to Kandersteg.

A Swiss New Year

We checked our large suitcases all the way to *Geneva* and hand carried several small bags for our three-day stopover in *Kandersteg*. These we stashed away for the day in a locker at *Interlaken* while we boarded another train to *Lauterbrunnen*, where we took a cable car and cog train up to the small mountainside town of *Murren*, which we had visited on our first trip in 1983, in sight of the mighty high peaks of the *Eiger and Jungfrau*. We had lunch at *Hotel Edelweiss*, the restaurant we remembered from before, which seemed to be built over the edge of the mountainside with a drop off of thousands of feet. As I recall, we tried to order the same meal as before, *Schnitzel, Pomme Frites and a European salad*. Then it was time to return to *Interlaken* and resume our journey to *Kandersteg*. Again, John hailed a taxi to take us to *Hotel Bernerhof* where we had reservations for three nights. We tried to get reservations at Hotel Victoria where we had stayed on our first trip, but they had been booked for months for the Christmas and New Year holidays. We found out from our travel agent that they only take bookings for a week during this time of the year. He was lucky to find us a room anywhere in Kandersteg, so we requested to be as near Hotel Victoria as possible. We thought we could at least eat our meals there and find our way over to the cable car lift up to the mountain top and ski lodge as we had done before.

Hotel Bernerhof, Kandersteg, Switzerland.

It was after dark and rather late when we arrived at Hotel Bernerhof, so we decided to stay in our room and snack on the cheese and crackers we had brought with us from the plane. When we opened the drapes the following morning, we couldn't believe our eyes! There right in front of us, perfectly centered within the drapes, was the picture of the lovely *little Chapel in the Snow,* the same picture which John had taken in January 1983. The picture had turned out so beautifully, we used it as the cover of our Christmas tapes that year which we gave as Christmas presents. Our room was located in the center of the hotel on the second floor right above the restaurant. It was amazing! Of all the hotel rooms in Kandersteg, I wondered, what would be the chances of our getting this particular room at this particular time of the year when most of the hotels were filled to capacity? One in 2,000, I suppose! What a miracle!

"The Little Chapel in the Snow," Kandersteg.

With all the hustle and bustle going on all around us, we fell right in with the celebration of the Christmas holidays and bringing in the New Year. Our three days in Kandersteg were well spent walking the trails again and having hot chocolate at the top of our mountain within sight of the mighty Jungfrau. We walked about a block down the street to have most of our dinners in the small restaurant of *Hotel Victoria,* which served great entrées and a great European salad with many different kinds of desserts. Although it wasn't the formal dining room inside the hotel which we remembered, the food was excellent and we enjoyed it tremendously. However, we stayed in our hotel to enjoy the New Year's Eve celebration and the wonderful New Year's dinner downstairs in the dining room. Outside our window below us, we could enjoy the laughter and joy of the children playing in the snow and families riding down the street in horse-drawn carriages or sleighs with bells on the horses. It was a joyous time of year!

A Majestic Scene of Kandersteg taken from The Ski Lodge high in the Swiss Alps.

On January 2nd, we caught the train for *Geneva* and stopped off for lunch in *Gstaad* where we again enjoyed our favorite *Wiener Schnitzel and pommes frites.* After our arrival in Geneva, we caught a taxi to the

Chantilly Hotel where we had reservations for four nights and spent the afternoon walking around the city trying to find some of our favorite restaurants. Hotel l'Arbalete had been demolished and another building was going up in its place, but we did find *A la Diligence,* where they still served their fabulous *Pepper Steak* and *Chocolate Mousse.* The second day, we bought a pizza, fresh fruit and a bottle of Chianti to celebrate John's 60th birthday and rested up from our trip. I washed out a few clothes and dried them on the radiators to repack for Spain.

The remainder of our time in Geneva, we walked around the downtown area and found our way over to the Olde Town. We walked through the historic cathedral to take pictures from the bell tower and read the history below the statues of Luther and Calvin regarding the *Reformation of the Church.* For lunch, we discovered a new restaurant in the Olde Town and ordered their special of the day, *Roast Beef with Noodles and Asparagus.* The food was excellent, so we added that to our list of good restaurants and continued our walk along the Corniche where we decided to take a boat ride out on *Lake Geneva* before going back to our hotel. The next morning, we were up bright and early for our train ride around the lake to Montreux to spend the day in one of our favorite cities. The weather was cold and cloudy, but the sun came out long enough to make a few good pictures. We walked down to *the Castle at Chillon* and took pictures of the lovely gardens around the *Riviera Hotel.* Our plans for taking the cog train up to *Rochers de Naye* were not possible due to bad weather, so we had an early dinner at the hotel and caught the train back to Geneva.

The following day, the bad weather continued, but we managed to enjoy breakfast and lunch in the hotel. That afternoon, we walked down the block with our umbrellas to buy more fruit and noticed a pizzeria around the corner with an Italian sounding name, *il Fornello Napolitano,* which opened its doors around 7:00 pm, so we decided to go back that evening and give it a try. Again, we ventured down the block under our umbrellas to find this Italian Restaurant and were immediately impressed when the host took our hats and threw them on top of a huge pile of hats in the corner. Then he seated us as far away from the door as possible. As we puzzled over the menu trying to figure it out and asked questions, the waiter took our orders. Finally, we understood the seating arrangement when at precisely 8:00 pm, the doors flung open wide and customers began to flood in filling up all the tables and chairs in a matter of minutes. It was fun to watch! We ordered a large Pepperoni & Cheese pizza with a few other ingredients, the wonderful European salad and a bottle of Chianti as we sat there eating and absorbing this very unusual *Italian* atmosphere. We lingered a bit longer than usual and promised ourselves to find this place again someday. The food was great and the Italian atmosphere very *amusing* and *enchanting* all at the same time.

Back in our hotel room, we received a phone call from Ginger and Mike telling us that Mother was in the hospital and the doctors were trying to *balance her electrolytes*. We didn't really understand, but Ginger assured us that Mother was in good hands and there was nothing we could do at this time. She said Mother told her to tell us not to hurry home but to finish our trip, and she would be ready to go home when we got there. We packed our clothes and left the following morning for Spain.

A Tour of Spain

We ran into some very strong head winds off the Atlantic just as we were crossing the mountains and making our descent into Malaga around 2:40 pm. After landing and retrieving all our baggage, John left me guarding everything while he walked over to the rental car desk to find us a suitable automobile for the week. Luckily, he found an English gentleman who ran his own rental car agency and gave him a good deal on a Ford Fiesta. Pleased with our good fortune, we loaded all our baggage into the small car and drove to Malaga where we had a room reserved for the night. The hotel manager suggested that we unload our car and bring everything into the hotel because the crime was very bad. After unloading our car, we ventured out to find a good restaurant for dinner only to find that none of the good restaurants opened their doors for dinner until 8:00 pm. We had to settle on a Tapas bar, where we ordered a couple of small, prepared pizzas, which we warmed up in a microwave oven and bought soft drinks. It was not good, but it had to suffice for our first day in Spain because we missed lunch and were too hungry to wait for dinner at 8:00.

As we ventured out further that afternoon exploring the area, we happened upon an ancient Roman Theatre, *Alcazaba Teatro Romano*, where we paid our entrance fee and walked through these very interesting Roman ruins. We were delighted with its history and the view of the city of *Malaga* from the high vantage point. Then it was time to find our way back to our hotel and settle in for the night. Our rather old, but recently renovated hotel on an industrial harbor had a nice balcony overlooking the busy seaport where many ships were docked. John took some fantastic pictures of the harbor that evening and the next morning at dawn, which are very expressive of the excitement we were feeling our first morning in Spain. The scene from our seventh floor balcony overlooking the industrial harbor was very peaceful and serene. The hotel did not have a restaurant for dinner, but they did serve a continental breakfast and some very good coffee for which we were most appreciative. After breakfast, we walked around the immediate vicinity of our hotel taking pictures of the lovely orange trees which lined the streets and filled the courtyard of the church across the street. Then it was time to rush back to the hotel to load the car again before check out time.

Malaga Harbor, Spain: Morning View from our Hotel Balcony.

After learning of the high crime rate in Spain, we decided to look for a hotel where we could rent our room by the week to avoid the problem of loading and unloading the car for overnight stays while trying to enjoy our vacation. Finally, we were on our way driving westward along the beautiful *Costa del Sol* on our way to *Marbella,* where we hoped to be located right in the center of the places we wanted to visit. We selected *Hotel Marvella-Dinamar* because we liked the looks of the place and we wanted to get settled quickly in our room before sunset. John went inside to check out the prices and made a good deal for the entire week which came with a breakfast buffet and a formal dinner in the evening. We were pleased to find that our hotel was located just a few blocks from a Marbella port and shopping center, which contained a bank where we might cash in our traveler's checks, and other facilities.

Hotel Marvella-Dinamar Entrance, Puerto Banus, Marbella, Spain.

Our room was comfortably furnished with a nice large bathroom, a complete bedroom suite with two large Queen-sized beds, two chests of drawers and a dresser for storing our clothing and a large closet for hanging our clothes and jackets. It had a nice, large balcony with a fantastic view of the grounds and swimming pool. We made ourselves comfortable in the room and went downstairs to have dinner, which we ordered from the menu and was served in courses. We brought with us a book written by a noted travel guide whose very interesting travels we had watched for years on TV and whose tapes we had purchased over the years. This book would prove invaluable to us as we planned our itinerary to see this part of Europe through the back door of Spain, which as yet remained somewhat undiscovered. It was going to be a glorious vacation!

Morning at the Harbor of Puerto Banus.

After our breakfast buffet, we walked down to the port to check out what we could find and discovered many international restaurants, a bank and other places of interest. We also discovered about that time that we were staying just a few blocks from Puerto Banus. That first morning, we drove north up the Ronda road to explore *Andalusia's Route of the White Villages.* The hour and a half drive was beautiful and, at times, very dangerous as we drove higher and higher around one hairpin curve after another. We stopped for scenic views and a couple of times had a tremendous, but very distant, view of the Rock of Gibraltar. Finally, after crossing the largest part of the mountains, the land leveled out a bit into a gently rolling plateau. When we arrived at Ronda, we drove straight through the small town in search of the routes to other places on our list recommended by our travel guide. We couldn't seem to find the *Cork Forest* through which one could see the small hidden city of *Grazalema,* but we did find the entrance to the *Pileta Caves.* However, we couldn't see anyone available to show us the cave, so we decided to leave these two places for another day. This day was one of exploring the area and becoming familiar with the roads and the places we knew we wanted to see on our travel guide's list of the *back doors of Spain.* It was getting rather late in the afternoon and we were anxious to get back to our hotel before sundown so back down the Ronda road we went.

On Monday morning, we drove back up the Ronda road and actually found the Cork Forest and saw through the trees what we believed to be the white washed village of Grazalema as described in the book. We drove around the cork forest to find the entrance to the tiny village nestled between mountains and were enchanted by what we found. It was like a *Brigadoon of Spain*, which was only lit up by the sun during mid-day and was overshadowed the rest of the time due to its location between the mountains. It was certainly stuck away from the outside world, but it was a city in every conceivable way, and we took many pictures of the local people as they walked through.

Grazalema in the mountains of southern Spain.

Passing the Town Square in Grazalema.

John parked the car, and we walked down the main street of *Grazalema* breathing in its charm and beauty. It was a tranquil little town and it didn't need a lot of tourists to spoil its eloquence. There wasn't room for them anyway. It was time for lunch and we were cold, so we found a small restaurant which wasn't quite open, but a young man saw us from across the street and ran over to open the door and invite us in. He didn't speak English and we couldn't understand his Spanish, but he was very polite and tried very hard to please us by taking our orders. The restaurant was colorfully decorated with a large, cozy fireplace and tastefully furnished with many tables covered with blue and white checkered tablecloths and matching blue napkins. They were obviously ready for the evening dinner crowd but opened up for lunch just for us. John ordered *Grilled Garlic Shrimp* with an appetizer of *Charizo Sausage*, and I ordered *Tuna Salad*, which turned out to be large chunks of tuna served on a bed of lettuce topped with a vinaigrette dressing, and, on the side, a large bowl of *Sopa Grazalema*. This soup was hot chicken broth drizzled with the broken yolk of an egg and served with a thick slice of French bread in the center. We each ordered a glass of white wine, and it was a moment to remember as we lingered in the small restaurant.

Then we walked around the lovely town again to drink in its beauty and take a few more pictures. John tried to capture its intricate features and some of the local color by including some of its people going about their daily business. It seemed to be getting late when we noticed the shadow of a mountain beginning to fall over Grazalema, so we decided it was time to head back down the Ronda road to make it back to the hotel before sunset. That evening, John and I enjoyed dinner in the hotel: *Pepper Steaks, spaetzel and creamed spinach.*

On Tuesday morning, it was raining so we drove down to the port to look for a bank to cash in some traveler's checks. This is when it dawned on us that this was "Puerto Banus," the world famous boat dock in which many of the large luxury liners of the rich and famous were docked. In fact, the Royal Family of Saudi Arabia had several luxury liners docked there and a few nearby villas, where they vacationed year-round. We decided to drive around Marbella to see what else we could find of interest in our proximity, and we made a very interesting discovery. Right there in Marbella on the coastal boardwalk we found *The Texas Bar & Grill,* blaring out American Country Music, *Deep in the Heart of Texas.* We decided to have lunch! Our Texas- size burgers were served with large stacks of crisp fried onion rings and french fries. That evening, we walked down to Puerto Banus and made a few pictures at sunset, then stopped in the Italian Restaurant for pizza and a glass of wine before returning to our hotel. We had developed a new flavor for the place we had selected in Marbella, and it was ideal for our desire to experience the exotic atmosphere of this area of Spain's Costa del Sol.

On Wednesday morning, the sun was shining brightly, so we got an early start for our next adventure up the Ronda road and across the mountain to *Arcos de la Frontera.* This time we by-passed Ronda and took a straighter route westward. Soon we saw our first sight of the ancient city sitting high on the escarpment before us and it grew larger and larger the closer we came until we were driving directly beneath the steep cliff of the city. Our road led us to the other side of the mountain where we turned up a very steep incline which would take us up into the city but it looked dangerous to John without being sure that this was the only way into the ancient city where we were to have lunch. He sent me walking up the steep incline to inquire! I couldn't find anyone on the street to speak English, so I entered a bank with a long line of people inside. Remembering my high school

Spanish, I asked, *"Habla usted Espanol?"* Everyone turned in my direction and said, *"Si, Si, Si!"*

Realizing my error, I tried again, *"Habla usted Englais?"* They all responded, *"No Englais."* Back on the street again, which was only *One Way* because there was only room enough for one car, I heard a voice coming from behind me, *"Hey lady, want a ride?"* It was John, of course. He finally mustered up the courage to drive straight up the steep incline to search for me, when he saw another car safely precede him all the way up with no problem. He noticed a young man at the top motioning him to come on up and turn right.

The City of Arcos de la Frontera, Spain.

The View from Arcos de la Frontera.

Our drive down the one road finally got us over to the scenic overlook where John parked the car and we walked through the old city looking for our restaurant. We found a very nice *Parador,* a place for visitors to stay overnight, right next door to the ancient cathedral. Finally, we found the entrance to *Hotel El Convento* on a side street and the *family-run restaurant,* recommended by our travel guide, right around the corner. We entered its arched doorway to find inside the restaurant long dining tables with smaller tables near the windows, all with nice clean tablecloths, cloth napkins and centerpieces of fresh flowers. We were finally able to sit down and relax as we studied the menu. Again, we followed his suggestions and ordered *"the house special"*: Garlic Roast Beef cooked with carrots and cauliflower in a rich beef broth and served with salad, bread and wine with a delicious vanilla cream dessert. The food was very well prepared and well served, and it was exceptionally good. We enjoyed the relaxed atmosphere and lingered over dessert and coffee. We hated to leave and thought we had found another place we must come back to someday, spend the night at the Parador and eat in this wonderful restaurant. However, we had to get back down the Ronda road to make it back across the mountains to Marbella before sunset. Since we already had such a wonderful dinner, we skipped dinner at the hotel and settled on cheese, crackers and fruit.

The Alhambra, Grenada, Spain.

After breakfast Thursday morning, we got an early start on our drive to *Granada* to see the famous *Muslim fortress of Alhambra*, built high above the city during the 9th Century. After driving north from Marbella through rain, we turned east and ran into sunshine just about the time we arrived in Granada. We found the ancient fortress, parked the car, and walked up a long sidewalk through lovely gardens into the magnificent structure built with Arabic architecture and a reddish hue, from which the fortress gets its name. *The Alhambra* was very impressive throughout with its intricate design and bold structure high above Granada. We were able to buy a very nice book inside the entrance which came in very handy as we found our way around and contains many beautiful pictures of the fortress and the city of Granada below.

Some places were inaccessible, or under renovation at the time we were there, but the book is very informative and gives the whole history of Alhambra and its many transitions over the years, including the *Spanish Inquisition* when the Muslims were expelled from Spain. We made many pictures inside and outside the fortress and of the many cats which live there to guard it from rodents. From the magnificent terrace of the fortress, we took many pictures of the city of Granada all spread out below. The tile rooftops of the buildings of Granada were of various hues of red, brown, and ochre and they, too, were very impressive. From the terrace, we tried to figure out the city center, the residential areas and other places of interest. On our way out, we walked down to *Hotel Alhambra,* just outside the fortress where we had parked the car, and decided to take a chance on dinner at the hotel. It was very good: *Pepper Steaks with mashed potatoes and steamed cauliflower, and Cream Caramel for dessert.* We drove back through the rolling hills down to the *Costa del Sol,* stopping briefly to take pictures of the gorgeous sunset. Both of us were able to get some very artistic shots before getting back on the main road to Marbella. Again, after a long day, we skipped dinner in the hotel and snacked on fresh fruit, cheese and crackers.

Near the Top of The Rock of Gibraltar.

After a hearty breakfast buffet early Friday morning, we were ready for our English-speaking bus tour of the *Rock of Gibraltar.* We had signed up for this tour a few days earlier because it was the only tour available for Gibraltar, and we didn't want to miss it. We were prepared for this bus-full of British vacationers and ex-pats, and content to enjoy the music and their wonderful witty British humor. It was quite an experience and we loved it! With all of John's recent driving, he was finally able to just sit back and enjoy the scenery as we drove along the coastline and approached *the Rock*, which became larger and larger until it was completely out of sight as we turned into the parking lot. We disembarked on *British soil* and boarded a smaller bus, which took us through the streets of Gibraltar and up and around the mountain to the *upper Rock*. From this high vantage point, we could see the faint *shoreline of Morocco* on the other side of the *Mediterranean Sea* with its isthmus jutting out from *Tangier*. We learned that, like in Holland, some of the land below was reclaimed from the sea, which highly increased its territory for the city and the expanded seaport of Gibraltar.

As one looks upward from the bottom level, the roads above are hidden from view, due to so much foliage on both sides of the mountain, and the Rock at the top of Gibraltar cannot be seen. However, from the top of the mountain below the Rock looking downward, the world below looks very minute with many ships and boats transiting the waters of the seaport, but the port itself cannot be seen. On the trip back down, we stopped twice: once to have a tour of *St. Michael's Cave* and once to see the world-famous *Rock of Apes*, a species of tailless monkeys there to greet us on the mountainside. John took a picture of me hanging over the rocky ledge to get a picture of a mother with a baby hanging on to the top of her head as she climbed up the steep ledge. Needless to say, we got more pictures of the monkeys than anything else.

I must, however, write something more about St. Michael's Cave, which was a very interesting place to visit and has a long history of its explorers and some who were never seen again. It consists of an *upper hall* connected with five passages, with drops of between 30 feet and 150 feet to a *smaller hall*. Beyond this point a series of narrow holes leads to a further succession of chambers, reaching a depth of some 250 feet below the entrance of the cave. Special guided tours to the smaller hall of St. Michael's Cave can be arranged by the Gibraltar Tourist Board. Our short stop didn't do it justice, and, in the 1960's, the *upper chamber*, now known as *Cathedral Cave*, was opened to tourists and serves as a theatre with a seating capacity of 400. It makes a unique auditorium for concerts, ballet and drama and can be hired for use through the Gibraltar Tourist Board. A fallen stalagmite, which fell thousands of years ago, now lies on its side cemented through the years by nature to the floor of the cave. A slice of the top portion was cut off in 1792 to reveal the interior structure of the stalagmite in a most dramatic way: Periods of heavy rainfall, light rain and glacier activity can be determined by the coloration of its rings of development, which are also partly translucent. To visitors, this centuries old stalagmite exhibits the unique beauty of crystallized nature.

Back in the old town at the bottom of the first tier, our bus dropped us off for a couple of hours to find a restaurant for lunch and shop around for souvenirs. John and I walked through the old town looking for a place *with atmosphere.* We finally found one in a remote area, which turned out to be an excellent choice, *Meson La Bodega de Gilbert,* which provided us both with great seafood dinners: fresh fish for me and a seafood platter for John, with Crème Caramel for dessert. Then it was time to find our bus, exit the city gate and prepare for the long drive back to Marbella. Again, we enjoyed the great British wit and humor in the videos they showed us on the way back.

The Welcoming Committee.

Scene of the Rock of Gibraltar Harbor.

We arrived back in Marbella around 4:00 pm and decided to walk down to Puerto Banus to get more pictures of the port at sunset and try the Italian food at *Restaurant de Paulo*. We ordered a large pizza, salad and two glasses of Chianti. The pizza was fantastic, and we lingered a while to enjoy the wonderful atmosphere and the beautiful sunset. After our long day, we needed the rest before walking the several long blocks back to our hotel. By this time, it was dark and we noticed the street lights were out along the main street leading into Puerto Banus as well as a few of the buildings lining the street. We passed a parked car with two men inside, just sitting there smoking, as we leisurely walked by, turning at the corner onto a side street, and then again onto another side street, on our way back to the hotel. We heard footsteps ... and then running and a shout by one of the men to the other, as if they lost pursuit of their targets.

John had become suspicious when he first saw them, and led us over an extra side street in the dark where they obviously lost track of us. He was holding a camera strap in each hand of our two cameras and was ready to use them as weapons if necessary. When we came out of the darkness into the light of a building, we pretended to be looking at the ads in the window as one of the guys casually walked by and entered our hotel. Then we walked in the front door and over to the lobby, where we pretended to be reading the list of available upcoming tours. We didn't see him inside the lobby until we passed by the pool room on our way to the elevator, and there we saw him, scuffling around as if he were setting up a game on the pool table. We walked on by him to the elevator and John pushed the button for the 2nd floor.

The Hallway to the Elevator at
Hotel Marvella-Dinamar.

We got off on the 2nd floor and ran up the steps to the 3rd floor. At the same time, we could hear him running up the steps to the 2nd floor. Quickly, we entered our room half-way down the hallway of the 3rd floor and closed the door. Since it was off-season, only a few rooms were occupied and most of them were on the 3rd floor. John told me to listen for his code by the number of knocks on the door, so I could identify him and let him back in. Then John stepped out into the hallway and saw the man coming around the corner.

When he saw John standing there looking for him, he stopped in his tracks and turned back around the corner and disappeared. That night we took every precaution to secure our room and fortify the balcony doors which did not lock securely for some reason. We did this with the empty drawers from the chests in our room, and John actually slept that night sitting up in bed with his camera weapons available just in case anyone tried to break in. The following morning, he stopped by the desk to report the incident to the hotel manager and gave him a full description of our would-be robber, but we never heard anything more about it.

As a precautionary measure the next day, we took our valuables with us and locked them in the glove compartment where we could keep better watch over them while we continued our last day adventures from Marbella. We drove back over to the vicinity of Grazalema and down the road to *Pileta Caverns.* This time we arrived early and parked the car to look down into the valley below where the cave owners lived and operated a small sheep farm. After several cars had accumulated, a young man came up from the farm house below to open the door to the cave. We were permitted to take pictures of the entrance and the steps leading up to it, but pictures were not allowed inside. The guide and a couple of the men in our group carried lanterns to light our way through the caverns which took about 45 minutes, as our young guide explained the very interesting history of Pileta Caves, which dates back thousands of years. These natural caverns, he explained, rich in beautiful stalagmite and stalactite formations, pools of water and pictures drawn on the walls by ancient cave dwellers in charcoal and other natural pigments, must be preserved for future generations. Therefore, no pictures are permitted inside the cave.

We made a picture of our young guide at the entrance, whose great, great, great grandfather had discovered the cave over a hundred years earlier when he bought the land to use as a sheep farm. And so it is in use today by his descendants, as a sheep farm. The ancient caverns were discovered some time later by members of his family who lived on the farm and tended the sheep. After telling him how much we enjoyed the tour of these very exciting caverns with so much history, we took his picture standing there at the entrance, waved goodbye and drove away with a great feeling of accomplishment. It would have been a terrible shame to have missed this wonderful adventure, which truly was the icing on the cake of our one visit to Spain. Then it was time to hit the Ronda road again, sadly for the last time, to drive back to Marbella for our last afternoon at beautiful Puerto Banus to try to capture its essence on film.

Puerto Banus, the Harbor at Sunset.

We spent our last evening in the exciting atmosphere of the Italian Restaurant De Paulo on the corner of the long line of international restaurants which lined Puerto Banus. This time, however, John parked our car directly in front of the restaurant. He ordered Chianti for us both and his usual pizza, *Quattro Staggioni, bread sticks and two salads.* I ordered *Lasagna.* After lingering with our wine and pizza, we lingered a while longer with our delicious *Strawberry Tortes and coffee.* Then we walked down the long line of restaurants overlooking the water with all its different sized boats containing names of all nationalities and watched the fish swimming in the water directly below us as they were drawn to the lights and lingered there hardly moving at all. We had fallen in love with another enchanting country and were saddened about having to leave the following morning knowing there was so much more of Spain remaining to be seen and its next-door neighbor, Portugal. We would have to come back again someday to see them both more thoroughly. On this particular evening, though, our last evening in Marbella, we took pictures of the beautiful sunset and lingered a while longer to say goodbye.

As we were leaving our hotel the following morning, we took pictures of the large, beautiful poinsettias in the courtyard, which grew in abundance and bloomed year round due to the agreeable climate. We drove back along the Costa del Sol to Malaga and returned our rental car before boarding our plane for Dublin.

A Short Visit to Ireland

We arrived in Dublin on Sunday and rented a car to drive to Howth where we spent two nights at our favorite B&B in the Dublin area, where we always had a wonderful full Irish breakfast with home-made Irish soda bread. Over the years, we had come to know the owner and her lovely family who started her B&B when she lost her husband many years earlier and found running a B&B for vacationers to be a good means of support for herself and her three children. Now her fine Irish Catholic family are grown and help her keep it going, but she continues making her delicious Irish soda bread a couple of times each week. Her son now prepares breakfast for all their guests.

We drove straight across Ireland to Killarney and stayed three nights there at our favorite B&B, so John could play his favorite golf courses. He also drove us around Dingle and the ring of Kerry as he usually did while we were visiting Killarney. Then we drove to Ennis where we spent the night at the Ennis Hotel to repack for the long flight home. As our plane backed out of the Shannon airport parking gate and headed out to the runway, we noticed two fire trucks lined up to spray water from their hoses in an archway over our plane. We heard over the intercom the announcement of the final flight of our pilot, the Delta Captain, who was retiring from Delta Airlines after 35 years of service. All the members of his family were on board to celebrate his retirement. We felt that somehow this celebration was meant for us, too, since it was our last flight home from our last job in Saudi Arabia. And so, we claimed it as well!

Mother, who had been in the hospital since the first of January, had come through her illness and was now stabilized and ready for us to take her home. Joseph and Erin met us at the airport and drove us directly to the Rehab Center where Mother was ready to be discharged. Michael and Ginger were there with Mother and her doctor when we arrived. John and I were tired and worn out from our series of trips, and Mother looked so cute and relaxed lying there fully dressed on top of her freshly made bed. It looked like she was smoking a pipe with the steam coming up around her head. Of course, Mother had never smoked anything in her life. She was inhaling mist to put moisture back into her lungs, but it looked like she was smoking a water pipe. Before the doctor released her, he asked, *"Mrs. G., if I send a video home with you, will you watch it?"* She responded, lying there on her bed with mist coming up all around her head, *"I just want to go home and watch 'The Young and the Restless.'"* Everyone had to laugh because Mother would turn 91 at the end of the month.

CHAPTER THIRTY-TWO

The DC Law Practice
1996-2000

Mother was happy to be home again where she could sleep in her own bed, watch television and resume her life as usual, and we were happy to be there to help her. Her neighbors came over to welcome her home, and everyone was glad to see her looking as well as she did after several weeks in the hospital. Mother's doctor set up an appointment for Michael and me to come in and speak with him about Mother's health and what we might expect over the months ahead. Confidentially, he told us that she was dying of a congested heart and might not make it through the year. He told us to live our lives as normally as possible, and no matter what we did or didn't do for her, not to allow ourselves to feel guilty because death is a natural part of life. Mainly, she needed to feel the stability of our love to be happy and feel secure. I planned to be with Mother as long as I could because I thought she needed me and wanted me to be there for her.

After the first month of resting up from our long journey home and getting Mother resettled, John was getting anxious to get back to work. He needed to get his law practice started and planned a trip up to northern Virginia to find a temporary office in DC where he could get established with a professional address. John made a reservation for us at the Holiday Inn for a few days while searching out the possibilities for an apartment. Within a few days, he found the perfect business organization within the District, which provided him with a DC address and private telephone number with answering service. This would enable him to get started with his law practice while we were still staying with Mother. It would also provide him with the use of a conference room for meetings and would suffice even after we were more settled in northern Virginia. We looked around Crystal City for an apartment with easy access to DC and the underground Metro system. We discovered a new high- rise apartment building with a fantastic view of the Jefferson Memorial and overlooking

National Airport. We were put on the waiting list for a small two-bedroom apartment at Crystal Place.

After accomplishing what we came up to do and were getting ready to leave, we received a phone call from Lorena's father in Mexico congratulating us on the birth of our *joint grandson*! We were anticipating the birth of the baby, but his call took us quite by surprise! Joshua was born on the 29th of February. How typical of Greg to be the father of a *Leap Year* baby! Nothing he ever did was *ordinary*, and it was certainly a date we would remember. We were thrilled about the birth of our only grandson and were happy to hear that Lorena and baby Joshua were doing fine. We were anxious to see him, so we quickly packed up our things and got on the road back to Alabama. We informed all the family about the birth of baby Josh and planned to see him as soon as possible. He was so cute and cuddly! And so full of energy! Finally, we got to hold him in our arms and talk to him. Little Josh was adorable!

When John and I finally got back to Mobile, Mother was feeling so well, she invited all the family over for Sunday dinner, as she had done in her younger years. She made out her grocery list, and I took her to the store to shop for a beautiful beef roast. She held on to the grocery cart using it as a *walker*, and we slowly moved through the store getting all the things she needed. Mother was up bright and early Sunday morning to start cooking her pot roast in her big iron Dutch oven with a little garlic and covered with onions, which made her beef gravy so good. When Erin and Ginger arrived around noon, they always pitched in to help by filling the iced tea glasses, getting the food on the table and the dessert ready to serve. We always enjoyed these family get-togethers around Mother's dining table with the beautiful view of Mobile Bay and the city in the far distance. It was like old times being together again enjoying one of Mother's delicious Sunday dinners and our conversation around the dinner table.

Mother often told us stories about the early days of life with Daddy when they were first married and many stories she remembered of her days as a young girl and playing her clarinet with the band during *the Roaring Twenties*. When she was 15, her mother, father and five children made their first trip back to Wisconsin to visit their relatives, and she had many stories to tell about that. It took them over a week to get there over two-lane dirt roads, with many stops along the way and overnights at campgrounds. My grandfather had built a storage cabinet on the side of their automobile to hold all their canned goods, which they opened and cooked over camp fires at the various campsites. It was the way everyone had to travel in those days by automobile, and they had no weather reports to inform them of bad weather ahead. One night, while they were trying to sleep at a campground, she thought a hurricane passed over them as they tried desperately to hold onto a tent which covered the car in which my grandmother and baby Charles were sleeping. They were all drenched and nobody got any sleep that night! I would write Mother's story about this trip from the notes she took in her diary as they made each leg of their journey. The roads were terribly muddy at times and they had to stop many times to *visit Mrs. Murphy* along the way. But one story she told which *kept us in stitches,* which I wish we could have gotten on tape, was about a trip up the mountain with my dad to buy a load of coal. She had a wonderful sense of humor and a great laugh! I'll try to remember how it went:

[In the 1930's, people burned coal in small furnaces, usually located in the center of the house, to keep warm during the cold winters. During the fall of their first year of marriage, my dad drove Mother and a friend up the mountain to get a load of coal in his roadster with a rumble seat in back. They loaded the whole back end of the car and the rumble seat and started the trip back down. Their friend, John Henry, had to hop on the running board because there was no room for him in the car. Well, the brakes gave way about halfway down the mountain and they started picking up speed when they noticed a train coming along the bottom of the hill. They would be crossing the tracks just about the time the train would be crossing the road. It was going to be a harrowing experience for everyone, especially the man on the running board, who was holding on for dear life! Mother said they were all scared to death and all my dad could do, as they approached the bottom of the hill and the on-coming train, was to make a sharp turn to ride alongside the train until the car came to a stop. When it did, he told his friend, *"Hop back on, and I'll give you a ride home."* John Henry responded, *"No thanks! I think I'll walk!"*]

[A cartoon caricature of this story was published in a magazine of the Pullman-Standard Car Manufacturing Company, Bessemer, AL, where my father worked in the 1940's, when they were making airplanes out of scraps of metal and crushed tin cans from households all over our Country during their combined contribution to the war effort of WWII.]

John sent out his announcements for the opening of his Law Office in the spring of 1996, and sometime in April, Ginger and I took Mother to look at an independent living facility in Mobile where she would have a private room, good supervision and good meals in the dining room. Ginger and Mike thought it would be a good place for Mother because she was an outgoing person and would enjoy the companionship of other people. They offered many activities and bus trips to wherever she needed to go. However, after what the doctor had shared with Michael and me, I questioned whether this was best for her because she loved her home and wanted to stay there. We thought she liked this place, but, after we left, she made it very clear that she didn't want to move away from her house. Her only comment was, *"There's nothin' there but old people."* Mother was not going to move away from her home -- and that was that!

Towards the end of May, after spending a few days at the Gulf fulfilling our condo rental agreement, John drove us up to Crystal City to move into our new apartment. It was tiny and we had wall to wall furniture, but at least he had all the operational privileges of a DC law office. We loved the view from our balcony and our proximity to the rest of Northern Virginia and Washington via subway. Our master bedroom was large enough to accommodate our five-piece rattan bedroom suite with small table and chairs, but the second small bedroom would have to serve as the law office for John to get started with his practice. We purchased a metal storage cabinet which fit snugly into the small closet to hold all our supplies and writing materials. John purchased a large filing cabinet and two work stations so we could both do our jobs as lawyer and secretary to keep up with all the incoming correspondence and phone calls. He ordered his very nice letterhead stationery and we proceeded to get to work establishing a business. When we were finished, John had all the amenities of a professional law office with the use of the conference room downtown in the District and the professional answering service, which relayed all his telephone calls and messages to the phone in our office. If we were away from the office, he could call in from anywhere in the world to get his messages and return his calls. It seemed like a perfect setup.

With nowhere to put our guests if we should have any, we invested in a double bed blow-up mattress for John and me to sleep on, which fit nicely into the floor space of our office. Our living room-dining area was so crowded with furniture I broke my toe for the second time bumping into things, but our small kitchen was very sufficient for our needs with a convenient counter space for moving food across it into our dining room. All our excessive boxes would be placed in large storage bins downstairs in the basement, which helped us clear out the small apartment to make room for all the office equipment. Eventually Maggie and Dave were able to borrow his brother's truck to drive up to get her queen-sized bed and chest of drawers, which we had purchased for her in Frankfurt. We had a wonderful visit with Maggie, Dave and Jenny when they came up for a couple of days to get the furniture, and John and I were able to try out the air-mattress for the first time. It worked!

Jenny was going on three, and so adorable! She seemed to take to John and me immediately after not seeing us for a long while. Her granddaddy showed her the train which passed below our balcony, and, when she heard it coming, she would run to him with her arms up so he could hold her up to see it pass on the tracks below. She talked to John asking him all sorts of questions, and she understood and remembered everything we said. The airplane path into National Airport also passed nearby and that also was a big attraction which prompted more questions. There was just so much little Jenny wanted to know, and her granddaddy loved telling her about all these things. She already knew the alphabet and could practically read, or recite, "*The Cat in the Hat*" books. Jenny was exceptionally bright!

Jenny also showed an interest in the *grandfather clock* standing in the small entrance way to our living room, and John explained that it didn't work because a very important part was missing, which of course, prompted more questions. He finally told her that we had to find the missing part before we could get it fixed, and we had to get it fixed before we could move again. Jenny remembered that and every time we talked about moving the next few months, she would say, "*But first, you have to get the clock fixed!*" It was adorable! And she never failed to say it. I had made a pumpkin pie for Thanksgiving, and Maggie expressed concern that she didn't know if Jenny would like it because she had never tasted pumpkin pie. I gave her a taste of it, and she shouted out in a very loud voice, "*I DO like pumpkin pie!*" She was so cute! When it was time for them to leave and we were passing down the hallway to the elevator, Maggie told talkative little Jenny to *shush* so we wouldn't disturb the people who lived in the other apartments. Jenny became terribly upset that other people lived in our apartment building, too, and exclaimed again in her very loud little voice, "*No! Just Mamama and Dadada!*" Even though our apartment was very small, it must have seemed to Jenny at the very young age of two that the whole building belonged to us.

Eventually, we were able to see Maria and Mark, who had kept their home in Maryland and rented it out while they were in Saudi Arabia. They had come back to the States when Mark entered Law School, and, when they heard we were back in the Washington area, they invited us over for dinner one Sunday afternoon. Maria served a wonderful baked chicken dinner, which we enjoyed tremendously as we chatted around the dinner table. Their second son, Jonah, born after they returned to the States, was about three, and we couldn't believe how much Beth and Benjamin had grown. Maria was very active in her church and told me about their new on-going projects. We invited them over to our apartment to watch the Washington Fourth of July Fireworks on the Mall, and, as always, they were spectacular!

I had hoped to get back to Mobile to be with Mother before the end of August. I knew she needed me and I talked to her every day on the phone, but a broken toe and a few other circumstances regarding the law office and out of town guests prevented me from going down during the summer. Besides trying to get the law practice started with potential clients and setting up a filing system, John bought us *season tickets for Wolf Trap and the Kennedy Center.* Then I made the mistake of wearing my lowest heels too soon and my toe suffered a setback. Occasionally, we would attend a concert or dinner theatre, but usually, our favorite pass-time was to walk across the street to the *Underground* to have chicken tacos at The San Antonio Grill. They had the most delicious shredded chicken kept hot in their taco stand for putting our tacos together ourselves the way we like them with all the condiments, freshly prepared on the side. These came free with our purchase of a dinner or margarita. They also made a great Chili Relleno which was well worth the price of dinner.

John had half a dozen great possibilities as clients to start with, and, at times, it seemed like we were starting to build a practice. However, nothing really seemed to get off the ground, but he had a lot of *pro bono* work to do for friends and some he was very glad to do for the *National League of Families, which dealt with the POW/MIA issues* from Vietnam. However, all his possibilities seemed to be just that – *possibilities* – with a lot of wasted time and effort. One of the good ones, which eventually fell through, was an opportunity to serve as financial coordinator to an internationally known architectural firm to find investors to back *a Unity House Redevelopment Project in Stoke-on-Trent, England.* It was a beautifully designed complex of hotels, a large shopping center, theatres, and other facilities designed by my brother Franklin and his architectural firm in Houston, but before they could get the financial backing, the city council sold the project to an English land developer. Another possibility was *African Fisheries,* which operated a fleet of fishing vessels off the coast of Africa. It could have been very profitable if successful, but it didn't get off the ground either. John had a few other cases, which he didn't feel had enough merit for him to represent in Court.

So many things came up to interfere with my plan of going home that summer. I knew Mother needed me, and she would ask me over the phone, *"Libby, when are you coming?"* I called her every day and remembered her in my prayers, but I never could seem to get away. John was busy with prospective clients and Aunt Grace and Uncle George were planning to come in October. John and I finally made it home the first week of November, and Mother was so glad to see me she gave me her biggest hug ever. We got home just in time to take her to visit my cousin, Edward, who I hadn't seen in years and was dying of *Mesothelioma,* a disease he acquired from working with asbestos in Florida as a volunteer to clean up after Hurricane Andrew. We escorted Mother to attend the visitation, which was held the following week at a Mobile funeral home. All our relatives and some of my old friends were there, and it was greatly attended by many people I didn't know. It was a terrible shame for this handsome young man to be taken from his lovely wife and two children in the prime of his life.

Mother seemed to be doing well for about two weeks, and then she became sick again, and John and I drove her back to the hospital. We were able to see Jimmy, Kathy and Katie for a day in Jackson and drive down to Baton Rouge to pick up Greg, Lorena and Josh to bring them to Mobile to visit Mother in the hospital. She had never seen her nine-month old great grandson, Joshua, so we brought them to Mobile for a few days and sat Josh on the side of her hospital bed just as I had placed Maggie on my grandmother's bed when she was in the hospital. Then, John and I drove Greg, Lorena and Josh back home and helped them buy a car in Baton Rouge. We also had to get the car registered and teach Lorena how to drive it before we left them there with the new car. Mother was expecting me to come back for my birthday party in her room and had Ginger buy a small birthday cake. I felt so bad about not making it back in time, and, by the time we got back, she had been released to go home with Ginger and Michael for Thanksgiving. I was very thankful to be there with Mother to share our last Thanksgiving Dinner together and help her with eating her food. Then she had trouble trying to keep it down and was still very ill the following day when Ginger and Mike took her back to the hospital.

John was busy loading the car with our winter clothing to take back to northern Virginia for the cold winter which was on its way, but I wanted to stay with Mother. Ginger insisted that I go with John as planned, so I decided to drive on up with him and fly back the following week after putting away all our clothes. On our way out of Mobile, we stopped by the hospital to say goodbye to Mother, and I kissed her goodbye on the forehead as I told her I would be back the following week. I had her bed and house all ready for her to come home just as she wanted, and I planned to stay with her for as long as she needed me. But, as usual, my plan was delayed again until after Christmas due to obligations for the holidays, and Mother was released back to the Rehab facility. I hoped to bring Maggie and Jenny back with me the first of January for a visit and bring Mother back to her house and her own bed. This time, I thought, John could manage by himself. I would stay with Mother as long as she needed me and put Maggie and Jenny on the plane back to Virginia when they needed to fly home.

One of our obligations for which we had a special invitation was to the home of COL Larry Thompson for his Christmas party. He and his wonderful wife, Laura, had been so kind to us while John was in training as a FAO student in Morocco, and John didn't want to miss this opportunity of seeing COL Thompson again. He had put John at the top of his list as the best FAO he ever had coming through the program. The US Ambassador to Morocco and his lovely wife were also there at the Christmas party, and I was greatly privileged to sit and chat with Mrs. Neuman most of the evening. She, of course, didn't remember me, but I reminded her of the wonderful baked salmon dinner they had served back in 1976 to an embassy crowd of about two dozen Americans. They did this quarterly each year to give all the US citizens an opportunity of being invited to the Ambassador's home for dinner. I also told her how much we enjoyed the wonderful Baked Alaska, which was passed around the long dinner table until it was totally consumed by all the guests. It was all so delicious and truly an evening to remember!

John and I drove down to Williamsburg Christmas Eve to be with Maggie, Dave and Jenny, and I remember reading *The Night before Christmas* to Jenny before she fell asleep and they put her into bed. Michael and Ginger brought Mother over to their house that Wednesday afternoon, so she would be with them and the rest of their family for Christmas Day. She died early Christmas morning while John and I were spending the night in a Williamsburg motel. Ginger said Mother was having a hard time getting to sleep that night, so Michael stayed up doing some work in a nearby room. Ginger stayed with her until she couldn't stay awake any longer and knew she had to get some sleep before the long day ahead when all the family were expected for Christmas Dinner. Michael called around mid-morning to tell us of Mother's passing during the night. I had awakened in the motel room where we were staying, and Kathy said Katie woke up about the same time and said a butterfly tickled her on the cheek. We wondered if it's possible for the spirits of people, in passing from their earthly bodies, to visit their loved ones on their way out of this world into heaven?

John and I enjoyed Christmas morning with Maggie and Dave watching Jenny find her presents and empty her stocking before handing out all the gifts under the tree. Jenny would hand the remaining gifts to her mom, and Maggie would hand them out to the rest of us while we all enjoyed the aroma of the delicious Christmas turkey cooking in the oven. We had gone through all the gifts and had breakfast when we received the phone call from Michael. We were glad we were all together there with Maggie, Dave and Jenny to receive the sad news that Christmas morning. After dinner, John and I had to drive back to Washington to prepare for our trip down to Mobile for Mother's funeral. Ginger did a great job making all the arrangements with her Methodist Church and she picked out her burial outfit. I think she had already been over some of these things with Mother in making preparations because they knew the time was getting close. At the same time, Ginger had to get herself and her family ready for the funeral. I had left one of my suits in Mother's closet and a suit for John. We arrived within a couple of days and the weather was unusually warm for the end of December. The ceremony was beautiful, and Mother would have been proud to see all our relatives from Houston to northern Virginia congregated there in her Methodist Church for the service and then her burial next to our dad in a Mobile cemetery where she had him and his first wife moved from one of the old cemeteries in Mobile.

I felt badly for not having been with Mother during her last days, but I knew her suffering was over and now she was with the Lord in a much better place. She had lived a good, long life, and I knew she loved God and had always been a faithful Christian. I sensed the celebration going on in heaven with all her family members who she hadn't seen for such a long time. Mother, the oldest of all her siblings, was the last one to make the journey except for her youngest brother, Charles, better known to me as *Uncle Charlie*, who followed her a few years later. Ginger touched Mother's beautiful clump of bouncy white hair above her forehead, and I couldn't resist the temptation to follow suit in my poor attempt to say goodbye. I knew Mother was no longer there in her broken body. She was in heaven in her new heavenly body with the Lord and all her family members who had gone on before her. I remembered what Mother once told me about the death of my great grandmother, whose relatives came over from England around 1850. According to my grandmother, her mother, who died at a ripe old age, sat up straight on her deathbed, looked up as though she were looking into heaven itself and said *"Glory to God in the heavens,"* before she lay back on her bed and fell asleep.

While we were busily engaged in trying to establish the Law Office one day, we received a phone call from Emory. He and Josee had just moved to Northern Virginia, and Emory was working at BDM Headquarters, where John had first signed up for BDM Saudi Arabia. He said that Josee would follow up with her cancer treatments in the US and we would be able to enjoy their company once again. We had received a Christmas card dated the 18th of December 1996 in Emory's handwriting, saying they were not happy with the way things were going in France, and they needed a change. Although the latest cat scan had shown some improvement and the radiation had killed one of the cells, they were still concerned about the other cell which continued to show up. We invited them over for dinner one night and made plans to take them to the West End Dinner Theatre to see *Seven Brides for Seven Brothers*. It was good to see them again, and Josee was just as beautiful as ever with her lovely smile and beautiful blue eyes. She and I visited over the telephone quite often, and she told me about the cute little dog that Emory had brought home one day to keep her company. She wondered how she could ever keep up with the little bundle of energy which required her supervision and constant care but was great for her spirit and got her outside in the fresh air and sunshine to get her exercise every day. Most importantly, the little dog furnished them with joy every day and took their minds off the underlying problem.

In March, Jim brought Kathy and Katie up for a visit to Washington for Katie's 5th birthday, and we all rode the subway into the District to spend the day. We got off at the South Building of the Department of Agriculture, where I used to have lunch sometimes when I worked with the Forest Service. We found the cafeteria for lunch and then walked around the mall to take a few pictures and then over to the museums. It was a great sunny day for us to be together in this very special place and enjoy the beauty of Washington and its Monuments and Museums. John and Jimmy took turns carrying Katie, who wore herself out very early in the day. Her favorite place, of course, was the Museum of Natural History with all the animals and dinosaurs. We have many great pictures of their time with us that summer, and I believe we also drove them around Washington using our special *Washington by Auto* tape.

On one of our trips to Mobile while we were trying to decide whether or not to buy Mother's house, John and I found a beautiful lot in a new housing development further south on the eastern shore of Mobile Bay. First we had to make the decision of whether or not we wanted to invest our money in renovating Mother's rather old house where John and I were married in 1957. It was still very nice with a wonderful view of Mobile Bay; however, Hurricane Danny came along that summer to make the decision for us. Danny sat out in the middle of Mobile Bay for over two days bringing torrents of rain to undermine the bluff, which had caused Mother so much worry over the years. John called from Washington to see how things looked at the Gulf and also at the bluff. I had just come home from the condo and told him everything was fine. He asked, *"How is the bluff holding up?"* I said, *"It looks good to me."* He asked, *"Did you go outside and look up under the bluff?"* I answered, *"Of course not, it's raining out there!"* When John came down the following week, he took one look up underneath the rim of the bluff and said, *"We're not buying this house! It isn't safe!"*

Mother always had trouble with the erosion of the bluff and had spent quite a bit of money on loads of dirt to fill in and pilings to be driven in place to hold the dirt, which seemed to be eroding down the bluff anyway. She also designed a concrete drainage ditch on both sides of her house for the run off of excessive rainfall, which carried the water out to disperse it over the end of the bluff. John didn't think it would hold up much longer after Hurricane Danny, and it certainly wouldn't hold the pool we wanted to put in the backyard. We had hired an architect in Montgomery to draw up a plan to renovate Mother's house. When we realized his cost analysis was more than a brand new home would cost, we decided to look for a better lot and build a new home. Eventually, a big chunk of Mother's backyard did fall off onto the highway down below her house a few years later, and the bluff is still a big problem to those who live there.

Maggie wanted us to look at new homes near them in Williamsburg, and, while we were there, we saw many very nice ones. We seriously considered one of the homes, but Williamsburg just wasn't home to me. We would have loved being close to Maggie, Dave and Jenny, but Williamsburg to us was more like an historical tourist attraction for people to bring their children to learn about Jamestown, the first English settlement, or the Revolutionary War, where the history of our Country began. It is a very interesting place to visit to learn how our great government had its beginning. But I didn't think it could ever be home to me since my heart has always been on the Gulf beach in South Alabama. Patrick Henry made his famous speech in 1775, shortly before war broke out against the British to gain our Independence from England. I loved American History and memorized most of his famous words.

[We must fight! I repeat it sir! We must fight!! They tell us sir, that we are weak. But when shall we be stronger? Will it be next week, or next year? Sir, we are not weak if we use the means by which the God of nature hath placed in our power. There is no retreat but in submission and slavery. Our chains are forged! Their clanking may be heard o'er the plains of Boston. The war is inevitable, and let it come. I repeat it, sir, let it come. Is life so dear, or peace so sweet, as to be purchased at the price of chains and slavery? I know not what course others may take; but as for me, give me liberty or give me death!]

They say history repeats itself! Well times may have changed and circumstances may be different, but we find ourselves in a war of unrest at home with a new world power spreading its venom across the Middle East, and into Europe, and eventually into the United States if we don't stop it. Today, we seem to be threatened from within by a subtle enemy which practices lies and deceit to spread hatred and division among the people of our once great nation. Could these lies be the *strong delusion* of which the Bible speaks, which will divide our nation according to our beliefs and divert people from the truth? (2 Thessalonians 2:1-12)

John and I loved being in Jamestown with the old world setting, watching actors dressed like the colonials. They played their roles so well that you would have thought they were actually living in the other world. They told the story of the first settlers and walked us through the historical places, including replicas of churches and historical buildings.

We actually felt the realm of history in the making and the need for the first Thanksgiving to give thanks for our bounty of plenty and the Native Americans who taught us how to grow enough crops to see us through the winter. We were also impressed with the glass-blowers and purchased a set of large green stemmed glassware made exactly like they did for use in early Jamestown. I found a good use for these heavy green glasses at Christmas time and sometimes used them to serve hot spiced apple cider. The whole tour of historical Jamestown was absolutely fantastic! It is certainly a great place to take the family on vacation and teach them about Colonial Days; however, I knew it would never be home to me. John had always promised to bring me *"home again,"* like the Irish song says. I was sorry that we would have to disappoint Maggie again and truly wished for her, Dave and Jenny to move down south with us.

Back in Crystal City, we invited Josee and Emory over for New Year's dinner in our tiny apartment, and Josee surprised me when she said she loved the black eyed peas, the traditional dish which went so well with our baked ham and candied sweet potatoes. She mentioned one day that she and Emory were thinking of buying a house in Florida because they needed another change. I don't know if it had anything to do with our plans to move south or if it was their desire to be closer to Emory's mother, but things were not going well for them because of her illness and the depression it was causing them both. They made the decision to return to France where Josee could get the treatment she needed from her original doctors who were more familiar with her case. I believe she also felt her days were numbered and she needed to be near her mother. My last letter from Josee was beautifully written in her own handwriting on the 8th day of July, 2001 answering all my questions about where we might find a place to stay near her if we stopped by for a visit on a trip we were planning to Normandy. Josee died on the 18th of December 2001, exactly five years to the day of Emory's handwritten Christmas card of 1996. We miss her and hope Emory and her mother are doing well.

During the following spring before we decided to move down to our condo, Maggie and Dave brought Jenny up for a visit to tour the Museum of Natural History just as Katie had done the previous year. They knew we might be moving away and they wanted to see Washington, too, while we were still there. At almost four years old, Jenny was still a little young, but still very smart, and she remembered everything. Like Katie, she loved the animals and wanted to see and learn all about them as well as the dinosaurs, which she had never seen before. She was very inquisitive and would have many questions which would need answers because she was a talker like her mom had been at that age. I made them a picnic lunch with homemade cookies to have on the Mall before visiting the museum because we knew from past experience with Katie, how quickly Jenny would become tired from so much walking, and she, too, would expect to be carried. Sure enough, when they returned home that evening, both Maggie and Dave were dead tired and ready for bed.

I realize now that in trying to buy Mother's house, I was trying to hold on to her and I couldn't let go until well after her death in summer of 1997. After finding our lot with *good vibes* and *wonderful bird sounds* coming from the trees, John and I were ready to focus our attention on building our dream home with a pool and screened in lanai, where we could enjoy swimming without bugs and mosquitoes, and where our children and grandchildren would love to come for visits. The house plan we chose fit our needs perfectly, and everything just seemed to fall in place. The lease on our Virginia apartment had run out, so we moved to our nice three-bedroom condo at Orange Beach. We loved living there although John brought his computer and files with him, and it was hard getting him out to enjoy the beach with me. Nevertheless, I loved having my early morning coffee outside on our 14th floor balcony with the pelicans, which were doing their V-shaped fly-bys about that time almost level with me.

I was always my happiest at the Gulf, *in my element so to speak,* walking through the surf kicking up the salty water with its spray hitting my face, and the waves lapping upon the shore and the wind blowing my hair. I loved melding into the natural elements of wind, water, sand and sunshine. I was in heaven just being there! The weather was always changing and the beach always beckoning for me to come out and enjoy what it had to offer that day. And each day was different! I even loved the stormy weather and the excitement of hurricane season. Sometimes, John and I would sit out on the rocks in the early morning watching the parade of boats going out through the pass into deeper waters for fishing. Sometimes we would go back in the afternoon to watch them come in again bringing their catch with them. Every day brought something new to the beach, and the changing weather, the birds and all the sea creatures brought it to life and kept it renewed daily. It was a great place to live while I was growing up as a teenager, and I cherish all the memories of the short time we had there while building our retirement home on the eastern shore. I really hated to leave!

Late one afternoon, when I finally got John out for a walk down the beach, something quite spectacular happened! It was a great surprise to both of us! And quite unexpected! He was focusing his camera on a bird flying over the setting sun when into his vision came a flight of birds he didn't recognize, so he snapped the picture. He could hardly believe it! This flock of birds just happened to be the Blue Angels turning right into the focus of his camera! He was elated and kept right on snapping as all six planes flew right past us on their way to the Naval Air Base at Pensacola. We hardly ever missed one of their air shows, especially the big spectacular event in November. We had already accumulated over a thousand pictures of this annual event, but these six pictures stand out as the most spectacular of all. They will always remind us of that one very special moment in time, which probably wouldn't happen again in a million years!

One of John's fraternity brothers from Ole Miss, called us one day as he and his wife were passing by from a vacation in Florida. John invited them to stop by our condo for a visit, and she and I became acquainted as we walked down the beach that afternoon. As we discussed many topics of interest, we found that we shared many Christian beliefs, and she shared many things she had learned through her Bible studies. We coaxed them into spending a few days with us at the Gulf and then a couple of days at our new home on the eastern shore since we had it partially furnished. I enclose in my bibliography the two books she sent me to reciprocate: One about the *Jewish Feasts*, which I found in The Jewish Holiday Kitchen, truly an *international cookbook* containing many wonderful recipes which evolved over many years of life in many different countries; and the second, The Gold of Exodus, *the discovery of the true Mount Sinai*.

After moving into our new home and just before we moved out of our condo, we invited my old best friend and high school buddy, Roberta, and her husband, Paul, to come down to the beach for a visit. We had sort of lost touch over the years, and I wanted to rectify the situation since we would be living nearby on the eastern shore of Mobile Bay. I invited them down to spend the day and prepared lunch for the four of us. Roberta and I enjoyed walking down the beach again kicking up the sand and water just as we used to do as teenagers. She and her husband, Paul, had also met at Gulf Shores and were married right after our graduation from high school.

We had a great day together at the beach, and our husbands finally got to know each other and discovered their mutual interest in football and other sports! Roberta and Paul lived a short distance from Mother's house and were greatly blessed with three grown children and five grandchildren, who all live close by in the greater Mobile area. We hoped to see more of our family and friends now that we were settled. Many vacationers, known as *Snow Birds*, were flocking in from the northern Midwest to escape the harsh winters, and some were even buying or building retirement homes. Our good friends, Hal and Marty, who we would very soon come to know in Egypt, would become two of these Snow Birds, and they would come down every winter to rent a condo on the beach for several months. John and I would always try to drive down to the Gulf to meet them somewhere for lunch, or they would drive up to spend the day with us. We usually found a good place for a fish dinner on the old causeway crossing of Mobile Bay.

While spending some time with us at the Gulf that summer, Jim, Kathy and Katie came down for a visit after one of our hurricanes, and a bulldozer was working the beach replacing some of the sand which had washed away. Katie didn't want to leave when it was time for them to go and said, quite prophetically, *"It'll never be like this again!"* They loved the beach, but there was something different about this time because of its changing appearance. It actually had a new and exciting characteristic, which was noticeably different. Large sea shells had washed up from the ocean's floor along with star fish, sea dollars and the shell-formed houses of other interesting sea creatures. The beach had taken such a pounding, some of it had washed away along the rocky seawall of the pass, and the shoreline had receded forming a cliff-like appearance where loads of new sand had been hauled in to fill the void. I think all of us shared Katie's sentiment of this last time on *our beach,* and it saddened us to think of them driving away and leaving us there without them. The following spring, before leaving the country to take another job overseas, John made the decision to sell the condo, and, just like Katie said, *It would never be like this again.*

We moved into our retirement home in May 1999, and, by March 2000, John had another job which would take us out of the country again and back to the Middle East, this time to Alexandria, Egypt. John was not looking for a job when his resume was discovered on the internet, but he was the only Civil Engineer they could find with a Law degree and Bar Accreditation, who spoke Arabic and who had years of experience in construction management in the Middle East. After a quick trip to the company home office in Boston and a telephone interview with the on-site project director, John received an offer, which I guess he couldn't refuse. So he accepted the position as Deputy Construction Manager of the wastewater program, a bilateral effort between the United States Agency for International Development (USAID) and the Government of Egypt (GOE). I would make many more trips across the ocean!

CHAPTER THIRTY-THREE

An Introduction to Egypt
2000

Before John could leave the country in April 2000, he felt he had to tie up all the loose ends, and one of them, to our disadvantage, was to sell the condo on our beautiful white sandy beach. We also bought a new Chevrolet Monte Carlo to replace the old Mercury Cougar, which we gave Jim to use as a second car. By this time, most of our family had come to see our new home in its pristine condition and try out the pool. Everyone seemed to love it, and it was fun having them visit. They would all come back many times over the next few years to enjoy it with us. I would miss the Gulf where I had planned to spend many of my older years on the beach, walking through the sand, picking up shells and enjoying the surf like Aunt Margaret had done in her older years. However, I was tired of making the trips back and forth to the beach, which lately seemed to be covered with lots of seaweed and jelly fish and flecks of oil from an oil rig somewhere out in the Gulf. In addition to all of that, I really smashed the middle toe of my left foot into the leg of a hard wood chair in our condo bedroom and was having trouble walking on the slant of the beach. Then I finished it off by walking through the deep sand from the beach to the condo, which seemed to pull the tendon loose entirely and was quite painful for a while. I resigned myself to my new job of getting settled in our new home and completing our many unfinished projects, which up until then had been packed away in boxes. I thought how nice it would be to have a home for once in our life where our children and grandchildren could come to enjoy being together with us as a family and where we might finally know where to find everything.

We had someone to cut the grass and take care of the yard, but we still needed someone to take care of the pool. John had tried several guys from local pool companies, but none of them seemed to work out. Without proper maintenance, it could become quite a problem, as we were soon to find out. Finally, he found someone from the Gulf to come up a couple of times each month to maintain the pool. This first summer, however, Katie wanted to bring some of her friends over before school started back in August, and Lorena wanted to bring Josh to see our new home and take him to the Gulf to play on the beach when the hot summer weather ended. Grace and George were also planning a trip down in the fall, and I really needed to be here for all of them. Also, I needed to prepare the house and cars for the long term before leaving for any length of time during the winter. While I was busy trying to accomplish all these things, John came home on his first *home leave* and wanted me to go back with him. I had to tell him that I just wasn't ready to leave yet with so much left to do in getting the house in order.

Jim brought his family down more often than the others because Katie was the oldest of our grandchildren and already knew how to swim. Greg and Lorena didn't have a car in those early days and Maggie lived so far away. Katie would always bring a friend, and they would do a dance routine around the Jacuzzi before jumping into the pool while the rest of us watched and took pictures. Maggie flew down with Jenny a couple of times to see our new home, and, of course, Jim drove his family down to visit while they were here. The girls, with an age gap of 3 ½ years, would have a great time together with Jenny following Katie around trying to do all the things Katie did, and it was so cute to hear Jenny trying to hit the high notes of *Annie* about an octave higher than Katie, who was just learning to sing *Tomorrow*. It was so much fun to watch and listen! Jenny was afraid of the pool at first and would sit on the top step in the water playing with her things. She would scream if anyone came near to try to coax her out into the water in her float. In fact, she would get out of the pool and run away from them screaming, and John would have to scold her because he was afraid she would slip down and get hurt. Jenny couldn't understand his concern for her safety, but, after a couple of years, she was swimming all over the pool with or without her little float.

Before John left for Egypt, we made a trip over to Baton Rouge to teach Lorena and Greg how to put together a German bed we had given them which no one could figure out because of the intricate German fixtures, which had to be snapped together at just the right place. It was Joshua's fourth birthday, and Lorena had planned a birthday party for him at a small park with sandwiches, cold drinks and a beautiful birthday cake. Everyone was standing around eating when we noticed little Josh standing beside his granddaddy, with his arms folded just like John, standing there looking out over a small pond at the birds flying around and floating in the water. When the party was over, we drove them home so John could show them how the bed snapped together. Little Josh was watching the whole procedure when he asked his granddaddy, who was sporting a mustache at the time, a very important and well-studied question, *"Granddaddy, when you were a little boy, did you have a mustache?"*

When Lorena brought Josh over the following August, she and I had a great time taking him to the city park, where I made many great pictures of him and a new friend he made there at the park. They tried out all the playground equipment and had a great time! The next day, Lorena and I took Josh to the beach, where I made many more pictures of him running all over chasing sea gulls and playing in the sand. He loved it! He found a rope which seemed to be anchored to something buried in the sand and worked on it for hours trying to dig it up. Greg joined us a few days later, and we all went back to the beach for more fun in the sun. Since we no longer had our condo, we bought a pizza and carried it down to Alabama State Park to have a picnic lunch with our cold drinks on the picnic tables. Then we parked the car at the beach pavilion and enjoyed the surf for the rest of the afternoon.

Aunt Grace and George came down in October for about a week, and I took them on a day trip to *Bellingrath Gardens*. I was surprised to learn that these gardens, which I had known all my life, are well known throughout the world and are one of the most popular tourist attractions in the United States. According to our brochure, they are *"a favorite among historic attractions of visitors from all over the world."* We followed the walking tour through the picturesque gardens and lakes passing the beautiful *Bellingrath Home*, where we stopped for a while to rest and take pictures. Then we boarded the river boat where we ate our picnic lunch we had brought with us as we cruised by the Bellingrath Home and down the river listening to our guide as he explained the natural habitats of birds and wild life in the area. He also pointed out the breeding grounds of the fish, which fill the waters of the Gulf of Mexico. Then we visited the Bellingrath museum and gift shop to see Mrs. Bellingrath's famous porcelain collection and her collections of crystal, silver, china and cut glass. The fifteen-room home, with its many antiques and collectables, was built in 1935 for the Bellingraths, the *"first bottlers of Coca Cola in Mobile, Alabama."* I'm so glad Aunt Grace and Uncle George came down when they did to enjoy this wonderful excursion because the very next year George started showing signs of Alzheimer's.

As the Memphis weather began to turn cold the following fall, George put on Grace's nice dinner jacket, which he found hanging over the back of a kitchen chair and just walked out the kitchen door. When Grace couldn't find him anywhere, she became worried and called 911 to report him missing. She had noticed a few warning signs of Alzheimer's earlier and was very concerned. Finally, she got a call from a service station two miles away telling her that George was there and didn't know where he lived or how to get home. They had also called 911 to inquire about the possibility of a missing person and were notified that the police were on their way to get him and bring him home. These *warning signs* had developed into progressive Alzheimer's and Grace started asking him questions, *"George, do you know who I am?"* He would answer, *"Yes, you're Mary Poppins,"* or *"Miss Clementine,"* or something equally as humorous, yet very disturbing. Grace had to keep all the doors locked with the keys in her pocket to rest assured that he would stay in the house and not wander off again.

After an intense year of caring for George herself, Grace needed some R&R time, so I coaxed her into coming down for a relaxing visit with me, while I was still at home. Her daughter, Sandi, and son, Jonathan, took turns staying with George while she was away, and Grace was finally able to relax and get some sound sleep without having to be on edge all the time. I drove her over to *Perdido Bay* to visit Ginger one day, and we ran into a terrible rainstorm. Although we had a good visit with Ginger inside her lovely home, we decided to head back to our place to get out of the rain, and we just happened to drive back into the sunshine. We were so happy to see the sun again we decided to stop off at our favorite Italian restaurant to enjoy their ambiance and their great Italian food before driving home. Grace and I enjoyed their wonderful salad and ordered *Chicken Parmesan* while listening to their piano player playing some of our old favorites. Our portions were so large we each brought half of our double chicken breast serving home with us to have the next day. It was great having this leisure time with Grace, so we could both just relax and spend this restful time together.

The day before Grace was scheduled to fly home, a *straight wind storm* hit Memphis with *hurricane force winds*, which knocked down trees and traffic lights all over the city. All flights into Memphis were cancelled!

So we had to rebook her flight home when they resumed a couple of days later. Sandi had a terrible time of consoling her dad, who didn't understand what was happening during the storm and got very upset when he couldn't find Grace. He called Sandi by other names, just as he had done Grace. And Jonathan had a very hard time meeting his mom at the airport when her plane came in with all the traffic lights still out all over town. Although this was terribly upsetting to Grace knowing she needed to get home quickly, the two extra days of rest and recuperation were good for her. However, she arrived home to find a large hole in the roof of her den where a tree had fallen during the terrible windstorm. Sandi was glad to have her mother home again after all she had been through with her dad, and now she needed a rest. A short time later, they found George a good rest home, where they could visit him every day and knew he was well taken care of.

When John came home to stay in 2004, we drove up to Memphis for a visit with Uncle George, and Grace took us to see him. When we arrived, we found him sitting out in the lobby of the rest home in a wheelchair with his hands folded in the air praying for Grace to come. George seemed to know us for a while and responded to our conversation, but when we came back after lunch, he didn't know us anymore and kept saying, *"They've taken away the ones I loved."* We kept saying, *"No, George, we're here!"* But he couldn't understand. George died the following year, and John gave a beautiful eulogy at his funeral. Having been an Army veteran of WWII driving supplies to the troops stuck in *the Battle of the Bulge,* he was buried *with Military honors* in Memphis Memorial Cemetery. It was a beautiful ceremony, which we will always remember, and when we visit Aunt Grace in Memphis, we usually drive her through this lovely memorial cemetery in remembrance of Uncle George.

As time passed, Katie brought more friends with her for visits to our home, and she always gave them a tour of our house and showed them *the Mary Kay Room* which, for lack of a better storage place, was under the bar area between our dining room and kitchen, where I stored my Mary Kay products. Of course, I had to follow up *the tour* with Mary Kay facials for all the girls around our kitchen table. After *the Skin Care* portion of the facial, they always had fun picking out their *Color Combination Cards* and applying the makeup to their faces to make themselves beautiful. Usually, they would end up in the pool anyway where all the color would wash off and they would return to their original youthful, and more refreshing, appearance. They always had fun in the pool, and Jim would throw them up in the air one at a time to try to teach the girls how to dive in. The rest of us would join in their fun by sitting outside on the lanai to watch and take pictures. When John brought Tiny Gamila home with him in 2004, TG would sit intensely inside the living room window watching the kids in the pool; always making sure to keep her distance. Once, when my brothers, Michael and Joe, were talking in our living room before leaving the house one day, TG rose up from the back of the couch to defend her territory pawing at them in the air and making her most ferocious hissing sound. It was so cute and hilarious, we all had to laugh! Quickly they moved away!

Josh caught up with the older kids after taking swimming lessons one summer in Baton Rouge. Then later, after spending most of his summers with me and having access to the pool, he learned many new strokes. He and Jenny became good friends when they were both here at the same time one summer and their 1 ½ year age gap seemed to shrink away. That summer, John and I took all the kids to the little Zoo at Gulf Shores, which became famous during the hurricane years 2003-2005, when hurricanes Ivan, Georges, Rita, Katrina, Danny and a few others all passed through this region at different intervals. Several TV specials about *The Little Zoo that Could* became very popular because of the tremendous efforts of the owner and her band of loyal workers, who had to work hard for days at a time without stopping to evacuate all the animals and birds further inland before the possibility of the flooding waters of the Gulf came crashing in upon them. After the receding tides of all these storms, the workers of the Gulf Shores Zoo had to find all the missing birds and reptiles, then rebuild the zoo and move the animals back.

Thanksgiving in Ireland

Finally, in November 2000, I was ready for my first trip to Alexandria. John and I planned to meet in Dublin for a few days to celebrate Thanksgiving Day and my birthday. He met me at the airport and drove me to our B&B where he had arranged for me to have breakfast after my 8:30 am arrival. We then drove to Howth golf course and walked up to the hilltop where we made pictures of the harbor below. After driving around a bit to see some of our favorite places, we drove back to King Sitric's seafood restaurant at the harbor for dinner. We remembered this restaurant from our first trip to Dublin for their great *seafood* and famous *dessert*, which they named, *"Chocolate Volcano."* It looked like a small *baked Alaska with an eruption of hot chocolate sauce* pouring down over it. We left Dublin the following morning and headed south to Waterford where we visited the Crystal Factory, which had been closed the afternoon of our first visit.

This time our trip was successful. We arrived in time to enjoy the whole tour and watched the skillful workers as they created each piece of crystal. If the object wasn't *perfect*, it would be scrapped and remade. That evening, we drove down to the waterfront for John to make night pictures of the port. We found a nice hotel restaurant overlooking the river where we ordered dessert and Irish coffee, so we could sit by the window and admire the lovely view. On our way back to the car, we discovered a *Zeil*, similar to the ones we remembered in Germany. We decided to go back the following day to take daylight pictures of the port and the Zeil, and planned on having lunch at a very nice Irish Pub we noticed near the entrance. After our walking tour, we stopped in the pub for a wonderful Roast Beef Dinner. Then John drove us across a bridge to the other side of Waterford and through the countryside down the eastern coastline which took us around a small peninsula. We stopped at a nice hotel for afternoon coffee before driving on back to our Waterford B&B.

The following morning, we enjoyed our full Irish breakfast and got an early start to Killarney where we stayed four days at the Redwood B&B. John played a little golf at several golf courses and I walked with him some of the time for exercise and picture taking. We also took time to drive to some of our favorite places: *Torc Waterfall, the Ladies View* half-way up the mountain, and then on up to the top for lunch and the lovely view of the *Three Lakes of Killarney* below. Then we drove south across the mountains to the little town of *Bantry* where we found a nice restaurant for a fish dinner, and then all the way back to Killarney.

The following day, we drove around Dingle Peninsula hoping to find a good restaurant for Thanksgiving Dinner, but the restaurants were all closed at 2:00 pm, so we drove back to Killarney to have dinner at *O'Leary's*. We noticed a sign in the window the previous day saying that they would be serving *Thanksgiving Dinner and welcomed Americans*. Thanksgiving dinner was very well prepared, although it was served a little differently: they served large plates of sliced turkey and sliced ham with delicious fresh vegetables and a large mixture of salad greens. The desserts were a la carte. Finally, the following day, it was time to drive back to Dublin to catch our flight to Frankfurt for our connecting flight to Alexandria on Lufthansa airlines.

Before boarding, we had time for a nice dinner in the airport restaurant.

My first Trip to Alexandria, Egypt

Our late flight across the Mediterranean Sea brought us into Egypt over the beautiful well-lighted City of Alexandria with its crescent-shaped port quite visible and all lit up below. We landed at a small airport outside the city, and there to meet us was our Egyptian driver, Hamid, who I came to know over the next few years as a very cheerful, kind and dependable person. I was glad to have John with me for my first trip through Egyptian Customs, which was pretty much like Saudi Arabian Customs with all my baggage opened and checked for questionable items. On the way over, John had told me about the beautiful apartment he had rented from a very nice retired lady of *the Faculty* of the *University of Alexandria*. She had been honored by the Administration to live in the apartment while teaching at the University and then, upon her retirement, the apartment was hers to keep as an investment. When John first arrived, *Dr. Daria* helped him find his way around and gave him advice about where to shop. Our apartment, with a partial view of the Mediterranean Sea, was located just a block away from the Corniche, where John loved to walk to get his exercise. He also told me about his life at work with all the wonderful people he had come to know, and I was very anxious to meet them.

We were very tired when we arrived and I chose to sleep in one of the twin beds in the small bedroom, while John took up most of his double bed in the larger bedroom with its open window and balcony door which let in the fresh sea air. My small bedroom had a window, slightly opened, and more my style with a more feminine touch. I fell asleep almost immediately between the smooth, cotton sheets and soft warm blankets. Dr. Daria came over the following day to meet me and welcome John back to Alex. She was a very prestigious lady about our age who had lost her husband several years earlier, and, upon her retirement, rented her apartment as another source of income. She had moved to another section of the city to be closer to her daughter's family and away from the high school which was located right in front of our apartment.

Dr. Daria was very nice and immediately took me under her wing to show me around the city. She was very selective about those to whom she

481

would rent her apartment and mentioned her previous tenant, a gentleman from Ireland, with great respect. One of the first things she asked of me was to take care of her lovely wooden schrank in the living room and told me to use only what sounded to me like *bleach*. I knew that couldn't be right and asked John about it! He laughed and said she was trying to say *Pledge*. He explained that there is no *P* in the Arabic alphabet, so it comes out sounding like *B*, and the *"dge"* sounds like *"ch"*. Dr. Daria was a very charming and caring person who made us feel at home in her lovely apartment. She even had her living room sofa and chairs re-covered to suit my taste in a solid color to blend in with the Oriental rugs. She went out of her way to please us and helped me learn my way around our vicinity by showing me where to shop for fresh vegetables in the nearby souks only a few blocks from our apartment. She would come over quite often to ask if we needed anything, and she would take me shopping in the near-by malls to show me where to shop for anything we might need. Whenever we did this, Dr. Daria would insist on taking me out to lunch at one of her favorite restaurants where she would order for both of us and never allow me to pay for anything.

Walk on the Corniche.

Since John was already sleeping in the large bedroom and had all his things in there, it seemed appropriate for me to make myself comfortable in the smaller bedroom which just fit my needs for the time I was there. It had a built-in schrank, where I could hang my clothes and store a few things, and a cute little vanity and chest of drawers with a night table between the twin beds with a drawer for my vitamins and meds. The extra bed offered me a place to put my suitcase while I was doing my packing, or unpacking, for our trips coming and going. All the sheets were of luxurious Egyptian cotton which washed beautifully. Our blankets were sufficient enough for the moderate climate. Our windows were always open to let in the fresh sea air unless, of course, there was a sand storm; in which case, we closed them up tightly. Our apartment came with an Egyptian maid who cleaned the house weekly and did the laundry. We paid her a small wage and she proved to be very loyal and trustworthy. She had been employed by Dr. Daria for years and still worked for her in her new apartment.

I loved walking around our neighborhood and down the street to buy vegetables about once a week, and I always came home with several bags full. The fruits and vegetables were very good, and I couldn't believe how large some of them had grown. Since I did all our cooking in the small kitchen, which was well stocked with everything I needed, I always had a sufficient supply of fresh fruits and vegetables. The green house watermelons and strawberries were tasteless, so I quickly learned to avoid them. A staple meal from Egypt was a dish called *Koshari*, a mixture of lentils and rice simmered together, with onions, garlic, chili pepper and chopped tomatoes and served over a plate of pasta. John liked it, but I didn't care for it well enough to prepare it myself: I preferred Italian Spaghetti prepared the old fashioned way, simmered for hours and served over pasta. I discovered a wonderful family-run bakery a few blocks away which always had a good assortment of small cakes with rich chocolate frosting and many other delicious desserts. They also liked Americans and were very nice to me when I came in and always mentioned how they hoped to visit our country someday.

Soon after my arrival, we were invited to an *Iftar*, the large meal during the Muslim holy month of Ramadan to celebrate the breaking of the all-day fast from sunup to sundown. It was sponsored by Metcalf & Eddy and held at a large restaurant in downtown Alexandria. It was my first opportunity to meet all of John's co-workers, and he walked me around introducing me to everyone. Although we were first seated with the mixed group of married couples, John and I ended up sitting at a large table with all the ladies who worked in his office. We were so busy talking and getting acquainted, I didn't realize that we were supposed to be eating the food before they took it away and placed other dishes before us. I especially enjoyed the hommous, and I hardly had time to finish one piece of chicken. John ended up sitting with me and the ladies instead of returning to our original mixed group. It was a memorable evening, and I felt right at home with these wonderful Egyptian people.

The Italian villa where John worked was originally the office of the Italian Consulate, but now was an Egyptian office building with the sole purpose of completing the rebuilding of the wastewater system for the city of Alexandria. The Italian villa was filled with the offices of many specialists and just as many computers, a receptionist, several secretaries, a large conference room and many engineers and support groups. There were many *drivers* and *tea boys* who brought in tea and ran errands, and a *cook* who prepared a wonderful Egyptian meal for everyone about once a week. When I first visited the office, one of the drivers presented me with a beautiful flower he had picked from the garden. The staff secretary to engineering and the office receptionist always gave me a warm welcome when I stopped by for a visit and took time out of their busy schedules to chat a while. The staff secretary to John's boss, the Director of the Project, joined the group shortly after my arrival and helped John save two lost baby kittens with the help of the other secretaries by feeding them with an eye dropper.

Brian Landers, the Director of the office, had five birds which he left in the care of his secretary while he was on vacation. While he was away, one of the birds died, and she was terribly upset and came to John with the terrible news. She thought she had killed the bird, but her boss assured her when he returned that the bird was very old and died of natural causes. She was so relieved! I'll always remember these secretaries and office managers who were kind and compassionate to raise funds to help the poor and underprivileged people in Alexandria. I remember the young computer engineer, who invited us to her home for tea and cookies shortly after her wedding, which I missed because it was a few days before my arrival. She and her husband made us feel welcome by sharing some of the amusing stories they had to tell of their honeymoon. All the young women at the office were very friendly, and they would take time out of their busy schedules to welcome me to the office and stop by to say hello and chat a bit.

Dr. Daria would drop by the apartment about once each week to make sure everything was going well and to see if I needed anything. Most of her extra linens, dishes and fixtures were packed inside the living room schrank, and she wanted me to feel free to look through them and use whatever I needed. She also invited me to go shopping with her and showed me all the right places in town to find the products we might need. She was a very courageous woman and would stop her car in the midst of traffic to move barriers to find a parking place, or she would stop traffic just to fix her windshield wipers! When crossing streets, she would take me by the hand and very protectively pull me through the midst of traffic. Sometimes, she would tell people to get out of the way! On one of our excursions to visit the Port of Alexandria, she was very protective of me when some school kids stopped to ask if I was American. She shooed them away, although they didn't appear to be threatening in any way. She also invited me down to her condo along the beautiful Mediterranean coastline on the west side of Alexandria, and we had a very enjoyable day walking the beach and having lunch together.

I noticed that Dr. Daria always dressed very modestly even on the beach or walking around the race track at the *Sporting Club.* She always wore a turban-like hat to cover the top of her head and a loose jacket with long sleeves and long pants, but she was attuned to the western ways and accepted me as I was. However, she showed me how to make a turban for myself one day at her apartment where she had invited me for lunch, hoping I would follow suit and make one for myself. She also encouraged me to wear a jacket. Dr. Daria prepared a wonderful meal for us that day, and I got a taste of her interesting lifestyle having to walk up two flights of stairs to her third floor apartment, which I believe kept her very healthy. And she was always on the go!

Our driver, Hamid, was a very cheerful person who was never in a bad mood, and when asked how he was doing, he would always answer, *"Everything is good!"* He picked us up very late at night to take us to the airport to see us off or meet our in-coming planes, and he was always on call for wherever we might need to go. He took us grocery shopping every week to Safeway and waited while we enjoyed a *Cappuccino* at the Coffee Bar before doing our grocery shopping. Other times, he would drive us out to the new large shopping center, a short distance outside the city, where we could find just about everything one could imagine. Hamid would also take us to the *Meat Store* whenever we wanted to go, about once a month, where we watched the butcher cut and prepare our orders exactly the way we wanted them. Then he would wrap each order individually for us to bring home and store in our freezers. John and I loved the Egyptian yogurts, which seemed to have more fruit and natural flavor than other yogurts, and we found the preserves just heavenly on our whole wheat toast in the morning. Our favorites were *Mango, Fig and Date*, which I wish we could import into our country. The breads were delicious and seemed to have more bite than our traditional American breads because they have more substance like the Italian breads. All the spices were plentiful and rather inexpensive, so we tried to load up on them before coming home.

A Tour of Cairo & Giza

Soon after my arrival, John had reservations for us to take the train from Alexandria to Cairo to see *the Pyramids at Giza*. Our Egyptian driver in Cairo, a very nice gentleman, met us at the train station and drove us to the Conrad Hilton Hotel, where we would spend two nights on the beautiful Nile River. We had wonderful international cuisine for dinner that evening and for breakfast the following morning. After having the traditional English breakfast, the first morning, I discovered that hommous and pita bread was also very good the second morning. Then our driver picked us up for a drive through the countryside to *Giza* to see the *Pyramids*. On the way, we passed carts filled with all sorts of fruits and vegetables on their way to market and some sheep being herded down the road. We took many pictures of the local color as we passed through, but one thing which caught our eye was the carrot cart stopped on the side of the road. Our driver didn't quite understand why we wanted him to stop to take pictures of the carrot wagon. It was so beautifully laden with bright orange carrots with lots of green plumage on the ends that it looked quite colorful and artistic in its arrangement. He didn't understand our *artistic interest* and pulled over to buy a few carrots for us to taste. He was a kind man and so very thoughtful to go out of his way to please us, so we had to oblige him and taste the carrots.

When we arrived at the Pyramids, there were many tourists and tour busses and many men riding upon camels and horses. John and I were taking pictures of the pyramids when a man led a camel over to where I was standing and wanted me to get on to have my picture taken. When I didn't oblige him, he picked me up and put me on the camel! I was glad

John saw me in that predicament and rushed over to take my picture and pay the man to get the camel to kneel down so I could get off. What an experience! We had taken many pictures of the pyramids, and then our driver drove us over to an area where vendors had spread out their wares for tourists to view and make their purchases. One of them actually chased us back to the car to give us a good deal on a heavy black marble bust of Queen Nefertiti. Then he drove us over to the great *Sphinx* guarding the entrance to the Pyramids, and, as I was focusing my camera on the Sphinx, an Egyptian walked up with his five children to pose for a picture. Before I could take the picture, a lady with a baby seemed to catch up with them to also stand for the picture, and I realized she had to be his wife, the mother of all the children. It made a great picture!

The Pyramids at Giza.

Our driver then drove us down to *Old Cairo* to visit *the Convent of St. George* where we received information about *the journey of the Holy Family in Egypt* and received a beautiful fold-up map of the places Joseph had led Mary and Jesus and where they sojourned at various places until God told them it was safe to return to their homeland. He also drove us to *The Pharaonic Village*, where we boarded a small boat for a ride up the river to see the different scenes along the river banks depicting the different lifestyles of the Egyptian people during different eras of history. The first was a depiction of baby Moses, hidden in the bulrushes, as he was discovered by an Egyptian maiden and taken to Pharaoh's daughter who spared his life. We disembarked to tour a few of the typical houses of a certain period and had a rest stop at a small outdoor restaurant where we were able to buy lunch. Then we boarded a small boat for the return trip to the exit of the Pharaonic Village. It was all very interesting.

After dinner that evening, our Egyptian driver picked us up again at the hotel and drove us back to the Pyramids for *the Sound & Light Show,* which was very similar to the one in Athens with the historic sites of Egypt being lit up as the history was being given to bring each place into focus. Staying at the International Conrad Hilton Hotel was always a great experience for John and me, and we appreciated all the excellent food! Sunday morning, we walked across the street to take pictures of *the Nile River* and encountered a group of young boys fishing. They saw us and immediately posed with big smiles on their faces for a group picture. One of them was holding a baggie full of water containing a minnow, and their ages ranged from about 8 to 12. They were so cute! Then our driver picked us up for a drive back through the city to the train station. Cairo, vast and heavily populated, is truly an International City, and we had only gotten a tiny taste of it. We would have to come back again and again to see more.

I was surprised to find Maria, Mark and the children in Alex when I arrived. John knew that Mark and his family were interested in coming to Egypt, and, when there was an opening in Personnel, John recommended Mark to fill the position. They were very excited to be in Egypt and would soon take advantage of some of the Egyptian tours. We invited them over to our apartment and out for a walk on the Corniche while they were staying in a hotel looking for a place to rent. It didn't take them long to find a suitable house on a corner lot just a few blocks down from us and about one minute by street car. Maria invited us over for a wonderful dinner she prepared in her new kitchen, and we enjoyed our time together on many occasions. Her kids were starting school after their arrival, so Maria asked me to go with her and the kids on a shopping trip into Alexandria to buy some things they needed. It was fun! I hopped on the street car at my stop about a minute after they boarded at theirs, and we all rode downtown together. They shopped for things they needed for school while I looked around for a good oil painting at some of the art shops to represent our time in Egypt. I selected one which was not exactly what I was looking for, but at least it showed a typical scene along the Nile River, and it would represent the cruises we would take later on. For lunch we stopped at an Arabic food stand along the street and enjoyed falafels and orange juice.

I rode the street car back with Maria and the children, and we all got off at their stop for an afternoon on the beach just a block from their house. The kids had fun playing in the sand while Maria and I visited for about an hour sitting on the sand watching them. After our beach time, I walked about a mile up the Corniche before having to cross under the busy street to our apartment. It was a beautiful day and I enjoyed the walk, and, as I was turning up through a little park, I saw a man standing there gazing out over the beautiful rocky coastline holding a cup of tea. When he saw me, he smiled really big and held up his cup as if making a toast or inviting me to take his picture since I had my camera hanging over my shoulder. He looked exactly like Omar Sharif, even to the point of having a small gap between his two front teeth. I sort of nodded back, smiled a little and walked on by. Was it he? If it wasn't, then it must have been his son or twin brother because he was *"the spittin' image!"* I'll always believe it was Omar Sharif! After all, he was Egyptian, and this was the beautiful Corniche of Alexandria! Where else would he be more likely to show up?

I first met Hal when John invited him to dinner one Saturday afternoon. His wife, Marty, had not yet arrived and I served *a spur of the moment potluck* dinner. I cannot remember what I served that day, but we enjoyed our day with Hal and loved having him over for dinner. Afterwards, we all three went for a long walk on the Corniche and made plans to sit together at the EgyptAir Promotional Dinner the following week. Everyone had received an invitation to the free dinner, sponsored by Egyptian Airlines, and it was very nice! Most of the gifts were advertisements for trips via EgyptAir, especially to the famous *Sharm El Sheikh* on the *Egyptian Riviera*. John told me later that Hal was working with Metcalf and Eddy when his name appeared as a possible candidate for the open position he had filled, and, since Hal was favorably impressed with John's work on the Peace Shield project with Boeing, he had endorsed John for the job. Now John was working directly for Hal on the Egyptian wastewater project as Deputy Construction Manager and Contracts Manager and would serve in Hal's place as Construction Manager whenever Hal was unavailable.

I returned to Mobile in mid-January, and Ginger was there to meet me in that unusually cold weather. She had watered our plants while I was gone and they looked good inside the house but were frozen outside. I was very thankful for my family, which was always supportive of our job efforts overseas, and they always had someone there to meet us at the airport. We really couldn't have done it without them and I couldn't have chosen two better sisters-in-law than Ginger and Erin. It was good to be home again to speak with all the kids and find out how they were doing, and it didn't take me long to get back in the routine of making my rounds over to Baton Rouge, Jackson and Memphis. I always felt that something was missing when I came home from overseas. I always missed Mother. I would fit into her schedule and knew what I needed to do with my time. Now, all I could do was get back to work on unfinished projects around the house, and, since I had no one to cook for, I took myself out to lunch quite often. I visited everyone as time permitted and often called them while I was home. I would also sometimes visit Virginia Beach when I visited Maggie, usually when I was enroute to, or from, Egypt via Atlanta. The time passed quickly, and, before I knew it, it was time for my return trip in March because John had us booked for the Nile River Cruise in April. John and Hamid were there to meet me as I exited Egyptian Customs trying to pull all my lined-up suitcases behind me quite unsuccessfully at times.

Something quite spectacular happened on this trip into Alexandria! As we were crossing the Aegean Sea, the pilot announced that we would be passing by, on the left hand side of the plane, what some people believe to be *the missing continent of Atlantis*. I just happened to be sitting on the left hand side right behind the left wing with a remarkably clean window and great visibility. The sun light couldn't have been better coming from the gradual descent of the sun in the northwest to dramatically light up the island. I had my camera ready to snap the shutter as soon as the Island of Santorini came into view. The result was a perfect picture which shows the complete outline of three crescent-shaped islands which were left after a volcanic eruption around 1500 BC blew out the center of a large round island, which once existed right there in the Aegean Sea, the circumference of which can be clearly defined from the air. One can even see the small islet being formed in the center of *the Crater of the Caldera,* where a new island is in the process of creation. It is incredible!! (The history of Santorini can be found on Pages 308-312 in Chapter 21, *A Tour of Greece.*)

The Island of Santorini: "The Missing Continent of Atlantis."

Finally, Marty arrived in Alexandria, and, just as Hal had promised, he invited us over to their apartment to meet her. We found Marty to be a great person and very easy to talk to. She was a retired school teacher from Minnesota and spoke with a northern, mid-western accent. She and Hal had a very interesting story about how they met while she was working her way through college at the Badlands National Monument managing the dining room at Cedar Pass Lodge. Hal was also working there as Project Manager for the National Park Service overseeing projects in the Dakotas, Wyoming and Nebraska. They started dating as they got to know each other because Hal often ate his meals there and they became acquainted. Eventually, they were married and chose to make their home in Illinois. Marty loved to walk as much as Hal and they made a great pair! The two of them seemed to be experts on where to find everything in Alexandria.

Hal prepared a wonderful s*moked cheese ball* for us to share that evening with *great crackers and a delicious white wine*. It was so good! We just couldn't stop eating, and I had to ask for the recipe. Hal said it was very simple to make: just soften a couple of packages of cream cheese with a little liquid smoke, *the secret ingredient,* add some coarsely chopped black kalamata olives, mix all together and roll into a round ball. Cover with wax paper and refrigerate overnight. Hamid picked up all four of us every Friday morning for grocery shopping, and Marty, being an avid coffee drinker, would coax the rest of us into stopping at the coffee bar for a Cappuccino before hitting the aisles. We found them to be great friends and enjoyed their company throughout the whole four years of the wastewater project in Alexandria. There was a period of almost two years, however, when Hal and Marty were stuck in the States and couldn't get back because of medical reasons.

While I was away from Alex on home leave, Hal and Marty were also in the States tending to family business following the death of Hal's father. Hal had a very serious heart attack, and his doctor wouldn't allow him to return to work until he had completely recovered. While Hal was recuperating, John took over his job as Construction Manager. Then Ray, another colleague of John's, arrived to replace Hal. The two of them worked closely together for the next two years monitoring the progress of the expansion of two wastewater treatment plants and six pumping stations. The wastewater project, begun in 1993, was doing its job of clearing up the pollution of the city of Alexandria and the entire Egyptian coastline.

The Corniche at Night.

CHAPTER THIRTY-FOUR

Cruises on the Nile
2001-2002

On the 6th of April 2001, John and I boarded the train to Cairo where we were met in the depot restaurant by our Egyptian driver and transported to the Conrad Hilton Hotel on the Nile River. We always enjoyed coming back to this beautiful international hotel even if it was only for one night. We loved the luxurious atmosphere and the great international cuisine. I always took advantage of my opportunity to order Chicken Curry and the delicious mango chutney and other accompaniments. Our driver picked us up after a very early breakfast the following morning and drove us to the airport where we boarded our EgyptAir flight to *Luxor for the Nile River Cruise to Aswan.* We were met at the airport and transported to the lobby of the Luxor Movenpick Hotel where we were presented a welcoming *hibiscus drink* while waiting to be checked in for one night at the hotel. After lunch, we had the afternoon free to walk around the lovely grounds and visit the small zoo and bird sanctuary. Later in the afternoon, we were invited to the amphitheatre on the eastern bank of the Nile River to hear classical music while watching the gorgeous sunset. John took many pictures of birds and people in silhouette as the sun slowly dropped over the Nile. We enjoyed a good dinner in the hotel restaurant that evening and met some people at the next table on vacation from Texas.

After breakfast in the hotel, we boarded the Radamis I and got settled for the first day of the Nile River Cruise. Shortly after boarding, we disembarked to board a bus which took us to *the Karnak and Thebes Temples,* where we had a guided tour through the ruins of ancient Luxor. We returned back to the Radamis I for lunch around noon and enjoyed a buffet of Arabic food in the galley. In the early afternoon, we re-boarded the bus for a guided tour of *the Valley of the Kings & Queens* and visited the *burial sites of ancient rulers at El-Bahari.* At one of the sites, our tour guide walked us down a narrow passageway which took us deep down inside one of the tombs where we were able to view a mummy still lying where it was discovered. Back at the entrance, he pointed out ancient ruins across the way where workers lived while working on these tombs. We were driven to the *Temple of Queen Hatshepsut at El-Deir, another site at El-Bahari, and then to the Colossi of Memnon to see more ancient burial sites*. On the way back to our cruiser, we returned to the *Temples of Karnak and Thebes* for those who wanted to see them again or missed seeing them that morning. We returned to the Radamis I for afternoon tea on deck followed by a very nice dinner while still docked in Luxor.

When we arose the second day, we found ourselves underway cruising up the Nile and rushed up on deck to take pictures as we left Luxor. We quickly returned below deck to get our morning coffee to take up on deck with us as we sat at a table to view the passing scenery along the river banks. We returned to the galley to find our table for the breakfast buffet, which was very enjoyable. Then we became fascinated by passing through *the locks at Esna* and took pictures of the rising and lowering of the water levels as we passed through. We had lunch on deck and then afternoon tea as we traveled on to *Edfu*. After docking at Edfu, we enjoyed a dinner buffet of Middle Eastern food on deck and spent our second night in the cabin. Following breakfast, the third day, we disembarked from the Radamis I to board donkey- pulled carriages, which took us through the dusty streets of Edfu to the outskirts of town to tour the magnificent ancient *Temple of Horus*. We had a guided tour through the temple and learned a little of the ancient religion of Egypt, which was very much like the mythical gods and goddesses we had just learned about on our trip to Greece. Our tour guide, a professor at the University of Cairo, was excellent and really knew his stuff about the ancient religion. I asked him some very important questions regarding Islam and Christianity, and he said that before Islam, Egypt was 85% Christian. The streets were lined with many small shops exhibiting their merchandise to attract the passing tourists.

While having lunch on board Radamis I, we sailed on to *Kom Ombo*, where we disembarked to visit *the Temple of two ancient gods, Sobek and Haeroeis*. Our tour guide had a lot to tell us about the ancient religion at Kom Ombo, and we took some really great pictures of the ancient temple. We also captured some of the *local color* of this very picturesque island, the street vendors and our cruise ship sitting in the harbor. As we were returning to Radamis I, we saw a snake charmer sitting cross legged on the sidewalk with several cobras performing as people were throwing money into his basket. After boarding, we continued our cruise to Aswan where we docked and boarded buses which drove us up to the high dam, the beginning of Lake Nasser. On the way down, we visited a granite quarry to see how the Egyptians cut the stone they favored in building their pyramids. We visited the *unfinished obelisk,* which remains abandoned where it lay when a crack in the granite brought the work to a halt. Had it been completed, it would have competed with the tallest obelisks on record. Then we visited the *Temple of Philae* and enjoyed a *felucca ride* on the river with an English speaking group to see *Elephantine Island,* where much of the trading was done in earlier times. The Island got its name from the shapes of the rocks, eroded by the waters of the Nile River over time, which resemble a group of elephants. We were then transported to *the Old Cataract Hotel for overnight in Aswan.* That evening we enjoyed venturing out around our very old, but very classical, hotel with a lovely view of the Nile River, filled with many small boats and feluccas. It was really quite luxurious and the dining room, serving great international cuisine, quite elegant for dinner as well as breakfast. The view from our balcony, overlooking the river and desert beyond, was really something to behold and very beautiful; something we would remember always. After breakfast the following morning, we were transported to the airport for our return flight to Cairo.

Nile Cruise: Tour of Ancient Egypt.

John and I flew home together in May for his home leave and arrived in Frankfurt during a Lufthansa strike, which really messed up our schedule: we had to be rerouted through Miami to Mobile. After being at home a few days to see everyone within driving distance, I accompanied John to Atlanta for a round-trip to Norfolk in early June where we visited Maggie, Dave and Jenny before John had to resume his flight back to Alexandria. During this visit at our Williamsburg motel, we enjoyed the swimming pool and the ducks and, of course, our continental breakfasts in the small breakfast room, which was separate from the larger buildings. Jenny always loved having cereal, muffins and juice in the little breakfast room, and we would always walk over to the lake to feed the ducks and geese. We did this several times during our travels back and forth to Egypt and always stayed in this same motel and made pictures of Jenny growing up. This time, Maggie, Jenny and Dave wore their bathing suits under their clothes and enjoyed the pool while John and I watched them having fun in the water. John took us all out for an Italian dinner at Olive Garden to celebrate our 44th anniversary the night before he left, and I flew back to Mobile several days later.

While I was home in July, Lorena brought Joshua over to spend a few days with me to see if he would be content staying overnight without his mother at the young age of five. He would be starting first grade the following year, and she was making plans for his summers while she was starting to work at her new job as a bi-lingual insurance agent. I thought surely he would want to go home in the middle of the night, but he did just fine and we found a lot of things to do together while he was staying with me. Lorena drove back over to spend her vacation with us, and we took him back to the beach again before she drove them both back to Baton Rouge. I returned to Alex on the 31st of August, less than two weeks before 9-11, and settled back into our apartment overlooking the beautiful Mediterranean Sea. Again, John and I walked the Corniche just about every day to take pictures and get our exercise. Dr. Daria planned to take us both down to her condo along the western Mediterranean coast the following Saturday and had already ordered her three fish dinners to be picked up on our way through a small nearby town, so we could all three spend the day together on her lovely beach.

However, on September 11, 2001, something quite unexpected happened to change everything. I turned on CNN to hear the afternoon news about 5:00 pm Egyptian time, when I noticed that a plane had crashed into one of the Twin Towers in New York City. A few minutes later, John was at the door coming in from work, and I called him to come quickly to see the terrible tragedy which had just occurred in New York. Just about the same time John entered our apartment, we saw another plane coming into focus as it swerved in the air to hit the other tower much lower down than the first. We knew then that this was no accident!! John told me to call Dr. Daria immediately to cancel our plans for Saturday, and she expressed her sorrow about the terrible accident. The next day, all the Egyptians down at John's office expressed how very sorry they were to hear of the terrible accident in New York. Dr. Daria was very disappointed, but she understood completely. We could not take a chance as Americans in a foreign country being so vulnerable to those who might want to kill us.

John and I were the only ones living on the 8th floor of our apartment building because there were only two apartments on each floor and the other one on our floor was vacant. Dr. Daria had told us that the person who owned the other apartment was living abroad and she didn't know when he would return. The people who lived directly above us decided to put in a picture window across the front of their apartment and started knocking holes in the wall and doing other jobs of renovation. The constant pounding was very irritating and it went on all day long from morning 'til night. Then we noticed a leak in our bathroom, and Dr. Daria called a plumber to come out to fix the leak. The plumber started doing the same thing — knocking holes in the bathroom wall to put in new pipes. Because of the leaks, he and his men started tearing up the wooden floor to haul out the dirt, which had become wet due to the leaking pipe. It had to be removed so that new dry dirt could be hauled in to replace it. I never could quite figure out why the dirt filling was necessary between the wooden floors, but I'm sure it was there for a very good reason; maybe insulation?

In spite of all the pounding going on day after day and my constant headache, we needed to move over closer to John's office for many reasons; not the least of which was his safety in getting back and forth to work each day. Hamid picked him up every morning and drove him back home every afternoon, which took about 20 minutes through heavy traffic each way. We considered his drive through the slow moving souk areas, where it would be easy for an ambush; which had happened to five of John's colleagues in foreign countries who had been killed in similar situations. In fact, we could be attacked at any time in our apartment building, and it just wasn't safe. There were many people right there in Egypt and other parts of the Arab world who hated Americans. Sometimes, when our elevator wasn't working, which happened occasionally, we had to walk up seven flights of stairs. We had seen blood stains on the floor of our elevator and figured that probably an animal had been killed on the way up to an Iftar. We had also noticed blood stains along the Corniche in a couple of places following Ramadan. They sometimes roasted an animal on the beach and kept the meat fresh as long as possible this way.

Ray told John about a vacancy on the third floor of his apartment building, just half a block from John's office. Hamid drove us both over to look at the apartment and we both liked it very much. We made our decision to move as quickly as possible and notified Dr. Daria about our plans to be closer to John's office. She was such a good lady and always understood our reasoning. It would give her plumber time to make the repairs to her apartment, and, at the same time, the people above would have time to finish their renovations. So we started moving our things over to the new apartment with the help of the *tea boys and several drivers of the large vans*. However, there was a hitch when John couldn't work out the TV situation with the owner of the new apartment, and, all of a sudden, he told the tea boys to take everything back to the first apartment. Well, I had already washed out the drawers of the two large chifforobes and sprayed them with Pinesol. I had aired them out and partially filled them with our nicely washed and folded clothing. I wasn't about to take everything out and move it back to the first apartment, which was giving me a headache every day and a floor which was partially not there anymore. The tea boys had made several trips to bring all our things over to this apartment, and now they were supposed to take everything back? When they started moving our bags back down the hall, I said, *"Wait a minute! Don't move anything until Mr. John comes back to have another look at this apartment!"*

Ahmed, the administrative manager of the office, was there overseeing the move to put things back when I told the guys to put everything down. Ahmed, a wonderful gentleman who had great respect for both John and me, said, *"Mrs. Libby, Mr. John has made up his mind, and he said to take everything back."* I responded, *"Well, just tell him to come and look one more time."* The tea boys were standing up and down the hallway not knowing what to do; some still holding bags in their hands. Ahmed repeated, *"Mr. John won't change his mind! He wants us to take everything back."* Again, I said, *"Well tell him to come back and look again."* The guys dropped everything right where they were standing and left for the day. Ahmed walked down the street to the office and told John what I said. John returned with a slight grin on his face and sat down to reason with Ahmed and me. I showed him how nicely everything fit into the drawers and hung in the closets. We had two double beds in our large bedroom and a queen-sized bed in the other bedroom. It was a much better and safer place for us to live out the remainder of our time in Egypt; and it was so much more convenient for him to just walk down the street to his office and even come home for lunch. We also had a nice, large storage room which we didn't have before, which we really needed for our growing files and accumulation. He had known all along that I was right, and he agreed to try to negotiate with the owner about the TV. Finally, he and Ahmed worked it out with the owner and everything worked out just fine. Later, Ahmed told John, whose pride wasn't wounded one bit, *"Well, at least Mrs. Libby was very respectful!"*

On the 25th of September, John, Ray and I attended *a Memorial Service held at St. Mark's Anglican Church in downtown Alexandria honoring those killed in the New York World Trade Center attack.* Hamid drove us downtown for this memorable event with both Christians and Muslims present. Many Americans and English speaking people were there and the church was filled to capacity. Ray also accompanied us to Christian church services at the American School and the graduation of the daughter of one of their co-workers, whose wife had recently died of cancer in the Alexandria German Hospital. I visited the office occasionally when I walked down to the little convenience store across the street. We were very fortunate to be able to order our bottled water from there, and they delivered cases of drinking water right to our door. Occasionally, Ray came to dinner, and he was always fun to be around and brightened up our day. Hamid continued to pick us all up for grocery shopping on Friday morning, and John usually played golf on Saturday mornings with his boss who picked him up on the corner of our building.

Our new apartment came with a *Boab,* an older gentleman who sat outside the building looking after the place. When we were first getting ready to move into the apartment and I was alone one-day cleaning, I found the bathroom door would not open from the inside and I was locked in and couldn't get out. John was at the office half a block away and I had no way to call him from the bathroom, so I had no recourse but to open the window and call out to anyone who could hear me. Luckily, a man working in the garden of the rest home next door heard me and notified the Boab, who came up the stairs and opened the door to our apartment. When he heard me calling from the bathroom for help, he opened the bathroom door and walked in to show me how to open the door. He didn't understand the problem, and I had to rush out through the door before he closed it and locked both of us inside. Sure enough, he had to close the door to understand the problem and I had to open the door to let him out. Finally, the landlord had the door repaired so it could be opened from both directions.

Through the windows of our third floor apartment, which stretched across the front of our living area, John and I were able to see many interesting things taking place in the streets below. One very memorable event was the paving of the streets: as the pavers came down the street with their large equipment, they moved quickly paving everything on the street and didn't miss a lick. If the limb of a tree got in their way, they just cut it off, pushed it aside and kept on going. By the time they were passing our place, it was time for lunch, and John was home to watch with me as their tea boys served them lunch right there in the middle of the street still sitting inside their big equipment. It was fun and amazing to watch the procedure, and, by the end of the day, they were finished with our street entirely. Another incident was a traffic accident involving a lady driver and a man in a wheelchair, which turned out very satisfactory for the man in the wheelchair, who was actually hit by the passing car. This scenario took all day to play out with an unexpected outcome: the wheelchair was damaged so it wouldn't move, but the man in the wheelchair was okay! He sat there for hours on the curb until the person who hit him brought him a brand new wheelchair, and off he went happily down the street with a much better wheelchair than he had before. Of course, there were other traffic accidents where the police were called in to write up accident reports and citations to be handled in court. These usually created a traffic jam on our street for most of the day. In watching all these incidents, I realized for the first time that there was *"a watchman"* sitting on the corner across the street from our apartment. John said that he had learned that this watchman was stationed there *to protect the old folks' home next door to us, John's office with the on-going wastewater project and the British and the Israeli Consulates a block away from us in two different directions.*

The wild Alexandria cats were everywhere and we could hear them at night in the courtyard below. It sounded sometimes as if they were killing one another and some really big fights seemed to be taking place, at least for a few minutes. The cats seemed to congregate in the courtyard of John's office, and John always had some dry cat food in his pockets to give them. The Alexandria cats were always hungry, and they seemed to know that Mr. John would always have something for them, so they looked for him every day and gathered around to be fed. The tea boys would sometimes mix up a batch of fish scraps and large cans of cheap mackerel, which John would buy in bulk from the store. They would mix breads and leftovers together with the fish to make it go further so all the cats could be fed. One day, a lady engineer from Cairo came into the office and said she heard a baby kitten crying outside in the garbage can where someone had placed it. She told the drivers about it and John and his secretary went out to see about the kitten and brought him in so they could feed him with an eye dropper. He was a newborn male the color of apricots, so they quite appropriately named him *Mishmish*, which in Arabic means apricot. Mishmish grew up to be king of the villa cats and drove away *old Blackie*, the meanest cat in the neighborhood. Blackie had been the cause of many cat fights in the courtyard and still dropped in occasionally to cause trouble, so Mishmish became their hero when he drove Blackie away. He loved John because he and one of the secretaries had saved his life as a baby and protected him as a small kitten from the other cats. Mishmish would walk into the Italian Villa through the front door like he owned the place and go straight under all the furniture to John's desk, crawl up in John's lap and sit there a good while watching the computer screen.

Since John had told all the ladies down at work that I was a Mary Kay Beauty Consultant before I came over, and they had each filled out one of my questionnaires regarding their skin problems, I had to follow through as promised to give them all facials. It was a good time for me to do this now that we lived right down the street from the office, and they could come over on their lunch hour. Also, I wanted them to feel at home in our apartment just as they made me feel at home down at the office. So, I set the time and invited them for lunch on a certain day. I had all the place settings ready so as not to waste time on their lunch hour, knowing full well that I could not sell them anything because of the Egyptian laws regarding the sale of American goods in Egypt. It was entirely a friendly gesture to be hospitable to my new friends. It went well, although I cannot remember what I served for lunch, but it was fun having them over for a Mary Kay facial and giving them a few samples to try out at home. I had brought over a good assortment of Mary Kay products for my own use and a little extra in case I ran into any Americans who might need some Mary Kay products while living in Egypt. I also gave Dr. Daria a facial and a few samples. At the end of our four years, I only had a few products left to ship home so it was quite an appropriate amount to bring over.

In order to get all our vitamins and supplements over and to save room in my suitcases, I once filled an electric coffee maker and an electric blender with all the pills out of their boxes in layers which I labeled, so that I could unload them into their empty bottles I had saved to accommodate them over there. This was quite puzzling to Egyptian Customs who saw them through their x-ray devices and asked me what they were without having to unpack everything. They were very nice and took my word about what they saw in the containers and let them through, thank goodness; or it would have been quite a predicament for me if they had not let them in. I also brought in some *Move Free* in the original boxes for Dr. Daria from time to time and always had room to squeeze them in somewhere. I tried not to over pack; but usually it was impossible, and I would come in with several suitcases on rollers all hooked together.

Dr. Daria continued to be my friend and introduced me to *the Sporting Club,* of which she was a member. She invited me to walk the race track with her for exercise and have lunch in the very exclusive restaurant where she ordered our dinner to be served at the appropriate time. She escorted me all around the lovely grounds to show me the two Olympic swimming pools and other very nice restaurants, and we would always walk the race track to get our exercise and see the beautiful horses. John visited the Sporting Club every weekend for a round of golf with his boss, Brian Landers, and it was the most popular place for sports in the area, including polo, soccer and field hockey. Always in the afternoon, when we were tired out from all our walking, we would have lemonade in the reading lounge before driving back home in the heavy traffic.

Dr. Daria was a very good friend during our whole four years in Alexandria and took me to see many of the historical places. On one occasion, she took me to see the famous *Lighthouse at the Port of Alexandria,* shooing away a few teenagers who stopped to ask if I was American. They seemed to be on a school excursion touring some of the historical places and were not bothering me at all. In fact, I found it delightful to be noticed in the crowd as an American. We also toured the large *Fortress* there which was *built in historical times for the protection of Alexandria and its famous seaport.* Dr. Daria reserved a table for us to have dinner at a very nice seafood restaurant right on the Mediterranean Sea *with a fantastic view of the famous Port and City of Alexandria.* On another occasion, I made some great pictures of Dr. Daria and her lovely daughter, who joined us for dinner at this same restaurant shortly before I left the country.

John and I flew to Shannon via London on the 16th of November 2001 for a few days' vacation in Ireland on my way home. I departed out of Dublin on the 25th, and he departed out of Shannon on the 26th via London on his way back to Alex. While at home, I made a round-trip airline reservation to Norfolk to visit Amanda and her family in Virginia Beach on my way to visit Maggie, Dave and Jenny in Williamsburg. Amanda met my plane when I arrived in Norfolk on the 19th of December. It just happened to be the evening of her two granddaughters' high school band concert. Stephanie played oboe in the School Orchestra and Suzanne served as an usher, who ushered us to our seats in the large auditorium. It was a fantastic performance! Later, Suzanne, the older of these two beautiful young ladies served her time in Iraq along with her new husband, and I was very happy to learn they both returned home safely. My wonderful sister, Amanda, had made a reservation just for the two of us to have dinner at a very nice restaurant down Virginia Beach right on the beautiful Atlantic Ocean where we could just relax and enjoy being together as we got away from all the problems and caught up on everything over the previous months. We both needed this restful time together to just get away from it all for a while. Then, Amanda's youngest daughter, Joanie, drove me to Williamsburg where she left me with Maggie, Dave and Jenny on her way to visit her older sister, Jill, who lived closer to Richmond.

Christmas 2001 was a very special time for me to share with Maggie and her family in Williamsburg, and I was sorry John could not be with us. Jenny was now 7 and still excited about getting up early Christmas morning to find her presents under the tree, and she and Maggie handed out all the gifts. After breakfast, we all dressed for church and Dave drove us to a large Methodist Church to see live animals in their beautiful Nativity Scene in front of the church. Then we went inside to hear the wonderful Christmas music and songs sung by the choir. Afterwards, Dave drove us out to his brother Ronny's home, where his sister, Liz, visiting from New York, and his wife, Beth, had prepared a wonderful Christmas Dinner. It was my first time to see their nice home on the lake and to meet Dave's sister Liz, who I found to be a very sweet and lovable person. I also enjoyed seeing Ronny and Beth again who had helped us find the Williamsburg motel we loved to stay in. I wasn't aware of it then, but Liz was suffering with cancer and only had a few months to live. I know it was very important for her to be there with her brothers for these last few months of her life, and I'm sure it inspired her to cook such a wonderful Christmas Dinner. Liz was the oldest of four children and Dave was only 8 when their mother died of cancer. I was very sad that last morning when I had to get up early and leave Maggie at home with Jenny to fly back to Mobile. Dave drove me to the Norfolk Airport and dropped me off before driving on to work that morning. The time passed much too quickly, but we all had a great Christmas visit with many happy memories of our time together.

Before my flight to Alexandria that spring, I had to work in another triangular trip to Memphis, Baton Rouge and Jackson for a special school project of Jenny's first grade class, taking with me a flat cardboard person on a stick called *Flat Stanley*. Jenny wanted me to write a story about *Flat Stanley's Vacation*. I decided I had time for another trip to see everyone before I left again so I planned my trip to Baton Rouge, Jackson and Memphis. Of course, everyone was greatly impressed with Flat Stanley. When I arrived in Memphis, Grace took us to the Memphis Zoo, where I held Flat Stanley up to see the Pandas, and Grace took pictures for me to send to Jenny. Uncle George was still living at home going through stages of Alzheimer's, and he called me by his daughter's name and held on to one of my arms and one of Grace's while walking through the Memphis Zoo. I got a picture of Flat Stanley sitting on the couch between Uncle George and one of his grandsons. When I returned home, I sent the whole story with pictures to Jenny for *Show & Tell*. I'm glad I took the time to do this because my trip to Memphis, especially, was long overdue, and I enjoyed being with all the family again. Of course, everyone was amused with the guy on the stick!

Back in Alexandria that spring I found that Ray had moved to Phoenix to accept another job offer and Hal and Marty were living downstairs in his apartment directly below us. This proved very convenient for Hamid to pick us all up at the same place for grocery shopping on Friday mornings, and he could leave the car parked outside our building, just around the corner from the office. We went back to our old routine of occasionally stopping off at the coffee counter for a Cappuccino before hitting the aisles with our grocery carts. It was great having them back in Alexandria! She and Hal resumed their walking, although Hal had to take it easy at first. Marty and I were able to visit more often while the guys were working, and we planned a few outings for the four of us and attended the usual office parties and get- togethers around Ramadan.

We both had housemaids who worked for us a couple of days each week to clean our wooden floors and hang the sheets out to dry on our clotheslines in the fresh air and sunshine. Most of our clothes, however, could be dried in our dryers, folded and put away, or ironed, if necessary, and hung up. They also washed the large windows across the front and sides of our building; they really needed it about once a month, especially after a dust storm. Our Egyptian maid would keep John supplied with stuffed grape leaves and other foods while I was away on home leave, and she did a very good job of cleaning our wooden floors. It was wonderful having her twice a week, and both Marty and I appreciated our maids enormously. Her maid had a very serious health problem, which Marty was very concerned about, and I hope she was able to recover after we left. We had all the modern conveniences of home in our spacious apartments, although our appliances were smaller and probably not up to US standards; which made it all the more interesting for our adventurous spirits. All we really lacked was a microwave oven and we did very well without one.

I accompanied John on his third *home trip* in April 2002, via Frankfurt and then from Mobile to Norfolk for a few days with Maggie's family in May before John returned back to Alex on the 18th. Then I returned back to Mobile and Lorena brought Joshua over to stay with me for about a month to sort of break him in for the following summers to come after school started that fall. Again, he did just fine and Lorena came to get him during her vacation in June. Josh began first grade in August at the Hosannah Christian Academy. The following summer, Josh was ready to come back for another visit with his grandmother and the precedent was set. One summer, Lorena took Josh with her to Mexico for a couple of weeks to meet his other grandfather and her very large family, and Josh came back speaking Spanish. A few years later, he was almost *fluent* between other trips to Mexico and hearing his mother speak Spanish with her sisters. Eventually, his summers became split between time with us, time for Christian Summer Camp and time with his cousins in Knoxville and Baton Rouge. As he grew older, he preferred staying in Baton Rouge most of the time with his friends taking part in all their summer activities. However, he was always ready to come here for visits and would bring his pet rabbit, *Nibbles*, with him with her cage, rabbit food and the rest of her paraphernalia. After John brought Tiny Gamila home with him, we had to keep a close watch on TG because she was quite suspicious of the rabbit, and I think she was also a little jealous and would smell under the door and around everywhere Nibbles had been after Joshua had taken her home.

Rothenburg & The Romantic Road

I left on the 16th of July 2002 to meet John in Frankfurt for a 10-day vacation in Germany. We rented a car in Frankfurt and spent a couple of days touring Rothenburg and taking pictures of its old medieval wall which surrounds the back portion of the city. We also took the walking tour of *the Night Watchman* to learn the very interesting history of Rothenburg. We enjoyed all the wonderful German food again, especially the Schnitzels, Spaetzel and the delicate European salads. We began our drive from Rothenburg down the *Romantic Road,* otherwise known as the *Romantische Strasse,* the route the Romans took when they first came into Germany.

Steps up to the City Wall, Rothenburg, Germany.

The Covered Walkway around the City, Rothenburg, Germany

"Tour of the Night Watchman," Rothenburg, Germany.

Our drive took us through Bavaria retracing our many other trips from Frankfurt over into Austria, where we visited the small salt mining town of Hallstatt for the second time and stayed in Hotel Gruner Baum. This time, we took the cruise around the lake and walked the many pathways much of the way up the steep mountainside. We then drove to Hall for another visit to this historic town which was once the salt-mining trading center of the world, which also housed *the Mint.* We spent a couple of days coming and going through Chiemsee, the US military recreation facility (AFRC), which once served as a Nazi hospital during WWII. On the 26th of July, we returned to Alexandria. On our next trip in November, John and I would have Thanksgiving Dinner with the troops at the AFRC at Chiemsee, which since then has been handed back to the Germans.

Chiemsee Armed Forces Recreation Center, Lake Chiemsee, Germany.

Our Second Nile River Cruise: Aswan to Luxor

Since we enjoyed the Old Cataract Hotel so much in Aswan, we made reservations for two nights and planned our second Nile River cruise in October in reverse of the first cruise. This time we would be cruising down stream going with the flow of the river from Aswan to Luxor and, of course, we would be making better time. We toured the same ancient tombs, relics and monuments of the first tour, but going through the locks, would be quite different. While stopping at one of the locks, the people on the bank below threw up packages of fancy dresses for us to purchase for the *Galabia Party* to be held on board that evening. Those interested could put the money in the enclosed container and throw it back down. I bought a fancy black dress trimmed in gold, although it was way too big for me. However, it was very pretty and inexpensive to keep as a souvenir, and we enjoyed a great evening at the Galabia dinner that night.

On the last day of the Cruise, *we repeated the tour of the ancient temples of Karnak and Thebes* as well as all the other places of the first tour. This time, however, John and I enjoyed the Movenpick Hotel much more than before because we took advantage of all the amenities we missed the first time just walking around the grounds, visiting the zoo, buying ice cream, and watching the women bake bread. And we didn't dare miss the amphitheatre with the beautiful classical music and the lovely sunset over the Nile taking pictures of the birds and people in silhouette. We also enjoyed our last dinner at the Movenpick restaurant and made it special by ordering a steak entrée with a glass of wine, taking time to relax before the rest of the trip home. Now, we had taken the Nile River Cruise in both directions and revisited its ancient monuments with the same tour guide we had come to know and respect. We learned more of the ancient religion which seemed to co-exist about the same time as the ancient Greek religion with all its different gods and goddesses and ancient folklore. The Egyptian tours were well protected by the Egyptian government with armed guards at all stops along the Nile. We flew back to Cairo the next day and spent two nights at the Conrad Hilton Hotel before returning to Alexandria on the train. Our short stay in Cairo with the great international food was always a pleasure, and our Egyptian driver in Cairo was always faithful to drive us wherever we wanted to go. Since the city of Cairo is so expansive, we only had time to see a very small part of it, mainly the downtown area along the Nile River, the Pyramids at Giza, and Old Cairo.

On the 27th of November, John and I flew back to Frankfurt for another 10- day vacation. On this trip, we repeated a portion of our previous trip during the summer, but we arranged to be at Chiemsee for Thanksgiving Dinner with the troops and their families. We enjoyed this tremendously and the food at the AFRC was excellent. Rothenburg was all lit up at night with bright Christmas lights in all the store windows, and it was so exhilarating to get into the Christmas spirit in such a holiday atmosphere of cold weather with a few flakes of snow. We enjoyed just walking around looking at the Christmas motifs and choosing a nice restaurant for dinner, or stopping in a café for a hot chocolate to get in out of the cold. It was always a joy traveling through Europe where people, although a little different from us in their traditions, were so much like us in sharing the Christmas spirit. We love the vigorous spirit of the German people and the intricate and artistic Christmas decorations and furniture they make.

Christmas at Rothenburg

I arrived back in the US on the 7th of December and John arrived back in Alex around the same time. Ginger met my plane at the Mobile airport, and again, I missed mother's not being there with her to meet me as always before. I felt very much alone in our big house without my family, so I made plans to fly to Portsmouth to spend Christmas with Maggie, Dave and Jenny. I left my car parked in long-term parking and let them know I was on my way. This time, it would be easier for them to meet my plane from Atlanta when I flew into Portsmouth. I brought a few gifts home with me from Germany and borrowed Maggie's car to do a little after Christmas shopping, and I also drove down to Virginia Beach to visit Amanda and her family. I remember doing a little grocery shopping there at the Norfolk Commissary to bring back for Maggie and Dave's kitchen. Again, I was very sad to leave them, but we had a very good visit which I would always remember. This time, Maggie and Jenny saw me off at the Portsmouth airport for Atlanta on my return flight to Mobile a few days following the New Year.

CHAPTER THIRTY-FIVE

A Cruise on Lake Nasser

2003-2004

While we were on *home leave,* John and I would make our triangular trip to Jackson, Memphis and Baton Rouge to see all the folks. We attended as many of Katie's dance recitals, plays and school functions as possible, and, after Joshua started to school, we tried to attend all of his school functions. Our time in Williamsburg with Maggie, Dave and Jenny was wonderful while it lasted, but when John came home to stay in 2004, we didn't pass through Atlanta anymore so our stopovers in Williamsburg seemed to end. After we were settled, it seemed better for them to come down to visit us. I'm very grateful that we had all those special times together in Williamsburg, and we will always cherish those memories. One year, Jenny's class made and served ice cream to all the parents, and then we went outside to watch the relay races in the school yard. We also enjoyed the art work which lined the walls in the hallway of the school and had fun finding Jenny's beautiful pictures. She was quite an artist! And she won a prize that year for designing a postage stamp depicting a ship coming up the James River with the first settlers of Jamestown, with the American Indians watching from a hillside. Maggie coached Jenny's softball team that year, and John and I were very happy to be sitting in the bleachers watching the kids out on the field playing ball. Maggie did a great job of teaching them good sportsmanship and how to play the game.

When Josh started coming over to spend his summers with me, I started him off with Bible school for the first two weeks. And I would meet him after Sunday school at the First Methodist Church for the church services. After several years, he had made many friends at the church and was invited to church events and to the homes of his friends. When my brother, Michael, built a pier to house his boat at their lovely home on Perdido Bay, he also built a large upper deck where we adults could sit to enjoy the sun and visit, while at the same time, supervise the kids having fun in the water below. Josh loved to visit Uncle Mike and Aunt Ginger, and his favorite thing was to swing out on a rope at the end of the pier and drop into the water. He also liked to swim and paddle around in the small boats they had for all the kids to play in. We all enjoyed the wonderful salty air of the Gulf and Perdido Bay there in the tranquil waters.

While very young, Josh spent all his Christmas vacations with us and I would try to balance out my time with all the grandchildren. When Lorena was here for Christmas with Josh, we would make it a point to attend church service to hear the Christmas carols at the various churches near us, and they were always very beautiful. After Josh got his pet rabbit, *Nibbles*, they had to bring over all her paraphernalia, and it started making sense to meet half-way and exchange passengers. Sometimes, we would have a picnic at the Mississippi Welcome Center and enjoy a family get-together, especially if Maggie and Jenny were visiting. After John came home from Egypt, we enjoyed having Josh with us for his summer vacation, and, one hot July, we took him to watch the Blue Angels fly over Pensacola Beach. Since we had to park the car a very long distance away and carry so much stuff with us to the beach, we found it was much easier to see them in November at the Naval Air Station. One summer, Josh flew to Kansas City with us to visit his Uncle Jim and Aunt Julie and brought his Nintendo game. Katie was also visiting at the time, and we all joined in to choose our characters for the sports games. It was practically the first time Josh and Katie had a chance to get to know each other, since there had always been a four-year age gap between them. On this trip, however, Josh, 12, and Katie, 16, seemed to get better acquainted while sharing this competitive family game. We all had fun! And the age gap was somewhat diminished. While in Kansas City, Josh attended a Royals Baseball Game with his granddad and Uncle Jim, and, due to his having won a door prize, Josh was interviewed on TV. John said he spoke up into the microphone very well, like his dad had done many years before at a Cub Scout pack meeting in Montgomery.

Ireland & the Aran Island of Inishmore

On the 9th of September, I left Mobile to meet John in Dublin for lunch at the Dublin Airport before renting a car to drive to Howth for overnight at our favorite B&B. We left the following day for Killarney where John played a little golf and we visited some of our favorite places. Then we planned the rest of our trip and decided to do something we had never done before. We drove around Galway Bay to the little town of Spiddal, where we spent the night in a lovely thatched roof cottage surrounded by a beautiful garden with many lovely hydrangeas. Our landlady was very hospitable and offered to hold our baggage in her storage house while John and I took the ferry over to *Inishmore Island* for overnight and a tour of the island the following day.

Our tour took us around the Island and up to the top of *Dun Aengus*, an ancient fortress, the origin of which is still a mystery. It was a long climb to the top of Dun Aengus, but once at the top of the rock-strewn slope, one notices a semicircular stone wall enclosing a space that ends at the edge of a 300-foot cliff, which drops off dramatically into the Atlantic Ocean. The *fortress* consists of three irregular semicircles, each originally thought to be a line of defense, but there seems to be a controversy today over whether or not this was indeed a fortress. Without any water supply or evidence of dwelling places, it was hardly suitable for holding out in a siege. Some speculate that it could have been used as a religious site for conducting pagan rituals or sacrifices. The climb up was quite treacherous over many rocks, but going down was much worse because the rocks had become slippery due to a passing rain. Back at the bottom of Dun Aengus, we found a restaurant and souvenir shop while awaiting our ride back into town. In *Kilronan*, we walked around the small town looking at the beautiful woolen capes and sweaters for sale in the many shops and then stopped to watch some kids having fun diving into the water at the port. Before catching our ferry back to the mainland, we had a wonderful fish dinner at the port restaurant.

Dun Aengus, Site of Ancient Fortress on Inishmore Island of the Aran Isles, Ireland.

Touring Inishmore Island by Donkey Cart.

During our three days stay at *Spiddal*, we discovered a small dirt road which led down to an inlet from Galway Bay. The road took us past two ancient cemeteries and both sides were laden with blackberries just right for picking and eating, so we picked some and took them back to our room. Our landlady served a full Irish breakfast every morning with wonderful homemade biscuits, or scones, which just melted in our mouths, and always a bowl of cut fresh fruit. The blackberries were a good addition. From Spiddal, we drove over to *Portumna* to check on the golf course and hotel, which had been up for sale the year before. John was seriously considering getting some of his friends together to invest in the reconstruction of a new hotel which would better serve the small town. However, another construction company beat him to it and we found a new hotel in its place. They had changed the overly modern looking building to one of a more traditional style, with meeting rooms and places for entertainment and sports events. We drove on to Dublin, returned our rental car and checked our baggage for our connecting flight back to Alexandria. We had come to depend on the good food at the Dublin airport restaurant and had plenty of time for dinner before boarding our Lufthansa flight to Frankfurt with connections to Alexandria.

I first met *Tiny Gamila* when she came bouncing out the door of the receptionist's office as I walked into the old Italian villa where John worked. We had just returned from Ireland and *Tiny* was about three weeks old and very lively for a small kitten. She was cute! But she was very scrawny and straggly looking with a rat-like tail. To me she was just one of the many cats of the compound, and I had no inclination of getting involved. John was planning another trip, which would take us down to the *Nubian Monuments with a Cruise on Lake Nasser* to view the ancient ruins of Nubia, and he asked Hal if he and Marty could watch out for the tiny kitten while we were away. The villa cats were always coming and going, and he thought she might try to venture outside the compound due to her inquisitive nature. And, as we had learned, the traffic on the streets was very dangerous for a small kitten.

John and the secretaries had saved Tiny's life as a newborn baby kitten just a few weeks before when one of the engineers discovered her trying to climb over some bricks in the courtyard, looking for her mother and crying to be fed. Somehow she had slipped away from her mother and was lost. Like Mishmish, someone heard her cries and brought her need for food to their attention. The first thing John did was to cross the street to buy her a small cup of plain yogurt. She sank her little face right into the yogurt and started lapping it up. Then he brought her inside his office and built her a cardboard house out of an old box like he had done for Mishmish. He sat it outside his office inside a terrace wall to protect her from the other cats. Here was another little mouth to be fed with the eye dropper, and John's secretary got right to it with the help of a few other secretaries. They all looked out for Tiny for the first couple of weeks, but now she was able to feed and care for herself within the boundaries of the walled terrace where she was safe and protected. Still, she was very inquisitive!

Lake Nasser & The Nubian Monuments

We hardly had time to turn around, when it was time for us to leave again. This time, John and I would fly down to *Abu Simbel* to see the *Nubian* monuments and take the three-day cruise on *Lake Nasser*. We left on the 7th of October on the morning train to Cairo, where we were picked up at the train station and taken to the *Movenpick Heliopolis Hotel in Cairo*. The next morning, we flew EgyptAir to *Aswan* and spent the night at the *Old Cataract Hotel*. Early the next morning, we flew to *Abu Simbel* arriving around 7:30, and we immediately boarded our cruiser, *the M.S. Kasr Ibrim* upon our arrival. From the cruise ship docked in the harbor, we visited the *Abu Simbel temple and the temple of Ramses II and his wife, Nefertari. Both temples were symbols of the international campaign for the salvage of the Nubian monuments, when the desert was flooded with water from the Aswan Dam to create Lake Nasser.*

Since the waters of the Nile River were not easily tamed and overflowed periodically, the English built the old dam around the turn of the 20th century. It became insufficient and the dam was enlarged to its present size in two stages: the first, in 1912, and the second in 1934. Still this was not enough to meet the demands of the Egyptian territory and the unpredictable river. A new dam would not only increase the amount of farmland, but irrigation would become a reality and the annual production of electricity would be dramatically increased. It was thus decided to embark upon the construction of a new barrier in the River: *"a barrier against hunger which would set Egypt on the road to modernity,"* as said by President Nasser. Construction was begun on the *High Dam* in January, 1960, and in 1964, the waters of the Nile were diverted into a branch canal; in 1972, the work of this enormous project was considered finished. The body of water thus formed is Lake Nasser, which is 500 kilometers long; 150 kilometers of which are in Sudanese territory.

Before the waters of the High Dam could be released, the numerous Nubian villages in the area had to be evacuated, and fourteen temples had to be dismantled and faithfully reconstructed on higher ground or they would have been submerged. The monuments had to be taken apart by cutting through stone and numbering the parts, so they could be put back together in their original form on the higher plateaus above the banks of the water. We would visit all of them on our trip across Lake Nasser which looked like an ocean as we were crossing it on our way back to Aswan.

Abu Simbel Nubian Temples.

Lake Nasser: Nubian Temples Re-Located.

After visiting the two very impressive temples at Abu Simbel that first morning in the early hours when the rays of the sun lit up the inside of the main temple, we re-boarded our cruise ship and took pictures from the deck as we sailed away and headed for *Kasr Ibrim,* where the tops of some of *"the vestiges of the distant past of Nubia"* could be seen slightly above the water. During the Pharaonic period and the Medieval Age, this hill was dominated by a citadel, and, on the summit of the hill, was a cathedral. We could see some of the Roman arches which were left in place, as the waters flooded the area. As we were not permitted entrance to the site, we could only view it from the sun deck of our cruise ship and listen to its history as we took pictures. Dinner was served on deck while sailing to *Amada.* After breakfast the following morning, we visited the *Temple of Amada of Dynasty XVIII, built during the reign of Thotmosis III, Amenophis III and Thotmosis IV, which were dedicated by Ramses II to the rising sun, and the tomb of Penout, Viceroy of Nubia.* Lunch was served while sailing to *Wadi El Seboua,* where we disembarked to visit *the Temple, dedicated by Ramses II to the two gods, Amon Ra and Ra Harmakis.* We also visited *the temple of Dakka, dedicated to the god Thot of Divine Wisdom, Lord of Time and Science, and Master of Literature.* We then visited the *Greco-Roman Temple of Maharakka* and had dinner on deck while sailing *to Aswan.*

The following morning, we disembarked after breakfast to visit *the Kalabsha temple, with its Pharaonic aspect, remodeled into the Greco-Roman style and dedicated to the god Mandoulis. We also visited Beit El Wah, erected by Ramses II in the beginning of his reign and the Kiosk of Kertassi, erected to honor the goddess Isis.* We then spent two nights at *the Old Cataract Hotel,* and on the morning of our departure as we were preparing to leave, a worker in the garden below caught my attention and threw up a bouquet of flowers he had just picked and entwined for me while I was standing out on our balcony looking one last time at the lovely view of the harbor and desert across the Nile River. There was only one other English speaking person on the cruise, a young vivacious Japanese woman who was on vacation by herself. The three of us got along very well as we disembarked at various stops in the desert to tour the furthermost Nubian sites. What a small world and how much we are all alike. She was very bold in allowing the guides to place a couple of live lizards and a scorpion in her hand for pictures. Everywhere we went, there were armed guards to protect us, so we felt very safe even far out in the desert. We flew *EgyptAir back to Cairo,* where we spent our last night at the Conrad Hilton Hotel before taking the train back to Alex on the 13th.

When John returned to the office, he learned that Hal, on his way home from work, had found Tiny, lying on the side of the busy street about a block from our apartment, obviously dying from a badly slit stomach wound. Hal went back to the office, found a platter to put her little body on, notified the secretary to call the Vet, and carried her up to his apartment. Hal and Marty turned their kitchen counter into a lab so the Veterinarian could work on her, and they saved her life. The lady Vet gave her shots of antibiotics and left them with medicine to shoot down her throat twice each day and salve to apply to her stomach wound each morning. We speculated on what happened: Some of the guys who disliked cats may have run them out of the compound, and she could have found a place to hide in the engine of a vehicle to get away from the terrifying traffic. As I had witnessed before, someone could have gotten into the vehicle and turned on the engine. I had seen this happen to another cat from our apartment window, but that time, the cat was run over by the back wheels of a truck which badly crushed her backside causing her to lie helplessly on the side of the street. Our Christian friend across the street went over and moved her onto the sidewalk. I called the office to notify John and his secretary, who both came down quickly but her body had already been moved and there was nothing more they could have done anyway. I think the lady called someone to come and get the cat, but she was so badly wounded she probably didn't make it. Tiny's wound looked like the blade of an engine could have cut her stomach and inside part of her upper right leg. The vet said she was a very lucky cat because none of her internal organs were damaged. The deep slit to her stomach would have to heal as an open wound.

Since Hal and Marty were ready to go on their vacation, John and I took over Tiny's treatment. It was hard to shoot the medication down her throat, but, once that was accomplished, all we had to do was catch her and wrap her in a towel so we could hold her tightly enough to apply the ointment and give it time to soak in. While John held her, I would place the gauze with the ointment over her wound and wrap the towel tightly around her and hold her for about 15 minutes like a *little baby bunting*. All of this sounds very simple, but doing it was quite a tedious matter. Once I had her all wrapped up securely in my arms, John would put on one of our favorite Elvis tapes and leave me sitting there holding TG while he left for work. She would listen quietly looking up at me until the 15 minutes passed and then she knew exactly when the time was up. She would start squirming to get loose, and then she would walk across the floor shaking off the gauze as she went. She loved to play with the wires of the TV, the computer and the telephone, so we tried to keep them up from the floor out of her reach as much as possible. TG was very suspicious of our cleaning lady. She would hide up under the furniture watching her every move with the vacuum cleaner and floor mop. As our maid moved forward through the apartment cleaning the rugs and wooden floors, TG stayed a couple of chairs ahead of her moving backwards sensing her every move.

Soon after the accident, we discovered TG's mother to be a one-eyed cat who looked very much like a picture we had of an Arabian Wild Cat. John had renamed her *Gamila* after his arrival when he heard people calling her *old one eye*. He thought that was terrible and asked one of the secretaries to help him come up with a name in Arabic which meant *beautiful*. When Gamila brought her other two siblings to the Villa to be fed, we noticed that one was apricot, like Mishmish, and the other had the same coloration as Tiny, except for the classic white and tan scarf-like appearance around her neck and the distinctive white upper chest. The rest of her coloration was a combination of black and gold which produced the same tortoiseshell effect. Tiny had a more classic look, as if she had been sprayed with white paint on one side of her chin and underneath her neck and upper chest. The other side of her chin and face was totally black. She also had tiny encirclements of light tan around the rims of her beautiful green eyes, which were a wonderful contrast to her mostly black and gold tortoiseshell appearance. She always wore a very serious look on her face, but she was very mischievous and fun loving. Always full of energy, she would plunge headfirst into the heavy fringe of our plush Egyptian carpet and try to chew and claw the fringe all at the same time. We had to put the carpet up out of her reach to save it.

Tiny Gamila remained full of life and energy and loved to chase a little ball outside on our balcony where John built her another little cardboard house to live in. She loved to jump out from behind a post to get the ball whenever one of us rolled it in front of her, and it became a game. Every time John would tell her to *"get ready,"* she would wriggle around on her little haunches behind the post ready to jump out and chase the ball. The vet told us to prepare good food for TG with vegetables and broth from our left over food all mashed up so she could easily digest it. One morning, we found her little toy mouse in her scrambled egg dish after she had finished eating most of it. Other times, while I was cooking in the kitchen, she would climb up the screen door or window to look in and cry for me to let her in. Finally, she made it in all by herself under the kitchen door which was only about two inches above the floor. She didn't let her open wound bother her one bit. We have pictures! When it turned cold outside at night, we brought her cardboard house inside and placed it in the entrance hall, or vestibule, where she had access to the half bath where her cat box was located. The tile floor of the small bathroom could be sprayed and washed out when needed. We also bought her a little bed to sleep in and closed the doors of the vestibule to the rest of the house at night when we went to bed, and she became well accustomed to her new environment and went to bed when we did. However, she couldn't wait for us to get up in the morning and would be standing up looking through the glass door down the long hallway for us to come and let her out.

One day, I noticed her open wound puffing up like a small leather football and called the Vet to come out and see what was wrong. The lady Vet, who spoke very little English, brought her husband with her, who spoke the language much better and explained that this is *"normal"* in the healing process of an open wound. It was just dead skin which needed to be trimmed off. She would give Tiny a light sedative so she could work on her, so we asked her to trim her nails as well while she was under. The Vet said she would give her a little stronger dose for the additional work and asked John to hold her while she gave TG the shot. TG wriggled loose with the needle still in her backside and jumped down from the kitchen lab to try to get away. Of course we didn't know how much of the medication went in, so the Vet gave her another shot. For fear of an overdose, I was up and down most of the night checking to see if TG was coming out of it. Finally, around 2:30 am, I started to see some movement. TG tried to get up, but fell back several times. When I could see that she was coming out of it, I was finally able to get some sleep. She was a little wobbly most of the morning but eventually came back to normal later in the day.

Marty and I remembered our plan to visit the very classic Cecil Hotel again overlooking the beautiful Port of Alexandria, where we had enjoyed their wonderful food at a memorable Iftar with our Egyptian friends. Since the food was so good and the view so lovely, we decided to do it again before we had to leave Egypt and return to the States. We made reservations for a table outside on the balcony. John and Hal invited a couple of gentlemen who were in Alexandria representing the Company to see how the wastewater project was going as it neared completion. It turned out to be a very memorable evening for all of us sitting together at a table outside on the balcony enjoying the gorgeous view before sunset and a wonderful seafood dinner. Again, we made some really great pictures. As we were leaving to go back down to the lobby, we noticed a newly renovated old-fashioned elevator shaft, which some people were using for exiting the top floor. John took a picture of Marty, Hal and me looking down the shaft in amazement, and it is quite hilarious! We were so fascinated by it, we eventually had to get on and ride it down! Now we laugh at the very thought of that picture.

The Bay of Alexandria from the Balcony of the Cecil Hotel.

Before Hal and Marty left Egypt to go back home, we invited them up for Thanksgiving Dinner. I prepared the closest thing I had to turkey, *a Chicken & Dressing Dinner,* which I prepared in a skillet from a recipe I found on a can of Campbell's soup using deboned chicken breasts, cream of chicken soup, sour cream and Stove Top dressing mix. It was very good, a great replacement for a turkey dinner, and I served it with peas and carrots, a mixed salad and dessert. Hal and Marty brought a beautiful floral centerpiece, and we all enjoyed our special day together.

They enjoyed playing with TG one more time before they had to leave the following day. We were sad to see them go, but our time was getting short, too. They had given us many things from their kitchen which they didn't want to ship back, including their bottle of *Liquid Smoke.* We would see them many more times in the future when they vacationed at the Gulf with some of their *snow bird* friends who came down every winter to get away from the ice and snow of the northern Mid-west. John and I would drive down to the beach to have lunch with them many times, and they would drive up to visit us. They were very gracious friends to offer to stay in our house with Tiny Gamila while John and I accompanied our son, Jim, and his new wife, Julie, to Ireland a few years later to celebrate our

50thAnniversary and their *First.* One of the items on *Jim's Bucket List* was to play golf with his dad in Ireland, so we met them there for a two-week golfing tour in July 2007.

In December 2003, John and I flew to Frankfurt for a second 10-day vacation, visiting Rothenburg and many of the places we had seen on our previous trip, and, on the 16th, he flew back to Alexandria and I flew to Mobile. John hired one of the tea boys to feed TG while he was away. Jim, Kathy and Katie invited me to spend Christmas in Jackson with them that year because I had missed them several years and Katie was growing up so quickly. I spoke with the rest of the family to let them know what I was doing that year and drove home a couple of days later. I flew back to Alex on the 5th of March. I noticed that the shower curtain around the tub was hanging in shreds. John said that after I left, TG would sit on the edge of the tub while he was showering to swipe the shower curtain with her sharp little claws and stick her head in to bite the water. Then she would follow him all over the house to help him get ready for work. While putting on his shoes, she would jump at his shoe laces and try to get them in her teeth while John was trying to tie them. Of course, I had seen this exhibition every morning before I left, and it was very amusing. She was so much fun! But while I was away, Tiny Gamila had grown up and was not quite as rambunctious as she was before I left. In fact, she had become quite demure.

Tiny Gamila at Six Months.

I was amazed to see how much TG had grown. She was beautiful! Her fur coat had become quite thick and lustrous and her tail with the white and tan end was full and fluffy as it curled around her while she was sitting. When she walked, it sorts of curled up gracefully behind her as it floated in the air waving to and fro demonstrating her happy disposition. She was glad to see me and would crawl up on my shoulder to bite my hair just as she had always done when I was lying on the couch. Tiny Gamila had grown into a very beautiful cat! The Vet said she would never be able to carry a litter of kittens with her stomach muscles having been severely damaged and advised us to have her spayed. In Egypt, the normal lifespan for a cat is only a few years, and we considered bringing her home with us. She loved us so much and would not be happy with anyone else. Ironically, our housemaid was the only person who volunteered to take her, but she didn't have much room for a cat, and we knew it wouldn't work out because TG didn't like her. It must have been the loud vacuum cleaner that scared her.

As we were preparing for our last few months in Alex, Dr. Daria took me shopping for Egyptian cotton sheets like she had in our first apartment to bring back with me for our new house which was now about five years old. She also took me to the Sporting Club my last time to walk around the race track and sit in the lounge to have lemonade with her before driving home. And just before we left, Dr. Daria and her very sweet and lovely daughter took me back to the restaurant at the Port of Alexandria for a wonderful seafood dinner. Then we picked up her vivacious granddaughter, a pretty young teenager of about 15, who was patiently waiting for us in front of her high school. She was very cute and seemed glad to meet me. She told me that Tiny Gamila is a very lucky cat if she gets to come home with us to America. They, too, wished to visit our country someday, and I invited them to spend some time with us if ever they could make the trip across the Atlantic. We said our goodbyes, and they knew this time I wouldn't be coming back. It was always sad to leave good friends behind knowing we might never see them again. We will always remember our Egyptian friends as very good and caring people who try to take care of the less fortunate. John's secretary collected funds on a regular basis for some of the needy charities in Alexandria as well as the many others we knew who worked in John's office. It was such a pleasure to get to know all of them, and we hope and pray they are all doing well.

While I had been at home the three months I was away from Egypt, I planned a wonderful trip home for John and me as our *grand finale,* visiting our favorite places and a few we had missed. I made numerous reservations at hotels throughout Germany, Switzerland and Austria for a month's tour of Europe with a 5 day Rhein River Cruise from Wiesbaden, Germany to Amsterdam with two two-night stops and one over-night in Arnhem, Netherlands, to see where *the Battle of the Bridge* took place during WWII. I even booked us on the Glacier Express for another trip from St. Moritz to Zermatt, four nights in Interlaken and four nights at Zell am See, Austria. We also hoped to rent a car somewhere along the way and drive to Normandy to visit the WWII battleground and cemetery, and to stand on the bluff looking out over the water to see where the US invasions took place back in 1945. It would have been a fantastic trip! However, we had become so attached to TG and couldn't find anyone who could give her a good home, so I cancelled all the above reservations and booked us on two separate flights home. First, I had to find a good cage which would hold TG all the way home, and I was finally able to get one sent to us from Lufthansa in Cairo. The cardboard cage which they provided us in Alex just wouldn't do for TG. She was a *feral cat* and would have destroyed it in no time. It was entirely too small for the long period of confinement. I flew home the first of May to get the house ready for John and our special feline guest.

John and Tiny Gamila arrived at the Mobile airport on the 3rd of June 2004, after a very lengthy 24 hours with TG caged in from Alex to Mobile via Frankfurt. John had given her a sedative before leaving Egypt and saw her briefly at the Atlanta airport. She had a brief crying spell when she saw him and made it very clear that she wanted out of that cage. I was happy to see them the morning they arrived. John drove us straight home with Tiny Gamila crying all the way. When we finally arrived at our house and John opened the cage door, she ran out quickly; glad to be out of the cage but mad at both of us. Then she ran all over the house from place to place, checking out every nook and cranny, with a growl now and then when she passed John. We left her alone to explore the house that evening while we closed our bedroom door and went to bed.

The following morning when I got up to open the blinds, Tiny G. ran with me from place to place looking out the windows, but it took her a whole day to get over her mad spell. When John got up to go outside on the lanai with his coffee, she went outside with him and checked all the planters, but she had a few more growls in her before the day was over. The third day she became herself again and seemed very happy with her new environment. She learned the morning routine of opening the blinds and would run as fast as she could to beat me to the back room when she saw me headed in that direction with my coffee. She would run around me and straight up the back of the couch to sit in the window and look out at the birds and squirrels. Eventually, she was talking to them with a clicking sound we had never heard before. We got the message quickly to leave her alone when she was busily engaged in conversation with one of her new friends who often came to sit on the outside of the windowsill.

Since I was an early riser, John usually slept a little longer, so when he got up in the mornings, he would feed TG and the two of them would go outside on the lanai where he would enjoy his morning coffee with the newspaper while she checked her jungles. Then she would wait patiently for the sound of the water pump to announce the flowing of water into the pool and would sit there watching for a while. Eventually, she was jumping over the weir, or walking across it when the water wasn't flowing. Sometimes I would join John and TG with my second cup out on the lanai, but I was usually involved with projects around the house. For them, however, it became the morning routine.

We received a letter from Ahmed written on 29 June 2004, with news about our shipment home and ended with a special note about the Villa cats. He said, *"Mishmish was in a very bad way the week of Mr. John's departure. He stopped eating entirely and was mostly sitting under Mr. John's desk waiting for him."* Ahmed said it was a great surprise to everyone. The other cats had the same feeling and looked for John every day. They would quickly walk into the office and smell around John's desk, look at his chair for a while and then walk out. Ahmed said, *"We keep feeding them, but they miss the warm and trusting feelings of Mr. John. We all do!"* John missed them, too!

I found out that I was extremely allergic to cat dander a few weeks after John left for Washington to work as a consultant for AECOM, who had been contracted to assist the US Government in the rebuilding of the Iraqi infrastructure. While he was away, I was TG's primary target as a companion, and she would climb up the back of the couch to sit on my shoulder and rub her head against my face or neck. I started itching terribly and eventually broke out in welts. Then I began to feel sick. It got so bad I thought I was dying and told John to come home and take care of us because TG shared her time with us equally while he was home. I made an appointment with an allergy specialist, and his first response to me was, *"Get rid of the cat."* I told him we couldn't because she was part of our family. She wouldn't be happy anywhere else, so I made the decision of accepting his program of *Immunotherapy*. The procedure required two shots per week the first year, and then one shot per week to be tapered off as needed for the next three years. I was also inoculated for my seasonal allergies and found the shots greatly beneficial. The medication started working after only a few weeks and cleared up my other allergies as well. After four years of inoculations, they were still working after four more years, and I'm still much better than I was before thanks to TG.

We enjoyed having Tiny Gamila with us all 11 years of her short life and lost her in August 2014 from kidney disease. We believe the real cause was a tumor which had been growing in her stomach, unnoticed at first, due to her injury in 2003 when she was only a month old. She was so beautiful and so much fun and gave us so much joy! We were greatly blessed to have known TG and her very unique kind of love. We will never forget her! We could never pet her as a normal cat but allowed her to climb up and sit in our laps and nestle her head against us or lick our hand or leg with her sandpaper tongue. Many times, she would sit, or lie, next to us while we watched TV with a paw touching an arm or a leg to make sure we were there and she was in control.

John heard from an Egyptian friend that after the work ended at the Italian Villa, a very nice gentleman from the office for whom he had great respect, took Mishmish home with him to live on his farm. We were relieved to hear this wonderful news about Mishmish having a good home in a safe place with such a kind man and his wonderful family. John would have brought Mishmish home with us if he could have, but Mishmish was King of the Villa cats, and he could take care of himself.

CHAPTER THIRTY-SIX

The Signs of the Times
THE 21ST CENTURY

At this time of our lives, when things seem to be moving along as usual, millions of people have been slaughtered all over the world to create havoc and instill fear in the hearts and minds of people everywhere. After murdering hundreds of thousands, the extremists are now driving millions from their homes to seek refuge in other countries whose economies were already in poor condition. How can these countries support all these refugees? Thousands of these women and young girls are being raped repeatedly while many more are sold into slave trafficking. The whole Middle East is in turmoil, and the horsemen of the Apocalypse are racing madly towards the climax of this world as we know it. Our Country, which once supported our allies and trained them to fight for world peace, has now shifted our monetary support to countries which appear to be our enemies and want to kill us. At the same time, our military has shrunk to drastic lows, so that we could easily be overtaken by an enemy. We once had missile batteries in strategic locations around the United States to protect us in case of an atomic attack, but today they seem to have vanished. What in the world is happening? Why have we allowed ourselves to become so vulnerable? And our young men and women who fought so bravely in Iraq and Afghanistan to set the people free from tyranny have come home to a country which fails to support their needs for proper medical care, rehabilitation and jobs. They see the land for which they fought so hard to save just given away as our troops were pulled out prematurely. There have never been more suicides taking place than today by our wonderful veterans who see all their sacrifices have been in vain.

As a nation, we cannot even defend ourselves much less train other countries to fight for world peace! Many of our ships are in dry dock, and our fighter planes are being repaired with parts taken from aircraft graveyards. We are so heavily in debt our children and grandchildren will never be able to pay it off without a miracle from God, and yet we are told by our leaders that, because of our heavy indebtedness, they have saved us from recession. How can we expect to survive without even trying to balance our country's budget? And how can we afford to give large sums of money to countries who are actually building nuclear weapons to destroy us? I've often wondered how the *Apocalypse* could ever come about when our great country was strong enough to protect us and our allies from the evils of the world. Today, it appears to be happening right before our eyes, just as the Bible predicts! Seven hundred years before Christ, Isaiah had a vision of what it would be like for Judah and Jerusalem in the days before the Jews were taken captive to Babylon, which was fulfilled shortly thereafter. Then he had visions far into the future of what it would be like for those living in the last days. The message is still the same. (Isaiah, Chapters One & Two)

We were once so greatly blessed as a Christian nation with so much to give the world because we were also a grateful nation and good stewards of what God provided. Our downfall began decades ago when we allowed our Christian God to be *kicked out* of the public schools, while opening the door to other religions and inviting them in. Since there is only *One Way* to God, and it's through his Son, *"Yeshua,"* the Jewish Messiah, our blessings began to diminish. Our God is *a jealous God*, and he will not share his throne with other gods. Jesus said, *"I am the way, the truth and the life: no man cometh unto the Father, but by me."* (John 14:6) God was with us during WWII, when we were truly a Christian nation and fought wars which took thousands of lives of men and women, who bravely fought for freedom from the tyrants who were trying to take over the world. President Harry S. Truman had a very tough decision to make after the bombing of Pearl Harbor, December 7, 1941. If he had not allowed the bombing of Hiroshima and Nagasaki for the cause of world peace, what might the outcome have been? The losses on all sides would have been catastrophic! Our young men were going through hell in the Pacific Islands where the Japanese were heavily entrenched. Truman made the right choice to stop the bloodshed quickly and end the war. Japan surrendered! And we can be very proud of the work we did in establishing world peace and assisting the war-torn countries to rebuild.

As long as America was in control of nuclear power, it was a deterrent to tyranny. Fascism and communism were stopped for a while, until communism raised its ugly head again in Russia, China, North Korea and

North Vietnam. We first heard about the atrocities in Asia from Dr. Tom Dooley, a Navy doctor in the late 1950's, who wrote three books about what was happening to the Montagnards of Vietnam. They were peaceful farmers in the mountainous areas who were being harassed and tortured by the Viet Cong from the North, who were coming down to take over the southern provinces. His books, <u>Deliver Us From Evil</u>, <u>The Edge of Tomorrow</u>, and <u>The Night They Burned the Mountain</u>, all tell the story about what was happening in that part of the world while communism tried to creep into the former colonies of French Indo-China. His mother's book, <u>Promises to Keep</u>, tells about his life as a medical doctor setting up refugee camps for the people fleeing the Viet Cong. It became a best seller in the 1960's and quotes a Robert Frost poem, *"Stopping by Woods on a Snowy Evening":*

"The woods are lovely, dark and deep; but I have promises to keep and miles to go before I sleep, and miles to go before I sleep."

Dr. Tom Dooley gave his life to help these poor people overcome their constant harassment from the Viet Cong, the atrocities they suffered and their loss of family members, who were tortured and murdered right before their eyes. He let their cause be known to the world. Tom Dooley became a legend before he died of cancer at the young age of 34. God tells us to fight the good fight of faith and defend those who cannot defend themselves.

The falling away from our Christian way of life began in the 1960's with the rebels of the *hippy* generation, who demonstrated against the war in Vietnam. This generation gravitated into drugs and heavy metal rock and almost destroyed Christian family life with its satanic vibes. Like the *Pied Piper,* they planted their seeds of destruction and led our young people blindly down that road to their oblivion. When their bombings didn't work, they came up with a new tactic: they would become *college professors* and teach their lies and deception in the major universities. They would rewrite the history books and blame all the ills of the world on our great Country calling us *War Mongers!* The real *war mongers* are the *terrorists and tyrants,* whose agenda is to take over the world for their own gain of power and wealth. They have *brain washed* millions of people into believing *lies* about Christianity and the United States of America. They have turned *their hate, prejudice, venom, and bigotry* against those who are trying to serve God and our great Country. They have *divided* our once peaceful Nation, greatly blessed by God, into *hotbeds of riots and racism* with the ultimate goal of destroying all that is precious and dear to us and our way of life. Our forefathers warned us what would happen if we neglected to use the Bible, *the holy Word of God*, along with our great *American Constitution*. Without God at the helm of our Nation, we could be headed down the road of destruction and not even know it.

One very important person who seems to have been written out of American History is Haym Salomon, a Jew who supported George Washington and the first American army by collecting funds to pay the troops and supply them with food, clothing and weaponry to see them through the terrible winter at Valley Forge. His story can be found in The Forgotten Patriot. Without Haym Salomon's help to finance General Washington and the first American Revolution, we might never have become the United States of America. Thank God for all his blessings and may we never forget all the American Patriots who made our Country great.

> *"Watch and pray always that ye may be counted worthy to escape all these things that shall come to pass and to stand before the Son of man... For as a snare shall it come on all them that dwell on the face of the whole earth."* (Luke 21:35-36)

We need another *Great Awakening* like the one which occurred in the 1850's, when people were being saved even aboard ships coming into our harbors. They could feel the presence of God as they neared our shores, as described in The New York City Noon Prayer Meeting, *a Simple Prayer Gathering that Changed the World.* Revival Fire tells the story of *The Reformation of the Church,* which was brought about by Martin Luther and John Calvin in the 1500's, and *The Great Awakening,* which occurred in the 1800's and was brought about by John and Charles Wesley, who were driven out of the Anglican Church to the highways and byways of England to preach the gospel. George Whitfield joined them by riding horseback across the United States to preach to thousands, and it was said you could hear his voice for miles around when he preached from cemeteries where the acoustics were very good. The Great Awakening spread across America, Ireland and England as far away as Australia.

In the 1960's, hate could have stemmed out of the *fear of death* for those not wanting to fight for the price of freedom. If they didn't understand the need to fight the war in Vietnam, they should have read Tom Dooley's books.

Although the political situation at home hampered our war effort and finally pulled us out of that war prematurely, we did accomplish one thing: we slowed down the communist movement and stopped the *"Domino Effect"* in Southeast Asia. But, in our Country, *hate* was being taught in the universities through the antagonists to stir up trouble and take advantage of all disasters and bad situations. They fanned the flames of unrest and racism and continue their agenda today against our government and our people. They amplify the sins of the past and allow *roots of bitterness* to fester and spring up again to cause trouble. God tells us to forgive one another so that we may be healed. This *unforgiving spirit* is the spirit of *the antichrist* at work in the world today. Paul teaches us in Romans:

> *"I beseech you brethren, by the mercies of God, that ye present your bodies a living sacrifice, holy, acceptable unto God, which is your reasonable service. And be not conformed to this world: but be transformed by the renewing of your mind; that you may prove that good, and acceptable, and perfect will of God....*
>
> *"Let love be without dissimulation. Abhor that which is evil; cleave to that which is good. Be kind to one another with brotherly love.... Bless them which persecute you: bless, and curse not. Rejoice with them that do rejoice, and weep with them that weep. Be of the same mind one toward another.... Recompense to no man evil for evil. Provide things honest in the sight of all men. If it be possible, as much as lieth in you, live peaceably with all men.*
>
> *"Dearly beloved, avenge not yourselves, but rather give place unto wrath: for it is written, 'Vengeance is mine; I will repay,' saith the Lord. Therefore if thine enemy hunger, feed him; if he thirst, give him drink: for in so doing thou shall heap coals of fire on his head. Be not overcome of evil, but overcome evil with good."* (Romans 12:1-4 & 9- 21)

In order for God's judgment to be withheld from the United States of America, it will require *a change in our lifestyles and turning back to God.* It will require *repentance* from all the abominations we have allowed to flourish in our land and *forgiveness for all the sins of the past.* It will also require *a spirit of thanksgiving* to God for all our blessings in appreciation for all he has done for us. We must acknowledge our sins and ask God to forgive us. Like King David, who was guilty of the most grievous sins, we must bow before God in prayer and ask him to *renew a right spirit within us.* (Psalm 51:10-17). God tells us if we draw near to him, he will draw near to us (James 4:8). If we will do this and truly repent, God promises to hear our prayers and heal our land.

> *"If my people, which are called by my name, shall humble themselves, and pray, and seek my face, and turn from their wicked ways; then will I hear from heaven, and will forgive their sins, and will heal their land."* (2 Chronicles 7:14)

The apostle Peter tells us:

> *"For he that will love life, and see good days, let him refrain his tongue from evil, and his lips that they will speak no guile: Let him eschew evil, and do good; let him seek peace, and ensue it.*
>
> *"For the eyes of the Lord are over the righteous, and his ears are open unto their prayers: but the face of the Lord is against them that do evil…. But and if ye suffer for righteousness' sake, happy are ye: and be not afraid of their terror, neither be troubled: But sanctify the Lord in your hearts: and be ready always to give an answer to every man that asketh you a reason of the hope that is in you with meekness and fear:*
>
> *"Having a good conscience; that, whereas they speak evil of you, as of evildoers, they may be ashamed that falsely accuse your good conversation in Christ. For it is better, if the will of God be so, that ye suffer for well doing, than for evil doing. For Christ also hath once suffered for sins, the just for the unjust, that he might bring us to God, being put to death in the flesh, but quickened by the Spirit….*
>
> *"FORASMUCH then as Christ has suffered for us in the flesh, arm yourselves likewise with the same mind: for he that has suffered in the flesh has ceased from sin; that he no longer should live the rest of his time in the flesh to the lusts of men, but to the will of God….*
>
> *"Beloved, think it not strange concerning the fiery trial which is to try you, as though some strange thing happened unto you: But rejoice, inasmuch as ye are partakers of Christ's sufferings; that when his glory shall be revealed, ye may be glad also with exceeding joy….*
>
> *"For the time is come that judgment must begin at the house of God: and if it first begin at us, what shall the end be of them that*

obey not the gospel of God? And if the righteous scarcely be saved, where shall the ungodly and the sinner appear?" (1 Peter, Chapters 3:11-18 & 4:1- 18)

In the Book of Revelation, Jesus appears to us in Judgment *with feet like unto fine brass, as if they burned in a furnace.* We must read again his *Message to the Churches* (Revelation, Chapters 2 & 3) and submit ourselves to *the washing of water by The Word* so that we may be clean. Jesus only had to die *once* to pay sin's debt, and after that, there is no more sacrifice. If our conscience reveals to us individually that we have *trampled the blood of Jesus* by not taking the blood of the Covenant seriously, we need to confess our sins before God and repent. We must humble ourselves by kneeling before the Lord in prayer and crying out to him like David did *with a broken and contrite heart* in sorrowful repentance. *"For godly sorrow worketh repentance to salvation not to be repented of: but the sorrow of the world worketh death."* (2 Corinthians 7:10)

> *"For if we sin willfully after we have received the knowledge of the truth, there remains no more sacrifice for sins, but a certain fearful looking for of judgment and fiery indignation, which shall devour the adversaries. He that despised Moses' law died without mercy under two or three witnesses:*
> *"Of how much sorer punishment, suppose ye, shall he be thought worthy, who hath trodden underfoot the Son of God and hath counted the blood of the covenant, wherewith he was sanctified, an unholy thing and hath done despite unto the Spirit of grace? ...*
> *"It is a fearful thing to fall into the hands of the living God."*
> (Hebrews 10:26-31)

King David's heartfelt prayers touched God's heart, and God forgave him even though he had committed the sins of murder and adultery. God said that David was a man after his own heart, and I believe God will do the same for all those who diligently seek him in prayer asking his forgiveness. (Psalm 51:1-19) Paul asks us in Romans, *"How can we who are dead to sin, live any longer therein?"* We cannot! But we can repent and turn our lives over to God's mercy praying for his forgiveness and a new beginning in Christ Jesus. (Romans 6:1-8)

> "Have mercy upon me, O God, according to thy loving kindness: according unto the multitude of thy tender mercies blot out my transgressions. Wash me thoroughly from mine iniquity, and cleanse me from my sin. For I acknowledge my transgressions: and my sin is ever before me....
>
> "Create in me a clean heart, O God; and renew a right spirit within me. Cast me not away from thy presence; and take not thy holy spirit from me. Restore unto me the joy of thy salvation; and uphold me with thy free spirit. Then will I teach transgressors thy ways; and sinners shall be converted unto thee....
>
> "O Lord, open thou my lips; and my mouth shall shew forth thy praise. For thou desirest not sacrifice; else would I give it: thou delightest not in burnt offering. The sacrifices of God are a broken spirit: a broken and a contrite heart, O God, thou wilt not despise.... Then shalt thou be pleased with the sacrifices of righteousness." (Psalm 51:1-19)

The Bible says that without godly sorrow, there can be no real repentance. As our *Kinsman Redeemer,* Jesus paid the full price for all who would ever believe and receive his *free gift* of eternal life. We need to wake up and come back to God before it's too late, or we may one day wake up to find ourselves *in the great and terrible Day of the Lord.* Our Country once stood for truth, justice and equality for all the people to live together peacefully and God's generous blessings were upon us. I pray that he will hear our prayer and restore our great Christian nation once again, so that we may *mount up with wings of eagles, with renewed strength and soar* once again. (Isaiah 40:31)

> "For I am not ashamed of the gospel of Christ: for it is the power of God unto salvation to everyone that believeth.... For therein is the power of God revealed from faith to faith: as it is written: The just shall live by faith.
>
> "For the wrath of God is revealed from heaven against all ungodliness and unrighteousness of men, who hold the truth in unrighteousness; because that which may be known of God is manifest in them; for God hath shown it unto them.
>
> "For the invisible things of him from the creation of the world are clearly seen, being understood by the things that are made, even

his eternal power and Godhead; so that they are without excuse." (Romans 1:18-32)

Without a doubt, our sinful lifestyles are reaching up into heaven! And God is not pleased! His *Truth* demands *Justice! And Justice must be done!* The only place *Justice* and *Truth* can meet together in perfect harmony and achieve *Peace* is at *the Cross of Jesus, the risen Messiah, our Lord and Redeemer.* (Psalm 85:10-11) In God's *Mercy* and *Grace,* he prepared *The Way* for us to be saved *through Faith* in the death of his beloved Son, *"The sacrificial Lamb of God who takes away the sin of the world."* (John 1: 29)

"The flesh profits nothing. The Words that I speak to you they are Spirit and they are Life." (John 6:63)

"Verily, verily I say unto you, the hour is coming, and now is, when the dead shall hear the voice of the Son of God: and they that hear shall live. For as the Father hath life in himself; so has he given to the Son to have life in himself; and has given him authority to execute judgment also, because he is the Son of man.… I can of my own self do nothing: as I hear, I judge: and my judgment is just; because I seek not my own will, but the will of the Father which has sent me." (John 5:25- 30)

There must be law and order in our Country, or we will destroy ourselves. Families need protection, and policemen are well loved by those who are threatened by evil doers. Criminals must be prosecuted and brought to justice, so that peace may prevail for all those innocent people who have suffered so much already by their crime and violence. Our Police Force must be respected if peace is allowed to prevail in our country ever again, and those who commit crime within the Force must be weeded out. We must always remember that their job is not easy, especially in areas of high crime and violence. Quick decisions must be made to save lives; and they are not always easy. Human beings make mistakes and sometimes jump to wrong conclusions, but if and when this happens, understanding must prevail because lives are at stake. Remember the words of Paul in his letters to the churches:

"And be not conformed to this world; but be ye transformed by the renewing of your mind, that ye may prove what is that good, and acceptable, and perfect will of God." (Romans 12:2)

> *"Bless them which persecute you: bless, and curse not. Rejoice with them that rejoice, and weep with them that weep. Be of the same mind one toward another.... Recompense to no man evil for evil. Provide things honest in the sight of all men. If it be possible, as much as lieth in you, live peaceably with all men."* (Romans 12:14-18)

Today, these s*eeds of destruction* are flourishing all over the earth, and they are being driven with satanic power. Only *"the Seed of Life" in Christ Jesus* can save us from eternal destruction. Our forefathers warned us about neglecting Biblical wisdom in running our great country in accordance with our Constitution, which was written by devout men of God *for the people* to establish *justice for all*. Without Biblical wisdom and God's leadership, our government is vulnerable and could easily crumble from within. We have never needed God's love and wisdom more than we do today.

> *"And I heard a loud voice saying in heaven: Now is come salvation, and strength, and the kingdom of our God, and the power of his Christ: for the accuser of our brethren is cast down, which accused them before our God day and night. And they overcame him by the blood of the Lamb, and by the word of their testimony; and they loved not their lives unto death."* (Revelation 12:10-11)

When the seventh seal is broken, there is silence in heaven while the seven trumpets are preparing to sound. And another angel came and stood before the altar with a golden censer filled with incense to be offered with the prayers of the saints. And the angel took the censer, filled it with fire from the altar and cast it upon the earth: God's judgment begins to fall as the seven trumpets begin to sound one after another. When the fifth trumpet sounds, demons are released from the bottomless pit to inhabit men without the seal of God, and when the sixth trumpet sounds, four angels, bound in the great river Euphrates, are set loose to slay the third part of men.

> *"And the rest of the men which were not killed by these plagues yet repented not of the works of their hands, that they should not worship devils and idols of gold, and silver, and brass, and stone, and of wood: which neither can see, nor hear, nor walk: Neither*

repented they of their murders, nor of their sorceries, nor of their fornication, nor of their thefts." (Revelation 9:20)

That little drop of wine which fell across the Lord's Supper in my Bible will always be there to remind me of my promises to God to get into *Bible Study* and to denounce *Astrology*. I know in my heart that God allowed me to get involved with this abomination to show me *how very real is the spiritual realm*. Without God's Word to teach us discernment and the Holy Spirit to lead us into all truth, we might never have known how to fight this battle of *Spiritual Warfare*. We would be totally vulnerable to an easy takeover by the devil and his forces of evil by helping him set his throne above God's with our habitual practice of sin and immorality. *Battles are taking place right now* between God's angels and the devil's, who are working overtime to destroy God's people because they know their time is short. It is *their mission* to take as many souls with them as they can to their eternal damnation. *God has told us the truth!*

"This know also, that in the last days, perilous times shall come. For men shall be lovers of their own selves, covetous, boasters, proud, blasphemers, disobedient to parents, unthankful, unholy, without natural affection, trucebreakers, false accusers, incontinent, fierce, despisers of those that are good, traitors, heady, high-minded, lovers of pleasures more than lovers of God;

"Having a form of godliness, but denying the power thereof: from such turn away. For of this sort are they which creep into houses and lead captive silly women laden with sins, led away with divers lusts; ever learning, and never able to come to the knowledge of the truth." (2nd Timothy 3:1-7)

"And when ye shall see Jerusalem compassed with armies, then know that desolation thereof is nigh. Then let them which are in Judea flee to the mountains; and let them which are in the midst of it depart out; and let not them that are in the countries enter there into. For these are the days of vengeance, that all things which are written shall be fulfilled....

"And there shall be signs in the sun, and in the moon, and in the stars; and upon the earth distress of nations, with perplexity; the sea and the waves roaring; men's hearts failing them for fear and for looking after those things which are coming on the earth: for the powers of heaven shall be shaken. And they shall see the Son of

man coming in a cloud with power and great glory. And when these things begin to come to pass, then look up, and lift up your heads; for your redemption draweth nigh.

"And he spake to them a parable; 'Behold the fig tree, and all the trees; when they now shoot forth, ye see and know of your own selves that summer is nigh at hand. So likewise ye, when ye see these things come to pass, know ye that the kingdom of God is nigh at hand. Verily I say unto you, This generation shall not pass away, till all be fulfilled. Heaven and earth shall pass away: but my words shall not pass away.

"'And take heed to yourselves, lest at any time your hearts be overcharged with surfeiting, and drunkenness, and cares of this life, and so that day come upon you unawares. For as a snare shall it come on all them that dwell on the face of the whole earth.

"'Watch ye therefore, and pray always, that ye may be accounted worthy to escape all these things that shall come to pass, and to stand before the Son of man.'" (Luke 21:20-36)

"And I say unto you my friends: Be not afraid of them that kill the body, and after that have no more that they can do. But I will forewarn you whom ye shall fear: Fear him, which after he hath killed hath power to cast both soul and body into hell; yea, I say unto you, Fear him....

"Also I say unto you: Whosoever shall confess me before men, him shall the Son of man also confess before the angels of God. But he that denies me before men shall be denied before the angels of God. And whosoever shall speak a word against the Son of man, it shall be forgiven him: but unto him that blasphemeth against the Holy Ghost it shall not be forgiven." (Luke 12:4-9)

"Let every soul be subject unto the higher powers. For there is no power but of God: the powers that be are ordained of God. Whosoever, therefore, resists the power, resists the ordinance of God: and they that resist shall to themselves receive damnation. For rulers are not a terror to good works, but to the evil.

"Wilt thou then be not afraid of the power? Do that which is good, and thou shalt have praise of the same: For he is the minister of God to thee for good. But if thou do that which is evil, be afraid;

for he beareth not the sword in vain: for he is the minister of God, a revenger to execute wrath upon him that doeth evil....

"*Render therefore to all their dues: tribute to whom tribute is due; custom to whom custom; fear to whom fear; honor to whom honor. Owe no man anything, but to love one another: for he that loveth another hath fulfilled the law.*" (Romans 12:1-8)

"*Let this mind be in you which was also in Christ Jesus: Who, being in the form of God, thought it not robbery to be equal with God: But made himself of no reputation, and took upon him the form of a servant, and was made in the likeness of men.*

"*And being found in fashion as a man, he humbled himself, and became obedient unto death, even the death of the cross. Wherefore, God also hath highly exalted him, and given him a name which is above every name: That at the name of Jesus, every knee should bow, of things in heaven, and things in earth, and things under the earth; and that every tongue should confess that Jesus Christ is Lord, to the glory of God the Father.*" (Philippians 2:5-11)

"*Rejoice in the Lord always: and again I say Rejoice. Let your moderation be known unto all men. The Lord is at hand. Be careful for nothing; but in everything by prayer and supplication with thanksgiving let your requests be made known unto God. And the peace of God, which passeth all understanding, shall keep your hearts and minds through Christ Jesus.*

"*Finally, brethren, whatsoever things are true, whatsoever things are honest, whatsoever things are just, whatsoever things are pure, whatsoever things are lovely, whatsoever things are of good report; if there be any virtue, and if there be any praise, think on these things.*" (Philippians 4:6-8)

CHAPTER THIRTY-SEVEN

Out of Egypt
2004

One day as I was filing away our Egyptian memorabilia, I came across the little book I received from the Convent of St. Mark in Old Cairo and the map of *The Holy Family's Journey through Egypt*. I sat down and started reading: it was a very difficult journey with Joseph leading the donkey on which Mary and Jesus were riding. There were many stops along the way where they rested and sojourned for a few days, places where wells sprang up to give them drinking water and a spring of water where Mary bathed Jesus. People still go there today for the healing waters. Of course, there are many stories and legends left behind by the people who witnessed the incredible journey of the Holy Family. Christian churches and monasteries sprang up to cover the route they took along the Nile River as far south as the land of Mallawi. And it is very interesting to note that thousands of monks took to the hills in the 4th and 5th Centuries to build monasteries and churches which are still there in the mountains. I'll try to recount the story written in the Egyptian ledger:

> [When Herod heard that a new king was born in Bethlehem, he ordered the death of all baby boys under the age of two. Jesus was a year old when Joseph was told by an angel to *"Take the young Child and his mother, and flee to Egypt, and remain there until I tell you, for Herod is about to search for the Child, to destroy him."* (Matthew 2:13)
>
> Joseph promptly obeyed the angel in the dream and *"took the Child and his mother by night and went to Egypt."* (Matthew 2:14) And this started the journey in which the land of Egypt was blessed according to Isaiah's prophecy, *"Blessed be Egypt my people."* (Isaiah 19:25)

Hurriedly, the small caravan left Bethlehem at night, and Salome, the old nursemaid, who was with Mary when Jesus was born, accompanied them. According to the Egyptian legend, when Salome witnessed the birth of Jesus, she pledged to accompany Mary throughout her life.

Again, the angel of the Lord appeared to Joseph in a dream informing him of the death of Herod and told him it was safe for them to return to their homeland. But when Joseph learned that Archelaus was reigning over Judea instead of his father, Herod, Joseph was afraid to take them back to Jerusalem. And being warned by God in another dream, he turned aside into the region of Galilee. And he came and dwelt in the city of Nazareth that it might be fulfilled that which was spoken by the prophets, *"He shall be called a Nazarene."* (Matthew 2:19-23)]

From this marvelous little book, <u>The Visit of the Holy Family to Mallawi</u>, I learned that Jesus was one-year-old when they started the journey and about five when they returned. They lived in Egypt approximately four years and journeyed most of the way by foot and donkey traveling along the Nile River. They stopped many times to rest a few days and journeyed on, but they continued south and sojourned quite a long time around Mallawi. When the word came to Joseph in a dream that it was safe to return home because Herod was dead, they returned the way they had come. The book describes the miracles which took place at the many stops along the way where they rested for a few days, and the evidence is overwhelming that the Biblical account of the Holy Family in Egypt is true. According to legend, miracles are said to have taken place when Jesus passed by including *trees bowing down and Egyptian idols smashing to the ground.* The many churches and monasteries active today attest to their visit and the fact that Christianity is still alive in Egypt.

"For unto us a child is born; unto us a Son is given; and the government shall be upon his shoulder; and his name shall be called: Wonderful Counselor, Mighty God, the everlasting Father, and Prince of Peace. Of the increase of his government and peace, there shall be no end." (Isaiah 9:6-7)

"For God so loved the world, that he gave his only begotten Son, that whosoever believeth in him should not perish, but have

everlasting life, For God sent not his Son into the world to condemn the world; but that the world through him might be saved. He that believeth on him is not condemned, but he that believeth not is condemned already, because he hath not believed on the name of the only begotten Son of God." (John 3:16-18)

"In the beginning was the Word, and the Word was with God, and the Word was God. The same was in the beginning with God. All things were made by him; and without him was not anything made that was made. In him was life; and the life was the light of men. And the light shineth in the darkness, and the darkness comprehended it not." (John 1:1-5)

"He was in the world, and the world was made by him, and the world knew him not. He came unto his own, and his own received him not. But as many as received him, to them gave he power to become the sons of God, even to them that believe on his name: Which were born, not of blood, nor of the will of the flesh, nor of the will of man, but of God.

"And the Word was made flesh, and dwelt among us, (and we beheld his glory, the glory as of the only begotten of the Father), full of grace and truth. John (the Baptist) bare witness of him, and cried, saying, 'This is he of whom I spake, he that comes after me is preferred before me: because he was before me.' And of his fullness have all we received, and grace for grace. For the law was given by Moses, but grace and truth came by Jesus Christ." (John 1:10-17)

"I am the true vine, and my Father is the husbandman. Every branch in me that bears not fruit, he takes away; and every branch that bears fruit he purges, that it brings forth more fruit. Now ye are clean through the word which I have spoken unto you. Abide in me, and I in you. As the branch cannot bear fruit of itself, except it abide in the vine; no more can ye except ye abide in me.

"I am the vine, ye are the branches: He that abides in me and I in him brings forth much fruit: for without me, ye can do nothing… If ye abide in me and my words abide in you, ask what ye will and it shall be given you. Herein is my Father glorified, that ye bear much fruit; so shall ye be my disciples. As the Father hath loved me, so have I loved you: Continue ye in my love.

"If ye keep my commandments, ye shall abide in my love; even as I have kept my Father's commandments and abide in his love. These things have I spoken unto you, that my joy might remain in you, and that your joy might be full. This is my commandment: That ye love one another as I have loved you. Greater love hath no man than this; that a man lay down his life for his friends." (John 15: 1-13)

"Verily, verily I say unto you, he that believes on me has everlasting life. I am that bread of life. Your fathers ate manna in the wilderness and are dead. This is the bread which comes down from heaven, that a man may eat thereof and not die. I am the living bread which came down from heaven: if any man eat of this bread, he shall live forever: and the bread that I will give is my flesh, which I will give for the life of the world." (John 6:35-37; 47-51)

"Verily, verily, I say unto you, 'Except ye eat the flesh of the Son of man and drink his blood, ye have no life in you. Whoso eats my flesh and drinks my blood has eternal life; and I will raise him up at the last day; for my flesh is meat indeed and my blood is drink indeed. He that eats my flesh and drinks my blood dwells in me, and I in him. … This is that bread which came down from heaven: not as your fathers did eat manna and are dead: he that eats of this bread shall live forever.'" (John 6:53-58)

Since it was against Jewish law to drink blood, the Jews strove among themselves saying, *"How can this man give us his flesh to eat? … This is a hard saying, and who can hear it?"* Jesus knew that some of his disciples murmured about this and said unto them, *"Doth this offend you? What if ye shall see the Son of man ascend up where he was before: It is the spirit that quickens; the flesh profits nothing: the words that I speak unto you they are spirit, and they are life."* (John 6:61-63)

At the last supper, when Jesus had given thanks, he broke the bread and said, *"Take, eat: This is my body, which is broken for you: Do this in remembrance of me."* After the same manner, he also took the cup and said, *"This cup is the New Testament in my blood: This do, as often as you drink it, in remembrance of me. For as often as you eat this bread and drink this cup, you show forth the Lord's death until he comes again."* (Matthew 15:38) Holy Communion is a sacred moment for all the people of the

Church, and therefore, it should be administered with quiet dignity as all have access to kneel before the altar in prayer before eating the bread and drinking the cup in memory of the body and blood of Jesus. He warned us not to eat the bread or drink the cup in an unworthy manner, or we shall be guilty of the body and blood of the Lord:

> *"But let a man examine himself... For he that eats and drinks unworthily, eats and drinks damnation to himself, not discerning the Lord's body. For this cause many are weak and sickly among you, and many sleep. For if we would judge ourselves, we should not be judged. But when we are judged, we are chastened of the Lord, that we should not be condemned with the world."* (1 Corinthians 11:29-32)

After speaking with his disciples about what was to happen because his time had come and they would all be scattered, Jesus said to them:

> *"Nevertheless, I tell you the truth; it is expedient for you that I go away: for if I go not away, the Comforter will not come unto you; but if I depart, I will send him unto you. And when he is come, he will reprove the world of sin, and of righteousness, and of judgment....*
>
> *"Howbeit when he, the Spirit of Truth, is come, he will guide you into all truth: for he shall not speak of himself; but whatsoever he shall hear, that shall he speak: and he will show you things to come. He shall glorify me; for he shall receive of mine, and shall show it unto you.... A little while, and ye shall not see me: and again, a little while, and ye shall see me, because I go to the Father."* (John 16:7-16)

> *"Behold, the hour cometh, yea, is now come, that ye shall be scattered, every man to his own, and shall leave me alone: and yet I will not be alone because the Father is with me. These things I have spoken unto you, that in me ye might have peace. In the world, ye shall have tribulation: but be of good cheer; I have overcome the world."* (John 16:32-33)

> *"These words spoke Jesus, and lifted up his eyes to heaven, and said: Father, the hour is come; glorify thy Son, that thy Son also*

may glorify thee: As thou hast given him power over all flesh, that he should give eternal life to as many as thou hast given him.

"And this is life eternal, that they might know thee the only true God, and Jesus Christ, whom thou hast sent. I have glorified thee on the earth: I have finished the work which thou gavest me to do. And now, O Father, glorify me with thine own self with the glory which I had with thee before the world was.

"I have manifested thy name unto the men which thou gavest me out of the world: thine they were, and thou gavest them me; and they have kept thy word. Now they have known that all things whatsoever thou hast given me are of thee. For I have given unto them the words which thou gavest me; and they have received them, and have known surely that I came out from thee, and they have believed that thou didst send me.

"I pray for them: I pray not for the world, but for them which thou hast given me; for they are thine.... And I come to thee, Holy Father, keep through thine own name those whom thou hast given me that they may be one, as we are.... And now come I to thee; and these things I speak in the world, that they might have my joy fulfilled in themselves.

"I have given them thy word; and the world hath hated them, because they are not of the world, even as I am not of the world. I pray not that thou should take them out of the world, but that thou should keep them from the evil. They are not of the world, even as I am not of the world. Sanctify them through thy truth: thy word is truth.

"As thou hast sent me into the world, even so have I also sent them into the world. And for their sakes, I sanctify myself that they also might be sanctified through the truth. Neither pray I for these alone, but for them also which shall believe on me through their word; that they all may be one; as you, Father, art in me, and I in thee, that they also may be one in us; that the world may believe that thou hast sent me....

"O righteous Father, the world hath not known thee: but I have known thee, and these have known thee, and these have known that you have sent me, and I have declared unto them thy name, and will declare it: that the love wherewith thou hast loved me may be

in them and I in them." (Jesus' prayer to the Father for his church: John, Chapter 17)

Paul wrote many letters to the existing churches of his day, more than any other author, but his last letter was written to his beloved adopted son, Timothy, from Rome while he was in prison awaiting martyrdom:

> *"I charge thee therefore before God and the Lord Jesus Christ, who shall judge the quick and the dead at his appearing and his kingdom:*
>
> *Preach the word; be instant in season, out of season; reprove, rebuke, exhort with all long suffering and doctrine.*
>
> *"For the time will come when they will not endure sound doctrine; but after their own lusts shall they heap to themselves teachers, having itching ears; and they shall turn away their ears from the truth, and shall be turned unto fables. But watch thou in all things, endure afflictions, do the work of an evangelist, make full proof of thy ministry;*
>
> *"For I am now ready to be offered and the time of my departure is at hand. I have fought a good fight; I have finished my course; I have kept the faith. Henceforth, there is laid up for me a crown of righteousness which the Lord, the righteous judge, shall give me at that day: and not to me only, but unto all them also that love his appearing."* (2 Timothy 4:1-8)

The Bible reveals *the apostasy,* the falling away from the truth of the gospel in these last days. A few years ago, laws were passed to make it unlawful for Bible reading in the public schools, and they tried to remove the Ten Commandments from public buildings. They also tried to destroy Christmas and other Christian traditions, but *"we the people,"* took a stand and resumed our Christmas traditions, because they couldn't remove the love of Jesus from our hearts and our love for one another in the celebration of His birth with the giving of gifts.

> *"Now we beseech you brethren, by the coming of our Lord Jesus Christ, and by our gathering together unto him, That ye be not soon shaken in mind, or be troubled, neither by spirit, nor by word, nor by letter as from us, as that the day of Christ is at hand.*

"Let no man deceive you by any means: for that day shall not come, except there comes a falling away first, and that the man of sin be revealed, the son of perdition, who opposes and exalts himself above all that is called God, or that is worshipped; so that he as God sitteth in the temple, showing himself that he is God....

"For the mystery of iniquity doth already work: only he who now lets, will let, until he be taken out of the way. And then shall that Wicked be revealed; whom the Lord will consume with the spirit of his mouth, and will destroy with the brightness of his coming: Even him, whose coming is after the working of Satan with all power and signs and lying wonders, and with all deceivableness of unrighteousness in them that perish; because they received not the love of the truth, that they might be saved.

"And for this cause, God shall send them strong delusion that they should believe a lie: That they all might be damned who believe not the truth, but had pleasure in unrighteousness.... Therefore, brethren, stand fast, and hold the traditions which you have been taught, whether by word, or our epistle." (2 Thessalonians 2:1-15)

"Love not the world, neither the things that are in the world. If any man loves the world, the love of the Father is not in him. For all that is in the world, the lust of the flesh, and the lust of the eyes, and the pride of life, is not of the Father, but is of the world. And the world will pass away, and the lust thereof: but he that doeth the will of God abideth forever." (1st John 2:15-17)

"If the world hates you, ye know it hated me before it hated you. If ye were of the world, the world would love its own; but because ye are not of the world, but I have chosen you out of the world, therefore, the world hates you. Remember the word I said to you: The servant is not greater than his lord. If they have persecuted me, they will also persecute you; if they have kept my saying, they will keep yours also. But all these things they will do unto you for my name's sake, because they know not him that sent me." (John 15:18-21)

"Jesus said unto them, 'If God were your father, ye would love me: for I proceeded forth and came from God; neither came I of myself; but he sent me. Why do ye not understand my speech? Ye

cannot hear my word because ye are of your father the devil, and the lusts of your father ye will do. He was a murderer from the beginning, and abode not in the truth, because there is no truth in him. When he speaks a lie, he speaks of his own: for he is a liar, and the father of lies.'" (John 8:42-44)

In the seventh Chapter of Revelation, we have an interlude while God seals the 144,000 Jews to take them through the tribulation. Then we have another glimpse into heaven: *"A great multitude of people from all nations and tongues who have come out of great tribulation and washed their robes and made them white in the blood of the Lamb."* When *"the Restrainer,"* the Holy Spirit, is taken out of the world with those caught away in the *Rapture* of the Church, all hell will break loose upon the earth and many will be tried and tested. Many lives will be sacrificed when they refuse to pay homage to the beast. *Mystery Babylon* will continue to make life miserable for all the earth until God destroys *the unholy trinity* composed of *the great dragon, Satan* (Revelation 12:9), *the beast with seven heads which comes up out of the sea* (Revelation 13:1) and *the false prophet who comes up out of the earth* (Revelation 13:11).

> *"And in the latter time of their kingdom, when the transgressors are come to the full, a king of fierce countenance, and understanding dark sentences, shall stand up. And his power shall be mighty, but not by his own power: and he shall destroy wonderfully, and shall prosper, and practice, and shall destroy the mighty and the holy people."* (Daniel 7:23-24)

> *"And the king shall do according to his will and he shall exalt himself, and magnify himself above every god and shall speak marvelous things against the God of gods, and shall prosper 'till the indignation be accomplished: for that that is determined shall be done."* (Daniel 11:36)

> *"And there shall be a time of trouble; such as never was since there was a nation even to that same time: and at that time, thy people shall be delivered, everyone that shall be found written in the book. And many of them that sleep in the dust of the earth shall awake, some to everlasting life, and some to shame and everlasting contempt.*

"And they that are wise shall shine as the brightness of the firmament; and they that turn many to righteousness as the stars forever and ever." (Daniel 12:1-3)

Mystery Babylon, which combines world commerce and religion, is depicted as *that great City* (Revelation, Chapter 18) under the control of the beast of Chapter 13, which by this time will have grown its eighth head (Revelation 17:11). The last World Empire, whose deadly wound is healed, is in coalition with the false prophet, who makes *an image to the beast* and causes the people to take a number to buy and sell. The false prophet will set up *the abomination of desolation* in the temple in Jerusalem, and the people will be expected to pay homage to *the beast* or be killed. (Daniel 11:31)

"And I heard a voice from heaven saying unto me, 'Write, Blessed are the dead which die in the Lord from henceforth: Yea, saith the Spirit, that they may rest from their labors; and their works do follow them.' And I looked, and behold a white cloud, and upon the cloud one sat like unto the Son of man, having on his head a golden crown, and in his hand a sharp sickle.

"And another angel came out of the temple, crying with a loud voice to him that sat on the cloud, 'Thrust in thy sickle and reap: for the time is come for thee to reap; for the harvest of the earth is ripe.' And he that sat on the cloud thrust in his sickle on the earth and the earth was reaped. And another angel came out of the temple which is in heaven, he also having a sharp sickle....

"And another angel came out from the altar, saying 'Thrust in thy sharp sickle and gather the clusters of the vine of the earth for her grapes are fully ripe.' And the angel thrust in his sickle unto the earth and gathered the vine of the earth and cast it into the great winepress of the wrath of God. And the winepress was trodden outside the city, and blood came out of the winepress, even unto the horse bridles, by the space of a thousand and six hundred furlongs." (Revelation 14:13)

"Who is this that comes from Edom, with dyed garments from Bozrah; this that is glorious in his apparel, traveling in the greatness of his strength? I that speak in righteousness, mighty to save: 'Why are you red in your apparel, and your garments like him that treads

in the winepress?' 'I have trodden the winepress alone; and of the people, there was none with me: for I will tread them in mine anger and trample them in my fury; and their blood shall be sprinkled upon my garments, and I will stain all my raiment: For the day of vengeance is in my heart, and the year of my redeemed is come.'" (Isaiah 63:1-4)

In Chapter 11, we see the holy city trodden down by the Gentiles for 3½ years, and God gives power to his two witnesses to work miracles and to prophesy. These are the two *Sons of Oil*, who God said he would send before the great and dreadful day of the Lord (Zechariah 4:14 & Malachi 4:5). These will have the power to shut heaven, so it will not rain in the days of their prophecy, and over the waters, to turn them to blood, and to smite the earth with all plagues as often as they will. These two prophets are thought to be Moses and Elijah who were translated back to earth since it is appointed unto man once to die and afterwards the judgment (Hebrews 9:27). Moses and Elijah were both seen talking with Jesus on the *Mount of Transfiguration* (2 Peter 1:16-18). Moses performed these same miracles against Pharaoh to get the people out of Egypt, and Elijah held back the rain against Baalam. Therefore, it stands to reason that these two witnesses are Moses and Elijah. (Matthew 17:1-9) (Luke 9:28-36)

> *"And when they shall have finished their testimony, the beast that ascends out of the bottomless pit shall make war against them, and shall overcome them and kill them. And their dead bodies shall lie in the street of the great city … where also our Lord was crucified.*
>
> *"And they of the people and kindreds and tongues and nations shall see their dead bodies three and a half days, and they shall not allow them to be put into graves. And they that dwell upon the earth shall rejoice over them and make merry, and send gifts to one another; because these two prophets tormented them that dwelt on the earth.*
>
> *"And after that, the Spirit of life from God entered into them, and they stood upon their feet; and great fear fell upon all them which saw them. And they heard a great voice from heaven saying unto them, 'Come up hither.' And they ascended up to heaven in a cloud; and their enemies beheld them. And the same hour, there was a great earthquake….*

"And the seventh angel sounded; and there were great voices in heaven saying, 'The kingdoms of this world are become the kingdoms of our Lord, and of his Christ; and he shall reign for ever and ever.'" (Revelation 11:1-15)

"The Mystery of God is finished!" (Revelation 10:7)

"And after these things, I heard a great voice of many people in heaven, saying 'Alleluia; Salvation, and glory, and honor, and power, unto the Lord our God: For true and righteous are his judgments: for he hath judged the great whore, which did corrupt the earth with her fornication, and hath avenged the blood of his servants at her hand.'

"And a voice came out of the throne, saying, 'Praise our God, all ye his servants and ye that fear him, both small and great.' And I heard as it were the voice of a great multitude, and as the voice of many waters, and as the voice of mighty thunderings, saying, 'Alleluia: for the Lord God omnipotent reigneth.

"'Let us be glad and rejoice, and give honor to him: for the marriage of the Lamb is come, and his wife hath made herself ready.' And to her was granted that she should be arrayed in fine linen, clean and white: for the fine linen is the righteousness of saints. And he said unto me, 'Write, Blessed are they which are called unto the marriage supper of the Lamb.' And he said unto me, 'These are the true sayings of God.'

"And I fell at his feet to worship him. And he said unto me 'See thou do it not: I am thy fellow servant, and of thy brethren that have the testimony of Jesus: Worship God: for the testimony of Jesus is the spirit of prophecy.'

"And I saw heaven opened, and behold a white horse; and he that sat upon him was called Faithful and True, and in righteousness he doth judge and make war. His eyes were as a flame of fire, and on his head were many crowns; and he had a name written that no man knew, but he himself.

"And he was clothed with a vesture dipped in blood: and his name is called The Word of God. And the armies which were in heaven followed him upon white horses, clothed in fine linen, white and clean. And out of his mouth goeth a sharp sword, that with it he should smite the nations: and he shall rule them with a rod of

iron: and he treadeth the winepress of the fierceness and wrath of Almighty God.

"And he hath on his vesture and on his thigh, a name written, KING OF KINGS, AND LORD OF LORDS." (Revelation 19:1-16)

"And I saw the beast, and the kings of the earth, and their armies, gathered together to make war against him that sat on the horse, and against his army. And the beast was taken, and with him the false prophet that wrought miracles before him, with which he deceived them which had received the mark of the beast, and them that worshipped his image. These both were cast alive into a lake of fire burning with brimstone. And the remnant were slain with the sword of him that sat upon the horse, which sword proceeded out of his mouth: and all the fowls were filled with their flesh." (Revelation 19:19-21)

"I am the Lord, and there is none else, there is no God beside me: I girded thee, thou hast not known me: That they may know from the rising of the sun, and from the west, that there is none beside me. I am the Lord and there is none else. I form the light and create darkness: I make peace and create evil: I the Lord do all these things." (Isaiah 45:5-7)

God describes *"the great whore that sits upon many waters,"* who is *"riding on the back of the beast with seven heads and ten horns."* She is *arrayed in purple and scarlet and decked with gold and precious stones and pearls, and in her hand is a golden cup full of the abominations and filthiness of her fornication:* This is *"Mystery Babylon the Great, the Mother of Harlots and Abominations of the Earth. And I saw the woman drunken with the blood of the saints and with the blood of the martyrs of Jesus."* When the kings of the earth see this spiritual adulteress for who she is and what she has wrought in the earth, *"they will hate her and burn her with fire for in one hour her judgment will come."* (Revelation, Chapters 17 & 18)

"And I heard another voice from heaven, saying, Come out of her, my people, that ye be not partakers of her sins, and that ye receive not of her plagues, For her sins have reached unto heaven and God hath remembered her iniquities. Reward her even as she

rewarded you, and double unto her double according to her works: in the cup which she hath filled fill to her double." (Revelation 18:4-10)

"And I saw a new heaven and a new earth: for the first heaven and the first earth were passed away; and there was no more sea. And I John, saw the holy city, New Jerusalem, coming down from God out of heaven, prepared as a bride adorned for her husband.

"And I heard a great voice out of heaven saying, 'Behold, the tabernacle of God is with men, and he will dwell with them and they shall be his people, and God himself shall be with them, and be their God. And God shall wipe away all tears from their eyes; and there shall be no more death, neither sorrow, nor crying, neither shall there be any more pain: for the former things are passed away.'

"And he that sat upon the throne said, 'Behold, I make all things new.' And he said unto me, 'Write: for these words are true and faithful.' And he said unto me, 'It is done. I am Alpha and Omega, the beginning and the end. I will give unto him that is athirst of the fountain of the water of life freely. He that overcomes shall inherit all things; and I will be his God, and he shall be my son.

"'But the fearful, and unbelieving, and the abominable, and murderers, and whoremongers, and sorcerers, and idolaters, and all liars, shall have their part in the lake which burneth with fire and brimstone: which is the second death.'

"And there came unto me one of the seven angels which had the seven vials full of the seven last plagues, and talked with me, saying, 'Come hither, I will show thee the bride, the Lamb's wife.' And he carried me away in the spirit to a great and high mountain, and showed me that great city, the holy Jerusalem, descending out of heaven from God....

"And I saw no temple therein: for the Lord God Almighty and the Lamb are the temple of it. And the city had no need for the sun, neither of the moon, to shine in it: for the glory of God did lighten it, and the Lamb is the light thereof. And the nations of them which are saved shall walk in the light of it: and the kings of the earth do bring their glory and honor into it. And the gates of it shall not be shut at all by day: for there shall be no night there.

> "And they shall bring the glory and honor of the nations into it. And there shall in no wise enter into it anything that defileth, neither whatsoever worketh abomination, or maketh a lie: but they which are written in the Lamb's book of life." (Revelation 21:1-27)

Then God shows us the *River of Life* flowing out from the throne of God and the Lamb and the *Tree of Life* growing on both sides of the river, *which bears twelve kinds of fruit, and yields its fruit every month.* (Ezekiel, Chapter 47)

> "And he showed me a pure river of water of life, clear as crystal, proceeding out of the throne of God and of the Lamb. In the midst of the street of it, and on either side of the river, was there the tree of life, which bare twelve manner of fruits, and yielded her fruit every month: And the leaves of the tree were for the healing of the nations.
>
> "And there shall be no more curse: but the throne of God and of the Lamb shall be in it; and his servants shall serve him: And they shall see his face; and his name shall be in their foreheads. And there shall be no night there; and they need no candle, neither light of the sun; for the Lord God giveth them light: and they shall reign for ever and ever. "And he said unto me, These sayings are faithful and true: and the Lord God of the holy prophets sent his angel to show unto his servants the things which must shortly be done. Behold, I come quickly: blessed is he that keepeth the saying of the prophecy of this book....
>
> "And he said unto me, Seal not the sayings of the prophecy of this book: for the time is at hand. He that is unjust, let him be unjust still: and he which is filthy, let him be filthy still: and he that is righteous, let him be righteous still: and he that is holy, let him be holy still.
>
> "And, behold, I come quickly; and my reward is with me, to give every man according as his work shall be. I am Alpha and Omega, the beginning and the end, the first and the last.
>
> "Blessed are they that do his commandments, that they may have right to the tree of life, and may enter in through the gates into the City. For without are dogs, and sorcerers, and whoremongers, and murderers, and idolaters, and whosoever loveth and maketh a lie.
>
> "I Jesus have sent mine angel to testify unto you these things in the churches. I am the root and the offspring of David, and the bright and morning star. And the Spirit and the Bride say, Come.

And let him that heareth say, Come. And let him that is athirst come. And whosoever will, let him take the water of life freely.

"For I testify unto every man that heareth the words of the prophecy of this book, If any man shall add unto these things, God shall add unto him the plagues that are written in this book. And if any man shall take away from the words of the book of this prophecy, God shall take away his part out of the book of life, and out of the holy city, and from the things which are written in this book.

"He which testifieth these things saith, **Surely I come quickly.** Amen. Even so, come, Lord Jesus." (Revelation 22:10-21)

Bibliography

Arthur, Kay, Lord, I Want to Know You, Multnoma Books, a division of Questar Publishers, Inc., Portland, OR. Copyright: 1992.

Arthur, Kay, Lord, Is it Warfare? Teach Me to Stand, Multnoma Books, a division of Questar Publishers, Inc. Portland, OR. Copyright: 1991.

Arthur, Kay, Lord, Teach Me to Pray...in 28 days, a Workbook on Praying, Precept Ministries of Reach Out, Inc., Chattanooga, TN.

Arthur, Kay, Revelation, Maranatha...Our Redemption Draweth Nigh, Precept Upon Precept, Reach Out's Inductive Bible Study Course, Chattanooga, TN, 1981.

Arthur, Kay, Romans, The Constitution of Your Faith, Precept Upon Precept, Reach Out's Inductive Bible Study Course, Chattanooga, TN 1981.

Arthur, Kay, The Peace & Power of Knowing God's Name, TBN Edition, Waterbrook Press, Colorado Springs, CO, a Division of Random house, Inc. Copyright: 2002.

Baron, David, ISRAEL In The Plan of God, Kregel Publications (2001) (P/B).

Blum, Howard, The Gold of Exodus, The Discovery of the True Mount Sinai, Simon & Schuster, Rockefeller Center, 1230 Avenue of the Americas, New York, NY 10020. Copyright: 1998.

Bouji, Anne, The Way to a Man's Heart, Traditional Lebanese Recipes Step by Step...for Beginners & Expatriates, Librairie du Liban Publishers, Riad Solh Square, Beirut, Lebanon, 1999.

Chambers, Talbot W., The New York City Noon Prayer Meeting, "A Simple Prayer Gathering that Changed the World," Published by Campus Renewal, Inc., San Antonio, Texas. Copyright: 2009.

Clancy, Tom, Into the Storm, On the Ground in Iraq, with GEN Fred Franks, Jr. (Ret.), Berkley Publishing Company, 200 Madison Avenue, New York 10016. Copyright: 1997.

Compton's Encyclopedia, F.E. Compton Co, Division of Encyclopedia Britannica, Inc. 1967 Edition.

Copeland, Gloria & Billye Brim: Their TV Ministry on "The Signs of His Coming," "The Great Awakening" and "The Restoration of Israel"; Kenneth Copeland TV Ministry (2004-2012).

Cragg, Kenneth. The Call of the Minaret, Oxford University Press, 1956, A Galaxy Book with Corrections 1964, Library of Congress Catalogue, Card Number 56.8005, Printed in the United States of America, Pages 69-94.

Cruz, Nicky, Run Baby Run, (P/B); Outreach, Bridge-Logos, Publishers, 1969: Latest Publication, 2001.

Duvenoy, Claude, The Prince and The Prophet: The Rebirth of Israel, (196 pp.); Reprint: Billye Brim Ministries, 2003 (P/B); Original Publisher: Land of Promise Productions. Copyright: 1975.

Dooley, Agnes W., Promises to Keep, the Life of Dr. Thomas A. Dooley, A signet Book, Published by the New American Library of World Literature, Inc., 501 Madison Avenue, New York, NY 10022. Copyright: 1962.

Dooley, Dr. Thomas A., Deliver Us From Evil, A signet Book, Published by the New American Library of World Literature, Inc., Published by the New American Library, Inc., 1301 Avenue of the Americas, New York, NY 10019. Copyright: 1956.

Dooley, Dr. Thomas A., The Edge of Tomorrow, A signet Book, New American Library, Inc., 1301 Avenue of the Americas, New York, NY 10019. Copyright: 1958.

Dooley, Dr. Thomas A., The Night They Burned The Mountain, Signet Book, New American Library, Avenue of the Americas, New York, NY 10019. Copyright 1960.

Duewel, Wesley L., REVIVAL FIRE, Zondervan, Grand Rapids, Michigan 49530. Copyright: 1995.

Gibb, H.A.R., Mohamedanism, An Historical Survey, Oxford University Press, Pages 16-23; Second Edition 1953; Paperback 1969.

Graham, Billy, <u>PEACE WITH GOD</u>, Doubleday & Company, Inc., Garden City, NY. Copyright 1953.

Graham, Billy, <u>JUST AS I AM</u>, The Autobiography of Billy Graham, Harper Collins Worldwide Publishers; Harper San Francisco and Zondervan. Copyright: 1997.

Harmon, M. Judd, <u>Political Thought from Plato to the Present</u>, Dept. of Political Science, Utah State University, McGraw-Hill Book Co., Pages 174- 195.

<u>THE HOLY BIBLE</u>, King James Version, Oral Roberts Edition, with Oral's Personal Commentary, Oral Roberts Evangelistic Assn., Inc., Tulsa, OK.

Jeremiah, Dr. David, <u>AGENTS OF THE APOCALYPSE</u>, A Riveting Look at the Key Players of the End Times, Tynsdale House Publishers, Inc. Copyright: 2014.

Jeremiah, Dr. David, <u>AGENTS OF BABYLON</u>, What the Prophecies of Daniel Tell Us About the End of Days, Tynsdale House Publishers, Inc. Copyright 2015.

Jeremiah, Dr. David, <u>ESCAPE THE COMING NIGHT</u>, A Message of Hope in a Time of Crisis, W Publishing Group, Nashville, TN. Copyright 2018.

Kennedy, Dr. D. James, <u>THE GOSPEL IN THE STARS</u>, Coral Ridge Ministries, Fort Lauderdale, FL. Sermon from the Pulpit: 1992.

Lewis, Dr, David Allen, <u>THE FORGOTTEN PATRIOT</u>, The Story of Haym Salomon, Reproduced from 1993 edition, Bridges for Peace International, P.O. Box 1093, Jerusalem, Israel. Copyright: 2007.

Lindsey, Hal, <u>The Late, Great Planet Earth,</u> with Carol C. Carlson, first published by Zondervan in 1970, (Hardback & Paperback); best-selling book, 1970.

Lindsey, Hal, <u>Satan is Alive and Well on Planet Earth,</u> Co-author, Carol C. Carlson; Bantam Books (P/B), 1973.

McBirnie, William Steuart PhD, <u>The Search for the Twelve Apostles</u>, Tyndale House Publishers, Inc., Carol Stream, Illinois; John, Pages 87-93. Copyright: 1973.

<u>Merriam-Webster's Collegiate Dictionary,</u> Tenth Edition, Springfield, Massachusetts.

Moore, Lt. Gen. Harold G., (Ret.), and Galloway, Joseph L., <u>WE WERE SOLDIERS ONCE...AND YOUNG</u>, Random House, Inc. Copyright: 1992.

Nathan, Joan, <u>The Jewish Holiday Kitchen</u>, 250 Recipes from Around the World to Make Your Celebration Special, Schocken Books, Inc., New York. Copyright: 1988.

National Transportation Safety Board, <u>Aircraft Accident Report: Air Florida 90, Jan. 13, 1982</u>, Washington, DC, Sep. 9, 1992.

Roberts, Frances J., <u>Come Away My Beloved</u>, Prophecies to The Church, New Edition: 1973; 31st Printing, King's Farspan, Inc., 1473 S. La Luna Ave., Ojai, CA 93023. Copyright: 1970.

Roberts, Oral, <u>The Miracle of Seed Faith,</u> (P/B), April 1, 1977, Oral Roberts University, Tulsa, OK; Publisher: Revel, 1977.

Robertson, Pat, <u>The Secret Kingdom</u>, Your Path to Love, Peace and Financial Security, World Publishing, Dallas, TX. Copyright: 1992.

Shayesteh, Daniel, <u>ISLAM: The House I Left Behind</u>, My Personal Testimony, 21st Century Press. Copyright: 2009.

Stevenson, Kenneth E., and Gary R. Habermas, <u>The Verdict on the Shroud</u>, Evidence for the Death and Resurrection of Jesus, "Yeshua," the Jewish Messiah, Servant Books, Ann Arbor, Michigan. Copyright: 1981.

Steves, Rick, <u>Europe Through the Back Door</u>, Eleventh Edition, John Muir Publications, Santa Fe, New Mexico. Copyright: 1993.

<u>Strong's Exhaustive Concordance of the Bible,</u> Hebrew, Chaldee and Greek with references to the English words, James Strong, S.T.D., LL.D., Riverside Book and Bible House, Iowa Falls, Iowa 50126. ten Boom, Corrie, <u>The Hiding Place</u>, Special Film Edition, World Wide Pictures.

Copyright: 1972. ten Boom, Corrie, <u>Tramp for the Lord.</u>, Sequel to <u>The Hiding Place</u>, Published by Christian Literature Crusade, Ft. Washington, Pennsylvania and Fleming H. Revell Company, Old Tappan, New Jersey. Copyright: 1974.

Torrey, Reuben A., <u>The Power of Prayer</u>, Original Publication by Fleming H. Revell Co.; Later Published by Olive Tree, A Zondervan Publication. Copyright: 1924.

<u>Vine's Expository Dictionary of Old and New Testament Words,</u> T. E. Vine, Old Testament Edited by F. F. Bruce, Fleming H. Revell Company, Old Tappan, New Jersey. Copyright: 1981.

<u>The Visit of the Holy Family to Mallawi - Egypt</u>, Prepared by: Bishop H.G. Demetrius of Mallawi, Hermopolis & Antenoepolis; Translated by: Rev. Father Kirillos Bassili Makar; Published by: Coptic Orthodox Diocese of Mallawi, Registered No. 13897/99, Third Edition 2001 AD.

Wilkerson, Rev. David R., <u>The Cross and the Switch Blade,</u> Original Publication by Pillar Books, New York, 1962; Publication by Zondervan, 2002.

Sue G Whitaker
as *Elizabeth (Wife)*

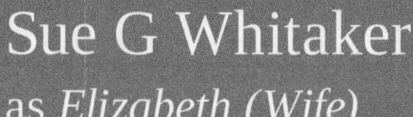

Sue Golemon Whitaker is a former legal secretary for a large DC firm, and a former secretary and computer programmer for the USDA Forest Service. She has raised three children through the turbulence of the '60s and '70s and the upheavel of 20 years of military life. She has moved over 40 times, including family moves to residences in 11 states and Morocco; she has lived in four foreign countries, including three in the Middle East and North America. She has been a devoted student of the Bible for over 30 years and sees the world running out of time.

Bobby V Whitaker
as *John (Husband)*

After his retirement from the army in 1982, Bob was hired by Litton Data Command Systems to build radar sites in Saudi Arabia and later by Boeing to build underground bunkers to house the Saudi Arabian Air force. Around the turn of the century, he was hired by the government of Egypt to finish a four year waste water project in Alexandria to clean up the pollution of that area around the Mediterranean Sea.

www.ingramcontent.com/pod-product-compliance
Lightning Source LLC
Chambersburg PA
CBHW07085120626
46546CB00001B/16